# THE MARILYN ENCYCLOPEDIA

# THE MARILYN ENCYCLOPEDIA

ADAM VICTOR

THE OVERLOOK PRESS
WOODSTOCK • NEW YORK

First published in the United States in 1999 by
The Overlook Press, Peter Mayer Publishers, Inc.
Lewis Hollow Road
Woodstock, New York 12498
Web: www.overlookpress.com



Library of Congress Cataloging-in-Publication Data

Victor, Adam.
The Marilyn Encyclopedia/ Adam Victor.
p. cm.
1. Monroe, Marilyn, 1926–1962 Encyclopedias. I. Title.
PN2287.M69V48 1999 791.43'028'092—dc21 99-37838

Bernard Schleifer, *Book Design and Type Formatting*
Albert DePetrillo, *Editorial Supervision*
Sara Carder, *Photo Research*
Abigail Luthin, *Copyediting*

The publisher wishes to thank
Bob Cosenza at The Kobal Collection and George Zeno

Manufactured in Spain
FIRST EDITION
1 3 5 7 9 8 6 4 2
ISBN 0-87951-718-2
D.L. TO: 1530 - 1999

PHOTO CREDITS

*Left to Right and Top to Bottom*

frontispiece: © 1999 Archives of Milton H. Greene L. L. C., //www.archivesmhg.com

Page viii: Photo by André de Dienes, 1949. (Copyright Mrs. André de Dienes.).1: Twentieth Century-Fox/Kobal. 2: Twentieth Century-Fox/Kobal; Courtesy of Archive Photos. 3: The George Zeno Collection. 4: Kobal. 5: Kobal; Kobal; Kobal. 6: The George Zeno Collection. 7: The George Zeno Collection. 8: The George Zeno Collection. 9: Kobal. 10: Twentieth Century-Fox/Kobal. 11: © Eve Arnold/Magnum Photos. 12: Frank Driggs/Archive Photos; Frank DriggsArchive Photos. 13: Kobal; RKO Radio/Kobal. 14: Kobal. 15: Photomosaic™ by Robert Silvers/www.photomosaic.com. 16: Corbis/Bettman. 17: © Eve Arnold/Magnum Photos. 18: Kobal; Kobal. 19: MGM/Kobal. 20: MGM/Kobal; MGM/Kobal. 21: Kobal. 22: 23: Kobal. 24: Corbis/Bettman; Kobal. 25: The George Zeno Collection. 26: The George Zeno Collection. 28: George Barris World copyright ©. 29: George Barris World copyright ©; Courtesy of Photofest; Courtesy of Photofest. 30: Courtesy of Photofest. 32: Twentieth Century-Fox/Kobal. 33: Courtesy of Archive Photos; Kobal; The George Zeno Collection. 34: Courtesy of Archive Photos. 35: The George Zeno Collection. 38: Courtesy of Photofest; Courtesy of Archive Photos. 39: © Eve Arnold/Magnum Photos. 40: Courtesy of Archive Photos. 41: The George Zeno Collection. 43: Twentieth Century-Fox/Kobal; Twentieth Century-Fox/Kobal. 44: Courtesy of Archive Photos. 45: Twentieth Century-Fox/Kobal. 46: Courtesy of The Cal-Neva Resort. 47: The George Zeno Collection. 48: Courtesy of Photofest. 49: Kobal. 50: © Henri Cartier-Bresson/Magnum Photos. 53: Courtesy of The Chateau Marmont Hotel. 54: Kobal; The George Zeno Collection; Courtesy of Archive Photos. 56: RKO Radio/Kobal; RKO Radio/Kobal. 58: United Artists/Kobal; The George Zeno Collection. 59: Twentieth Century-Fox/Kobal. 61: Corbis/Bettman. 62: Courtesy of The Hotel del Coronado. 63: Courtesy of Photofest. 64: Courtesy of Photofest. 65: The George Zeno Collection. 66: United Artists/Kobal. 67: Twentieth Century-Fox/Kobal. 68: Courtesy of Archive Photos; Twentieth Century-Fox/Kobal; Twentieth Century-Fox/Kobal. 69: Twentieth Century-Fox/Kobal. 70: © Bruce Davidson/Magnum Photos. 72: Copyright Mrs. André de Dienes. 73: The George Zeno Collection. 74: Kobal. 76: The George Zeno Collection. 77: Kobal. 78: Corbis/Bettman; Courtesy of Archive Photos. 79: Kobal. 82: Courtesy of Photofest; The George Zeno Collection. 83: The George Zeno Collection. 85: Twentieth Century-Fox/Kobal. 86: Twentieth Century-Fox/Kobal. 88: Kobal. 89: Kobal. 91: Kobal. 92: Corbis/Bettman; The George Zeno Collection. 93: Kobal. 94: © Elliott Erwitt/Magnum Photos. 95: Twentieth Century-Fox/Kobal. 96: Twentieth Century-Fox/The George Zeno Collection. 98: Corbis/Bettman; RKO Radio/Kobal; © Bob Henriques/Magnum Photos. 99: M. Garrett/Archive Photos. 100: George Barris World copyright ©. 102: Kobal. 103: Kobal. 108: Courtesy of Photofest. 109: Columbia Pictures/Kobal. 112: © *The New York Times*. 113: Twentieth Century-Fox/Kobal. 114: United Artists/Kobal. 115: Corbis/Bettman. 116: © Eve Arnold/Magnum Photos. 117: Courtesy of Photofest. 118: Twentieth Century-Fox/The George Zeno Collection. 119: Twentieth Century-Fox/Kobal. 120: Courtesy of Archive Photos. 121: Kobal. 123: Kobal. 124: Twentieth Century-Fox/Kobal; M. Garrett/Archive Photos. 125: Twentieth Century-Fox/Kobal. 126: Corbis/Bettman; Courtesy of Archive Photos. 127: © 1999 Archives of Milton H. Greene L. L. C., //www.archivesmhg.com. 128: © 1999 Archives of Milton H. Greene L. L. C., //www.archivesmhg.com. 129: Courtesy of Archive Photos. 130: © 1999 Archives of Milton H. Greene L. L. C., //www .archivesmhg.com. 133: Twentieth Century-Fox/Kobal. 134: Courtesy of Archive Photos. 135: The George Zeno Collection; RKO Radio/Kobal; Twentieth Century-Fox/Kobal; The George Zeno Collection. 137: The George Zeno Collection; Twentieth Century-Fox/Kobal. 138: The George Zeno Collection. 140: The George Zeno Collection; The George Zeno Collection; The George Zeno Collection. 141: MGM/Kobal. 142: The George Zeno Collection; The George Zeno Collection. 143: Corbis/Bettman. 144: Corbis/Bettman; Twentieth Century-Fox/Kobal. 145: Twentieth Century-Fox/Kobal. 146: Courtesy of Photofest. 147: M. Garrett/Archive Photos; Kobal. 149: George Barris World copyright ©. 151: Twentieth Century-Fox/Kobal; Courtesy of Archive Photos. 153: Twentieth Century-Fox/Kobal. 154: Courtesy of Photofest. 155: Courtesy of Photofest; The George Zeno Collection. 157: The George Zeno Collection. 159: Twentieth Century-Fox/Kobal; Courtesy of Archive Photos. 160: Courtesy of Archive Photos. 161: Kobal. 162: Columbia Pictures/Kobal; Columbia Pictures/Kobal. 163: Courtesy of Photofest; Courtesy of Photofest. 164: Courtesy of Photofest. 166: Courtesy of Photofest; United Artists/Kobal. 167: Twentieth Century-Fox/Kobal. 168: Twentieth Century-Fox/Kobal; Courtesy of Archive Photos. 169: Twentieth Century-Fox/Kobal. 170: Courtesy of Archive Photos; Frank Driggs/Archive Photos. 171: Frank Driggs/Archive Photos; Courtesy of Photofest. 172: Courtesy of Photofest. 173: Courtesy of Photofest. 174: Twentieth Century-Fox/Kobal; The George Zeno Collection. 175: Courtesy of Photofest. 177: Twentieth Century-Fox/Kobal. 178: Courtesy of Photofest; Courtesy of Photofest. 179: The George Zeno Collection; The George Zeno Collection; The George Zeno Collection; The George Zeno Collection; Courtesy of Photofest. 181: Courtesy of Photofest; The George Zeno Collection. 182: The George Zeno Collection. 183: © 1999 Archives of Milton H. Greene L. L. C., //www.archivesmhg.com. 184: The George Zeno Collection. 185: Kobal; Courtesy of Photofest. 186: The George Zeno Collection. 188: © 1999 Christie's Images, Ltd. 189: Courtesy of Photofest. 191: George Barris World copyright ©. 192: Kobal; Express Newspapers/Archive Photos. 193: Kobal. 194: Courtesy of Photofest; Kobal. 195: © 1987 Sam Shaw. 197: United Artists/Kobal; The George Zeno Collection. 198: © Eve Arnold/Magnum Photos. 199: United Artists/Kobal; Courtesy of Archive Photos. 200: Kobal. 201: Kobal; Courtesy of Archive Photos. 203: Twentieth Century-Fox/Kobal; Courtesy of Photofest. 204: Kobal. 205: The George Zeno Collection. 206: Courtesy of Photofest. 207: © Inge Morath/Magnum Photos. 208: Twentieth Century-Fox/Kobal. 209: Courtesy of Archive Photos; The George Zeno Collection. 211: The George Zeno Collection. 212: Courtesy of Photofest. 213: Courtesy of Photofest. 214: Twentieth Century-Fox/Kobal; Courtesy of Photofest. 215: Twentieth Century-Fox/Kobal. 216: Courtesy of Photofest; Courtesy of Photofest. 218: Kobal. 219: © 1999 Bert Stern. 220: © 1999 Bert Stern. 223: © Eve Arnold/Magnum Photos. 224: Twentieth Century-Fox/Kobal; Courtesy of Photofest. 225: © 1987 Sam Shaw. 226: Courtesy of Photofest. 229: Kobal. 230: Twentieth Century-Fox/Kobal; The George Zeno Collection; Courtesy of Photofest. 231: Kobal. 233: © 1999 Archives of Milton H. Greene L. L. C., //www.archivesmhg.com. 234: M. Garrett/Archive Photos; Courtesy of Photofest; Courtesy of Archive Photos. 235: Kobal. 237: The George Zeno Collection; The George Zeno Collection. 239: Courtesy of Photofest. 240: Courtesy of Archive Photos. 241: The George Zeno Collection. 242: Copyright Mrs. André de Dienes. 243: Warner Bros./Kobal. 244: The George Zeno Collection; The George Zeno Collection. 245: Courtesy of Photofest. 246: The George Zeno Collection. 248: The George Zeno Collection. 249: The George Zeno Collection. 250: The George Zeno Collection. 251: Courtesy of Photofest; Kobal. 252: Twentieth Century-Fox/Kobal; Twentieth Century-Fox/Kobal. 253: Kobal; Frank Driggs/Archive Photos. 255: United Artists/Kobal. 256: The George Zeno Collection. 257: The George Zeno Collection; Courtesy of Archive Photos. 259: Kobal. 261: The George Zeno Collection; Courtesy of Archive Photos. 262: The George Zeno Collection. 263: The George Zeno Collection. 264: Twentieth Century-Fox/Kobal. 265: Twentieth Century-Fox/Kobal; Twentieth Century-Fox/Kobal; Courtesy of Archive Photos. 266: Courtesy of Archive Photos; The George Zeno Collection. 267: Warner Bros./Kobal; Kobal. 268: © Eve Arnold/Magnum Photos. 271: Twentieth Century-Fox/Kobal; Twentieth Century-Fox/Kobal; Twentieth Century-Fox/Kobal. 272: © 1987 Sam Shaw. 273: Darlene Hammond/Archive Photos. 274: The George Zeno Collection. 275: Courtesy of Archive Photos; Courtesy of Photofest. 277: Kobal. 278: © Eve Arnold/Magnum Photos. 280: Ted Baron. 281: The George Zeno Collection. 282: United Artists/Kobal. 283: United Artists/Kobal; United Artists/Kobal; Courtesy of the Hotel del Coronado. 284: Courtesy of Photofest; Courtesy of Photofest. 286: Courtesy of Archive Photos. 287: M. Garrett/Archive Photos; Corbis/Bettman. 289: © 1999 Bert Stern. 290: © 1999 Bert Stern. 292: The George Zeno Collection. 293: Courtesy of Photofest. 295: Twentieth Century-Fox/Kobal. 296: Twentieth Century-Fox/Archive Photos. 297: Twentieth Century-Fox/Kobal; Twentieth Century-Fox/Kobal. 300: The George Zeno Collection. 301: Kobal. 302: Twentieth Century-Fox/Kobal. 303: Courtesy of Photofest. 304: Twentieth Century-Fox/Kobal. 305: Twentieth Century-Fox/Kobal; Twentieth Century-Fox/Kobal; Twentieth Century-Fox/Kobal. 306: Courtesy of Photofest. 307: Copyright Mrs. André de Dienes. 308: The George Zeno Collection; The George Zeno Collection. 310: Twentieth Century-Fox/The George Zeno Collection. 311: Twentieth Century-Fox/Kobal. 313: Twentieth Century-Fox/Kobal. 314: Twentieth Century-Fox/Kobal; United Artists/Kobal. 315: Kobal. 316: The George Zeno Collection. 317: Courtesy of Archive Photos. 318: The George Zeno Collection. 319: Twentieth Century-Fox/Kobal; Twentieth Century-Fox/Kobal; Courtesy of Photofest. 320: © Madame Tussaud's, London; The George Zeno Collection. 321: The George Zeno Collection; Twentieth Century-Fox/Kobal. 323: Courtesy of Archive Photos; The George Zeno Collection. 324: Courtesy of Photofest. 325: © 1999 Sam Shaw. 326: The George Zeno Collection. 328: The George Zeno Collection. 329: The George Zeno Collection. 331: Twentieth Century-Fox/Kobal. 332: Columbia Pictures/Kobal. 333: George Barris World copyright ©. 335: © 1999 Archives of Milton H. Greene L. L. C., //www.archivesmhg.com. 342: Photo by André de Dienes, 1949. (Copyright Mrs. André de Dienes.)

*To the memory of Marilyn Monroe,*
*and all who hold a good thought for her*

# ACKNOWLEDGMENTS

One author's name on the cover, a whole team behind it—

My thanks and gratitude to the many people who have helped in the genesis, research and publication of *The Marilyn Encyclopedia*. First, my wife Patrizia, who tolerated such a formidable rival as Marilyn for such a long time; Overlook Publisher Peter Mayer, who knew a good idea when he saw it; Publishing Director Tracy Carns, who kept her faith as deadlines crumbled; Ed Victor and Michelene Wandor, without whom my life and this book would not have been possible; my agent, David Miller, for ably handling the small and not so small print; Eve Arnold, for her reminiscences, guidance, and for being Eve; countless librarians at the British Library, British Library Newspaper Library, and British Film Institute Library who helped me to trace obscure material and long-since out of print Marilyn paraphernalia, as well as second-hand book dealers on two continents; Sara Todd, for sharing my Marilyn mania and checking the not so niceties of my prose; and all the staff at The Overlook Press, who set new standards and records in their fields: Sara Carder for her unstinting photo detective work, Albert DePetrillo for his gargantuan task wrangling all my words, Abigail Luthin's wary eye for picking up on errors, Bernard Schleifer for his crystal-clear design, Chris Morran who along with Tracy managed this complicated production, and Nancy Freeman and her colleagues at Mondadori who did a great job keeping the tightest of deadlines.

Thanks also to the many loved ones, friends, and colleagues who have helped me through the research, organization, and endeavor of this book, and, ultimately, thanks to Marilyn's millions of fans, still avid to find out everything they can about this extraordinary and unique woman.

# CONTENTS

# INTRODUCTION

ALMOST FOUR DECADES AFTER HER MYSTERIOUS DEATH, THE LEGEND OF Marilyn Monroe is larger than ever. The popularity of other screen stars may wax and wane, but Marilyn's beacon continues to shine, primed with her unique, dazzling luminosity.

*The Marilyn Encyclopedia* has been written to bring a little order to the copious and chaotic body of literature about Hollywood's greatest female icon, the most written about woman of the twentieth century.

Unlike Marilyn biographies—some of which are scrupulously researched, others of which are little more than scurrilous pamphlets—this book does not claim to have a monopoly on the truth of Marilyn's life. For a woman whose shining success and incredible longevity is because of and thanks to her fans, it is only apt for the fans to seek out their own truths about Marilyn. *The Marilyn Encyclopedia* is a repository of the "truths" about Marilyn's life and times, her friends and family, films and acting achievements, as well as anecdotes, "half-truths," gossip, famous Marilyn sayings, suppositions, fantasies, trivia, and a selection of photos that document the thirty-six years of her exceptional life.

*The Marilyn Encyclopedia* aims to be a work of reference and an entertaining read. For this reason, the categories we have chosen are broad; copious cross-references provide quick access to the people, places, and details of Marilyn's life (words referring the reader to other entries in the book are set in small captital letters). References are given for further reading, and a comprehensive bibliography rounds off the work.

Photograpy by André De Dienes, 1949.

A

## ACADEMY AWARDS

Although there is no more enduring Hollywood star or icon of the film industry than Marilyn, she never received an Academy Award in recognition of her talent, either in her own lifetime or posthumously. Recognition was more forthcoming from other countries (France and Italy) than from her own. (*see* AWARDS)

The closest Marilyn ever got to an Oscar was in 1951, a year before she had graduated to top-star billing, when she went to the Pantages Theater (6233 Hollywood Boulevard, Hollywood) to present the Best Achievement in Sound Oscar to Thomas Moulton for his work on *ALL ABOUT EVE* (1950). For the occasion she looked resplendent in a lavender-colored off-the-shoulder gown borrowed from the Fox wardrobe department. There was drama just before she was due to go on stage, when she noticed a small rip in the dress. A bevy of Fox handlers had to fix the rip and calm her nerves sufficiently for her to conquer her stage fright.

The closest Marilyn came to winning on her own merits was rumors of a Best Actress nomination for her performance in *BUS STOP* (1956), and then two years later for *SOME LIKE IT HOT* (1959). On neither occasion did the nomination materialize; the Oscars going in 1956 to Ingrid Bergman (*Anastasia*) and in 1959 to SIMONE SIGNORET (*Room at the Top*).

On two separate occasions, film columnists have suggested giving Marilyn a special posthumous career Oscar, first in 1963, then ten years later.

In the early nineties a cartoon artist named Ross Gathercole created an animated Marilyn and sought Academy interest in using this Marilyn to present one of the awards. Despite lobbying by fans, nothing ever came of this.

## ACTING

"How I wanted to learn, to change, to improve! I didn't want anything else. Not men, not money, not love, but the ability to act."

The last Twentieth Century-Fox publicity portrait of Marilyn that was ever done, for *Let's Make Love* (1960).

One of Marilyn's first Twentieth Century-Fox publicity portraits, 1950.

Acting was Marilyn's art, the skill to which she dedicated her life with a commitment and seriousness many critics found hard to believe. To pursue her art Marilyn had to fight many battles: with a studio system intent on using her only in "dumb blonde" roles, with critics who would not give her a break however well she performed, but mainly with her own desperate fears of forgetting her lines, disappointing people she respected, and falling short of her own high standards.

Her first big challenge was getting into the movie business. Once she achieved this, she went about getting the ACTING LESSONS and advice she needed to do her job well. Throughout her career she studied under many coaches and was always eager to learn and develop her craft. Her performances improved immensely; she showed her sternest critics that not only did the camera and her countless fans love her, but she had masterful comic timing [*HOW TO MARRY A MILLIONAIRE* (1953), *GENTLEMAN PREFER BLONDES* (1953), and *SOME LIKE IT HOT* (1959)] and a talent for high drama [*BUS STOP* (1956)]. Yet somehow Marilyn was never satisfied. Receiving accolades wasn't enough to boost her confidence. Anxieties over getting the performance right remained a torment to Marilyn until the end: too many people to please (not least of whom her perfectionist self), and concerns that she did not look good enough, were compounded by a brief reappearance of red blotches, and the stutter she suffered as a child.

Yet Marilyn's ability to "turn it on" for the camera was legendary. Despite her on-set difficulties, her paralyzing stage fright, her nervousness about learning lines, and lack of self-confidence, despite the many takes often required to satisfy herself and her directors, Marilyn had a skill that few others have matched in doing just what was right for the camera. JEAN NEGULESCO, who directed her in *How to Marry a Millionaire*, summed it up as "a love affair nobody around her was aware of. It was a language of looks, a forbidden intimacy. . . . The lenses were the audience."

In her later films, when she had more control over her choice of roles, Marilyn perfected her spellbinding style of "micro" acting, her eyes and mouth registering a flickering range of emotions, from vulnerability to hope to fear to love to bewilderment to coital pouts all in the space of a few seconds.

Marilyn very much wanted to prove that she could also show her acting talent on the stage—LEE STRASBERG and his wife PAULA were very encouraging in this respect ("All I want is to play something different. The Strasbergs say I can."). In some ways Marilyn saw the THEATER as her salvation, a way of proving beyond doubt to the world that she could stand on her acting merits alone—plus the fact that, as she once said, "You can go on forever in the theater"—but there was always the problem of self-doubt to overcome.

Ultimately, Marilyn never did get the chance to prove herself in the footlights, although many of her movies were screen adaptations of successful Broadway plays.

Following events at FOX in 1962, when she was kicked off *SOMETHING'S GOT TO GIVE*, Marilyn made several oblique comments to interviewers that life might be easier out of the movie business. Nevertheless, days before her death she was happy to hear the studio was thinking of reinstating her to the movie.

MARILYN:

Of herself as a child: "I'd listen to *The Lone Ranger* and get terribly excited. Not at the horses and chases and the guns but . . . the drama. The wondering of how it would be for each person in the situation. . . . There are techniques to be learned, and it's hard work. But it still seems sort of like play to me, and something you want terribly to do."

"I think if other girls know how bad I was when I started they'll be encouraged. I finally made up my mind I wanted to be an actress and I was not going to let my lack of confidence ruin my chances."

1952, to Aline Mosby, sanguine about the acclaim for her performance in her first starring role, the crazed babysitter of *Don't Bother to Knock*: "I'm trying to find myself now, to be a good actress and a good person. Sometimes I feel strong inside but I have to reach in and pull it up. It isn't easy. Nothing's easy. But you go on."

1953 in a *New York Times* interview: "My dramatic coach, Natasha Lytess, tells everybody that I have great soul—but so far nobody's interested in it. Someday, though, someday—" By this time Marilyn had appeared in almost twenty movies, invariably playing a beautiful blonde temptress who uses her looks to obtain her sly and calculating goal, generally tempting an older man who, in time, realizes the error of his ways.

1955: "The thing I'd like the most is to become a real actress. I remember when I was a kid at the movies on Saturday afternoon. I'd sit in the front row and I'd think how wonderful it would be to be an actress, you know. But I didn't really realize about acting. I appreciated what I saw. Bad, good, it didn't matter, I enjoyed it very much. Anything that would move on the screen. However, you know, I realize more and more the responsibility, and as I say, 'I would like to be a good actress.'"

1958, to columnist Hedda Hopper: "I'm not a quick study, but I'm very serious about my work and am not experienced enough as an actress to chat with friends and workers on the set and then go into a dramatic scene. I like to go directly from a scene into my dressing-room and concentrate on the next one and keep my mind in one channel. I envy these people who can meet all comers and go from a bright quip and gay laugh into a scene before the camera. All I'm thinking of is my performance, and I try to make it as good as I know how."



Marilyn at The Academy Awards ceremony, 1951.

1961: "Being a movie actress was never as much fun as dreaming of being one. When I'd nearly given up, I got a break. Then when I didn't want the studio kind of star roles, I was showered with them."

The difference between theater and movies: "There's no audience watching you. There's nobody to act for except yourself. It's like the games you play when you are a child and pretend to be someone else. Usually, it's almost the same sort of story you made up as a child."

1962: "I really am trying to find myself and the best way for me to do that is to try to prove to myself that I am an actress. . . . My work is the only ground I've ever had to stand on. To put it bluntly, I seem to have a whole superstructure with no foundation. But I'm working on the foundation."

### ACTING LESSONS

Marilyn studied drama with:
1947–1949: The Actors Lab (Phoebe Brand and Morris Carnovsky)
1948–1955: Natasha Lytess
1951–53: Michael Chekhov
1953: Lotte Goslar
1955: Constance Collier
1955–1961: The Actors Studio (Lee Strasberg, Paula Strasberg)
as well as dozens of voice coaches, singing teachers, and choreographers.

The methods Marilyn followed, through all her drama teachers, focused to some degree on inner questing to find the strength and breadth of emotion to play a character. This meant reaching deep within, and in later years it involved frequent sessions with psychoanalysts. As biographer DONALD SPOTO notes, this was not without danger: "The efforts required made Marilyn ever more self-conscious and unfree in acting and effected a kind of paralysis. Instead of seeking the role within herself, Marilyn was urged by her teachers to seek herself in the role, and in so doing she was thrown back on her own insecurities and insufficiencies."

At the ACTORS LAB Marilyn was infused with the wonder of theater. NATASHA LYTESS, who guided Marilyn's drama development for the first half of her career, believed very strongly in the motivation of characters, seeking through introspection the reasons for every action, movement, and even changes in tone of voice.

Exercises with MICHAEL CHEKHOV were designed to free Marilyn up, to make her body more pliant and malleable, among other things by using stretching and breathing exercises and developing self-awareness.

In 1955 Marilyn moved to New York and made a clean break with her Los Angeles past. She became the most famous student of THE METHOD, as taught at the ACTORS STUDIO. One significant change was that Marilyn's diction became clearer after working with drama coach Lytess, who taught her to emphasize her enunciation. *Bus Stop* was Marilyn's first movie after joining the Actors Studio, a change that added great depth and a studied spontaneity to her technique. Many people consider this to be her finest dramatic performance.

Not everybody was in favor of Marilyn taking up The Method. At the time, BILLY WILDER said, "If she sets out to be artistic and dedicated, and she carries it so far that she's willing to wear sloppy-Joe sweaters and go without makeup and let her hair hang straight as a string, this is not what has made her great to date. I don't say that its beyond her realm of possibility that she can establish herself as a straight dramatic actress—but it will be another career for her, a starting over."

GEORGE AXELROD, who wrote *THE SEVEN YEAR ITCH* and the screen adaptation of *Bus Stop*, saw her in action on set before and after the 1955 watershed. One thing remained the same: "Although she was full of aspirations and frantic to succeed, she had no technical vocabulary about acting for filmmaking, and that gave her 'protectors' the advantage over her. They taught and encouraged her—although not too much, or they'd have been out of work."

## ACTORS LAB
CRESCENT HEIGHTS BOULEVARD, LOS ANGELES

Marilyn and a clutch of Fox starlets were sent by the studio to the Actors Laboratory to learn their craft from Morris Carnovsky and his wife Phoebe Brand, East Coast theater folk who had founded and ran the place. The Actors Lab had come into being as the West Coast outpost of the Group Theater in New York, founded by, among others, LEE STRASBERG. Students generally studied plays which explored the plight of working men and women, offering criticisms of the dangers of capitalism. This material appealed greatly to Marilyn, who had grown up in precisely the kind of environment portrayed on the stage.

Throughout 1947 Marilyn attended classes, read plays, and studied scenes, paid for at first by TWENTIETH CENTURY-FOX, and then after Fox failed to renew her contract, by new benefactors JOHN CARROLL and LUCILLE RYMAN. She met the major figures in New York theater and for the first time came into contact with the social and political issues she was to espouse throughout her life. She later recalled: "It was as far from *Scudda-Hoo* [Marilyn's first movie appearance] as you could get. It was my first taste of what real acting in real drama could be, and I was hooked."

However much an impression her time at the Actors Lab may have made on young Marilyn, her shyness prevented her from taking a vociferous role in activities. Phoebe Brand, an actress in her own right, remem-

Marilyn Monroe at the Actors Studio, ca. 1956.

bered Marilyn as a conscientious student: "I remember her for her beautiful long blonde hair. I tried to get through to her and find out more about her, but I couldn't do it. She was extremely retiring. What I failed to see in her acting was her wit, her sense of humor. It was there all the time—this lovely comedic style, but I was blind to it."

One of the plays Marilyn read was CLASH BY NIGHT, in which she was later to have a screen role.

## ACTORS STUDIO

Located in a former Greek Orthodox church at 432 West Forty-fourth Street between Ninth and Tenth Avenues, New York.

The Actors Studio was a workshop where performers met to learn and practice THE METHOD, an acting technique based on eliciting emotions developed from the teachings of Russian thespian KONSTANTIN STANISLAVSKI. Marilyn began attending in May 1955, four years after LEE STRASBERG became artistic director. Until the 1970s, actors flocked to this celebrated temple of drama to expand their experience and range, to expose themselves to the opinions and searing analysis of their fellow actors, and the critique of Strasberg himself. The atmosphere could be tense with emotion, and tears were not uncommon.

Sessions took place twice a week, on Tuesdays and Fridays. Actors would present a scene to the group and then explain what they were trying to accomplish with it. Anybody attending the class, or in the audience, was free to comment, encourage, or criticize. Once comments from the floor were finished, Strasberg would have his say.

Before joining the studio actors had to audition for Lee Strasberg. Once in, they were free to work as much or as little as they wanted—there was no strict timetable. Although Marilyn was one of the studio's highest-profile alumni, she was never an official member, a title awarded to just a dozen or so of the thousand-plus actors who auditioned for membership each year.

When she attended sessions, rather than the private lessons she had with Lee at his apartment, Marilyn sat unobtrusively at the back of the room, occasionally taking notes. She was very much in "Norma Jeane mode"—no makeup, a simple blouse and slacks, and a scarf over her trademark hair. Fellow student Frank Corsaro commented, "She was invariably late, but she listened and observed the critiques with a steadfast gaze."

A fundamental part of The Method was "freeing" the actor through PSYCHOANALYSIS. Between 1955 and 1960, when she was in New York, Marilyn's daily routine revolved around drama classes with Strasberg and sessions with her psychoanalyst. Among the various drama exercises, Marilyn played the lead role in a scene from ANNA CHRISTIE—although clapping was not generally the done thing, Marilyn's performance on that occasion elicited a heartfelt round of applause. In another exercise Marilyn had to "be a kitten." Never one to do things by half measures, Marilyn borrowed a kitten from a grocery store where she used to shop, and studied and mimicked the little creature's behavior for a week until she felt she was ready.

Over the years Marilyn could always be counted on for Actors Studio fundraisers. In December 1956 she was a star usherette at the premier of *Baby Doll* (held at the Victoria theater on Broadway). In 1961, just a week after getting out of the hospital, Marilyn put in an appearance at a benefit raising money for the Actors Studio held at Roseland in New York.

Theresa Russell in *Insignificance* (1985).

Ashley Judd as Norma Jeane (above) and Mira Sorvino as Marilyn (below) in *Norma Jean and Marilyn* (1996).

Marilyn continued to take lessons from Lee Strasberg until the year of her death. It is thought that she was intending to finally become an official member later on that year.

Following Marilyn's death the Actors Studio launched its Marilyn Monroe Fund campaign, designed to raise a minimum contribution of $2,500 from one hundred members. The proceeds went to build a brand-new studio and rehearsal area in Los Angeles, and to endow a scholarship fund for promising young talent. The Marilyn Monroe Theater is located at the Strasberg Institute in West Hollywood, California. The Actors Studio also commemorated their most famous student by raising finance for a Broadway season.

### FAMOUS ACTORS STUDIO ALUMNI

Anne Bancroft, Marlon Brando, Ellen Burstyn, Montgomery Clift, James Dean, Robert De Niro, Robert Duvall, Sally Field, Jane Fonda, Julie Harris, Dustin Hoffman, Anne Jackson, Karl Malden, Steve McQueen, Paul Newman, Al Pacino, Geraldine Page, Sidney Poitier, Eva Marie Saint, Maureen Stapleton, Rod Steiger, Eli Wallach, Shelley Winters, and Joanne Woodward.

Not all who came to these hallowed portals were allowed to enter: three not welcomed were Jack Nicholson, George C. Scott, and Barbra Streisand.

MARILYN:
"They work so hard with me on the essentials—like a pianist and his scales. Projection, movement, breath control—all those things."

## ACTRESSES WHO HAVE PORTRAYED MARILYN OR MARILYN-BASED CHARACTERS

Melody Anderson, *Marilyn and Bobby* (1993, TV movie)
Stephanie Anderson, *Death Becomes Her* (1992) and *Calendar Girl* (1993)
Patricia Arquette, *Holy Matrimony* (1994)
Jennifer Austin, *My Fellow Americans* (1996)
Holly Butler, *Netherworld* (1992)
Judy Davis, *Insignificance* (1982 play)
Sondra Dickenson, *Legend* (1974)
FAYE DUNAWAY, *After the Fall* (1974, TV movie)
Patty Duke, *The Goddess* (1958)
Sherilyn Fenn, *Ruby* (1992)
Brigitte Fonda, *Graceland* (1998)
Constance Forslund, *Moviola: This Year's Blonde* (1980)
Eve Gordon, *A Woman Named Jackie* (1991, TV movie)
Susan Griffiths, *Legends in Concert* (1992), *Marilyn and Me* (1991, TV movie), *Pulp Fiction* (1994)
Marcia Gay Harden, *Used People* (1992)
Sunshine H. Hernandez, *With Honors* (1994)
Catherine Hicks, *Marilyn: The Untold Story* (1980, TV movie)
Jane Horrocks, *Self Catering* (1993) and *Little Voice* (1998)
Joyce Jameson, *Venus at Large* (1962)
Ashley Judd, *Norma Jean and Marilyn* (1996, TV movie)
Linda Kerridge, *Fade to Black* (1980)
Sally Kirkland, *The Island* (1999)

Shirley Knight, *Kennedy's Children* (1975 play)
Paula Lane, *Goodnight, Sweet Marilyn* (1989)
Linda Lavin, *Cop-Out* (1969 play)
Stephanie Lawrence, *Marilyn!* (1983 play)
Phoebe Legere, *Mondo New York* (1987)
Barbara Loden, *After the Fall* (1964 play)
Julie London, *The Eleventh Hour: Like A Diamond in the Sky* (1963)
Arlene Lorre, *Another Chance* (1989)
Kate Mailer, *Strawhead* (1986 play)
JAYNE MANSFIELD, *Will Success Spoil Rock Hunter?* (1955 play, 1957 movie)
Barbara Niven, *The Rat Pack* (1998, TV movie)
Kerri Randles, *Introducing Dorothy Dandridge* (1999, TV movie)
Alyson Reed, *Marilyn: An American Fable* (1983 play)
Misty Rowe, *Goodbye Norma Jean* (1976)
Theresa Russell, INSIGNIFICANCE (1985)
Mira Sorvino, *Norma Jean and Marilyn* (1996, TV movie)
Ginger Spice, *Spiceworld* (1998)
KIM STANLEY, *The Goddess* (1958)
Connie Stevens, *The Sex Symbol* (1974)
Heather Thomas, *Hoover vs. the Kennedys: The Second Civil War* (1987, TV movie)

## ADAMS, CASEY
(B. 1917, MAX SHOWALTER)

Character actor Adams twice worked with Marilyn, in *Niagara* (1953) and *Bus Stop* (1956). He has been quoted as saying that during location work on *Niagara* Marilyn appeared naked at her hotel window, quickly gathering a crowd of male admirers, and then at night jumped into bed with Adams with the words, "Don't do anything but just hold me!"

## ADLER, BUDDY
(1906–1960, B. MAURICE ADLER)

A producer at COLUMBIA STUDIOS from 1948, before moving to TWENTIETH CENTURY-FOX. In 1956 he replaced DARRYL ZANUCK as studio head, until his death at age fifty-one in 1960. He has a producer credit on *Bus Stop*.

Other movies: *The Dark Past* (1948), *From Here to Eternity* (1953), *Love Is a Many Splendored Thing* (1955), *Anastasia* (1956), *The Inn of Sixth Happiness* (1958).

## ADVERTISEMENTS

Before accolades for her screen performances began rolling in, Marilyn had already been named "The Most Advertised Girl in the World" by the Advertising Association of the West.

During her starlet days Norma Jeane supplemented her income with a number of print advertisements. The only known TV commercial she made was for Royal Triton Oil in 1950. In it, Marilyn breathlessly pitched, "This is the first car I ever owned. I call it Cynthia. She's going to have the best care a car ever had. Put Royal Triton in Cynthia's little tummy. . . . Cynthia will just love that Royal Triton."

Some of the products Marilyn promoted:

American Airlines
City Club Shoes

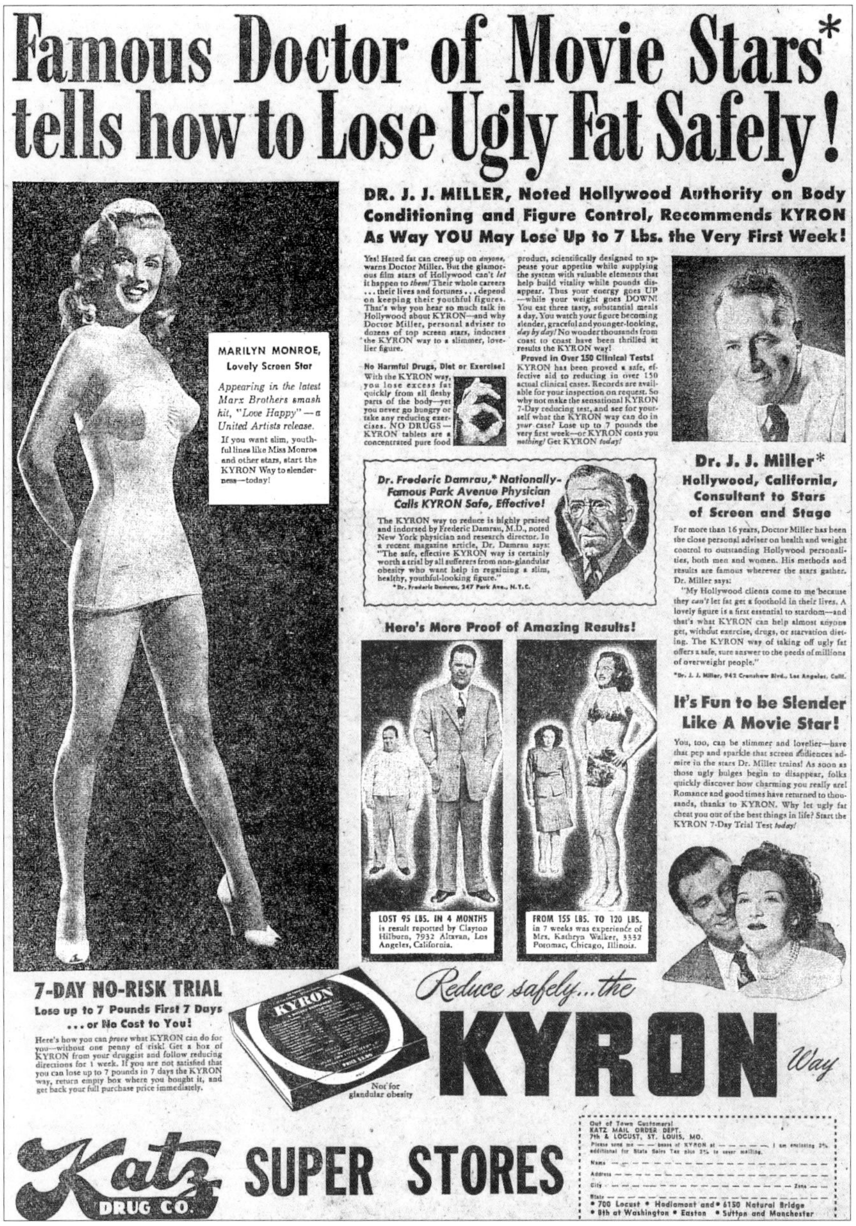


An advertisement for Kyron diet pills, 1950.

Close-Up Perfect Kiss-Tested Lipstick
Hiltone Hair Coloring
Jantzen Swimwear
Kyron Way Diet Pills
Louis Creative Hairdressers
Lustre-Creme Shampoo
Pabst Beer
Rayve Shampoo
Roi-Tan Cigars
Tar-Tan Suntan Lotion
Westmore's Tru-Glo liquid makeup

Since her death Marilyn's image has been used for a vast number of products, licensed by the Marilyn Monroe ESTATE. These include:

Absolut Vodka
American Airlines
Chanel No. 5
Hershey's candy
Max Factor
Maxell Tapes
Levi's
Mercedes Benz

The name Marilyn Monroe has also been licensed for all manner of products and MEMORABILIA. One of the strangest has to be underwear, considering that Marilyn regularly abstained from wearing these garments.

## ADVISERS

From the moment she became a star, Marilyn seemed to acquire advisers of all types. To add to her drama coach of the moment (see ACTING LESSONS), Marilyn had a long succession of AGENTS, LAWYERS, psychoanalysts, DOCTORS, and business partners, not to mention strong-willed HUSBANDS, all of whom had opinions on how she should run her life and handle her professional engagements. According to Fox studio boss PETER LEVATHES, "Her so-called advisers created the difficulties and caused her a terrible identity crisis."

An advertisement for Tru-Glo liquid makeup, 1953.

An advertisement for Lustre-Creme Shampoo, 1953.

## AFTER THE FALL

ARTHUR MILLER's first play after Marilyn's death centered on the tortured relationship between Quentin, a lawyer, and his wife, Maggie, a singer. Many critics saw the play as Miller's attempt to exorcise the ghost of Marilyn and show the world that he had done everything a man could reasonably do to save a doomed woman. This was only Miller's second completed work after his marriage to Marilyn, and it revealed the darkest side of her, after the hardly glowing character of Roslyn he wrote for Marilyn in *THE MISFITS* (1961). As Marilyn biographer FRED LAWRENCE GUILES states, "Both works derive from his life, the most legitimate source any writer has, and taken together they give us as complete a portrait of Marilyn as we are ever likely to get."

The writer's block Miller suffered during his marriage had lifted, and in the process he revealed a sense of the development of this unlikely relationship between "egghead and hourglass," the terrible strife and pain both he and Marilyn experienced.

*After the Fall* was the inaugural play of the Repertory Theater of Lincoln Center, opening on January 23, 1964. Jason Robards played Quentin, Barbara Loden was Maggie, ELIA KAZAN directed, and Robert Whitehead produced the play. Regardless of protestations by writer and director, the parallels between the lives of Marilyn and Maggie are unmistakable. Maggie is plucked from obscurity working at a switchboard to become a famous pop singer. The Miller character is not a writer but a lawyer, and he becomes as much a father figure as husband to his new wife. Soon after they marry, Maggie shows a hidden side: a crippling lack of self-esteem, a constant fear that people are trying to keep her down, a well of emotional pain and rising hatred for a man she feels has turned into a traitor. As she begins to regret the marriage, she finds solace in drink and pills, eventually threatening suicide in order to get Quentin to save her. Despite his attempts to prevent it, Maggie inevitably makes good on her threat.

QUENTIN:
"The first honor was that I hadn't tried to go to bed with her! She took it for a tribute to her 'value,' and I was only afraid! God, the hypocrisy!"

"You want to die, Maggie, and I really don't know how to prevent it."

* * *

MAGGIE:
"You tried to kill me, mister. I been killed by a lot of people, some couldn't hardly spell, but it's the same, mister."

Miller's defense, expressed eloquently in his autobiography *Timebends*, is that only as he neared completion of the play shortly after Marilyn's death did he realize that everybody would equate the character of Maggie with Marilyn. The title *After the Fall* refers to *The Fall*, a novella by Albert Camus in which a man comes to learn that he cannot save the woman he loves, that salvation lies only within herself. Miller also claims that it was the actress Barbara Loden who suggested wearing a blonde wig; he did not say no, much to his later regret.

**Reviews:**

*The Herald Tribune*
"*After the Fall* resembles a confessional which Arthur Miller enters as a penitent and from which he emerges as a priest. It is a tricky quick change . . . but it constitutes neither an especially attractive nor especially persuasive performance."

*The New Republic*
"A confessional autobiography of embarrassing explicitness . . . a three and one half hour breach of taste."

*Life*
"He tears from himself a confession that when Maggie, with whom married life had become unbearable, was on the brink of death from an overdose of sleeping pills he felt a wave of gratitude that his ordeal with her was ending."

A screen version of *After the Fall* appeared as an NBC television movie on December 10, 1974, adapted by Miller himself and directed by Gilbert Cates. The lead characters were played by FAYE DUNAWAY (who had a small part in the original stage play) and Christopher Plummer. In the ten years between Broadway debut and television premiere, both MGM and Paramount attempted to make the movie, at various times placing Sophia Loren and BRIGITTE BARDOT in the role of Maggie.

## AGENCIES

In her fifteen years in Hollywood, Marilyn had almost as many agents. These are the people responsible for making sure that Marilyn got noticed:

MODELING:
BLUE BOOK MODELING AGENCY, run by EMMELINE SNIVELY.

MOVIES:
The National Concert Artists Corporation, West Coast Office, (9059 Sunset Boulevard) became Norma Jeane's first movie agents in 1946 after Emmeline Snively contacted her

This early modeling shot of Marilyn was taken by an unknown photographer in 1946.

friend HELEN AINSWORTH and recommended she see this keen young girl. Ainsworth was assisted by HARRY LIPTON.

The William Morris Agency (then at 202 North Canon Drive, Beverly Hills) took Marilyn on in 1949 after top agent JOHNNY HYDE became completely enamored of her. Although Marilyn offically remained on the agency's books for the next four years, Hyde's death in late 1950 led to Marilyn seeking representation elsewhere.

The Famous Artists Agency signed Marilyn two years after CHARLES FELDMAN helped Marilyn negotiate her second contract with TWENTIETH CENTURY-FOX in 1951. Feldman was assisted on the Marilyn account by Hugh French and Jack Gordeen. When Marilyn left Hollywood in 1955 to form her own production company, on the advice of business partner MILTON GREENE, she severed ties with Famous Artists.

MCA, the Music Corporation of America, took over from the Famous Artists Agency to mastermind renegotiation of Marilyn's restrictive 1951 contract with Fox. Marilyn and Milton agreed that the best policy for independent MARILYN MONROE PRODUCTIONS was to draw on agency chief LEW WASSERMAN's contacts to make distribution deals. MCA took a guiding role in Marilyn's film career after she wound up MARILYN MONROE PRODUCTIONS in 1958. George Chasin assisted on the account. Amid some acrimony, MCA ceased to represent Marilyn in the last year of her life, when she instructed attorney Milton Rudin to take over.

## AGING

MARILYN:
"I sit in front of the mirror for hours looking for signs of age. Yet I like old people; they have great qualities younger people don't have. I want to grow old without face-lifts. They take the life out of a face, the character. I want to have the courage to be loyal to the face I've made. Sometimes I think it would be easier to avoid old age, to die young, but then you'd never complete your life, would you? You'd never wholly know yourself."

"Real beauty and femininity are ageless and can't be contrived. Glamour can be manufactured."

"Thirty-six is great when kids twelve to seventeen still whistle."

Marilyn never had the chance to grow old. And yet by the age of thirty-six, time was beginning to take its toll on her body. She tried a number of hormone creams and questionable "youth" injections in her later years in an attempt to delay the effects of aging. She had also taken to wearing gloves to camouflage signs of aging on her hands.

In 1992 *McCall's* magazine published a computerized picture of what Marilyn may have looked like at the age of sixty-six.

## AINSWORTH, HELEN

Recommended by EMMELINE SNIVELY, Norma Jeane was signed by the head of the West Coast branch of the National Artists Corporation, an imposing woman known in the trade as "Cupid" Ainsworth. Norma Jeane signed to this agency on March 11, 1946. Ainsworth, who worked on the account with colleague HARRY LIPTON, arranged the vital introduction to BEN LYON, an executive at the TWENTIETH CENTURY-FOX Studios on Pico Boulevard.

## ALEXANDER, WILLIAM

In 1962 Bill Alexander was owner of The Mart, a designer home furnishings shop in West Hollywood. A few days before her death, Marilyn went with EUNICE MURRAY to the store to buy a wall hanging and a small table. Only when Marilyn wrote out a check did Bill realize who she was. He was so overwhelmed that on the spot her asked her to marry him. Marilyn responded that she would think it over. Although she did not give him her hand in marriage, she did give him an autograph, believed to be the last of her life, on the check she handed over for the merchandise (though she may have signed other checks afterward). At least that's one version of events. In another, Marilyn cryptically informed him that she was very happy because she was about to remarry. William Alexander died in 1997.

## *ALL ABOUT EVE* (1950)

One of the all-time great Hollywood movies, skewering the world of New York theater, with a script as sharp as they come. In 1950 this movie swept all before it, picking up four Academy Awards (including Best Picture) out of a total eleven nominations. Thanks to JOHNNY HYDE, Marilyn rode the triumph.

The role Marilyn plays only required two brief appearances, but her character was important for the way it highlighted the central character of Eve. Studio head DARRYL ZANUCK thought so too, signing her to a long-term contract on the strength of the rushes. Developed out of a short story by Mary Orr ("The Wisdom of Eve"), during production the working title was *Best Performance*. Marilyn's contract, marking a return to Fox, was for $500 for a week's work.

At one point GEORGE SANDERS, playing caustic critic Addison De Witt, appears with Marilyn Monroe on his arm and introduces her as "a graduate of the Copacabana school of acting." Just a few months after *THE ASPHALT JUNGLE*, Marilyn appeared in a minor role alongside a highly-distinguished cast of actors.

One of Marilyn's two scenes was a location shoot at the Curran Theater in San Francisco, the other was a complex party scene shot at the studio. For the hotel sequence Marilyn wore one of her own clinging sweater-dresses which she had already used in *THE FIREBALL* (1950) and *HOMETOWN STORY* (1950). In her other scene she is the epitome of effortless seduction in a strapless white gown.

If he wanted to page Marilyn without causing any fuss, SIDNEY SKOLSKY would use the name of Marilyn's character, "Miss Caswell."

**Nominations:**
ACADEMY AWARDS:
Best Actress: Anne Baxter, Bette Davis
Best Art Direction–Set Decoration, Black and White: George W. Davis, Thomas Little, Walter M. Scott, Lyle R. Wheeler
Best Cinematography, Black and White: Milton R. Krasner
Best Film Editing: Barbara McLean

Best Music, Scoring of a Dramatic or Comedy Picture: Alfred Newman
Best Supporting Actress: Celeste Holm, Thelma Ritter

**Awards:**
ACADEMY AWARDS:
Best Costume Design, Black and White: Edith Head, Charles Le Maire
Best Director: Joseph L. Mankiewicz
Best Picture: Darryl F. Zanuck
Best Supporting Actor: George Sanders
Best Writing, Screenplay: Joseph L. Mankiewicz
Best Sound Recording

GOLDEN GLOBE:
Best Screenplay: Joseph L. Mankiewicz

BRITISH ACADEMY AWARDS:
Best Film from any Source

CANNES:
Best Actress: Bette Davis
Jury Special Prize: Joseph L. Mankiewicz

**Taglines:**
"The most provocative picture of the year!"
"It's all about women... and their men."

**Credits:**
20th Century-Fox, Black and White
Length: 138 minutes
Released: October 14, 1950

Directed by: Joseph L. Mankiewicz
Produced by: Darryl F. Zanuck
Written by: Joseph L. Mankiewicz, Mary Orr (from her story "The Wisdom of Eve")
Cinematography by: Milton R. Krasner
Music by: Franz Liszt (from "Liebestraum"), Alfred Newman
Production Design by: George W. Davis, Lyle R. Wheeler
Costume Design by: Edith Head, Charles Le Maire
Film Editing by: Barbara McLean

**Cast (credits order):**
Bette Davis . . . Margo Channing
Anne Baxter . . . Eve Harrington
George Sanders . . . Addison De Witt
Celeste Holm . . . Karen Richards
Gary Merrill . . . Bill Sampson

In this photo taken on the set of *The Misfits* by Eve Arnold in 1961 it is possible to detect the first signs of aging on Marilyn's face.

Gregory Ratoff, Anne Baxter, Gary Merrill, Celeste Holm, George Sanders and Marilyn (left to right) in *All About Eve* (1950).

A publicity photo of Marilyn for *All About Eve* (1950).

Hugh Marlowe . . . Lloyd Richards
Gregory Ratoff . . . Max Fabian
Barbara Bates . . . Phoebe
Marilyn Monroe . . . Claudia Caswell
Thelma Ritter . . . Birdie
Walter Hampden . . . Aged Actor (Speaker at Dinner)
Randy Stuart . . . Girl
Craig Hill . . . Leading Man
Leland Harris . . . Doorman
Barbara White . . . Autograph Hunter
Eddie Fisher . . . Stage Manager
William Pullen . . . Clerk
Claude Stroud . . . Pianist
Eugene Borden.... Frenchman
Helen Mowery . . . Reporter
Steven Geray . . . Captain of Waiters
Bess Flowers. . . . Well-Wisher

**Crew:**
W. D. Flick . . . sound
Gaston Glass. . . . assistant director
Roger Heman . . . sound
Erich Kästner . . . dialogues in German version
Charles Le Maire . . . wardrobe director
Thomas Little . . . set decorator
Ben Nye . . . makeup
Edward B. Powell . . . orchestration
Walter M. Scott . . . set decorator
Fred Sersen . . . special photographic effects
Lyle R. Wheeler . . . art director

**Plot:**
An ordinary tale of everyday theater folk . . . revolving around cold hard calculation with a touch of ambitious ruthlessness.

Theatrical grande dame Margo Channing (Bette Davis) is perhaps a little beyond the high point of her career, but when she is presented with devoted fan Eve Harrington (Anne Baxter) she decides the girl has had such a hard time she could do with a break, and hires her as her secretary. From this position Eve assiduously studies everything the actress says and does, gradually insinuating herself into the confidences of her theater friends, including drama critic Addison De Witt, the story's original narrative voice, a man of great importance whose "protégé" is aspiring actress Miss Caswell, played by Marilyn Monroe.

Using Margo's wealthy friend Karen (Celeste Holm), who is incidentally married to playwright Lloyd (Hugh Marlowe), Eve obtains the role of understudy to Margo. Karen then makes sure that Eve gets to play the part, by ensuring that there is not enough gas in the car tank for Margo to make it back to town in time for the performance that night. The show and Eve go on to rapturous success, and Eve makes an unsuccessful pass at the play's director (and Margo's long-time boyfriend) Bill Sampson. Next Eve tries to persuade Karen to get her husband to give her the lead in his latest play—blackmailing her with the very help she provided. In the end, Karen's crisis is averted when Margo pulls out of the play to marry Bill.

Eve is not finished. She declares to critic De Witt that she is about to marry Lloyd. De Witt, who knows a thing or two about sleaze, puts her off by letting her know he is aware of her sordid past—a far cry from the story she had told her new friends. Nevertheless, Eve receives the Sarah Siddons Award for her performance in Lloyd's new play. The action ends with young hopeful Phoebe, a woman not unlike the Eve we saw at the beginning of the story, taking delivery of the award statuette which De Witt presents.

**Reviews:**
*The New York Herald Tribune*
"A brilliant writing-directing stint by Joseph L. Mankiewicz has brightened up the autumn screen....As a director, he has spiced every foot of the film with pointed or amusing detail, and he has summoned a round of tip-top performances from Bette Davis, Anne Baxter, George Sanders, Celeste Holm and the others. The result is one of the finest and most mature pictures to emerge from Hollywood or anywhere else in years."

Leo Mishkin
"The wittiest, the most devastating, the most adult and literate motion picture ever made that had any thing to do with the New York stage."

*New York Times*
"A withering satire—witty, mature and worldly-wise . . . the movies are letting Broadway have it with claws out and no holds barred. If Thespis doesn't want to take a beating, he'd better yell for George Kaufman and Moss Hart.

As a matter of fact, Mr Kaufman and Mr Hart might even find themselves outclassed by the dazzling and devastating mockery that is brilliantly packed into this film. For obviously, Mr Mankiewicz, who wrote and directed it, had been sharpening his wits and talents a long, long time for just this go. Obviously, he had been observing the theater and its charming folks for years with something less than an idolater's rosy illusions and zeal. And now, with the excellent assistance of Bette Davis and a truly sterling cast, he is wading into the theater's middle with all claws slashing and settling a lot of scores."

## ALLAN, RUPERT

Marilyn's PRESS aide, a former journalist for *Look* magazine, Allan was both a friend and shrewd publicist. U.S. born and British educated, he knew everybody there was to know in Hollywood and was a great favorite on the social circuit. He was also appreciated for his skills as a publicist, at one time or another representing MARLENE DIETRICH, BETTE DAVIS, GREGORY PECK, and GRACE KELLY.

Allan was a confidant of Marilyn's from 1949, when she met him through her boyfriend, agent JOHNNY HYDE. While West Coast editor of *Look* magazine, he was responsible for Marilyn's first *Look* cover in 1952. Soon after, Allan became Marilyn's official publicist, a job he held until the end of shooting on *THE MISFITS* in 1960, when he accepted an offer too good to refuse: Grace Kelly, with whom he had been good friends in

Hollywood, asked him to come to Monaco and serve as her personal publicist.

(*see* ARTHUR JACOBS)

## ALLEN, ANGELA

Script supervisor on *THE MISFITS* (1961). Angela spent much of her time typing the endless rewrites ARTHUR MILLER composed at the end of every day. Marilyn and Angela did not see eye to eye: Marilyn suspected that there was something between the script girl and her husband, and accused her of as much on set.

Although they did not get along on a personal level, Allen was quite ready to acknowledge Marilyn's prowess on screen. Years later she told biographer FRED LAWRENCE GUILES: "When I saw her up there, it was nearly incredible. The legend, which I thought a kind of joke in questionable taste, suddenly made sense. I could understand why all the fuss had been made. . . . I never came to really like her, but I realized her worth as an actress, her value to any production. . . . What was so amazing about her was the thing she projected on the screen. She seemed so ordinary when doing a scene, and then you go to the rushes and see her up there, so different, like no one else."

## AMAGANSETT, LONG ISLAND

In 1957, while work was being done on the new house in ROXBURY, Marilyn and ARTHUR MILLER rented a house in Amagansett, Long Island, a couple of hours drive from New York City. It was here that Miller wrote the short story that later became *THE MISFITS* (1961).

(*see* HOMES)

## AMBASSADOR HOTEL
3400 WILSHIRE BOULEVARD, LOS ANGELES

This building housed the offices of Marilyn's first agency, the BLUE BOOK MODELING AGENCY run by EMMELINE SNIVELY. Nineteen-year-old Norma Jeane was a regular visitor between 1945 and 1947, until her film career began to take off.

This was not the first time she had come to the hotel. As a little girl her mother Gladys and legal guardian GRACE MCKEE GODDARD sometimes brought her to the hotel for a weekend lunch as a treat. Gladys returned years later to thank Snively.

In 1968, six years after Marilyn's death, ROBERT KENNEDY was assassinated outside the Ambassador as he was leaving a celebration for his success in the California primary.

(*see* HOTELS)

## AMBULANCE

One of the many mysteries surrounding Marilyn's DEATH concerns allegations about an ambulance being called to her home on the night of August 5, 1962.

Some biographers state that a private ambulance answered an anonymous call early on the morning of August 5 and arrived at Marilyn's FIFTH HELENA DRIVE home. The story has been told in several versions: In one, the ambulance, sent out by the Schaefer Ambulance Service, driven by Ken Hunter and colleague Murray Leibowitz, picked up a comatose Marilyn but resuscitated her on the way to SANTA MONICA HOSPITAL. At this point, DR. RALPH GREENSON took over, administered a massive injection, had them take her back home and swore the ambulance men to secrecy.

In May 1986 a man called James E. Hall wrote an article for *Hustler* magazine in which he stated that he had been driving the Schaefer ambulance that night, but that Dr. Greenson prevented them from taking Marilyn away from the house.

One of the many theories surrounding Marilyn's death runs that after Dr. Greenson discovered Marilyn's lifeless body and failed to reach her usual DOCTOR Hyman Engelberg. He then placed a call to the ambulance service, which arrived too late to pump her stomach or revive her. The ambulance crew was then dismissed.

## *AND GOD CREATED WOMAN* (1956)

The film that made BRIGITTE BARDOT an international sensation, directed by Roger Vadim, is all about a beautiful young orphan girl who grows up in a foster family and seeks love wherever she can find it. The most willing accomplices are a succession of men, though in the end 1950s mores prevail as the nubile Bardot arries a respectable young fellow. The plot closely resembles the life of Marilyn Monroe. The sight of Bardot's beautiful tanned young body made this movie a scandal and huge success, and crowned Bardot France's answer to Marilyn.

Twenty years later Vadim attempted to generate a second bolt of lightning with a film of the same name (but different plot).

## ANDES, KEITH

Born in 1920, Andes played Joe Doyle, Marilyn's love interest in *CLASH BY NIGHT* (1952). This actor appeared in around twenty films, and was often on television during the sixties, and starred in his own cop series, *This Man Dawson*.

Keith Andes with Marilyn in *Clash by Night* (1952).

Marilyn meets Lassie at a party at musician Ray Anthony's home in 1952.

## ANIMALS

"I like animals. If you talk to a dog or a cat it doesn't tell you to shut up."

Marilyn always loved and empathized with animals. Throughout her life she had a succession of PETS, and she would be deeply affected if she ever came across an animal suffering or the victim of cruelty.

This sensitivity was evident during her marriage to JAMES DOUGHERTY: when he once came home with a rabbit ready to skin and eat, Norma Jeane refused to touch the animal and was inconsolable for hours. Things were worse when he came home after a hunting trip with a deer that was still alive. Heartbroken, Norma Jeane pleaded with him not to harm the mortally wounded creature, but it was already too late to save its life. One rainy day Norma Jeane reputedly took pity on a neighbor's cow tethered outside the house and tried to bring it into her own house so it could dry off. Dougherty was not amused and prevented this plan from being put into action. On Norma Jeane's very first extended photo shoot in 1946, touring the California desert with Army photographer DAVID CONOVER, she came across an injured terrier and insisted that they take it to a vet.

Stardom did nothing to diminish her sympathy for defenseless creatures. ARTHUR MILLER tells of Marilyn being moved to tears at the sight of a wounded seagull. One day along the beach at Amagansett she ran herself almost to exhaustion, picking up fish—which fishermen had left on the sand because they could not sell them—and throwing them back into the sea.

In the late fifties in New York Marilyn frequently went to Central Park to feed the birds and squirrels. One day she came across some boys who were trapping pigeons. She tried to reason with them, to no avail, and then resorted to a second plan: she bought the birds' freedom. Pigeons were not even her favorite—she once told a friend that she identified far more with the timid sparrows—but she simply could not bear to see violence being done to animals.

Marilyn's love of animals, and indeed abhorrence of killing any living thing, even plants, extended to her literary tastes. She could not abide Hemingway, who glorified the deeds of bullfighters and hunters. Arthur Miller's screenplay for *THE MISFITS* (her character, Roslyn, is appalled to learn that the cowboys who are rounding up wild mustangs intend to sell them for dog food) and his short story entitled "Please Don't Kill Any Thing" touched upon Marilyn's empathy for all living things.

## ANN-MARGRET
(B. 1941, ANN-MARGRET OLSSON)

"She was a very healthy girl when she came on the scene, physically and mentally... people picked on her, she was terribly abused for no reason. She became sick—and posthumously they gave her acclaim."

Discovered by George Burns, Ann-Margret's career began as Marilyn's ended, and she was TWENTIETH CENTURY-FOX's main hope to take over Marilyn's recently vacated position as the nation's number-one bombshell.

Ann-Margret and Marilyn may never have met, but they came very close: the Swedish star visited the set of *THE MISFITS* (1961) while on a tour with a singing group in Reno; apparently Marilyn's exacting eye picked out the pretty young blonde from her trailer. Incidentally, Ann-Margret played at least one of the roles that Marilyn so much wanted, that of Blanche DuBois, in a 1984 TV version of *A STREETCAR NAMED DESIRE*. She also worked with Marilyn's former stand-in, EVELYN MORIARTY. However, she declined the "Marilyn" role in the screen version of ARTHUR MILLER's play *AFTER THE FALL*.

## *ANNA CHRISTIE*

After almost a year at the ACTORS STUDIO, on February 17, 1956 Marilyn finally took the plunge and went on stage in front of class. Her role: Anna Christie, the title character in Eugene O'Neill's play, described in the play notes as "a blond, fully developed girl of twenty, handsome but now run down in health and painfully showing all the outward evidences of belonging to the world's oldest profession," who falls in love with a young sailor. This role was more than demanding—it had been practically immortalized by GRETA GARBO in the 1930 Hollywood movie, in which she uttered her first words in a talkie: "Gimme a whisky—ginger ale on the side—and don't be stingy, baby." Marilyn reprised this scene opposite MAUREEN STAPLETON, an affirmed Broadway actress who had starred in the TENNESSEE WILLIAMS play *The Rose Tattoo*.

Marilyn was petrified before going on stage: "I couldn't feel anything. I couldn't remember one line. All I wanted to do was lie down and die. I was in these impossible circumstances and I suddenly thought to myself, 'Good God, what am I doing here?' Then I just had to go out and do it." Marilyn's performance elicited a heartfelt round of applause—a rarity at the Actors Studio, where the students were actually told not to clap. Ever the perfectionist, after the scene Marilyn broke down in tears at how wretched she had been, and remained tearful for the rest of the day. Later that evening Lee and Paula told her she was a great new talent.

## ANNIVERSARIES

Marilyn's wedding anniversaries:
JAMES DOUGHERTY: June 19
JOE DIMAGGIO: January 14
ARTHUR MILLER: June 29 (civil ceremony), July 1 (Jewish ceremony)

## ANTHONY, RAY

Big band leader Ray Anthony recorded a SONG, "Marilyn," in 1952, written by Ervin Drake and Jimmy Shirl. Marilyn attended a party thrown by her studio at bandleader Anthony's home in late 1952, at which, coached by MICKEY ROONEY, Marilyn played the drums.

## *APPLES, KNOCKERS AND COKES*

Also known as *Apples, Knockers and the Coke Bottle*, this is an X-rated film that has been falsely attributed to the young Marilyn. In the film the actress—in fact, the buxom 1954 *Playboy* playmate ARLINE HUNTER—suggestively removes her clothes, rolls an apple around her breasts, and then provocatively sips from a Coke bottle.

## ARBOL STREET

The only period of any length—almost a year—in which Norma Jeane lived with her mother GLADYS BAKER was in a three-bedroom house at 6812 Arbol Street, not far from the Hollywood Bowl. In order to afford the house, Gladys rented it out to actor GEORGE ATKINSON and his wife and daughter (according to FRED LAWRENCE GUILES; other biographers leave this family unnamed), keeping one or two rooms (biographers disagree) for herself and her daughter. According to Guiles, the couple worked as extras in Hollywood, with the husband working as stand-in to English actor George Arliss. It was from this house that Gladys was taken into institutional care in early 1934. The English couple continued to look after little Norma Jeane even after the house was repossessed, but when they decided to return to England, GRACE MCKEE GODDARD took over.

The house itself was demolished during expansion of the Hollywood Bowl gardens, and the street is now called Arbol Drive.

(*see* HOMES)

## ARCHWOOD STREET

Norma Jeane lived at two addresses along this Van Nuys street.

First, in 1940 and 1941, she lived with GRACE GODDARD and husband Doc at number 14743. It was here that guardian Grace hatched the plan for Norma Jeane to marry the boy next door, JAMES DOUGHERTY. The newlyweds moved into a one-bedroom apartment on nearby Vista Del Monte Street, but returned to the Dougherty family home in the summer of 1942 (1943 in some accounts) at 14747 Archwood Street, briefly house-sitting the three bedroom premises while Jim Dougherty's parents were away. The house was recently put up for rent at $900 per month.

(*see* HOMES)

## ARMY

Norma Jeane got her first break thanks to Army Air Corps photographer DAVID CONOVER, on a 1945 mission to the RADIO PLANE MUNITIONS FACTORY to find morale-boosting women at work for the war effort. His photos appeared in *Yank* magazine.

Marilyn had a huge following in the military, picking up numerous awards from soldiers' magazines ("Miss Cheesecake of the Year") and from individual corps ("The Girl Most Likely to Thaw Alaska," "The Girl They Would Most Like to Intercept," and many more unprintable private accolades.)

In September 1952 Marilyn was asked for a repeat performance by another army photographer, this time with uniformed service women, as part of a campaign to encourage more women to join the U.S. armed forces. Wearing a white summer dress with red polka dots, Marilyn was photographed leaning forward over a balcony, showing so much well-developed womanhood that almost as soon as the picture was distributed, an army official canceled the campaign and withdrew the pic-

Marilyn singing to troops in Korea, 1954.

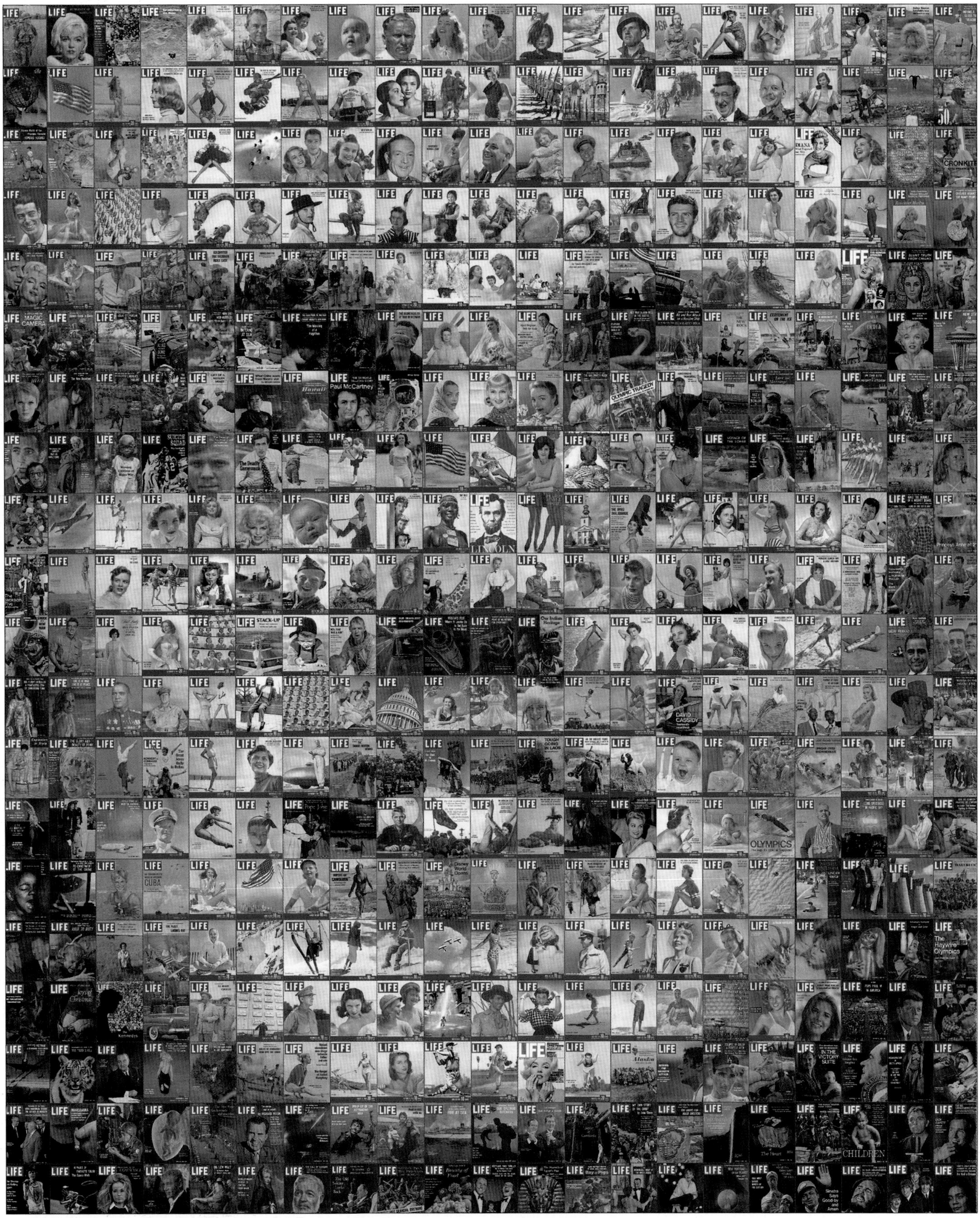

Robert Silvers's photomosaic of Marilyn Monroe for the cover of the June 1996 issue of *Life* magazine.

ture. With some embarrassment he stated, "This picture might give parents of potential women recruits a wrong conception." Marilyn countered, "That dress I wore was designed for eye-level—not for photographers who stand on a balcony and shoot downward."

Earlier that same year Marilyn had performed before the marines at CAMP PENDLETON, south of Los Angeles, and then in early 1954, soon after her marriage to JOE DIMAGGIO, she made a triumphant tour of U.S. troops stationed in KOREA.

## ARNOLD, EVE

Arnold first worked with Marilyn in 1952, and had her last photo session with Marilyn not long before her death. They developed a friendship which spanned the years of her stardom, and Marilyn invited Eve Arnold along on some of her engagements, including her 1955 trip to BEMENT, ILLINOIS. Arnold was one of the MAGNUM agency photographers who worked on the set of *THE MISFITS* (1961). It was Arnold who Marilyn initially invited to accompany her to MADISON SQUARE GARDEN for her serenade of President KENNEDY. When Arnold couldn't make it, Marilyn called Isidore Miller instead.

In her warm 1987 book *Marilyn Monroe: An Appreciation*, Arnold detailed their personal and professional relationship, stating: "I never knew anyone who even came close to Marilyn in natural ability to use both photographer and still camera . . . she has remained the measuring rod by which I have—unconsciously—judged other subjects."

## ART

For a woman known as inspiration for art—De Kooning, ANDY WARHOL, Claes Oldenburg and Salvador Dali are the most famous of the thousands of artists to have depicted Marilyn in every artistic medium—Marilyn had a strong interest in art. She attended an art appreciation class at UCLA in 1951, by which time she already had reproductions of works by Fra Angelico, Dürer, and Botticelli hanging on the walls. These replaced earlier Titian School illustrations she had taken from a sixteenth-century treatise on human anatomy.

In 1955 she told reporters her favorite artists were Goya, Picasso, and El Greco. That same year she went with NORMAN ROSTEN to a Rodin exhibition in New York, where she was particularly moved by his sculptures *The Hand of God* and *Pygmalion and Galatea*. In the last year of her life Marilyn bought a Rodin statue for her Brentwood home.

Marilyn once gave an original Chagall sketch as a birthday gift to SUSAN STRASBERG. Strasberg writes of handing Marilyn a sketch pad and watching as Marilyn quickly and economically made a self-portrait "depicting a feline sensual grace and movement."

A Warhol silk screen print, *Orange Marilyn*, was bought by an anonymous buyer for $17.3 million at auction in May 1998, three times its expected price and four times the previous highest price for a Warhol, also paid for another Marilyn inspired item.

Marilyn is also a favorite subject for thousands of amateur artists, and artists working with new techniques, technologies and media. One such work, a photomosaic by Robert Silvers, was featured recently on the cover of *Life* MAGAZINE.

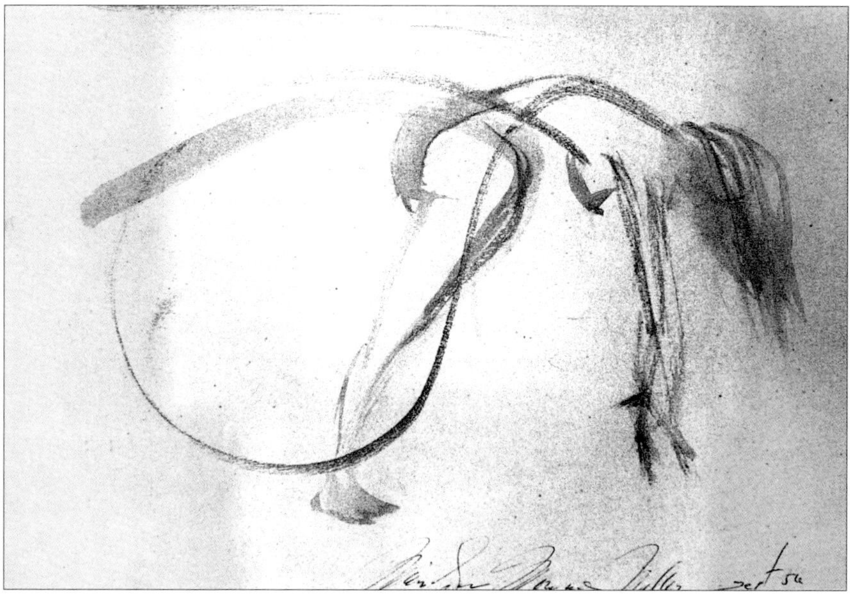

A self-portrait by Marilyn Monroe, ca. 1957.

BOOKS:

*Marilyn in Art*, compiled by Roger C. Taylor. NH: Salem House, 1984.

A comprehensive survey of the artists who have drawn, painted, sculpted, and etched Marilyn.

*Elvis + Marilyn: 2 x Immortal*, Geri DePaoli ed. New York: Rizzoli International, 1994.

Catalog to an art exhibition documenting the lives of the two biggest American cultural icons of this century.

## *ART AND MRS. BOTTLE*

Schoolgirl love and not a higher calling attracted Norma Jeane Baker to the world of theater, in the form of this play at Van Nuys High School. She auditioned but didn't get a part. Years later she told biographer MAURICE ZOLOTOW, "I wanted to be in it because a boy I had a crush on, Warren Peek, was playing the lead."

## ARTHRITIS AND RHEUMATISM FOUNDATION

In 1955 Marilyn made an appearance at MADISON SQUARE GARDEN perched on a pink elephant, during a benefit evening organized by the Mike Todd Circus for this charitable foundation.

## ARTICHOKES

Perhaps not the first thing Marilyn conjures up in most people's minds, but the edible thistle provided one small step on Marilyn's starlet route to fame. On February 20, 1948 Marilyn was crowned California Artichoke Queen of Salinas, California, an area renowned for its artichokes. To mark the fiftieth anniversary of this event, in 1998 the City of Hollywood officially declared February 20th "California Artichoke Day," and Chasen's, one of Marilyn's favorite Los Angeles RESTAURANTS, created a special artichoke-based dish called *The Monroe*. Head chef Andreas Kisler explained: "*The Monroe* is a tribute to Marilyn.... Sliced artichoke shaped like a star. In the center there are soba noodles representing Marilyn's blonde hair, and on the sides there are shrimp, which with a little imagination resemble Marilyn's shapely legs."

## *AS YOUNG AS YOU FEEL* (1951)
(ORIGINAL TITLE: *Will You Love Me in December?*)

Although she had a minor and unremarkable part as a secretary in this film, Marilyn received above-the-title billing to capitalize on her rising success. However, Marilyn's spirits were very low at this time; mentor JOHNNY HYDE, responsible for Marilyn's return to Fox, had only recently died. First time director Harmon Jones was worried: "Every time I need her, she's crying. It puffs up her eyes!"

During this production Marilyn had a romance with director ELIA KAZAN, who had come to the set specifically to meet her. More importantly, she met a friend of his on a trip from New York, writer ARTHUR MILLER.

**Credits:**
20th Century-Fox, Black and White
Length: 77 minutes
Release date: August 2, 1951

Directed by: Harmon Jones
Produced by: Lamar Trotti
Written by: Lamar Trotti, from an original story by Paddy Chayefsky
Cinematography by: Joseph MacDonald
Music by: Cyril J. Mockridge
Film Editing by: Robert E. Simpson

**Cast (credits order):**
Monty Woolley . . . John Hodges
Thelma Ritter . . . Della Hughes
David Wayne . . . Joe Elliott
Jean Peters. . . . Alice Hodges
Constance Bennett . . . Lucille McKinley
Marilyn Monroe . . . Harriet
Allyn Joslyn . . . George Hodges

This photograph was taken by Eve Arnold on the set of *The Misfits* (1961).

Marilyn and Albert Dekker in *As Young as You Feel* (1951).

Marilyn and Wallace Brown in *As Young as You Feel* (1951).

Albert Dekker . . . Louis McKinley
Clinton Sundberg . . . Frank Erickson
Minor Watson . . . Cleveland
Ludwig Stössel . . . Conductor
Renie Riano . . . Harpist
Wally Brown . . . Gallagher
Russ Tamblyn . . . Willie
Don Beddoe . . . Head of Sales
Helen Brown . . . Clancy
Paul E. Burns . . . Printer
Charles Cane . . . Rogell
Harry Cheshire . . . President, Chamber of Commerce
David Clarke . . . Chauffeur
Dick Cogan . . . Benson
Charles J. Conrad . . . Information Clerk
Robert Dudley . . . Old Man
Raymond Greenleaf . . . Vice President
James Griffith . . . Cashier
Billy Lechner . . . Mailboy
Harry McKim . . . Page Boy
Roger Moore . . . Saltonstall
Renie Riano . . . Harpist
Carol Savage . . . Librarian
Harry Shannon . . . Kleinbaum
Gerald Oliver Smith . . . Butler
Houseley Stevenson . . . Old Man
Emerson Treacy . . . Director, Public Relations
Ann Tyrrell . . . Secretary
Frank Wilcox . . . Lawyer

**Crew:**
Maurice Ransford . . . art director
Lyle R. Wheeler . . . art director
Thomas Little . . . set decoration
Bruce MacDonald . . . set decoration
Renié . . . costume design
Ben Nye . . . makeup
W. D. Flick . . . sound
Roger Heman Sr. . . . sound
Maurice De Packh . . . orchestrator
Charles Le Maire . . . wardrobe director
Lionel Newman . . . musical director
Fred Sersen . . . special photographic effects

**Plot:**
A moral tale in which we learn that age is no barrier to business performance.

On reaching sixty-five, John Hodges (Monty Woolley) has to step down from his job at the Acme Printing Services because of a compulsory retirement policy of parent company Consolidated Motors. On the advice of his daughter's fiancé Joe Elliott (David Wayne) who also works at the company, he writes a letter to the president, a man called Cleveland who is something of a recluse.

It's all part of a plan that involves him posing as the president and arranging a surprise visit to Acme that puts the Acme boss Louis McKinley (Albert Dekker) in a complete panic, regardless of his beautiful secretary Harriet (Marilyn, in her first role during her second spell with Fox).

Hodges' plan works rather too well—not only does he instigate a new policy whereby retirees can keep their jobs as long as they want, but his former boss's wife Lucille (Constance Bennett) falls in love with him. That's before things start to unravel: his speech causes the company's stock to rise, he is unmasked as an imposter, the real Cleveland (Minor Watson) seeks him out, and so does Lucille. McKinley arrives at the Hodges house to reclaim his wife, in the process berating the real Cleveland (who he has never met). McKinley faints when his wife lets him know of the horrible mistake he has just made. Cleveland offers Hodges a high powered job with the parent company, but all Hodges wants is his old job back. And so it all ends happily ever after.

**Reviews:**
*New York Post*
"It is an uncommonly pleasing picture if no critical solvents are applied to it. Being short on probability and long on popular laugh devices of plot and character, it can be recommended highly to most of the people most of the time."

*The New York Times*
"This unpretentious little picture, which Lamar Trotti has written and produced and which Harmon Jones has directed in a deliciously nimble comic style, is a vastly superior entertainment so far as ingenuity and taste are concerned, and it certainly confronts its audience on a much more appropriately adult plane. . . . Albert Dekker is mighty amusing as a fatheaded small-business boss, Marilyn Monroe is superb as his secretary..."

## ASPHALT JUNGLE, THE (1950)

JOHNNY HYDE lobbied hard to get Marilyn a break in this landmark caper movie, celebrated among other things for being the first ever told from the criminal's point of view. Written and directed by JOHN HUSTON, *The Asphalt Jungle* received great critical acclaim and four Academy Award nominations.

Hyde was right to insist: the role was made for Marilyn. In the novel on which the movie was based, author W. R. Burnett describes the Angela Phinlay character as "voluptuously made; and there was something about her walk—something lazy, careless and insolently assured—that was impossible to ignore." Marilyn acquitted herself admirably in her three brief scenes, bringing poise and confidence to the role of the carnal yet girlishly vulnerable mistress. In her final scene, shot in only two takes, she runs through a gamut of emotions as her loyalty unravels under police interrogation, causing the film's tragic denouement.

Marilyn always considered this to be one of her finest performances, and it was certainly the first of which she felt she could be proud. After the wrap on her last scene, she said to drama coach NATASHA LYTESS, "I don't know what I did, but I do know it felt wonderful."

The behind-the-scenes networking of smitten agent Hyde was in fact just one of the reasons why Marilyn landed the role of Angela Phinlay. There are several stories about exactly how it all happened over the two auditions it took. One story runs that at the first call Marilyn turned up in a padded bra. John Houston is reputed to have reached into her sweater, pulled out the falsies and said, "You've got the part, Marilyn." In Huston's own autobiography he states, "Marilyn didn't get the part because of Johnny Hyde. She got it because she was damned good."

This, however, is most probably apocryphal, and it certainly clashes with Marilyn's recollection a few years later of her second performance before the renowned director:

> "When I first read for him I was so scared I shook. I'd studied my lines all night but when

I came in to read I just couldn't relax. He asked me to sit down but there were only straight-backed chairs all around the room so I asked him if I could sit on the floor—just to get comfortable. But I was still nervous so I asked if I could take off my shoes. 'Anything, anything,' he said. Then I read for him—and I was sure I was awful—but before I had a chance to say anything he kind of smiled and said I had the part, all right. Then he said I'd probably turn into a very good actress—which is really what I want to be."

At least one biographer, however, considers that Marilyn got the part not because of her audition and not because of Hyde's solicitation, but because Huston was subjected to a piece of "friendly" blackmail. Huston, a keen horseman, had been stabling his horses on a ranch belonging to JOHN CARROLL and LUCILLE RYMAN, who the year before had helped struggling starlet Marilyn financially and with contacts. As Huston had fallen seriously in arrears with his payments, Ryman threatened to sell his stallions to liquidate the debt . . . unless he gave Marilyn the part.

First husband JAMES DOUGHERTY got a close look at how far his wife had come after leaving him, when he was posted with fellow police officers to restrain fans outside the theater where *The Asphalt Jungle* premiered.

MEMORABLE COSTUME:
Off-the-shoulder black cocktail dress

**Nominations:**
ACADEMY AWARDS:
Best Cinematography, Black and White: Harold Rosson
Best Director: John Huston
Best Supporting Actor: Sam Jaffe
Best Writing, Screenplay: John Huston, Ben Maddow
BRITISH ACADEMY AWARDS:
Best Film from any Source

**Awards:**
VENICE FILM FESTIVAL:
Best Actor: Sam Jaffe

**Credits:**
MGM, Black and White
Length: 112 minutes
Release date: May 23, 1950

Directed by: John Huston
Produced by: Arthur Hornblow Jr.
Written by: John Huston and Ben Maddow, from a novel by W. R. Burnett
Cinematography by: Harold Rosson
Music by: HaroFilm
Editing by: George Boemler

**Cast** (credits order):
Sterling Hayden . . . Dix Handley
Louis Calhern . . . Alonzo D. Emmerich
Jean Hagen . . . Doll Conovan
James Whitmore . . . Gus Minissi
Sam Jaffe . . . Doc Riedenschneider
John McIntire . . . Police Commissioner Hardy
Marc Lawrence . . . "Cobby" Cobb
Barry Kelley . . . Lt. Ditrich
Anthony Caruso . . . Louis Ciavelli
Teresa Celli . . . Maria Ciavelli
Marilyn Monroe . . . Angela Phinlay
William B. Davis . . . Timmons
Dorothy Tree . . . May Emmerich
Brad Dexter . . . Bob Brannom
John Maxwell . . . Dr. Swanson
Benny Burt . . . Driver
Frank Cady . . . Night Clerk
Jean Carter . . . Woman
John Cliff . . . Policeman
Henry Corden . . . William Doldy
Charles Courtney . . . Red
Ralph Dunn . . . Policeman
Pat Flaherty . . . Policeman
Alex Gerry . . . Maxwell
Sol Gorss . . . Policeman
Fred Graham . . . Truck Driver
Don Haggerty . . . Detective Andrews
Eloise Hardt . . . Vivian
Thomas Browne Henry . . . James X. Connery
David Hydes . . . Evans
Fred Marlow . . . Reporter
Strother Martin . . . Karl Anton Smith
Patricia Miller . . . Girl
Howard Mitchell . . . Secretary
Alberto Morin . . . Eddie Donato
Kerry O'Day . . . Girl
Raymond Roe . . . Tallboy
Henry Rowland . . . Frank Schurz
Tim Ryan . . . Jack; Police Clerk
James Seay . . . Officer Janocek
Jack Shea . . . Policeman
Joseph Darr Smith . . . Reporter
Helene Stanley . . . Jeannie
Ray Teal . . . Policeman
Leah Wakefield . . . Girl
William Washington . . . Suspect
Constance Weiler . . . Woman
Judith Wood . . . Woman
Wilson Wood . . . Man

**Crew:**
Jack Dawn . . . makeup
Randall Duell . . . art director
Cedric Gibbons . . . art director
Sydney Guilaroff . . . hairstyles
Jack D. Moore . . . set decorator
Douglas Shearer . . . sound
Edwin B. Willis . . . set decorator

REMADE AS: *Cool Breeze* (1972)

**Plot:**
A meticulously planned heist goes wrong because of dishonor and double-crossing among thieves.

Veteran thief Doc Riedenschneider (Sam Jaffe) may be just out of jail, but he is itching to heist a jewelry store with a gang of hand-picked men, in an operation financed by a bookie named Cobby (Marc Lawrence). The plan is to off-load the hot property to a man above suspicion, society lawyer Alonzo D. Emmerich (Louis Calhern), who is ideally placed to fence the jewels. Aided by his mistress Angela Phinlay (Marilyn Monroe) whom he coyly refers to as his niece—such was the convention of the day—he is planning a double cross.

The robbery goes like clockwork until the

A French poster for *The Asphalt Jungle* (1950).

Marilyn and Sterling Hayden in *The Asphalt Jungle* (1950).

central alarm is tripped. A watchman's gun is knocked to the floor, it fires and one of the robbers is hit. At Emmerich's place Doc realizes that the lawyer is playing false when he claims not to have the money for the jewels; a tussle ensues and Emmerich's henchman is killed. The body of the dead robber makes it a cinch for the police to round up the others. In this consummately executed moral tale, none of the plotters comes out well . . . except Angela, who decides to come clean and precipitates the arrest of her sugar daddy.

**Reviews:**
*The New York Times*
"Louis Calhern as the big lawyer who tries to pull a double cross and muffs it is exceptionally fluid and adroit, and Sterling Hayden is sure-fire as a brazen hoodlum who just wants to go back home. . . . But, then, everyone in the picture—which was produced, incidentally, by MGM—gives an unimpeachable performance. If only it all weren't so corrupt."

*Photoplay*
"This brutally frank story of crime and punishment in a Midwestern city . . . packed with stand-out performances. . . . There's a beautiful blonde, too, name of Marilyn Monroe, who plays Calhern's girlfriend, and makes the most of her footage."

*New York Herald Tribune*
"It is a violent exhibition, dedicated to sluggings and large-scale jewel robberies, but Huston has made it a taut and engrossing melodrama.... Sterling Hayden is excellent in the part of the fast shooting Dix. . . . Incidentally, Jean Hagen is very good as the Doll who gets mixed up in a major robbery, James Whitmore gives a good account of himself as the sidekick of Dix and John McIntire, Marilyn Monroe and Anthony Caruso lend a documentary effect to a lurid exposition."

*New York Post*
"This picture has the authority of a blow in your solar plexus. It leaves you physically tired with sheer tension, participation and belief. It is the crime picture of this decade, and it may be the best one ever made."

## ASTROLOGY

"I was born under the sign of Gemini. That stands for intellect."

Marilyn summed up her star sign as "Jekyll and Hyde. Two in one."

Astrologer Carroll Righter once asked Marilyn if she knew she shared her sign of Gemini with Rosalind Russell, JUDY GARLAND, and Rosemary Clooney. Marilyn retorted, "I know nothing of these people. I was born under the same sign as Ralph Waldo Emerson, Queen Victoria and Walt Whitman."

Marilyn was born at 9:30 A.M. on June 1, 1926 in Los Angeles, California, at location 34' 04" North and 118' 15" West, with the sun in Gemini and the moon in Aquarius. Her rising sign was Leo.

## ATKINSON, GEORGE

English actor who, with his wife and daughter, lived in the same Arbol Street house as Norma Jeane and her mother from 1933—according to biographer FRED LAWRENCE GUILES. The whole family acted, though their fortunes were mixed: he had landed a few small roles in George Arliss productions (as well have serving as a stand-in), his wife was an extra in crowd scenes, and his daughter occasionally worked as a stand-in for Madeleine Carroll. After GLADYS BAKER was taken into an institution, the Atkinsons looked after little Norma Jeane for a while, until they decided to move back to Britain.

## AUSTRALIA

An entrepreneur named Lee Gordon offered

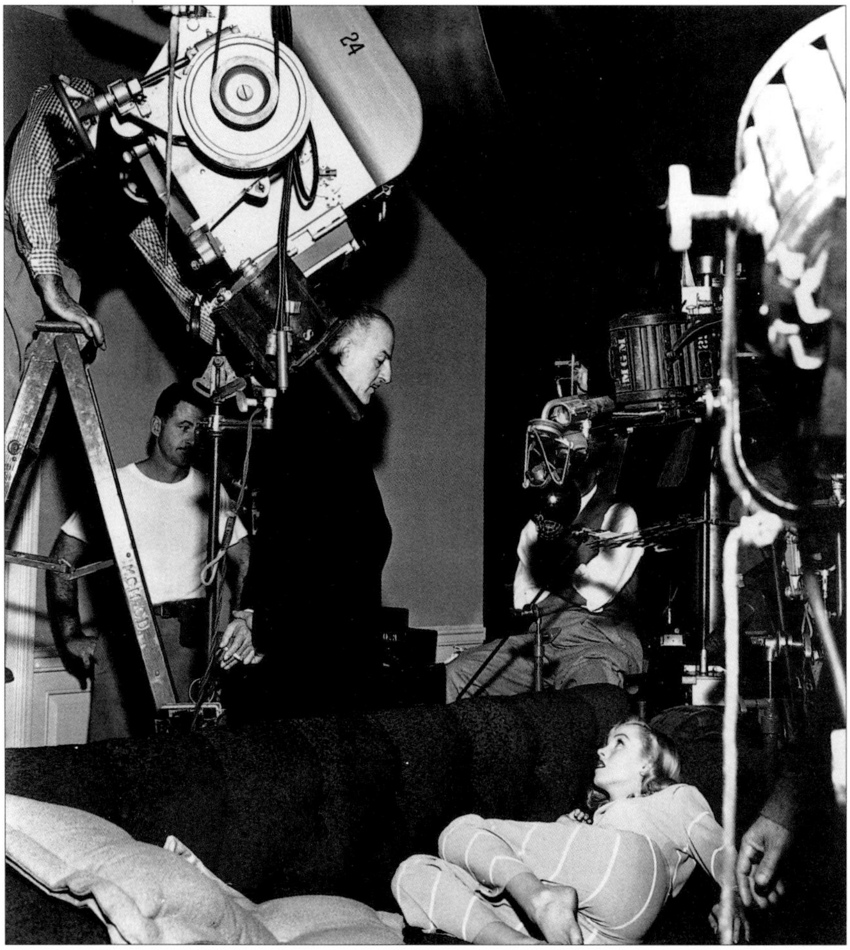

Marilyn and Louis Calhern on the set of *The Asphalt Jungle* (1950).

A close-up of Marilyn on the set of *How to Marry a Millionaire* (1953).

Marilyn $200,000 for a twenty-five day tour of Australia in 1955. Marilyn, then living in New York, was too focused on setting up her own production company and exploring her acting potential with LEE STRASBERG and the ACTORS STUDIO to accept.

## AVEDON, RICHARD

After the strains and rigors of working on *SOME LIKE IT HOT* (1959), Marilyn was relieved to get back to the still camera. Avedon shot a sequence of Marilyn posing as film stars MARLENE DIETRICH, Lillian Russell, JEAN HARLOW, Theda Bara, and Clara Bow, for a feature first published in *LIFE* on December 22, 1958. Avedon found her easy to work with: "She gave more to the still camera than any actress—any woman—I've ever photographed; infinitely more patient, more demanding of herself and more comfortable in front of the camera than away from it."

In ARTHUR MILLER's accompanying text, he wrote about "the spontaneous joy she takes in anything a child does, her quick sympathy and respect for old people. . . . The child in her catches the fun and the promise, and the old person in her the mortality."

Two years later Marilyn told SIMONE SIGNORET that this photo session was one of the greatest moments of her career; this was a typical Monroe performance, changing herself for the camera not into her own persona, but into that of film goddesses who had come before. In her autobiography Signoret says, "She talked about these photography sessions the way other actors talk about their films. She seemed to have no other happy professional memories."

## AWARDS

Marilyn may not have ever picked up an Oscar, but her many talents were recognized in a variety of ways during her lifetime.

During her SCHOOL days, Norma Jeane won a fountain pen for her essay "Dog, Man's Best Friend." She also received a certificate "in recognition of the personal service rendered by her as a member of the School Safety Committee" at the Sawtelle Boulevard School.

Working for the war effort at the RADIO PLANE MUNITIONS FACTORY in 1945, Norma Jeane Dougherty, won an "E" certificate for excellence.
"Miss Press Club" 1948, from the Los Angeles Press Club
"Miss Cheesecake of the Year," 1951 *Stars and Stripes*
"The Present All GIs Would Like To Find in Their Christmas Stocking," 1951
"The Best Young Box Office Personality," 1951 Henrietta Awards
"The Girl Most Likely to Thaw Alaska," Soldiers posted to the Aleutians
"The Girl Most Wanted to Examine," the 7th Division Medical Corps
"The Girl They Would Most Like to Intercept," the All Weather Fighter Squadron 3, San Diego
"Cheesecake Queen of 1952," *Stars and Stripes*
"Most Promising Female Newcomer," 1952 *Look* MAGAZINE Achievement Awards
"The Most Advertised Girl in the World," February 1953, Advertising Association of the West
"Fastest Rising Star of 1952," PHOTOPLAY Magazine Awards, March 9, 1953
"Best Young Box Office Personality," Spring, 1953, *Redbook* magazine
"The Best Friend a Diamond Ever Had," July 1953, the Jewelry Academy
"Female World Film Favorite 1953," March 1954 Golden Globe Awards
"Best Actress," March, 1954 *Photoplay* Magazine awards for *GENTLEMEN PREFER BLONDES* and *HOW TO MARRY A MILLIONAIRE*
"The Thank-God Award: To Marilyn Monroe, who in a sweeping public service has made no movies this year," 1958, *Harvard Lampoon*
Nomination for 1956 British Academy Award, "Best Foreign Actress," for *THE SEVEN YEAR ITCH*
Nomination for 1958 British Academy Award, "Best Foreign Actress," for *THE PRINCE AND THE SHOWGIRL*
"Best Foreign Actress of 1958," 1959, DAVID DI DONATELLO Prize (Italian equivalent of the Oscar), for *The Prince and the Showgirl*
"Best Foreign Actress," March 1959, CRYSTAL STAR AWARD (French equivalent of the Oscar) for *The Prince and the Showgirl*
"1959 Best Actress in a Comedy," March 8, 1960 GOLDEN GLOBE AWARDS, for *SOME LIKE IT HOT*
"Female World Film Favorite 1961," March 1962 Golden Globe Awards

*Some Like It Hot* and *All About Eve* scored positions fourteen and sixteen respectively in the American Film Institute's 1998 list of America's 100 Greatest Movies. In June 1999

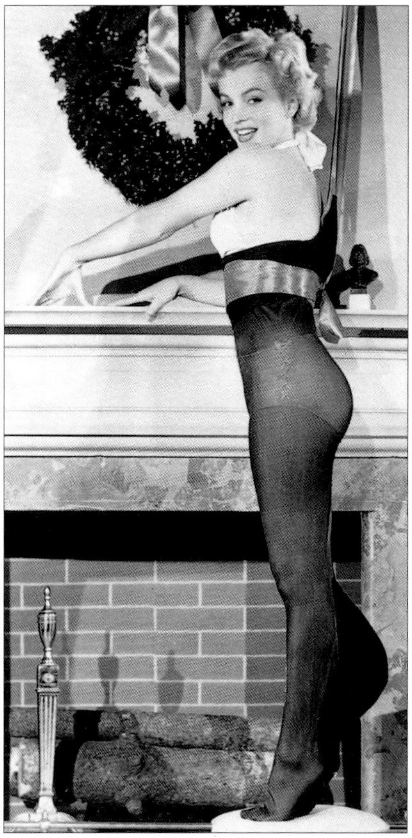

Marilyn as "The Present All GIs Would Like To Find in Their Christmas Stocking," 1951.

Marilyn with her Henrietta Award for "Best Young Box Office Personality," 1951.

Marilyn came sixth in the American Film Institute's list of the top twenty-five female stars of all time.

Since her death, Marilyn continues to top lists and polls of sex symbols. Sporadic suggestions that she should be awarded a posthumous Academy Award continue to fall on deaf ears.

## AXELROD, GEORGE (B. 1922)

After a showbiz debut as an actor and stage manager, George Axelrod became a successful Broadway comedy writer. Hollywood called, and after his first film, *Phffft*, he adapted his Broadway hit *THE SEVEN YEAR ITCH* for Marilyn in 1954. Two years later he wrote the screen version of WILLIAM INGE's Broadway play *BUS STOP*, a movie many believe is Marilyn's finest dramatic performance. *Bus Stop* director JOSHUA LOGAN said Axelrod wrote the adaptation "expressly for her, and let the entire story be guided by his feelings for her. . . . The girl was half Inge and half Monroe."

If Marilyn had been the kind of person to bear a grudge, she may not even have worked with Axelrod. After *The Seven Year Itch* he set to work on his 1955 farce *WILL SUCCESS SPOIL ROCK HUNTER?*, a tongue-in-cheek take on a screen siren called Rita Marlowe whose life was a carbon copy of Marilyn's—recently divorced from a legendary sportsman, launching her own production company, and making proclamations of how important acting was to her. On Broadway the play was a big hit, notching up 444 performances for JAYNE MANSFIELD in the lead role, who reprised this success in the 1957 film version.

Before her death, Fox was lining Marilyn up to star in a screen version of another Axelrod stage hit, *Goodbye Charlie*, which was eventually directed by Vincente Minelli and released in 1964.

Axelrod's writing credits include *Breakfast at Tiffany's* and *The Manchurian Candidate*. In the mid-sixties he began to direct as well as write. He also penned some searing memoirs of Hollywood and Broadway life.

# B

## Babysitting

In her first star vehicle, *Don't Bother to Knock* (1952), Marilyn was the babysitter from hell, attacking the little girl she was looking after in a fit of madness. Oddly enough, when Marilyn was first signed to Twentieth Century-Fox, the publicity department invented a story of how she had been "discovered" when babysitting for a Hollywood talent agent.

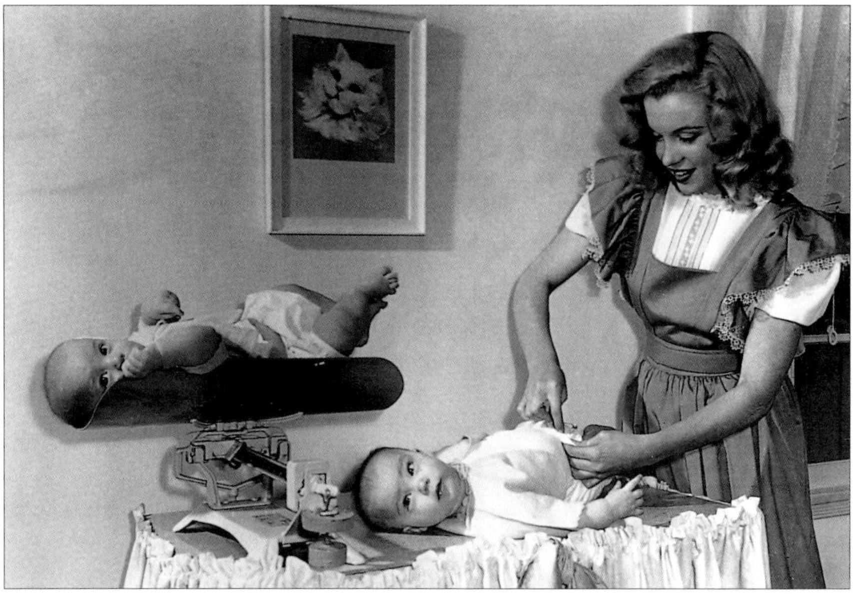

This publicity photo was intended to promote Twentieth-Century Fox's story that Marilyn had been "discovered" when she showed up to babysit for a casting director.

## Bacall, Lauren
(b. 1924, Betty Jean Perske)

"Slinky, sultry, sensational!" said the studio. Bacall found rapid success at a young age, opposite Humphrey Bogart in *To Have and Have Not* (1944). Dubbed simply "The Look" by Warners Brothers, Bacall put in a performance that was enough to win plaudits and her older co-star's hand in marriage. Like Marilyn, Bacall's childhood included escapes to the movies—she would skip lessons to go and watch screen favorite Bette Davis. Also like Marilyn, she had a devil of a time getting parts she wanted to do; she was suspended by her studio no less than twelve times. Bacall's movies include *The Big Sleep* (1946), *Key Largo* (1948), *Young Man with a Horn* (1950), *Written on the Wind* (1956), *Sex and Single Girl* (1964), *Harper* (1966), *Murder on the Orient Express* (1974), and *Ready to Wear* (1994).

In 1953 Bacall was one of the three husband hunters in *How to Marry a Millionaire*, competing with Marilyn and Betty Grable. Like many people who worked with Marilyn, she found the experience at times frustrating. In her 1979 biography *By Myself*, she wrote: "During our scenes she'd look at my forehead instead of my eyes; at the end of a take, [she'd] look to her coach, standing behind Jean Negulesco, for approval. If the headshake was no, she'd insist on another take. A scene often went to fifteen or more takes, which meant I'd have to be good in all of them as no one knew which one would be used."

These frustrations, however, did not prevent her from being won over: "I couldn't dislike Marilyn. She had no meanness in her—no bitchery. She just had to concentrate on herself and the people who were there only for her."

On set for *How To Marry a Millionaire* Marilyn apparently told her co-star that all she wanted "was to be in San Francisco with Joe DiMaggio in some spaghetti joint."

## Bachrach, Ernest

Gloria Swanson's favorite studio photographer, Bachrach was chief portrait photographer at RKO when Marilyn was shooting *Clash by Night* (1952).

Lauren Bacall, Humphrey Bogart, and Marilyn at the premiere of *How to Marry a Millionaire* (1953).

## Bacon, James

Bacon was a Hollywood journalist and author who wrote about an early affair with Marilyn in his 1977 article "The Night I Made It with Marilyn Monroe." In it, he describes how they met at a Hollywood party in 1948, after which then she invited him back to her home at the time, Joseph Schenck's pool house. Their affair lasted two years: "I knew she was promiscuous in those early days. She admitted it helped, and I had no illusion she was after me for me. She liked me, sure, but she was also after all the newspapers my syndicated column appeared in." Bacon was also responsible for some memorable quotes about the effect Marilyn had when she dressed to impress (*see* Clothes, 1953).

## Baker, Carroll (b. 1931)

Elia Kazan overlooked Marilyn for fellow Actors Studio colleague Carroll Baker in the role of the young, ill-treated wife in *Baby Doll* (1956). Trained as a dancer before joining Strasberg's academy, she is described by critic David Thompson as "a splendidly vulgar creature, capable of a specially daft sexiness." Baker also starred in *Harlow*, a project Marilyn long held dear to her heart and which was finally made in 1965.

## Baker, Gladys Pearl
(1902–1984, maiden name Gladys Monroe, also Gladys Mortensen, Gladys Eley)

Marilyn:
"I just want to forget about all the unhappiness, all the misery she had in her life, and I had in mine. I can't forget it, but I'd like to try. When I am Marilyn Monroe and don't think about Norma Jeane, then sometimes it works."

"For a long time I was scared I'd find out that I was like my mother and end up in the crazy house. I won der when I break down if I'm not tough enough—like her. But I'm hoping to get stronger."

MRS. LEILA FIELDS, former colleague at RKO: "She was a beautiful woman, one of the most beautiful women it was ever my privilege to know. She had a good heart and was a good friend and was always happy until she got this sickness."

INEZ MELSON:
"Marilyn's mother was overly taken up with her religion, Christian Science, and with evil. That was her area of disturbance. She figured she had done something wrong in her life, and was being punished for it."

Norma Jeane's mother was born Gladys Pearl Monroe in Piedras Negras, MEXICO (then known as Porfirio Diaz, in honor of the nation's incumbent president), on May 27, 1902. Her early childhood, about which little is known, was spent in various locations in booming Southern California, as her parents DELLA MAE HOGAN and OTIS ELMER MONROE moved from town to town picking up what work they could find. In 1908, when Gladys was six, her father was admitted to a mental institution; whether this was because of mental illness, heavy drinking, or the advanced syphilis he was suffering is still a matter of conjecture. He died only months after entering the institution. Two years later Gladys's mother remarried, but soon after she took up with another man.

At the age of fourteen Gladys saw her chance to get out of the broken maternal home, in the shape of JOHN (JACK) NEWTON BAKER, a twenty-six-year-old businessman (or gas station attendant, or gas meter reader, depending on biographers) from Kentucky. The two were married on May 17, 1917, after Gladys's mother falsely declared her daughter to be eighteen years of age, explaining that there was no proof of this because they had only recently arrived in California from Oregon. Seven months later Gladys gave birth to a son, Jack, followed in July 1919 by a daughter, Berniece Inez Gladys (*see under* MIRACLE).

Gladys's own recent childhood had been a troubled and transient affair, in a succession of different homes and with a number of different father figures, and this invariably affected her motherhood. Still only seventeen, she was far more interested in living it up, going out to dance halls, and having a good time than looking after her two young children. Her marriage broke down in 1921—Gladys filed for divorce on the grounds of "extreme cruelty by abusing and calling her vile names and using profane language at and in her presence, by striking and kicking." John countered with accusations of lewd and lascivious conduct. Gladys moved out of their home and went to share a rented bungalow with her mother at 46 Rose Avenue, Venice, but this could only be a short term solution, as the two women did not get along. Gladys's divorce was finalized in May 1923; John took the children and returned to Kentucky. For a time Gladys visited infrequently, and then she lost touch altogether.

Gladys found a measure of stability in work. One of thousands to be employed by the thriving film industry, she found a job as a film cutter, working for CONSOLIDATED FILM INDUSTRIES, COLUMBIA, and then RKO.

At Consolidated, Gladys soon became close friends with a supervisor named GRACE MCKEE (*see under* GODDARD). Within months they were sharing an apartment at 1211 Hyperion Avenue, in what is now the Silver Lake district of Los Angeles, a few miles east of Hollywood. Gladys dyed her hair a shocking hue of red, and the two girls would often be seen out on the town, on the lookout for good times. Or as Vernon S. Harbin, a colleague of hers, put it, "she was known as a barfly."

In the summer of 1924 Gladys attracted the attentions of a man named MARTIN EDWARD MORTENSEN, whose proposals of marriage she finally accepted on October 11, 1924. Mortensen was a good catch, a man with a steady job, handsome looks, and a generous nature, but Gladys was either not willing or not able to settle down. Four months later she was back living with Grace, and divorce was to follow. Once more, Gladys dedicated herself to the carefree pursuits of a twenties girl, meeting men, courting popularity, and having fun. Then, in late 1925, she became pregnant again. When she went into hospital to give birth to Norma Jeane, her third child, she listed her first two as dead. Her stay in hospital was paid for through a collection taken by her fellow workers. Norma Jeane Mortensen was born on June 1, 1926. At this time Gladys was living at 5454 Wilshire Boulevard, the home to which she returned with her newborn girl. Though on the birth certificate her mother listed Martin as the father, any number of men could have been responsible: Mortensen himself, or Gladys's colleague CHARLES STANLEY GIFFORD. Some Marilyn biographers have added names of other potential fathers: co-workers Harold Rooney and Clayton MacNamara, and Raymond Guthrie, a film developer who pursued Gladys for months that year.

Less than two weeks after her baby girl was born, Gladys took Norma Jeane to live with a foster family, the BOLENDERS, some sixteen miles away in Hawthorn, not far from where her mother, Della Mae, was living. Gladys had a full-time job, and her hedonistic lifestyle would have been severely compromised by an infant; she had already "failed" in her mothering of her first family, and her own experience growing up had been one where her well-being had come a distant second to the desires and aspirations of her mother. She did, however, meet her financial responsibilities for her daughter, making regular $5-a-week payments to the devout Bolenders for Norma Jeane's bed and board. During the years she lived with the Bolender foster family, Marilyn recalled that when her mother came to visit, she never smiled, never kissed her, never cuddled her, and hardly spoke to her.

Though Gladys visited her daughter, taking her out for an occasional weekend treat, she was not actually to live with Norma Jeane for seven years, until 1933 when she temporarily moved into the Bolender house to nurse Norma Jeane as she recovered from a bout of whooping cough. Later that year she picked up Norma Jeane from the Bolenders for good; her little girl was in a state of almost inconsolable distress after her pet dog Tippy had been shot dead by a neighbor unhappy with its forays into his yard.

Gladys took her little girl to live in an apartment at 6021 Afton Place, close to the studios in Hollywood where she and best friend Grace were still working as freelance film cutters. The two women often took the girl out to see the local Hollywood sights—movie palaces whose facades resembled the architectural wonders of the world—and of course they took her to the movies too.

Gladys Monroe Baker with two-year-old Norma Jeane at Santa Monica Beach, 1928.

That fall Gladys obtained a $5000 loan from the Mortgage Guarantee Company of California to purchase a three-bedroom furnished house at 6812 ARBOL STREET, quite close to the Hollywood Bowl—indeed close enough to be swallowed up during expansion of the Bowl's grounds in the 1930s. Gladys fell in love with the house at first sight. What sold her, though, was a WHITE PIANO, a Franklin baby grand. To afford the mortgage repayments, Gladys rented out the whole house to a married couple, English film actor GEORGE ATKINSON and family, reserving one room for herself and her daughter.

Marilyn later described the impact of this enormous change in lifestyle: "Life became pretty casual and tumultuous, quite a change from the first family. They worked hard when they worked, and they enjoyed life the rest of the time. They liked to dance and sing, they drank and played cards, and they had a lot of friends. Because of that religious upbringing I'd had, I was kind of shocked—I thought they were all going to hell. I spent hours praying for them." Nonetheless, it was during this period that Norma Jeane first felt the allure of the movies and the film industry. For long periods during school vacations she would be parked at one of Hollywood's spectacular movie palaces where she watched the big screen all day long: "There I'd sit, all day and sometimes way into the night—up in front, there with the screen so big, a little kid all alone, and I loved it. I didn't miss anything that happened—and there was no popcorn, either."

This idyll time only lasted a matter of months. In May 1933 Gladys was informed that her grandfather Tilford Hogan—whom she had never met—had hanged himself. This in itself may not be enough to explain her slide into deep and debilitating depression, but for Gladys it was yet another sign that there was no escape; both her mother and father had perished in mental institutions, and she was con-

Gladys Baker and Norma Jeane, 1933.

vinced that her hold on her own sanity was tenuous at best.

The drugs she was prescribed did not help to bring her back to her functioning self, and in January 1934 (January 1935 for some biographers), the English couple who had rented the house on Arbol Street called an ambulance to take a hysterical Gladys, cowering, petrified under the staircase, to hospital by force. This was to be the beginning of forty years in and out of institutions. Marilyn later recalled that for a long time afterward, "I kept hearing the terrible noise on the stairs and my mother screaming and laughing as they led her out of the home she had tried to build for me."

The most widely-held view among Marilyn biographers is that Gladys suffered from mental illness and was, inevitably, taken to live in an institution. However, biographer DONALD SPOTO argues that more than suffering from actual clinical psychiatric illness, she was pushed into depression by circumstance, and then swallowed up in a system where mental health care was rudimentary, if not brutal; misdiagnosis and unsuitable medication turned a temporary crisis into a lifelong illness.

Gladys was admitted to a rest home in Santa Monica in early 1934, and then transferred to Los Angeles General Hospital. Depending on accounts, either the Atkinsons or Gladys's best friend Grace McKee Goddard looked after Norma Jeane, and once again the little girl only saw her mother on rare weekends when Gladys was allowed temporary leave as a way to assess whether or not she was ready to leave the hospital. On some weekends Gladys and Grace took Norma Jeane for lunch at the AMBASSADOR HOTEL, where a decade later she was to sign up with the BLUE BOOK MODELING AGENCY.

By the end of 1934 Gladys was formally pronounced insane—a paranoid schizophrenic—by the doctors at Los Angeles General Hospital. From there she was transferred to NORWALK STATE HOSPITAL, where her mother had died a few years earlier. The chief medical officer's report states: "Her illnesses have been characterized by (1) preoccupation with religion at times, and (2) at other times deep depression and agitation. This appears to be a chronic state."

Gladys Baker's estate, now legally represented by Goddard, was liquidated in April 1935. She had $60 in a bank account, $90 in unendorsed insurance checks, one table radio (value $25, $15 of which was still owed to the store), a $250 debt on a 1933 Plymouth sedan, plus $200 outstanding on the white piano. Grace sold the car back to its original owner, offloaded the piano for $235, and arranged for the house to be returned to the mortgagee.

After an attempted escape from Norwalk in 1938, Gladys was moved to the Agnew State Asylum, a secure hospital near San Francisco. Gladys's escape attempt was precipitated by a series of telephone calls she claimed to have received from her last husband, Martin Edward Mortensen. Though there is nothing strange about this in itself, hospital staff had been informed that Mortensen had been killed nine years previously, in a 1929 motorcycle accident in Ohio, so these phone calls were pure delusion. Confusion over Mortensen was to affect not only poor Gladys, but also Marilyn's many biographers, particularly since another man called Martin Edward Mortensen who lived in Riverside Country, California and died as recently as February 10, 1981, long claimed he was Marilyn's father.

In any event, the staff at Norwalk saw Gladys's attempt to leave the hospital as a typical schizophrenic delusion, and Agnew was specialized in this kind of condition.

After 1938 Norma Jeane only saw her mother a handful of times. One occasion was soon after her thirteenth birthday, when McKee took her up to the clinic-supervised boarding house in San Francisco where Gladys was living at that time. Her mother had not a word to say the entire visit, until it was time for her visitors to leave, when she plaintively murmured, "You used to have such tiny little feet."

Gladys was similarly taciturn in 1945, when Norma Jeane, accompanied by photographer ANDRÉ DE DIENES, turned up to visit her in the grimy hotel room where she was then living in downtown Portland, Oregon, after the hospital had decided she was no longer a danger to herself or others. De Dienes describes the uneasy occasion in his book *Marilyn Mon Amour*:

> "The reunion between mother and daughter lacked warmth. They had nothing to say to each other. Mrs. Baker was a woman of uncertain age, emaciated and apathetic, making no effort to put us at our ease. Norma Jeane put on a cheerful front. She had unpacked the presents we had brought: a scarf, scent, chocolates. They stayed where they were on the table. A silence ensued. Then Mrs. Baker buried her face in her hands and seemed to forget all about us. It was distressing."

This behavior was at odds with Gladys's avowed desire to put an end to her aimless wanderings around the Pacific Northwest, and come and live with her daughter. The very thought put Norma Jeane into a panic. At last she had succeeded in wresting some measure of control over her own life, after the years living with guardian Grace McKee and now the end of her marriage to JAMES DOUGHERTY. In 1945 Norma Jeane felt she was on the brink of an exciting career in MODELING, which she fervently hoped would prove to be a passport into the world of film. The thought of having to look after a woman who had spent most of the previous decade in mental institutions, a woman who to all intents was a stranger to her, must have filled her with dread. Gladys continued to plead with her daughter, and in April 1946 Norma Jeane caved in and sent money for the journey. Gladys came to share the two small rooms Norma Jeane had taken on Nebraska Avenue, below "Aunt" ANA LOWER's apartment.

Gladys was not in good shape. ELEANOR (BEEBE) GODDARD recalls her behavior: "She wandered and she was unpredictable. She was docile, but she was not 'there.'" One day Gladys dressed up all in white to make an unannounced visit to her daughter's modeling agency, where she said to Emmeline Snively, "I only came so I could thank you personally for what you've been doing for Norma Jeane. You have given her a whole new life."

But within a few weeks (a few months in some accounts) Gladys was back at the Norwalk State Asylum. Out of her still modest earnings Norma Jeane sent money to supplement the rather Dickensian basic free care.

On April 20, 1949 Marilyn received a note from Grace informing her that her mother had married a man called John Stewart Eley. Marilyn continued to send money to her mother, the sums increasing as she earned more. Eley, an electrician, died of heart disease at the age of sixty-two on April 23, 1952.

In 1951 Marilyn's new business manager INEZ MELSON began to make regular visits to see Gladys on Marilyn's behalf, in order to make sure that she had sufficient money for her life as she drifted in and out of sheltered facilities. The following year Melson persuaded Marilyn to appoint her as Gladys's legal guardian. By this time, quite unexpectedly for all concerned, Marilyn's mother had suddenly become national news. TWENTIETH CENTURY-FOX had touted its latest star as a poor orphan who despite adversity had made good, but that was before an inquisitive journalist found out that Marilyn's mother was alive, and, what's more, had recently been released from the latest in a long line of institutions and was working at a private nursing home called Homestead Lodge, not far from Pasadena. Perhaps on its own this news would not have represented a threat; however, it came just one month after the huge scandal surrounding revelations that Marilyn had posed nude. Once again the studio went into damage control mode, and an "exclusive interview" was granted to columnist Erskine Johnson. In fact Marilyn's "confession" was crafted by her friend SIDNEY SKOLSKY, who so often helped her out of tricky situations.

MARILYN MONROE CONFESSES MOTHER ALIVE, LIVING HERE

*by Erskine Johnson*

Marilyn Monroe—Hollywood's confessing glamour doll who made recent headlines with the admission that she was a nude calendar cutie—confessed again today.

Highly publicized by Hollywood press agents as an orphan waif who never knew her parents, Marilyn admitted that she's the daughter of a one-time RKO studio film cutter, Gladys Baker, and that "I am helping her and want to continue to help her when she needs me."

Recovering form an appendectomy in a Los Angeles hospital, Marilyn gave me an exclusive statement through the Twentieth Century-Fox studio following the appearances at the studio of five women claiming Marilyn as their "long-lost daughter."

Said Hollywood's new glamour queen:

"My close friends know that my mother is alive.

Unbeknown to me as a child, my mother spent many years as an invalid in a state hospital.

I was raised in a series of foster homes arranged by a guardian through the County of Los Angeles and I spent more than a year in the Los Angeles Orphans Home.

I haven't known my mother intimately, but since I have become grown and able to help her I have contacted her.

I am helping her and want to continue to help her when she needs me."

Hollywood friends of her mother supplied the rest of the story:

"When Marilyn was a small child her father was killed in an automobile accident and her mother subsequently suffered a nervous breakdown. A friend of her mother was appointed her legal guardian.

Marilyn's mother recovered from her illness in 1945 and lived with her daughter for a short time in 1946. In the same year her mother remarried and became a widow for the second time last week when her husband died following a short illness.

The news that Marilyn's mother is alive and in Hollywood came as an eyebrow-lifting surprise because of extensive studio publicity that Marilyn had never known her mother or her father.

But the new star's confession that her twice-widowed mother is in Hollywood and that "I am helping her" came as a relief to the Twentieth Century-Fox legal department, which has been confronted with wild claims by women insisting that Marilyn is their "daughter."

Soon after this article appeared, Marilyn received an imploring letter from her mother, in which she said, simply, "Please dear child, I'd like to receive a letter from you. Things are very annoying around here and I'd like to move away as soon as possible. I'd like to have my child's love instead of hatred." The letter was signed "with love, Mother." But Marilyn's energies were totally focused on her career, and she felt she could do no more than make sure her mother's financial needs were met. On the advice of Grace Goddard, in February 1953 Gladys was taken back to hospital, this time the more comfortable ROCKHAVEN SANITARIUM at Verdugo City.

Marilyn completely secured her mother's financial future by setting up a trust fund in 1959.

Gladys was reportedly highly disturbed after Marilyn's death, on more than one occasion attempting suicide. In 1963 she escaped from Rockhaven but was found a day later in a San Fernando Valley church, clutching a Bible and a Christian Science prayer book.

On her final release in 1967, Gladys went to live with her daughter Berniece in Florida. In 1970 she moved to a retirement home. When asked at that time about her famous daughter, she reputedly said, "Don't mention that woman to me!" In 1972 she told Marilyn fan JAMES HASPIEL, "I never wanted her to go into that business!"

Gladys Baker lived the final years of her life at the Collins Court old age home (4201 S.W. Twenty-first Place, Gainesville, Florida), registered under the name Gladys Eley. She died at the age of eighty-one, in March 1984, outliving her daughter by more than two decades.

## BAKER, HERMITT JACK

Marilyn's half brother, born in 1918. Little is known about beyond the fact that, according to most biographers, he died of tuberculosis as a young child. Other biograhers, however, have claimed that he died at thirteen.

## BAKER, JACK (1891—?)

GLADYS BAKER married first husband Jack (referred to by some sources as John Newton or Jasper) on May 17, 1917. The marriage lasted four years, in which time they had two children. Their marriage ended in acrimonious divorce, with both parties claiming infidelities by the other. In one account, Jack kidnapped their two children the day after the divorce was granted. Marilyn later wrote, "My mother spent all of her savings trying to get the children back. Finally, she traced them to Kentucky where they were . . . living in a fine house. The father was married again and well off. She met with him but didn't ask him for anything, not even to kiss the children she had been hunting for so long." Biographer DONALD WOLFE painted a picture of a violent man in his book, *The Last Days of Marilyn Monroe*.

## BAKER, ROY WARD (B. 1916)

British-born director who guided Marilyn through her first starring role, *DON'T BOTHER TO KNOCK* (1952). Other films he made: *The October Man* (1947), *Morning Departure* (1950), *The One That Got Away* (1957), *Quatermass and the Pit* (1967).

## BANCROFT, ANNE
(B. 1931, ANNA MARIA LUISA ITALIANO)

Bancroft worked in television before Hollywood called in 1952, putting her opposite Marilyn's first star vehicle, *DON'T BOTHER TO KNOCK*:

> "It was a remarkable experience. Because it was one of those very few times in all my experiences in Hollywood when I felt that give and take—that can only happen when you are working with good actors. There was just this scene of one woman seeing another woman who was helpless and in pain, and she was helpless and in pain. It was so real, I responded. I really reacted to her. She moved me so that tears came into my eyes. Believe me, such moments happened rarely, if ever again, in the early things I was doing."

In the space of four years Bancroft made eleven movies before returning to her native New York and triumphing on Broadway in *Two for the Seesaw* and *The Miracle Worker*, a role that won her an Oscar in its 1962 film version.

Other movies: *The Pumpkin Eater* (1964), *The Graduate* (1968), *The Turning Point* (1977), *The Elephant Man* (1980), *84 Charing Cross Road* (1987).

## BANFF SPRINGS HOTEL
SPRAY AVENUE, BANFF

Marilyn stayed in room 816 during the arduous location shooting for *RIVER OF NO RETURN* (1954) on and around the Athabasca River. She stayed here for several weeks, and returned to Los Angeles on September 1, 1953. She caused a minor local scandal not for clothes she wasn't wearing but for the ones she was—she was turned away from the dining-room after arriving in slacks.

(*see* HOTELS)

## BAPTISM

On December 6, 1926 Marilyn's grandmother DELLA MAE MONROE and foster mother IDA BOLENDER took Norma Jeane to be baptized (Norma Jeane Baker) at the Foursquare Gospel Church, in Sister AIMEE SEMPLE MCPHERSON's Angelus Temple, at 4503 West Broadway, in Hawthorne, California.

## BARBITURATES

Marilyn took barbiturates because she thought they would help her SLEEP. After her second miscarriage, Marilyn was consumed with fear that she had brought this on by her intake of Amytal, (medical name amobarbital). Amytal and Nembutal, the barbiturates she took most regularly, are not only sedatives but depressants. By the late fifties, Marilyn was trapped into a dangerous spiral of having to take drugs to get to sleep, different drugs in the morning to battle through the grogginess, and then more pills during the day to control her anxiety. Typically, Marilyn scheduled no appointments before midday; the hangover from Nembutal took all morning to clear. During shooting on many of her movies she was simply too groggy to make it to work in the mornings—one reason for her legendary LATENESS. As her dependency worsened, her entourage made sure that she had nothing scheduled in the morning hours.

Tests conducted by the coroner's office following her DEATH revealed levels of 8 mg of chloral hydrate and 4.5 mg of Nembutal in Marilyn's blood, but a toxicological examination of her liver revealed a much higher 13 mg of concentration of Nembutal.

## BARDOT, BRIGITTE
(B. 1934, CAMILLE JAVAL)

Dubbed the French answer to Marilyn, Bardot was discovered as a young model by director Roger Vadim. Like Marilyn, Bardot was originally a brunette, and she made headlines for her beautiful body and her willingness to expose it. Her 1956 film *AND*

Marilyn with George Barris at the party to celebrate Marilyn's 36th birthday on the set of *Something's Got to Give*, 1962.

GOD CREATED WOMAN, partly based on the Marilyn story, turned her into an international star. She made many movies over the following fifteen years, including the 1963 Jean-Luc Godard classic *Contempt*.

Bardot stood with Marilyn in the line of actresses on October 29, 1956 at the Leicester Square Empire Theatre in London, waiting to be presented to Queen ELIZABETH II, at the royal command performance.

## BARNHART, SYLVIA

Hairdresser at FRANK AND JOSEPH'S BEAUTY SALON on Hollywood Boulevard who straightened Norma Jeane's hair and slowly, over a few weeks of applying the harsh chemicals of the day in small doses so as not to ruin her hair, turned her brunette locks blonde for the first time in late 1946.

## BARRIS, GEORGE

George Barris first encountered Marilyn as one of the many PHOTOGRAPHERS during location shooting of the infamous *SEVEN YEAR ITCH* (1955) skirt scene.

Barris was one of the last PHOTOGRAPHERS to photograph Marilyn, between June 29 and July 1, 1962, on Santa Monica beach, by the pool at PETER LAWFORD's home in some accounts, and at another home near Marilyn's. This was originally destined to be a photo feature for *Cosmopolitan*. There is also a home movie of Barris and Marilyn on the beach, with Marilyn cavorting in a green towel.

Some of these photographs appeared in NORMAN MAILER's 1973 biography *Marilyn*, with many more featured in his 1986 collaboration with GLORIA STEINEM (*Marilyn Norma Jeane*). In 1995 he published *Marilyn: Her Life in Her Own Words*, the text of which consists of notes he scribbled down after their photo sessions, reputedly in preparation for a joint autobiography project which Marilyn said would "set the record straight."

George Barris's images of Marilyn at Santa Monica Beach in 1962 are some of the most famous photographs ever taken of her.

## BATES, JOHN

On the weekend of Marilyn's death, ROBERT KENNEDY and his family were staying with the Bates family at their ranch near Gilroy, California, several hundred miles north of Los Angeles. Bates was at this time a respected attorney in a San Francisco law firm, who had been offered (and turned down) a prestigious job with the Kennedy administration. CONSPIRACY theory accounts of Marilyn's death question the movements of Kennedy during this weekend, claiming that he took a helicopter flight to Los Angeles on the night of August 4, 1962. Bates has gone on record to say that the Kennedys were in Gilroy the entire weekend. This has not satisfied conspiracy theorists who point out that he did not see Robert between 11 P.M. on August 4 and 8 A.M. on August 5.

## BATTELLE, KENNETH

The "Hairdresser to the Stars" also known as "Mrs. Kennedy's Kenneth," or just plain "Mr. Kenneth," first started working with Marilyn on the *SOME LIKE IT HOT* set in 1958, and continued to style Marilyn's hair on and off until her death, especially when she was in New York.

## BAXTER, ANNE (1923–1985)

Granddaughter of architect Frank Lloyd Wright (*see* ROXBURY), Baxter's first screen success was in Walter Lang's *The Great Profile* (1940), followed by *The Magnificent Ambersons* (1942), and an Oscar-winning performance in *The Razor's Edge* (1946). Contracted to Fox, she had leading roles in three early Marilyn movies: *ALL ABOUT EVE* (1950), *TICKET TO TOMAHAWK* (1950), and *O. HENRY'S FULL HOUSE* (1952). Baxter was originally cast for a part in *NIAGARA* (1953), one of Marilyn's first star vehicles, but pulled out of the project before filming began.

## BEACHES

Norma Jeane was a California girl who regularly went to the beach during her teenage years, most often to Santa Monica beach. Her first photographers regularly took her to the beach for photographs, either to Santa Monica, Malibu, or Zuma beach. It was at, BEN LYON's beach house that Norma Jeane was renamed Marilyn Monroe, and at PETER LAWFORD's Santa Monica beach house that she dined with the Kennedy brothers.

## BEACH STREET

2150 BEACH STREET, MARINA DISTRICT, SAN FRANCISCO

Immediately after their marriage in early 1954, JOE DIMAGGIO and Marilyn went to live at the two-story DiMaggio home in San Francisco. Marilyn soon missed Los Angeles life, and the couple agreed to return in May 1954.

(*see* HOMES)

While in New York on a promotional tour for *Love Happy* in 1949 Marilyn took a trip out to Jones Beach on Long Island.

A Twentieth Century-Fox publicity shot, 1947.

Marilyn takes a bath in *The Seven Year Itch* (1955). Marilyn was particularly fond of ice baths scented with Chanel No. 5.

## BEATON, SIR CECIL WALTER HARDY (1904–1980)

"Miss Marilyn Monroe calls to mind the bouquet of a fireworks display," he said. He also described her as "artless, high-spirited, infectiously gay."

English PHOTOGRAPHER and theater designer who broke new ground with his early fashion photographs for *Vogue* magazine and collaborated on artistic design for films such as *Gigi* and *My Fair Lady*. One of Marilyn's favorite photos of herself was taken by Beaton: Marilyn in a white gown on a bed of white sheets, holding a long-stemmed carnation to her breast. It hung on her living room wall at her East FIFTY-SEVENTH STREET apartment in New York.

## BEAUTY

MILTON GREENE:
"You don't just wake up in the morning and wash your face and comb your hair and go out in the street and look like Marilyn Monroe. She knows every trick of the beauty trade."

Norma Jeane was schooled in the arts of cosmetics and beauty tricks from a very early age by her mom's best friend (later her legal guardian) GRACE McKEE GODDARD. As a little girl she would be dressed up, taken to the hairdressers, and paraded around in makeup. One of her only fond memories from the time she lived at the LOS ANGELES ORPHANS HOME was when the director allowed her to try out some makeup.

ALLAN "WHITEY" SNYDER, the man who did Norma Jeane's makeup for her first ever screen test and continued to do her cosmetics throughout her career, said: "She knew every trick of the makeup trade—how to line her eyes, what oils and color bases to use, how to create the right color for her lips. She looked fantastic, of course, but it was all an illusion: in person, out of makeup, she was very pretty but in a plain way, and she knew it." To biographer MAURICE ZOLOTOW he said, "She has certain ways of lining and shadowing her eyes that no other actress can do. She puts on a special kind of lipstick. It's a secret blend of three different shades. I get that moist look to her lips for when she's going to do a sexy seen by first putting on the lipstick and then putting on a gloss [a mixture of Vaseline and wax]." WILLIAM TRAVILLA said that Marilyn used up to five shades of lipstick to achieve the contour and shadowing she wanted.

To make Marilyn up for the movies, Snyder first applied a light base. He highlighted under her eyes and out, over and across the cheekbones. Next he added toning to the eye-shadow, working lightly out toward the hairline, followed by a pencil outline round the eyes; her brows would be pointed slightly to make her forehead look broader, with more toning added beneath her cheekbones; further shadings were added to match costume and lighting. Lipstick colors vary depending on what was needed for a particular scene.

It took Marilyn and Snyder anywhere between one and a half and a full three hours to work the magic that turned her from Norma Jeane to the Marilyn fans wanted and expected.

When doing her own makeup, Marilyn would use a base stick to darken the flesh tones of her face and chest, and then take most of it off, using witch hazel and tissue.

During her first marriage Norma Jeane would wash and scrub her face many times a day with soap and water to prevent blemishes and, she hoped, to improve the circulation. Her then husband JAMES DOUGHERTY later told a reporter: "She was a perfectionist about her appearance. If anything she was too critical of herself."

When living with NATASHA LYTESS in the early fifties, Marilyn washed her face several times a day to prevent clogged pores, took long baths, and made frequent visits to the dentist to make sure that her teeth were in perfect gleaming health.

Marilyn loved taking baths. Sometimes these were ice baths scented with Chanel No. 5. More often she spent hours soaking in hot perfumed baths: "Sometimes I know the truth of what I'm doing. It isn't Marilyn Monroe in the tub but Norma Jeane. . . . And it seems that Norma can't get enough of fresh bath water that smells of real perfume."

During her struggling starlet years Marilyn had a trick of applying a little saliva to her cheekbones to give them an extra sheen.

She also studiously avoided the sun to keep her skin as white as possible—thirty years before it became generally acknowledged that a "healthy" tan is anything but. Marilyn's motives were less skin protection than to keep the colors right for her look and hair. At various times during her life Marilyn protected her face by smearing it with Vaseline, cold cream, or hormone cream. Partly as a consequence of using hormone creams, by her mid-thirties Marilyn had a fine down on her cheeks.

In early 1953 Marilyn discovered what she described as "a trick to lose weight quickly"—colonic irrigation, an enema that flushes out the bowels. Marilyn used this rather unpleasant technique throughout the rest of her life. Some biographers report that she resorted to a one-a-day regime of enemas when she felt she needed to slim down to fit into a dress.

As early as 1943, with Dougherty on Catalina Island, Marilyn improved her FITNESS by working out with free weights and machines. A 1952 *Life* photo feature shows her stretching and using barbells.

In later years, Marilyn slept in a bra to maintain breast muscle tone; she also told a friend that she put on a bra immediately after lovemaking.

In her last years, Marilyn apparently was taking hormonal injections to delay the effects of AGING. She also took to wearing gloves to protect her hands.

## BEL AIR HOTEL
701 STONE CANYON ROAD, BEL AIR

On several occasions Marilyn stayed at this secluded and luxurious HOTEL. Her very first taste of luxury living was in 1948, when COLUMBIA PICTURES billeted her there during her six month contract. She returned in 1952, paying her own way from the proceeds of her first starring role, in *DON'T BOTHER TO KNOCK*; her poolside suite came with a garden terrace, and set her back what for the time was the very high price of $750 per month. She spent her twenty-sixth birthday alone in her suite, dining on steak and drinking champagne, celebrating the fact she had landed the Lorelei Lee role in *GENTLEMEN PREFER BLONDES* (1953)—a role that had originally been reserved for top female star of the day, BETTY GRABLE.

Marilyn stayed at Suites 133–135 in 1958 when she returned from New York to Los Angeles for studio scenes of *SOME LIKE IT HOT* (1959).

The last time she patronized the hotel was June 1962 for the BERT STERN photo session that has come to be known as the "Last Sitting"—in suite 261 and then bungalow 96.

Previous page: Marilyn on the beach, 1949.

## BEMENT, ILLINOIS

In August 1955 Marilyn traveled to this town to inaugurate a museum in honor of ABRAHAM LINCOLN. Her traveling companion that day was photographer EVE ARNOLD, whom Marilyn had invited along to record the event. Marilyn was upbeat about her trip to small-town America: "I'm going to bring art to the masses."

## BENEFACTORS

People who helped Marilyn financially and professionally to get her break:

- JOHN CARROLL
- HARRY COHN
- JOHNNY HYDE
- LUCILLE RYMAN
- JOSEPH SCHENCK

## BENNY, JACK
(1894–1974, B. BENJAMIN KUBELSKY)

Marilyn made her television debut on September 13, 1953, with Benny, in a show recorded at the Shrine Auditorium soon after the release of *GENTLEMEN PREFER BLONDES*. She performed in a comedy sketch with the host, and sang the song "Bye Bye Baby" from the film; the sketch, in which Marilyn vamps host Benny, ends with a kiss that leaves Marilyn cold and Benny, in his own words, "a wreck."

Because Marilyn's contract with Fox prohibited any cash payment for publicity performances, her payment for the appearance was a black Cadillac convertible with red leather interior, of which Marilyn was very proud. The presenter was very complimentary of her performance: "She was superb. She knew the hard-to-learn secret of reading comedy lines as if they were in a drama and letting the humor speak for itself."

The sketch, called "The Honolulu Trip," aired on CBS.

According to JEANNE CARMEN, Benny and Marilyn once went for a day trip to a nude beach, with Benny disguised in a black beard and Marilyn incognito in a black wig. Carmen has also told of how the three of them went together to a massage parlor on Sunset Boulevard for facial treatments.

Marilyn with Jack Benny, 1953.

Benny and Marilyn shared the limelight once more in 1962, at MADISON SQUARE GARDEN where he hosted President JOHN F. KENNEDY's birthday festivities.

Marilyn and Irving Berlin on the set of *There's No Business Like Show Business* (1954).

## BERGEN, EDGAR
(AND CHARLIE MCCARTHY)

Edgar Bergen and his wooden dummy pal Charlie were great favorites in the fifties. In the thirty-minute episode of the Edgar Bergen and Charlie McCarthy radio show in 1952 that featured Marilyn, Charlie schemes to marry Marilyn, unperturbed by the fact that he is a wooden puppet. Marilyn is surprisingly keen on the idea too, but there is stiff opposition from Marilyn's fans; even Winston Churchill is worried: "Never has anyone so little taken so much from so many."

Marilyn with Edgar Bergen and Charlie McCarthy, 1952.

## BERLE, MILTON
(B. 1908, MILTON BERLINGER)

One of America's best-known TV entertainers met starlet Marilyn on the Columbia lot in her first co-starring role, *LADIES OF THE CHORUS* (1949). According to his 1974 autobiography, he had an affair with the young actress, though at the time he was romantically linked with Adele Jergens, the star of the movie.

Marilyn and Milton met again in 1955 at MADISON SQUARE GARDEN; she was riding a pink elephant at a circus benefit, and he was ringmaster for the day. He announced Marilyn with the immortal words: "Here comes the only girl in the world who makes Jane Russell look like a boy!" The crowd of 18,000 roared in delight.

Berle also made a cameo as himself in one of Marilyn's last pictures, *LET'S MAKE LOVE* (1960).

## BERLIN, IRVING
(1888–1989, B. ISIDORE BALINE)

Self-taught composer who wrote more than 1,500 songs for Broadway musicals and films, remembered for his sharp lyrics and catchy melodies. Marilyn's 1954 musical *THERE'S NO BUSINESS LIKE SHOW BUSINESS* was a showcase for Berlin's songs, including the title tune. According to writer Henry Ephron, Berlin himself wanted Marilyn in *There's No Business Like Show Business* after seeing her nude CALENDAR photo on top of JOSEPH SCHENCK's piano.

Berlin and Marilyn met at the party she gave for completion of *THE SEVEN YEAR ITCH* (1955).

## BERNARD OF HOLLYWOOD (1912–1987)

One of Hollywood's best-known portrait and glamour PHOTOGRAPHERS worked with Marilyn many times in her early modeling career, as well as taking the well-known photographs of her in the red dress she wore for *NIAGARA* (1953).

BOOK:
*Bernard of Hollywood's Marilyn*, Susan Bernard, ed. New York: St. Martins Press 1993.

## BERNSTEIN, WALTER (B. 1919)

Bernstein was the third or fourth screenwriter to be called in to sort out the script for *SOMETHING'S GOT TO GIVE*. Like those who went before, he made little headway. He went several times to Marilyn's new home, and remembered she was particularly keen and proud to give him a tour of the house. When they discussed the screenplay at hand, Bernstein found "she was very shrewd about what would play and what wouldn't. . . . I remember her saying, 'Remember, you've got Marilyn Monroe. You've got to use her.'"

In a 1973 article, he wrote, "She was not glamorous; she was not even pretty, but her appeal was genuine, a child's appeal—sweet and disarming."

## BESSEMER STREET
VAN NUYS, CALIFORNIA

Norma Jeane and husband JAMES DOUGHERTY moved into a house here in 1943, before he joined the Marines and was posted to CATALINA ISLAND.

(*see* HOMES)

## BEVERLY CARLTON HOTEL
(NOW CALLED THE AVALON)
9400 WEST OLYMPIC BOULEVARD

Marilyn's first spell of residence at this HOTEL did not see her using the bed very much; in 1949 and 1950 she paid for and used the place as an official residence while living with agent JOHNNY HYDE in their "love nest" on North Palm Drive.

It has been said that one of the reasons why Marilyn decided to do her infamous nude CALENDAR photographs was to keep up with payments on her room at the hotel, as well as on her car.

Marilyn returned to the Beverly Carlton in 1951 after a spell living first with Hyde, then with drama coach NATASHA LYTESS. The hotel reputedly decorated her room in burgundy, white, and gray. Marilyn spent a lot of time in her room, reflecting on past disappointments and future hopes, reading her burgeoning collection of books, with her baby grand piano to keep her company. Apparently at one moment she wrote the Latin word *nunc*, which means "now," on the mirror in her apartment during her stay. She was right: 1952 was the year she became a superstar.

## BEVERLY HILLS HOTEL
9641 WEST SUNSET BOULEVARD, BEVERLY HILLS

Marilyn first moved in to a third-floor room at this HOTEL in late 1952, after a brief lease had run out on a Hollywood Hills house she had co-rented with JOE DIMAGGIO. It was to this room that she returned from the studio party that year, to spend what she later told friends was her best-ever Christmas; rather than spending it alone, as she had expected, she found DiMaggio had not gone to be with his family in San Francisco but had flown in as a surprise. He had brought a tree and decorations, put the champagne on ice, and prepared a blazing fire to welcome her home. Marilyn was still living at the Beverly Hills Hotel on March 9, 1953, which was very convenient for an evening engagement she had to pick up her *PHOTOPLAY* magazine award for Hollywood's Fastest Rising Star at the hotel's Crystal Room. That evening her vampish attire caused great scandal and, to the more prudish members of the audience, even offense.

Marilyn and Joe stayed at the hotel soon after they were married, in early 1954, while waiting for decorators to finish work on their home on Palm Drive. She was back once more on March 8, 1954 to pick up another *Photoplay* award—this time she dressed more demurely and did not cause an outburst. Later that year, after she split up with DiMaggio, Marilyn may have stayed a few days at this hotel as she worked out her next move.

Marilyn at the Beverly Carlton Hotel, ca. 1950.



A 1955 issue of *Movie Stars* magazine featured a piece on Marilyn's "big scenes" in *The Seven Year Itch*.

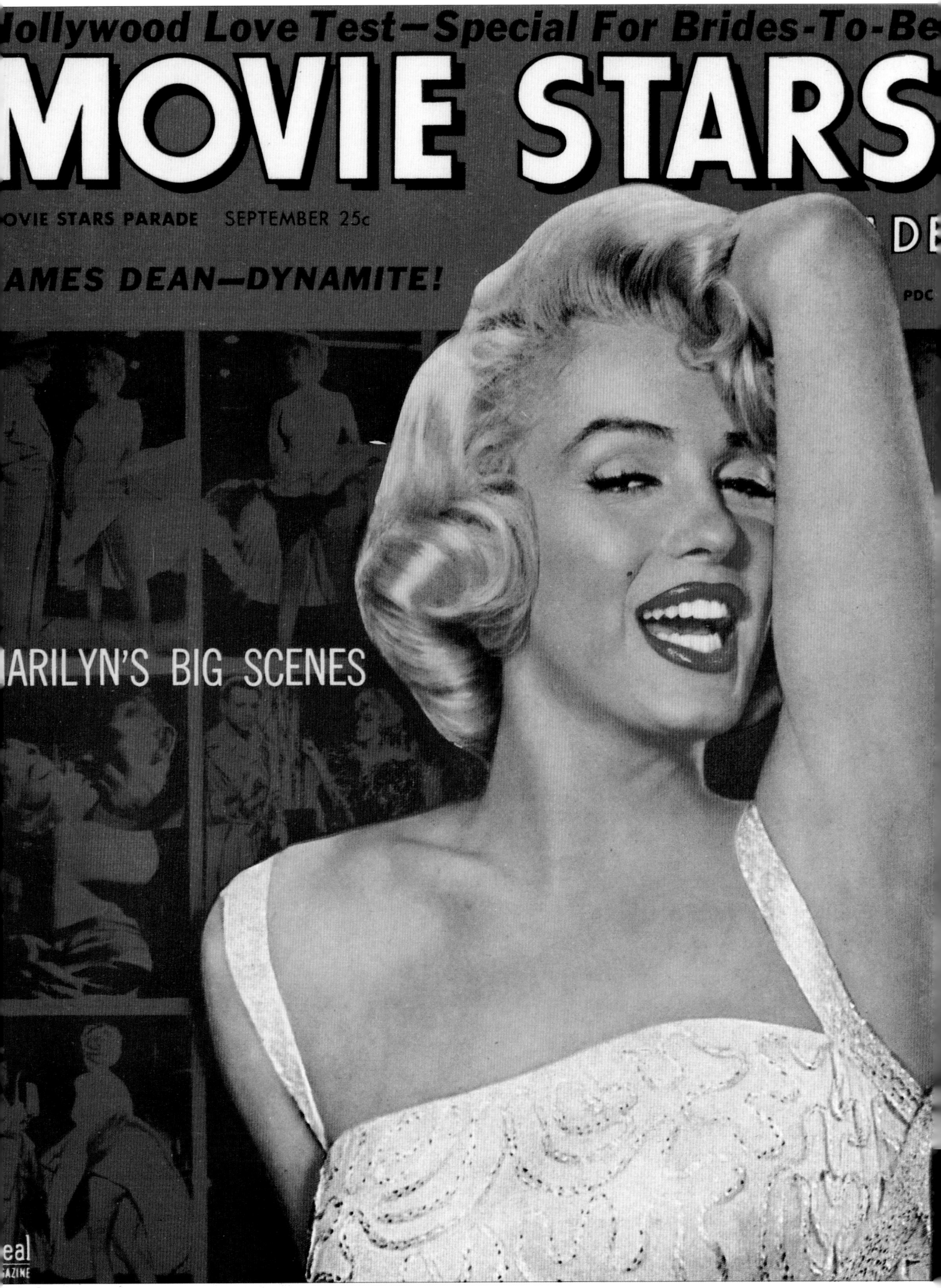
Hollywood Love Test—Special For Brides-To-Be
MOVIE STARS
OVIE STARS PARADE
SEPTEMBER 25c
DE
AMES DEAN—DYNAMITE!
PDC
ARILYN'S BIG SCENES

During the years she was based in New York, the Beverly Hills Hotel was where she stayed when filming commitments took her to Los Angeles: in 1958, shooting for SOME LIKE IT HOT, and in 1960 for LET'S MAKE LOVE—perhaps her longest sojourn when for four months she and husband ARTHUR MILLER lived in neighboring bungalows with YVES MONTAND and his wife, actress SIMONE SIGNORET. Biographers do not agree on which couple had which bungalow, some putting Marilyn and Arthur in bungalow 20, others in bungalow 21, while Montand and Signoret were either in bungalow 21 or 22—the majority agree, however, that Marilyn and Arthur were in no. 21. During this time Marilyn and Montand had an affair.

## BIOGRAPHERS

More books have been written about Marilyn Monroe than any other entertainer. The most conservative estimates are in the low hundreds; more accurate guesses exceed the six-hundred mark, and at least half a dozen new Marilyn books are published every year in the English language alone. Marilyn biographers come in every possible form: the scholarly, the investigative, the sensational, the kiss-and-tell, the "Marilyn that I knew" memoirists, not to mention those by fiction writers, film historians, and even those who worked with Marilyn on autobiographical projects.

Currently the die-hard Marilyn fans are likely to nominate as the most realistic—in other words the one with the highest fact to fiction quotient—DONALD SPOTO's *Marilyn Monroe: The Biography*, which has perhaps superseded previous favorite *Legend: The Life and Death of Marilyn Monroe* by FRED LAWRENCE GUILES. Believers in the conspiracy theories surrounding Marilyn's death tend to prefer works like *Goddess: The Secret Lives of Marilyn Monroe* by ANTHONY SUMMERS and *The Last Days of Marilyn Monroe* by DONALD WOLFE. Ultimately, it seems that perceptions of a biography are based more on whether the biographer is a suicide or murder theorist than on the quality and depth of their research and interviews.

### FIRST BIOGRAPHERS

The earliest Marilyn biographies were more massaged than written, under the watchful eye of Fox publicist Harry Brand. The first book-length work was intended as a Marilyn autobiography, ghost written by Ben Hecht. Contractual problems with Hecht's agent and then two decades of oblivion passed before a version of this work appeared, in 1974, under the title *My Story*. Marilyn's friend, ally and round-about-town companion Sidney Skolsky made up for the abandonment of the Hecht project by quickly putting together his own biography, which came out in 1954. This was not, however, the first book to appear on Marilyn. That honor goes to Joe Franklin and Laurie Palmer, who produced a slender hundred-page Marilyn biography stitched together from the bulging collection of articles lavished on the nation's most popular female star of the time.

The first thorough Marilyn biography, *Marilyn Monroe*, based on extensive interviews with the star, was written by Maurice Zolotow and published in 1960. Though Marilyn actively participated in the genesis of this book, it was not an authorized biography, and after it came out Marilyn expressed some reservations.

## BIOGRAPHIES

Here is a chronological list of the main English-language works wholly dedicated to Marilyn. Her life story also appears in various guises in most general books about Hollywood stars or sex symbols, and there is almost always a biographical component to the hundreds of Marilyn photo books that have been published.

It is safe to say that there have been at least as many Marilyn biographies written in other languages, only a few of which have been translated into English. As well as the following biographies, a host of books have been written about specific films and relationships in Marilyn's life, not to mention reflections on Marilyn in the autobiographies of major Hollywood columnists, film stars, directors, and studio heads of the day.

*The Marilyn Monroe Story*, Joe Franklin and Laurie Palmer. New York: Rudolf Field Company, 1953.

The first Marilyn biography could have been written by the studio.

*Marilyn*, SYDNEY SKOLSKY. New York: Dell Publishing, 1954.

Magazine-style treatment of Marilyn by her friend and confidant.

*Will Acting Spoil Marilyn Monroe?*, Peter Martin. New York Doubleday, 1956.

Adapted from interviews in *Saturday Evening Post*.

*Marilyn Monroe*, MAURICE ZOLOTOW. New York: Harcourt, Brace and Co., 1960; revised edition, Harper and Row, 1990.

The result of a series of 1955 interviews with Marilyn, considered the first comprehensive Marilyn biography.

*Marilyn Monroe: Her Own Story*, George Carpozi Jr. New York: Belmont Books, 1961.

Based on a series of interviews from 1955.

*Violations of the Child Marilyn Monroe*, Her Psychiatrist Friend. New York: Bridgehead Books, 1962.

An anonymous and discredited book that did not take long to appear after Marilyn's death.

*The Strange Death of Marilyn Monroe*, Frank A. Capell. Staten Island: Herald of Freedom, 1964.

The first book to question the circumstances surrounding Marilyn's death, from the publisher of a right-wing magazine.

*Marilyn, The Tragic Venus*, Edwin P. Hoyt. New York: Chilton Books, 1965.

An unfavorable biography based substantially on the testimony of Nunnally Johnson.

*Who Killed Marilyn Monroe?*, Charles Hamblett. Leslie Frewin, 1966.

Only one chapter actually about Marilyn.

*The Mysterious Death of Marilyn Monroe*, James A. Hudson. New York: Volitant Books, 1968.

One of the first books to probe a KENNEDY involvement in Marilyn's death.

*Marilyn Monroe: A Composite View*, Edward Wagenknecht, ed. Chilton Books, 1969.

An anthology of writings about Marilyn, including late interviews.

*Norma Jeane: The Life of Marilyn Monroe*, FRED LAWRENCE GUILES. New York: McGraw Hill, 1969. Revised edition, 1984.

Well-researched and highly regarded biography, appearing in a revised 1984 version.

*Marilyn, Barven Screen Greats No. 4*, Milburn Smith, ed. New York: Barven Publications, 1971.

Magazine treatment of Marilyn's life.

*Marilyn*, LAWRENCE SCHILLER, ed., text by NORMAN MAILER. New York: Grosset and Dunlap, 1973.

A fictional biography, accompanied with photographs by twenty-four of Marilyn's finest photographers.

*Marilyn: An Untold Story*, NORMAN ROSTEN. New York: Signet Books, 1973.

What it was like to be a long-term friend, by her poet pal.

*Marilyn Monroe*, Joan Mellen. New York: Pyramid Books, 1973.

Comprehensive biography, part of "The Pyramid Illustrated History of the Movies" series.

*The Life and Curious Death of Marilyn Monroe*, ROBERT SLATZER. New York: Pinnacle Books, 1974.

One of the most controversial Marilyn books, the lodestone for conspiracy theorists, a fabrication for many others.

MY STORY, Marilyn Monroe. New York: Stein and Day, 1974.

Much massaged autobiography ghosted by BEN HECHT and finally published through MILTON GREENE.

*Marilyn: The Last Months*, EUNICE MURRAY. New York: Pyramid Books, 1975.

Marilyn's housekeeper pleads her case.

*Conversations with Marilyn*, W. J. WEATHERBY. London: Sphere Books, 1976.

Marilyn spills her heart to a British journalist in the right place at the right time.

*The Secret Happiness of Marilyn Monroe*, JAMES E. DOUGHERTY. Chicago: Playboy Press, 1976.

First husband Dougherty attempts to set the record straight.

*Who Killed Marilyn?*, Anthony Sciacca. New York: Manor Books, 1976.

All the usual suspects and more in this conspiracy theory favorite. (*see* SCADUTO)

*Marilyn and Joe DiMaggio*, Robin Moore and Gene Schoor. New York: Manor Books, 1977.

Tale of the romance from a fan's perspective.

*Diary of a Lover of Marilyn Monroe*, Hans Jorgen Lembourn. New York: Arbor House, 1979.

Forty days that shook a Danish journalist.

*The Joy of Marilyn in the Camera Eye*, SAM SHAW. New York: Exeter, 1979.

Many photos of Marilyn's time in and around New York.

*Marilyn Monroe Confidential*, LENA PEPITONE and William Stadiem. New York: Simon & Schuster, 1979.

Marilyn's New York maid dishes the dirt.

*Finding Marilyn: A Romance*, DAVID CONOVER. New York: Grosset & Dunlap, 1981.

Story of the photographer credited with "discovering" young Norma Jeane.

*Marilyn Lives!*, Joel Oppenheimer. New York: Delilah, 1981.

A fan's-eye view of their heroine.

*Marilyn Monroe: Murder Cover-up*, MILO SPERIGLIO. New York: Seville, 1982.

Whodunnit points finger at top suspects.

*The Screen Greats: Marilyn Monroe*, Tom Hutchinson. New York: Exeter, 1982.

The Marilyn episode of a series.

*Marilyn Monroe*, Janice Anderson. London: Hamlyn, 1983.

Illustrated biography marking twenty-one years since Marilyn's death.

*Marilyn Monroe: In Her Own Words*, Roger Taylor. Salem, NH, 1983.

The best quotes, in one place, a formula repeated over the years.

*Legend: The Life and Death of Marilyn Monroe*, Fred Lawrence Guiles. New York: Stein and Day, 1984.

Updated version with additional interviews, with explicit references to Marilyn's relationship with ROBERT KENNEDY.

*Goddess: The Secret Lives of Marilyn Monroe*, ANTHONY SUMMERS. New York: Macmillan, 1985.

Copious biography that puts the Kennedys in the hot seat.

*Requiem for Marilyn*, Bernard of Hollywood. London: Kensal Press, 1986.

Photograph-driven biography.

*The Marilyn Conspiracy*, Milo Speriglio. New York: Seville, 1986.

Updated version of earlier book.

*Marilyn Norma Jeane*, GLORIA STEINEM, photos by GEORGE BARRIS. New York: Henry Holt, 1986.

A feminist analysis of Marilyn, alongside some of the last photos taken of her.

*Joe and Marilyn: A Memory of Love*, Roger Kahn. New York: William Morrow & Co., 1986.

Written by baseball writer, with more focus on the ball player than the actress.

*Marilyn Monroe: A Life of the Actress*, Carl E. Rollyson Jr. Ann Arbor: UMI Press, 1986.

Assessment of Marilyn's screen performances.

*The Marilyn Scandal: Her True Life Revealed by Those Who Knew Her*, Sandra Shevy. New York: William Morrow & Co., 1987.

Concentrates on the many theories surrounding the death.

*Marilyn Among Friends*, Sam Shaw and Norman Rosten. New York: Henry Holt, 1987.

Two of Marilyn's friends tell of their friendships with her in words and pictures.

*Marilyn Monroe*, Graham McCann. NJ: Rutgers University Press, 1988.

A critical analysis of Marilyn's life and image.

*Marilyn on Location*, Bart Mills. London: Sidgwick and Jackson, 1989.

More a general biography than specifically about locations.

*Norma Jean: My Secret Life with Marilyn Monroe*, TED JORDAN. New York: William Morrow & Co., 1989.

Tales of a passionate early affair while he was working as a lifeguard at the AMBASSADOR HOTEL.

*Marilyn: The Last Take*, Peter Brown and Patte Barham. New York: Dutton, 1992.

Focuses on the last four months of Marilyn's life, implicating Bobby Kennedy in her death.

*Why Norma Jeane Killed Marilyn Monroe*, Lucy Freeman. Chicago: Global Rights Limited, 1992.

The reasons behind the suicide.

*Marilyn's Men: The Private Life of Marilyn Monroe*, Jane Ellen Wayne. New York: St. Martin's Press, 1992.

Revealing her character through the men in her life.

*Marilyn Monroe: The Biography*, DONALD SPOTO. New York: HarperCollins, 1993.

The most thorough Marilyn biography to date, discounting most (but not all) CONSPIRACY theories.

*My Sister Marilyn*, BERNIECE BAKER MIRACLE. Chapel Hill, NC: Algonquin Books, 1994.

Marilyn's half-sister tells what she knows, including new letters and photos.

*Marilyn Monroe, Quote Unquote*, Janice Anderson. New York: Crescent Books, 1995.

Marilyn's best lines with photos.

*Marilyn Monroe: The Life, The Myth*, Giovan Battista Brambilla, ed. New York: Rizzoli, 1996.

Collection of international MEMORABILIA accompanying an Italian traveling exhibition, with reminiscences on Marilyn.

*The Last Days of Marilyn Monroe*, also titled *The Assassination of Marilyn Monroe*, DONALD H. WOLFE. New York: William Morrow & Co., 1998.

Reopening the Kennedy conspiracy and naming names.

*Marilyn Monroe*, BARBARA LEAMING. New York: Crown, 1998.

Particularly strong on the film business and how Marilyn went through the TWENTIETH CENTURY-FOX mill.

### MARILYN BIOGRAHIES IN COMIC BOOK FORM

*Marilyn Monroe*, Steven Spire, Bill O'Neill and Bob Dignan. Massapequa, NY: Personality Classics, 1991.

*Son of Celluloid,* Clive Barker. Forestville, CA: Eclipse, 1991.

*The Marilyn Monroe Conspiracy*, Todd Loren. San Diego, CA: Conspiracy Comics, 1991.

*Monroe & DiMaggio*, Alfonso Alfonso, ed. Miami: Conquest Comics, 1992.

*Marilyn Monroe: Suicide or Murder?*, Jay Sanford. San Diego, CA: Revolutionary Comics, 1993.

*Tragic Goddess: Marilyn Monroe*, Adam Post. Westport CT: POP comics, 1995

*Marilyn: The Story of a Woman*, Katherine Hyatt. New York: Seven Stories Press, 1996.

## BIRTH

Norma Jeane Mortensen was born to Gladys Pearl Mortensen (*see* GLADYS BAKER) on June 1, 1926 at 9:30 A.M. in the Charity Ward of Los Angeles General HOSPITAL. The doctor who delivered her was Herman M. Beerman.

## BLUE BOOK MODELING AGENCY

THE AMBASSADOR HOTEL,
3400 WILSHIRE BOULEVARD

EMMELINE SNIVELY's agency groomed girls "for careers in motion pictures, photographic modeling and fashion modeling, [with] personalized instruction in charm and poise, success and beauty and personalized development."

English-born Miss Snively had opened the business initially in 1937, under the name the "Village School" in Westwood, but then moved to her Sunset Boulevard premises in January 1944. Nineteen-year-old Norma Jeane put on her best clothes for her interview—a white shark skin dress with an orange yoke, plus white suede shoes—and signed on to the agency's books on August 2, 1945, joining another twenty or so young and not so young hopefuls. The Norma Jeane file listed her height at 5' 5", weight 118 pounds, measurements 36-24-34, size 12, hair color medium blonde ("too curly to manage, recommend bleach and permanent"), blue eyes, and "perfect teeth." Additional information supplied by the aspiring model was that she could "dance a little and sing." Quite possibly, the $25 fee Norma Jeane paid that day was the best investment she ever made.

Norma Jeane attended fashion modeling classes with Mrs Gavin Beardsley, makeup and grooming with Maria Smith, and posing instruction with Miss Snively. The $100 cost of these courses was defrayed against her first modeling assignment—ten days work for the Holga Steel Company at an industrial show in the Pan-Pacific Auditorium. Next came a job modeling in the Montgomery Ward clothing catalog and at a Hollywood fashion show, but then Miss Snively told Norma Jeane she had a "problem": nobody was paying attention to the clothes she was supposed to be modeling, they couldn't take their eyes of the body in the clothes. As a result, the agency sent Norma Jeane to pose for magazine covers and advertising agencies—her cheesecake career began with her first advertising placement, in which she was dressed in a sheer black negligee. Within six months Norma Jeane collected an incredible thirty-three covers (though some biographers put this figure much lower) in MAGAZINES such as *Peek*, *See*, *U.S. Camera*, *Parade*, *Glamorous Models*, *Personal Romances*, *Pageant*, and *Laff*. She may even have been too successful, for the next six months the offers dried up out of fear that she had been seen too often.

(see AGENCIES)

## BODY

Marilyn referred to her body has her "magic friend." Her last psychoanalyst, RALPH GREENSON, commented that the attractiveness

Marilyn with two other hopefuls from Emmeline Snively's Blue Book Modeling Agency, ca. 1945.

of her body was the main mechanism she used to bring some feeling of stability and significance to her life. In her last years, however, GLORIA STEINEM wrote, "Her body became her prison."

Marilyn worked hard to make the best of her natural assets, but there were some features she was never happy with. She once told SIMONE SIGNORET, "They all think I've got beautiful long legs; I have knobby knees and my legs are too short." She also thought that her hands were too fat; she avoided wearing rings because she didn't want to draw any attention to them.

The Artists Institute of America also highlighted imperfections in Marilyn's anatomy, in 1952, when they awarded their top pinup prize to actress Janice Rule because they considered Marilyn's legs to be too short and rear too sloping.

However, many people had flattering things to say, and at the time when direct reference to certain parts of the anatomy was avoided in polite company and in print, a surprising amount of press comment focused on Marilyn's more prominent features.

Actress Constance Bennett, who worked with Marilyn on *AS YOUNG AS YOU FEEL* (1951), said, "There's a broad with her future behind her."

PHILIPPE HALSMAN commented, "With every step her derriere seemed to wink at the onlooker."

JACK CARDIFF, who worked with Marilyn on *THE PRINCE AND THE SHOWGIRL* (1957), recalled, "Her whole body had a touch of overripeness—how Renoir would have adored her!"

BILLY WILDER, who worked with Marilyn on two films, said, "Her bosom was a miracle of shape, density, and an apparent lack of gravity."

Some people thought that the miracle was just a little too improbable. Journalist Pete Martin asked Marilyn if she had ever been accused of wearing falsies. Marilyn replied, "My answer to that is, quote: Those who know me better know better. That's all. Unquote."

## BOLAÑOS, JOSÉ

Marilyn met screenwriter Bolaños during her 1962 trip to Mexico, and then brought him back to Los Angeles as an escort to the GOLDEN GLOBE AWARDS. Soon after, with JOE DIMAGGIO back in town, he departed. According to LENA PEPITONE, Marilyn's New York maid, Marilyn referred to Bolaños as "the greatest lover in the whole wide world."

After Marilyn's death Bolaños claimed that he and Marilyn were planning to get married. In some biographies he is among the many people to have called Marilyn on her last night alive.

## BOLENDERS
### WAYNE, IDA, AND LESTER

On June 13, 1926, when Norma Jeane was less than two weeks old, her mother placed her with a foster family, the Bolenders, who lived on the same road as grandmother DELLA MAE MONROE, at 459 East Rhode Island Street in Hawthorne, California. This was sixteen miles away from where GLADYS BAKER was sharing an apartment with her friend GRACE MCKEE GODDARD. Norma Jeane spent the first seven years of her life with this devout family, during which time over a dozen other children arrived and departed. The family was poor—Wayne delivered mail—but more interested in religious propriety than wealth. Gladys kept up the weekly $5 payments for her daughter's board and lodging, but she was absent from her daughter's day-to-day existence.

Devout members of the United Pentecostal Church, an offshoot of the Los Angeles Apostolic Faith Gospel Mission, the Bolenders adhered to the belief that true religion was manifest in strict obedience to a specific code of behavior. The world was divided up into good and bad; drinking, smoking, dancing, and card-playing were works of the devil: neatness, order, and discipline were signs of virtue. Children were calmly and carefully told what it was they should and should not do, with no allowances made for childish exuberance or mischievousness. The Bolenders, like Marilyn's

Marilyn with screenwriter José Bolaños, 1962.

Eve Arnold took this photograph of Marilyn—a revealing look at her body—during filming of *The Misfits* (1961).

grandmother Della Mae, had also been followers of evangelist AIMEE SEMPLE MCPHERSON, founder of the controversial Foursquare Gospel Church where Norma Jeane was baptized.

One day little Norma Jeane called Ida Bolender "mother"; Mrs. Bolender politely told her to call her "aunt" instead. For young Norma Jeane, this must have been a source of great confusion. Her mother Gladys visited infrequently to take her out on weekends, and to her baby girl she was simply "the woman with the red hair."

The Bolenders were strict, God-fearing people, for whom morality and religious responsibilities were the cornerstones of any child's upbringing. In later life, Marilyn recalled Ida saying to her, "If the world came to an end with you sitting in the movies, do you know what would happen? You'd burn along with all the bad people. We are church-goers, not moviegoers."

While living with the Bolenders, Norma Jeane made her first public stage appearance as one of fifty black-clad youngsters, part of a religious ceremony for Easter 1932 held at the Hollywood Bowl:

> "We all had on white tunics under the black robes and at a given signal we were supposed to throw off the robes, changing the cross from black to white. But I got so interested in looking at the people, the orchestra, the hills and the stars in the sky that I forgot to watch the conductor for the signal. And there I was—the only black mark on a white cross. The family I was living with never forgave me."

The Bolenders taught Norma Jeane to pray every night; she had to say, "I promise, God helping me, not to buy, drink, sell or give alcohol while I live. From all tobacco I'll abstain, and never take God's name in vain." And yet when her mother came for weekend visits, she would be taken out to the picture palaces in Hollywood to see matinee movies.

In such a meticulously regimented life, young Norma Jeane took refuge in an inner world, revealed by Marilyn in later life to a biographer: "I dreamed that I was standing up in church without any clothes on, and all the people there were lying at my feet on the floor of the church, and I walked naked, with a sense of freedom, over their prostrate forms, being careful not to step on anyone."

Most likely the last time Norma Jeane saw the Bolenders was at her 1942 wedding to JAMES DOUGHERTY.

In adult life Marilyn said of the Bolenders, "They were terribly strict. They didn't mean any harm—it was their religion. They brought me up harshly." Biographers agree that Norma Jeane's years with the Bolenders, the first seven years of her life, left her feeling she was not quite one of the family, never quite good enough, always failing in something.

A publicity photo of Marilyn reading in her apartment, 1951.

## BOLENDER, LESTER

Two months older than Norma Jean, Lester was legally adopted by the Bolenders. In the first seven years of their lives the two children were so inseparable they were known as "the twins"; they would walk to school together and play with each other when they got home.

## BOOKS

Marilyn was the best read "dumb blonde" in movie history. Acutely conscious of her lack of official education, in adult life Marilyn was eager to read as much and as widely as she could. As a starlet she was seen touting major classics onto the set, and she continued to take reading matter—"heavy books, not light and flight books," as her stand-in EVELYN MORIARTY once said—with her when shooting her last films.

Marilyn was eclectic in her literary tastes. When Marilyn first met ARTHUR MILLER in 1951, they went together to a bookshop where she bought poetry by Frost, Whitman, and e.e. cummings. In his autobiography *Timebends*, Miller observes, "With no cultural pretensions to maintain, she felt no need to bother with anything that did not sweep her away. She could not suspend her disbelief toward fiction, wanting only the literal truth as though from a document." He also notes, "With the possible exception of Colette's *Cheri* and a few short stories, however, I had not known her to read any thing all the way through. There was no need to: she thought she could get the *idea* of a book—and often did—in a few pages."

On her first publicity tour in 1949 for *LOVE HAPPY* Marilyn retired to her hotel room to read novels by Proust and Thomas Wolfe, as well as Freud's writings on dreams. For entertainment she dipped into DOSTOEVSKY's *The Brothers Karamazov*. During shooting she had often been seen intently studying a copy of *De Humanis Corporis Fabrica*, a sixteenth-century treatise on human anatomy.

Writer/director JOSEPH L. MANKIEWICZ, who worked with Marilyn on *ALL ABOUT EVE*, noticed her carrying around a copy of Rilke's *Letters to a Young Poet* on the set. Marilyn told him, "Every now and then I go into the Pickwick [a Beverly Hills bookshop] and just look around. I leaf through some books, and when I read something that interests me, I buy the book. So last night I bought this one." After the director agreed that this was this best way to buy books, she sent him a copy the very next day. A shocked Mankiewicz said he would have been "less taken aback to come upon Herr Rilke studying a Marilyn Monroe nude calendar." There was more to come. Another book she was reading, *The Autobiography of Lincoln Steffens* (1866–1936), earned her a word of friendly advice from Mr. Mankiewicz, that she would get into trouble if people saw her reading such radical material. Soon after, when asked by the studio publicity department to give a list of her ten greatest men in the world, she put Steffens at the top of the list, only for him to be omitted as too politically dangerous.

Marilyn was particularly enamoured of Russian literature, an interest she developed during her early years in the film business, partly through her early professional exposure to the ACTORS LAB, partly as a reflection of the interests of her drama coach NATASHA LYTESS. She read Tolstoy and Chekhov short stories, Dostoevsky and Turgenev novels, and poetry by Pushkin and Andreyev.

In 1952 photographer PHILIPPE HALSMAN went to Marilyn's modest L.A. apartment on an assignment for Marilyn's first *Life* cover. He was struck by "the obvious striving for self-improvement," and a stack of books that included the history of Fabian socialism, as well as works by Dostoevsky and Freud, Shaw, Steinbeck, Ibsen, Wilde, Zola and her collection of Russian novels. He also found a number of books of art criticism, dealing with Goya, Botticelli, and Leonardo da Vinci.

During shooting of *NIAGARA*, Marilyn told photographer JOCK CARROLL what she had been reading recently: *The Thinking Body* by Mabel Ellsworth Todd (recommended to her by drama coach MICHAEL CHEKHOV), *Letters to a Young Poet* by Rainer Maria Rilke, and *The Prophet* by Kahlil Gibran. She also told him that she was a great fan of Whitman and Thomas Wolfe. On the set between takes she was seen scribbling down notes of passages she felt were particularly salient.

Marilyn treasured Antoine de Saint-Exupéry's *The Little Prince*. When married to JOE DIMAGGIO, she gave him a gold medal with a maxim from this book engraved on it: "True love is visible not to the eyes, but to the heart, for eyes may be deceived." DiMaggio's reported response was "What the hell does that mean?"

In the course of her studies with LEE STRASBERG at the ACTORS STUDIO Marilyn read widely, from Shakespeare sonnets to Colette. After one shopping trip in March 1955 she returned home with half a library, including *Ulysses* by James Joyce, *Fallen Angels* by Noel Coward, Shaw's *Letters to Ellen Terry* and *Letters to Mrs. Patrick Campbell*, and Richard Aldrich's biography of his wife Gertrude Lawrence.

With British poet EDITH SITWELL, Marilyn discussed the book she was reading at the time they first met, Rudolph Steiner's *Course of My Life*, and then, when Marilyn went to visit Dame Edith in England, they talked of Dylan Thomas and Gerard Manley Hopkins, a poet whose work Marilyn knew well enough to recite some lines.

Perhaps one of the most original excuses Marilyn ever came up with for her LATENESS was during shooting of *SOME LIKE IT HOT*, when she was so engrossed reading Paine's *The Rights of Man* that she reputedly told the assistant director, who had come to pick her up, to "fuck off."

In 1961 Marilyn was still avidly reading up on psychiatry and psychoanalysis. During her three-week stay in the HOSPITAL that February, she spent sleepless nights reading the letters of Sigmund Freud. She also read Sean O'Casey's autobiography.

To help Marilyn through her extreme nerves at having to sing to president KENNEDY at MADISON SQUARE GARDEN, Joan Greenson, daughter of her psychiatrist, gave her the children's book *The Little Engine That Could* to take along.

### SELECTED LIST OF BOOKS MARILYN READ

ACTING
*An Actor Prepares*, Kostantin Stanislavsky
*Biography of Eleanor Duse*, William Weaver
*How Stanislavsky Directs*, Michael Gorchakov
*The Thinking Body*, Mabel Ellsworth Todd
*To the Actor*, Michael Chekhov

FICTION/POETRY
*The Brothers Karamazov*, Fyodor Dostoevsky
*Leaves of Grass*, Walt Whitman
*Life Among the Savages*, Shirley Jackson
*The Little Prince*, Antoine de Saint-Exupéry
*Look Homeward Angel*, Thomas Wolfe
*Magnificent Obsession*, Lloyd Douglas
*The Old Man and the Sea*, Ernest Hemingway
*The Prophet*, Kahlil Gibran
*The Rebel*, Albert Camus
*Swann's Way*, Marcel Proust
*The Trial*, Franz Kafka
*Ulysses*, James Joyce
*War and Peace*, Leo Tolstoy

NON-FICTION/HISTORY
*Abraham Lincoln* (vols. 1–6), Carl Sandburg
*The Autobiography of Lincoln Steffens*
*The Course of My Life*, Rudolph Steiner
*Essays*, Ralph Waldo Emerson
*Letters to Ellen Terry*, George Bernard Shaw
*Letters to a Young Poet*, Rainer Maria Rilke
*The Rights of Man*, Thomas Paine

Marilyn and Brando at the premiere for *The Rose Tattoo* in 1955.

PSYCHOLOGY/SELP-HELP
*The Importance of Living*, Lin Yutang
*Psychology of Everyday Life*, Sigmund Freud
*Your Key to Happiness*, Harold Sherman

RELIGION
The Bible
*Science and Health with Key to the Scriptures*, Mary Baker Eddy

## BOX OFFICE

It seems that no two biographers agree on exactly how successful Marilyn's movies were in gross terms, though there is no disputing that she was the biggest female draw throughout the 1950s. Estimates of the total amount her films grossed during her lifetime range from $45 million to $250 million—impressive figures considering that movie theater tickets cost just fifty cents in the 1950s.

In 1982 *Film Magazine* listed the following gross figures for the original runs of Marilyn's movies (in order of release):

*HOW TO MARRY A MILLIONAIRE*—$7.3 million
*NIAGARA*—$2.5 million
*GENTLEMEN PREFER BLONDES*—$5.1 million
*RIVER OF NO RETURN*—$3.8 million
*THERE'S NO BUSINESS LIKE SHOW BUSINESS*—$5 million
*THE SEVEN YEAR ITCH*—$6 million
*BUS STOP*—$4.5 million
*THE PRINCE AND THE SHOWGIRL*—$1.6 million
*SOME LIKE IT HOT*—$7.9 million
*LET'S MAKE LOVE*—$3 million
*THE MISFITS*—$4.1 million.

Other estimates put the gross takes at roughly twice this level, in other words four or five times budget costs. For all but three of these movies, Marilyn was on unfavorably low fixed-earnings contracts with TWENTIETH CENTURY-FOX. However, Marilyn earned a 10 percent share of profits from *The Prince and the Showgirl*, *Some Like It Hot*, and *The Misfits*. To this day in these films continue to earn money for the beneficiaries of the ESTATE of Marilyn Monroe. Incidentally, *Some Like It Hot* was one of the most financially successful movies of the decade.

## BRAND, HARRY

The head of publicity at TWENTIETH CENTURY-FOX and the man who, together with ROY CRAFT, masterminded the promotional campaign that made a promising starlet into a legend. The first national feature on Fox's latest star, which appeared in *Collier's* magazine in September 1951, quotes Brand as saying, "She's the biggest thing we've had at the studio since SHIRLEY TEMPLE and BETTY GRABLE," even though at that time Marilyn had yet to play a lead role.

When all the hard work to portray Marilyn as a meek orphan made good was endangered after news leaked that she had posed nude for the infamous "Golden Dreams" calendar, unlike his studio bosses, Brand did not panic. At the crisis meeting his opinion was, "This isn't going to kill her. It's going to make her." Never a truer word was spoken by a publicity man.

In the heyday of the studio, the head of publicity at Fox wielded considerable power—he may not have been able to direct events, but he could certainly delay and massage the way that news was presented to the public. Marilyn called him, for instance, to inform him of her whirlwind marriage ceremony to JOE DIMAGGIO; then, nine months later, she called him so that he could arrange the most favorable possible tone for news of the divorce proceedings she was instituting against him.

## BRANDO, MARLON (B. 1924)

MARILYN:
"Personally, I react to Marlon Brando. He's a favorite of mine."

"[He is] one of the most attractive men I've ever met."

BRANDO:
"Do you remember when Marilyn Monroe died? Everybody stopped work, and you could see all that day the same expressions on their faces, the same thought: 'How can a girl with success, fame, youth, money, beauty... how could she kill herself?' Nobody could understand it because those are the things that everybody wants, and they can't believe that life wasn't important to Marilyn Monroe, or that her life was elsewhere."

There are conflicting reports about exactly when the two most famous alumni of the ACTORS STUDIO first met. Some biographers claim it was in 1951, when Marilyn was having an affair with director ELIA KAZAN, at a time when he was working with Brando on *A STREETCAR NAMED DESIRE*. In other accounts they didn't meet until 1954, on the Fox lot where she was working on *THERE'S NO BUSINESS LIKE SHOW BUSINESS* (1954) and Brando was shooting *Désirée*. They met frequently in 1955, after Marilyn moved to New York; he may well have been instrumental in persuading her of the benefits of working with LEE STRASBERG. Rumors did the rounds of an affair between these two stars, based on the many times they were seen out on the town, going to the theater or restaurants. In December 1955 Marilyn was Brando's guest at the premiere of *The Rose Tattoo*, after which they went to a celebration dinner at the Sheraton Astor Hotel on Forty-forth Street. In his biography of Marilyn, ANTHONY SUMMERS writes that Marilyn told her friend AMY GREENE that she secretly referred to Brando as "Carlo," and that he was "sweet, tender." The intriguing screen pairing of Marilyn and Brando never came closer than when Brando asked Marilyn if she would co-star in jazz movie *Paris Blue*, before himself pulling out of the project. They remained friends for life.

## BRENNAN, WALTER (1894–1974)

Three time Oscar-winning actor who specialized in playing toothless old men after a 1932 accident that knocked out his front teeth. Marilyn had bit parts in two movies with Brennan, *SCUDDA HOO! SCUDDA HAY!* (1948) and *A TICKET TO TOMAHAWK* (1950). In a career spanning from the twenties to the seventies, Brennan made well over one hundred movies.

## BROOKLYN, NEW YORK

In early 1955, not long after her break-up with JOE DIMAGGIO, Marilyn improbably told radio interviewer Dave Garroway, "I want to retire to Brooklyn." What she really meant was that she enjoyed her clandestine meetings with ARTHUR MILLER, who at that time was living in Brooklyn Heights with first wife Mary Slattery Miller. Photographer SAM SHAW said of Marilyn in late 1955 and early 1956, as she visited her new beau Arthur, that "Brooklyn became Nirvana to her, a magical place, her true home."

(*see* NEW YORK)

## BROTHERS

For an only child, Marilyn acquired a large collection of brothers in all shapes and sizes:

Half-Brother: Hermitt Jack Baker
Foster Brother: LESTER BOLENDER
Brothers-In-Law:
- Thomas DiMaggio
- Michael DiMaggio
- Vincent DiMaggio
- Dominic DiMaggio
- Marion Dougherty
- Tom Dougherty
- Kermit Miller

## BRYSON, JOHN

A PHOTOGRAPHER who worked for many years at *Life* magazine, and often did stills on movie sets. In 1960 Bryson documented Marilyn during shooting of *LET'S MAKE LOVE* for a cover feature in *Life* and a piece in *Paris-Match*.

## BUGGING

In the last months of her life Marilyn reputedly told friends that she knew her home was bugged; as evidence, it has been said that she went out with plenty of change so that she could make and receive calls from public phones. A wiretap specialist named BERNARD SPINDEL claimed that this was the case. The bugs may have been planted by Mafia interests, JIMMY HOFFA, the CIA, and possibly even a jealous and concerned JOE DIMAGGIO.

## BURNSIDE, BILL

"She was very aware of how she affected men. If I took her to a restaurant, however elegant, the waiters were ready to jump at her bidding. She had it all there, that star quality."

A Scottish PHOTOGRAPHER who worked a number of times with Norma Jeane between 1946 and 1948. Burnside received her favors as they made the raw material to sell her image. He was attracted, he said, by "the lost look in the middle of a smile. . . . A kiss took two weeks to achieve. She did not like to be touched too soon."

## *BUS STOP* (1956)
(ALSO KNOWN AS: *The Wrong Kind of Girl*)

After resolving her bitter wrangle with TWENTIETH CENTURY-FOX and forming her own production company, Marilyn was tempted back to Hollywood to play the lead in a screen adaptation of WILLIAM INGE's 1955 Broadway hit. The result was what many considered to be Marilyn's finest dramatic performance.

Marilyn's business partner MILTON GREENE, did much to design the look of the picture. Under the terms of her new contract with Fox, Marilyn had approval not only of the script but of the director and cinematographer as well. First choice JOHN HUSTON, who had directed her so well in *THE ASPHALT JUNGLE*, was unavailable. LEW WASSERMAN suggested JOSHUA LOGAN, who was persuaded to take on the project when his friend LEE STRASBERG vouched for Marilyn's abundance of talent. Initially, PAULA STRASBERG was not allowed onto the set. However, Marilyn's intercession, and Lee's behind-the-scenes insistence, led to his wife being hired (for a whopping $1,500 per week) for the first time to steady the star's nerves and help her perfect her accent.

Location shooting took place in the first part of 1956 in Phoenix, Arizona for the rodeo footage and SUN VALLEY, IDAHO for mountain exteriors. The enormous temperature difference between the desert and the mountain gave Marilyn a nasty case of bronchitis, and shooting had to be suspended as Marilyn was admitted to hospital in early April.

Marilyn, as ever, was "difficult" during shooting. It wasn't just her old bugbears, fear of failure, and low self-esteem; she had an increasing dependency on BARBITURATES to contend with. She was also, for the first time, in a position of executive power. Co-star DON MURRAY, for one, found that she was not always a caring boss. The only actor on the set with whom Marilyn struck up a friendship was Eileen Heckart, who had recently starred in the ARTHUR MILLER play *A View from the Bridge*.

With scope at last to express her creativity, Marilyn made some brilliant decisions. She vetoed the sumptuous costumes that wardrobe came up with, picking out a shabby dress and deliberately laddering a pair of fishnet stockings. Marilyn also gave the "chantoose" character of Cherie a stutter in moments of high tension (a detail from Marilyn's own life), and a tendency to forget her lines at important moments.

In the final version, much of Marilyn's monologue with HOPE LANGE in the bus, in which she gives a highly dramatic performance, was cut after Logan was put under pressure to shorten the movie. Marilyn believed that this cut cost her an Oscar nomination.

Screenwriter GEORGE AXELROD had Marilyn very much in mind when he adapted the original stage play. In the character's revealing speech to young Lange on the bus, she says:

> "I've been goin' with boys since I was twelve—them Ozarks don't waste much time—and I've been losin' my head about some guy ever since. Of course I'd like to get married and have a family and all them things... Maybe I don't know what love is. I want a guy I can look up to and admire. But I don't want him to browbeat me. I want a guy who'll be sweet with me. But I don't want him to baby me, either. I just gotta feel that whoever I marry has some real regard for me—aside from all that lovin' stuff."

Several copies of the black dress in which Marilyn sang her "Old Black Magic" number are in collectors' hands: one is owned by model JERRY HALL, one is on display at the Costa Mesa (California) Planet Hollywood restaurant, and another is in the Debbie Reynolds Las Vegas museum.

This is perhaps the only one of the movies in which Marilyn stars that has not been available on video in the United States, as a result of legal wrangles with the estate of playwright William Inge.

MEMORABLE COSTUME:
Midnight blue and green sequined "Old Black Magic" dress, fishnet stockings with runs, and a removable black sequined tailpiece.

**Tagline:**
"The coming of age of Bo Decker . . . and the girl who made him a man!"

**Nominations:**
ACADEMY AWARDS:
Best Supporting Actor: Don Murray

BRITISH ACADEMY AWARDS:
Most Promising Newcomer: Don Murray

**Credits:**
Twentieth Century-Fox, CinemaScope & Color (DeLuxe)
Length: 96 minutes
Release date: August 31, 1956

Directed by: Joshua Logan
Produced by: Buddy Adler
Written by: George Axelrod from a William Inge play
Cinematography by: Milton R. Krasner
Music by: Cyril J. Mockridge, Alfred Newman plus a song by Ken Darby
Film editing by: William Reynolds

**Cast (credits order):**
Marilyn Monroe . . . Cherie
Don Murray . . . Beauregard "Bo" Decker
Arthur O'Connell . . . Virgil "Virge" Blessing
Betty Field . . . Grace
Eileen Heckart . . . Vera
Robert Bray . . . Carl
Hope Lange . . . Elma Duckworth
Hans Conried . . . Photographer
Max Showalter (aka Casey Adams) . . . *Life* Reporter
Henry Slate . . . Manager of Nightclub
Terry Kelman . . . Gerald
Linda Brace . . . Evelyn
Greta Thyssen . . . Cover Girl
Helen Mayon . . . Landlady
Lucille Knox . . . Blonde on Street
Kate MacKenna . . . Elderly Passenger
Budd Buster . . . Elderly Passenger
Mary Carroll . . . Cashier

Marilyn and Don Murray in *Bus Stop* (1956).

J. M. Dunlap . . . Orville
Fay L. Ivor . . . Usher
Phil J. Munch . . . Preacher
Jim Katugi Noda . . . Japanese Cook

**Crew:**
Mark-Lee Kirk . . . art director
Lyle R. Wheeler . . . art director
Paul S. Fox . . . set decoration
Walter M. Scott . . . set decoration
Travilla . . . costume design
Charles Le Maire . . . wardrobe designer
Ben Nye . . . makeup
Helen Turpin . . . hair
Ben Kadish . . . assistant director
Alfred Bruzlin . . . sound
Harry M. Leonard . . . sound
Ray Kellogg . . . special effects

**Plot:**
Bo Decker (Don Murray) has grown up on an isolated Montana ranch with guardian Virgil (Arthur O'Connell). He may know a thing or two about riding horses and roping cattle, but on his way to Phoenix with Virgil for a rodeo he is all wide-eyed innocence.

In town Bo follows Virgil into the Blue Dragon Café, where he hears singer Cherie (Marilyn Monroe), originally from the Ozarks, haltingly delivering "That Old Black Magic" while being heckled by the grizzled drinkers. Bo springs to his feet and silences the crowd. Cherie, we learn, has a life plan to continue her journey West until she hits Hollywood, where who knows what will start to happen for her.

Bo mistakes Cherie's grateful kiss for the sign that this is the woman he wants for his wife. No matter what Virgil has to say, he won't be shaken in his belief that he has found an angel.

Bo tracks Cherie down and wakens her the following morning with the news that later that day, after he has ridden in the rodeo, they'll be getting married. Cherie and her

Marilyn and Don Murray in *Bus Stop* (1956).

friend Vera (Eileen Heckart) go to the rodeo and watch as Bo wins everything, spurred on by his love for Cherie and a green scarf he has purloined from her. Cherie realizes Bo is serious and wants to go through with his crazy marriage plans, and that she needs to take evasive action. She borrows some money from Virgil and she goes to the bus station, bound for Los Angeles, but Bo spots her and pushes her onto his bus back to Montana. In a poignant speech, Cherie reveals her battered hopes and her checkered life to a young girl on the bus, Elma (played by Hope Lange, making her debut). Then, because of snow up ahead, the bus is forced to make an overnight layoff at Grace's Diner. While Bo and Virgil are sleeping, Cherie goes into the diner, and Elma explains that she has been put on the bus against her will.

Bo comes in indignant that Cherie is trying to make another break for it, and picks her up in a fireman's lift to carry her off to the nearest minister. Bus driver Carl (Robert Bray) has heard what is going on and challenges Bo to a fight—the older man leaves the younger man unconscious in the snow.

Bo is so ashamed of losing that he can't face Cherie. Virgil tells him he has to apologize, and finally he does. Cherie lets him know that he is better off without her—he knows nothing of her past. The road has been cleared, it is time for Bo to move on. He gently asks if he may kiss Cherie goodbye. She says yes, only to find that she is deeply moved. Bo says he still wants to marry her, and this time Cherie says yes. The couple get onto the bus and wait for Virgil, but Virgil, seeing that his work is done and now Bo will have a wife, decides to stay behind.

**Reviews:**

*The Saturday Review*
"Speaking of artists, it is beginning to appear that we have a very real one right in our midst... in *Bus Stop* Marilyn Monroe effectively dispels once and for all the notion that she is merely a glamour personality, a shapely body with tremulous lips and come-hither blue eyes."

*The Los Angeles Examiner*
"This is Marilyn's show, and, my friend, she shows plenty in figure, beauty and talent. The girl is a terrific comedienne as the bewildered little 'chantoose' of the honky-tonk circuit. Her stint at the Actors Studio in New York certainly didn't hurt our girl."

*New York Herald Tribune*
"Eighteen months ago Marilyn Monroe quit Hollywood and came East to study 'serious' acting. Now she is back on the screen . . . and everybody can see what the 'new' Marilyn is like.

In *Bus Stop* she has a wonderful role, and she plays it with a mixture of humor and pain that is very touching. This is also the special genius of the movie. One minute it is uproariously funny, the next minute tender and fragile, and somehow director Joshua Logan preserved the delicate balance."

*The New York Times*
"Hold onto your chairs, everybody, and get set for a rattling surprise. Marilyn Monroe has finally proved herself an actress in *Bus Stop*. She and the picture are swell!

. . . Mr. Logan has got her to do a great deal more than wiggle and pout and pop her big eyes and play the synthetic vamp in this film. He has got her to be the beat-up B-girl of Mr. Inge's play, even down to the Ozark accent and the look of pellagra about her skin.

He has got her to be the tinseled floozie, the semi-moronic doll who is found in a Phoenix clip-joint by a cowboy of equally limited brains and is hotly pursued by this suitor to a snow-bound bus stop in the Arizona wilds. And, what's most important, he has got her to light the small flame of dignity that sputters pathetically in this chippie and to make a rather moving sort of her.

Fortunately for her and for the tradition of diligence leading to success, she gives a performance in this picture that marks her as a genuine acting star, not just a plushy personality and a sex symbol, as she has previously been."

C

The Cal-Neva Lodge, ca. 1960.

## CAL-NEVA LODGE

NUMBER 2 STATE LINE, CRYSTAL BAY, NEVADA

This Lake Tahoe casino resort, named after its location on the border between California and Nevada, was reputedly owned by FRANK SINATRA and MAFIA boss SAM GIANCANA and features in all accounts of the last week of Marilyn's life. But that's where agreement ends. Depending on the biographer, Marilyn either spent the weekend there in a drug- and drink-induced state, went there and attempted suicide, stayed there as a guest of the LAWFORDS (as she regularly did), had sex there with Giancana, went there for a quiet reunion with JOE DIMAGGIO (the two deciding that they wanted to remarry), or never went there at all but the story was put out as a cover for a secret abortion. A recent addition to these theories is a suggestion that Sinatra was considering marrying Marilyn to try and pull her out of her depression. Marilyn stayed in chalet 52. The hotel advertises that the suite has been kept as she left it ever since, with a pink, round bed and wicker furniture.

## CALENDAR

Before posing for her famous calendar shots, Marilyn had turned down many offers to pose nude. It seems she accepted only when her need was dire and immediate; her contracts with TWENTIETH CENTURY-FOX and COLUMBIA had not been renewed, she was out of work, and she had a certain level of lifestyle to maintain. The $50 she was paid was exactly the amount she needed to get back her car which had been impounded; she was also at that time living in a rather expensive room at the BEVERLY CARLTON HOTEL.

The photographs that became the infamous "Golden Dreams" calendar were taken on May 27, 1949, the day that Marilyn walked into TOM KELLEY's photo studio. Kelley's wife Natalie helped him to prepare the red velvet backdrop and the cameras. So that his model could relax, he put Artie Shaw's "Begin the Beguine" on the record player. The shoot lasted two hours, while Kelley, assisted by his wife Natalie, shot a sequence of photographs from a ten-foot ladder. Only two of the twenty-four shots Kelley took with his Deardorff View camera actually made it into print. "A New Wrinkle" graced one Baumgarth Company calendar, but the picture that captured a nation's imagination was "Golden Dreams."

Kelley received $500 for all publication rights, and Marilyn went home with $50, but not before going out with the photographer (and maybe Natalie too) for a meal. This left John Baumgarth, according to an estimate in a 1956 issue of *Time* magazine, with a profit of around $750,000 from that one photo.

The remaining unpublished nudes mysteriously disappeared from Kelley's office, and have never resurfaced (though recently some photographs from the Kelley session may have been unearthed and put on sale, with alluring titles such as "On the Knees, Close #6"). Kelley also shot an additional roll, which he gave to Marilyn; she in turn reputedly gave this roll as a wedding gift to second husband JOE DIMAGGIO.

The story that Hollywood's hottest new property Marilyn Monroe was in fact the girl in the "Golden Dreams" calendar was broken by wire journalist Aline Mosby in March 1952.

There are at least two versions of how she managed to get this scoop. One runs that she had been tipped off by JERRY WALD and NORMAN KRASNA, who had produced *CLASH BY NIGHT* (1952) for RKO pictures and wanted to generate a little extra free publicity. Mosby contacted Fox for confirmation or denial. Twentieth Century-Fox executives—Marilyn had only been loaned to RKO for one picture and was under contract to Fox—went into panic mode and confronted Marilyn, who admitted that she had indeed posed for the nude calendar shots. An interview was arranged so that at least the studio could manage the seemingly disastrous situation.

The second version of events has Marilyn, with tears in her eyes, taking Mosby to one side at the end of a quite innocent, run-of-the-mill interview, and confessing that she had posed nude for the calendar and desperately needed a sympathetic hearing.

The studio's initial reaction was to deny everything. No Hollywood star had ever been proven to have done such a thing; whatever people did in private, the early fifties was a time of strait-laced public morals. Biographers agree that Marilyn was instrumental in persuading the studio that their natural inclination to deny the whole thing was the wrong way to handle the situation. Fox publicity director HARRY BRAND concurred that ably managed, this potentially lethal piece of news could be turned to the studio and star's advantage. An exclusive interview was arranged and the following confession ran in U.S. newspapers on March 13, 1952.

---

### MARILYN MONROE ADMITS SHE'S NUDE BLONDE OF CALENDAR

*by Aline Mosby*

A photograph of a beautiful nude blonde on a 1952 calendar is hanging in garages and barbershops all over the nation today.

Marilyn Monroe admitted today that the beauty is she.

She posed, stretched out on rumpled red velvet, for the artistic photo three years ago because "I was broke and needed the money.

"Oh, the calendar's hanging in garages all over town," said Marilyn. "Why deny it? You can get one any place.

"Besides, I'm not ashamed of it. I've done nothing wrong."

The beautiful blonde now gets a fat paycheck every week from an excited Twentieth Century-Fox Studio. She's rated the most sensational sweater girl since Lana Turner.... she lives in an expensive hotel room.... She dines at Romanoff's.

LIVED IN ORPHANAGE

But in 1949 she was just another scared young blonde, struggling to find fame in the magic city, and all alone. As a child she lived in a Hollywood orphanage. She was pushed around among twelve sets of foster parents before she turned an insecure sixteen.

After an unsuccessful marriage, she moved into Hollywood's famed Studio Club, home of hopeful actresses.

"I was a week behind on my rent," she explained. "I had to have the money. A photographer, Tom Kelley, had asked me before to pose but I'd never do it. This time I called him and said I would as soon as possible, to get it over with.

"His wife was there. They're both very nice. We did two poses, one standing up with my head turned profile, and another lying on some red velvet."

Marilyn speaks in a breathless, soft voice, and she's always very serious about every word she says.

"Tom didn't think anyone would recognize me," she said. "My hair was long then. But when the picture came out, everybody knew me. I'd never have done it if I'd known things would happen in Hollywood so fast for me."

Marilyn's bosses at plushy Fox Studio reached for the ulcer tablets when the calendar blossomed out in January.

"I was told I should deny I'd posed... but I'd rather be honest about it. I've gotten a lot of fan letters on it. The men like the picture and want copies. The women, well...

"One gossip columnist said I autographed the pictures and handed them out and said 'Art for Art's Sake.' I never said that."

"Why, I only gave two away," said Marilyn, and blinked those big, blue eyes.

---

In the aftermath of the calendar confession, Marilyn was harangued by journalists. In typical fashion, when asked if it was true she had nothing on when she posed for the calendar, she replied "Oh no, I had the radio on."

For the following weeks Marilyn dutifully did interview after interview, letting the world know that she was an honest girl who had found an honest way to make a crust when in need. She succeeded in turning this desperate act into an episode of populism: "I've been on a calendar. I don't want to be just for the few, I want to be for the many, the kind of people I come from. I want a man to come home after a hard day's work, look at this picture and feel inspired to say 'Wow!'"

For a while in 1953 America lapsed into high comedy as hundreds of thousands of calendars flew out of the stores while hard-pressed police departments tried unsuccessfully to stem the flood of what was officially branded a dangerous, obscene, and erotic publication. Camera store owner Phil Max, of Wilshire Boulevard in L.A., was arrested and fined for displaying the "New Wrinkle" calendar in his shop window. In December 1953 an astute man named HUGH HEFNER bought the rights to reproduce the "Golden Dreams" photograph as the first centerfold in the first ever issue of *Playboy* magazine.

The calendar was reprinted many times in the early fifties—estimates run at a total of around four million copies sold by 1955. "Original" calendars, the ones that do not have Marilyn's name on them, exchange hands for over $500. Later specimens can be bought for substantially less.

This was not Marilyn's calendar debut. A year or two earlier she had posed for EARL MORAN "photo illustrations" which appeared on a calendar for the Brown and Bigelow Calendar Company, distributed in the U.S. and Mexico.

## CALHERN, LOUIS
(1895–1956, B. CARL VOGT)

An accomplished stage actor who made the switch into film during the silent era. In 1950 Calhern played Alonzo D. Emmerich, Marilyn's sugar daddy in *THE ASPHALT JUNGLE*. He also shared the screen with Marilyn in 1952, though in a different episode of the segment film *WE'RE NOT MARRIED*. Calhern is best remembered for his bumper year of 1950, when as well as his performance opposite Marilyn he starred in *Annie Get Your Gun* (1950), and received an Oscar nomination for his work in *The Magnificent Yankee* (1950). His last screen appearance, shortly before he died, was in *High Society* (1956).

## CALHOUN, RORY
(1922–1999, B. FRANCIS TIMOTHY DURGIN)

Discovered riding the trails above Hollywood, Calhoun was roped into the movie world as an archetypal cowboy. He worked with Marilyn three times, in *A TICKET TO TOMAHAWK* (1950), *HOW TO MARRY A MILLIONAIRE* (1953), and *RIVER OF NO RETURN* (1954).

## CAMEOS

Marilyn's demise did not stop her from appearing in a hundred movies since 1962—as an image in a newspaper, a face on a movie screen, or a name on a movie house billboard. Here are a few of Marilyn's "cameo" appearances:

FILMS:

*Cool World* (1992): Scenes from *LET'S MAKE LOVE* (1960) are shown.
*Destiny Turns on the Radio* (1995): Marilyn in neon at the Marilyn Monroe Motel.
*Guilty by Suspicion* (1990): *GENTLEMEN PREFER BLONDES* (1953)is being shot during events.
*Hercules* (1997): Marilyn is one of three constellations visible at the end of the song "Zero to Hero."
*Jigsaw Murders* (1988): Marilyn's photos cover a bedroom wall.
*L. A. Confidential* (1997): Marilyn, in front of Grauman's Theater, features in the opening scene.
*Myra Breckinridge* (1970): Fox film starring MAE WEST and Raquel Welch, in which Marilyn made a posthumous appearance in the form a clip of her bathing suit scene from the unfinished *SOMETHING'S GOT TO GIVE*.
*Milk Money* (1994): Marilyn's photos decorate a fifties dancehall.
*Night People* (1954): German movie posters promoting *NIAGARA* (1952) are visible at a movie house.
*Okinawa* (1952): COLOMBIA recycled Marilyn's performance of "Every Baby Needs a Da-Da-Daddy" in this war movie set in the Pacific.
*Pretty in Pink* (1986): A *MISFITS* poster.
*Riders of the Whistling Pines* (1949): A cowboy sings a lament to a photo of his dead wife – and the picture is Marilyn.
*Tommy* (1975): Mass is celebrated before a statue of Marilyn.
*Valley of the Dolls* (1967): Marilyn's laugh was "borrowed" from *Something's Got to Give*.
*Venice/Venice* (1992): Poster of the *THE SEVEN YEAR ITCH* (1955) skirt scene in the opening minutes.
*White Palace* (1990): Susan Sarandon's home is full of Marilyn memorabilia.

TV SHOWS:

*I Love Lucy*: Episode titled "Ricky's Movie Offer" has Lucille Ball doing a Marilyn impression (November 8, 1954).
*Roseanne*: The yacht scene with guest TONY CURTIS; Sandra Bernhard does a Marilyn in a Halloween special.
*Quantum Leap*: A Marilyn episode.
*MASH*: "Bombshells" episode
*Benson*: "Boys Night Out" episode
*Matt Houston*: "Marilyn" episode

Truman Capote and Marilyn at the El Morocco, 1955.

## CAMP PENDLETON

In early 1952 Marilyn performed before ten thousand spellbound Marines at this military base south of Los Angeles. Marilyn was at the time vying for the role of Lorelei Lee in GENTLEMEN PREFER BLONDES (1953). There was speculation that she performed there to prove to FOX boss DARRYL ZANUCK she could sing. Her repertoire for the boys that day consisted of "Somebody Loves You" and "Do It Again." Between songs, Marilyn whipped up excitement with provocative lines such as: "I don't know why you boys are always getting so excited about sweater girls. Take away their sweaters—and what have they got?"

Marilyn recorded "Do It Again," composed by George Gershwin and written by G. DeSylva, in January 1953.

## CAPELL, FRANK A.

Former investigator into subversive activities at Westchester County, publisher of virulently anti-Communist newspaper *Herald of Freedom*, Capell was friends with columnist WALTER WINCHELL and with policeman JACK CLEMMONS, the first to arrive at Marilyn's house after her death. Capell's 1964 seventy-page publication *The Strange Death of Marilyn Monroe* was among the first to make allegations implicating ROBERT KENNEDY in Marilyn's death. It was Capell's thesis that Kennedy had promised to marry Marilyn, changed his mind and then deployed "his personal Gestapo" to get rid of her.

## CAPOTE, TRUMAN
(1924–1984, B. TRUMAN PERSONS)

"There was something exceptional about Marilyn Monroe. Sometimes she could be ethereal and sometimes like a waitress in a coffee shop."

"She labors like a field hand to please everybody."

Southern writer to whom success came early, and continued through novels, essays, short stories, and screenplays, some focusing on homosexuality. Capote wrote the screenplays for his own novels: *Breakfast at Tiffany's* (1961), for which he originally wanted Marilyn [*see* FILMS MARILYN CONSIDERED OR WANTED], and *In Cold Blood* (1967).

Capote and Marilyn first met in 1950, during shooting of *THE ASPHALT JUNGLE*. He said they immediately became friends, and recalled an occasion when Marilyn danced nude in CECIL BEATON's New York hotel suite. Just months before she died, Capote found Marilyn "had never looked better... and there was a new maturity about her eyes. She wasn't so giggly any more."

Like Marilyn, Capote is buried in the WESTWOOD MEMORIAL PARK CEMETERY.

BOOK:
*Music for Chameleons*. New York: Random House, 1980.
Contains a chapter on Marilyn called "A Beautiful Child."

## CARDIFF, JACK (B. 1914)

"She wasn't a great actress, she was a genius. She had a talent that in most cases was not seen until it was on the screen. She had this extraordinary magic that came over on camera.... However, she had this double side. Larry [Olivier] called her schizoid, and she was."

Marilyn specifically requested Cardiff's services for *THE PRINCE AND THE SHOWGIRL* after hearing that this British cinematographer was the best in the business, unrivalled in his handling of color. His credentials were an Oscar for *Black Narcissus* (1946), as well as credits on *A Matter of Life and Death* (1946), *The African Queen* (1951), *War and Peace* (1956), and many more. In the late fifties Cardiff tried his hand at directing. On the set of *The Prince and the Showgirl,* Cardiff took a number of photographs of Marilyn, including one as a Renoir girl.

BOOK:
*Magic Hour*. New York and London: Faber & Faber, 1996.
Contains a twenty-page chapter on Marilyn.

## CARLYLE HOTEL
35 EAST SEVENTY-SIXTH STREET, NEW YORK

This was the HOTEL that President JOHN F. KENNEDY used when staying in New York. His affair with Marilyn reputedly took place here, according to, among others, biographer ANTHONY SUMMERS.

## CARMEN, JEANNE (B. 1930)

Jeanne Carmen, actress and friend of Marilyn Monroe, does not tend to get good press. The facts of where and when she was born vary from one biographer to the next. Carmen has been a regular on Marilyn-related TV shows, where she discusses the confidences Marilyn allegedly shared with her after they struck up a close friendship in 1961 at the apartment building on DOHENY DRIVE.

Biographer DONALD SPOTO confirms that Carmen was indeed a neighbor of Marilyn's in 1961, but that they never met beyond usual neighborly contact, and she was certainly not "Marilyn's roommate" as she later claimed. Her name does not appear in any of Marilyn's address books, and Marilyn's close friends had never heard of her when, in the 1980s, she began to talk about nude swimming parties and evidence of the romance between the president and Marilyn.

For GLORIA STEINEM, Carmen was one of only two women with whom Marilyn was close at the end of her life, the other being publicist PATRICIA NEWCOMB. ANTHONY SUMMERS cites her as an important witness to BOBBY KENNEDY's alleged clandestine visits to Marilyn. Carmen has gone on record to back up ROBERT SLATZER's claims to a lifelong friendship with Marilyn, though she denies that Slatzer and Marilyn were ever married. In a 1991 interview in the *Ladies' Home Journal* Carmen says that the day Marilyn died they were due to go out golfing, and Marilyn had very much been looking forward to it.

John Carroll

Carmen's acting credits include *Striporama* (1954), *Untamed Youth* (1957), *Born Reckless* (1958), and *The Devil's Hand* (1962).

## CAROLWOOD DRIVE

In early 1949, before meeting JOHNNY HYDE, Marilyn lived in a pool house cottage on the estate belonging to FOX mogul JOSEPH SCHENCK, address 141 South Carolwood Drive, Beverly Hills.

(*see* HOMES)

## CARROLL, JOCK

A Canadian PHOTOGRAPHER who did an extended photo spread on Marilyn during production of NIAGARA (1952) for *Weekend* MAGAZINE. His photographs were published posthumously in 1996 in *Falling for Marilyn: The Lost Niagara Collection*.

## CARROLL, JOHN
(1906–1979, B. JULIAN LA FAYE)

An actor with a passing resemblance to CLARK GABLE, whose film career spanned thirty years from his first appearance in the 1929 film *Marianne*. He and wife LUCILLE RYMAN took Marilyn in to live with them in their "El Palacio" apartment, West Hollywood, when she was out of contract and going hungry in 1947. For the next five months they looked after her financially and emotionally.

The actor first met Marilyn at an annual celebrity golf tournament held at the Cheviot Hills Country Club (Motor Avenue, Rancho Park, just opposite the TWENTIETH CENTURY-FOX Studios), when Marilyn was assigned as his caddy. After the tournament John Carroll gave her a lift back to the

A Twentieth Century-Fox publicity photo, 1953.

Harrah's

rundown apartment where she was living; apparently Marilyn asked him in but he declined. Soon afterward he and Ryman, who were known for helping struggling actresses out of difficult moments, took Marilyn in, provided her a weekly allowance of $100, and introduced her to their impressive circle of friends in L.A. and at their ranch out of town in the Granada Hills. The Carrolls were well connected—well enough to appear in gossip magazine *Confidential*, which alleged that the couple threw all-nude parties.

Reputedly Carroll became Marilyn's lover, though this is something that the actor later denied. In FRED LAWRENCE GUILES's biography *Norma Jeane: The Life and Death of Marilyn Monroe*, Ryman describes an incident when Marilyn took her to one side, "Lucille, I want to have a little talk with you. You don't love John. If you did, you wouldn't be off working all the time. I think I'm in love with him. . . . Would you divorce him so we can marry?" Marilyn apparently believed that anybody who showed such a degree of kindness wanted something in return. For his part, Carroll is quoted by ROBERT SLATZER as saying, "The only thing I ever did with Marilyn was to try to teach her how to sing,"—though he did sign her to a personal management contract in late 1947, which later had to be voluntarily rescinded.

The Carrolls ceased being Marilyn's benefactor in 1949, around the time that Marilyn began seeing top Hollywood agent JOHNNY HYDE. The last installments of their allowance were redirected to cover repayments for Marilyn's convertible.

Marilyn repaid the Carrolls' kindness with a gift from her paycheck for her work in the film *LOVE HAPPY* (1950).

## CARS

Marilyn was taught to drive either by first husband JAMES DOUGHERTY, or by his mother Ethel, while her husband was away on service during World War II. Marilyn always loved driving, but her record was not unblemished. She apparently first met photographer TOM KELLEY in the aftermath of a fender bender on Sunset Boulevard in 1948.

On May 21, 1954 a rather distraught Marilyn was charged with reckless driving after driving her 1952 Cadillac convertible into the back of a car belonging to a man called Bart Antinora, at the corner of Sunset Boulevard and Beverly Drive. The court awarded the plaintiff $500, against Antinora's claim of $3000 from Marilyn and passenger JOE DIMAGGIO.

On February 28, 1956 Marilyn was charged for driving without a license after being stopped on Wilshire Boulevard two years earlier. W. C. Fields Jr., son of the famous actor, provided her with legal counsel on this occasion. Judge Charles J. Griffin, who had issued two warrants for Marilyn Monroe's arrest before she finally appeared in court, fined her fifty-five dollars and reminded her, "Laws are made for all of us, rich or poor, without race or creed or whether your name happens to be Miss Monroe or not, and this kind of acting won't win you an Oscar."

This photograph was taken by Henri Cartier-Bresson on the set of *The Misfits* (1961).

### CARS IN MARILYN'S LIFE

Norma Jeane was wooed by Jim Dougherty in his blue 1940 coupé; on her divorce from Dougherty, her settlement was the 1935 Ford coupé they then had.

As soon as she had enough money, Marilyn splurged on a 1948 Ford convertible—soon repossessed when she fell behind in her payments.

Her next car was a 1950 Pontiac convertible.

1953: For her appearance on the "Jack Benny Show," Marilyn was paid with a black Cadillac convertible with red leather upholstery.

1954: Joe DiMaggio's black Cadillac (license "Joe D") sped off with them after their wedding.

1955: Milton H. Greene may have purchased the black Thunderbird sports car Marilyn drove after moving to New York. She later gave this car as a gift to John Strasberg.

With Arthur Miller, she used his Jaguar.

1960: Marilyn's transportation during location shooting for *The Misfits* was a white Cadillac.

1961: On moving back to Los Angeles, Marilyn did not bother buying a car; she hired a chauffeur-driven black limo if and when she needed it. For errands housekeeper Eunice Murray's green Dodge, or the car that belonged to Murray's nephew, did just fine.

## CARTIER-BRESSON, HENRI (B. 1908)

One of the most influential PHOTOGRAPHERS of the twentieth century, Cartier-Bresson was one of a number of MAGNUM photographers who worked on the set of *THE MISFITS* (1961).

## CASTILIAN DRIVE

In the fall of 1952, Marilyn and JOE DIMAGGIO took out a short lease on a house at 2393 Castilian Drive, on Outpost Estates in the Hollywood Hills, as a safe haven from the reporters who followed their every move at the BEL AIR HOTEL, where Marilyn was living at the time.

(*see* HOMES)

## CATALINA ISLAND

In late 1943 Norma Jeane and JAMES DOUGHERTY moved to this island off the California coast, after Jim was transferred to the maritime service training base. Before being converted into a military training ground at the start of World War II, Catalina had been something of a playground for Hollywood moguls, who enjoyed sailing their yachts the twenty-seven miles from the mainland to preview their latest offerings in the world's first movie theater equipped for projecting sound films. Jim was not happy that his young, attractive wife wore tight-fitting fashions, causing quite a stir on an island inhabited almost exclusively by Marine recruits. Norma Jeane left Catalina in the spring of 1944 after Jim was posted to Southeast Asia.

(*see* HOMES)

## CENSORSHIP

MARILYN:
"The Johnston Office spends a lot of time worrying whether a girl has cleavage or not. They ought to worry if she doesn't have any."

There have been far more claims of censorship regarding the way Marilyn died than how she did her job. Considering how far Marilyn's upfront sensuality clashed with the prudish morals of her day, it may seem strange that none of her movies fell foul of the censors, with the exception of the yacht seduction scene in *SOME LIKE IT HOT (1959)* in the state of Kansas. Provocative as Marilyn could be, her directors and film studios succeeded in their intent to sail as close to the wind as possible. For example, the flesh-colored dress in her "Heat Wave" number from *THERE'S NO BUSINESS LIKE SHOW BUSINESS* (1954) is technically a covering, but it leaves nothing to the imagination.

During Marilyn's stay in ENGLAND, she struck a small blow against censorship by becoming a founder member of the Watergate Theatre Club, formed to put on plays which had been banned by the British censorship office. The Club's first production was by her husband ARTHUR MILLER, *A View from the Bridge*.

While shooting *THE MISFITS* (1961), in one scene where CLARK GABLE wakes Marilyn in the night, Marilyn let the bed sheet drop far enough to reveal a breast as the cameras rolled. Huston called, "Cut! I've seen 'em before." Marilyn suggested they keep the take to make a stand against censorship. She is reputed to have said, "Gradually they'll let down the censorship—though probably not in my lifetime."

## CENTRAL PARK WEST

During 1957 and 1958 Marilyn spent much of her day in the building at 135 Central Park West in Manhattan. Every morning she went for a session with her new analyst, DR. MARIANNE KRIS, before taking the elevator to LEE STRASBERG's apartment for acting lessons.

## CHAPLIN, CHARLIE

During his partnership with Marilyn in MARILYN MONROE PRODUCTIONS, MILTON GREENE had the idea of pairing up Marilyn and Chaplin in a movie. Chaplin and Marilyn had a number of things in common: both made a success of themselves despite growing up without a father, and both had a mother whose sanity was constantly on edge. Alas, the project with Chaplin was abandoned in the wake of a fallout between Marilyn and Greene.

## CHAPLIN, CHARLES JR.

Biographer ANTHONY SUMMERS writes that in 1947 Marilyn had an affair with two of Charlie Chaplin's sons, Charlie Junior and Sydney. At this time Marilyn allegedly also had an abortion.

## CHARACTER TRAITS

"Someone said to me, 'If 50 percent of the experts in Hollywood said you had no talent and should give up, what would you do?' My answer was then and still is, 'If a 100 percent told me that, all 100 percent would be wrong.'"

RUPERT ALLAN:
"In Marilyn's case, admiration was always linked to love."

"Under all the frailty was a will of steel."

PAT NEWCOMB:
"At the core of her, she was really strong . . . and that was something we tended to forget, because she seemed so vulnerable, and one always felt it necessary to watch out for her."

ARTHUR MILLER:
"What she wanted most was not to judge but to win recognition from a sentimentally cruel profession, and from men blinded to her humanity by her perfect beauty. She was part queen, part waif, sometimes on her knees before her own body and sometimes despairing because of it."

"It was impossible to sense at all what she was feeling and what her mood was until she spoke."

"She never stopped probing the world and people around her for the least sign of hostility, and everyone sensed the desperation for reassurance, witty and quick to laugh and winning as she was, and so they reassured, and truth moved further and further away."

SAM SHAW:
"Everybody knows about her insecurities, but not everybody knows what fun she was, that she never complained about the ordinary things of life, that she never had a bad word to say about anyone, and that she had a wonderful spontaneous sense of humor."

PHILIPPE HALSMAN:
"The trait that struck me most was a general absence of envy and jealousy, which in an actress was astonishing."

Yes, but what was Marilyn really like?

Marilyn's single-mindedness in pursuit of a screen career extended to every part of her activities—the people she met and cultivated, the BOOKS she read, her physical exercise, the people she slept with—in a constant process of seeking approval, and attention. She could never be satisfied, not even when she achieved what, since a child, she had set as a goal.

Not surprisingly, throughout her life Marilyn suffered from a terrible inferiority complex. More than one biographer notes that from her earliest days, Marilyn's sense of self worth was undermined by her mother, for whom a fatherless child was a major complication, if not to say an outright source of shame. Marilyn was always extremely conscious of her lack of formal EDUCATION. She always sought out the educated and intellectual, as if contact with them could fill her with at least some of the knowledge she felt she lacked. Her feelings of intellectual inadequacy were compounded in her starlet years, as she consorted with much older and more worldly-wise men who carelessly belittled anything she said. And yet so many people who met Marilyn had their preconceptions overturned. Photographer ELLIOTT ERWITT, for example, was surprised by how he "had always thought that all those amusing remarks she was supposed to have made for the press had probably been manufactured and mimeographed by her press agent, but they weren't. She was a very bright person, an instinctive type."

Marilyn almost always felt uneasy with journalists in "live" situations, despite her skill at using certain columnists to express her opinions. The counterpoint to this personal timidity was a streak of exhibitionism that enabled her to parade in front of photographers and fans in dresses which were scandalously revealing for the day. Impersonal public exhibitionism before a crowd was one thing; relating to individuals, or even having to give an impromptu interview, was quite another, as she greatly feared appearing dumb or lacking in social skills.

Marilyn's lack of self-confidence in her acting, which continued even after masterful performances in her later work, was the result of years of important Hollywood people writing off her talents, and possibly the promptings of people in her entourage whose interests lay in Marilyn requiring their services and succor for as long as possible.

Marilyn's compassion for others, her sense of feeling sorry for people who seemed shy, defenseless, in need of support and love, may well have included her husbands. After divorcing JOE DIMAGGIO, Marilyn told a friend that she married him "because I felt sorry for him," because "he seemed so lonely and shy." Marilyn's empathy with ANIMALS and her GENEROSITY are well-known.

Although many friends have testified to Marilyn's generosity and graciousness to friends, and biographers note that Marilyn never gave voice to ill-feeling against people she felt had slighted her in the press, she was quite capable of being manipulative. On several occasions during her life she resorted to fabrications in order to elicit sympathy (to JOHN CARROLL and LUCILLE RYMAN, who took her in, that there had been an intruder in her bedroom; to FRED KARGER that she was living in a seedy rundown apartment when in fact she was at the tony HOLLYWOOD STUDIO CLUB), and so she would, effectively, find people and families to foster her, at least for a short while, until the deception ran hollow. Not surprisingly, after her falsifications were discovered she had a hard time making people believe her.

And when angry, Marilyn sometimes flew into a rage which ARTHUR MILLER described as " slashing, out to destroy."

The Marilyn the world adored was a character she turned on and off at will. Many times with friends she announced she was going to "do a Marilyn." SUSAN STRASBERG describes an occasion when the two of them were walking up to her New York hotel and Marilyn said, "Do you want to see me be her?" and turned the character on. ELI WALLACH had a similar experience walking along with Marilyn in New York.

Marilyn occasionally spoke of herself in the third person, sometimes with bitterness. She did this in one of her later interviews (with journalist Vernon Scott), but she was already doing this in the mid-fifties, commenting on the kind of things Marilyn would and wouldn't do, how she would look and move.

And yet a host of people—friends and journalists as well as star-struck fans—found that when they were in Marilyn's presence, some of her vitality, her wit, and her talent for having a good time rubbed off on them.

On the intensity and sincerity of her emotions, GLORIA STEINEM writes, "Even when she tried to pretend an emotion—for instance, to be confident or gay when she did not feel it—some underlying honesty still gave her away." This honesty extended to declining countless proposals of marriage, which would have made her financially secure during her penniless starlet days, because she would only marry for love.

Biographer DONALD SPOTO writes, "The intensity of her desires clashed with her deepest emotional and spiritual needs. She was someone with a vivid inner life whose desire for recognition caused an outer-directed life: In this regard, Marilyn Monroe may indeed be the ultimate movie actress."

Throughout her life Marilyn was intellectually curious, eager for knowledge and learning. In 1955 this curiosity took an inward turn as she left Hollywood for New York and experimented with acting technique at the ACTOR'S LAB. She began what would be seven years of intense psychotherapy, met new people, and tried to explore what lay behind the persona of Marilyn she had been supporting all those years.

## CHARITABLE WORKS

Marilyn donated time and/or money to:

A 1953 benefit for underprivileged children at Jude's Hospital, Memphis, Tennessee—singing with Jane Russell at the Hollywood Bowl.

WAIF—an organization that placed abandoned children in homes, after Jane Russell enlisted Marilyn's help in 1955.

The Arthritis and Rheumatism Foundation in 1955—astride a pink elephant at a benefit for given by Mike Todd's Circus at Madison Square Garden, New York.

The Milk Fund for Babies in 1957—Marilyn decided to give earnings from the world premiere of *The Prince and the Showgirl* to this charity.

Marilyn was one of the models in the 1958 March of Dimes fashion parade, that aided children with polio—held at the Waldorf-Astoria Hotel in New York.

A children's welfare organization that gave free breakfasts to underprivileged youngsters—a donation of $1000.

An orphanage Marilyn visited during her 1962 trip to Mexico—she ripped up her initial check of $1000 and donated $10,000. That night was one of the few nights in her later life that she recalled sleeping without the aid of sleeping pills.

S.A.N.E.—an organization dedicated to eliminating nuclear weapons.

In 1982 German Bruno Bernard set up the Marilyn Monroe Memorial Fund to benefit struggling young actors.

A muscular dystrophy benefit held at Chavez Ravin Dodger Stadium, Los Angeles, on her thirty-sixth birthday—This was Marilyn's last public appearance.

Marilyn's final donation to charity was the biggest. In her last WILL she left 25 percent of her ESTATE (after provisions for her mother and legacies for some friends) to a former psychiatrist, DR. MARIANNE KRIS, "to be used for the furtherance of the work of such psychiatric institutions or groups as she shall elect." Knowing Marilyn's enormous love for children, Kris chose the Anna Freud Children's Clinic of London. This behest has been used to set up the Monroe Young Family Centre, in Daleham Gardens, London.

Among friends and colleagues, Marilyn was renowned for her GENEROSITY in helping people wherever she could; stand-in EVELYN

MORIARTY remembers Marilyn making an anonymous donation of $1,000 to a crew member on *LET'S MAKE LOVE* (1960) who needed the money to cover funeral expenses for his wife.

In recognition of Marilyn's love for and connection with children, writer GLORIA STEINEM and photographer GEORGE BARRIS set up a trust fund to help children in need, starting it off with the proceeds from their book *Marilyn Norma Jeane*.

## CHATEAU MARMONT HOTEL
8221 SUNSET BOULEVARD, WEST HOLLYWOOD

A luxury HOTEL popular with movie and rock stars. Marilyn lived at the Chateau Marmont for a number of weeks in 1956, using it as her Los Angeles base during shooting on *BUS STOP*. Her occasional companion was ARTHUR MILLER, who at the time was living near RENO to qualify for a Nevada divorce from first wife Mary Slattery.

BRAD DARRACH interviewed Marilyn at the hotel for *Time* magazine during the same period. The FBI, who had been tailing Miller, opened its file on Marilyn.

The Chateau Marmont Hotel, Hollywood

## CHAUFFEURS

Until she moved to New York in 1955, Marilyn generally drove herself. In New York PETER LEONARDI, who was also her hairdresser, drove her around until they parted company. Then it was "Johnnie," who Marilyn called "The Sheik." In Los Angeles Rudy Kautzky chauffeured her when she needed. (*see* CARS)

## CHAYEFSKY, PADDY
(1923–1981, B. SIDNEY AARON STUCHEVSKY)

This renowned playwright, screenplay and television writer made his movie debut with *AS YOUNG AS YOU FEEL* in 1951, one of Marilyn's early films.

In 1956 Marilyn briefly entered discussions with Chayefsky about her company MARILYN MONROE PRODUCTIONS producing the film version of his play *Middle of the Night*, which she saw in New York starring Edward G. Robinson and Gena Rowlands. Marilyn would have taken the lead role. It seems that Chayefsky was not happy with the way negotiations went, and not only withdrew the property but wrote a bleak version of Marilyn in his next film, *The Goddess*. ARTHUR MILLER unsuccessfully tried to dissuade him from doing the film, which was released in 1958 starring KIM STANLEY as the celestial lead.

Chayefsky won two Oscars during his career, for *The Hospital* (1971) and *Marty* (1955), as well as an Oscar nomination for *The Goddess* (1958).

## CHEKHOV, MICHAEL (1891–1955)

MARILYN:
"His name should be world famous. There should be statues of him. Yet hardly anyone knows about him.... I thought of paying for a statue of him myself, to put up in New York."

Michael Chekhov became Marilyn's supplementary drama coach from late 1951, on the recommendation of her main coach NATASHA LYTESS. Marilyn was introduced to him by Jack Palance, then best known as a Broadway actor, and began studying with him twice a week. Chekhov was reportedly most impressed by her talents; he was also one of the first people to actually tell her this, to help her to build up some belief in her abilities, and begin to undo the harm done by the many important men who had mistreated her.

Chekhov's credentials were impeccable. Not only had he himself put in an Oscar-nominated acting performance in Hitchcock's *Spellbound* (1945), he came from a theatrical dynasty; he was the nephew of playwright Anton Chekhov, and had worked with KONSTANTIN STANISLAVSKY at the Moscow Art Theater. When Marilyn started lessons with him he was sixty and had worked with many of the leading theater actors of the twentieth century. He had also build up a stable of students including GREGORY PECK, Joan Caulfield, Yul Brynner, and Cornell Wilde.

Early on in their relationship Chekhov told her, "Our bodies can be either our best friends or worst enemies. You must try to consider your body as an instrument for expressing creative ideas. You must strive for complete harmony between body and psychology." He quickly recognized that for Marilyn to put his advice into practice, she needed to have a broader pool of experience on which to draw. To this end he advised her to enlarge her circle of interests, to learn more of the psychology of her characters, taking up the basic tenet of the Moscow Art Theater ethos. It was his contention that the only way to really enter a dramatic character, to be possessed by that character, was to use creative imagination, to make "will and feelings... want to be another character."

Marilyn studied his seminal book, *To the Actor: On the Technique of Acting*, and for some years considered it to be her bible on acting. He also recommended she read Mabel Elsworth's *The Thinking Body*, a rather obtuse book of theories on the relationship between anatomy, psychology, and the emotions. Unfortunately the complexity of this work only fed the feelings of intellectual inadequacy that often lurked just beneath Marilyn's not-so-thick skin.

Their working relationship sometimes suffered from Marilyn's chronic LATENESS. In 1952, when he commented she was creating difficulties, she wrote him a letter telling him how much she appreciated his patience and valued his friendship. In one class Marilyn played Cordelia to Chekhov's King Lear. Years later she told a reporter, "He gave the greatest performance I have ever seen. It was so wonderful."

In 1952 she gave him an engraving of ABRAHAM LINCOLN, with a note, "Lincoln was the man I admired most all through school. Now that man is you." In 1954, she referred to him as "the most brilliant man I have ever met."

When she heard that Chekhov had died, Marilyn asked Arthur to read with her from *The Brothers Karamazov*.

## CHEKHOV, XENIA

As she did so often, Marilyn became firm friends with the family of the person she admired. Marilyn kept in touch with her teacher's widow, and on a number of occasions helped her out financially. Soon after Michael Chekhov died, Marilyn wrote a WILL in which she left $10,000 to Xenia. In a later will she converted this into a trust fund which was to pay out a minimum annual sum of $2,500, though legal complications prevented any money being paid before Xenia died in 1970.

## CHILDHOOD

MARILYN:
"No one ever told me I was pretty when I was a little girl. All little girls should be told they're pretty, even if they aren't."

"This sad bitter child who grew up too fast is hardly ever out of my heart. With success all around me, I can still feel her frightened eyes looking out of mine."

"When I was a kid, the world often seemed a pretty grim place. I loved to escape through games and make-believe. You can do that even better as an actress, but sometimes it seems you escape altogether and people never let you come back."

"The world around me then was kind of grim. I had to learn to pretend in order to—I don't know—block the grimness. The whole world seemed sort of closed to me. . . . [I felt] on the outside of everything, and all I could do was to dream up any kind of pretend-game." —Aged eleven or so, after the orphanage

Though she sometimes painted it as more grim and than it actually was, Norma Jeane's childhood could by no stretch of the imagination be described as happy or filled with love. Before she was two weeks old her mother GLADYS BAKER boarded her baby with a foster family, the BOLENDERS, who lived sixteen miles away in Hawthorne. Seven years later, for a brief spell, Norma Jeane lived with her mother, but after Gladys was taken into a mental hospital Norma Jeane began to be shuttled around between a number of FOSTER PARENTS and "aunts," and spent some time in the Los Angeles ORPHANAGE.

The insecurity of such an upbringing, the lack of love and a perennial feeling of not being wanted manifested itself in extreme

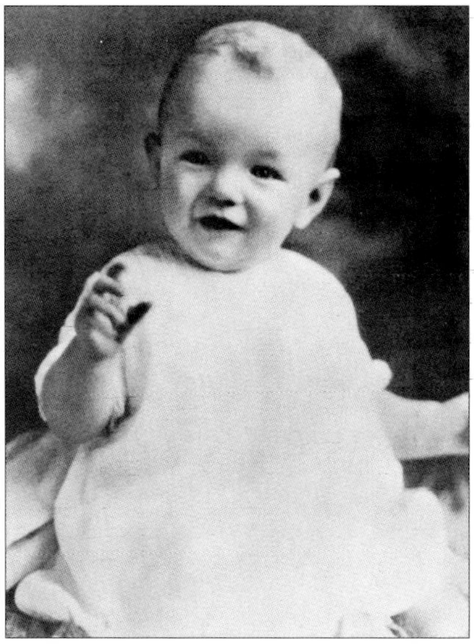

Norma Jeane at six-months-old, 1926.

Marilyn, two-years-old, on the beach in Santa Monica, 1928.

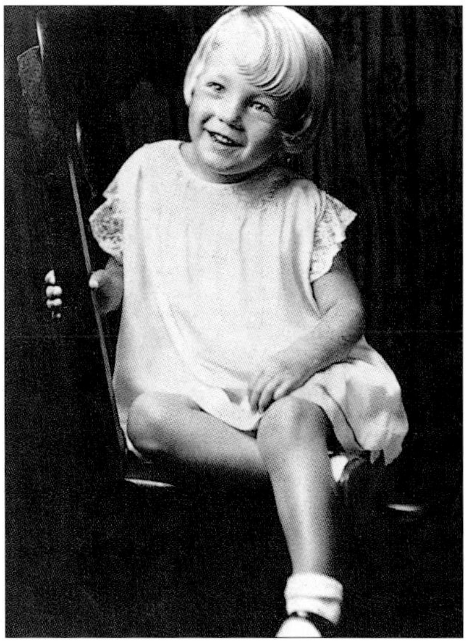

Norma Jeane Baker, age three, 1929.

shyness (the GODDARDS nicknamed her "The Mouse"), a stammer, a very active fantasy life, and then, as she matured physically, a realization that her sexy looks could bring her the appreciation and interest that had eluded her for so long. Many biographers note that in her adult years Marilyn's relationships were often a reflection of child/parent relationships, as she sought approval and confirmation from parent figures—husbands, drama coaches, or psychoanalysts.

## CHILDREN

ARTHUR MILLER:
"To understand Marilyn best, you have to see her around children. They love her; her whole approach to life has their kind of simplicity and directness."

Marilyn loved children. She went out of her way to befriend and play with the children of people she knew. Newly married Norma Jeane, barely out of childhood herself, fed, bathed, and played with the nephews and nieces of first husband JAMES DOUGHERTY. Soon after landing her first film contract, Marilyn confided to fellow actress Clarice Evans that she wanted to have four children, two her own and two adopted. Later she was indulgent with the children of many of the important people in her life: FRED KARGER's child, JOE DIMAGGIO's son, ARTHUR MILLER's children, the offspring of the STRASBERGS, and of her psychoanalyst, DR. RALPH GREENSON.

Long after the relationships had ended with her former husbands, Marilyn was still in close touch with the step-children she acquired through marriage. In 1962 she told a reporter from *Redbook* magazine just how important Joe DiMaggio Jr., and Jane and Robert Miller were to her: "I take a lot of pride in them. Because they're from broken homes too, and I think I can understand them. I've always said to them that I didn't want to be their mother or stepmother and such. . . . I just wanted to be their friend. . . . I can't explain it, but I think I love them more than I love anyone."

That she suffered MEDICAL problems or fertility problems and was unable to have children of her own was a great source of sadness. In the last year of her life Marilyn was asked what she wanted, more than anything else. She replied, "The thing I want more than anything else? I want to have children. I used to feel for every child I had, I would adopt another." Makeup man and confidant ALLAN SNYDER remembered, "She loved children so much—my daughter, other people's children—she went for them all. If she'd had one of her own to care for, to grow up with, I'm sure it would have helped her immensely."

In 1957, after miscarrying in the early stages of a pregnancy, Marilyn often went to a small park near her New York apartment, where she sat on a bench and watched the children play. She struck up a friendship with one of the young mothers in particular, a young Israeli woman called Dalia Leeds, and asked her about everything she could think having to do with pregnancy and motherhood. Leeds found she was "not glamorous, but just an ordinary woman who was shy, curious and lonely." She played with the children too. The kids adored her, and even after they had discovered the name of the woman who came to the park wrapped up in a head scarf and dark glasses, the mothers enjoyed her company and interest.

Although Marilyn did not have her own offspring, she did leave a legacy to children: money she left in her will to psychiatrist MARIANNE KRIS was used to set up the Monroe Young Family Unit in London.

Over the years a number of people have come forward claiming to be Marilyn's long-lost child. Marilyn supposedly told at least three people (ROBERT SLATZER, JEANNE CARMEN, and AMY GREENE) that she had a child when she was still a teenager, either just before or just after her marriage to Jim Dougherty, but was forced to give the baby up for adoption. Amy Greene has said that Marilyn felt her inability to have children in later life was a punishment for this earlier mistake. A similar assertion that Norma Jeane gave birth in her early teens was also made by Marilyn's former New York maid LENA PEPITONE, in her book *Marilyn Monroe Confidential*, though in this case the father was an unnamed "foster parent" who raped her.

In 1986 a woman called Nancy Green told lawyer LAWRENCE CUSACK that she was Marilyn's long lost daughter, and subsequently changed her last name to Miracle. Cusack said that at the time he dismissed Green as a fabulist.

It is highly unlikely that in her starlet years Marilyn would have risked a pregnancy—her contract with TWENTIETH CENTURY-FOX would have been cancelled the moment such a thing was discovered. Stories of her having a child after she became famous—a woman called Janet Raymond once claimed she was Marilyn's daughter, born during her 1952 visit to hospital for an appendectomy—have never been corroborated. Claims that Marilyn had an abortion just two weeks before her death are also unsubstantiated and seem particularly unlikely in the light of how much she wanted a child of her own.

## CHRISTIAN SCIENCE

For eight years of her life, until the late forties and her break into the film business, Norma Jeane, like her idol JEAN HARLOW before her, was brought up as a Christian Scientist, after being taken along to Sherman Oaks Christian Science Church by "Aunt" ANA LOWER. In 1938 there were around 270,000 members of the Christian Science church in America.

Christian Science was founded in 1879 by Mary Baker Eddy, whose belief that God is the loving and all-powerful Father of all people led her to question the fundamental realities of the evils and sufferings people encounter in human life. The goal of the religion is to bring the unreal material body into perfect harmony with man's real spiritual condition through prayer and study. In Christian Science the faithful can seek help in their prayers from registered practitioners of Christian Science healing (especially in moments of illness, as a basic tenet of the religion is to instill healing through prayer, and not through conventional medicine). Lower, with whom Norma Jeane lived on and off from 1938 to 1946, was one such practitioner.

Christian Science denies the reality of the senses. People do not sin, suffer, or die; they are victims of unhealthy delusions, particularly "malicious animal magnetism," a term for evil thought that appears real only because people erroneously give it credence. Part of the faith is the conviction that rather than medicines, there is a way to defeat sickness (not to mention sin) though prayerful thinking, healing, and abiding by Mrs. Eddy's commentaries on the scriptures.

Norma Jeane continued to study Christian Science throughout her marriage to JAMES DOUGHERTY. On her earliest modeling assignments, Marilyn sat quietly at mealtimes with her prayer book keeping her company.

## CHRONOLOGY

This is a list of some of the major events in Marilyn's life. The dates quoted are those most commonly associated with events; particularly in the early part of her life, biographers often disagree, sometimes by many months, about specific dates.

| | |
|---|---|
| **1926** | |
| June 1 | BIRTH at Los Angeles General HOSPITAL |
| June 13 | Taken to live with foster family, the BOLENDERS |
| **1933** | |
| Fall | Mother GLADYS BAKER takes Norma Jeane to live with her |
| **1934** | |
| February | Gladys Baker taken to an institution |
| **1935** | |
| June 1 | Grace McKee becomes legal guardian |
| September 13 | Norma Jeane is left at the orphanage |
| **1937** | |
| June 26 | Grace McKee takes her away from the orphanage |
| **1938** | |
| November | Goes to live with "Aunt" ANA LOWER |
| **1942** | |
| June 19 | Marries JAMES E. DOUGHERTY |
| **1944** | |
| April | Norma Jeane starts work at the RADIO PLANE MUNITIONS FACTORY |
| **1946** | |
| April 26 | First national MAGAZINE cover, in *Family Circle* |
| June 26 | Photographed by DAVID CONOVER for *Yank* magazine |
| July 19 | First SCREEN TEST, for TWENTIETH CENTURY-FOX |
| July 23 | First six-month studio contract, renewed in January |
| July 29 | First mention in a Hollywood gossip column (HEDDA HOPPER) |
| August 2 | Norma Jeane Dougherty applies to join the BLUE BOOK MODELING AGENCY |
| September 13 | DIVORCE granted from James E. Dougherty |
| **1947** | |
| August 25 | Fox contract not renewed for a second time |
| **1948** | |
| February | Marilyn befriends mogul JOSEPH M. SCHENCK |
| March 9 | Contract with COLUMBIA PICTURES |
| September 8 | Dropped by Columbia |
| December 31 | Meets agent JOHNNY HYDE, who dedicates himself to promoting her |
| **1949** | |
| May 27 | Poses for photographer TOM KELLEY—the nude CALENDAR shots |
| July 24 | First interview with EARL WILSON |
| August 15 | Starts shooting *A TICKET TO TOMAHAWK* |
| October | Signs contract with MGM for breakthrough role in *THE ASPHALT JUNGLE* |
| **1950** | |
| January 5 | Starts shooting *THE FIREBALL* |
| April | Lands small but perfectly-formed part in *ALL ABOUT EVE* |
| December 18 | Johnny Hyde dies |
| **1951** | |
| March 29 | Presents an Oscar at the ACADEMY AWARDS ceremony |
| April 18 | Shooting starts on *LOVE NEST* |
| May 11 | Latest six-month contract and Fox converted to seven-year deal |
| September 8 | First full-length national magazine feature in *Collier's* |
| **1952** | |
| March | Marilyn and JOE DIMAGGIO go out on a first date |
| March 13 | Nude calendar story broken to the public |
| April 7 | First *Life* cover, snapped by PHILIPPE HALSMAN |
| June 1 | On her birthday learns she is to be Lorelei Lee in *GENTLEMEN PREFER BLONDES* |
| August 31 | Live radio debut |
| September 2 | Grand marshal at the MISS AMERICA pageant |
| **1953** | |
| January 21 | *NIAGARA* released, Marilyn is a star |
| March 9 | JOAN CRAWFORD's prudish sensibilities offended as Marilyn picks up her *PHOTOPLAY* magazine award |
| June 26 | Marilyn and co-star JANE RUSSELL leave their prints for posterity outside GRAUMAN'S CHINESE THEATER |
| September 13 | First TV appearance, in "The JACK BENNY Show" |
| November 4 | *HOW TO MARRY A MILLIONAIRE* premieres |
| December 15 | Marilyn fails to turn up for first day of shooting on *Girl in Pink Tights* |
| **1954** | |
| January 4 | Fox suspends Marilyn |
| January 14 | Marries Joe DiMaggio at San Francisco City Hall |
| February 2 | HONEYMOON couple mobbed by fans upon arrival in Tokyo |
| February 16 | Marilyn starts ten-venue tour of troops in KOREA |
| September 15 | Infamous skirt-blowing scene shot for *THE SEVEN YEAR ITCH* |
| October 5 | Officially separates from Joe DiMaggio |
| October 27 | First divorce hearing held |
| November 5 | Joe and FRANK SINATRA go on "WRONG DOOR RAID" |
| November 6 | Agent CHARLES FELDMAN throws Hollywood party at Romanoff's, in Marilyn's honor |
| **1955** | |
| January 7 | Marilyn and MILTON GREENE hold press conference announcing the creation of MARILYN MONROE PRODUCTIONS |
| January 15 | Fox suspends Marilyn |
| February | Meets and begins studying with LEE STRASBERG |
| March 31 | Rides a pink elephant at MADISON SQUARE GARDEN for arthritis benefit |
| April 8 | EDWARD R. MURROW interviews Marilyn live on "Person to Person" |
| June 1 | *The Seven Year Itch* premieres |
| October 31 | Granted final divorce decree from Joe DiMaggio |
| **1956** | |
| January 4 | Announcement of reconciliation between Marilyn and Fox studios |
| February 9 | Press conference with LAURENCE OLIVIER to announce their joint project, *THE PRINCE AND THE SHOWGIRL* |
| February 17 | Performs bar room scene from *ANNA CHRISTIE* at the ACTORS STUDIO, New York |
| February 25 | Returns to Hollywood after more than one year away |
| May 3 | *BUS STOP* starts shooting |
| June 29 | Marries ARTHUR MILLER in a civil ceremony |
| July 1 | Marries Arthur Miller in a Jewish ceremony |
| July 14 | Arrives in London to begin work with Olivier on *The Prince and the Showgirl* |
| August | Becomes pregnant but loses baby |
| October 29 | Presented to Queen ELIZABETH II at the royal command film performance |
| November 20 | Returns to U.S. |
| December 18 | Radio show from WALDORF-ASTORIA |
| **1957** | |
| June 13 | *The Prince and the Showgirl* premieres |
| August 1 | Ectopic pregnancy has to be terminated |
| **1958** | |
| August 4 | Starts work on *SOME LIKE IT HOT* |
| November 6 | Finishes *Some Like It Hot* |
| December 17 | Miscarries again |
| **1959** | |
| March 29 | *Some Like It Hot* premieres |
| May 13 | Receives Italy's top acting award, the DAVID DI DONATELLO |
| **1960** | |
| March 8 | Receives GOLDEN GLOBE AWARD for "Best Actress in a Comedy" for *Some Like It Hot* |
| June | Begins seeing psychoanalyst RALPH GREENSON on a daily basis |
| July 18 | Shooting starts on *THE MISFITS* |
| August 26 | Flies to L.A. because of nervous breakdown during shooting |
| November 11 | Public announcement that Marilyn and Miller are to divorce |
| November 16 | Clark Gable dies of heart attack |
| **1961** | |
| January 20 | Mexican divorce from Arthur Miller granted |
| January 31 | Premiere of *The Misfits* |
| February 7 | Enters Payne Whitney Psychiatric Clinic, New York Hospital |
| February 11 | Joe DiMaggio arranges for Marilyn to be transferred to the much less intimidating Columbia Presbyterian Hospital |
| March 5 | Discharged from Columbia Presbyterian Hospital |
| Early October | Meets ROBERT KENNEDY at PETER LAWFORD's beach house |

| | |
|---|---|
| November 19 | Attends a dinner at Peter Lawford's beach house with President KENNEDY |
| **1962** | |
| February | Moves into HOME she has bought in the Brentwood district of Los Angeles |
| February 1 | Dinner in honor of Robert F. Kennedy |
| March 5 | Golden Globe Award, "World's Film Favorite" |
| March 24 | Marilyn and JFK spend weekend together in PALM SPRINGS |
| April 23 | Begins work on *SOMETHING'S GOT TO GIVE* |
| May 19 | Sings "Happy Birthday" to President Kennedy at Madison Square Garden |
| May 28 | Nude pool sequence shot on *Something's Got to Give* |
| June 1 | Marilyn's last day of work at Fox and final public appearance |
| June 7 | Fox fires Marilyn for breach of contract |
| June 23 | BERT STERN begins first of three photo sessions for *Vogue*, "The Last Sitting" |
| June 28 | Negotiations resumed with Fox about continuation of *Something's Got to Give* |
| June 29 | GEORGE BARRIS spends three days shooting Marilyn for *Cosmpolitan* |
| July 4 | Begins extensive interview, her last, with RICHARD MERYMAN |
| July 12 | Meets Fox studio chiefs |
| July 20 | Enters Cedars of Lebanon Hospital for endometriosis—or abortion, say CONSPIRACY theorists |
| July 28 | Weekend at CAL-NEVA LODGE |
| August 1 | Fox rewrites Marilyn's contract for double her previous salary and agrees to restart production of *Something's Got to Give* |
| August 3 | Appears on the cover of *Life* for the last time |
| August 4 | Marilyn's LAST DAY ALIVE, includes a six hour session with Dr. Ralph Greenson |
| August 5 | POLICE called to Marilyn's home; Official day of death; Autopsy performed |
| August 8 | Funeral at WESTWOOD MEMORIAL PARK CEMETERY |

A number of resources exist relating events in Marilyn's life to days of the year. See "The Marilyn Monroe Collector's Diary," by Jane Guy (1997), or on the Web, the site maintained by "Marilyn: Then and Now" Fan Club President Ray Zweidinger (http://www.geocities.com/Hollywood/Chateau/3987/).

## CINEMATOGRAPHY

If Marilyn's life was a love affair with the camera, her cinematographers served as matchmaker. Part of the complex negotiations over her renewed contract with Fox in 1955 regarded her insistence on approval of the cinematographer as well as the director. Four made it onto her list: Harry Stradling, Harold Rosson, James Wong Howe, and MILTON KRASNER.

Robert Ryan (left) and Keith Andes (right) with Marilyn in *Clash by Night* (1952).

### MARILYN'S CINEMATOGRAPHERS

Lloyd Ahern—*Love Nest* (1951), *O. Henry's Full House* (1952)
Lucien Andriot—*Hometown Story* (1951)
Lucien Ballard—*Let's Make It Legal* (1951), *Don't Bother to Knock* (1952)
Norbert Brodine—*Right Cross* (1950)
Jack Cardiff—*The Prince and the Showgirl* (1957)
William Daniels—*Something's Got to Give* (1962)
Daniel L. Fapp—*Let's Make Love* (1960)
Harry Jackson—*A Ticket to Tomahawk* (1950)
Benjamin Kline—*Dangerous Years* (1947)
Milton Krasner—*All About Eve* (1950), *Monkey Business* (1952), *The Seven Year Itch* (1955), *Bus Stop* (1956)
Charles Lang Jr.—*Some Like It Hot* (1959), *Something's Got to Give* (1962)
Joseph La Shelle—*River of No Return* (1954)
Joe MacDonald—*As Young As You Feel* (1951), *Niagara* (1953), *How to Marry a Millionaire* (1953)
William C. Mellor—*Love Happy* (1950)
Russell Metty—*The Misfits* (1961)
Nicholas Musuraca—*Clash by Night* (1952)
Ernest Palmer—*Scudda Hoo! Scudda Hay!* (1948)
Franz Planer—*Something's Got to Give* (1962)
Frank Redman—*Ladies of the Chorus* (1948)
Harold Rosson—*The Asphalt Jungle* (1950)
Leon Shamroy—*There's No Business Like Show Business* (1954)
Leo Tover—*We're Not Married* (1952), *Something's Got to Give* (1962)
Lester White—*The Fireball* (1950)
Harry J. Wild—*Gentlemen Prefer Blondes* (1953)

Note: No less than four cinematographers are recorded for Marilyn's final, incomplete film, *Something's Got to Give*.

## *CLASH BY NIGHT* (1952)

Marilyn's thirteenth film was on loan to RKO (the studio whose water tower she could see out of the L.A. county ORPHANAGE window during her years there as a child). SIDNEY SKOLSKY is generally credited with persuading producer JERRY WALD to give Marilyn what

Keith Andes with Marilyn in *Clash by Night* (1952).

proved to be an important role in this gritty drama based on a CLIFFORD ODETS play. Marilyn had first read the play *Clash by Night* years earlier, during her first year of acting lessons at the ACTORS LAB. For the first time Marilyn had a chance to act, rising above the secretary and decorative blonde roles she had landed until then. She insisted that throughout filming drama coach NATASHA LYTESS was on hand to help her wring the most from the role.

Location shooting was in Monterey, California, and filming was a trial for Marilyn and director FRITZ LANG. Marilyn suffered such intense nerves that she would vomit before scenes, and her hands and face broke out in red blotches. Even if director Lang was happy with a scene, Marilyn often thought she could do it better. Her sense of perfectionism, her desire to act to her utmost ability, even extended to her costumes and props. Wardrobe mistress MARJORIE PLECHER later recalled, "She didn't think the costume jewelry engagement ring given her for the part was right, but she liked mine—

so that's the one she wore in the picture."

Lang took exception to the fuss made over this rather minor player in his movie, particularly the fact that she had her own drama coach who would second-guess his directions. He was quoted at the time as saying, "I do not want anybody directing behind my back. I want this Lytess woman kept off my set." He issued orders to this effect, but in the end Marilyn's need to have personal back-up won the day, a compromise was reached, and filming continued.

One day during shooting on the RKO lot, Marilyn made an attempt to locate the orphanage where she had lived as a girl for a year and a half. In pre-release publicity for the film the studio made much of the fact that the little orphan girl would gaze out longingly at the studio water tower, dreaming of happier times ahead—until the story broke of Marilyn's nude CALENDAR shots, giving the picture enormous free publicity and ensuring that Marilyn was more in the news than the headline stars.

This film was produced by Harriet Parsons, sister to Louella, one of Hollywood's most important columnists and one of Marilyn's most important "friendly" PRESS allies.

**Tagline:**

"Livin' in my house! Lovin' another man! Is that what you call bein' honest? That's just givin' it a nice name!"

**Credits:**

Wald-Krasna Productions Inc., RKO Radio Pictures, Black and White
Length: 105 minutes
Release date: June 18, 1952

Directed by: Fritz Lang
Produced by: Harriet Parsons
Written by: Alfred Hayes, from a Clifford Odets play
Cinematography by: Nicholas Musuraca
Music by: Roy Webb
Film Editing by: George J. Amy

**Cast** (credits order):
Barbara Stanwyck . . . Mae Doyle D'Amato
Paul Douglas . . . Jerry D'Amato
Robert Ryan . . . Earl Pfeiffer
Marilyn Monroe . . . Peggy
J. Carrol Naish . . . Uncle Vince
Keith Andes . . . Joe Doyle
Silvio Minciotti . . . Papa D'Amato
Diane Stewart . . . Baby
Deborah Stewart . . . Baby
Roy D'Armour . . . Man
Gilbert Frye . . . Man
Nancy Duke . . . Guest
Sally Yarnell . . . Guest
Irene Crosby . . . Guest
Helen Hansen . . . Guest
Dan Bernaducci . . . Guest
Dick Coe . . . Guest
Al Cavens . . . Guest
Julius Tannen . . . Waiter
William Bailey . . . Waiter
Bert Stevens . . . Bartender
Mario Siletti . . . Bartender
Bill Slack . . . Customer
Art Dupuis . . . Customer
Frank Kreig . . . Artist
Tony Dante . . . Fisherman

**Crew:**
C. Bakaleinikoff . . . musical director
Mel Berns . . . makeup
Carroll Clark . . . art director
Albert S. D'Agostino . . . art director
Larry Germain . . . hairstylist
Jack Mills . . . set decorator
Clem Portman . . . sound
Darrell Silvera . . . set decorator
Jean L. Speak . . . sound
Harold E. Wellman . . . special effects
Michael Woulfe . . . wardrobe
Jack Baker . . . songwriter for "Hear a Rhapsody"
Joe Gasparre . . . songwriter "I Hear a Rhapsody"

**Plot:**

After many years Mae Doyle (Barbara Stanwyck) returns to her hometown. Brother Joe (Keith Andes), in love with fish cannery worker Peggy (Marilyn), is none too pleased to see her. Mae falls for down-to-earth, honest trawler skipper Jerry (Paul Douglas), they marry and have a child. Danger lurks in the form of Jerry's pal Earl (Robert Ryan), a movie projectionist at the local theater—they start an affair and Mae decides to leave her husband.

Jerry refuses to believe that his wife has been up to no good, but when she comes clean he tracks Earl down and comes within a whisker of killing him. Then he takes the baby onto his boat and heads for the high seas. Earl tries to get Mae to leave town with him, and forget about the baby; Mae realizes Earl is only concerned with himself, and that her place is with the man she loves, Jerry. She pleads for him to take her back, he finally relents, and peace is restored in the homestead.

**Reviews:**

*Variety*
"While Marilyn Monroe is reduced to what is tantamount to a bit role, despite her star billing, she does manage to get over her blonde sexiness in one or two scenes, and the film could have used more of her."

*New York Post*
"That gorgeous example of bathing beauty art (in denim), Marilyn Monroe, is a real acting threat to the season's screen blondes. Miss Stanwyck looks remarkably youthful—though not when she's face to face with Miss Monroe, a real charmer."

*New York Daily News*
"'Clash by Night', which Harriet Parsons produced for the Wald-Krasna unit at RKO, is a tense, dramatic film based on a domestic problem.... Marilyn Monroe, who is the new blonde bombshell of Hollywood, manages to look alluring in blue jeans. She plays the secondary role of the cannery worker, Peggy, with complete assurance, and she and young Andes make their marks on the screen against the stiff competition given them by the three principals."

*Time*
"Also on hand, in a minor role, shapely Marilyn Monroe as a fish-cannery employee who bounces around in a succession of slacks, bathing suits and sweaters."

*New York World Telegram and Sun*
"Barbara Stanwyck is off on another of her expert emotional rampages in 'Clash by Night' at the Paramount. This Clifford Odets play gives her much more than her usual substance in the way of story and character.

Before going on any further with a report on 'Clash by Night', perhaps we should mention the first full-length glimpse the picture gives us of Marilyn Monroe as an actress. The verdict is gratifyingly good.

This girl has a refreshing exuberance, an abundance of girlish high spirits. She is a forceful actress, too, when crisis comes along. She has definitely stamped herself as a gifted new star, worthy of all that fantastic press agentry. Her role here is not very big but she makes it dominant."

*The New Yorker*
"*Clash by Night* also gives us a glimpse of Marilyn Monroe and Keith Andes, who play a pair of lovers. Both are quite handsome, but neither can act."

## CLEMMONS, SERGEANT JACK

Acting commander at the West Los Angeles police station. Sergeant Clemmons was the first policeman to arrive on the scene at Marilyn's home after her DEATH, ten minutes after receiving a call at 4:25 A.M. on August 5, 1962 from Dr. Hyman Engelberg, informing the authorities that Marilyn Monroe had committed suicide.

At Marilyn's home he found her body face down under a sheet. Initially, he was told by EUNICE MURRAY that the body had been discovered at midnight. When he asked why it had taken so long to call the police, DR. RALPH GREENSON said that permission was required from the studio before they were allowed to notify outside agencies. Clemmons was relieved by a superior officer within half an hour, and then, according to biographer FRED LAWRENCE GUILES, called colleague JIM DOUGHERTY, Marilyn's first husband, to inform him of Marilyn's death.

Clemmons has long been one of the voices calling foul in the death of Marilyn Monroe. Part of a far-right group called The Police and Fire Research Organization, he assisted FRANK A. CAPELL in the inquiries which led to a 1964 book indicating ROBERT KENNEDY and a Communist plot in Marilyn's death.

Clemmons has gone on record to say that in his opinion Marilyn died at least eight hours before he was called to the scene. He has long said that Marilyn was murdered, and called for official investigations into the crime.

## CLIFT, MONTGOMERY (1920-1966)

CLIFT ON MARILYN:
"Marilyn was an incredible person to act with... the most marvelous I ever worked with, and I have been working for twenty-nine years."

"I have the same problem as Marilyn. We attract people the way honey does bees, but they're generally the wrong kind of people. People who want something from us—if only our energy. We need a period of being alone to become ourselves."

MARILYN ON CLIFT:
"He is the only person I know who's in worse shape than I am."

FRANK TAYLOR:
"Monty and Marilyn were psychic twins. They were on the same wavelength. They recognized disaster in each other's faces and giggled about it."

Montgomery Clift and Marilyn in *The Misfits* (1960).

Alongside MARLON BRANDO and James Dean, Montgomery Clift was the most forceful actor to arrive in Hollywood during the 1950s. From a wealthy background, Clift made his Broadway debut when he was just fifteen, though he did not land his first film role until thirteen years later—in HOWARD HAWKS's *Red River* (1948). Thereafter he played a string of leading roles as a tortured outsider in films like *A Place in the Sun* (1951) and *From Here to Eternity* (1953). After *THE MISFITS* (1961), Clift, who was nominated four times for Academy Awards during his life, made three more movies before he died: *Judgment at Nuremberg* (1961), *Freud* (1963), and *The Defector* (1966).

A serious car crash in 1956 left his face—the prettiest male visage on the screen—scarred and in need of cosmetic surgery. From this point, according to biographer Patricia Bosworth he "crushed his life and career under an avalanche of booze, pills and inexplicable anguish." Perhaps one of the reasons behind this anguish was accepting his homosexuality at a time when open expression of single-sex preferences was simply not an option.

Marilyn and Monty had been good friends for many years by the time they teamed up on *The Misfits*. They met up regularly during the years when Marilyn lived in New York, and would drink vodka together at Marilyn's apartment. Their friendship survived a difference of opinion about LEE STRASBERG—Clift thought he was something of a charlatan. According to Marilyn's maid LENA PEPITONE, Marilyn once attempted to seduce Clift; this was not a success.

ARTHUR MILLER and JOHN HUSTON agreed that Clift would be perfect for the part of troubled rodeo rider Perce Howland. They almost didn't get him, not because he didn't want the part, but because with his history of alcoholism and unpredictable behavior, no insurance company wanted to cover him. On Miller and Huston's insistence he got the role. Not only did he put in a good performance, but his diligence was one of the few points of stability in a production which lurched from one major problem to another.

## CLIFTON MOTEL
PASO ROBLES, CALIFORNIA

In January 1954, Marilyn and JOE DIMAGGIO spent the first day (some sources say two days) of their honeymoon in this perfectly unassuming way station at Paso Robles, California. DiMaggio picked up the check for room 15 at a cost of $6.50 per night (or $4 in some reports). The plan to stay incognito worked perfectly; not even HOTEL owner Ernest Sharp recognized them. Nevertheless, newspapers managed to report that they had stayed fifteen hours in their room without emerging, and that the room, as DiMaggio requested, did have a television. Ever since that day, the room has been adorned with a plaque reading "Joe and Marilyn Slept Here."

## CLOTHES

Marilyn may have been dressed by the leading FASHION DESIGNERS of her day, but even in a sweater and slacks she could, if she chose, be voluptuousness incarnate. As she once said, (referring to her wartime job at

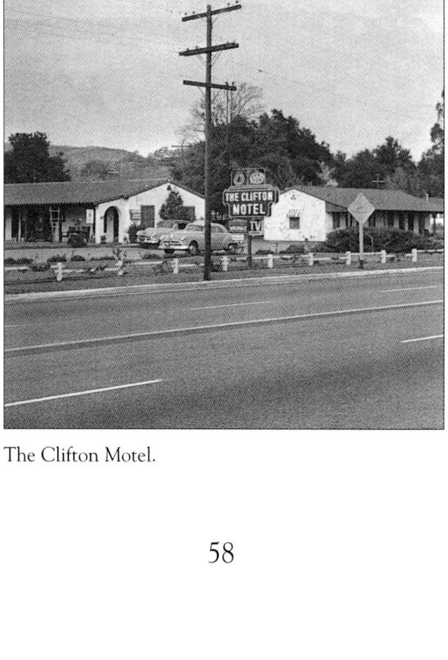


The Clifton Motel.

the RADIO PLANE MUNITIONS FACTORY), "Putting a girl in overalls is like having her work in tights, particularly if a girl knows how to wear them."

In the early days, right up to the film that made her a national success, Marilyn wore what she could find—mainly by borrowing from the studio wardrobe. Director HENRY HATHAWAY asked her to wear her own clothes for her part in *NIAGARA* (1953). Marilyn told him she didn't have any, and invited him to her room where he saw for himself she had nothing.

When she was off-duty, lounging at home, welcoming guests, or doing press interviews, Marilyn kept it comfortable and simple. She could quite happily spend all day in her favored white terry-cloth bathrobe. A number of journalists over the years came to interview Marilyn at home and found themselves sitting on the end of her bed, pencil and paper at the ready, while Marilyn lounged in her bathrobe. Otherwise, she might relax in a blouse or sweater, slacks, and loafers or moccasins.

In New York, if she had errands to run, she went out in a baggy sweater, a black "teddy bear" coat, or a black cape and headscarf. In wintertime, it was more likely a fur coat. She was seen in a full-length black mink and a blue sapphire mink, and a white ermine coat worth $25,000 was among her personal effects after her death.

When it came to colors, Marilyn played the field. The first evening gown she bought with her own money was a bright red low-cut dress, and she continued to wear red to dazzling effect on many occasions and in many movies. Black was a favorite for more sombre, official occasions. There were days when Marilyn dressed down to look demure, such as the time she wore a grey skirt and black blouse to meet ARTHUR MILLER's parents. Purple was popular—she referred to one purple dress with matching purple scarf as her "Purple People-Eater Wardrobe," and green worked well too.

### A SELECTION OF MARILYN MONROE OUTFITS

1941
First date with Jim Dougherty: Norma Jeane borrowed a red silk party dress from friend Beebe Goddard.

1943
With Jim Dougherty in service with the marines, on Catalina Island, Norma Jeane made plenty of friends wearing tight sweaters, tight skirts, white shorts, white blouses, and ribbons in her hair. Jim was not amused.

1945
Interview at Blue Book Modeling Agency: Norma Jeane took her first step into showbiz wearing a white sharkskin dress with an orange yoke, and white suede shoes.

1947
Caddying for John Carroll at a celebrity golf tournament, she wore a bathing costume and platform shoes.

1949
*Love Happy* publicity tour: On Marilyn's first trip to New York she arrived at Grand Central Station wearing a navy blue suit, blue blouse, and a beret. The three wool suits she had packed were so unsuitable for the torrid summer heat that she went straight out to buy a blue polka-dot cotton dress with a low-cut neckline and decorative red velvet belt.

1950
One of Marilyn's favorite sweater dresses is on show in three of Marilyn's movies (*All About Eve, The Fireball*, and *Hometown Story*).

1951
Presenting an Academy Award: a lavender-colored off-the-shoulder dress.

In one of the most bizarre publicity stunts ever, Twentieth Century-Fox decided the world needed to know that Marilyn was sexy in anything, absolutely anything. They cut arm and leg holes in an burlap Idaho potato sack and took the photos to prove their point.

1952
First date with Joe DiMaggio: a blue tailored suit, low-cut white shantung blouse.

"Grand Marshal" of the Miss America Pageant, Marilyn waved to the cheering crowds wearing a black dress cut to the navel.

1953
*Photoplay* Awards for "Fastest Rising Star": Scandal! Marilyn turned up in the gold lamé gown borrowed from the studio that had to be sewn on. It was a Travilla design that was too risqué to make more than a cameo appearance in *Gentlemen Prefer Blondes*. Apparently the seams did not hold through the awards, and required an emergency re-stitch. "When she wiggled through the audience to come up to the podium, her derriere looked like two puppies fighting under a silk sheet" was the comment of one journalist; another remarked that it looked "as if it had been painted on."

1954
Golden Globe Awards, to pick up the first of her two "World Film Favorite" awards, Marilyn wore a red velvet evening gown.

Wedding to Joe DiMaggio, a dark brown suit with ermine collar.

Flying to Tokyo with Joe on honeymoon: a staid black suit with leopard skin choker, carrying a mink coat.

In Korea, Marilyn was decked out in army fatigues and wore a leather jacket. She performed for the boys in a low-cut, plum-colored sequined gown which she kept for the rest of her life as a souvenir.

DiMaggio divorce: In court Marilyn wore a black silk dress suit, a black straw hat worn at an angle, white gloves, and white pearls.

To pick up her *Photoplay* Award for *Gentleman Prefer Blondes*: white satin sheath, and a new short hairstyle.

Party at Romanoff's thrown in Marilyn's honor: a spectacular red chiffon gown borrowed from the Fox wardrobe.

1955
Press conference announcing formation of Marilyn Monroe Productions: all in white—an ermine coat over a white satin dress.

Attending classes at the Actors Studio: jeans and a baggy sweater.

1956
Returning to Los Angeles, after a year-long absence, to start work on *Bus Stop*, she wore a brown two-piece suit with a high-necked black blouse. A reporter asked if the high-necked suit was the "New Marilyn." Her answer was, "Well, I'm the same person—it's just a different suit."

Press conference announcing production of *The Prince and the Showgirl*: a black low-cut velvet dress designed by John Moore, with the thinnest of shoulder straps, one of which snapped right on cue.

In 1951 Twentieth Century-Fox set out to prove that Marilyn even looked good in an Idaho potato sack.

Party for President Sukarno of Indonesia: a figure-hugging black wool dress.

Arrival at London Airport, July 1956: a tight fitting dress, fawn raincoat, and matching leather hand-bag.

Press conference with Laurence Olivier at the Savoy: a tight two-piece dress joined by revealing chiffon insert.

Meeting the Queen: sewn into a red velvet dress.

London premiere of *A View from the Bridge* at the Comedy Theater in London, she wore a tight red strapless satin number. The Associated Press reported, "Marilyn Monroe's close-fitting dress turned the London opening of her husband's latest play into a near riot."

1958
Marilyn was criticized for being photographed wearing the less than figure-hugging "sack dress" popular that year—a style that was very good at covering up the extra twenty pounds she had put on.

Arriving in Los Angeles for shooting on *Some Like It Hot,* Marilyn was a vision in white—white shoes, white gloves, white skirt, white silk shirt, and white bleached hair.

1959
Picking up her David di Donatello Award from the Italian Consulate, she wore a black cocktail dress with matching jacket, and black patent leather heels.

Lunch with Khrushchev: a black net dress with translucent insert.

Twentieth Century-Fox party in honor of Frankie Vaughan and Yves Montand: a champagne-colored chiffon cocktail dress.

1960
Relaxing at her Beverly Hills Hotel bungalow with Miller, Montand, and Signoret: a Woolworth's blue polka-dotted rayon dressing gown, or for special occasions, a long crimson velvet bathrobe Miller gave her for New Year's Day, 1960.

1961
One of her favorite outfits—a black Norman Norell dress with a matching black broadcloth jacket—got an outing to a dinner party at Peter Lawford's house. Her nipples reputedly protruded through the little holes in the eyelet gown.

1962
Golden Globe Awards: sewn into a green backless floor-length dress.

To sing "Happy Birthday" to John F. Kennedy, Marilyn was sheathed in a sheer flesh-colored gown shimmering with hand-sewn rhinestones, designed by Jean-Louis. Marilyn worked very closely with the designer; his brief was to "make this a dress that only Marilyn Monroe would dare to wear." The $12,000 dress did precisely that. When the spotlights hit Marilyn, the silk became almost transparent and she looked like she was glistening and nude.

Marilyn was buried in one of her favorite outfits, a pale green Pucci dress.

## COHN, HARRY (1891–1958)

Harry Cohn, the archetypal movie mogul, was the son of a German tailor, whose first jobs were as a trolley conductor and vaudeville singer. In the early twenties, together with Joe Brandt and brother Jack, he formed a movie studio which in 1924 changed its name to COLUMBIA. Bitter boardroom battles followed. Harry managed to take full control of the studio, and became the single most powerful mogul in Hollywood. Cohn was almost universally hated for his ruthlessness and vulgarity—he was quoted as saying among other things, "I don't have ulcers, I give them!"—but he was also a master in finding and using talent to make Columbia Studios one of the most powerful forces in Hollywood for decades.

From an initial reputation as churning out second-rate pictures, the studio went up-market after Cohn gave Frank Capra his chance in the thirties. Rita Hayworth was the studio's greatest draw in the forties. The fifties saw Cohn working with the biggest directors and launching the careers of KIM NOVAK, Judy Holliday, JACK LEMMON, and others.

Marilyn was put in touch with the head of Columbia Studios by close friend and new-found patron, JOSEPH SCHENCK, head of TWENTIETH CENTURY-FOX. On Schenck's recommendation Cohn hired Marilyn on a six-month contract at $125 per week, starting March 9, 1948. The other version is that Cohn was persuaded to hire the young starlet not because of trading favors, but because Marilyn, like his wife, was a follower of CHRISTIAN SCIENCE.

Before allowing Marilyn to appear in the one film she made for Columbia, *LADIES OF THE CHORUS* (1948), Cohn sampled her singing talents in the office, accompanied on the piano by FRED KARGER. She did enough to get the part, but Cohn was apparently less than impressed with what he saw of Marilyn in the film, and her six-month contract was not renewed. Most biographers cite the real reason for the brush-off was less to do with Marilyn's acting talents than the fact that she turned down his offer to join him on his yacht for a quiet little weekend jaunt, just the two of them. Marilyn said she would only accept the invitation if his wife came along too.

Many years later, Marilyn still remembered the incident enough to sarcastically send him an autographed photo from *GENTLEMAN PREFER BLONDES* (1953), inscribed, "To my great benefactor, Harry Cohn."

Cohn's funeral in 1958 proved to be an occasion for memorable quotes. Red Skelton quipped, "It proves what they always say: Give the public what they want to see and there'll come out for it." HEDDA HOPPER noted, "You had to stand in line to hate him."

Cohn gave back as well as taking from the industry. He provided the inspiration for model film moguls in *All the King's Men* (1949), *Born Yesterday* (1950), *The Big Knife* (1955), and *The Godfather* (1972).

## COLE, JACK (1914–1974)

Dancer Jack Cole choreographed Marilyn in all her song and dance routines starting in 1953 with *GENTLEMEN PREFER BLONDES* and including *RIVER OF NO RETURN* (1954), *THERE'S NO BUSINESS LIKE SHOW BUSINESS* (1954), and *LET'S MAKE LOVE* (1960). He also helped Marilyn without credit for her "Running Wild" number in *SOME LIKE IT HOT* (1959).

Marilyn implicitly trusted Cole's guidance, and after the first time they worked together they became firm friends. Cole's function was very much like that of Marilyn's drama coaches, giving her step-by-step help through filming. Cole stood next to the camera and performed the steps, Marilyn mirrored his movements in front of the camera.

Cole worked especially hard with Marilyn for her numbers in *Let's Make Love*. More than anything else, Marilyn dreaded the dance numbers. Afterward Marilyn showed her gratitude by giving him a card into which she had slipped a $1500 check and a note, "I really was awful, it must have been a difficult experience, please go someplace nice for a couple of weeks and act like it all never happened." A couple of days later Cole received another check, this time for $500, in a card which said, "Stay three more days."

Cole later said, "She was just a terribly pretty girl whom all this had happened to, and all of a sudden she was a star, she was going to have to go out and do it and everybody was going to look at her. And she was just terrified! She knew that she was not equal to it."

As well as his work as a choreographer, Cole danced on film in *Moon over Miami* (1941) and *Kismet* (1944). His choreographer credits grace more than ten movies, including *Gilda* (1946) and the *Gentleman Prefer Blondes* follow-up, *Gentlemen Marry Brunettes* (1955).

## COLLIER, CONSTANCE (1878–1955, B. LAURA CONSTANCE HARDIE)

In later life this renowned British stage actress moved to Hollywood to play a succession of eccentric dames, including roles in *Anna Karenina* (1935), *Little Lord Fauntleroy* (1936), *Stage Door* (1937), *Kitty* (1945), and *An Ideal Husband* (1948). After 1950 she began coaching, and in the five years before her death worked not only with Marilyn but Katharine Hepburn, AUDREY HEPBURN, and VIVIEN LEIGH. Collier was the first drama teacher Marilyn began to study with after moving to New York, before coming under the tutelage of LEE STRASBERG. If Collier had not died just a few months later, in April that year, Marilyn may never have joined the ACTORS STUDIO. Marilyn was accompanied to Collier's funeral by TRUMAN CAPOTE.

Collier's estimation of Marilyn was extremely acute: "She is a beautiful child. I don't think she's an actress at all, not in any traditional sense. What she has—this presence, this luminosity, this flickering intelligence—could never surface on the stage. It's so fragile and subtle, it can only be caught by the camera. . . . But anyone who thinks this girl is simply another Harlow harlot or whatever, is mad. I hope, I really pray, that she survives long enough to free the strange lovely talent that's wandering through her like a jailed spirit."

## COLLINS, JOAN (B. 1933)

Joan Collins had already arrived in Hollywood but had not yet landed a lead until Marilyn inadvertently did her a favor by refusing to follow up *THE SEVEN YEAR ITCH* (1955) with Fox's next planned movie vehicle, *The Girl in the Red Velvet Swing*. When Marilyn stonewalled, Fox pulled Collins out of its bag of tricks for her first major starring role.

In her 1996 autobiography *Second Act*, Collins describes how she met Marilyn at a party thrown by GENE KELLY; when Marilyn saw her sitting all alone, she went over to make friends.

Collins was initially approached to portray Marilyn in the 1974 British stage play *Legend*. The part went to Sondra Dickinson.

## COLUMBIA PICTURES
1438 GOWER STREET, HOLLYWOOD
(NOW AT BURBANK STUDIOS,
4000 WARNER BOULEVARD, BURBANK)

On March 9, 1948, two decades after her mother had worked there as a film cutter, studio chief HARRY COHN signed Marilyn to Columbia on a $125 per week six-month contract, on the recommendation of Fox chief JOSEPH M. SCHENCK. Although she only appeared in one film, *LADIES OF THE CHORUS*, her time there was significant. The first thing the studio did was remodel Marilyn's hairline by using electrolysis to move it higher; they also peroxided her hair from ash blonde to Harlow platinum. More importantly, head of talent, Max Arnow, introduced Marilyn to drama coach NATASHA LYTESS, with whom she worked for seven years, and voice coach FRED KARGER, referred to by many biographers as Marilyn's first true love.

## CONNERS, HAL

Helicopter pilot who, it has been alleged, flew ROBERT KENNEDY from PETER LAWFORD's beach house to the TWA departure gate at LAX early in the morning of August 5, 1962, when Marilyn was found dead. According to Conner's former partner Jim Zonlick, Conners picked Kennedy up between midnight and 2:00 A.M. as he made his return to Gilroy, California, where he was staying with friends.

## CONOVER, DAVID (1919–1983)

In the fall of 1944 (or spring 1945, as he says in his own memoir of his "discovery" of Marilyn Monroe), Conover was seconded from the Hal Roach Studios to the Army's 1st Motion Picture Unit, at that time commanded by actor RONALD REAGAN. Conover was assigned to go to the RADIO PLANE MUNITIONS FACTORY, where he was instructed to shoot "Moving Pictures" for an army training film, and get some stills of "morale booster types" for the boys on the front line, to show them that their efforts were being supported by the loveliest of girls back home. Norma Jeane, who was working at Radio Plane, either pushed or was pushed to the front in these shots. Corporal Conover expressed his interest in taking some color shots of her, Norma Jeane jumped at the opportunity, and for the next couple of weeks he commuted from Culver City to the Radio Plane plant. Conover writes that what captivated him was "a luminous quality to her face, a fragility combined with astonishing vibrancy."

Norma Jeane described her first, unexpected break to guardian GRACE MCKEE GODDARD in a letter dated June 4, 1945:

> "The first I know [the photographers] had me out there, taking pictures of me. . . . They all asked where in the H—I had been hiding. . . . They took a lot of moving pictures of me, and some of them asked for dates, etc. (Naturally I refused). . . . After they finished with some of the pictures, an army corporal by the name of David Conover told me he would be interested in getting some color still shots of me. He used to have a studio on the Strip on Sunset. He said he would make arrangements with the plant superintendent if I would agree, so I said okay. He told me what to wear and what shade of lipstick, etc., so the next couple of weeks I posed for him at different times. . . . He said all the pictures came out perfect. Also, he said that I should by all means go into the modeling profession . . . that I photographed very well and that he wants to take a lot more. Also he said he had a lot of contacts he wanted me to look into.
>
> I told him I would rather not work when Jimmie was here, so he said he would wait, so I'm expecting to hear from him most any time again.
>
> He is awfully nice and is married and is strictly business, which is the way I like it. Jimmie seems to like the idea of me modeling, so I'm glad about that."

Conover's photographs were Norma Jeane's first small step to stardom. Conover showed the shots to a commercial photographer Marilyn identified in a late interview as Potter Hueth, for whom she did some modeling. It was Hueth who later showed pictures to EMMELINE SNIVELY, who ran the BLUE BOOK MODELING AGENCY.

Norma Jeane's first magazine cover photo, in *Yank* magazine in 1945 or in *Douglas Air Review* in January 1946, depending on sources, was taken by Conover during the early summer of 1945 as they toured California for shots against dramatic backdrops. He writes in *Finding Marilyn: A Romance*, that during these trips young Norma Jeane seduced him and they became lovers. He also writes that he lent her $100 to cover the cost of a course she took at Blue Book.

Conover and Marilyn met up six years later, after Marilyn had made it, on the set of *GENTLEMEN PREFER BLONDES*.

BOOKS:

*Finding Marilyn: A Romance*. New York: Grosset & Dunlap, 1981.

*The Discovery Photos, Summer 1945*. Ontario: Norma Jeane Enterprises, 1990.

Private detective and author of *The Marilyn Conspiracy* Milo Speriglio and a Marilyn look-alike at a 1982 press conference called by Speriglio to demand that the coroner's office reopen the case.

## CONSOLIDATED FILM INDUSTRIES
MELROSE AVENUE, HOLLYWOOD

GLADYS BAKER worked at this Hollywood processing lab as a film cutter starting in 1923. Her job, performed six days a week, was to cut up the film marked by studio editors, before it was passed along to splicers who made up the final negative. This is where she was working around the time she became pregnant with Norma Jeane. A fellow employee, C. STANLEY GIFFORD, is one of the two men thought most likely to have been Marilyn's FATHER. Speculation has also fallen on the possible paternal responsibilities of other male colleagues of Gladys.

## CONSPIRACY

. . . theories abound. The mystery of Marilyn's DEATH just gets more mysterious as the years go by. Almost forty years on, the circumstances of how she died still make tabloid headlines. One recent story revealed that Marilyn didn't really die, she simply lives on under an FBI witness protection program somewhere in the Midwest; another claims that JOHN F. KENNEDY, fearing she was about to go public, had Marilyn kidnapped, drugged, and shipped out to Australia, where to this day she suffers amnesia and lives as a sheep farmer. There have even been stories that Marilyn's death was in some way connected to the cover-up surrounding alleged alien landings in Roswell, New Mexico.

More credence has been given to theories that have provided the basis for TV DOCUMENTARIES and sensational books: Marilyn was killed by the MAFIA on behalf of the Kennedys; ROBERT KENNEDY stifled her with a pillow in her Brentwood home after she threatened to expose her affair with his brother to the press; a cast of characters ranging from RALPH GREENSON to PETER LAWFORD administered a lethal dose of drugs for a wide variety of reasons.

This wealth of conspiracy stories has not prevented speculators from casting the net of suspicion as wide as teamsters leader JIMMY HOFFA (suspected of BUGGING Marilyn's home), FBI boss J. EDGAR HOOVER, and Fidel Castro.

Even unbelievers agree on one point: whatever the circumstances of Marilyn's death, somebody, quite possibly a number of persons, perpetrated a COVER-UP that has lasted to this day.

DONALD SPOTO traces the genesis of conspiracy theories about a shadowy Kennedy hand in Marilyn's death all the way back to a gossip column tidbit (Marilyn was supposedly "vastly alluring to a handsome gentleman who is a bigger name than JOE DIMAGGIO") written by DOROTHY KILGALLEN the day before Marilyn died. This juicy morsel was taken up by rival columnist WALTER WINCHELL, in a story planted by a right-wing colleague FRANK A. CAPELL. Here the genealogy becomes intriguing. Capell was a friend of JACK CLEMMONS, the first policeman to arrive at Marilyn's house after her death, who was a member of a far-right Emergency Services organization called The Police and Fire Research Organization, whose mission was to root out anti-American subversive activities. Spoto says that Capell's book implicating Robert Kennedy was just too appealing for later authors to ignore. Without naming names, FRED LAWRENCE GUILES's 1969 biography of Marilyn hints at the presence of Bobby Kennedy, but it was NORMAN MAILER's 1973 book that brought these allegations to full public notice. Since 1974, when he published the first of his Marilyn books, ROBERT SLATZER became a vociferous proponent of the Kennedy theory. His theories have been developed further in the books published by private detective MILO SPERIGLIO. ANTHONY SUMMERS's 1986 biography pointed an accusing finger at Kennedy once more, spawning a number of television documentaries and interest. Seymour Hersch's 1998 Kennedy biography brought yet more attention to the Kennedy brothers and their antics, and DONALD WOLFE's Marilyn biography that same year indicted Kennedy once more.

Only one thing is for sure: for a long time to come rumor-mongers and conspiracy theorists will continue to weave Marilyn's death into the backdrop of events during the 1960s.

## CONTINENTAL HILTON HOTEL
PASEO DE LA REFORMA, MEXICO CITY

This was where Marilyn stayed in February 1962 on her Mexican furniture-buying spree. It was here that she entertained handsome Mexican screenwriter JOSÉ BOLAÑOS. On February 26, 1962 Marilyn gave a press conference at this HOTEL. The hotel was destroyed in 1985 by the earthquake that ravaged Mexico City.

## COOKING

Marilyn's many talents did not include culinary prowess. As a career woman, she far more often ate what other people prepared.

First husband JAMES DOUGHERTY thought cooking was Norma Jeane's worst quality. He would have seen quite a lot of her favorite dish—peas and carrots—which she liked for the pretty combination of colors. Eager as she may have been as a sixteen-year-old to please her new husband, in later years Dougherty revealed to reporters several culinary disasters, including a trout served virtually raw, salt in the coffee, and an unvarying menu of egg sandwiches in the lunchbox she packed for him to take to work every day.

SHELLEY WINTERS, who reputedly shared an apartment with Marilyn in 1951, recalled that Marilyn's culinary skills were minimal: "Her idea of making a salad was to scrub each lettuce leaf with a Brillo pad."

Marilyn's second and third husbands had a slightly better time as she picked up cooking skills along the way. The FOOD she made included hearty pasta dishes for JOE DIMAGGIO, which she learned from Mama DiMaggio during her time living with Joe's family in San Francisco immediately after their wedding. For ARTHUR MILLER she made all kinds of traditional Jewish delicacies—she herself having just converted.

Marilyn's time with the home-cooking DiMaggios was probably when she learned most about cooking. She had grown up during the Depression, with a succession of foster families, and without a mother to show her the basics of cooking. Over the years, she did learn a few recipes. For example, during shooting of *LET'S MAKE LOVE*, when Marilyn and Arthur Miller lived in a bungalow at the BEVERLY HILLS HOTEL next to co-star YVES MONTAND and wife SIMONE SIGNORET, Marilyn occasionally cooked up spaghetti as party fare.

In a December 1960 *Cosmopolitan* interview with Jon Whitcomb, Marilyn had food on her mind. She talked about how she enjoyed cooking bread, but revealed that "some people seem to find cooking quite tedious." She also talked of an occasion on Long Island, with Arthur Miller, when she set to work in the kitchen:

> "For homemade noodles, I roll the dough out very thin, then I slice it into narrow strips . . . then, the book says, 'Wait till they dry.' We were expecting guests for dinner. I waited and waited. The noodles didn't dry. The guests arrived; I gave them a drink; I said, 'You have to wait for dinner until the noodles dry. Then we'll eat.' I had to give them another drink. In desperation, I went and got my little portable hair dryer and turned it on. It blew the noodles off the counter, and I had to gather them all up and try again. This time I put my hand over the strips, with my fingers outspread, and aimed the dryer through them. Well . . . the noodles finally dried. So they *do* leave out a few instructions. I've wanted to write in and ask, 'Please, let people know how long it takes to dry noodles.' But I never did."

However, in his book *Marilyn: An Untold Story*, NORMAN ROSTEN reveals that Marilyn loved to cook for her friends, and made tasty stews, roast beef and bouillabaisse.

## CORONADO BEACH, CALIFORNIA

Marilyn came here for a week's shooting of exteriors in September 1958 at the HOTEL DEL CORONADO (1500 Orange Avenue) for *SOME LIKE IT HOT* (1959), a couple of hours' drive south of Los Angeles. She stayed in the "Vista Mar Cottage."

Marilyn and Jack Lemmon on the set of *Some Like it Hot* (1959) at the Hotel del Coronado in Coronado Beach, California.

## CORONERS

Head Coroner of Los Angeles County: Theodore J. Curphey
Deputy Medical Examiner: Thomas Noguchi
Assistant to Deputy Medical Examiner: Eddy Day
Suicide Investigation Team: Dr. Robert Litman, Dr. Norman Farberow
Coroner's Aide: LIONEL GRANDISON
Coroner's Case Number: 81128; Coroner's Crypt No.: 33

Head coroner Curphey's statement, August 18, 1962: "It is my conclusion that the death of Marilyn Monroe was caused by self-administered sedative drugs, that the mode of death is 'probable suicide.'"

Head Toxicologist R. J. Abernethy's finding on Marilyn's DEATH, delivered on August 27, 1962, was "acute barbiturate poisoning—ingestion of overdose."

The autopsy revealed no external signs of violence on Marilyn's body. Blood tests showed 8 mg of chloral hydrate and 4.5 mg of Nembutal. Examination of the liver revealed a much higher 13 milligram concentration of Nembutal.

Dr. Litman, who worked in the coroner's office at that time, told biographer DONALD SPOTO, "We wanted to get this over with, to come to a decision, close the case, issue a death certificate and move on. But, of course, that turned out to be a misplaced hope."

### AUTOPSY:

Performed at 10:30 A.M. on August 5, 1962 by Deputy Medical Examiner Thomas Noguchi, assisted by Eddy Day.

### REPORT:

External examination: The unenbalmed body is that of a 36-year-old well-developed, well-nourished Caucasian female weighing 117 pounds and measuring 65 1/2 inches in length. The scalp is covered with bleached blond hair. The eyes are blue. The fixed lividity is noted in the face, neck, chest, upper portions of the arms and the right side of the abdomen. The faint lividity which disappears upon pressure is noted in the back and posterior aspect of the arms and legs. A slight ecchymotic area is noted in the left hip and left side of lower back. The breast shows no significant lesion. There is a horizontal 3-inch long surgical scar in the right upper quadrant of the abdomen. A suprapublic surgical scar measuring 5 inches in length is noted.

The conjunctivae are markedly congested; however, no ecchymosis or petechiae are noted. The nose shows no evidence of fracture. The external auditory canals are not remarkable. No evidence of trauma is noted in the scalp, forehead, cheeks, lips or chin. The neck shows no evidence of trauma. Examination of the hands and nails shows no defects. The lower extremities show no evidence of trauma.

Body cavity: The usual Y-shaped incision is made to open the thoracic and abdominal cavities. The pleural and abdominal cavities contain no excess of fluid or blood. The mediastinum shows no shifting or widening. The diaphragm is within normal limits. The lower edge of the liver is within the costal margin. The organs are in normal position and relationship.

Cardiovascular system: The heart weighs 300 grams. The pericardial cavity contains no excess of fluid. The epicardium and pericardium are smooth and glistening. The left ventricular wall measures 1.1 cm and the right 0.2 cm. The papillary muscles are not hypertrophic. The chordae tendinae are not thickened or shortened. The valves have the usual number of leaflets which are thin and pliable. The tricuspid valve measures 10 cm, the pulmonary valve 6.5 cm, mitral valve 9.5 cm and aortic valve 7 cm in circumference. There is no septal defect. The formane ovale is closed.

The coronary arteries arise from the usual location and are distributed in normal fashion. Multiple sections of the anterior descending branch of the left coronary artery with a 5 mm interval demonstrate a patent lumen throughout. The circumflex branch and the right coronary artery also demonstrate a patent lumen. The pulmonary artery contains no thrombus.

The aorta has a bright yellow smooth intima.

Respiratory system: The right lung weighs 465 grams and the left 420 grams. Both lungs are moderately congested with some edema. The surface is dark and red with mottling. The posterior portion of the lungs show severe congestion. The tracheobronchial tree contains no aspirated material or blood. Multiple sections of the lungs show congestion and edematous fluid exuding from the cut surface. No consolidation or suppuration is noted. The mucosa of the larynx is grayish white.

Liver and biliary system: The liver weighs 1890 grams. The surface is dark brown and smooth. There are marked adhesions through the omentum and abdominal wall in the lower portion of the liver as the gallbladder has been removed. No calculus or obstructive material is found. Multiple sections of the liver show slight exaggeration of the lobular pattern; however, no haemorrhage or tumor is found.

Hemic and lymphatic system: The spleen weighs 190 grams. The surface is dark red and smooth. Section shows dark red homogeneous firm cut surface. The Malpighian bodies are not clearly identified. There is no evidence of lymphadenopathy. The bone-marrow is dark red in color.

Endocrine system: The adrenal glands have the usual architectural cortex and medulla. The thyroid glands are of normal size, color and consistency.

Urinary system: The kidneys together weigh 350 grams. Their capsules can be stripped without difficulty. Dissection shows a moderately congested parenchyma. The cortical surface is smooth. The pelves and ureters are not dilated or stenosed. The urinary bladder contains approximately 150 cc of clear straw colored fluid. The mucosa is not altered.

Genital system: The external genitalia shows no gross abnormality. Distribution of the pubic hair is of female pattern. The uterus is of the usual size. Multiple sections of the uterus show the usual thickness of the uterine wall without tumor nodules. The endometrium is grayish yellow, measuring up to 0.2 cm in thickness. No polyp or tumor is found. The cervix is clear, showing no nabothian cysts. The tubes are intact. The right ovary demonstrates recent corpus luteum haemorrhagicum. The left ovary shows corpora lutea and albicantia. A vagina smear is taken.

Digestive system: The esophagus has a longitudinal folding mucosa. The stomach is almost completely empty. The contents is brownish mucoid fluid. The volume is estimated to be no more than 20 cc. No residue of the pills is noted. A smear made from the gastric contents and examined under the polarized microscope shows no refractile crystals. The mucosa shows marked congestion and submucosal petechial haemorrhage diffusely. The duodenum shows no ulcer. The contents of the duodenum is also examined under polarized microscope and shows no refractile crystals. The remainder of the small intestinal shows no gross abnormality. The appendix is absent. The colon shows marked congestion and purplish discoloration.

The pancreas has a tan lobular architecture. Multiple sections show a patent duct.

Skeletomuscular system: The clavicle, ribs, vertebrae and pelvic bones show no fracture lines. All bones of the extremities are examined by palpation showing no evidence of fracture.

Head and central nervous system: The brain weighs 1440 grams. Upon reflection of the scalp there is no evidence of contusion or haemorrhage. The temporal muscles are intact. Upon removal of the dura mater the cerbrospinal fluid is clear. The superficial vessels are slightly congested. The convolutions of the brain are not flattened. The contour of the brain is not distorted. No blood is found in the epidural, subdural or subarachnoid spaces. Multiple sections of the brain show the usual symmetrical ventricles and basal ganglia. Examination of the cerebellum and brain stem shows no gross abnormality. Following removal of the dura mater from the base of the skull and calvarium no skull fracture is demonstrated.

Liver temperature taken at 10.30 a.m. registered 89 degrees F.

Specimen: Unembalmed blood is taken for alcohol and barbiturate examination. Liver, kidney, stomach and contents, urine and intestine are saved for further toxicological study. A vagina smear is made.

## COSMETIC SURGERY

Legends are not born fully formed. They take work, and Marilyn was no exception. The precise details of who persuaded, took, or paid for Marilyn to have these minor operations varies from one biography to the next, but the salient facts are as follows:

In March 1948 COLUMBIA Studios arranged for Marilyn, whose HAIR had been dyed blonde a couple of years earlier, to have her hairline raised by electrolysis; at the same time her hair color was lightened from ash blonde to platinum.

FRED KARGER sent Marilyn to Dr. Walter Taylor, a specialist in cosmetic dentistry, before the shooting of *LADIES OF THE CHORUS* in 1948. The orthodontist corrected Marilyn's slightly protruding front teeth, it seems by giving her a corrective brace to wear at night. Early photographer LASZLO WILLINGER also claims credit for fixing her "one bad front tooth."

In 1950 (1949 in some accounts) JOHNNY HYDE arranged for Marilyn to have her nose and chin touched up. On this occasion Beverly Hills plastic surgeon Michael Gurdin excised a slight bump of cartilage from the tip of her nose, and inserted a crescent-shaped silicone prosthesis into her lower jaw to "pad out" and soften the line of her chin.

The main difference, though, between the budding starlet and the accomplished star, was practice. Marilyn's great skill in front of the camera was her ability to use what she had to maximum effect. When she "did a Marilyn" she angled her head in a certain way, set her lips into her trademark pout, walked her walk, and seduced the lens.

Some apocryphal reports of cosmetic work have circulated about Marilyn too. There has been recent speculation that Marilyn had her breasts enhanced around the time she had her minor cosmetic surgery. This has never been confirmed, and appears highly unlikely, partly because she had a perfectly fine pair of breasts as a young girl, and partly because breast enhancement surgery was not readily available at that time. Silicon implants began to be used in the early sixties, though much cruder forms of breast enhancement had been experimented with prior to then: polyurethane injections in the early fifties, implantation of fatty tissues from other parts of the body (actress Tallulah Bankhead is reputed to have resorted to this in the 1930s), and even injections of paraffin. In her book *Lift*, Joan Kron says that a few years after operating on her chin, doctor John Pangman gave Marilyn silicone implants, which became a source of illness towards the end of her life. This would not seem to be borne out in topless pictures of Marilyn taken in the late 1940s by EARL MORAN and in 1962 by BERT STERN.

Early Norma Jeane photographer JOSEPH JASGUR stated in his book that young Norma Jeane had an extra little toe on her left foot which was surgically removed. His photos of her on Zuma beach are rather blurry and inconclusive in the sixth toe region, mainly because alleged toe number six is a small ridge of sand.

Marilyn in a costume for *Gentlemen Prefer Blondes* (1953) designed by William Travilla.

## COSTUME DESIGNERS

Bonnie Cashin—*Scudda Hoo! Scudda Hay!* (1948)
Carey Cline—*O. Henry's Full House* (1952)
Beatrice Dawson—*The Prince and the Showgirl* (1957)
Edith Head—*All About Eve* (1950)
Grace Houston—*Love Happy* (1950)
Rene Hubert—*A Ticket to Tomahawk* (1950)
Dorothy Jeakins—*Niagara* (1953), *Let's Make Love* (1960)
Elois Jenssen—*We're Not Married* (1952)
ORRY-KELLY—*Some Like It Hot* (1959)
CHARLES LEMAIRE (head of wardrobe at Fox)—*Dangerous Years* (1947), *The Fireball* (1950)
JEAN-LOUIS—*Ladies of the Chorus* (1948), *The Misfits* (1961), *Something's Got to Give* (1962–incomplete)
Renie—*As Young As You Feel* (1951), *Love Nest* (1951), *Let's Make It Legal* (1951)
Helen Rose—*The Asphalt Jungle* (1950), *Right Cross* (1950), *Hometown Story* (1950)
WILLIAM TRAVILLA—*Don't Bother to Knock* (1952), *Monkey Business* (1952), *Gentlemen Prefer Blondes* (1953), *How to Marry a Millionaire* (1953), *River of No Return* (1954), *There's No Business Like Show Business* (1954), *The Seven Year Itch* (1955), *Bus Stop* (1956)
Michael Woulfe—*Clash By Night* (1952)

[For information on specific costumes, see individual film entries. Also see FASHION.]

## COTTEN, JOSEPH (1905–1994)

"Everything that girl does is sexy. A lot of people—the ones who haven't met Marilyn—will tell you it's all publicity. That's malarkey. They've tried to give a hundred girls the same publicity build-up. It didn't take with them. This girl's really got it!"

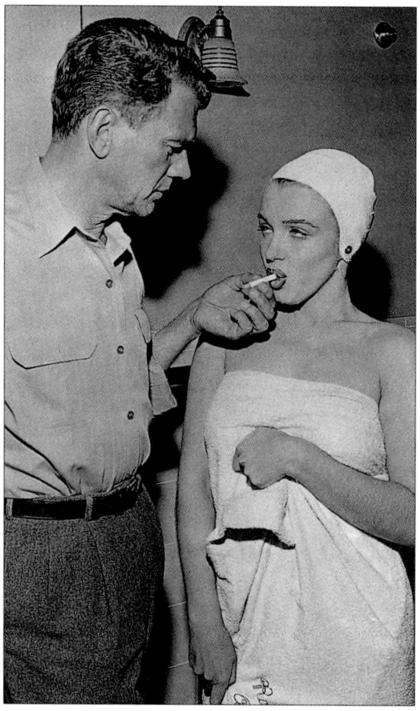

Joseph Cotten with Marilyn in the eyebrow-raising shower scene in *Niagara* (1953).

Leading actor who came to the movies after a spell first as a drama critic, then as a Broadway star, Cotten starred opposite Marilyn in NIAGARA (1953), and got on well with her during filming: "If you wanted to talk about yourself, she listened. If you wanted to talk about her, she blushed. A rather lost little girl, I found her to be."

Orson Welles cast Cotten in *Citizen Kane* (1941), *The Magnificent Ambersons* (1942), and *The Third Man* (1949). The man many believe is America's finest director once paid Cotten the double-edged compliment, "I'm afraid you'll never make it as an actor. But as a star, I think you might well hit the jackpot."

## Court Appearances

Marilyn's court appearances were mainly for DIVORCE. Her Herculean battles against the studio system kept a phalanx of LAWYERS busy for two years, but never made it to court. In 1951 or 1952 she was sued for unpaid phone bills in her name, at NATASHA LYTESS's house on NORTH CRESCENT DRIVE. This too was resolved out of court.

On June 26, 1952 Marilyn was called to testify before presiding judge Kenneth Holaday in a trial against defendants Jerry Karpman and Morrie Kaplen, charged with conducting a nude photo mail-order business. The partners had used the name "Marilyn Monroe" in their advertising.

Marilyn's 1952 fender bender resulted in an enormous claim for damages by the owner of the car she allegedly ran into. This dispute was settled out of court. (*see* CARS)

On February 28, 1956, after many delays, Marilyn appeared at the Beverly Hills City Hall to answer charges of driving without a license on Sunset Boulevard on November 21, 1954. Judge Charles J. Griffin not only fined her $55, he pointedly reminded her that the law was the same for everyone.

## Cover-up

There is perhaps only one aspect of Marilyn's death about which all her biographers agree: On the night of August 4, 1962 a cover-up was perpetrated to hide evidence about the true circumstances of Marilyn's death.

GLORIA STEINEM describes it as "a cover-up of a non-crime: the personal relationship between Marilyn and John and Robert Kennedy." Her thesis includes PETER LAWFORD sweeping Marilyn's house for any incriminating evidence, including a suicide note, and housekeeper EUNICE MURRAY tidying things up even after the police arrived—the first policeman on the death scene noticed that she was running the washing machine.

ROBERT KENNEDY and Lawford may have been involved in an attempt to resuscitate Marilyn after she took an overdose; ambulance drivers from a local company told biographer ANTHONY SUMMERS of an unsuccessful attempt to rush her to the hospital, only to deposit her dead body back at her house. The police arrived on the scene five or six hours after Marilyn's probable time of death.

For DONALD SPOTO, the people involved in cleaning up Marilyn and her apartment before the arrival of the police include DR. RALPH GREENSON, Dr. Hyman Engelberg, and Eunice Murray. What they were covering up, according to this biographer, was evidence of a fatal enema administered as a means of sedating a distraught Marilyn. This involved concocting a story about Greenson breaking into Marilyn's locked bedroom through the window, which itself would have meant removing the heavy black material Marilyn had tacked up against the window to block out all light, and then destroying traces of administration of an enema which had killed Marilyn by mistake.

Other people reputedly involved in a cover-up include HAL CONNERS, a helicopter pilot who allegedly flew Robert Kennedy out of Los Angeles, and, for advanced CONSPIRACY theory believers, a small army of spooks, MAFIA men, and underworld enforcers.

## Cowan, Lester (1907–1990)

The producer of 1950 Marx brothers caper LOVE HAPPY did his agent friend JOHNNY HYDE a favor by adding Marilyn to the movie and drumming up a little favorable publicity for the starlet. Marilyn's side of the deal was to go out on a nationwide tour to promote a film in which she had a rather microscopic role. Cowan took credit for dubbing her "The MMMMMM GIRL" and maneuvered a press piece into LOUELLA PARSONS's *Los Angeles Examiner* column saying he was going to make her a star. Marilyn had other ideas. Half way through the publicity tour for the film Marilyn decided she had had enough and returned home to Los Angeles.

## Cox, Wally (1924–1973)

Marilyn specifically requested that her friend Wally Cox get a part in SOMETHING'S GOT TO GIVE. Until then, Cox had worked in television, including his best known role, "Mr Peepers," between 1952 and 1955. Marilyn's man won the day, overruling the producers who had intended to cast Don Knotts in the role. Wally Cox was also the voice of cartoon anti-hero *Underdog*.

Cox was very good friends with MARLON BRANDO, and a good friend of Marilyn's after she returned to Los Angeles in 1960.

## Craft, Roy

"She had such magnetism that if fifteen men were in a room with her, each man would be convinced he was the one she'd be waiting for after the others left."

As assistant to HARRY BRAND in the Fox publicity department. From Norma Jeane's first studio contract to the CALENDAR scandal, Craft was involved in drumming up publicity for the studio's latest sex symbol and helped to forge a legend. Craft's job was to make sure that Marilyn stayed in the public eye by feeding the press tidbits, STUDIO BIOGRAPHIES and—in the case of the scandal of Marilyn's mother (the studio had claimed she was an orphan) and the nude calendar—limit the damage. One of Craft's most successful publicity stunts, at least as far as Marilyn's personal life was concerned, was her photo session with Chicago White Sox players that first piqued JOE DIMAGGIO's interest. It has also been rumored that Craft was responsible for a number of Marilyn's snappiest answers to the press.

## Crawford, Joan
(1904–1977, B. LUCILLE FAY LE SUEUR, ALSO KNOWN AS BILLIE CASSIN)

Like Marilyn, Joan was a poor girl from an unstable background who glimpsed salvation in the movies. The story goes that in her youth she was prepared to go to considerable lengths, including dancing the Charleston nude in speakeasies, and appearing in porn movies. Many years later Crawford spent a great deal of time and effort buying back the porn films—one aptly called *The Casting Couch*. Rumor has it that MGM paid out half a million dollars in its bid to buy up every single surviving copy.

After first being put under contract by MGM in 1925, the magazine *Movie Weekly* held a competition to name the studio's latest starlet—"Joan Crawford" was the winning entry (Marilyn too was renamed immediately after being signed to her first studio contract). That was the start of a forty-five-year career, during which Joan remained a top box office star, whether as a young romantic heroine, a worldly wise femme fatale, or even as a camp icon. *Mommie Dearest*, written by Crawford's adopted daughter, added domineering parenthood to her legend. Crawford won an Oscar for *Mildred Pierce* in 1945, and starred in many memorable films such as *Grand Hotel* and *Rain* (both 1932), *Possessed* (1947), *Sudden Fear* (1952), and *Whatever Happened to Baby Jane?* (1962).

Marilyn first met Joan Crawford in her starlet years, at the home of JOSEPH SCHENCK.

By that time a star of twenty years standing, Crawford apparently offered to help Marilyn and give her advice. Marilyn accepted the star's invitation to her home, but was not too happy to find that Crawford was intent on giving her strict lessons on what and what not to wear. FRED LAWRENCE GUILES writes that Crawford's intentions didn't stop there; she used the opportunity to make a pass at the young hopeful.

Several years elapsed before they next met, during which time Marilyn had gone from obscurity to Hollywood's hottest new property. At the ceremony to pick up her 1952 *Photoplay* magazine award for "Fastest Rising Star of 1952" (held on March 9, 1953) Marilyn was sewn into an adventurously low-cut gold lamé gown. Nobody had eyes for anything else all evening. The next day's headlines crackled with Hollywood spite. Surprisingly, considering her own past, Crawford led the attack on Marilyn through the syndicated Bob Thomas column: "The publicity has gone too far. She is making the mistake of believing her publicity. Someone should make her see the light. She should be told that the public likes provocative feminine personalities; but it also likes to know that underneath it all, the actresses are ladies." Crawford more bluntly told an AP journalist, "There is nothing wrong with my tits, but I don't go around throwing them in people's faces."

Marilyn's counter-statement, voiced through the LOUELLA PARSONS column, succeeded in defusing the whole matter, "Although I don't know Miss Crawford very well, she was a symbol to me of kindness and understanding to those who need help. At first, all I could think of was WHY should she select me to blast? She is a great star. I'm just starting. And then, when the first hurt began to die down, I told myself she must have spoken to Mr. Thomas impulsively, without thinking."

This was enough to placate the furor in the press, but not the feud between Crawford and Hollywood's latest sex siren. Crawford was notably absent on the night of the party thrown for Marilyn at Romanoff's RESTAURANT, in November 1954, at which all of Hollywood consecrated her arrival as a major star.

## CROSBY, BING
(1905–1977, B. HARRY LILLIS CROSBY)

This crooner whose Hollywood career spanned forty years made an uncredited cameo (as himself) in Marilyn movie *LET'S MAKE LOVE* (1960).

Marilyn reputedly had a tryst with JOHN F. KENNEDY with Bing's connivance, when on the weekend of March 24, 1962 she allegedly went with the president to Crosby's PALM SPRINGS residence.

## CRYSTAL STAR AWARD

In 1959 Marilyn was given the top French Crystal Star Award for "Best Foreign Actress." The presentation was made at the French Film Institute in recognition of her performance in *THE PRINCE AND THE SHOWGIRL* (1957).

ARTHUR MILLER once commented that only the French really appreciated his wife—Americans were too puritanical to ascribe talent and intelligence to a woman of beauty, a mere sex symbol.

George Cukor with Marilyn on the set of *Something's Got to Give*, 1962.

## CUKOR, GEORGE (1899–1983)

"She had this absolute unerring touch with comedy. . . . she acted as if she didn't quite understand why it was funny. Which is what made it so funny."

"There may be an exact psychiatric term for what was wrong with her. I don't know—but truth to tell, I think she was quite mad. The mother was mad and poor Marilyn was mad."

Cukor learned his trade on Broadway stage before Hollywood called. Over five decades he built up a reputation as a director of sensitive and literary material. He is also remembered as an excellent handler of sometimes highly-strung leading ladies: Katharine Hepburn, Constance Bennett, VIVIEN LEIGH, Ingrid Bergman, Ava Gardner, Sophia Loren, and JUDY GARLAND all featured on his resumé before he worked, rather disappointingly, with Marilyn on *LET'S MAKE LOVE* (1960), and then disastrously on the aborted *SOMETHING'S GOT TO GIVE*.

Cukor was one of the select group of approved DIRECTORS on the list Marilyn handed Fox in late 1955. Although she had never worked with him, she was impressed by his reputation. Many years earlier, during her brief sojourn at COLUMBIA, Marilyn had unsuccessfully screen-tested for *Born Yesterday*.

Cukor was penciled in to direct *THE PRINCE AND THE SHOWGIRL* (1957) before LAURENCE OLIVIER got the job. Four years later he and Marilyn got their chance to work together, on *Let's Make Love*. As ever with Marilyn, tension reigned on set. After the event Cukor admitted he had "no real communication with her at all . . . and very little influence. All I could do was make a climate that was agreeable to her." He also recognized her greatness. He found her to be "quite dazzling on the screen, and at the end of the picture very generous to everyone she had worked with."

If anything, things got worse on *Something's Got to Give*. Marilyn's faith in Cukor—he was her suggestion to the studio—soon vanished as they disagreed over script changes and he struggled to cope with her lengthy absences from the set. According to NUNNALLY JOHNSON, who wrote the original script, Marilyn "dreaded Cukor, and he loathed her." The studio gave Cukor his walking papers from the movie and called in JEAN NEGULESCO before firing Marilyn and closing down the production.

Cukor won an Oscar for *My Fair Lady* (1964). He was Oscar-nominated for *Little Women* (1933), *The Philadelphia Story* (1940), *A Double Life* (1947), and *Born Yesterday* (1950). He also directed *Dinner at Eight* (1933), *David Copperfield* (1934), *Holiday* (1938), *Adam's Rib* (1939), and *A Star is Born* (1954).

## CURTIS, TONY
(B. 1925, BERNARD SCHWARZ)

Curtis came to Hollywood after growing up in the Bronx, serving in the navy, and putting himself through drama school. His film career began with *Criss Cross* (1949), two years after Marilyn's debut appearance. In the fifties he was a popular leading man in action movies, before BILLY WILDER revealed his comic potential by putting him and JACK LEMMON in drag and on the lam, with Marilyn at their side. Curtis was Oscar-nominated in 1958 for *The Defiant Ones*, and made acclaimed performances in *Spartacus* (1960) and *The Boston Strangler* (1968).

Tony Curtis's remark, after working with Marilyn on *SOME LIKE IT HOT* (1959), that "Kissing Marilyn was like kissing Hitler," has

Marilyn and Tony Curtis in *Some Like It Hot* (1959).

earned him at least as much notoriety as his memorable performance in the movie. It seems that his frustration boiled over and he made his comment to the press after many hours either waiting for Marilyn to show up on set, or enduring upwards of fifty takes until Marilyn got relatively simple lines right. In *Tony Curtis: The Autobiography* he says that at that time Marilyn was in a state of nervous exhaustion, and suffering the all too evident effects of pills and alcohol. He also writes that his Hitler remark was "just a throwaway line" to which people have paid far too much attention. And, perhaps going against the evidence of the public feud, he has claimed that Marilyn and he once spent a night together at the Malibu house of an unnamed friend.

Following such an infamous put-down, Marilyn was understandably upset with Curtis. Never one to fight her battles in public, Marilyn's cool response was, "He only said that about 'kissing Hitler' because I wore prettier dresses than he did." In a more serious vein, she later told reporter RICHARD MERYMAN, "You've read there was some actor that once said about me that kissing me was like kissing Hitler. Well, I think that's his problem. If I have to do intimate love scenes with somebody who really has these kinds of feelings towards me, then my fantasy can come into play. In other words, out with him, in with my fantasy. He was never there."

Tony Curtis was featured opposite Marilyn one more time, in Nicholas Roeg's 1985 film adaptation of *INSIGNIFICANCE*. On this occasion the Marilyn character was played by Theresa Russell; Curtis featured as a character resembling Senator Joe McCarthy.

## CUSACK, LAWRENCE

A lawyer who claimed his father, Lawrence Cusack Sr. provided secret legal counsel to President JOHN F. KENNEDY during the sixties, before in 1980 becoming legal guardian of Marilyn's mother, GLADYS BAKER. Cusack Jr. claimed to have stumbled across a file of handwritten documents chronicling relationships between Kennedy, his brother ROBERT KENNEDY, and Marilyn Monroe. The documents appeared to show alleged dealings between the president and underworld boss SAM GIANCANA, as well as an attempt by Kennedy to silence a distraught Marilyn by offering her hush money.

Between 1993 and 1997 Cusack sold these documents to collectors, in the process netting an estimated $7 million. The forgery was only uncovered during final verification checks on a book about the Kennedys by Pulitzer Prize-winning journalist Seymour Hersch. The giveaway was a typewritten document which bore signs of lift-off correction, a technology not available in the early 1960s, and the use of zip codes, which were not introduced until 1963.

# D

## DANCING

First husband JAMES DOUGHERTY spoke in an article of how his young, shy wife transformed before his eyes when they had friends around and put some records on the phonograph—she turned into a natural performer gyrating tirelessly and energetically.

On her application form to sign up with the BLUE BOOK MODELING AGENCY, among her skills Norma Jeane wrote she "could dance a little."

And yet her ability to perform well during her dance numbers was the source of great fear for Marilyn on set, one of the things that made her most nervous during shooting. After *GENTLEMAN PREFER BLONDES* (1953) Marilyn worked exclusively with choreographer and friend JACK COLE, who would take her through scenes at a pace she felt comfortable with.

Marilyn dancing in *Let's Make Love* (1960).

Choreographer Jack Cole worked extensively with Marilyn on the dance numbers in *Let's Make Love* (1960).

Dance teacher Arthur Murray invented what he called "The Marilyn Monroe Mamba", inspired by her spectacular "Heat Wave" number in *THERE'S NO BUSINESS LIKE SHOW BUSINESS* (1954).

DANCE COACHES

- Jack Cole
- Charles Henderson
- Mara Lynn
- Mildred Ann Mauldin

## *DANGEROUS YEARS* (1947)

During her initial contract at TWENTIETH-CENTURY FOX, Marilyn's first speaking part was in this movie, shot in May 1947. Marilyn played a waitress who could look after herself, working at a the local hangout for badly-behaved young men called the Gopher Hole.

Although this was not the first movie Marilyn worked on, it was the first movie in which she acted to be released nationally (in December 1947, by which time the studio had declined to renew her contract).

Marilyn ranked fourteenth billing in the credits.

**Credits:**
20th Century Fox, Black and White
Length: 62 minutes
Release date: December 7, 1947

Directed by: Arthur Pierson
Produced by: Sol M. Wurtzel, Howard Sheehan (associate)
Written by: Arnold Belgard (script and story)
Cinematography by: Benjamin H. Kline
Music by: Rudy Schrager
Film Editing: Frank Baldridge

**Cast (credits order):**
William Halop . . . Danny Jones
Ann E. Todd . . . Doris Martin
Jerome Cowan . . . Weston
Anabel Shaw . . . Connie Burns
Richard Gaines . . . Edgar Burns
Scotty Beckett . . . Willy Miller

William Halop with Marilyn in *Dangerous Years* (1947).

Darryl Hickman . . . Leo Emerson
Harry Shannon . . . Judge Raymond
Dickie Moore . . . Gene Spooner
Donald Curtis . . . Jeff Carter
Harry Harvey Jr. . . . Phil Kenny
Gil Stratton Jr. . . . Tammy McDonald
Joseph Vitale . . . August Miller
Marilyn Monroe . . . Evie
Nana Bryant . . . Miss Templeton

**Cast (uncredited):**
Mimi Doyle . . . Reporter
Tom Kennedy . . . Adamson
Lee Shumway . . . Alec
Claire Whitney . . . Woman

**Other crew:**
Walter Koessler . . . art director
William F. Claxton . . . editing assistant

**Plot:**
Danny Jones is a young delinquent (William Halop) who undermines the positive influence of a boy's club in keeping small-town delinquents off the streets during their "dangerous years." Jones recruits others to help him pull a heist. Marilyn has a minor role in the proceedings as a feisty waitress (Eve) who works in the bar where the bad boys meet up. A murder takes place, Danny is arrested, and owing to complicated family shenanigans of orphans and previously undiscovered parentage, he takes the rap.

**Reviews:**
*Motion Picture Herald*
"Some of the causes of juvenile delinquency, and some of the adult policies designed to offset them, are explored interestingly here in a melodrama forcefully directed by Arthur Pierson."

## DARBY, KEN (1909–1992)

Darby worked with Marilyn as voice coach and lyricist on *GENTLEMEN PREFER BLONDES* (1953), *RIVER OF NO RETURN* (1954), *THERE'S NO BUSINESS LIKE SHOW BUSINESS* (1954), and *BUS STOP* (1956). Over a long career as composer and arranger, much of it for TWENTIETH CENTURY-FOX, Darby was Oscar-nominated many times, including for his work on *Bus Stop*, and won Academy Awards for his work on *The King and I* (1956), *Porgy and Bess* (1959), and *Camelot* (1967).

## D'ARCY, ALEX
(1908–1996, B. ALEXANDER SARRUF)

Egyptian-born actor who worked with Marilyn on *HOW TO MARRY A MILLIONAIRE* (1953), though he had met Marilyn when she was still Norma Jeane and working with D'Arcy's friend, photographer ANDRÉ DE DIENES.

During shooting D'Arcy tried to shore up Marilyn's lack of self-confidence by praising her comic timing. One evening when they went out to dinner, "I looked in those famous liquid eyes and saw only a little scared child. I had to avert my gaze to hide the twinge of pity I felt."

Alex D'Arcy and Marilyn in *How to Marry a Millionaire* (1953).

## DARRACH, BRAD

In 1956, as part of the publicity for the film she was shooting at the time, *BUS STOP*, this *Time* magazine journalist had the pleasure of interviewing Marilyn in bed, at her CHATEAU MARMONT HOTEL suite. Darrach told biographer ANTHONY SUMMERS:

> "She was Marilyn, and reasonably pretty. And of course there were those extraordinary jutting breasts and jutting behind. I've never seen a behind like hers; it was really remarkable, it was a very subtly composed ass. Yet I never felt for a moment any sexual temptation. There was nothing about her skin that made me want to touch it. She looked strained and a little unhealthy, as though there was some nervous inner heat that dried the skin. But there was no sexual feeling emanating from her. I am sure that was something that she put on for the camera."

## DAVID DI DONATELLO AWARD

Italy's most prestigious award for acting—"Best Actress in a Foreign Film"—was presented to Marilyn at the Italian Cultural Institute in New York (686 Park Avenue) on May 13, 1959 for Marilyn's performance in *THE PRINCE AND THE SHOWGIRL* (1957). Four hundred watched as institute director Filippo Donini gave Marilyn one of the few acting awards she won.

## DAVIDSON, BRUCE

MAGNUM photographer who shot stills on two Marilyn movies, *LET'S MAKE LOVE* (1960) and *THE MISFITS* (1961). His best-known Marilyn photographs are of the Millers and Montands relaxing together.

## DAVIS, BETTE
(1908–1989, B. RUTH ELIZABETH DAVIS)

Bette Davis was one of Hollywood's most bankable stars for a decade up until the late forties. Renowned for her dramatic intensity, Davis was still a huge box office draw in 1950 when she starred in *ALL ABOUT EVE*. Marilyn's small but high-profile role in the movie brought her face-to-face with Davis in a few scenes.

Davis's career brought her a half dozen Oscar nominations—*Dark Victory* (1939), *The Letter* (1940), *The Little Foxes* (1941), *Now Voyager* (1942), *Mr. Skeffington* (1944), *All About Eve* (1950), *The Star* (1952), and *Whatever Happened to Baby Jane?* (1962). Her two Academy Awards were for *Dangerous* (1935) and *Jezebel* (1938).

## DAVIS, SAMMY JR. (1925–1990)

This popular all-round entertainer, who once described himself as "a one-eyed Jewish Negro," allegedly had an affair with Marilyn some time around 1954–55. It has been said that just before her death, Marilyn was in negotiations with Davis and other members of the RAT PACK to star in a heist film.

After her death, he offered the memorable if off-beat quote, "Still she hangs like a bat in the heads of men who have met her, and none of us will ever forget her."

Anne Baxter, Bette Davis, Marilyn, and George Sanders (left to right) in *All About Eve* (1950).

Magnum photographer Bruce Davidson took these famous photographs of Marilyn, Arthur Miller, Simone Signoret, and Yves Montand dining together in a bungalow at the Beverly Hills Hotel during filming of *Let's Make Love* (1960).

## DAY, DORIS
(B. 1924, DORIS VON KAPPELHOFF)

Doris Day was in some ways the anti-Marilyn. After a boisterous film debut in *Romance on the High Seas* (1948), Day's image was honed into the perennial virgin of a string of innocent 1960s sex comedies. GROUCHO MARX once quipped, "I've been around so long I can remember Doris Day before she was a virgin."

Although they generally played very different roles, Day and Marilyn's career paths crossed at least twice. Over a year before Marilyn announced that her production company MARILYN MONROE PRODUCTIONS had obtained rights to work with LAURENCE OLIVIER on a film version of the Terence Rattigan play *The Sleeping Prince*, Doris Day and her producer husband Marty Melcher had been planning to make this her next movie. Day got partial revenge by winning her only Oscar nomination for *Pillow Talk* (1959), a movie that Marilyn apparently originally wanted for herself.

After Marilyn's death, TWENTIETH CENTURY-FOX revised and recast Marilyn's abandoned last film project *SOMETHING'S GOT TO GIVE* and turned it into the Doris Day vehicle *Move Over Darling* (1963).

Day's best-regarded performances came in *Moonlight Bay (1951)*, *Calamity Jane* (1953), *The Pajama Game* (1957), and *That Touch of Mink* (1962), and she landed her own TV show between 1968 and 1972.

## DEATH

ARTHUR MILLER:
"Beneath all her insouciance and wit, death was her companion everywhere and at all times, and it may be that its unacknowledged presence was what lent her poignancy, dancing at the edge of oblivion as she was."

GLORIA STEINEM:
"Most tragic of all, the time, effort, and obsession that has gone into explaining Marilyn's death has done little to explain her life."

Would Marilyn's legend have grown and endured if she had not met an untimely and mysterious end? We are no more likely to find out the answer to this hypothetical question than to achieve a definitive answer about how Marilyn died. Marilyn biographies continue to appear at the rate of several a year; many of them lavish hundreds of pages on her death and reserve just a few dozen on her life. Almost four decades later, incredibly enough, "new evidence" is touted on a regular basis.

For such a public event, one of the rare occasions in the public sphere where, years afterward, people recall exactly where they were when they first head the news, there is a remarkably small body of evidence on which all biographers agree.

Even the day of Marilyn's death is a source of contention. On the official CORONER's report Marilyn was pronounced dead by her general doctor, Hyman Engelberg, at 3:50 A.M. on August 5, 1962. However, owing to the advanced state of rigor mortis at that time, it is generally believed that Marilyn died some time during the evening of August 4, as perhaps as many as eight hours before the official time. The first chapter of ANTHONY SUMMERS's 1986 biography *Goddess* opens with publicist ARTHUR JACOBS being called out of a Hollywood Bowl concert some time between 10 P.M. and 11 P.M. on August 4 to deal with the repercussions of Marilyn's death.

The first police officer on the scene was Sergeant JACK CLEMMONS. Detective Sergeant Robert E. Byron then arrived and took statements from DR. RALPH GREENSON, Dr. Engelberg, and EUNICE MURRAY. Officer Don Marshall arrived and searched unsuccessfully for a suicide note. He also interviewed Marilyn's closest neighbors, Mr. and Mrs. Abe Landau, who reported they had heard no disturbance during the night. Allegations that during the morning after Marilyn's death her personal papers were tampered with and destroyed have been denied by police officers who were on the scene throughout the day. However, in the notes to his biography, DONALD SPOTO makes reference to papers he acquired from the INEZ MELSON estate, including documents which Marilyn's business manager removed from her house the day after her death.

Tests conducted by the coroner's office revealed levels of 8 mg of chloral hydrate and 4.5 mg of Nembutal in Marilyn's blood, but a toxicological examination of her liver revealed a much higher 13 mg concentration of Nembutal. The official explanations that the motive of Marilyn's death was "probable suicide," given by coroner Theodore J. Curphey and toxicologist R. J. Abernethy, substantially reflect the testimonies of Greenson and Murray. However, critics have seized on the failure to fully examine Marilyn's intestinal area, which would have helped to prove the way in which the fatal overdose was administered, plus missing confirmation of a heavy bruise on Marilyn's lower lumbar region.

Inconsistencies in the accounts of the people present that night, and suspicions that other people played a shadowy role in the proceedings, have led to no end of CONSPIRACY theories. Practically all biographers agree that whether or not a criminal act was committed, some kind of COVER-UP did take place. Proponents of the "Marilyn was murdered" theory have seized on the discrepancy between the levels of lethal drugs in Marilyn's blood and liver, as well as the lack of pill residue in her stomach. However, explanations have been put forward for this. In 1976 Thomas Noguchi, the man who performed the autopsy on Marilyn's body, told a *Oui* magazine reporter that because Marilyn's system was so accustomed to the use of DRUGS, especially Nembutal, it was not surprising that it had so rapidly assimilated the thrity or forty tablets she took.

Nevertheless, it has been inferred that the fatal overdose of barbiturates was administered in some other way, against Marilyn's will, either by injection or, more probably, by enema, which would explain substantial colon discoloration. However, if an attempt had been made to revive Marilyn after she ingested the pills, as has been claimed by drivers who worked for the Schaefer AMBULANCE Service, including the use of a stomach pump, then no pill residue would have been found.

As if there were not enough competing theories already in circulation, some sources have ventured that Marilyn's body manifested symptoms of poisoning, perhaps from cyanide.

### HOW MARILYN DIED: THE THEORIES

Suicide is the official verdict. Marilyn had a history of drug abuse, ready access to large quantities of pills, and had attempted suicide a number of times during her life. Supporters of the suicide theory point to Marilyn's depression over troubles in her career, loneliness in her personal life, or despair that one or both of the Kennedy brothers had dumped her. Coroner Thomas J. Noguchi described Marilyn as a typical suicide risk. Whether or not Marilyn really intended to kill herself is another matter; all previous attempts were cries for help in which somebody rescued her. Authors who subscribe to the suicide theory include Fred Lawrence Guiles ("Marilyn was a compulsive potential suicide . . . And on that last weekend she was in the group of some final compulsion—a compulsion that had become determination") and Barbara Leaming (as a gesture of despair after her psychiatrist left her for the evening).

Many more theories cry murder. It has been argued by many people that Marilyn was positive about her future and had no reason to take her life. Just a month before she died, Marilyn told photographer George Barris, "As far as I'm concerned, the happiest time is now. There's a future and I can't wait to get to it."

The usual suspects in this case, either directly or indirectly, are the Kennedys. This is popular territory, first mapped out by right-wing author Frank A. Capell, who as early as 1964 pointed the finger at Robert Kennedy, aided and abetted by fellow "Communist conspirators." According to Robert Slatzer and others, Kennedy was desperate to silence Marilyn before she told the world about her affairs with both the Attorney General and President. Anthony Summers offers conflicting scenarios, one of which has Robert Kennedy at the scene of the crime, before concluding, "In all probability, no serious crime was committed that night, although the return of Marilyn's body to her home was highly irregular, and Lawford's destruction of the note clearly unlawful." James Haspiel cites tapes obtained from bugging Marilyn's home as proof that Kennedy personally smothered Marilyn with a pillow. Peter Harry Brown and Patte B. Barham come to a similar conlusion, and Donald Wolfe is also persuaded that Robert Kennedy's prints are all over the case.

Bobby is not the only Kennedy to stand accused. Brother John Fitzgerald Kennedy has been implicated as the man who sent killers to silence Marilyn, as has patriarch Joseph Kennedy, in allegations raised by Milo Speriglio, an author who has also put forward theories of mob involvement in Marilyn's death. Mafia death theories received a boost in 1992 when Chuck Giancana brought out a book on the involvement of his brother, mobster Sam Giancana, in a gangland assassination of Marilyn in order to get at the Kennedys. Teamster boss Jimmy Hoffa, Fidel Castro, CIA mavericks, left-wing splinter groups, and J. Edgar Hoover have all, at some time, been connected with the death of Marilyn, in some theories coming together in bizarre and unholy alliances to do the deed.

Another strand of murder suspicions centers on Marilyn's psychoanalyst Ralph Greenson, though in some accounts it is incompetence, not malice, that motivated his acts. In many of the theories involving the Kennedys, Greenson is accused of administering the lethal dose of barbiturates. Donald Spoto is of the opinion that the moral responsibility at least is Greenson's, as he either gave Marilyn (or had housekeeper Eunice Murray giver her) an enema administration of drugs which, because he was unaware of the amount of barbiturates she had already taken that day, was to kill her: "To the horror of everyone involved, what may have been intended as Marilyn's long, deep sleep became her death." Greenson's name was also mentioned in 1986, when a driver from the Schaefer Ambulance Service claimed that he and a colleague had resuscitated a comatose Marilyn only for Dr. Greenson to appear with an enormous hypodermic needle and give her a lethal injection.

This photo by André de Dienes was taken in 1945 when Norma Jeane was 19 years old.

## DE DIENES, ANDRÉ (1913–1985)

Born in Hungarian Transylvania, De Dienes was thirty-two, muscular and blue-eyed when he met Marilyn. Before David O. Selznick called him to Hollywood, De Dienes had lived and worked in Rome, Paris, and London.

De Dienes was the first photographer to have a long relationship with Norma Jeane, both with and without the camera as go-between. The time he first met her, he recalls in his book *Marilyn Mon Amour*, she was wearing "a skimpy pink sweater, her curly hair tied with a ribbon to match, and carried a hat box. With child-like smile and clear gaze, she was absolutely enchanting."

De Dienes took his first shots of Norma Jeane in 1945. They were typical sweater-girl fare: along Route 101 in North Hollywood, in a field with a newborn lamb, in blue jeans and a red blouse; at Malibu Beach, with Norma Jeane in shorts and a sweater.

Later they went on extended photo shoots. Norma Jeane turned down his requests for her to pose nude, just as she initially refused his compliments, advances, and notes slipped under the door saying things like "Come to me, we'll make love. You won't be disappointed." But as they worked together, scouring the American West, South and North, from the beaches around L.A. as far north as Mount Hood, taking in Las Vegas, the Mojave Desert, Yosemite, and Oregon—where De Dienes accompanied her on a rare visit to her mother—the inevitable finally happened between model and photographer. It was one night when they could not find a motel with two separate rooms. Marilyn later recalled, "The truth is, that I began the trip with only business in mind [she was paid a flat $200 fee]. But André had other ideas." Actor ALEX D'ARCY, an acquaintance of De Dienes at that time, was in little doubt that it was a case of a photographer exploiting a young girl.

De Dienes wrote a rather fulsome account of that night in his book:

> "In my dreams I had explored her body. Reality far surpassed my imagination. . . . She slipped into the big bed, where I joined her. It seemed the most natural thing in the world. The night was ours. Everything she felt for me, trust, gratitude, even admiration, was fused in her surrender. Everything was so simple, so wonderful. Why had we hesitated, waited, denied ourselves so long? Our bodies were so well matched, made for each other. I could not get enough of that silky skin, of her supple body both docile and demanding, of our shared, repeated pleasure and, suddenly, as my cheek brushed hers, I realized she was crying."

By his account, De Dienes was greatly smitten with young Norma Jeane, and wanted to marry her. There was talk of her moving East to be with him in New York, where he lived, of Norma Jeane possibly studying law at Columbia University, but it must have been apparent to him that she was unlikely to tie herself down just at the moment she was beginning to make headway toward her dream; besides, she had only just divorced first husband JAMES DOUGHERTY. As Norma Jeane said in a letter to a friend in late 1946, she was "a little bit leery about this marriage business now and besides at the studio they want me single at least until I have become well known (when and if!)."

De Dienes photographed Marilyn once again in 1949, when she was in New York promoting the Marx brothers movie *LOVE HAPPY*. The shots he took at Tobey Beach are vintage fresh-faced Marilyn, cavorting on the beach in a white one-piece swimsuit. On this occasion, though, Marilyn rejected his attempts to rekindle their love affair, preferring to stay faithful to her then beau, JOHNNY HYDE.

The last time they met was on Marilyn's thirty-fifth birthday, at the BEVERLY HILLS HOTEL.

BOOKS:

*Marilyn Mon Amour*, André De Dienes. New York: St. Martin's Press, 1986.

## DECORATING

Just as gentleman prefer blondes, Marilyn favored white, white, white in the places she lived. In the early part of her career, when her home was more likely to be a hotel room than an apartment, she created her own atmosphere by hanging up her favorite pictures (works of art and portraits of her HEROES and great men she admired). Reputedly, in 1951 she persuaded management at the BEVERLY CARLTON HOTEL to redecorate her room in burgundy, white, and gray. In later years, when she had the space, wherever she lived she took with her a large WHITE PIANO to set on her deep white carpets in white-painted rooms.

Marilyn enthusiastically remodeled the country house she and ARTHUR MILLER bought near ROXBURY, Connecticut. She had dormer windows put in, raised the roof to make a room above the kitchen, and tended to interior decoration details. She had more ambitious plans too: In the late fifties she contacted famous architect FRANK LLOYD WRIGHT, by then in his ninties, to draw up a blueprint for a new house on a hill opposite.

Marilyn also worked with designer JOHN MOORE on redesigning her and Arthur's New York home at East FIFTY-SEVENTH STREET, including covering several walls with floor-to-ceiling MIRRORS.

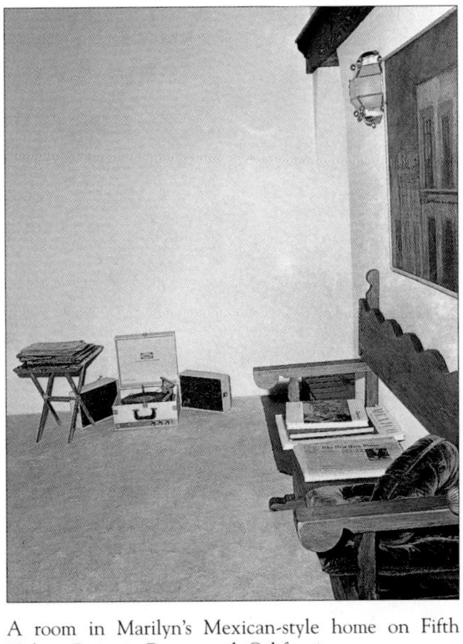

A room in Marilyn's Mexican-style home on Fifth Helena Drive in Brentwood, California.

The last place where Marilyn lived, FIFTH HELENA DRIVE, which was also the first home she ever owned, was a three-bedroom hacienda-style bungalow decorated with Mexican-style furnishings, many of whilch she bought on her 1962 trip to MEXICO.

## DELONGPRE AVENUE

On November 1, 1954 Marilyn moved out of the Palm Drive home she had shared with JOE DIMAGGIO, and took up residence at this luxury duplex, number 8336 DeLongpre Avenue. She stayed there for little over a month, hatching plans to quit Hollywood for NEW YORK.

## DENEUVE, CATHERINE
(B. 1943, CATHERINE DORLÉAC)

France's most famous cool blonde, Deneuve began her film career in 1960, though she is perhaps better known outside France for her cosmetics promotion than her stunning performances in films like *Les Parapluis de Cherbourg* (1964) and *Belle de Jour* (1967).

Deneuve once narrated a Marilyn DOCUMENTARY, *Norma Jeane alias Marilyn Monroe*, based on a 1960 interview by Georges Belmont.

## DENNY, REGINALD
(1891-1967, B. REGINALD LEIGH DAYMORE)

British-born actor who, as well as pursuing a long and successful career on stage and screen, invented the first viable unpiloted drone aircraft. Denny then founded a factory—the RADIO PLANE MUNITIONS FACTORY—to produce his invention for anti-aircraft training. It was at this factory that Marilyn was working when she was spotted by army photographer DAVID CONOVER, who featured her prominently in his footage of women working wartime assembly lines. Marilyn was soon MODELING fulltime.

Denny's films included *The Leather Pushers* (1922), *Rebecca* (1940), *Mr Blandings Builds His Dream House* (1948), *Around the World in Eighty Days* (1956), and *Cat Ballou* (1965).

## DIAMOND, I. A. L.
(1915–1988, B. ITEK DOMMNICI)

"Sometimes I would run into her and get a big greeting; other times, she would look at me blankly, as if she'd never seen me before in her life.It was like trying to communicate with someone through a plate-glass window."

This Romanian-born screenwriter is best remembered for his comic work, much of which was with director BILLY WILDER. Diamond wrote or co-wrote the screenplays of four Marilyn films—*LOVE NEST* (1951), *LET'S MAKE IT LEGAL* (1951), *MONKEY*

BUSINESS (1952), and SOME LIKE IT HOT (1959). Diamond was awarded an Oscar for *The Apartment* (1960).

## DIANA, PRINCESS (1961–1997)

In the wake of her tragic death in August 1997, endless parallels have been drawn between Diana Spencer and Marilyn. The most photographed personalities of their respective days, the deaths of both women elicited enormous public response.

Both women had their every move followed by the PRESS, both had a consuming love of children, and both died in tragic circumstances at the age of thirty-six (in fact, there was just a three day difference in their ages at death). In interviews Diana had, more than once, compared herself to Marilyn. The centerpiece of Princess Diana's funeral was a revised version of ELTON JOHN's song "Candle in the Wind," originally written about Marilyn.

## DIARY

Since her death, Marilyn's biographers have been searching for their own Holy Grail: the red diary which, reputedly, Marilyn bought in the summer of 1962, in which she wrote about her dates with ROBERT KENNEDY, including information on important political matters he had revealed to her. ROBERT SLATZER said that she showed this diary to him. After her death, coroner's aide LIONEL GRANDISON said he saw it in the coroner's offices, but then its trail goes mysteriously cold. Although the diary has never resurfaced, several people have claimed to have it in their possession. In 1982, antiques dealer Doug Villiers made an offer, on behalf of a client, of $150,000 to anybody who could bring the diary to him.

However, the people closest to Marilyn—publicist PAT NEWCOMB, psychiatrist DR. RALPH GREENSON and housekeeper EUNICE MURRAY - all deny that Marilyn kept such a diary; indeed, they suggest that she was far too disorganized a person to do something regular like keep a journal. Biographer DONALD SPOTO traces reports of the diary back to an article written by ANTHONY SCADUTO in 1975.

## DIETRICH, MARLENE
(1901–1992, B. MARIA MAGDALENA VON LOSCH)

Great German-born screen icon who after a spate of silent successes in her home country took Hollywood by storm with her sultry and brooding sensuality. She came to Hollywood with director Josef Von Sternberg, and is best remembered for *The Blue Angel* (1930), *Shanghai Express* (1932), *The Scarlet Empress* (1934), *Desire* (1936), *Destry Rides Again* (1939), and *A Foreign Affair* (1948). She concluded her screen career with an appearance in the David Bowie vehicle *Just a Gigolo* (1978).

According to some reports Marlene was present at the press conference called at lawyer Frank Delaney's apartment in January 1955 to announce the foundation of MARILYN MONROE PRODUCTIONS. Later that night Marilyn and the Greenes went to Dietrich's Park Avenue apartment to continue celebrations.

Marilyn with Marlene Dietrich and Milton Greene following the announcement to the press that she and Greene would be forming Marilyn Monroe Productions, 1955.

It was after seeing photographs of Dietrich taken by EVE ARNOLD that Marilyn enthusiastically approached the photographer at a party, with a line that would have set any photographer's heart racing: "Imagine what you could do with me!" Later in her career, Marilyn was portrayed as Dietrich by RICHARD AVEDON for *Life* magazine's Christmas 1958 issue.

## DIMAGGIO, JOE (1915–1999)

ALLAN "WHITEY" SNYDER:
"Joe DiMaggio may not have made a good husband for Marilyn, but no one cared more for her. He was always, before the divorce, and after the divorce, her best friend."

EDWARD BENNETT WILLIAMS,
close friend of DiMaggio's:
"He carried a torch bigger than the Statue of Liberty. His love for her never diminished through the years."

Joe DiMaggio was born Joseph Paul DiMaggio to Sicilian immigrants in the Northern California town of Martinez, on November 25, 1914, the eighth of nine children. His father, Giuseppe, also known as Zio Pepe, was a crab fisherman who worked from a boat called the *Rosalie*, named after Joe's mother. Joe grew up in a strict Catholic household, where devotion, honesty, and hard work were prized. Between the ages of six and eight he was a rather withdrawn boy, an outsider who felt different from his peers because of the leg braces he had to wear to rectify weak ankles. This experience had a lasting effect on DiMaggio; he understood what it was like to suffer and be shunned, a corollary to feelings Norma Jeane experienced during years in foster care. As soon as Joe was able to run around again, he made up for lost time and played as much baseball as he could with his closest brothers Vincent and Dominic. All three of them dreamed of playing the sport professionally—dreams that came true for them all.

Like Marilyn, Joe never completed high school. He left in tenth grade to go and work in an orange juice bottling plant, to help support the family. By the age of eighteen he had been spotted and signed as shortstop by the San Francisco Seals. His rise to national fame was meteoric. Within three years he was practically a folk hero, the highest profile rookie in the nation, earning a top-notch salary with the New York Yankees and living a fast and glamorous life. As soon as he had the money, he bought his parents a nice house in San Francisco and opened up a seafood restaurant for them to run, Joe DiMaggio's Grotto, located in the city's popular Fisherman's Wharf area. By his early twenties he had picked up three successive Most Valued Player awards. Off the field he lived a celebrity life, was lionized wherever he went, and toured the most fashionable night spots in the company of a string of beautiful woman.

In 1939 Joe married a blonde actress named Dorothy Arnoldine Olsen (1917–1984), whom he had met on set during a cameo appearance he made in the 1937 movie *Manhattan Merry-Go-Round*. His new wife, however, did not see their future life in the same terms as he. As DiMaggio was to discover with Marilyn too, it is hard to persuade an ambitious actress to take a back seat, forget about the career, and become a traditional housewife.

JOE DIMAGGIO JR. was born on October 23, 1941, but by this time Joe's first marriage had already begun to unravel. In 1942 Joe's previously impeccable batting averages dropped dismally. He walked away from baseball in early 1943 to join the war effort as a physical training supervisor for the Army Air Force. Joe returned to baseball after the end

*Previous page:* This photo of Marilyn was taken in her apartment during an interview with Sidney Skolsky for *Modern Screen* magazine in 1954.

of the war. After his divorce came through, Dorothy married a New York stockbroker, though this too was a short-lived marriage. Joe kept in touch with Dorothy, and during breaks in the baseball season he lived at the family home in San Francisco. During the season he lived in New York's finest hotels, and spent evenings out with his pals at his favorite joints, more often than not TOOTS SHOR'S. He went out with many women, but none of these relationships lasted.

By the late forties, Joe was suffering from sports injuries and nagging anxiety. He responded by resurrecting his career with a performance that put him in the record books, hitting four home runs in three games and going on to score an amazing 114 runs in 139 games in the 1950 season. In late 1951 he finally threw in the towel, at the age of thirty-seven succumbing to a whole catalog of sports-related injuries including arthritis and bone spurs, not to mention the perennial ulcers that troubled this outwardly placid man. During his career he had become baseball's biggest star. The "Yankee Clipper" was the first player to earn a six figure salary, he led his team to ten American league pennants and eight World Series championships, and he established hitting records that would take years to be broken. His fifty-six game hitting streak in 1941 has never been surpassed. In honor of his achievements, the New York Yankees officially retired the "No. 5" uniform the season after he gave up the game. He was elected to the Baseball Hall of Fame in 1955.

Joe was very keen to meet Marilyn Monroe after he saw a photograph of her in a newspaper, posing with Chicago White Sox players Joe Dobson and Gus Zernial. The sight of Marilyn, in a pair of figure-hugging white hot pants, a tight jersey blouse, and of course a baseball cap, prompted him to ask Zernial, "Who's the blonde?" When Joe found out that one of his drinking pals at Toots Shor's, DAVID MARCH, knew Marilyn personally, he pestered him to set up a double date, with March's current belle, actress Peggy Rabe. This took place in March 1952 at the Villa Nova Italian restaurant on Sunset Boulevard—though in Marilyn's ghost written autobiography *MY STORY* she says the restaurant where they first met was Chasen's. Marilyn apparently arrived two hours late, but Joe waited for her all the same. Many accounts of the event, however, maintain that the evening out was just Joe and Marilyn, and not a double date at all.

There are conflicting reports as to how the evening went. Marilyn's official version, as told to a friend, was, "I expected a flashy New York sports type, and instead I met this reserved guy who didn't make a pass at me right away. I had dinner with him almost every night for two weeks. He treated me like something special. Joe is a very decent man, and he makes other people feel decent, too." Another version has March calling Marilyn the following morning to hear what Marilyn had thought of Joe, and she told him that DiMaggio had "struck out" after making a clumsy pass at her when she had driven him back to his Hollywood hotel, the KNICKERBOCKER. The most scabrous version of events had them making love on the backseat of her car, followed by an instant proposal of marriage from the baseball legend, which was ably parried by Hollywood's fastest rising star.

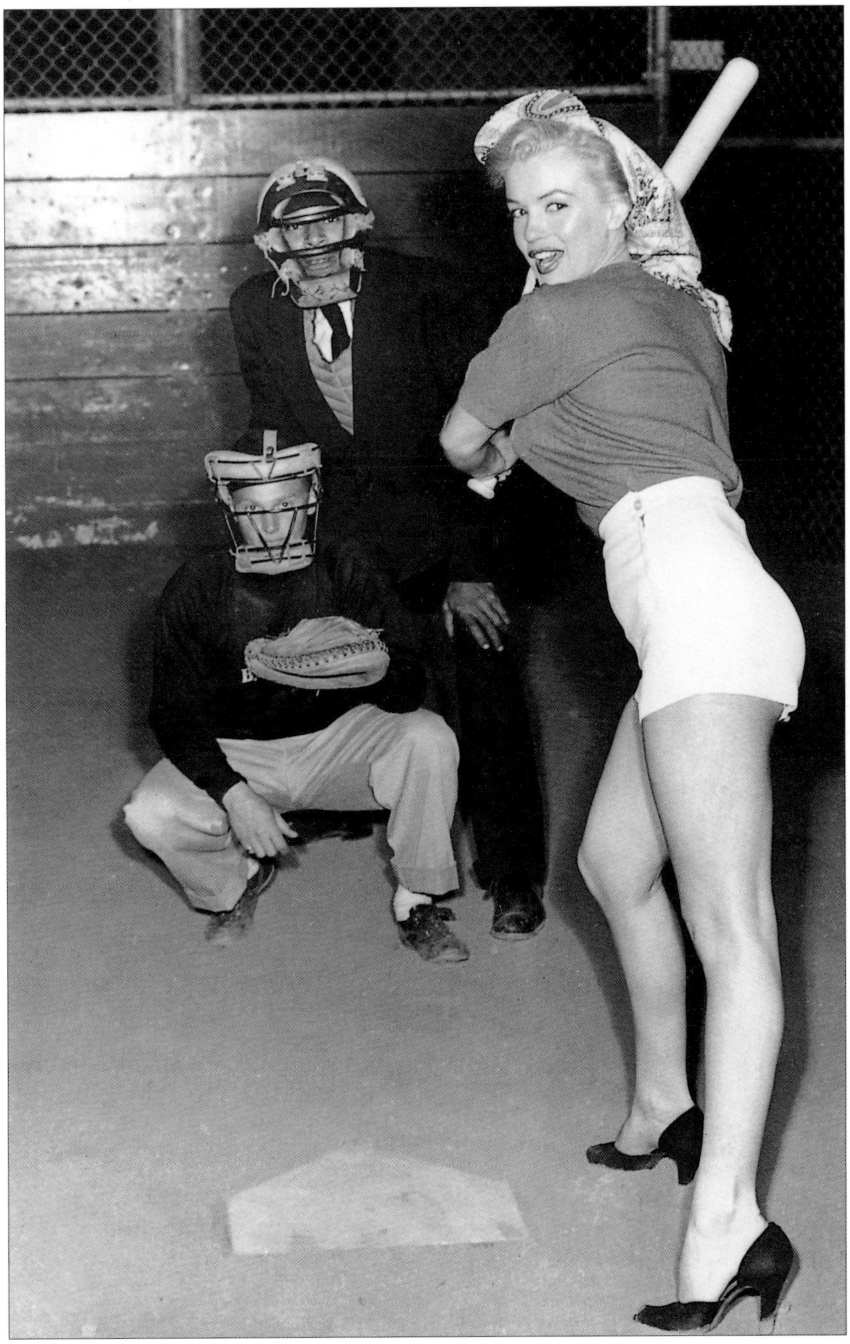

In 1951 a newspaper ran photos of Marilyn "playing ball" with Chicago White Sox players Joe Dobson and Gus Zernial. Smitten with the blonde in the photo, DiMaggio contacted Dobson and Zernial to ask for an introduction.

When Marilyn and DiMaggio met in early 1952, she was a twenty-five-year-old film star poised to make it to the top of her profession. He was thirty-seven years old and recently retired after the most glorious baseball career of his day. He had been a household name for more than fifteen years, and as a result was often suspicious that people were interested in him because of his image, not for himself; he was often heard to lament the fact that "everybody who calls me wants something."

Whichever version of their first date is true, DiMaggio called Marilyn every day after their first date, until Marilyn said she'd like to go out again. They soon became the nation's most famous dating couple, a storybook romance documented by paparazzi at all the swankiest locations on both coasts. Joe went to see Marilyn at the final day's shooting of *MONKEY BUSINESS* (1952); Marilyn was taken to her first baseball game; and on many weekends during the early months of their relationship Marilyn flew out to New York to be with Joe, who after retiring from baseball had taken up a contract as a broadcaster.

Four months after they met, Joe took Marilyn home to San Francisco to meet the family. Marilyn must have loved the warmth of such a close-knit home, but also been concerned at what, as a wife, would be expected of her. Quite apart from the practicalities of homemaking, Joe was not happy that his girl was being leered at and fantasized about by practically every male in the nation. Marilyn later told MILTON GREENE that Joe "wanted me to be the beautiful ex-actress, just like he was the great former ballplayer. We were to ride into some sunset together. But I wasn't

Marilyn and Joe on their wedding day, January 14, 1954.

ready for that journey yet. I wasn't even thirty, for heaven's sake!" Just as Joe was withdrawing from the public eye after a long and glorious career, Marilyn was at last achieving the stardom she had craved, and gloried in being in constant demand.

DiMaggio may have realized that a relationship with Marilyn would not be simple. Within a month of their meeting, the whole of the nation was titillated by the news that she had posed nude during her struggling starlet days. Another scandal followed soon after during that hectic first half of 1952, when it was revealed that Marilyn was not, as her STUDIO BIOGRAPHIES had said, an orphan, but that her mother was still alive, although hardly well, living in a mental institution. And yet Marilyn was smitten: "He has the grace and beauty of a Michelangelo," she said soon after they met. "He moves like a living statue."

During their courtship, DiMaggio was plagued by the jealousy that would ultimately undo their marriage. The plunging necklines Marilyn wore, her sexy pouting poses in public for the paparazzi, clashed with his straight-laced values. Marilyn had nothing but pride in her body and no shame in exposing it to the world; Joe simply didn't want it on display. He started to duck out of public occasions. He wasn't there when Marilyn was poured into a scandalously tight dress to pick up her *PHOTOPLAY* Award for "Fastest-Rising Star"; Marilyn was escorted to the premiere of *GENTLEMEN PREFER BLONDES* (1953) by BETTY GRABLE, not by her famous boyfriend. He would agree to squire her around town if she went out decorously attired, but then would stay away after the latest pictures of his girlfriend—leaving little to the imagination—had been splashed over the nation's papers. His jealousy also prompted him to make spontaneous visits to Marilyn on set, for example in August 1953 flying out with buddy George Solotaire to visit Marilyn on location in Canada where she was shooting *RIVER OF NO RETURN* (1954). It was jealousy in some reports, concern for her in others, that prompted this visit after she had sprained her ankle, while shooting a rafting scene. Joe stayed on with Marilyn, spending the days fishing and hunting while Marilyn worked.

Marilyn's makeup artist ALLAN "WHITEY" SNYDER gives an idea of what the atmosphere was like while Joe was on set: "Joe could be very hard to get along with—surly and withdrawn—and he was awfully jealous. Marilyn liked to invite a few people for coffee or a drink at the end of the day, but when Joe was around the mood was dark. He hated the movies and everything to do with them."

However, Joe did appear to be excellent husband material, and the tabloid press gleefully published blow-by-blow reports of this ideal romance. The courting couple spent time together in his modest San Francisco home; they went fishing together; Marilyn even learned from Mama DiMaggio and Joe's unmarried sister Marie how to cook the baseball hero his favorite spaghetti sauce. Marilyn also saw his passionate side—their sex life was full and satisfying—and his emotional depths, when for weeks he was inconsolable after one of his brothers drowned in an accident.

Despite the fireworks in their pre-marriage relationship, Marilyn considered that Joe's love and loyalty outweighed his jealousy (not only about her wearing revealing garments in public, but even about doing a film with FRANK SINATRA, well known for getting his leading ladies into bed). To Marilyn, Joe was a protective figure, an adviser, an ally against the narcissism and ruthlessness of Hollywood—he was her "Slugger," her "Giuseppe," admired by millions, loved by his close-knit family, and now a man who was resolutely on her side. Marilyn told friends that her best ever Christmas was in 1953, when DiMaggio threw her a wonderful surprise after telling her he was going to spend the festive period with his family in San Francisco; instead, he decorated her BEVERLY HILLS HOTEL apartment with a tree, put champagne on ice, and welcomed her when she arrived back, alone, after the studio party.

It was Joe who first pushed Marilyn to start doing something about her salary, which despite her headline billing were still pegged to the flat weekly rates of the contract she signed with Fox in 1951. Marilyn began to turn down projects the studio wanted her to do, starting with *The Girl in Pink Tights*, the film the studio had cast her in to follow *River of No Return*. Marilyn failed to turn up for the first day of shooting, and a week later was on the midnight plane to San Francisco to spend the rest of the holiday Christmas with her fiancé and his family.

On January 14, 1954, Joe whisked Marilyn off to City Hall in San Francisco for an impromptu wedding. Although they had been thinking of tying the knot for some time, they made the actual decision just a couple of days earlier. Despite the couple's initial intention to keep the occasion as low-key as possible, over a hundred (some reports put the number at closer to two hundred) newsmen and photographers found out—tipped off by the studio, which Marilyn had only informed one hour before the event—and thronged the entrance and corridors of the municipal building. Inside, the bride had no guests at all; Joe's friends and family looked on as Judge Charles S. Perry pronounced Joe and Marilyn man and wife. As they tried to make their exit they were way-

Marilyn and Joe on their honeymoon in Japan, 1954.

laid by reporters who asked, among other things, how many children they planned on having. Marilyn replied, "I'd like to have six." Joe, at the same moment, said "One." Then the couple raced out through the rear entrance, jumped into Joe's dark blue Cadillac and sped off to their honeymoon: one night at the modest CLIFTON MOTEL in Paso Robles, before driving on to a tranquil mountain hideaway outside Idyllwild, near PALM SPRINGS, where they stayed for two weeks. Marilyn went fishing with her new husband, she learned to play billiards, and they enjoyed the rare luxury of time alone together.

Marilyn's wedding gift to her possessive Italian husband was a nude photo from the legendary CALENDAR set, one that had never been published because it was deemed too risqué—as a token that her nude body was his and his alone. The studio tried to put a positive gloss on the whole business. A Fox executive quipped, "We haven't lost a star, we've gained a center fielder."

Life together ran no smoother than before marriage, even though they were prepared to overlook major personality differences and make a go of living together. Joe was punctilious in the way he kept his home clean and his financial affairs in order; Marilyn was just the opposite. He preferred to live in the calm of San Francisco; Marilyn had to be in Los Angeles. He was taciturn and outwardly impassive; Marilyn was impulsive and prone to emotional outbursts. He preferred spending time with family and old friends at home, or even just watching television all evening, while Marilyn, who had given up the Hollywood party circuit, craved intellectual stimulation. For the first time in her life, Marilyn was in the position of trying to pass on her literary knowledge and interests. She attempted to get Joe to take an interest in BOOKS, from Saint-Exupéry to Mickey Spillane to Jules Verne, but television addict Joe DiMaggio would not be swayed.

Even during the first weeks of the marriage, when Marilyn's career was not an issue as she was under suspension from her studio, the couple's trip to JAPAN brought a share of problems as reporters hounded the couple and fans mobbed them, first in Honolulu, then on arrival in Tokyo. *Time* magazine reported that Joe "went virtually unnoticed by the Japanese as the thousands swarmed to meet his bride. Marilyn's fans pressed so thickly about the arriving couple that both were forced to scramble back into the airplane, escaping later through its baggage hatch." And this was on a tour arranged for baseball hero Joe. The mass hysteria continued at their hotel. So many people wanted to get a glimpse of Marilyn that the couple decided to risk going out only on official engagements.

Things between the couple soured considerably when Marilyn accepted an invitation to fly out to KOREA and entertain the troops. Joe did not want her to go, but Marilyn decided she wanted to do her bit for the boys. She left with Jean O'Doul, wife of Joe's friend Lefty O'Doul, for a four-day, ten-show marathon, which she was to remember as the most carefree and successful performance of her life.

The marriage was already in trouble by the time the couple returned to California.

Marilyn and DiMaggio at the premiere of *The Seven Year Itch* (1955).

DiMaggio refused to accompany his wife to the *Photoplay* Awards for the second year running. Marilyn went along with her friend SIDNEY SKOLSKY, to whom she confided, just weeks after her wedding, that one day she was going to marry ARTHUR MILLER.

Back in Los Angeles, Marilyn sorted out her wrangles with the studio and returned to work soon after the couple moved into a $700-a-month mansion on NORTH PALM DRIVE. Joe preferred being in San Francisco, so in April and May Marilyn spent most of her time at the DiMaggio family home on BEACH STREET. Marilyn apparently enjoyed the family atmosphere and boat trips with Joe on his yacht the *Yankee Clipper*, but there were also reports that Joe's temper got the better of him, and that he was sometimes violent too. NATASHA LYTESS writes that Marilyn would call her in the middle of the night, desperate after he "was being so filthy to her, when he beat her."

Joe continued in his crusade against the public and personal exposure of Marilyn. It wasn't long before he was complaining, "It's no fun being married to an electric light." In August 1954 he was so incensed by the skimpy costume and suggestive choreography of the grand finale "Heat Wave" number in *THERE'S NO BUSINESS LIKE SHOW BUSINESS* that he stormed off the set in a fit of jealous rage. Despite his strong protestations, the number stayed in the movie. Worse, DARRYL ZANUCK had Joe barred from the Fox lot for making trouble.

Then Joe's jealousy found a focus: rumors that his wife was having a romance with voice coach HAL SCHAEFER, who in July 1954 narrowly survived a suicide attempt. Columnist LOUELLA PARSONS wrote at the time that Joe was "very unhappy when Marilyn went to the hospital many times to see Hal Schaefer when he was critically ill. . . . He was just as jealous of Marilyn's relationship with Natasha Lytess, whom he once ordered out of their house." Joe did not even like Marilyn having friends come to their rented home. As Marilyn later said, "He didn't talk to me. He was cold. He was indifferent to me as a human being and an artist. He didn't want me to have friends of my own. He didn't want me to do my work. He watched television instead of talking to me."

The watershed came the day when WALTER WINCHELL persuaded DiMaggio to join a crowd of several hundred onlookers watching Marilyn's dress being blown over her head for two hours on a New York street corner. If columnist Winchell had brought Joe along to the set of *THE SEVEN YEAR ITCH (1955)* because he wanted some hot copy, he was not disappointed. In Winchell's next column, he faithfully records Joe hollering out, "What the hell's going on around here?" before turning on his heels and heading back to the hotel. When Marilyn returned to their room, they had a vicious fight. The film's hairdresser Gladys Whitten, who saw Marilyn the next day, says, "Joe was very, very mad with her and he beat her up a little bit. There were bruises on her shoulders, but we covered them with makeup." This was confirmed by friend Amy Greene, "Her back was black and blue."

The couple flew back to Los Angeles, but almost immediately Joe was back in New York to broadcast commentary for the World Series. When he returned on October 2, Marilyn informed him that their marriage of eight months and thirteen days was over; she had instructed her attorney to file DIVORCE papers. That night neighbors heard the noises of a huge and prolonged argument, and saw the sight of Marilyn stomping around the darkened streets, holding a fur coat tightly around herself.

Two days later Fox publicity chief Harry Brand announced to the world that the nation's most glamorous couple was to separate amicably. Their North Palm Drive home was immediately besieged by photographs and reporters, who then watched and waited to see who would come out and what would happen. Both Marilyn and Joe were at home, Marilyn being attended by her physician and lawyer, while Joe was holed up in the basement den, watching television. He moved himself and his stuff out at 10 P.M., aided by his pal Reno Barsocchini. From the car Joe told reporters he was getting out of L.A., "I'll never come back here." At least one biographer, however, claims that in fact Joe spent the next six weeks in Los Angeles, a secret guest of Marilyn's doctor, Leon Krohn.

The press went into a frenzy of speculation about what went wrong between the country's most famous sweethearts. Natasha Lytess blamed Joe for preventing Marilyn from fully expressing her talent. Close friend Sidney Skolsky wrote in his memoirs, "Joe DiMaggio bored Marilyn. His life-style added up to beer, TV and the old lady—the wife who ran third to *Gunsmoke* or *The Late Show* and a can of beer, night after night after night." Donald Spoto quotes Marilyn as saying, "He didn't like the women I played—he thought they were sluts. I don't know what movies he was thinking about! He didn't like the actors kissing me, and he didn't like my costumes. He didn't like anything about my movies, and he hated all my clothes. When I told him I had to dress the way I did, that it was part of my job, he said I should quit that job. But who did he think he was marrying when he was marrying me? To tell the truth our marriage was a sort of crazy, difficult friendship with sexual privileges. Later I learned that's what marriages often are."

Then again, it takes two. Hollywood columnist Sheilah Graham wrote, "You could find Marilyn by following the trail of her stockings, her bra, her handkerchief, and her handbag, all dropped as she went. He was always trying to train her. And he could not. They reached a point where they could not speak without screaming." And not everything was bad about their marriage. Marilyn told several people that DiMaggio was the greatest lover, "If our marriage was only sex it would last forever."

Joe did not take the divorce proceedings as final. He was convinced that he could win Marilyn back, that she was simply "being misled by the wrong friends." The day before the writ was due to be read out in court, Joe made a last ditch attempt, enlisted Skolsky's help, and went to try and persuade Marilyn to reconsider. She would not be swayed.

On October 27, 1954, dressed in black from head to toe, Marilyn appeared before Judge Orlando H. Rhodes. Joe stayed away from the interlocutory divorce proceedings. Marilyn later recounted to biographer Maurice Zolotow what she told the court: "My husband would get in moods where he wouldn't speak to me for five to seven days at a time—sometimes longer, ten days. I would ask him what was wrong. He wouldn't answer, or he would say 'Stop nagging me!' I was permitted to have visitors no more than three times in the nine months we were married. On one occasion, it was when I was sick. . . . I hoped to have out of my marriage love, warmth, affection and understanding. But the relationship was mostly one of coldness and indifference."

Less than two weeks after this court appearance, Joe thought that the private detectives he had hired to keep tabs on Marilyn (Philip Irwin and Barney Ruditsky) had come up with something well worth their retainer. Several times one of the PIs had followed Marilyn to the same address, 8122 Waring Avenue, home of Sheila Stuart, who was both a student and friend of Hal Schaefer. Crazed with jealousy, DiMaggio, his PIs, Frank Sinatra (who later denied being there), and some brawny buddies burst into the offending apartment to catch Marilyn *in flagrante* and teach her lover a lesson—but they had broken down the wrong door. Marilyn and Schaefer, who DiMaggio claimed were in the next-door apartment, had plenty of time to make good their escape, if indeed they had been there at all. Ever after known as the "Wrong Door Raid," the ill-conceived punitive expedition became public knowledge and led to at least one lawsuit.

And yet after months of tension and the high drama of a very public divorce, Joe and Marilyn continued to spend time together. Joe not only visited her every single day in early November, during the five days she was in the HOSPITAL for an operation to remedy her chronic endometriosis, he practically camped out in the hospital building. The bottle of Chanel No. 5 he delivered to Marilyn as a gift set off rumors that they would be getting back together, until Marilyn told the press, "There's no chance of that, but we'll always be friends." Confidant Rupert Allan backed this up, giving the reasons too: "Marilyn told me that Joe had been a great friend to her after the divorce, but that while they were married he had beaten and abused her and believed her unfaithful."

Joe is reported to have spent a night with Marilyn at her New York hotel room over Christmas 1954, making him one of the very few people who knew that she had quit Hollywood. In the following months he continued to stay close to Marilyn wherever she was. He turned up at Marilyn and Milton Greene's hotel in Boston, and then he whisked her off for five days at his brother's home in Wellesley, Massachusetts. Marilyn regularly sought his advice as she put in practice what Joe had been telling her do all along, namely renegotiate her contract with Fox. In June 1955, for the first time ever, Joe escorted Marilyn to the premiere of one of her movies, *The Seven Year Itch*—though the party he threw afterward at Toots Shor's was an unmitigated failure, as Marilyn stormed out in a rage. However, with Marilyn's increasing interest in next-husband-to-be Arthur Miller, press hopes of a fairy tale reconciliation waned. The divorce was finalized on October 31, 1955. Around this time Marilyn confessed to Amy Greene, "I never should have married him. I couldn't be the Italian housewife he wanted me to be. I married him because I felt sorry for him, he seemed so lonely and shy." And yet Marilyn also said, "I never loved any guy more."

After their divorce Joe continued with his television commentary and then landed a job as a representative for a military supply company, V. H. Monette. He never remarried, though he apparently came close in 1957, to Marian McKnight, a woman who was later elected Miss America.

Although it seems that they did not meet up for some years after this, Joe and Marilyn remained in touch and were in each other's thoughts. Joe reputedly took Marilyn's advice and went to see a psychotherapist which, he is said to have told her, "saved his life."

Then, when Marilyn most needed him, Joe was there. In 1961 a highly distraught Marilyn called Joe from the psychiatric ward of the Payne Whitney HOSPITAL in New York, where she had gone after her psychoanalyst Marianne Kris recommended she needed a rest. Joe flew up immediately from Florida and demanded that Marilyn be released from the secure ward. Marilyn was driven back to her apartment by friend Ralph Roberts, where DiMaggio was waiting. Joe organized for Marilyn to recuperate in a far more conducive hospital environment, the Columbia University-Presbyterian Hospital Medical Center, where Marilyn remained from February 10 to March 5, 1961. Joe was with her every day. Soon after Marilyn left the hospital, he took her to the Yankees training camp, and then on to the Florida resort town of Redington Beach. Not only could Marilyn relax, she knew that she had somebody on her side, somebody she could count on.

Joe was there after her divorce from Arthur Miller, helping Marilyn out and keeping her company. After Marilyn moved back to Los Angeles they spent Christmas and New Year's 1961 together at her North Doheny Drive apartment. Almost in a repeat performance of Christmas 1953, Joe arrived bearing champagne and caviar, with a Christmas tree for good measure. When he wasn't traveling abroad for work, Joe made a point of visiting Marilyn in Los Angeles. In early 1962 he helped her move into her new home at Fifth Helena Drive.

They met at least once in June and twice in July 1962, either for an intimate supper at Marilyn's new home, or to go shopping or cycling together. According to Donald Spoto, in late July they met secretly at the Cal-Neva Lodge in Lake Tahoe, where they hatched plans for a secret wedding. As evidence, Spoto cites Joe's employer at the time, Valmore Morette, and Susan Strasberg, who told him, "She was getting out of relationships that were not good for her and back into one that was. She knew she needed some sort of emotional and spiritual anchor." At this time Marilyn was also in the process of commissioning designer Jean-Louis to make her a gown, which Spoto says would have been for this wedding.

The day after Marilyn died, a note was found folded up in her address book, that she had started writing to Joe. It read:

> "Dear Joe,
>
> If I can only succeed in making you happy, I will have succeeded in the biggest and most

difficult thing there is—that is, to make *one person completely happy*. Your happiness means my happiness, and..."

Whether or not a wedding was in their plans, Joe came to Marilyn's assistance one final time. After her DEATH he stepped in to organize Marilyn's FUNERAL, issuing invites, arranging the ceremony, and enlisting Marilyn's half-sister BERNEICE MIRACLE to help. He spent the night before the funeral holding a private vigil over Marilyn's body at the Westwood Village Mortuary.

Following the funeral, Joe DiMaggio placed a twenty-year order with the local PARISIAN FLORISTS for a long-stemmed red rose to be delivered to Marilyn's grave twice a week (three times in some accounts). In doing this he fulfilled a promise he had made to Marilyn on their wedding day, when he pledged that he would be as loyal to her as William Powell had been to JEAN HARLOW. After this order expired, Joe made a donation to a children's charity in Marilyn's memory, convinced that she would have been happier he remembered her in this way.

DiMaggio always maintained a respectful silence about his time with Marilyn. He is the only major figure in Marilyn's adult life not to have written a "Marilyn book," though from time to time rumors circulated that he did write a book but placed a publication embargo on it for fifty years after his death.

Joe lived out his retirement with the same elegance and grace he had brought to the world of baseball. Apart from advertising appearances as a spokesman for Mr. Coffee coffeemakers, he kept out of the public eye. DiMaggio died at his Florida home on March 8, 1999, five months after an operation for lung cancer. He was buried at the Holy Cross Cemetery.

### DIMAGGIO'S FRIENDS

BARSOCCHINI, RENO
The friend Joe DiMaggio chose to be best man for his wedding with Marilyn. Nine months later Barsocchini helped DiMaggio move his things out of the couple's North Palm Drive residence, the marriage in tatters.

O'DOUL, FRANK "LEFTY"
Lefty O'Doul was Joe DiMaggio's friend, baseball manager, and drinking buddy. Lefty and his wife Jean accompanied newlywed Joe and Marilyn on the international part of their honeymoon, the trip to Japan. Jean O'Doul went with Marilyn on her triumphant tour to entertain U.S. troops stationed in Korea.

SOLOTAIRE, GEORGE
Owner of the Adelphi Theater Ticket Agency, Brownsville-born Solotaire was Joe DiMaggio's best buddy in New York. Solotaire had the "in" to all the happenings in New York. He has also been credited with coining the words "dullsville" for a boring play and "splitsville" for divorce. Solotaire and DiMaggio were regulars at Toots Shor's New York eatery.

In 1953 Solotaire went with DiMaggio to Canada to visit Marilyn while she was shooting location scenes for *River of No Return*. He also accompanied Joe on other occasions to watch Marilyn making movies; he was with him in August 1954 when Joe stormed off the set of *There's No Business Like Show Business*, scandalized by Marilyn's skimpy "Heatwave" costume.

Solotaire was one of the few people invited to Marilyn's funeral in 1962.

SHOR, TOOTS
Toots Shor was a larger than life New York character, known for his hard drinking and companionability. His bar/restaurant was a magnet for top sports stars, newspapermen, and theater folk, and a regular haunt over the years for Babe Ruth, Jack Dempsey, and Ernest Hemingway.

WINCHELL, WALTER
Influential right-wing columnist and old friend of Joe's. See individual entry.

## DIMAGGIO, JOE JR. (1942–1999)

Marilyn maintained a warm relationship with Joe's son from his previous marriage to Dorothy Arnold. Joe Jr. called Marilyn's home a number of times on her last day alive, from nearby Orange County where he was serving with the marines. He did not get through the first couple of times—he was told Marilyn was either not at home or unavailable. Around 7 P.M. that evening he finally got through, and told Marilyn the news that he had broken off his engagement to his then fiancée, which put Marilyn in a good mood as she had not taken to the girl.

## DIRECTORS

MARILYN:
"I worked in some pictures where I was directed by men who never directed before or didn't know a thing about character motivation or how to speak lines. Do you ever see on the screen 'this pictures was directed by an ignorant director with no taste'? No, the public always blames the star. Me. I had directors so stupid all they can do is repeat the lines of the script to me like they're reading a timetable. So I didn't get help from them. I had to find it elsewhere."

Marilyn was not an easy actor to direct. Because she was such a perfectionist, and because she had such a dread of failing to live up to people's expectations, directorial assistance had to be gentle yet firm if it was not to set off floods of tears and lowered self-esteem. Marilyn's legendary LATENESS was a function of this; sometimes she did not think that she was ready for the camera, she found fault with her face, her hair, or her costumes, or else she did not feel sufficiently confident with her lines, or with the moves she had been rehearsing. Add to that the permanent on-set presence of a drama coach—first NATASHA LYTESS, then PAULA STRASBERG—and Marilyn picked up quite a reputation. In her twenty-nine films Marilyn worked with some of the finest directors in the business, almost all of whom provided a string of memorable quotes.

### MARILYN'S DIRECTORS

| | |
|---|---|
| Roy Baker | *Don't Bother to Knock* (1952) |
| George Cukor | *Let's Make Love* (1960) |
| | *Something's Got to Give* (1962) |
| Tay Garnett | *The Fireball* (1950) |
| Edmund Goulding | *We're Not Married* (1952) |
| Henry Hathaway | *Niagara* (1953) |
| Howard Hawks | *Monkey Business* (1952) |
| | *Gentlemen Prefer Blondes* (1953) |
| F. Hugh Herbert | *Scudda Hoo! Scudda Hay!* (1948) |
| John Huston | *The Asphalt Jungle* (1950) |
| | *The Misfits* (1961) |
| Harmon Jones | *As Young As You Feel* (1951) |
| Phil Karlson | *Ladies of the Chorus* (1948) |
| Henry Koster | *O. Henry's Full House* (1952) |
| Fritz Lang | *Clash By Night* (1952) |
| Walter Lang | *There's No Business Like Show Business* (1954) |
| Joshua Logan | *Bus Stop* (1956) |
| Joseph L. Mankiewicz | *All About Eve* (1950) |
| David Miller | *Love Happy* (1950) |
| Jean Negulesco | *How to Marry a Millionaire* (1953) |
| Joseph Newman | *Love Nest* (1951) |
| Laurence Olivier | *The Prince and the Showgirl* (1957) |
| Arthur Pierson | *Dangerous Years* (1947) |
| | *Hometown Story* (1951) |
| Otto Preminger | *River of No Return* (1954) |
| Richard Sale | *A Ticket to Tomahawk* (1950) |
| | *Let's Make It Legal* (1951) |
| John Sturges | *Right Cross* (1950) |
| Billy Wilder | *The Seven Year Itch* (1955) |
| | *Some Like It Hot* (1959) |

One of the greatest sticking points during renegotiation of her contract with TWENTIETH CENTURY-FOX, lasting throughout 1955, was Marilyn's insistence on approval of her directors. Although this is commonplace nowadays, at the time it was very rare for a studio to hand over such power to a star. Marilyn and business partner MILTON GREENE held firm, and were rewarded in early 1956 with a new contract.

### MARILYN'S LIST OF APPROVED DIRECTORS

George Cukor
Vittorio De Sica
John Ford
Alfred Hitchcock
John Huston
Elia Kazan
David Lean
Joshua Logan
Joseph L. Mankiewicz
Vincente Minnelli
Carol Reed
George Stevens
Lee Strasberg
Billy Wilder
William Wyler
Fred Zinnemann

Marilyn herself never worked on the other side of the camera, though she had an excellent understanding of what made a movie work. For example, during shooting on *THE PRINCE AND THE SHOWGIRL* (1957), she routinely watched the rushes of the previous day's shooting, making comments to director LAURENCE OLIVIER and Milton Greene. In the latter part of her career she was always keen to participate in the pre-production process, take part in script conferences and make suggestions not just about her character but the shape of the film she was working on.

## DISCOVERERS

DARRYL ZANUCK:
"Nobody discovered her; she earned her own way to stardom."

But plenty of people have claimed they did:

First photographer: DAVID CONOVER
First modeling contract: EMMELINE SNIVELY
First agent: HARRY LIPTON
First studio talent scout to take a chance on Norma Jeane: BEN LYON
First mogul to help her: JOSEPH M. SCHENCK
First agent to really get her career on track: JOHNNY HYDE
First long-term drama coach: NATASHA LYTESS

## DISGUISE

After 1952 and national stardom, being Marilyn Monroe was pretty much a full-time occupation, not only on the set but when going out to restaurants and doing the round of publicity engagements. When Marilyn abandoned Hollywood for New York in 1955–56 she discovered that she could quite effectively get around town incognito by slipping on an old coat, a baggy sweater, and dark glasses, and then knotting a scarf beneath her chin—and easy on the makeup. When that didn't work, she resorted to wearing a black wig as well.

## DIVORCE

JAMES DOUGHERTY
September 13, 1946: After living out the statutory waiting period under Nevada law, Norma Jeane's divorce from her first husband in Clark County came through just one month before she signed her first studio contract. As part of their settlement, Norma Jeane got the CAR.

JOE DIMAGGIO
October 4, 1954: Studio publicist HARRY BRAND announces that Joe and Marilyn are to divorce.

October 27, 1954: Marilyn obtains an interlocutory divorce from Judge Orlando Rhodes. The official reason was, "since the marriage of the parties defendant has inflicted upon plaintiff grievous mental cruelty, causing her grievous mental suffering and anguish, all of which acts and conduct on the part of defendant were without the fault of plaintiff, and by reason of which defendant has caused plaintiff grievous mental distress, suffering and anguish."

October 31, 1955: Judge Elmer Doyle grants the Final Decree.

ARTHUR MILLER
November 11, 1960: Marilyn announces she is separating from Arthur Miller

January 20, 1961: In Juarez, MEXICO, Marilyn obtains divorce from Judge Miguel Gomez Guerra, on the grounds of "incompatibility of character." Press attention that day was focused on President Kennedy's inauguration, not on Marilyn's day trip to Mexico.

## DOCTORS

JOHN HUSTON:
"Marilyn wasn't killed by Hollywood. It was the goddam doctors who killed her. If she was a pill addict, they made her so."

(NOTE: this quote appears in at least three different forms depending on biography. Compare with DRUGS version.)

During her lifetime Marilyn collected a long list of doctors and psychoanalysts to tend to her physical and mental needs. She suffered many recurring medical complaints including frequent bouts of bronchitis and endometriosis requiring stays in the HOSPITAL.

It was rare for any one doctor to collaborate with others who were seeing her at the time. So, while seeing a psychoanalyst who might prescribe her one type of pill, Marilyn would also be getting prescriptions for drugs from her regular doctor, and sometimes the studio doctor too. Even if one doctor refused to write out a prescription, there was always another more than willing to do so. In the end, nobody except Marilyn was in control of the stronger pills and dangerous combinations of drugs that she used to combat her debilitating insomnia.

By the last year of her life, before beginning shooting on *SOMETHING'S GOT TO GIVE*, Marilyn's daily routine revolved around seeing her medical entourage, typically one or even two daily sessions with psychoanalyst Dr. RALPH GREENSON, followed by visits either to Dr. Hyman Engelberg or Dr. Lee Seigel.

PHYSICIANS

CORDAY, DR. ELLIOT
Marilyn's doctor from 1948 to the mid-fifties.
In an interview with Anthony Summers this doctor explained why he stopped treating Marilyn: "I eventually withdrew from the case because she would not employ a decent psychiatrist. People would understand her death better had they been listening to her in my office back then. There had been many suicide attempts, more than were known. And by 1954 she was using drugs—I think the hard stuff as well as the sleeping pills. In the end I told her I was not going to be around to witness what was happen."

ENGELBERG, DR. HYMAN
Office at 9730 Wilshire Boulevard, Beverly Hills.
Dr. Ralph Greenson recommended Dr. Engelberg to Marilyn soon after she began seeing Greenson in 1960. Engelberg coordinated Marilyn's hospitalization during shooting of *The Misfits* that year. He flew out to New York to prepare her for her 1961 gallbladder operation,

On October 6, 1954 Marilyn and attorney Jerry Geisler met the press in front of Marilyn and Joe DiMaggio's house in Beverly Hills to announce that a suit for divorce had been filed.

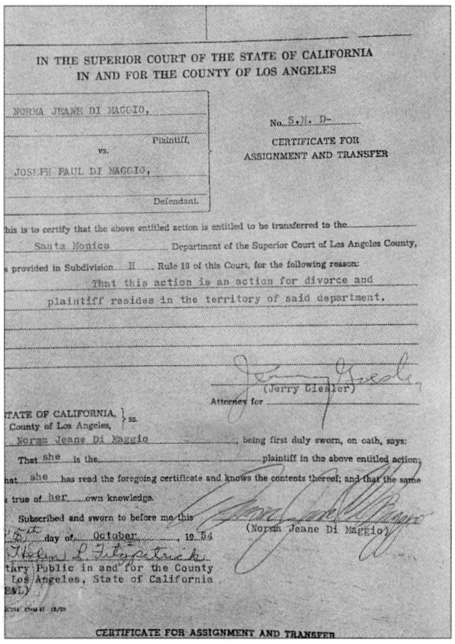

IN THE SUPERIOR COURT OF THE STATE OF CALIFORNIA
IN AND FOR THE COUNTY OF LOS ANGELES

NORMA JEANE DI MAGGIO, Plaintiff,
vs.
JOSEPH PAUL DI MAGGIO, Defendant.

No. S.M. D-
CERTIFICATE FOR ASSIGNMENT AND TRANSFER

This is to certify that the above entitled action is entitled to be transferred to the Santa Monica Department of the Superior Court of Los Angeles County, as provided in Subdivision H, Rule 18 of this Court, for the following reason:
That this action is an action for divorce and plaintiff resides in the territory of said department.

(Jerry Giesler)
Attorney for

STATE OF CALIFORNIA, County of Los Angeles, } ss.
Norma Jeane Di Maggio, being first duly sworn, on oath, says:
That she is the plaintiff in the above entitled action; that she has read the foregoing certificate and knows the contents thereof; and that the same is true of her own knowledge.

(Norma Jeane Di Maggio)

Subscribed and sworn to before me this 25th day of October, 1954
Helen L. Fitzpatrick
Notary Public in and for the County of Los Angeles, State of California
(SEAL)

CERTIFICATE FOR ASSIGNMENT AND TRANSFER

Final divorce papers.

ANC
MOVIE SECRETS
A STERLING PUBLICATION
EXCLUSIVE: What Made Joe Go?
SIX PAGES OF SENSATIONAL PIX
February • 25¢
DORIS DAY'S Picture Life Story
BOB WAGNER Why He Won't Marry
GLENN FORD What Has His Wife Got?
AVA GARDNER Little Girl Lost
HOLLYWOOD'S HE-MEN—Real or phony?
• Portraits

and he treated her for the viral infection that prevented her from fulfilling her contractual obligations during shooting of *Something's Got to Give* (1962).

As Marilyn's general doctor, Dr. Engelberg was also responsible for writing out prescriptions for sleeping pills. In the six weeks before her death, Marilyn saw Dr. Engelberg a total of twenty-nine times. Many biographers write that Engelberg gave Marilyn injections on August 1 and August 3—either sedatives or so-called "youth shots"—but that these needle marks (which should have still been in evidence on Marilyn's body) did not feature on the official autopsy report.

Engelberg was in close contact with Marilyn's psychoanalyst Dr. Ralph Greenson, from whom he would receive calls and then go to Marilyn's house (Marilyn had given him the keys) to administer sedatives and other drugs.

On August 3, 1962, Engelberg wrote out a prescription for twenty-five Nembutal capsules, which Marilyn obtained from the San Vicente pharmacy in Brentwood. On Saturday, August 4, the day of Marilyn's death, Engelberg reputedly received two requests from Dr. Greenson to go to Marilyn's home and administer a sedative, but owing to personal problems—he was separating from his wife at the time—he was unable to make a house call on his most famous patient. He was called much later by Dr. Greenson. It was Engelberg who placed the call to the police from Marilyn's home, and who officially pronounced Marilyn Monroe dead at 3:40 a.m. on August 5, 1962.

HEADLEY, DR. NATHAN
Treated Marilyn for bronchitis and a viral infection in April 1956, after she suffered through freezing temperatures during location shooting for *Bus Stop*.

ROSENFELD, DR. ROBERT
Doctor who treated Marilyn in 1954, during her illness while shooting *There's No Business Like Show Business*.

RUBIN, DR. PHILLIP
Called in for a second opinion about the viral infection preventing Marilyn from working on *Something's Got to Give*, Dr. Rubin recommended that Marilyn stay home to recover.

SEIGEL, DR. LEE (also spelled Siegel)
The studio doctor at Twentieth Century-Fox, Seigel first treated Marilyn in the early fifties. He was on hand during *The Seven Year Itch* (1954) and *Bus Stop* (1956). During *Itch* Marilyn worked on despite a lung infection and the impending breakdown of her marriage to Joe DiMaggio. Dr. Seigel gave her sleeping pills to help her rest. He also treated her for bronchitis, as he did again during shooting of *Bus Stop*. Later, in 1962, Seigel treated Marilyn during the filming on *Something's Got to Give*.

SHAPIRO, DR. PHILLIP
Marilyn's physician in New York, 1955, who looked after her and wrote out prescriptions for sedatives and barbiturates

OTHER PHYSICIANS:
Dr. Myron Prinzmetal—1952
Marilyn continued to see JOHNNY HYDE's physician for two or three years after Hyde died.
Dr. Verne Mason—1954

### GYNECOLOGISTS

BERGLASS, DR. BERNARD
Gynecologist during 1957, including operation for ectopic pregnancy in August that year.

DUBROW, DR. HILLIARD
Gynecologist who operated on Marilyn at time of her ectopic pregnancy, New York, August 1, 1957.

KROHN, DR. LEON "RED"
Marilyn's long-term gynecologist was brought in by surgeon Marcus Rabwin to assist in an operation to remove Marilyn's appendix in May 1952. From that time on, she consulted him about her chronic reproductive problems (*see* MEDICAL HISTORY). Krohn became a friend, somebody who Marilyn felt she could turn to when she needed help and advice
on matters both medical and personal. One such occasion was October 1954, when her marriage to Joe DiMaggio broke down; Krohn went to their house to help manage the situation that was exacerbated by hundreds of journalists camped outside. Some sources say that after Joe drove off, he didn't go to San Francisco as he told journalists he would, but actually went to stay at Krohn's house. After Marilyn moved to New York, she found another gynecologist, but she continued to see Krohn when she was back in Los Angeles. It was as much as a friend as a doctor that he spent a lot of time on set with Marilyn as she worked on *Some Like It Hot*.

Dr. Krohn went on record to deny rumors of Marilyn's abortions, as many as fourteen according to some sources: "She never had even one. Later there were two miscarriages and an ectopic pregnancy requiring emergency termination, but no abortion."

He also warned her of the dangers of her addictions: "She often told me how she longed for a child, but I cautioned her that she would kill a baby with the drink and the pills—the effects of those barbiturates accumulated, I told her, and it would be impossible to predict when just one drink will then precipitate an spontaneous abortion."

### SURGEONS

GURDIN, DR. MICHAEL
Plastic surgeon who in 1949 or 1950 performed minor cosmetic surgery on Marilyn. It has also been written that psychoanalyst Dr. Greenson took Marilyn to Gurdin a couple of months before her death, after she apparently fell over in the shower; Gurdin examined Marilyn but found that she had not broken her nose.

RABWIN, DR. MARK
In April 1952 Dr. Rabwin removed Marilyn's appendix. Marilyn, concerned that this operation might compromise her ability to have children, taped a poignant note to her abdomen pleading with him to be very careful in his work (*see* MEDICAL HISTORY).

RODGERS, DR. MORTIMER
Doctor who performed surgery on Marilyn for her chronic endometriosis in June 1959.

## DOCUMENTARIES

The first Marilyn documentary was broadcast just five days after she died. The most recent was probably shown by a TV station in your area within the last six months. Here is a list of Marilyn documentaries over the years, many of which have been recut and expanded and then shown under different names at different times in different areas. As well as in these programs, Marilyn is a popular addition to any documentary about the history of Hollywood, tragic stars, cinema greats, the most important people of the twentieth century, doomed marriages, and any other TV fare that needs a bit of star allure.

*Marilyn Monroe, Why?* (CBS, 1962), 30 minutes.
Charles Collingwood interviews people who knew Marilyn on this *Eyewitness* program slot, August 10, 1962. Originally titled, *Who Killed Marilyn Monroe?*

*Marilyn* (Twentieth Century-Fox, 1963), 83 minutes.
ROCK HUDSON narrates this anthology of Marilyn's fifteen at Fox plus material from the unfinished *SOMETHING'S GOT TO GIVE*. FRANK SINATRA was originally slated to narrate. First released April 18, 1963.

*The Marilyn Monroe Story*, (ABC, 1963), 30 minutes. Also known as *The Story of Marilyn Monroe*.
Mike Wallace narrates brief treatment of Marilyn's life.

*The Legend of Marilyn Monroe*, (ABC, 1966), 60 minutes. Also known as *Portrait: Marilyn Monroe* and the *Marilyn Monroe Story*.
Narrated by JOHN HUSTON.

*Marilyn Remembered* (ABC, 1974), 60 minutes.
Extended version of 1966 ABC documentary.

*Marvellous Marilyn* (syndicated, 1979), 30 minutes.
Tom Bosley narrates this feature that went out on the syndicated *That's Hollywood!* show.

*In Search of: The Death of Marilyn Monroe* (syndicated, 1980), 30 minutes.
An episode of Alan Lansburg's syndicated show.

*Marilyn, In Search of a Dream* (ABC, 1983), 30 minutes.
Kevin McCarthy narrated feature on the *Hollywood Close-Up* series.

*The Last Days of Marilyn Monroe*, (BBC, 1985), 60 minutes. Also known as *Say Goodbye to the President* and *Marilyn, Say Goodbye to the President.*
UK-produced documentary based on ANTHONY SUMMERS' 1986 biography *Goddess*.

*Marilyn Monroe: Beyond the Legend* (Cinemax, 1986), 60 minutes.
RICHARD WIDMARK narrates this documentary on which JAMES HASPIEL served as a consultant.

*Norma Jeane Alias Marilyn Monroe* (1987).
CATHERINE DENEUVE narrates this original French look at Marilyn Monroe.

*Remembering Marilyn* (ABC, 1988), 60 minutes.
LEE REMICK hosts this look at Marilyn.

*Two Tragic Blondes: The True Stories of Harlow and Monroe* (Hollywood Select, 1989), 53 minutes.
Comparison of the parallel lives of these actresses.

*Marilyn: Something's Got to Give* (Twentieth Century-Fox, 1990), 60 minutes.
Featuring material from Marilyn's abandoned final film project.

*Marilyn Monroe, The Early Years* (Ashley Entertainment Productions, 1991), 50 minutes. Also known as *The Discovery of Marilyn Monroe*.
Focusing on Marilyn's first photographer, DAVID CONOVER.

*Marilyn: The Last Interview* (HBO, 1992), 30 minutes.
Journalist RICHARD MERYMAN and the interviews for Marilyn's final press feature.

*The Marilyn Files* (syndicated, 1991), 120 minutes.
Bill Bixby and Jane Wallace host a two-hour special.

*Marilyn: The Last Word* (Paramount, 1993), 57 minutes.
Barry Marilyn and Terry Murphy help reconstructs Marilyn's movements during her last days. First appeared on *Hard Copy*.

*Marilyn Monroe, Life after Death* (Showtime, 1994) 90 minutes.
MILTON GREENE's photographs feature in this recent documentary, narrated by Roscoe Lee Brown.

*We Remember Marilyn*, (Passport Video, 1996) 100 minutes.
Two cassette tribute.

*Marilyn, The Mortal Goddess* (A&E, 1996), 120 minutes.
In-depth treatment of Marilyn's life.

*Marilyn Monroe Loss of Innocence* (World Vision Entertainment, 1997), 60 minutes.
Includes excerpts from the adult movie Marilyn allegedly made.

*Intimate Portrait: Marilyn Monroe* (Unapix, 1998), 60 minutes.
Part of series looking at Hollywood actresses.

Over the years, a number of dramatizations of Marilyn's life have been made too. (*See* ACTRESSES WHO HAVE PORTRAYED MARILYN).

For more detailed information about these documentaries, see *The Ultimate Marilyn* by Ernest W. Cunningham, *The Unabridged Marilyn* by Randall Riese and Neal Hitchins, or the Web site "Where She Lives," (http://www.plutarch.com/marilyn.html) which has a detailed rundown on the footage featured in TV documentaries.

## DOHENY DRIVE

APARTMENT 3, 882 NORTH DOHENY DRIVE, BEVERLY HILLS

Between early 1953 and January 1954, Marilyn lived at this address between Sunset and Santa Monica Boulevards, in a modern three-room first-floor apartment rented from a Miss Violet Mertz. JANE RUSSELL helped Marilyn with the DECORATION scheme of white, with thick carpets and a baby grand WHITE PIANO. This was where Marilyn lived while dating JOE DIMAGGIO, and when she moved out it was as Mrs DiMaggio.

In 1961, after her separation from ARTHUR MILLER and return to Los Angeles, Marilyn moved back to the very same apartment. To keep away unwanted interlopers, Marilyn put the name "Marjorie Stengel" on the mailbox—Stengel had once worked as her secretary. Since her previous stay, the decoration had changed to feature blue, with floor-to-ceiling mirrors in the dressing room and a black enameled front door. This time, Marilyn kept her changes to a minimum, adding just a few personal effects—her BOOKS, makeup, and a suitcase of clothes—and for once she did not put up on the walls the pictures that had made her feel at home in so many places.

That Christmas Marilyn must have felt a strong sense of déjà vu; Joe DiMaggio spent the festive season with her at this modest apartment, as he had done in 1953, when he threw a surprise Christmas party for just the two of them.

(*see* HOMES)

Marilyn as deranged babysitter Nell Forbes in *Don't Bother to Knock* (1952).

## DON'T BOTHER TO KNOCK (1952)

(WORKING TITLE: *Night Without Sleep*)

After loaning Marilyn out to other studios, TWENTIETH CENTURY-FOX chose a rather unlikely vehicle to give their latest sex symbol her first lead role. Hot on the heels of the fish cannery employee she played in CLASH BY NIGHT (1952), Marilyn is a deranged and ultimately psychotic babysitter, two roles a million miles away from the string of bubbly and decorative blondes she played in almost all of her previous fourteen movies. *Don't Bother to Knock* was adapted from a serial suspense story called "Mischief," written by Charlotte Armstrong and originally published in *Good Housekeeping* magazine.

The star potential in Marilyn's performance was spotted by some (but not all) reviewers. *Variety* called her "a surefire money attraction"; the *Motion Picture Herald* recognized in her "the kind of big new star for which exhibitors are always asking." Years later, Marilyn still considered this movie one of her best dramatic efforts.

Playing Nell Forbes must have been something of an emotional trial for Marilyn. To portray the character, Marilyn may well have drawn upon her own deprived CHILDHOOD, and used the asylums in which she had visited her mother as a way of understanding the character's loneliness and the damage inflicted by years of institutionalization. From her own life Marilyn knew of the allure of a fantasy existence, and the hurt that pushes people to the brink of suicide.

The film was shot with tight budget constraints, so English director ROY BAKER went with the first take of every shot. Considering Marilyn's great nervousness, the result is impressive indeed. Drama coach NATASHA LYTESS, who Marilyn insisted having on set with her, recalled, "Actually, I had very little to do. She was terrified of the entire project, but she knew exactly what the role required and how to do it. I simply tried to infuse her with some confidence."

RICHARD WIDMARK's pilot Jed Towers hits the mark in the film when he says of Marilyn's character, "You're a gal with a lot of variations," and sums her up as "silk on one side and sandpaper on the other."

The film was remade for television in 1991, this time entitled *The Sitter*.

**Tagline:**
"You never met her type before..."

**Credits:**
Twentieth Century-Fox, Black and White
Length: 76 minutes
Release date: July 18, 1952

Directed by: Roy Ward Baker
Produced by: Julian Blaustein
Written by: Daniel Taradash, from "*Mischief*," a story by Charlotte Armstrong
Cinematography by: Lucien Ballard
Music by: Lionel Newman
Costume Design by: Travilla
Film Editing by: George A. Gittens

**Cast (credits order):**
Richard Widmark . . . Jed Towers
Marilyn Monroe . . . Nell Forbes
Anne Bancroft . . . Lyn Leslie
Donna Corcoran . . . Bunny Jones
Jeanne Cagney . . . Rochelle
Lurene Tuttle . . . Mrs. Jones
Elisha Cook Jr. . . . Eddie Forbes
Jim Backus . . . Peter Jones
Verna Felton . . . Mrs. Ballew
Willis Bouchey . . . Bartender Joe
Gloria Blondell . . . Girl Photographer
Don Beddoe . . . Mr. Ballew
Grace Hayle . . . Mrs. McMurdock
Michael Ross . . . Pat the House Detective

**Cast (uncredited):**
Eda Reiss Merin . . . Maid
Vic Perrin . . . Elevator Operator
Dick Cogan . . . Bell Captain
Robert Foulk . . . Doorman

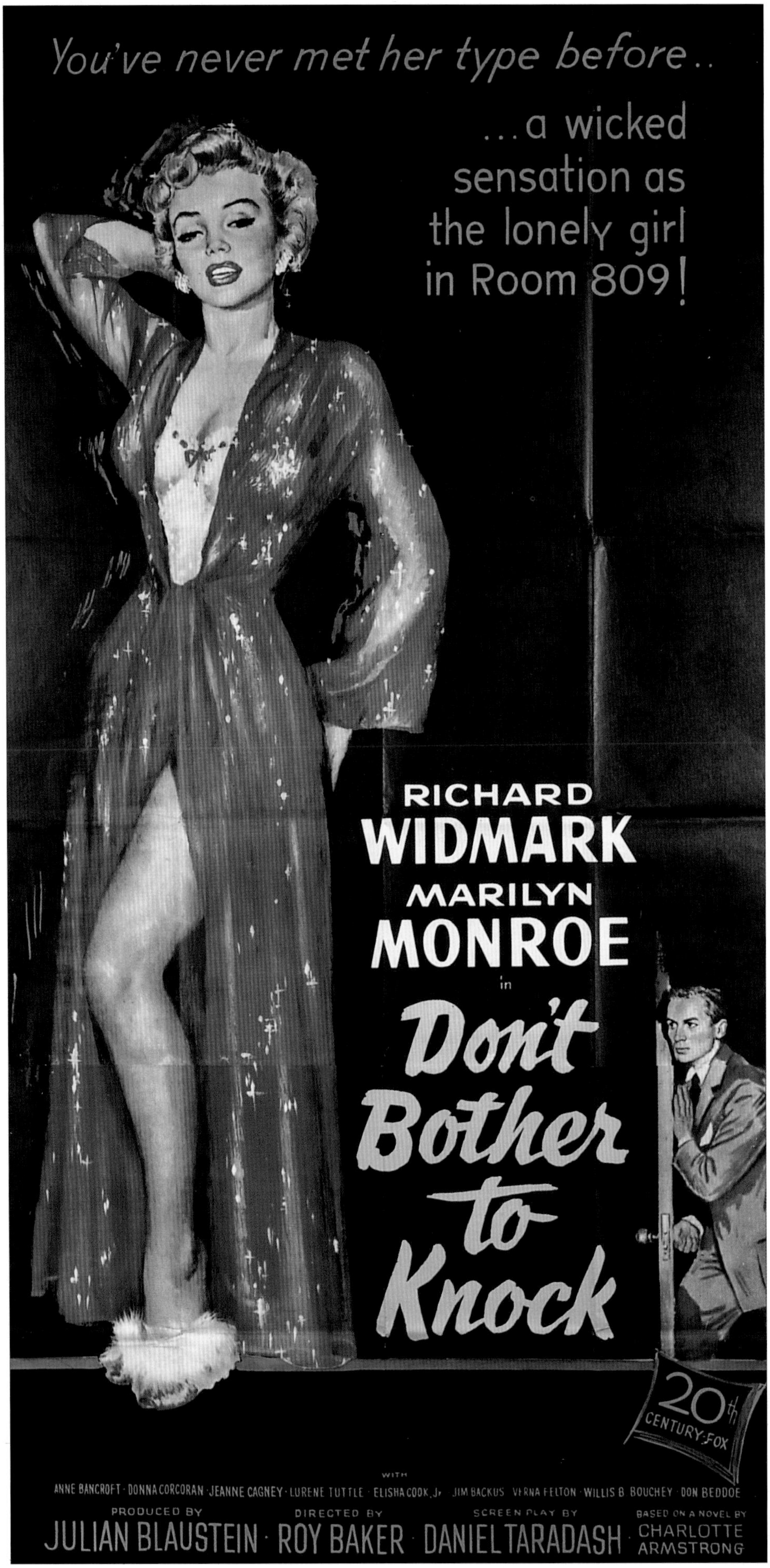
You've never met her type before..
...a wicked sensation as the lonely girl in Room 809!
RICHARD WIDMARK
MARILYN MONROE
in
Don't Bother to Knock
20th CENTURY-FOX
WITH
ANNE BANCROFT · DONNA CORCORAN · JEANNE CAGNEY · LURENE TUTTLE · ELISHA COOK, Jr. · JIM BACKUS · VERNA FELTON · WILLIS B. BOUCHEY · DON BEDDOE
PRODUCED BY JULIAN BLAUSTEIN
DIRECTED BY ROY BAKER
SCREEN PLAY BY DANIEL TARADASH
BASED ON A NOVEL BY CHARLOTTE ARMSTRONG

Olan Soule . . . Desk Clerk
Emmett Vogan . . . Toastmaster

**Crew:**
Paul S. Fox . . . set decorator
Richard Irvine . . . art director
Charles Le Maire . . . wardrobe supervisor
Thomas Little . . . set decorator
Lyle R. Wheeler . . . art director
Jerry Goldsmith . . . music (uncredited)
Alfred Newman . . . theme from Panic in the Streets (1950), (uncredited)
Ben Nye . . . makeup
Bernard Freericks . . . sound
Harry M. Leonard . . . sound
Earle H. Hagen . . . orchestrator
Ray Kellogg . . . special effects
Charles Le Maire . . . wardrobe director

**Plot:**
Jed Towers (Richard Widmark) is a pilot staying at a New York hotel where his girl, singer Lyn Leslie (played by Anne Bancroft in her feature film debut), works. Lyn gives him the brush off, but he immediately finds a rebound candidate in the provocative blonde who is staying in the room opposite. Marilyn's Nell, however, is not all she seems. As innocent as she may have seemed to the couple who gave her a job babysitting for their little girl Bunny (Donna Corcoran) that evening, in reality she never recovered after her pilot fiancé left her. . . . Nell entices Jed into her room, and does her best to minimize any distractions, particularly those coming from Bunny. Any doubts that Nell is not functioning with a full deck disappear when she becomes angry with her uncle Eddie, the elevator operator, for talking about her fiancé. Jed, meanwhile, makes good his escape, and makes a play for Lyn again. When he realizes that the little girl with the mad babysitter is in grave danger, he goes back upstairs, where the girl has been tied up and Nell is fighting with Bunny's mother. Nell runs off, but Jed tracks her down—she is threatening suicide with a razor, but his intervention is sufficient to get her to hand over the blades. Nell is led away, docile, to the hospital, while Jed's compassion wins back the girl who at the start had judged him too unemotional.

**Reviews:**
*New York Daily Mirror*
"Marilyn Monroe, whose screen roles had had little import except to show her natural physical attributes, now emerges in 'Don't Bother to Knock'... as more than a sexy dame. She has good dramatic promise.

Richard Widmark shares star billing in the Twentieth Century-Fox melodrama but fizzles in the light of the new beauty. She is a provocative woman even in the drab costume of a poor hireling. She is what the movies need, a few more like her and the industry would thrive."

*New York Post*
"In *Don't Bother to Knock*... they've thrown Marilyn Monroe into the deep dramatic waters, sink or swim, and while she doesn't really do either, you might say that she floats. With that figure, what else can she do."

*Motion Picture Herald Tribune*
"It proves conclusively that she is the kind of big new star for which exhibitors are always asking."

## DORS, DIANA
(1931–1984, B. DIANA FLUCK)

"Britain's Marilyn Monroe" was the undisputed top screen blonde on her own side of the Atlantic, who like Marilyn sailed very close to the prevailing ideals of decency. Dors tried her hand in Hollywood but found limited success. It was during this period that Marilyn was in England working on *THE PRINCE AND THE SHOWGIRL* (1957), thereby depriving the British tabloid press of the "battle of the blondes" they had been hoping for.

## DOSTOEVSKY, FYODOR (1821–1881)

The great nineteenth-century Russian novelist was one of Marilyn's favorite authors. Marilyn probably first came across Dostoevsky when studying drama at the ACTOR'S LAB in 1947.

Her favorite Dostoevsky novel was *The Brothers Karamazov*. Early lover JOHNNY HYDE once compared Marilyn to the lusty Grushenka, and after this she harbored a lifelong ambition to play this role. Some years later, Marilyn described the story of Grushenka's sacrifice in loving Dmitri Karamazov as, "the most touching thing I'd ever read or heard of. I asked Natasha [Lytess] whether it would make a good movie. She said yes, but not for me—yet." Acting coach MICHAEL CHEKHOV also encouraged Marilyn in this desire, as did ARTHUR MILLER, who once said that he would adapt a version of the novel for her. BILLY WILDER thought Marilyn would have been great: "People who haven't read the book don't know that Grushenka is a sex pot... [Marilyn] would be a Grushenka to end all Grushenkas."

Sadly for Marilyn, this ambition was never to be realized. Maria Schell took the role in the 1958 MGM version of this classic. Columnist SHEILAH GRAHAM was one of many disappointed that Marilyn didn't get the part: "[Marilyn] would have been superb as Dostoyevsky's sensual, confused heroine. She was born for the part, and Maria Schell with her assured smile was completely wrong."

## DOUGHERTY, JAMES (JIM) (B. 1921)

MARILYN:
"My marriage brought me neither happiness nor pain. My husband and I hardly spoke to each other. This wasn't because we were angry. We had nothing to say."

JIM DOUGHERTY:
"She was a most responsive bride—a perfect bride in every respect—except the cooking department."

"Our marriage was a good marriage.... I wonder if she's forgotten how much in love we really were."

Born in Los Angeles on April 12, 1921, making him five years Norma Jeane's senior, Jim Dougherty was a typical local boy from a working family who happened to live down the road from the future star when she was fifteen years old. At school Jim was a popular if not overly academic pupil; he was a star on the football team and served a spell as student president. His football skills won him a scholarship to college, but he turned it down to get a job and bring in the money his family needed. In 1941, the year he first started spending time with neighbor Norma Jeane, he had a job at Lockheed Aircraft which paid well enough for him to drive around in a blue Ford coupe that impressed the local girls. At that time he was working the day shift—later he worked nights—and living so close to VAN NUYS HIGH SCHOOL that his mom Ethel, good friend of Norma Jeane's legal guardian GRACE GODDARD, frequently asked him to drive Norma Jeane and friend BEEBE GODDARD home from school.

If Norma Jeane was impressed by this young man's CAR, the feature that probably most attracted her was his moustache; ever since as a little girl she had caught sight of a photo of a mustachioed man her mother said was her father, she had felt a fascination for men with moustaches.

Dougherty's initial intentions were apparently not of a romantic nature. He had a steady girlfriend, Santa Barbara beauty queen Doris Ingram, and Norma Jeane was just fifteen years old: "I noticed she was a pretty little thing, and she thought I looked angelic in white shirts, but she was only a child so far as I was concerned." But his intentions were less important than the plans of Grace Goddard, who had her reasons when she asked him to squire Norma Jeane to a Christmas dance at Adel Precision Products (231 South Olive Street, Burbank) where DOC GODDARD was working at the time—though some sources say the dance was at the Lockheed factory. This was a double date, with a pal of Jimmy's and Norma Jeane's step-sister Beebe. Through early 1942 the young couple courted, going on hikes in the Hollywood Hills, drives to local beauty spots, and occasional evenings parked on Mulholland Drive looking out over the shimmering lights of L.A, and the San Fernando Valley, during which "She very neatly held things in check."

THE WEDDING INVITATION SENT OUT BY MISS ANA LOWER:

Miss Ana Lower
requests the honor of your presence
at the marriage of her niece
Norma Jean [sic] Baker
to
Mr. James E. Dougherty,
Friday, the nineteenth of June
nineteen hundred and forty-two
at 8:30 o'clock P.M.
at the home of
Mr. and Mrs. Chester Howell
432 South Bentley Avenue
Los Angeles, California
Reception immediately after ceremony,
432 South Bentley Avenue,
Los Angeles, California.

The idea of marriage was not necessarily uppermost in the young man's mind, until one day his mother told him bluntly, "The Goddards are going to Virginia, and they're not taking Norma Jeane. She can't stay with Mrs. Lower [ANA LOWER, who was suffering heart problems], and that means she goes back to the orphanage until she's 18 ... Grace wants to know if you'd be interested in marrying her." Jim weighed it up, but it seems that this was an inevitable match. Apparently before he even asked her to marry him, he took her shopping for the ring.

Immediately after Norma Jeane's sixteenth birthday they found a miniscule place to live, a one-room bungalow at 4525 VISTA DEL MONTE, in the Sherman Oaks district, and moved in their scant possessions before the wedding day. Grace Goddard chose the home of some friends, apparently because she liked the winding staircase which she thought would make the ceremony "just like in the movies."

On the appointed evening, the ceremony was officiated by non-denominational minister Benjamin Lingenfelder. Conspicuously absent from the ceremony was Norma Jeane's mother, and, tellingly, the whole Goddard clan. Jim's brother Marion was best man, while Norma Jeane invited a girl she had only recently met at University High to be her matron of honor. Jim recalled that his bride "was shaking so she could hardly stand... She never let go of my arm all afternoon, and even then she looked at me as though she was afraid I might disappear while she was out of the room."

Marilyn later said she had six mothers weeping as she marched down the aisle. This was a forgivable exaggeration, but there were at least two in attendance. She was given away by Ana Lower, and the ceremony was attended by the BOLENDERS, her first foster parents.

Marrying at sixteen kept Norma Jeane out of the orphanage. It also meant she left school and suddenly found herself on her own in the world, an adult in the eyes of society. In a 1953 article "Marilyn Monroe Was My Wife," Jim Dougherty admitted, "She was so sensitive and insecure I realized I wasn't prepared to handle her. I knew she was too young, and that her feelings were very easily hurt. She thought I was mad at her if I didn't kiss her good-bye every time I left the house. When we had an argument—and there were plenty—I'd often say, 'Just shut up!' and go out to sleep on the couch. An hour later, I woke up to find her sleeping alongside me, or sitting nearby on the floor. She was very forgiving... I thought I knew what she wanted, but what I thought was never what she wanted. She seemed to be playing some kind of a part, rehearsing for a future I couldn't figure out."

The couple did not go away on a honeymoon. Norma Jeane did her best to be a housewife, though she did not particularly like housework and had practically no idea about cooking. Meanwhile, husband Jim continued his carefree carousing with his pals.

Dougherty always maintained that their sex life was full and satisfying. One *Playboy* article on their marriage paints a picture of Norma Jeane as a highly sexed young woman who was keen on sex in unusual, public places. Marilyn's recollections were different: "I wasn't very well informed about sex. Let's just say that some things seemed more natural to me than others. I just wanted to please him, and at first I found it all a little strange. I didn't know if I was doing it right."

In early 1943 the newlyweds moved from their cramped quarters to Jim's parents place at 14747 ARCHWOOD STREET in Van Nuys, to look after the property while the in-laws were away. Later that year they moved once again, not far away to a house on BESSEMER STREET.

Jim Dougherty and Norma Jeane Baker were married on June 19, 1942.

In late 1943 the young couple moved once more, as a result of Jim's joining the Merchant Marine. He was billeted to CATALINA ISLAND, off the California coast. They lived in the island's main town of Avalon where he supervised the training of new recruits. "I had more reason to be jealous of her that year on Catalina," said Jim. "Norma Jeane realized very well that she had a beautiful body and knew men liked it. She took Muggsy [her PET dog] for walks wearing a tight white blouse and tight white shorts, with a ribbon in her hair for a touch of color. It was just like a dream walking down the street." Their relationship deteriorated as he accused her of dressing too provocatively. Norma Jeane, though, who had no thoughts of being unfaithful, protested her innocence. His jealousy continued to mount after her enormous popularity at a big dance, fired up by Stan Kenton's famous band, at the Catalina Casino ballroom.

In the spring of 1944 Jim Dougherty was posted on to the Pacific, where he took active part in the South-East Asian war effort. Norma Jeane begged him not to go, fearing yet another abandonment after the many times during her childhood when she had been left or forced to move as a result of decisions beyond her power. According to some biographers, when she saw that there was nothing he could do, she suggested that they have a baby. Jim assured her that they would start a family on his return after the war. In 1976 Dougherty told *People* magazine, "If I hadn't gone into the Merchant Marine during World War II, she would still be Mrs. Dougherty today."

Norma Jeane moved in with her mother-in-law, who got her a job helping the war effort at the RADIO PLANE MUNITIONS FACTORY. Jim came home on leave for the Christmas and New Year break. After a long absence, they enjoyed each other's company, but this was to be the last time they ever lived together as man and wife. A few months earlier, Norma Jeane had posed for photographer DAVID CONOVER of the Army First Motion Picture Unit, and taken the very first steps towards a show business career. Warned by his mother that his wife was flirting dangerously with a career unbecoming to a young married woman, Jim wrote to Norma Jeane, "All this business of modeling is fine, but when I get out of the service we're going to have a family and you're going to settle down. You can only have one career, and a woman can't be two places at once."

He was quite right. As she told friends, at that time, "All I wanted was to find out what I was. Jim thought he knew, and that I should've been satisfied. But I wasn't. That marriage was over long before the war ended." The death-knell came on August 2, 1945, when Norma Jeane applied to join the BLUE BOOK MODELING AGENCY. When he returned from active duty for Christmas 1945, Jim realized exactly how things stood: "She was an hour late. She embraced me and kissed me, but it was a little cool. I had two weeks off before resuming shipboard duties along the California coast, but I don't think we had two nights together during that time. She was busy modeling, earning good money." Norma Jeane spent much of that time touring California beauty spots as a model for, and then lover of, Transylvanian-born photographer ANDRÉ DE DIENES. Before he returned to Asia to help the Merchant Marine complete its clean up operations after the war, Jim issued his wife with an ultimatum which she then ignored. Their marriage effectively over, Norma Jeane moved out of her mother-in-law's house.

His next leave, in April, brought the shock of finding his wife no longer living alone... but sharing her accommodation with her mother GLADYS BAKER, who had come down to Los Angeles after being released from the institution where she had been living. Dougherty apparently thought this was a cunning ruse by Norma Jeane to get rid of him: "She had made sure that Gladys would be living there on NEBRASKA AVENUE, that her mother would have my place in the only bed in the apartment." In fact, Norma Jeane had only succumbed under duress to her mother's repeated requests to come and stay.

Norma Jeane was well aware that the title "Mrs." was a severe handicap to her chances for making her Hollywood dreams come true. On May 14, 1946 Norma Jeane left L.A. to go and stay with another aunt of her guardian Grace McKee Goddard's, a widow called Minnie Willette who lived in Las Vegas. A

Marilyn and Jim Dougherty, 1943.

quick divorce could be obtained after fulfilling the relatively easy Nevada state residency requirement. It took two weeks for Jim, in Shanghai, to receive notification that his wife had filed for divorce. Jim made arrangements to return, and severed payment of the allowance he had been sending her regularly.

Jim was not present at the court hearing, held at 2 P.M. on September 13, 1946 before District Judge A. S. Henderson in Las Vegas. Norma Jeane filed for and obtained a DIVORCE on the formula grounds of "extreme mental cruelty that has impaired the plaintiff's health." Court records show that Norma Jeane played her role with aplomb: "My husband didn't support me and he objected to my working, criticized me for it and he also had a bad temper and would fly into rages and he left me on three different occasions and criticized me and embarrassed me in front of my friends and he didn't try to make a home for me."

Four years later Marilyn succinctly summed up the whole marriage to a reporter: "I married and was divorced. It was a mistake and he has since remarried."

Dougherty got a chance to see exactly what his first wife left him for some years later. After leaving military service he joined the police and was one of the police officers assigned to hold back the fans outside GRAUMAN'S EGYPTIAN THEATER as the stars arrived for the premiere of *THE ASPHALT JUNGLE* in 1950. Luckily Jim was spared the irony of actually coming face to face with his former wife, as Marilyn did not attend that night.

In a TV interview marking the thirty-fifth anniversary of Marilyn's death, Dougherty stated his belief that she died accidentally as a result of an overdose of sleeping pills taken out of desperation to get some sleep. As a one-time member of the Los Angeles Police Department, his acquaintances included Sergeant JACK CLEMMONS, the first police officer to arrive at Marilyn's Brentwood home after her death. Clemmons had actually called Dougherty that night to let him know what had befallen his first wife.

After Marilyn, Jim Dougherty married twice more. With Patricia Scoman Dougherty, to whom he was married between 1947 and 1972, he had three daughters, and a rule that his first wife's name could not be mentioned in the house. Dougherty's third wife was named Rita.

BOOKS:

*The Secret Happiness of Marilyn Monroe*, James E. Dougherty. Chicago: Playboy Press, 1976.

### JIM DOUGHERTY'S FAMILY

DOUGHERTY, BILLIE
Norma Jeane's sister in law, who under the name Elyda Nelson wrote an article on Marilyn that appeared in the 1952 issue of *Modern Screen*.

DOUGHERTY, EDWARD
Father.

DOUGHERTY, ETHEL MARY
Jim's mother was instrumental in carrying out the plan of her good friend Grace Goddard to arrange the marriage between Norma Jeane and her son Jim.

Norma Jeane moved in with her mother-in-law at 5254 Hermitage Street (now Avenue) in North Hollywood when her husband Jim was posted to Asia on a World War II tour of duty. At that time Ethel Dougherty had a job as a nurse at the Radio Plane Company in nearby Burbank. Mrs. Dougherty taught Norma Jeane how to drive and managed to get her a job at the Radio Plane Company, unwittingly putting her in the right place to be discovered by Army photographer David Conover later that year. Marilyn moved out of her mother-in-law's home in 1945, after her modeling aspirations were becoming concrete action and she started to go off on jaunts with Conover around California. Jim's mom voiced her disapproval, fearing that this was no way for a married woman to carry on. The obvious place for Norma Jeane to move to was back with Ana Lower, with whom she had remained in close contact all along.

DOUGHERTY, MARION
Jim's older brother was best man at his 1942 wedding to Norma Jeane.

DOUGHERTY, TOM
Jim's brother.

## DRAKE HOTEL
440 PARK AVENUE, NEW YORK

New York HOTEL where Marilyn took time off shooting of *NIAGARA* to spend a week with JOE DIMAGGIO in 1952. Although the couple each had a room for the sake of propriety, they spent their time in one.

## DREAMS

As a devout follower of Freudian PSYCHOANALYSIS, Marilyn was very attentive to her dreams and their hidden meanings. She read a great deal of Freud's writings on the subject.

Marilyn told biographers of a recurring dream she had in childhood which continued through her adult life:

> "I dreamed that I was standing up in church without any clothes on, and all the people there were lying at my feet on the floor of the church, and I walked naked, with a sense of freedom, over their prostrate forms, being careful not to step on anyone."

Another childhood dream is equally revealing: "I dreamed of myself walking proudly in beautiful clothes and being admired by everyone and overhearing words of praise."

## DRESSLER, MARIE
(1869–1934, B. LEILA MARIE KOERBER)

Marilyn often said she admired this actress more than any other. She was not alone—Louis B. Mayer once said that he had only worked with three great actors: GRETA GARBO, Spencer Tracy, and Marie Dressler.

Born in Canada, Dressler has a long and distinguished career in silent comedy movies before takes on a slew of starring roles in MGM comedy dramas during the thirties, around the time when young Norma Jeane went regularly to the movie matinees. Dressler's film credits include *Anna Christie* (1930), *Min and Bill* (for which she won an Oscar for Best Actress, 1930), *Tugboat Annie* (1933) and, opposite JEAN HARLOW, *Dinner at Eight* (1933). Perhaps her best remembered contribution to Hollywood lore, however, is the line "You're only as good as your last picture."

## DRINK

Given the choice, it was always champagne. She drank a little too much of the stuff at her first WEDDING, aged sixteen, and never looked back. She was still drinking copious amounts the last days she was alive. Her favorite champagne was vintage Dom Pérignon 1953. At other times Marilyn ran on plenty of water and a constant supply of coffee.

There were times during her life when Marilyn drank very heavily. In 1958, for example, she fell down a flight of stairs, bruised her ankle and cut her hand on a broken whisky tumbler. Often, Marilyn drank not so much to forget as to somehow numb herself into SLEEP. The effects of her drinking, mixed with her intake of BARBITURATES were not always predictable or controllable. Many of the occasions when people thought she was drunk, she was actually groggy from the drugs she had been ingesting.

At varying times in her life Marilyn imbibed:

BREAKFAST DRINKS:

coffee
milk
carrot juice
tea with gin
Bloody Marys
grapefruit juice

SOFT DRINKS:

Ginger ale

HARD DRINKS:

vodka martinis
scotch whisky
bourbon
vermouth
wine
daiquiris
sherry

## DRUGS

MARILYN:
"When you're on a film you've got to look good in the morning so you've got to get some sleep. That's why I take pills."

JOHN HUSTON:
"The girl was an addict of sleeping tablets and she was made so by the goddam doctors."

ARTHUR MILLER:
"Doctors had gone along with her demands for new and stronger sleeping pills even though they knew perfectly well how dangerous this was... there were always new doctors willing to help her into oblivion."

According to DONALD SPOTO, Marilyn began to be addicted to sleeping pills in early 1954, after she took some to combat jetlag-induced sleeplessness. However, the evidence is that by that time she had already been using pills for as many as eight years—Marilyn told AMY GREENE that she had been taking pills since the age of seventeen or eighteen. Certainly by 1950, on the threshold of her big break, Marilyn resorted to drugs to combat the overwhelming anxiety she suffered before screen tests. Since 1950 Marilyn had had a ready source of pills from her friend, confidant, and sometime mouthpiece, columnist SIDNEY SKOLSKY, who worked out of Schwab's drugstore and could be relied on to provide sleeping pills and the like. JOE DIMAGGIO reputedly referred to Sidney and Marilyn as "pill-pals."

The use of BARBITURATES, amphetamines, and narcotics was common in Hollywood. It was an exciting and dangerous thing to do, and there was far less awareness of the harmful long-term effects of substance abuse. Drugs ultimately claimed the careers and lives of many famous stars, from Errol Flynn to JUDY GARLAND and MONTGOMERY CLIFT.

Marilyn used barbiturates, hypnotics, and anti-anxiety drugs. Apart from one documented occasion in 1962, when she met DR. TIMOTHY LEARY, she did not take pills for recreation or thrill-seeking, but as a way of combating her crippling inability to SLEEP, to calm her frayed nerves, or to tackle the debilitating FEAR and anxieties which assailed her. SUSAN STRASBERG writes, "People mixed champagne and pills all the time, to increase the effectiveness of the pills. As for Marilyn, she had the burdens of her fear, her timidity, her insecurity and her unusually agonizing monthly periods that rendered her literally incapable of moving." Once the addictive spiral began, she began to take yet more pills to counteract the effects of other drugs she had taken.

Marilyn was visibly affected by the aftereffects of sleeping pills in 1954, when she regularly turned up late and groggy to work on *THERE'S NO BUSINESS LIKE SHOW BUSINESS*—this was a time of high emotional tension as her recent marriage to Joe DiMaggio was running anything but smoothly.

After escaping the immediate dangers of Hollywood and moving to New York in late 1954, Marilyn embarked on a year of self-discovery and acting experimentation, but she still needed sedatives and barbiturates to sleep. She continued to wash down the barbiturates with champagne, hoping that this would give her the chance of a good night's rest. Eight years later, on the set of *SOMETHING'S GOT TO GIVE*, Marilyn was still fraught enough to swallow valium pills with champagne.

Despite warnings about the dangers of her drug abuse, Marilyn seemed unable to cut down her intake except for short periods—there was always some new crisis or her perennial insomnia to bring her back. Gynecologist Leon Krohn (*see* DOCTORS) warned Marilyn that if she wanted to have children, she should do something about her intake of drink and drugs. After her second miscarriage, Marilyn was consumed with fear that she had brought this on by her intake of Amytal, a barbiturate (medical name amobarbital). By the late fifties, Marilyn was trapped in a dangerous spiral of having to take drugs to sleep, different drugs in the morning to battle through the grogginess, and then take more pills during the day to control her anxiety. Typically, Marilyn scheduled no appointments before midday; the hangover from Nembutal took all morning to clear.

Marilyn's dependence on barbiturates and sleeping pills increased even further during tumultuous shooting on *THE MISFITS* in 1960. Her Los Angeles doctors sent out stronger drugs, 300 milligram doses of Nembutal (sodium pentobarbital), three times the standard dosage for treating insomnia, and so strong that just seven of these pills would have been enough to kill a person without her tolerance. When she felt that these weren't enough, she persuaded doctors to inject Amytal directly, in quantities not far off those administered for general anesthetics. In the mornings Marilyn was so groggy that makeup man ALLAN "WHITEY" SNYDER had to start making her up while she lay in bed. Rumors circulated that Marilyn had to be walked around her bedroom for hours to get her sufficiently clear-headed, and some biographers write that the only way to get her to actually wake up was to put her in the shower.

In the last years of her life, Marilyn increasingly switched to chloral hydrate, more commonly known as "Mickey Finn" knockout drops. These were prescribed to her by psychoanalyst RALPH GREENSON in an attempt to reduce her dependency on the barbiturates she habitually took. Greenson apparently also prescribed Dexamyl, a potent combination of Dexedrine (a now banned stimulant) and amobarbital, a barbiturate. He remarked in correspondence that her dependence was such that she resembled an addict, yet "did not seem to be the usual addict." There were times, though, when her behavior was very much that of the addict, seeking new ways to administer the drugs she craved, including injection. Reputedly in the last month of her life, Marilyn's regular doctor, Dr. Hyman Engelberg, attended Marilyn almost daily to give her so-called "youth shots," which altered her mood and gave her redoubled energy.

On August 3, 1962, just two days before her death, Marilyn had two prescriptions for Nembutal, her regular barbiturate sleeping pills, filled at her local pharmacy, from two different doctors (Dr. Engelberg and Dr. Seigel) at the San Vicente pharmacy on 12025 San Vicente Boulevard.

On her last day alive, Marilyn probably took pills of phenobarbital and chloral hydrate. By mid-afternoon that day, she was seen on the beach walking with a little difficulty, and her speech was slurred. The autopsy showed levels 10 times the normal dose of the first drug and 20 times the normal dose of the second drug: blood levels of 4.5 mg Nembutal and 8 mg of chloral hydrate, and a much higher concentration of 13 mg of Nembutal in Marilyn's liver. Disparities in these figures have been used to support allegations of foul play in Marilyn's DEATH and speculation that the lethal dose of drugs was administered either by injection or by enema. Controversy has even surrounded the exact list of drugs that Marilyn had in her bedroom at the time, with some commentators suggesting that only half of the pill bottles found on the bedside table were ever listed by the coroner on his toxicology report (Librium, Nembutal, chloral hydrate, Phenergan and others without labels).

## DUNAWAY, FAYE (B. 1941)

Faye Dunaway played the Marilyn character of Maggie in the 1974 TV version of ARTHUR MILLER's 1964 play, *AFTER THE FALL*. Like Marilyn, Dunaway was an actress with a reputation for being "difficult." She also played Hollywood legend JOAN CRAWFORD in *Mommie Dearest* (1981). She won an Oscar for *Network* (1976), and was nominated two other times for *Bonnie and Clyde* (1967) and *Chinatown* (1974).

## DUSE, ELEANORA (1858–1924)

Italian actress Eleonara Duse was considered one of the greatest talents of the stage, along with French actress Sarah Bernhardt. Marilyn greatly admired Duse; she read her biographies and, it is said, identified with her. For many years, Marilyn put up a photograph of "La Duse," along with images of her other HEROES, in the hotels and homes where she lived. Eleanora Duse was often cited as an exemplar of the dramatic arts by LEE STRASBERG.

E

Marilyn attended the premiere of *East of Eden* (1955) in the role of celebrity usherette.

## EAST OF EDEN

Marilyn attended the premiere of the James Dean movie *East of Eden* at the Astor Theater in New York on March 9, 1955 as a celebrity usherette. Proceeds from the occasion were donated by director ELIA KAZAN to the ACTORS STUDIO. The movie was worth an Oscar to lead Jo Van Fleet, and brought nominations for Kazan, Dean, and writer Paul Osborn.

## EDUCATION

Marilyn's formal education was piecemeal to say the least. During her itinerant CHILDHOOD she attended no less than nine different SCHOOLS before dropping out of tenth grade to marry first husband JAMES DOUGHERTY.

While she was in school, academic achievement was not on top of her list of priorities. She once told photographer JOCK CARROLL, "I remember in mathematics I used to write down figures, just any figures, instead of trying to do the questions. I used to think it was a waste of my brain, using it up with mathematics, when I could be imagining all sorts of wonderful things."

Marilyn was embarrassed about her lack of formal education. She felt ashamed of making elementary spelling and punctuation mistakes, knowing that legions of reporters and detractors would be only too happy to conclude that she was no more than the dumb blonde of her screen image.

Yet Marilyn was actually very smart and curious. She had a real turn of wit, and throughout her adult life she voraciously pursued knowledge, following an eclectic path outlined by her various BENEFACTORS, DRAMA COACHES, and by the intellectuals she was drawn to, starting with ARTHUR MILLER. NATASHA LYTESS described Marilyn as "a mental beachcomber, picking the minds of others and scooping up knowledge and opinions."

GLORIA STEINEM paints this quest in a more desperate light: "Her searches after knowledge were arbitrary and without context. It was as if she was shining a small flashlight of curiosity into the dark room of the world."

## EGHAM, ENGLAND

Between July and November 1956, while in England during shooting of *THE PRINCE AND THE SHOWGIRL* (1957), Marilyn and ARTHUR MILLER made their home at Parkside House, on the Englefield Green estate in Egham, not far from the Queen's second home at Windsor and about an hour's drive from London. They rented a Georgian mansion from Lord North, publisher of the *Financial Times*, and his actress wife Joan Carr. As well as a verdant and mature ten acres complete with rose garden, the five-bedroom house had oak beams. Before they arrived, MILTON GREENE made sure that one of the bedrooms was repainted white for Marilyn, and that blackout blinds were fixed over the windows to help ensure that Marilyn could get her beauty sleep. In true British door-stop journalism style, the gates to the property were besieged by newsmen for most of Marilyn's stay.

Pictures splashed over all the newspapers were not enough for a sixty-strong gang of blazer-clad students from the nearby Shoreditch Training College. Three days after Marilyn arrived, they sneaked into the grounds and congregated beneath Marilyn's bedroom window in the hope of enticing her out—in some reports, they serenaded her too. Marilyn, under strict orders from bodyguards, did not appear.

## EINSTEIN, ALBERT (1879–1955)

Einstein was a man Marilyn could look up to, so along with her other HEROES she had a photograph of him on display in the many places she lived. This photo even had a personal inscription: "To Marilyn, with respect and love and thanks, Albert Einstein," though this was most probably a practical joke perpetrated by actor ELI WALLACH. According to JAMES HASPIEL, Marilyn's suite at New York's Waldorf Towers in 1955 contained not one but two photographs of the scientist. According to SHELLEY WINTERS, Albert Einstein made it onto Marilyn's list of men she would most like to sleep with.

The two eventually met in Terry Johnson's 1982 stage play *INSIGNIFICANCE*, made for the screen in 1985.

## EISENSTAEDT, ALFRED

Polish-born photographer who emigrated to the United States where he became a leading photographer for *Life* magazine. "Eisie," as he was known in the trade, photographed Marilyn for the magazine in 1953.

## EL PALACIO APARTMENTS,
8491-8499 FOUNTAIN AVENUE, APARTMENT F

In 1947, down on her luck starlet Marilyn Monroe was invited to stay with LUCILLE RYMAN and JOHN CARROLL at their Hollywood apartment on La Cienega Boulevard and Fountain Avenue.

## ELIZABETH II, QUEEN
(B. 1926, ELIZABETH ALEXANDRA MARY WINDSOR)

Marilyn was presented to the newly crowned Queen Elizabeth II during her trip to England to film *THE PRINCE AND THE SHOWGIRL* (1957), at the Royal Command Performance of *The Battle of the River Plate* (known in the U.S. as *The Pursuit of the Graf Spee*) on October 29, 1956. It was held at the Empire Theater in Leicester Square. Even for royalty Marilyn contrived to arrive late, slipping in only just before the doors were closed. Twenty screen stars lined up to be presented to the queen—including JOAN CRAWFORD, BRIGITTE BARDOT, and Anita Ekberg—but Marilyn as ever stole the show. The queen complimented Marilyn on her fine curtsey and asked her, "How do you like living in Windsor?" A rather nervous Marilyn replied "What?... I understand we lived at Englefield Green." The queen explained

Marilyn met Queen Elizabeth II on October 29, 1956. Next in line to meet the Queen is Victor Mature.

that this was next door, so they were neighbors—and indeed Marilyn and Arthur's house at EGHAM abutted Windsor Great Park.

## EMERSON JUNIOR HIGH SCHOOL

Norma Jeane Baker attended grades seven through nine at this SCHOOL on 1650 Selby Avenue, West Los Angeles, repeating part of the seventh grade to make up for time she had lost because of being in and out of so many schools. There is some dispute among biographers whether she started in the school in 1938 or 1939, but they all agree she graduated on June 27, 1941. The school drew its pupils from a wide area of West Los Angeles, from the working-class area of Sawtelle where Norma Jeane lived with ANA LOWER, to the prosperous gated community of Bel Air. The pupils from the wrong side of the tracks—of which Norma Jeane was one—had a certain stigma attached to them. Elementary biology teacher Mable Ella Campbell remembered Norma Jeane as "very much an average student, but she looked as though she wasn't well cared for. Her clothes separated her a little bit from the rest of the girls. In 1938 she wasn't well developed. Norma Jeane was a nice child, but not at all outgoing."

Twenty years later Marilyn recalled, "I was very quiet, and some of the other kids used to call me The Mouse. The first year at Emerson, all I had was the two light blue dress-suits from the orphanage. Aunt Ana let them out because I'd grown a little, but they didn't fit right. I wore tennis shoes a lot, because you could get them for 98 cents—and Mexican sandals. They were even cheaper. I sure didn't make any best-dressed list. You could say I wasn't very popular."

Puberty changed all that. In 1939 Norma Jeane put on a growth spurt and reached her adult height of 5 feet 5 inches. She filled out too, and soon people took notice of her. "Even the girls paid a little attention to me just because they thought, 'Hmmm, she's to be dealt with!' I had to walk to school, and it was just sheer pleasure. Every fellow honked his horn, you know, workers driving to work, waving, and I'd wave back. The world became friendly."

To her precocious physical development Norma Jeane added her childhood familiarity with the arts of cosmetics, taught her by legal guardian GRACE MCKEE GODDARD. She would spend hours preparing herself before school, and it paid dividends as suddenly she became very popular with the boys, who would take her out for sodas, or perhaps entice her up into the hills for a night-time view of the twinkling city lights in the hope of a kiss.

Her earliest known boyfriend was Chuck Moran, who introduced Norma Jeane to the delights of dancing at the pier. Marilyn told a biographer, "We danced until we thought we'd drop, and then, when we headed outside for a Coca-Cola and a walk in the cool breeze, Chuckie let me know he wanted more than just a dance partner. Suddenly his hands were everywhere! But that made me afraid, and I was glad I knew how to scrape with the best of them—life at the orphanage taught me that. Poor Chuck, all he got was tired feet and a fight with me. But I thought, well, he isn't entitled to anything else. Besides, I really wasn't so smart about sex, which was probably a good thing."

The final meeting of the English press with Arthur Miller, Marilyn, Vivien Leigh, and Laurence Olivier before Marilyn and Miller flew back home to New York, 1956.

When she graduated from ninth grade in June 1941, her grades were not impressive; not surprisingly, with her shyness in speaking up and the stammer she had, she came perilously close to failing Rhetoric and Spoken Arts. She did, however, shine in Journalism, a course given by a Miss Crane. One of many features Norma Jeane wrote that year for the school newspaper, *The Emersonian*, according to biographer DONALD SPOTO, had an air of prophecy about it:

> "After tabulating some 500-odd questionnaires, we have found that 53 percent of the gentlemen prefer blondes as their dream girl. Forty percent like brunettes with blue eyes, and a weak seven percent say they would like to be marooned on a desert island with a redhead.... According to the general consensus of opinion, the perfect girl would be a honey blonde with deep blue eyes, well modeled figure, classic features, a swell personality, intelligence, athletic ability (but still feminine) and she would be a loyal friend. Well, we can still dream about it."

At this school Norma Jeane had parts in two school plays. She was a king in *Petronella*, and a prince in a Valentine's Day musical production.

## ENGLAND

On July 14, 1956, less than two weeks after their wedding, Marilyn and ARTHUR MILLER flew to England. Arthur had a British production of his play *A View from the Bridge* to attend, while Marilyn was getting ready for production of *THE PRINCE AND THE SHOWGIRL* (1957) at PINEWOOD STUDIOS.

A scrimmage of over two hundred newsmen (four hundred in some reports) awaited them at the airport, barely restrained by more than seventy police officers who also had to handle three thousand fans who had gathered to welcome the world's best-known newlyweds. Heading the welcome party were LAURENCE OLIVIER and his wife VIVIEN LEIGH. None of them could leave until Marilyn gave the baying crowds an impromptu press conference, described at the time as "the largest conference in English history."

The day after her arrival, Marilyn battled her way through four thousand adoring fans to the Savoy Hotel, for a press conference with Olivier about *The Prince and the Showgirl*, while police officers had to join hands to restrain the boisterous crowds.

This level of interest continued for the duration of Marilyn's stay in the U.K.; wherever she went and whatever she did, it made the front pages. While she was in the country, *BUS STOP* (1956) opened to rapturous reviews. *The Times* called her, "a talented comedienne, and her sense of timing never forsakes her.... There is about her a waif-like quality, an underlying note of pathos which can be strangely moving." Regular trips to the theater were well documented, as were the couple's cycle ride around Windsor Great Park and trip to Brighton, where they strolled along the seaside promenade.

Marilyn couldn't even go SHOPPING without being mobbed; after fainting in Regent Street on August 25, she arranged her shopping expeditions outside regular business hours.

During their English sojourn Arthur and Marilyn lived in Parkside House, EGHAM. The house was spacious, set in beautiful grounds, and a convenient distance from the studios. It was also next door to the country home of Queen ELIZABETH II at Windsor.

Magnum photographer Elliott Erwitt took this picture of Marilyn during a break in the filming of *The Seven Year Itch* (1955).

## ERWITT, ELLIOTT (B. 1928)

PHOTOGRAPHER who took what is perhaps the best-known still from the many great pictures taken by MAGNUM photographers during filming of *THE MISFITS* (1961), with Marilyn sitting between CLARK GABLE and MONTGOMERY CLIFT; behind are JOHN HUSTON, ELI WALLACH, FRANK TAYLOR, and ARTHUR MILLER.

In common with almost all of Marilyn's photographers and cinematographers, Erwitt was struck by the way she bewitched the camera: "In spite of the fact that she wasn't terribly attractive to look at, she usually came out extremely well in photographs."

## ESTATE, THE

When she died, Marilyn left an estate estimated at $930,626, to be divided up among the beneficiaries of her last WILL: $183,941 was held in actual monies, $65,400 in real and personal property in Los Angeles, $2,200 in her checking account at the Beverly Hills branch of the City National Bank. The bulk of the estate consisted of Marilyn's interest in MARILYN MONROE PRODUCTIONS and her 10 percent profit share of *SOME LIKE IT HOT* (1959), *THE PRINCE AND THE SHOWGIRL* (1957), and *THE MISFITS* (1961).

During the sixties the estate continued to increase as monies came in from deferred salaries and profit share, but these sums were later dwarfed by the vast amounts made through licensing of the Marilyn name and image and worldwide merchandising.

Yet three years after Marilyn's DEATH, rumors circulated that far from dying a millionaire, Marilyn's wealth was just a "one million dollar myth." None of her beneficiaries had been paid, there were many outstanding claims, and almost all of the money was being paid in taxes. FRED LAWRENCE GUILES writes, "Marilyn's estate at the time of her death was insolvent. However, those films she had produced herself or in which she owned an interest would bail out her estate and put it solidly in the black." None of the beneficiaries named by Marilyn in her will received any money until 1971.

Columnist SHEILAH GRAHAM asked, "All that insecurity and agony, for what?" Some people believed that even in death, Marilyn was still being exploited by advisers and representatives. Long-time executor Aaron R. Frosch successfully fought a 1981 lawsuit accusing him of embezzling $200,000 from the Marilyn estate.

In 1982 attorney Roger Richman put the affairs of the estate in order, registered trademarks and copyright on Marilyn's likeness, and licensed her image for an enormous spread of merchandise and the modern day campaign of selling Marilyn.

Tom Ewell and Marilyn in *The Seven Year Itch* (1955).

The main beneficiary of the millions of dollars that have accrued from sales of Marilyn merchandise is ANNA STRASBERG (LEE STRASBERG's second wife, who never knew Marilyn but was bequeathed the legacy when Lee died in 1982).

Today the Curtis Management Group Worldwide (CMG) represent the Marilyn estate and are responsible for authorizing all "licensed" Marilyn merchandise. They introduce themselves on their Web site as "the home of properties and personalities considered to be among the most prestigious in the licensing industry. . . . CMG Worldwide secured its position during the 1970s as the premier company for representing the families and estates of deceased celebrities."

The company has copyrighted the names "Marilyn" and "Norma Jeane," so in theory it is a breach of copyright to even write this movie star's name. CMG is also being proactive in prohibiting the publication of any photos (for merchandising purposes) of Marilyn in which she is depicted wearing either fur or feathers, or photographs of her smoking; one Internet photo vendor had to retouch a photo they were selling to change the feathers to a satin sheet. There are unconfirmed reports that the estate is also trying to ban any references to Marilyn's marriages and divorces, her physical problems, and "alleged chemical dependencies," and of course, the circumstances of her death.

## EWELL, TOM
(1909–1994, B. S. YEWELL TOMPKINS)

The man led sorely into temptation by the happy-go-lucky girl upstairs, Marilyn Monroe, in *THE SEVEN YEAR ITCH* (1955). Ewell found Marilyn professional and courteous—during a kissing scene she apologized to him for the smell of cough medicine she was taking after picking up a lung infection while shooting the famous white skirt scene. Marilyn's professionalism was all the more surprising considering the great emotional upheaval in her life, as her marriage to JOE DIMAGGIO was in its final throes.

Ewell began his career in the theater. The mid-fifties saw him reprising his own Broadway roles on film not just with Marilyn, but with JAYNE MANSFIELD as well, in *The Girl Can't Help It*. As well as his own TV show in the early 60s, highlights of his career include *Adam's Rib* (1949) and *The Great Gatsby* (1974).

# F

Two classic Marilyn expressions: Left, publicity picture, 1950. Right, publicity shot for *Clash by Night*, 1951.

## FACE

BERT STERN:
"My eye roved her face, searching. I couldn't find the secret of her beauty in any one feature. She didn't have a great nose like Liz Taylor, or perfect lips like Brigitte Bardot. She didn't have gorgeous almond-shaped eyes like Sophia Loren. And yet she was more to me than all of them put together."

WILLIAM TRAVILLA:
"She adored her own face, constantly wanted to make it better and different. Everything she did in that regard, by the way, was right at the time. She once told me, 'I can make my face do anything, same as you can take a white board and build from that and make a painting.'"

PAULINE KAEL:
"Her face looked as if, when nobody was paying attention to her, it would go utterly slack— as if she died between wolf calls."

Marilyn's BODY may have attracted more than its fair share of attention, but to countless camera lenses her face shone with a luminescence that few, if any, actresses have ever matched. According to SUSAN STRASBERG, "A fine mist of down on her face captured a kind of halo, a nimbus of light around her: photographs seemed to canonize her, to offer a creature almost ethereal as well as sensual." Journalist A. T. McIntyre was equally struck by his gaze upon her countenance: "It is not special lighting which brings out Monroe and leaves her supporting actors to fade into the woodwork—she is astonishingly white, so radically pale that in her presence you can look at others about as easily as you can explore the darkness around the moon."

Marilyn's trademark quivering pout was apparently the result of a friendly piece of advice from EMMELINE SNIVELY, who ran the modeling agency she first signed up to. Because "there isn't enough upper lip between the end of your nose and your mouth," Ms. Snively told Marilyn to lower her smile by pushing her top lip downwards. It worked.

GEORGE MASTERS, Marilyn's longtime hairdresser, considered that "Marilyn Monroe had the most beautiful mouth ever. No one has ever been able to convey so much sex appeal with just one feature." Photographer RICHARD AVEDON agreed: "Marilyn never closed her mouth. A lot of girls had great laughs, but she took it to the furthest point, so that it became iconic—the gasping mouth, the laughing mouth, the open mouth, which represented the possibility of pleasure."

According to ARTHUR MILLER, when nervous Marilyn's top lip would flick, "like the lip of a bridled horse, a prideful tick of self-possession."

Her other trademark feature, the beauty mark on her upper lip, had its secrets too. Makeup man ALLAN "WHITEY" SNYDER said, "We wouldn't always put it in the same spot. Sometimes we had it on the other side. If we hadn't darkened it, nobody would know it was there. But she thought she could see it."

Her cornflower blue eyes blazed in Technicolor and glowed in black and white photography. George Masters reported she made sure that he prepared hand-trimmed eyelashes for her. However, Marilyn thought that her ears were on the large side, and generally kept them covered up.

## FAME

MARILYN:
"I think when you are famous every weakness is exaggerated."

Marilyn wanted the adulation of millions, and that's exactly what she got. Survey after

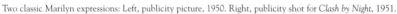

Marilyn waves to the crowds at Ebbets Field, 1959. Photograph by Bob Henriques.

survey places Marilyn as both the century's most popular female performer (the American Film Institute) and greatest sex symbol (*Playboy*).

"I want to be a big star more than anything. It's something precious," Marilyn said during filming for GENTLEMAN PREFER BLONDES (1953). And yet fame was part of the cocktail that fed Marilyn's FEARS, something she desperately wanted but which repelled her too.

ALLAN "WHITEY" SNYDER, referring to that period, said, "She was frightened to death of the very public that thought her so sexy. My God, if only they knew how hard it was for her."

Publicly, Marilyn played the fame game and did the publicity campaigns. Out and about to promote *Gentlemen Prefer Blondes*, she told a *New York Times* journalist what fame felt like: "I'm thrilled of course. Everything's so wonderful—people are so kind—but I feel as though it's all happening to someone right next to me. I'm close—I can feel it—I can hear it—but it isn't really me."

Friend and newspaper columnist SIDNEY SKOLSKY, who was Marilyn's regular escort to public engagements when JOE DIMAGGIO didn't want to go, wrote in mid-1953, "Success has helped The Monroe. But she hasn't lost that rare combination of being part of the crowd as well as aloof at the same time."

By 1955, the burden of fame had begun to weigh more heavily: "I guess nobody trusts a movie star. Or at least this movie star. Maybe in those first few years I didn't do anything to deserve other people's trust. I don't know much about these things. I just tried not to hurt anybody, and to help myself."

After a decade of being America's most recognizable woman, Marilyn became desperately protective of her privacy. In 1961, when photographers came to her apartment in Los Angeles, she made them swear they would never divulge her address.

In the last years of her life, Marilyn increasingly reflected on fame. In her last interview with *Life* journalist RICHARD MERYMAN, she reflected on its ultimate effects: "Fame is certainly only a cause for temporary and partial happiness—not really for a daily diet. That's not what fulfils you. It warms you a bit, but the warming is temporary. It's like caviar, but not when you have it every meal."

In the same article Marilyn pronounced what many people perceive to be an adieu to her film career: "Fame will go by and—so long, fame, I've had you! I've always known it was fickle. It was something I experienced, but it's not where I live."

Marilyn was one of a very small number of the famous to become a legend in their own lifetime. Two weeks before her death, Marilyn told studio executive PETER LEVATHES, "in a way I'm a very unfortunate woman. All this nonsense about being a legend, all this glamor and publicity. Somehow I'm always a disappointment to people."

Not everyone thought that fame was a bad thing for Marilyn, though. BEN HECHT, with whom she worked on an autobiography project in 1954, felt that Marilyn was "*saved* by Hollywood. Fame saved her. The spotlight beating on her twenty-four hours a day made the world seem livable to her.... It was the only world in which she could thrive. The real world held only hobgoblins for her, terrors that harried her nights."

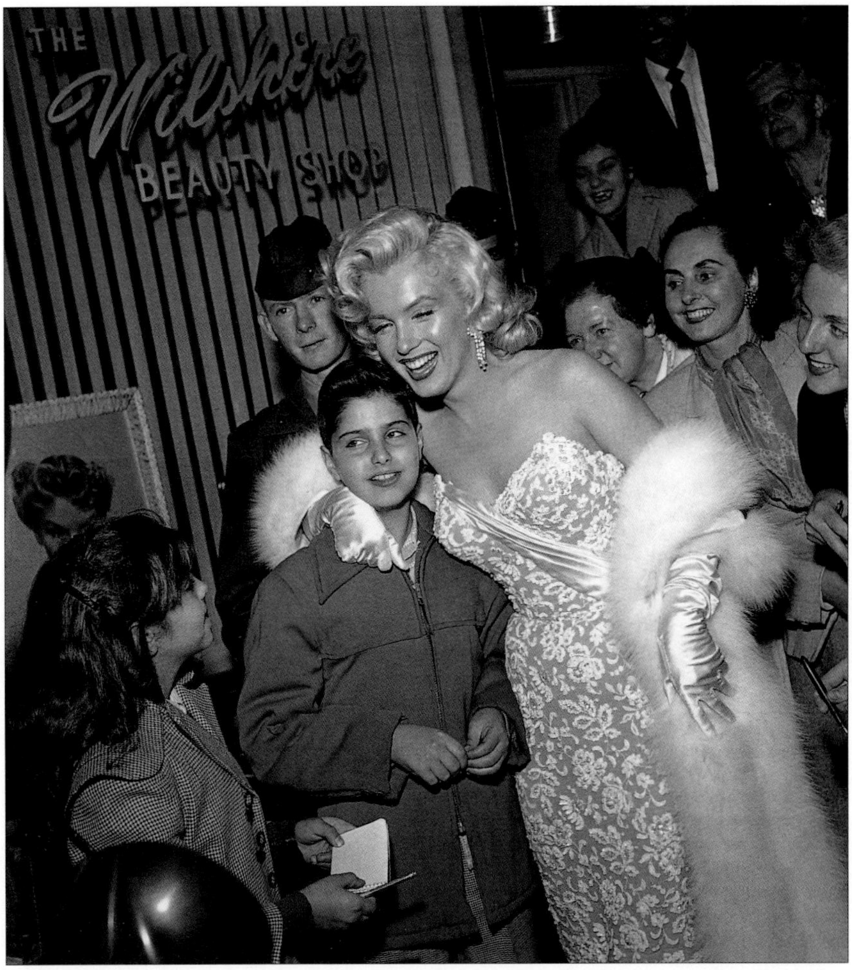


Marilyn surrounded by fans outside The Wilshire Beauty Shop before the premiere of *How to Marry A Millionaire* (1953).

## FAMILY

Marilyn said her ancestry was Irish, Scottish, and Norwegian. Grandmother DELLA MAE HOGAN's roots went back to Dublin, Ireland, while grandfather OTIS ELMORE MONROE was of Scottish stock. The Norwegian origins are only true if Marilyn's real father was MARTIN EDWARD MORTENSEN, but this has never been proven. Marilyn occasionally claimed that she was a descendant of U.S. President James Monroe.

The ancient history of Marilyn's family is one of the areas where biographers disagree.

Because of her troubled CHILDHOOD on the fringes of many families, and less than a year spent living with her mother GLADYS BAKER, as a young adult, Marilyn relished the glimpses of "normal" family life opened up to her through relationships. Friendships with the mother and sister of early love FRED KARGER, JOE DIMAGGIO's son, the STRASBERG family, ARTHUR MILLER's father and, in the last years of her life, the family of psychiatrist RALPH GREENSON, were very important to Marilyn.

In the absence of her own stable family, like many stars Marilyn gathered an entourage around her, her own traveling (and hired) care structure. On the day she first reported for work in Nevada to shoot her final completed motion picture, *THE MISFITS* (1961), this consisted of coach PAULA STRASBERG, secretary MAY REIS, personal masseur RALPH ROBERTS (whom she sometimes referred to as "the brother"), publicist RUPERT ALLAN, personal make up artist ALLAN "WHITEY" SNYDER, hairdresser AGNES FLANAGAN, chauffeur Rudy Kautzky, wardrobe supervisor Sherlee Strahm, and body makeup artist Bunny Gardel. PAT NEWCOMB took over after Allan resigned.

## FANS

MARILYN:
"I like people. The 'public' scares me, but people I trust."

Marilyn was almost always happy to sign autographs, pose for photographs, or do a twirl for an 8mm movie camera. Wherever she went, the fans were there. Within hours of her arrival at a hotel, the PRESS got wind of the fact, and soon enough there were hundreds of fans outside. They were waiting for her to appear, hoping to catch a glimpse, snap a photo, or get an autograph. She was known to be pursued into restrooms, with fans passing autograph books under the cubicle. In New York, Marilyn even had a group of hardened fans known as the "MARILYN SIX," who kept up a vigil for Marilyn whenever she was in town. JAMES HASPIEL, who did not belong to this group, also spent many hours waiting for Marilyn to appear, and was

*Next page*: Marilyn photographed by George Barris in one of her many Pucci blouses, 1962.

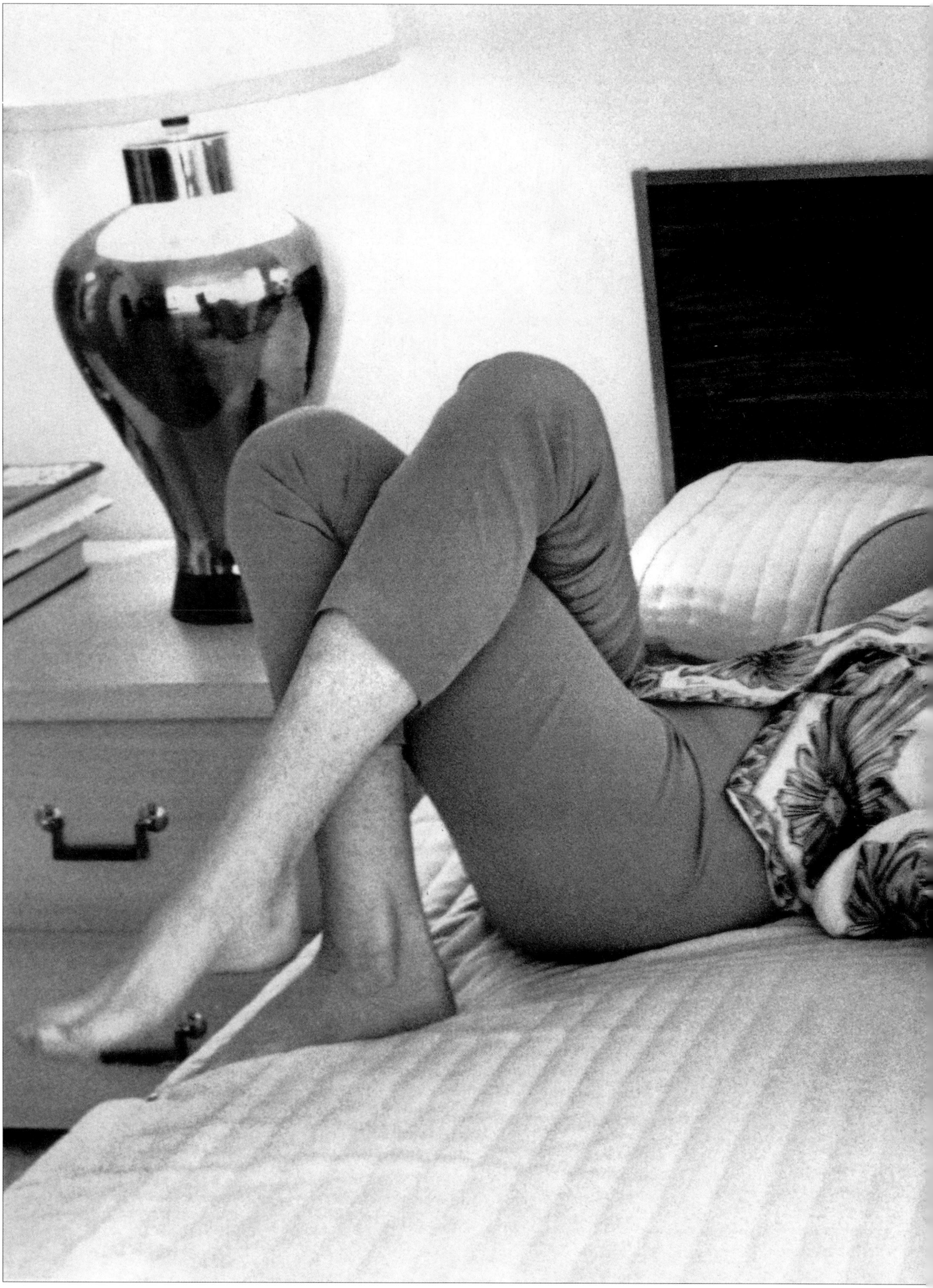

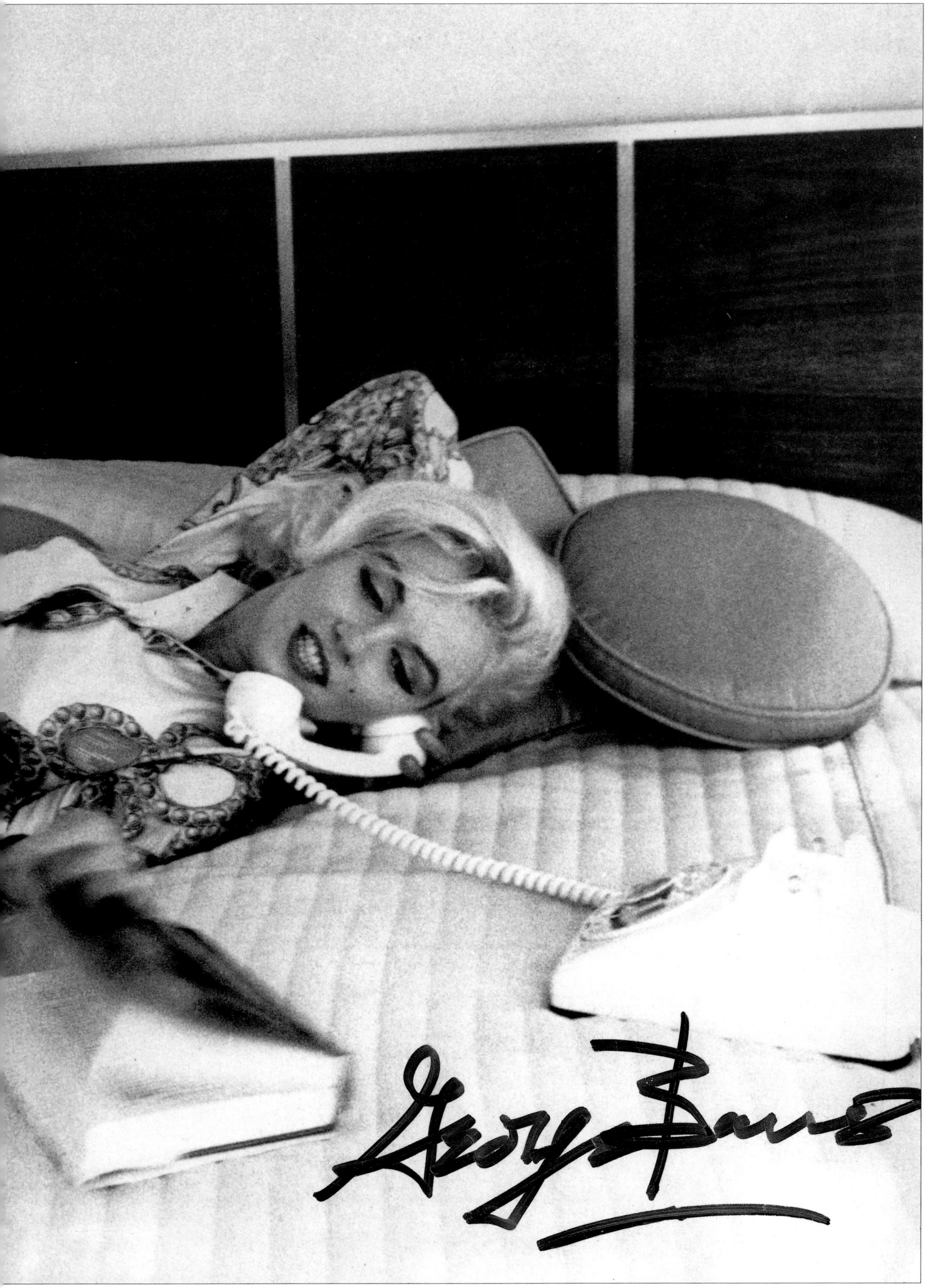

rewarded with taxi rides and peeks into the star's private life.

Even before she began landing leading roles, her small but perfectly formed appearances in THE ASPHALT JUNGLE (1950) and ALL ABOUT EVE (1950) had led to an avalanche of fan mail at Fox studios. Bulging with up to three thousand letters a week, Marilyn's mailbag was already heavier than all but the studio's most established stars.

In 1952, the year Marilyn made top billing, she was receiving five thousand fan letters a week. By the summer of 1953, after HOW TO MARRY A MILLIONAIRE, this had swollen to over twenty-five thousand fan letters a week.

In his autobiography *Timebends*, ARTHUR MILLER described how Marilyn worked her fans: she could handle a crowd "as easily and joyfully as a minister moving among his congregation. Sometimes it was as though the crowd had given her birth; I never saw her unhappy in a crowd, even some that ripped pieces of her clothes off as souvenirs."

Marilyn was genuinely aware of her fans' adulation, which at times was a definite antidote to her lifelong feelings of low self-esteem: "I love them for it. Somehow they know that I mean what I do, both when I'm acting on the screen and when I meet them in person."

Miller explains, "She relied on the most ordinary layer of the audience, the working people, the guys in the bars, the housewives in the trailer bedeviled by unpaid bills, the high school kids mystified by explanations they could not understand, the ignorant and—as she saw them—tricked and manipulated masses. She wanted them to feel they'd gotten their money's worth when they saw a picture of hers."

But there were times, more frequent after the novelty wore off, when the last thing Marilyn wanted, as she went about her personal business, was to have to turn on the smile and "do a Marilyn." At times like these Marilyn resorted to a DISGUISE—usually a headscarf and dark glasses, in later years supplemented by a black wig—to conserve some degree of freedom. Even then, however, anonymity was a question of luck. Near her New York apartment, people recognized her. Sometimes, when passers-by stopped to ask if she was Marilyn Monroe, she answered, "No, I'm Mamie Van Doren," or "SHEREE NORTH," who at that was time being touted as the "new" Marilyn. Some biographers relate that even in disguise, Marilyn had a secret urge to be recognized—she reputedly once berated a taxi driver who failed to spot the woman behind the wig.

The well-intentioned fans who loitered outside Marilyn's hotels or gathered to get a glimpse of her before and after premieres and press conferences, also thronged the entrance to the hospital where she was recovering from nervous exhaustion.

Marilyn continues to receive the adulation and devotion of millions of fans. Almost every nation has its fan clubs; the Internet offers hundreds of fan sites and dozens of Marilyn discussion groups. Every year the Marilyn Remembered Fan Club holds a memorial service at the WESTWOOD MEMORIAL PARK CEMETARY where Marilyn is buried, attracting visitors from around the world as well as people who knew Marilyn and wish to pay their continuing respects.

### A Few Fan Clubs

Marilyn Remembered
contact: Greg Schreiner
1237 Carmona Street
Los Angeles, CA 90019
USA

Marilyn Then and Now International
contact: Ray Zweidinger
97-07 63rd Road, Suite 15H
Rego Park, NY 11374
http://www.geocities.com/Hollywood/Chateau/3987/

The Legend Club For Marilyn Monroe
contact: Dale Notinelli
2401 Artesia Blvd. #185
Redondo Beach, CA 90278
USA

Marilyn Monroe International Fan Club
contact: Ernie Garcia
842 Linden Avenue
Long Beach, CA 90813
USA

Marilyn Reporter
contact: Debbie Jasgur
1648 S. Crystal Lake Dr., Suite 40
Orlando, FL 32806
USA

Marilyn Monroe Australian Fan Club
contact: Jane Guy
P.O. Box 60
Richmond, Victoria 3121
Australia

The Marilyn Lives Society
contact: Michelle Finn
14 Clifton Square
Corby, Northants NN17 2DB
UK
http://www.doheny.demon.co.uk/mls.html

Many of these clubs produce newsletters full of Marilyn facts, interviews with people who knew her, information on "Marilyn sightings" on TV screens and in magazines book reviews, etc.

The Internet offers many sites where Marilyn fans rendezvous to exchange news and views about their heroine. The oldest such forum is the Marilyn Monroe mailing list, run by Peggy Wilkins (http://www.glamournet.com/legends/Marilyn/index.html).

## FASHION

Marilyn's style of dress, both on and off screen, was scandalous to many self-proclaimed upholders of society's morals. But while some women looked on in shock at Marilyn's revealing outfits, many more were paying attention to the styles she wore and went right out to buy something similar. Marilyn helped to push the boundaries of what was acceptable to wear. There was collateral damage—no less than JOAN CRAWFORD cried scandal at the sight of Marilyn slinking to pick up a PHOTOPLAY award in 1953—but the stores couldn't get in enough copies of the white, pleated dress that billows up around her in THE SEVEN YEAR ITCH (1955). Marilyn was one of the first female icons to be photographed wearing jeans; she had been wearing them ever since her wartime job at the RADIO PLANE MUNITIONS FACTORY, she wore them to her UCLA evening classes, and she most famously appeared in a jeans outfit in THE MISFITS (1961).

Marilyn in the famous sheer gold lamé Travilla gown in which she appeared briefly in *Gentlemen Prefer Blondes* and then later wore to the Photoplay Awards where she took home the award for "Fastest Rising Star of 1952."

Marilyn expressed her fashion philosophy succinctly in a 1960 interview with *Cosmopolitan*: "I like to be really dressed up, or really undressed. I don't bother with anything in between." Sometimes her outfits were a combination of the two, as studio designers and seamstresses spent hours sewing Marilyn into creations a size too small precisely to create the effect that she was unclothed. Notoriously, Marilyn often went without UNDERWEAR altogether in order to avoid pantylines. She flouted the staid conventions of the post-war years by appearing in dresses with plunging necklines, strapless gowns, skimpy shorts, and tight skirts. But whatever CLOTHES she happened to be wearing—or not wearing—the effect was calculated and devastating.

BOOKS:

*Hollywood Costume Design*, David Chierichetti. New York: Harmony Books, 1976.
Features Marilyn costumes by Rene Hubert, Orry-Kelly, and Travilla.

*Marilyn Monroe Paper Dolls*, by Tom Tierney. New York: Dover Publications, 1979.
Thirty-one outfits from Marilyn's movies to be cut out and attached to a Marilyn paper doll.

*Fashion in Film*, Regine and Peter W. Engelmeier, eds.; Eileen Martin, trans. Munich: Prestel-Verlag, 1990.

*Star Style—Hollywood Legends as Fashion Icons*, Patty Fox. Los Angeles: Angel City Press, 1995.

The impact of fashions worn by ten top actresses, including Marilyn.

## FASHION DESIGNERS

In addition to the top movie COSTUME DESIGNERS, many of whose creations she wore to industry events and premieres, Marilyn wore CLOTHES designed by other fashion creators:

Elgee Bove
Ceil Chapman
JEAN-LOUIS
John Loper
JOHN MOORE
George Nardiello
Norman Norell
Emilo Pucci
WILLIAM TRAVILLA

Marilyn leant herself to the backlash against Christian Dior when he introduced the H-line, otherwise known as the flat look, claiming that it was a personal offense to women like her.

## FATHER

Most biographers ascribe paternity of Norma Jeane either to MARTIN EDWARD MORTENSEN, married to GLADYS BAKER at the time she conceived, or CHARLES STANLEY GIFFORD, a fellow worker at Consolidated Film Industries, with Gifford the more likely candidate. GLORIA STEINEM has no doubt that it was C. Stanley Gifford; in her opinion, he left Gladys on Christmas Eve, the day she told him she was pregnant, after offering her money and then advising her to count her blessings that she was already married.

The full list of potential fathers is considerably longer: Gladys was not short of male admirers at work, so the names of Raymond Guthrie, Clayton MacNamara, and Harold Rooney have also been mentioned.

As a young girl Norma Jeane latched onto a handsome man with a mustache in a photograph her mother kept, which Gladys had once told her was a picture of her father. In her make-believe world, this man became a fantasy presence in her life, waiting for her at home as she walked home from school, or visiting her in hospital the time she had her tonsils out. Later, Marilyn wrote, "I could never get him in my largest, deepest daydream to take off his hat and sit down."

Biographers continue to cast doubt that Marilyn had concrete knowledge of who her father really was. This opinion is contradicted in part by a letter Norma Jeane wrote to GRACE MCKEE GODDARD in February 1943, revealing plans to meet her daddy:

> "Oh Gracie, you just can't imagine how excited I am, to think I am really going to see him at last. Golly I just hope that he will want to see me. I think he might though, after he gets used to the idea. Ever since I have found out, it has practically made a brand new person of me. It's something I have to look forward to with the greatest pleasure, seeing him I mean. I had my fortune told by a friend just for fun and guess what? My fortune read that I was going to come in contact with him and he was going to become very fond of me etc. Oh doesn't that sound wonderful, if only things would work out that way, I'm just praying with all my heart and soul they will..."

The man Marilyn believed to be her father was Gifford. Although she made numerous attempts to contact him, there is no hard evidence that they ever met or spoke, with some biographers speculating that these attempts always took place at times when Marilyn felt particularly insecure or feared she was about to be abandoned by the people she loved.

On the first occasion, when husband JAMES DOUGHERTY was on leave in 1944, Norma Jeane called a number, said her name, and announced that she was Gladys's daughter. Soon after, she put the phone back in its cradle and told Jim that the man had hung up on her. In Jim's words, after the call, "We were closer than ever. I was her lover, husband, and father, the whole tamale."

The second time was in early 1951, just weeks after lover and benefactor JOHNNY HYDE had died of heart disease. Marilyn told her drama coach, NATASHA LYTESS, that she had learned the true identity of her father and wanted moral support as she went to meet him. They drove out beyond PALM SPRINGS, until Marilyn pulled up at a service station, from where she placed a call to her father. She returned to the car in tears because he had refused to see her. A similar sequence of events was repeated a few weeks later, this time with SIDNEY SKOLSKY. In 1961 Marilyn twice drove back to the Red Rock Dairy near PALM SPRINGS, once with RALPH ROBERTS, once with publicist PAT NEWCOMB.

## FATHER FIGURES

Foster fathers ALBERT WAYNE BOLENDER, ERWIN "DOC" GODDARD, HARVEY GIFFEN, and SAM KNEBELCAMP were the male influences in young Norma Jeane's life, but this imaginative young girl had a more romantic solution in her mind's eye. Norma Jeane fantasized that her real father was CLARK GABLE, the handsome actor who bore more than a passing resemblance to the photo her mother had once told her was of her father.

Marilyn had a pet name she used with all the most important lovers in her life: "Daddy." She called first husband, JAMES DOUGHERTY, by this name, especially in moments of insecurity. Hollywood agent JOHNNY HYDE, who at the age of fifty-three, dedicated the last year of his life to advancing Marilyn's career, was very much in the father figure mold. Marilyn's second and third husbands were paternal figures too: twelve years older than Marilyn, JOE DIMAGGIO had traditional views on the roles of men and women, and was a man used to being in control. ARTHUR MILLER, eleven years older than Marilyn, was an intellectual mentor par excellence.

After moving to New York, acting guru LEE STRASBERG was a major father figure to Marilyn. A man notoriously parsimonious in his compliments, Strasberg nevertheless publicly and privately expressed his belief in her talent. In exchange for this esteem-boosting belief, Marilyn trusted him implicitly, both in acting and in life. Indeed, Marilyn asked Lee to "give her away" to Arthur Miller at their Jewish wedding ceremony.

A friend of Marilyn's from her New York days told one biographer of a fantasy Marilyn revealed during a party game. It consisted of dressing up in a black wig, finding and seducing her father, and then asking him, "How do you feel now to have a daughter that you made love to?"

GLORIA STEINEM claims that a recurrent theme in Marilyn's life was guilt at leaving or killing a father figure. It happened with Johnny Hyde, and it happened again after filming of *THE MISFITS* (1961)—Clark Gable died of a heart attack less than two weeks after they had finished working together. Marilyn's feelings of guilt were exacerbated by public comment about her: Hollywood gossip the first time, Hollywood columnists the second time. On both occasions she was so upset that she made SUICIDE ATTEMPTS.

## FAVORITES

The following is a list of some of Marilyn's favorite things. Like anyone else, Marilyn's tastes changed over the years, so not all of these "favorites" were long-term loves in Marilyn's life.

Actors: John Barrymore, MARLON BRANDO, CHARLIE CHAPLIN, JOAN CRAWFORD, Olivia de Havilland, MARIE DRESSLER, CLARK GABLE, GRETA GARBO, CARY GRANT, JEAN HARLOW, CHARLES LAUGHTON, Tyrone Power, GINGER ROGERS, Will Rogers, and RICHARD WIDMARK
Artists: Botticelli, El Greco, Goya, Michelangelo, and Picasso,
Book: *How Stanislavsky Directs* by Michael Gorchakov
Colors: beige, black, red, and white
Drink: Dom Pérignon 1953
Film Performances: *THE ASPHALT JUNGLE* (1950) and *DON'T BOTHER TO KNOCK* (1952)
Food: Cavier
Italian dinner: fettuccini Leon and veal piccata
Musicians: Louis Armstrong, Earl Bostick, Ludwig von Beethoven, and Wolfgang Amadeus Mozart
Perfume: Chanel No. 5

Marilyn's favorite beverage was Dom Pérignon 1953.

Photograph: Cecil Beaton's photo of Marilyn in her white dress
Restaurant: Romanoff's
Singers: Ella Fitzgerald and Frank Sinatra
Snack (when not dieting): hot dogs
Store: Bloomingdale's
Writers: Fyodor Dostoyevsky, John Keats, Arthur Miller, J. D. Salinger, George Bernard Shaw, Walt Whitman, Tennessee Williams, and Thomas Wolfe

## FBI

Marilyn came under intense FBI scrutiny in 1955, when she began to be frequently seen in the company of Arthur Miller, then under investigation by the House Un-American Activities Committee. After that date her movements were meticulously documented, from the people she saw in New York to her continuing interest in all things Russian. Donald Spoto records that J. Edgar Hoover himself ordered special monitoring of any attempt by Marilyn to leave the country. Marilyn's business partner Milton Greene and his wife Amy were also temporarily suspected to be subversives.

At the time of writing, eighty pages of FBI files are available for public consultation on the Web at http://www.fbi.gov/foipa/foipa.html. These consist mainly of summaries and photocopies of articles written about Marilyn in the press. Many of the comments are taken from Walter Winchell's column. The first file is dated April 27, 1956; paragraphs deemed too sensitive are blacked out. There is a great deal of material about her relationship with Miller, including allegations that Marilyn Monroe Productions was filtering money through to the Communist Party.

## Fears

Marilyn:
"I've always been frightened by an audience—any audience. My stomach pounds, my head gets dizzy and I'm sure my voice has left me."

Allan "Whitey" Snyder:
"She's frightened to death of the public who think she is so sexy. My God, if they only knew."

Arthur Miller:
"She seemed able to see only that she had been victimized and betrayed by others, as though she were a mere passenger in her life. But like everyone else, she was also the driver, and how could it be otherwise?"

In the movie industry, Marilyn's performance anxiety was the stuff of legend. The mere idea of learning lines sent her into paroxysms of fear. Much of her infamous lateness on set was because it took her an eternity to get herself confident enough to overcome her fears. She would break out in red blotches over her chest and arms and neck, and she would start stammering. Almost all of her directors had to struggle to keep her on track during the laborious process of shooting. George Cukor once tried to soothe her frayed nerves by reassuring her and telling her not to be nervous. Marilyn replied, "I was born nervous!" Things were compounded on later films by Marilyn's growing conviction that her director was victimizing her, deliberately mentally torturing her, and no amount of reasoning would persuade her otherwise. The incredible thing is that despite the crushing burden of fear she carried, Marilyn's performances belie no sign of nerves.

Marilyn's performance anxiety and underlying low self-esteem were not reserved just for the cameras—live audiences and the assorted ranks of the press could be even more intimidating. Marilyn suffered a tearful panic attack minutes before presenting an Academy Award in 1951. She was almost paralyzed by fear during filming of *Clash by Night* (1952) that same year. Louella Parsons had Marilyn on her radio show a number of times, and on almost every occasion she vomited just before going on the air. Even with experience and accolades, Marilyn's nerves did not go away. Henry Weinstein, producer of *Something's Got to Give*, recalled that Marilyn was so petrified that she sometimes stopped her car on the way into the studio, got out, and threw up.

The only time she performed in front of enormous adoring crowds and felt completely at ease was the time she was far, far from Hollywood, on a tour entertaining U.S. troops stationed in Korea. On this occasion she also conquered the agoraphobia which periodically made it difficult for her to go out.

Marilyn's lifelong fear of abandonment was not surprising after a childhood in which her guardians came and went with bewildering frequency, often without explanation. Norma Jeane was desperate when first husband James Dougherty was due to be sent away to Asia with the Marines. He recalled, "Each time I left it was a destructive thing that hit her extremely hard. She wanted something, *someone* that she could hold onto all the time."

Further legacies of childhood were unquenchable feelings of inadequacy, a desire for perfection she could never achieve, and fear of disappointing the people around her.

Donald Spoto writes that from when she left to live in New York, "The fear that she was not indeed herself, that there were major parts of her person unknown and unexplored, was her central concern."

Allan "Whitey" Snyder pins down one source of Marilyn's anxiety to a fear that her attractiveness and reputation as a sex symbol was pure sham. It was only after the hours of makeup and ministrations, as she put on the Marilyn mask, that she was able to perform the role the world expected of her.

Marilyn was also afraid that despite getting more of life's experience under her belt, she was not getting any wiser; on the contrary, she sometimes believed that her mistakes just got bigger in her personal life, particularly in her relationships. She was very concerned that this was a sign of "weak-mindedness," the mental illness that she feared she had inherited from her mother. Arthur Miller seems to concur, at least in part, that Marilyn's demons were innate, when he says in his autobiography that she suffered "the terrors she was born to."

## Feingersh, Ed

Photojournalist who shot "A Day in the Life of Marilyn Monroe" for the July 1955 issue of *Redbook* magazine, including famous shots of Marilyn waiting for the subway. Feingersh actually spent an entire week with Marilyn in March 1955, documenting among other things her elephant ride at the circus (*see* Madison Square Garden) and a trip to Broadway to see the Tennessee Williams play *Cat on a Hot Tin Roof*.

## Feldman, Charles K. (1904–1968)

Marilyn officially signed with the Feldman's Famous Artists Agency only after her contract with William Morris lapsed at the end of 1953, but Feldman had already been instrumental in negotiating Marilyn's second contract with Twentieth Century-Fox in 1951. Originally trained as a lawyer, Feldman had a high profile in Hollywood, combining his talent agency duties with a producing role. With Billy Wilder he co-produced Marilyn's 1954 movie *The Seven Year Itch*, as well as earning credits on films such as *The Big Sleep* (1946), *A Streetcar Named Desire* (1951), and *What's New Pussy Cat?* (1965).

Feldman's colleague Hugh French handled Marilyn's 1953 "separation" from longtime drama coach Natasha Lytess.

Feldman reputedly lent Marilyn more than just his professional guidance; her alleged affair with director Elia Kazan is said to have taken place at Feldman's home, and there have even been rumors that Marilyn and Feldman had an affair of their own many years later, not long after her divorce from Arthur Miller.

Feldman was the driving force behind the huge party for Marilyn at fashionable Romanoff's restaurant in November 1954. The sight of Hollywood's elite turning out to celebrate her must have delighted Marilyn at a time of great upheaval in her life—divorce from Joe DiMaggio, and increasing bitterness with Fox.

It was probably Feldman's ability to wear several hats at the same time that hastened Marilyn's decision to look elsewhere for representation. As well as being her agent and producer, Feldman's agency worked almost exclusively with Fox, which did not necessarily work to her benefit as she battled to rewrite her distinctly disadvantageous contract.

At the suggestion of new business partner Milton Greene, with whom she was starting Marilyn Monroe Productions at the same time, Marilyn left Feldman and the Famous Artists Agency to join MCA. In breaking her contract, Marilyn had to repay a $23,000 advance Feldman had given her to sustain the various expenses of finding a suitable new film project, to pay off Natasha Lytess, and to cover other professional needs. It took Feldman five years to recoup this money.

## Fiction

Not only has Marilyn provided inspiration for numerous characters of stage and film but she has also inspired countless characters in fiction. Thinly-veiled versions of Marilyn are likely to appear in the majority of novels set in Hollywood during the fifties, in stories about vulnerable and suicidal movie stars, and in many of the fictionalized accounts of the KENNEDYS. A good clue that Marilyn is the inspiration behind a character is the name: if both first name and last name begin with the same letter, chances are it's a pseudo-Marilyn.

SOME FICTIONAL MARILYNS

*The Sensualists.* Ben Hecht. New York: Messner, 1959.
*The Shy Photographer*, Jock Carroll. New York: Stein and Day, 1964.
*The Symbol*, Alvah Bessie. New York: Random House, 1966.
*The Golden Venus*, Martin Ryerson. New York: Award Books, 1968.
*The Director*, Henry Denker. New York: Richard Baron Publishing, 1970.
*Kill All the Young Girls.* Brett Halliday. New York: Bantam Doubleday Dell, 1973.
*The Idolators*, William Hegner. New York: Trident Press, 1973.
*Tinsel*, William Golding. New York: Delacorte Press, 1979.
*Moviola*, Garson Kanin. New York: Simon and Schuster, 1979.
*The Missing Person*, Doris Grumbach. New York: Putnam, 1981.
*Double Take*, Vadis Margener. New York: Playboy Press, 1982.
*Marilyn's Daughter*, John Rechy. New York: Carroll and Graf, 1988.
*Atomic Candy*, Phyllis Burke. New York: Atlantic Monthly Press, 1989.
*Candle in the Wind*, George Bernau. New York: Warner Books, 1990.
*MMII: The Return of Marilyn Monroe*, Ben Staggs. New York: Donald Fine, 1991.
*The Immortals*, Michael Korda. New York: Poseidon Press, 1992.
*Queen of Desire*, Sam Toperoff. New York: HarperCollins, 1992.
*The Angel Carver*, Roseanne Daryl Thomas. New York Random House, 1993.
*Shades of Blonde*, ed. Carole Nelson Douglas. New York: Forge, 1997.
*Mondo Marilyn: An Anthology of Fiction and Poetry*, ed. Lucinda Ebersole and Richard Peabody. New York: St. Martin's Press, 1995.
*The Marilyn Tapes*, E. J. Gorman. New York: Tom Doherty Associates, 1995.
*The Elvis and Marilyn Affair*, Robert S. Levinson. New York: Forge, 1999.
*Blonde,* Joyce Carol Oates. New York: Ecco Press/HarperCollins, 2000.

## FIELD, FRED VANDERBILT

This member of the prominent New York family and his Mexican wife, Nieves, acted as guides to Marilyn on her furniture buying trip to MEXICO in February 1962. This association was closely monitored by the FBI, apparently concerned about her liaison with "America's foremost silver-spoon Communist," who was in voluntary exile in Mexico City. The Fields found Marilyn to be "warm, attractive, bright, and witty; curious about things, people, and ideas—also incredibly complicated."

In his biography, *Goddess*, ANTHONY SUMMERS reports that Field discussed politics with Marilyn, and learned that "she and Robert Kennedy discussed the Kennedys' desire to fire J. Edgar Hoover."

## FIFTH HELENA DRIVE

With the help of JOE DIMAGGIO, on the weekend of March 8–9, 1962 (February in some accounts), Marilyn moved into her last residence—and the only house she ever owned—at 12305 Fifth Helena Drive, off Carmelina Avenue in Brentwood, Los Angeles. She bought the 2300 square foot one-storey three-bedroom house with a view over Los Angeles for just under $90,000 ($77,500 is sometimes quoted) from previous owners William and Doris Pagan. She paid for the premises with a $37,500 fifteen-year mortgage from City National Bank of Beverly Hills on which she was making monthly payments of $320.

Marilyn bought this home after encouragement from her analyst Dr. RALPH GREENSON, who was perhaps trying to instill some permanence in Marilyn's dangerously unstable existence. EUNICE MURRAY, who was the person who actually found the property, said, "The doctor thought the house would take the place of a baby or a husband, and that it would protect her." Marilyn's stand-in EVELYN MORIARTY puts a more sinister slant on this turn of events: "She was talked into this house—by Mrs. Murray and by Dr. Greenson, as she told us several times while we were filming *SOMETHING'S GOT TO GIVE*." Whatever the circumstances of how she came to buy the property, a rather modest home for one of Hollywood's most bankable stars, Marilyn was very proud of the house and the improvements she made, and keenly showed visitors around. She enjoyed the seclusion of the place, she happily shopped for furnishings and plants, and enjoyed working in the large garden. Although a number of photographers took pictures of her outside the house, notably GEORGE BARRIS, Marilyn refused permission to take photographs of her inside, saying, "I don't want everybody to see exactly where I live."

Set on a quiet cul-de-sac, "this fortress where I can feel safe from the world," as Marilyn once called it, was an L-shaped Spanish colonial-style construction very similar to the home of Dr. Greenson, with an oval swimming pool, a small guest house, and a garage. The Latin motto "cursum perficio" laid in Mexican-style tiles outside the front door has been seized upon by some biographers as some sign of Marilyn's desire to be laid to rest at this house. It was in fact installed by the original builders thirty years before Marilyn moved in. The expression, meaning "My journey's end" in some translations, "I complete the course" in others, originally comes from the Bible.

The interior decoration also took its lead from Dr. Greenson's house, following a Mexican theme and featuring furniture which Marilyn bought in Mexico during the trip in February 1962. Many of the authentic pieces had not yet been delivered by the time Marilyn died. The interior was characterized by adobe stucco walls, cathedral-beamed ceilings, fireplaces in both the living room and master bedroom, and casement windows. Like many of the places where Marilyn lived, the predominant color scheme was white: white walls, and white wool carpets in the bedrooms and living area. The kitchen Marilyn installed had a brick floor, wooden cabinets, Mexican ceramic wall tiles and a blue refrigerator. Sadly, she did not live there long enough to complete the project, as was evident by the piles of papers and personal possessions that built up in the corners.

Since Marilyn's death the home has changed hands many times. The first inquiry was registered by Mrs. Betty Nunez and her husband Gilbert on the day that Marilyn's death was announced. It took them seven months and a court battle to be given the go-ahead to complete the purchase, at five times the asking price of similar properties in the district. When they bought the house they purchased much of the furnishings Marilyn had bought and installed. In May 1997 Mrs. Nunez's children sold many pieces of Marilyn's original furniture at auction, with Marilyn's gardening hat fetching between $4,000 and $6,000, and her dressing-room mirror changing hands for between $15,000 and $20,000.

A number of owners have indicated that they had intentions to turn the house into a Marilyn museum. Although this has never transpired, the location remains a place of pilgrimage for Marilyn's greatest fans.

The last time the house was sold, its asking price was $1.3 million. It was completely remodeled and refurbished in 1998.

For a virtual tour, go to http://home1.gte.net/omrgav/tourwelcome.html.

(*see* HOMES)

## FIFTY-SEVENTH STREET APARTMENT
444 E. 57TH STREET, NEW YORK

In January 1957 Marilyn and ARTHUR MILLER moved into this thirteenth floor apartment with dramatic views over the East River. With the help of designer JOHN MOORE, Marilyn's remodeling work included painting all the walls white and installing floor to ceiling mirrors in the living room/dining area, created by knocking two rooms together. The sofa, deep chairs and furniture were also white, providing a perfect setting for the WHITE PIANO that accompanied Marilyn to many of the places she lived. In Arthur's studio he hung a photograph of Marilyn taken by JACK CARDIFF during their time in England working on *THE PRINCE AND THE SHOWGIRL* (1957). Although he had said that this was his favorite photograph of Marilyn, he left it behind. It has been said that Marilyn never quite felt that the place looked finished, even though she was to keep this apartment after Arthur moved out in 1960, and was often having decoration work done. For almost all of the time Marilyn used this apartment she had a live-in maid named LENA PEPITONE.

Marilyn once confided to RUPERT ALLAN that one day she had come close to throwing herself off the ledge of this thirteenth floor apartment, in distress after the break up of her marriage, and apparently after reading press allegations that CLARK GABLE's wife believed Marilyn responsible for the actor's death. What stopped her was that she saw a woman in a brown tweed suit, on the sidewalk and didn't want to "do her in too," though in one account she said she didn't throw herself out because she knew the woman.

(*see* HOMES)

## FILMS

Marilyn appeared in twenty-nine completed films and was working on number thirty when she died. She made twenty-four of those movies during the first half of her fifteen year career, up to and including 1954, before she rebelled against the studio system for greater control over the material she performed.

Some confusion surrounds which was Marilyn's first picture. *DANGEROUS YEARS* (1947) was made after *SCUDDA HOO! SCUDDA HAY!* (1948) but was released first. Some sources affirm that Marilyn's first film appearance was not in either of these movies, but in *THE SHOCKING MISS PILGRIM* (1947); if this was the case, her performance as a switchboard operator wound up on the cutting room floor. Other films in production at this time, in which contract player Marilyn may have featured, were *YOU WERE MEANT FOR ME* (Marilyn was reputed to be part of the chorus line during dance numbers), *The Challenge*, *Mother Wore Tights*, and *Green Grass of Wyoming*.

### FILM FIRSTS

First screen test: July 19, 1946
First movie she worked on: *Scudda Hoo! Scudda Hay!*
First close-up: *Dangerous Years*
First songs: *Ladies of the Chorus*
First screen kiss: *Ladies of the Chorus*
First mention in a review: *Ladies of the Chorus*
First lead role: *Don't Bother to Knock*

### MARILYN'S FILMS

(dates refer to first release):

*Dangerous Years* (1947)
*Scudda Hoo! Scudda Hay!* (1948)
*Ladies of the Chorus* (1948)
*Love Happy* (1950)
*A Ticket to Tomahawk* (1950)
*The Asphalt Jungle* (1950)
*All About Eve* (1950)
*The Fireball* (1950)
*Right Cross* (1950)
*Hometown Story* (1951)
*As Young As You Feel* (1951)
*Love Nest* (1951)
*Let's Make It Legal* (1951)
*Clash by Night* (1952)
*We're Not Married* (1952)
*Don't Bother to Knock* (1952)
*Monkey Business* (1952)
*O. Henry's Full House* (1952)
*Niagara* (1953)
*Gentlemen Prefer Blondes* (1953)
*How to Marry a Millionaire* (1953)
*River of No Return* (1954)
*There's No Business Like Show Business* (1954)
*The Seven Year Itch* (1955)
*Bus Stop* (1956)
*The Prince and the Showgirl* (1957)
*Some Like It Hot* (1959)
*Let's Make Love* (1960)
*The Misfits* (1961)

INCOMPLETE:
*Something's Got to Give* (Filming in 1962)

BOOKS:
*The Films of Marilyn Monroe*, Michael Conway and Mark Ricci. New York: The Citadel Press, 1964, 1988.
*Marilyn Monroe: A Life on Film*, John Kobal London: Hamlyn, 1974.
*The Films of Marilyn Monroe*, Richard Buskin. Lincolnwood, IL: Publications International, 1992.

## FILMS MARILYN CONSIDERED OR WANTED

***Baby Doll***
Marilyn was very keen to land the role of a Southern child bride of a cotton miller that made a star of CARROLL BAKER, in this 1956 Warner Brothers production directed by ELIA KAZAN and starring Karl Malden and ELI WALLACH. Apparently TENNESSEE WILLIAMS, who adapted his own play for the screen, wanted Marilyn, but Kazan said it had to be Baker. Marilyn worked as a "star usherette" at the December 4, 1956 premiere of *Baby Doll*, a benefit for the ACTORS STUDIO.

***The Blue Angel***
This was a project Fox proposed to Marilyn after *THE PRINCE AND THE SHOWGIRL* (1957)—or one which ARTHUR MILLER briefly considered working on, depending on the source. The modernized version of MARLENE DIETRICH's 1930 classic starring May Britt came out in 1959.

***Born Yesterday***
Judy Holliday won an Oscar in this 1950 GEORGE CUKOR-directed screen version of a popular Garson Kanin play. Holliday, who had played the role on Broadway, was third choice after Rita Hayworth and Jean Parker. Marilyn apparently screen tested for the role of Billie Dawn during her brief six month contract at Columbia, but studio chief HARRY COHN had already decided not to renew their option. A decade later Marilyn had a second chance, when FRANK SINATRA tried to interest her in a musical remake of the movie.

***Breakfast at Tiffany's***
AUDREY HEPBURN was nominated for a best actress Oscar in 1961, but it could have been Marilyn. TRUMAN CAPOTE, who wrote the original novel, wanted Marilyn to play Holly Golightly, but Paramount preferred Hepburn in the Blake Edwards movie. Producer Martin Jurow has said that Marilyn was sounded out and appeared to be very interested before PAULA STRASBERG advised her against playing a lady of dubious virtue.

***The Brothers Karamazov***
For as long as she was an actress, Marilyn had the ambition of playing Grushenka. JOHNNY HYDE, NATASHA LYTESS, and MICHAEL CHEKHOV had all encouraged her in this desire. As early as 1950, Johnny Hyde reputedly spoke with DORE SCHARY, head of production at MGM, about Marilyn playing this character. Marilyn corresponded with Arthur Miller about the possibility, years before they became romantically involved. At the 1956 press conference when Marilyn announced that her production company had hired Laurence for *The Prince and the Showgirl*, she repeated her wish to play the part of Grushenka, only to be ridiculed by a smart-alec journalist who asked her to spell "Grushenka." Not long after they married, there was preliminary talk of Miller writing a screenplay version of the novel for Marilyn. Instead, Marilyn was a spectator when MGM brought out the movie in 1958, in an adaptation written and directed by Richard Brooks, with Maria Schell as Grushenka. Gracious as ever, Marilyn's comment on Schell's performance was, "Maria was wonderful in it."

***Can-Can***
In 1958 TWENTIETH CENTURY-FOX asked Marilyn to star opposite Maurice Chevalier in this musical version of a Broadway show. The 1960 finished product starred Frank Sinatra, SHIRLEY MACLAINE, Maurice Chevalier, and Juliet Prowse.

***Clara Bow***
Marilyn apparently attempted to secure the rights to the life story of this famous 1920s actress, perhaps the first sex symbol with mass market appeal, the original "It" girl. Clara Bow (1905–1965), whose career was brought to an end by mental illness, did not want her story to be told on-screen and refused her permission. The closest Marilyn came to portraying her predecessor was in RICHARD AVEDON's *Life* photo feature of famous sirens of yesteryear.

***Cold Shoulder***
In 1950 Marilyn auditioned for this Fox movie, soon after filming *ALL ABOUT EVE* (1950). She didn't get the part opposite Richard Conte because the project was scrapped. However, her screen test impressed studio chief DARRYL ZANUCK sufficiently for him to assign her to *AS YOUNG AS YOU FEEL* (1951) and write out a long-awaited studio contract.

***The Egyptian***
Marilyn could have been forgiven for thinking that the ancient Egyptians had it in for her. Almost a decade before the studio pulled the plug on *SOMETHING'S GOT TO GIVE*, partly because of the enormous expenses on Egyptian blockbuster *Cleopatra*, as a follow-up to her success in *HOW TO MARRY A MILLIONAIRE* (1953), Marilyn unsuccessfully tried to get on board Twentieth Century-Fox's planned costume drama *The Egyptian*. Studio boss Zanuck had different ideas and didn't even let her test for the part. Bella Darvi was preferred for the role Marilyn coveted. Michael Curtiz directed the 1954 movie, which starred Jean Simmons, Victor Mature, Gene Tierney, Edward Purdom, and Peter Ustinov. Cinematographer Leon Shamroy picked up an Oscar nomination.

***Freud***
John Huston was very keen to land Marilyn for his movie on the man who invented psychoanalysis, but Marilyn's analyst RALPH GREENSON thought that this was not an appropriate project for her at this rather emotionally volatile time of her life. An alternative story runs that Marilyn refused to take on the project because she believed that ANNA FREUD was not happy that a movie was being made about her father. The 1962 Universal movie starred MONTGOMERY CLIFT and Susannah York.

***The Girl in Pink Tights***
(ALSO KNOWN AS *Pink Tights*)

This picture about a schoolteacher who becomes a saloon dancer was offered to Marilyn by Twentieth Century-Fox in late 1953 after Darryl Zanuck turned her down for *The Egyptian*. Frank Sinatra was attached to the project. Marilyn demanded to read the script before signing. Zanuck refused; as far as he was concerned, she was contracted to the studio and would do whatever movie the studio decided she would do. Marilyn didn't like either the movie or the fact that she was being offered yet another remake; fiancé JOE DIMAGGIO helped her make up her mind to say no. The studio issued threats. They publicly announced that the film would go ahead, starring the unknown SHEREE NORTH. In this to and fro battle, the next development was Marilyn marrying DiMaggio. The studio sent her the script and told her that the picture was still hers after all. She read it and her worst suspicions were confirmed. Marilyn's judgement prevailed and the picture was never made.

***The Girl in the Red Velvet Swing***
In early 1954 notices appeared in the Hollywood trade press that Marilyn was set to star in the cinematic version of the infamous Harry K. Thaw case involving the killing of famous architect Stanford White. Fox duly announced that *The Girl in the Red Velvet Swing* was to be Marilyn's next picture following completion of *THE SEVEN YEAR ITCH* (1955). They should have checked with Marilyn first, as she was preparing to quit Los Angeles for New York and set up her own company, MARILYN MONROE PRODUCTIONS, with MILTON GREENE. Fox made *The Girl in the Red Velvet Swing* in 1955, starring young British hopeful JOAN COLLINS, directed by Richard Fleischer. The story has been retold more recently in *Ragtime*, both in a movie and a Broadway musical version.

***The Goddess***
This 1958 movie written by PADDY CHAYEFSKY tells a story very familiar to Marilyn, about a troubled little girl who struggles, then makes it big in Hollywood and marries a famous sports star. Directed by John Cromwell, starring KIM STANLEY and Lloyd Bridges, COLUMBIA PICTURES denied that this movie was based on any living personage. But in a biography of Chayefsky it is clear that the writer, who won an Oscar nomination for his script, was settling a score with Marilyn after he felt she had wronged him by promising (and then failing) to buy his script for *Middle of the Night*. There are stories that Marilyn was briefly interested in playing the lead role, before husband Arthur Miller persuaded her against it. Arthur's sister, Joan Copeland, also stars in this movie, playing the role of a drama coach said to be modeled on Natasha Lytess.

***Goodbye Charlie***
Twentieth Century-Fox tried and failed to interest Marilyn in this adaptation of GEORGE AXELROD's Broadway comedy, originally starring LAUREN BACALL, about a womanizing gangster who is killed only to be transferred into the body of an attractive blonde. Vincente Minnelli directed the 1964 film starring DEBBIE REYNOLDS, Pat Boone, TONY CURTIS, and Walter Matthau.

***Guys and Dolls***
This MGM version of a Broadway smash hit came out in 1955, not long after Marilyn told columnist Earl Wilson that the role she most wanted was the one Vivian Blaine had played onstage in the Broadway adaptation of Damon Runyon's short stories about colorful, loveable New York lowlifes. The lavish production starred two of Marilyn's favorite actors, MARLON BRANDO and Frank Sinatra, alongside Vivian Blaine and Jean Simmons. It was written and directed by JOSEPH L. MANKIEWICZ and photographed by Harry Stradling.

***How to be Very, Very Popular***
One of the movies after *The Seven Year Itch* that Marilyn turned her back on to skip to New York and form her own production company. Originally conceived as a vehicle written for Marilyn—she was scheduled to play a belly dancer on the run who takes refuge in a college—Fox was understandably keen not to relinquish their intended star. However when Marilyn refused to touch the project, the studio turned to the unlikely combination of BETTY GRABLE (in her final film performance) and budding starlet Sheree North, paired opposite Charles Coburn and TOMMY NOONAN. The movie, when it came out in 1955, received lukewarm reviews.

***I Love Louisa***
After her suspension from *Something's Got to Give*, Marilyn made plans to team up with DEAN MARTIN in a dark comedy about a young woman whose string of rich husbands come to an untimely end, making her enormously wealthy. Marilyn's publicist ARTHUR P. JACOBS produced the package, directed by J. Lee Thompson and released as *What a Way to Go* by Fox in 1964, starring Shirley MacLaine, Martin, ROBERT MITCHUM, Dick Van Dyke, GENE KELLY, and Paul Newman.

***Irma La Douce***
BILLY WILDER, who swore after *SOME LIKE IT HOT* (1959) that he would never work again with Marilyn, is said to have offered her the title role. Marilyn had long since said no to prostitute roles on principle. Marilyn's loss was Shirley MacLaine's gain, in her Oscar-nominated performance as the prostitute who wins the attentions of a Paris *gendarme* in this 1963 United Artists version of a Broadway musical.

***The Jean Harlow Story***
A lifelong ambition unfulfilled, despite several false starts. In 1952 Marilyn told *Life* magazine that this was a possible project. In 1955 both Marilyn and BUDDY ADLER at Fox hinted that a film of JEAN HARLOW's life was in the works. Marilyn had been discussing the possibility of such a film for years with SIDNEY SKOLSKY—who as well as writing his weekly column produced two biopics—and she had apparently returned to the project during the last year of her life. A *Hollywood Reporter* article in 1964 claimed that Marilyn had decided not to proceed with the earlier Fox project, scripted by Adela Rogers St. John, because Arthur Miller did not think it suitable for her "new image." A rather saccharine version of the film was made as *Harlow* (Paramount, 1965) starring Carrol Baker in the title role and directed by Gordon Douglas. That same year a television version also aired, starring Carol Lynley.

***The Last Man on the Wagon Mound***
Fox apparently lined Marilyn up to play a frontier widow as one of the flurry of movies she made after signing a new contract with the studio in 1951. The putative project, slated to star Mitzi Gaynor, Debra Paget, and Jean Peters, never materialized.

***The Lieutenant Wore Skirts***
*Seven Year Itch* co-star TOM EWELL starred opposite Sheree North in this 1956 Fox farce, which began as a Marilyn vehicle. North joins the Air Force to be near her husband, who she does not know has been turned down for service, and winds up living on the military base.

***Middle of the Night***
Marilyn conducted negotiations with writer Paddy Chayefsky to play the lead in this cinema version of his television play. Chayefsky was all for it, but then Marilyn's interest cooled. KIM NOVAK eventually landed the lead, opposite FREDERIC MARCH, in this well-received 1959 Columbia production telling the story of the predicament of an elderly New York clothes manufacturer who falls in love with a much younger woman.

***The Naked Truth***
One of the projects Marilyn was considering in 1961, a film project with the Mirisch Brothers, producers of her most successful film ever, *Some Like It Hot* (1959).

***Of Human Bondage***
W. Somerset Maugham's tale of a prim Englishman who falls disastrously for a poor waitress, ably interpreted on screen by BETTE DAVIS in 1934, was reportedly suggested to Zanuck by HENRY HATHAWAY in 1954, not long after he had directed Marilyn in *NIAGARA* (1953). Zanuck was not interested in a putative pairing of Marilyn Monroe and James Dean. The movie was made in 1964 (the second remake, after a 1946 version) starring Kim Novak and Laurence Harvey.

***Pillow Talk***
DORIS DAY beat Marilyn to star opposite ROCK HUDSON in this Oscar-winning 1959 Universal comedy. The Day-Hudson pairing graced a host of films in the sixties after this success, in which they play two people who hate each other but somehow manage to fall in love through their shared telephone line.

***The Revolt of Mamie Stover***
One of the movies Twentieth Century-Fox wanted to showcase Marilyn in after *The Seven Year Itch* (1955) was this tale of a prostitute who leaves San Francisco for Honolulu, where she is redeemed by the love of a literary type. JANE RUSSELL got the role in this 1956 production, after Marilyn declined.

***Rain***
A planned TV project, to be directed by LEE STRASBERG in 1961, in which Marilyn was cast first opposite JOHN GIELGUD, then Frederic March. Somerset Maugham agreed that Marilyn would be "splendid" in the role of Sadie Thompson, a character played previously by Gloria Swanson, Joan Crawford, Rita Hayworth, and Tallulah Bankhead. Marilyn described the role, one she long

Marilyn with James Brown and Mickey Rooney in *The Fireball* (1950).

cherished, as that of "a girl who knew how to be gay, even when she was sad, and that's important." The project fizzled out when NBC was unwilling to entrust the drama to Strasberg. Marilyn's loyalty was never in question, and she wouldn't consider an alternative director.

***Some Came Running***
Marilyn was offered the role that went to Shirley MacLaine, opposite Frank Sinatra, in this screen adaptation of a novel about the travails of a writer who returns home after the war and finds it hard to re-adapt. The movie was made by MGM and released in 1958.

***The Sound and the Fury***
After the unsuccessful conclusion of Marilyn's experiment as an independent producer, one of the projects Twentieth Century-Fox offered her was this adaptation of the William Faulkner novel. Martin Ritt directed the 1959 movie about a Southern family fighting ruin, starring Yul Brynner, Joanne Woodward, and Margaret Leighton. Marilyn preferred one of the other offers on the table, *Some Like It Hot* (1959).

***The Story on Page One***
In 1959 this project was proposed to Marilyn by JERRY WALD, with whom she had worked many years earlier on CLASH BY NIGHT (1952). The story line revolved around lead character Jo Morris, a woman whose life bears more than a passing resemblance to Marilyn's—a childhood spent with foster parents, growing up into a beautiful young woman, longing for love, and then marrying, only for her husband to turn violent. Marilyn told Wald and writer CLIFFORD ODETS that she needed to see the finished script before she took any decision. She saw it and said no. Rita Hayworth took the lead role opposite Tony Franciosa in this 1960 Twentieth Century-Fox production.

***The Stripper***
Producer Jerry Wald approached Marilyn once again about taking the lead role in this screen adaptation of WILLIAM INGE's Broadway play *A Loss of Roses*, which tells the story of Lila, a small-town girl raised by foster parents whose dreams of Hollywood end in ignominy as she is forced to strip for a living. Joanne Woodward played the part, with Richard Beymer and Claire Trevor, in Twentieth Century-Fox's 1963 production.

***They Shoot Horses, Don't They?***
Jane Fonda's performance in this 1969 Palomar movie about a six-day dance marathon during the Depression was worth a Best Actress Oscar nomination. SIMONE SIGNORET, who had worked on a radio version of the drama many years earlier, advised Marilyn to buy the rights in 1960.

***A Tree Grows in Brooklyn***
Shortly before her death Marilyn was in talks with composer Jule Styne about a musical version of *A Tree Grows in Brooklyn*, originally filmed in 1945 starring Peggy Ann Garner and James Dunn, and directed by Elia Kazan. Marilyn was scheduled to meet Styne on August 9, 1962 to finalize arrangements. A non-musical version of Betty Smith's novel was made for television by Twentieth Century-Fox in 1974.

***We Were Strangers***
JOHN HUSTON apparently wanted to screen test Marilyn for this 1949 movie, about Cuban rebels plotting to kill a politician, which he was making at the time that Marilyn was at COLOMBIA PICTURES. Producer Sam Spiegel was not willing to spend the money to find out if she was up to the role.

Critic PAULINE KAEL, who was not one of Marilyn's greatest fans, grudgingly wrote that she "might have been right" in *Daisy Miller* (1974), *Candy* (1968), *Sweet Charity* (1969), *Lord Love a Duck* (1966), *Born Yesterday*, *Bombshell* (1933), *Red Dust* (1932), *Breakfast at Tiffany's* (1974), *Period of Adjustment* (1962), and *Bonnie and Clyde* (1967).

## FIREBALL, THE (1950)
(ALSO KNOWN AS: *The Challenge*)

MICKEY ROONEY vehicle in which Marilyn streaks through for a few seconds as a roller derby groupie.

**Credits:**
A Thor Production released through Twentieth Century-Fox, Black and White
Length: 84 minutes
Release date: November 9, 1950

Directed by: Tay Garnett
Produced by: Bert E. Friedlob
Written by: Tay Garnett, Horace McCoy
Cinematography by: Lester White
Music by: Victor Young
Film Editing by: Frank Sullivan

**Cast (credits order):**
Mickey Rooney . . . Johnny Casar
Pat O'Brien . . . Father O'Hara
Beverly Tyler . . . Mary Reeves
Glenn Corbett . . . Mack Miller
James Brown . . . Allen
Marilyn Monroe . . . Polly
Ralph Dumke . . . Bruno Crystal
Bert Begley . . . Shilling
Milburn Stone . . . Jeff Davis
Tom Flint . . . Dr. Barton
John Hedloe . . . Ullman
Larry Holden . . . Alan (uncredited)

**Plot:**
A sports flick about roller ball fifties-style in which true love and teamwork are learned the hard way by star Mickey Rooney, playing orphanage runaway Johnny Casar. After finding a job, Casar gets drawn into the world of competitive roller skating. It takes dedication, but he manages to beat his rival and land a job with roller skating speedway champions The Bears. Father O'Hara (Pat O'Brien) tracks down his former charge and expresses his pride that Johnny is making something of himself. Unfortunately, success starts to go to Casar's head. He starts thinking and playing for himself and not the team, and begins a wild new life that includes pretty girls like Polly (Marilyn Monroe) who are only interested in him because of his celebrity status. Old flame Mary (Beverly Tyler), who first took him to the Rollerbowl, is the one who nurses him through a bout of polio... so that he can take part in the championship game, in which, realizing the truth about life, he helps a young teammate to win the race for their team and take all the glory.

**Reviews:**
*The New York Times*
"As a trimly budgeted, fairly picturesque handling of a new sports angle, *The Fireball* has a few good moments in the skating sequences, in Pat O'Brien's droll portrayal of the priest, and, paradoxically, during the early scenes of Mr. Rooney's vagrancy."

## FITNESS

Forty years before the fitness craze came out of California, at a time when most women simply did not exercise, Marilyn was quick to realize that to further her screen dreams, a little body toning was a sound investment. In 1943, when still married to first husband JAMES DOUGHERTY and living with him at the CATALINA ISLAND maritime service training base, former Olympic weightlifting champion Howard Carrington taught her to use weights for fitness.

According to ANTHONY SUMMERS, after separating from Dougherty, Marilyn spent a lot of time on the beach with expert swimmer and lifeguard, TOMMY ZAHN. However, ARTHUR MILLER says she never learned to swim properly: "It was the only awkward thing she ever did."

At the start of her MODELING career Norma Jeane applied herself to learning the mechanics of how to walk and move. She read up on human anatomy and bought drawings of human musculature by Renaissance anatomist Vesalius. Using this as a basis, she developed an exercise program designed specifically to develop certain muscle groups: a regular forty-minute-a-day exercise program, including a workout with a pair of five-pound dumbbells.

In 1952, the year she became an A-list star, Marilyn revealed some of her exercise secrets in a *Pageant* magazine article entitled "How I Stay In Shape," accompanied by photographs by ANDRÉ DE DIENES which, truth be told, were posed more to show off her trim body than her weights technique. *Life* also featured Marilyn working out in a 1952 photo feature (pictures of which appeared in the summer 1998 issue of *Women's Sports and Fitness* magazine). PHILIPPE HALSMAN's pictures, taken in Marilyn's apartment, show Marilyn in blue jeans and a bikini top, bench pressing dumbbells and doing a head-stand. Marilyn explained to the photographer her exercise ethos: "I'm fighting gravity. If you don't fight gravity, you sag." A rather dubious photograph, reproduced in Anthony Summers' biography, supposedly shows Marilyn jogging through Beverly Hills service alleys.

This dedication paid off. It is not clear whether Marilyn kept up a regular exercise regime for the rest of her life—in the late fifties her weight fluctuated by as much as twenty pounds—though she did try her hand at a number of SPORTS. Her remarkable physical endurance and stamina served her n other ways, allowing her to recover from the increasing doses of DRUGS she took for insomnia and anxiety much faster than her doctors were used to seeing in other patients.

In her last year alive, Marilyn took up yoga as a means of trying to relax and be better able to SLEEP.

## FITZGERALD, ELLA (1917–1996)

Marilyn's favorite female singer, and one of the greatest of all jazz voices, known at the height of her career as "The First Lady of Song." Discovered at sixteen, Ella was a world renowned singer for over half a century. Marilyn was an avid listener, with a more than passing interest in Ella's remarkable clarity and phrasing. Music coach HAL SCHAEFER recalled that Marilyn "loved to sing, she sang well, and she just adored her idol, Ella. The most important influence on Marilyn's vocal art was, in fact, a recording I gave her called 'Ella Sings Gershwin.'"

Marilyn had an opportunity to show her appreciation in a unique way. Ella told the story in an August 1972 article in MS magazine:

> "I owe Marilyn Monroe a real debt. It was because of her that I played Mocambo [an L.A. club]. She personally called the owner of the Mocambo, and told him she wanted me booked immediately, and if he would do it, she would take a front table every night. She told him—and it was true, due to Marilyn's superstar status—that the press would go wild. The owner said yes, and Marilyn was there, front table, every night. The press went overboard. . . . After that, I never had to play a small jazz club again. She was an unusual woman—a little ahead of her times. And she didn't know it."

During filming of *Ladies of the Chorus* (1948), Columbia Pictures took photos of the young starlet exercising for a publicity piece on "How to Exercise."

## FLANAGAN, AGNES

Marilyn's personal hairdresser for over a decade, after they first met working together on the unmemorable 1950 Fox movie *THE FIREBALL*. Flanagan worked with Marilyn over the years on other movies, such as *SOME LIKE IT HOT* (1959) and *THE MISFITS* (1961), and often went to Marilyn's home to do her hair before social occasions, photo shoots, and business meetings. More importantly to Marilyn, she became a friend, part of the small entourage of people she felt she could count on. Marilyn was a frequent visitor to the Flanagan home, and something of an auntie to her two children. The last time Flanagan did Marilyn's hair was for her FUNERAL.

## FLOWERS

The details change from source to source about JOE DIMAGGIO's twenty year floral tribute to Marilyn. After her funeral DiMaggio placed an order with local PARISIAN FLORISTS for a long-stemmed red rose or six red roses to be delivered to Marilyn's grave twice (some reports say three times) a week. In so doing, he was making good on a promise made immediately after their wedding ceremony at San Francisco City Hall in January 1954: as Marilyn clutched three orchids in her hand, he swore that if she died before him, he would be as devoted in sending a floral sign of his affection as William Powell had been for JEAN HARLOW.

When DiMaggio's order expired, ROBERT SLATZER publicly announced he would be taking over the mantle, but his largesse only lasted three months. . . . Parisian Florists stopped its deliveries due to unpaid bills. However, Marilyn's crypt at the WESTWOOD MEMORIAL PARK CEMETARY always has fresh flowers, delivered or brought personally every week by devoted fans; sometimes there are so many that they have to be laid on the pavement.

## FONTAINEBLEAU HOTEL
4441 COLLINS AVENUE, MIAMI, FLORIDA

In February 1962 Marilyn stayed at this renowned Florida HOTEL, and visited with ARTHUR MILLER's father, Isidore.

## FOOD

As a child, Norma Jeane's love for all living creatures meant that she wouldn't eat fish, and she had a hard time eating chicken. She once told a photographer on location for *NIAGARA* (1953) that if she saw a chicken leg she would imagine the whole animal, and that would spoil the whole meal for her.

In the struggling starlet years she didn't have the money to eat properly. In 1948 she told FRED KARGER, "I have grapefruit and coffee for breakfast, and cottage cheese for lunch. Some days I get by with just a little over a dollar a day for food." As work began to pick up, she would have a kick-start morning drink of orange juice fortified with gelatin. There are stories that all she could afford in the worst of this period was peanut butter and raw hamburger (not necessarily together). When she lived with NATASHA LYTESS, every day she would breakfast on cold oatmeal porridge with milk, and then eat two eggs, washed down with orange juice and gelatin.

Marilyn was a very big steak fan, enjoying them on special occasions such as birthdays and for her wedding dinner with JOE DIMAGGIO. He and his family introduced her to the delights of Italian cooking; Mama DiMaggio taught her how to make a spaghetti sauce to satisfy her Italian-American husband's appetite.

In a 1953 interview Marilyn talked about the demands fame had made on her diet: "I've turned anemic since all this happened—I have to drink raw liver juice and stir uncooked eggs into my milk. And I eat steak for breakfast every morning."

This sort of menu is not too different from some of today's high protein weight loss diets. But Marilyn's preferred method of (temporary) weight reduction was in fact colonic irrigation, which she reputedly practiced on a regular basis.

Marilyn tended to eat plenty of proteins (meat and eggs), some greens, and as few carbohydrates as possible. For most of her adult life she ate irregularly; in the periods when she was taking DRUGS her appetite and eating habits were disturbed. Until her 1961 gallbladder operation, Marilyn suffered acute and recurring digestive problems.

When she lived in New York during the mid-fifties, AMY GREENE recalled that Marilyn was constantly on and off diets. When she was off, she did things like eat hot dogs purchased from a street vendor with ARTHUR MILLER as he showed her around town. Marilyn also enjoyed eating caviar—big pots of caviar—washed down with champagne. During 1957 and 1958 MONTGOMERY CLIFT used to come to her apartment for caviar and vodka. He never brought olives—Marilyn couldn't stand them.

Few memoirs about Marilyn have anything good to say about her COOKING. First husband JAMES DOUGHERTY complained of the colorful but tasteless peas and carrots placed in front of him, and in interviews where she talked about cooking Marilyn made it clear that she was more experimental than accomplished in the kitchen.

In 1960 when working on *LET'S MAKE LOVE*, Marilyn and Arthur Miller generally dined with next door neighbors YVES MONTAND and SIMONE SIGNORET after shooting. They took turns cooking and eating wholesome fare such as spaghetti or lamb stew.

### WHAT MARILYN ATE

During the lean years: raw hamburgers, peanut butter, hot dogs, chili, crackers
Typical breakfast, 1951: warm milk, two raw eggs, a dash of sherry
Typical dinner, 1951: broiled steak, lamb chop or liver, raw carrots
On first date with Joe DiMaggio: anchovies on pimento, spaghetti al dente, scallopini of veal
For her 1952 birthday dinner at the Bel-Air Hotel: steak
Favorite appetizer circa 1952: tiny tomatoes stuffed with cream cheese and caviar
While filming *River of No Return* (1954): lobster
For her DiMaggio wedding dinner: steak, cooked medium-well
While in Korea: cheese sandwiches
At the Romanoff's party in her honor: Chateaubriand
While shooting *Bus Stop* (1956): raw steaks
Typical breakfast, 1957: three poached eggs, toast, a Bloody Mary
Typical lunch at the Roxbury farm, 1957: salami and cheese sandwiches
What Lena Pepitone cooked for Marilyn: spaghetti, lasagna, sausages, peppers
Dinner following her split with Yves Montand: lasagna, hamburger, chocolate pudding
On New Year's Eve, 1960: spaghetti with sweet Italian sausages
While shooting *The Misfits* (1961): buttermilk, borscht
Typical breakfast, 1961: egg whites, poached in safflower oil (Marilyn had Eunice Murray regularly save the egg yolks to use in the holiday pound cakes.)
Typical breakfast, 1962: hard-boiled eggs, toast
Typical lunch, 1962: a broiled steak
Favorite Italian dinner, 1962: fettuccini Leon and veal piccata
Favorite snack when not dieting: hot dogs
On a 1962 picnic in the backseat of her Cadillac: cold steak sandwiches
The last breakfast, on August 3, 1962: a grapefruit
What Marilyn especially disliked: olives

## FOSTER PARENTS

Official STUDIO BIOGRAPHIES of Marilyn in the early fifties stated that as a girl she had been shuttled to as many as a fourteen foster families. The number increased in proportion to the amount of sympathy elicited. This does not change the fact that Norma Jeane's childhood took place against a disorienting backdrop of homes and parent figures, some for years, some for just a matter of weeks. The first seven years of her life were the most settled, living in the same place with the BOLENDER family. For a short spell Norma Jeane moved in to live with her mother GLADYS BAKER. After Gladys was taken to an institution, Gladys's best friend GRACE MCKEE GODDARD became the little girl's legal guardian and was responsible for the logistics of Norma Jeane's life. Immediately after Gladys's institutionalization it appears that the little girl was looked after by the lodgers where Gladys had been living with her daughter, an English actor called GEORGE ATKINSON and his family. Grace then temporarily placed Norma Jeane with the GIFFEN FAMILY and then with her mother EMMA WILLETTE ATCHINSON. Then for almost two years came the infamous spell at the Los Angeles ORPHANAGE. After 1937 Norma Jeane moved in with Goddard, and spent the remaining years of her youth, until her 1942 marriage to JAMES DOUGHERTY, either with Grace or living with her "aunt," ANA LOWER. Other brief foster parents were ENID AND SAM KNEBELCAMP, and IDA MARTIN, Norma Jeane's great aunt, with whom she lived soon after coming out of the orphanage.

## FRANK AND JOSEPH'S SALON
6513 HOLLYWOOD BOULEVARD

Popular Hollywood Boulevard hair salon into which Norma Jeane walked in as a brunette and came out a golden blonde in either late 1945 or late 1946, depending on the source. Sylvia Barnhart, the beautician who effected this change (and continued to do Marilyn's hair until her hair needs were taken over by the stylists at TWENTIETH CENTURY-FOX), recalled: "She'd come in like two or three hours late and still expect to be taken care of. If the truth be known, she was a user. I don't think she cared who she walked over. [But] she was just magnificent and breathtaking to look at." The salon was so taken with her that they photographed her to show off their skills.

## FRANKLIN AVENUE

For a short time during 1948, after moving on from the home of JOHN CARROLL and LUCILLE RYMAN, Marilyn lived in an apartment on Franklin Avenue, Hollywood, before returning for a second spell at the Hollywood STUDIO CLUB.

## FREUD, ANNA (1895–1982)

On the recommendation of her then psychoanalyst MARGARET HOHENBERG, who was flown in to see Marilyn when she was in working on *THE PRINCE AND THE SHOWGIRL* (1957), Marilyn had a number of therapy sessions with Sigmund Freud's daughter Anna, who continued her father's work with a special emphasis on the treatment of children. Anna Freud later recommended a new New York analyst for her to see, MARIANNE KRIS.

Marilyn's will included a provision for Kris, to be used as best she thought fit in a therapeutic manner. Kris chose the Anna Freud Foundation in London, which set up a special child treatment center in Marilyn's name.

## FREUD, SIGMUND (1856–1939)

Marilyn read a great deal of the writings of the founder of PSYCHOANALYSIS, after embarking on an intensive program of analysis and self-discovery in the mid-fifties that was to accompany her through the remainder of her life.

On seeing a photo of Freud inside a collection of his letters, Marilyn exclaimed that he looked "as if he died a disappointed man."

Marilyn was offered but rejected a role in a film about Freud, being put together by JOHN HUSTON in the early sixties (*see* FILMS MARILYN CONSIDERED OR WANTED).

## FRIENDS

MARILYN:
"Sometimes I think the only people who stay with me and really listen are people I hire, people I pay. And that makes me sad. Why can't I have friends around me all the time, friends who want nothing from me?"

EZRA GOODMAN, journalist:
"Monroe has a neat habit of latching onto people, of having them mother and father her, and then dumping them unceremoniously by the wayside when she has done with them.... She likes to change people like other women change hats."

JOE DIMAGGIO:
"If it hadn't been for her friends she might still be alive."

LAUREN BACALL:
"She was a taker in a way because every time she gave, she got rapped for it. There were a lot of leeches in her life... And she made a lot of blunders in accepting the wrong people."

It has often been said that the biggest tragedy of Marilyn's life is that she put her trust in the wrong people. After a childhood filled with a bewildering array of adults who were in *loco parentis* one day, out of her life the next, putting her personal faith and trust in anybody must have seemed a very risky business. In particular, Marilyn always found it hard to make friends with women her own age. In the words of Elyda Dougherty, sister of her first husband JAMES DOUGHERTY, "She was just too beautiful. She couldn't help it that men's wives looked at her and got so jealous they wanted to throw rocks!" Friendships with older women were much easier. Marilyn maintained lifelong relationships with XENIA CHEKHOV and Mary Karger Short, though in ARTHUR MILLER's view these bonds were not without their own complications, "veering from sentimental idealization to black suspicions that they disapproved of her." For the most part, Marilyn's friendships with women were only with those who she did not consider to be sexual competitors.

During her young adult life Marilyn was so driven in her desire to become a star, that the people she associated with all had something that could help her achieve her dream. They tended to be studio bosses (JOSEPH M. SCHENCK) or agents (JOHNNY HYDE); at least these are the relationships that have been documented by biographers. Even after she became an established star, Marilyn continued to seek out the company of people she felt could be useful to her intellectually or professionally, or whom she admired (for example MICHAEL CHEKHOV). Undoubtedly her initial attraction to Arthur Miller had much to do with his status as a prominent left-leaning intellectual; her devotion to LEE and PAULA STRASBERG also had a hint of this. Marilyn's longest friendships, surviving the length of her career, were with a select group of journalists and photographers, such as SIDNEY SKOLSKY and EVE ARNOLD, on whom she felt she could rely for allegiance, support and, sometimes, guidance.

Fickle as she may have been in choosing and losing her friends, Marilyn was loyal, kind, and dedicated to those she considered to be her friends. Marilyn's GENEROSITY is well-known. If, while out shopping, a friend expressed admiration for some item, she quite often made a mental note, called back later, and had the item delivered. She was also very solicitous of friends who were sick, and would make caring visits to make sure ill friends had everything they needed. This generosity of spirit extended to a loyalty to people she respected. For example, Marilyn refused to play along with the Fox publicity ploy of rivalry with fellow actresses BETTY GRABLE and JANE RUSSELL, with whom she was working on *GENTLEMAN PREFER BLONDES* (1953). Marilyn also stayed very close to the children of her ex-husbands, long after her relationships with their fathers had failed.

Several times in her life Marilyn dropped a whole set of friends, either because she felt she had moved beyond them, or because she thought that they were no good for her. Journalist W. J. WEATHERBY put it to her directly that she discarded people. Marilyn replied, "I've never dropped anyone I believed in. My trouble is, I trust people too much. I believe in them too much and I go on believing in them when the signs are already there. You get a lot of disappointments." And indeed, there were plenty of people, men and women, with whom she came into contact who were not interested in Marilyn the person, but Marilyn the trophy, Marilyn the status symbol, Marilyn the source of anecdotes. To this day, a number of people who claim to have been Marilyn's "intimate friends," despite little evidence to back this up, make a decent living from the Marilyn chat show circuit.

Marilyn was not, it seems, one to talk around an issue. If she was upset, or when she fell out with friends, she spoke her mind to the person concerned, and that was that. However, she avoided the many opportunities available to her to voice her personal grievances in public, or to respond to accusations made publicly against her.

Biographers agree that Marilyn's most loyal friend of all was former husband JOE DIMAGGIO. Either side of their bitter nine-month married life together, Joe was always there for her when she needed him; he never exploited her for his own ends, and he cherished her memory in death by maintaining a complete and respectful silence about their relationship.

Marilyn had many actor friends: ROBERT MITCHUM, DEAN MARTIN, MONTGOMERY CLIFT, TOM EWELL, ALEX D'ARCY, DAVID WAYNE, Frankie Vaughan, CASEY ADAMS, Zero Mostel, WALLY COX, MARLON BRANDO, ELI WALLACH, JANE RUSSELL, PETER LAWFORD, and FRANK SINATRA. Montgomery Clift was a special friend. He once said, "Maybe Marilyn and I would have got together one day if we weren't so much alike."

Arthur Miller experienced the full course of Marilyn's affections from admiration to friendship to love to disappointment to loathing. Referring to the first year they were together, 1955, Miller writes, "She was at this point incapable of condemning or even of judging people who had damaged her, and to be with her was to be accepted, like moving out into a kind of sanctifying light from a life where suspicion was common sense." By the end of their relationship, he too had become one of the traitors: "She had no means of preventing the complete unraveling of her belief in a person once a single thread was broken, and if her childhood made this understandable, it didn't make it easier for her or anyone around her to bear."

To some degree, Marilyn's psychoanalysts fulfilled the listening ear function of friendship from 1955, when she first began regular sessions. In the last years of her life she was having sessions with DR. RALPH GREENSON almost every day of the week, sometimes even twice a day. Add to this brew Marilyn's sometimes debilitating feelings of low self-esteem, occasional feelings of being unworthy of true friendship or incapable of reciprocating it, and friendship becomes part of a general equation of unhappiness.

Marilyn was a big phone fan, particularly during nights when she could not sleep. She would call at the oddest hours and seek solace or just some chat from her friends.

A major source of support for Marilyn was the entourage she built up around her, a family of people who were there for her partly out of genuine feeling, but originally because she paid their wages: her hairdressers, maids, masseur, publicists, and secretaries. With these people Marilyn indulged her intense curiosity about social behavior, about how "normal" families are and behave. She was constantly asking her New York maid LENA PEPITONE about her routine, her family in Italy, and her husband and sons, almost as if she was desperately seeking to learn the lines for a role she wanted so much to fill.

Marilyn used to ask her friends to "hold a good thought" for her. To this day, countless fans around the world continue to do so.

## FUNERAL

JOE DIMAGGIO flew in to look after arrangements for Marilyn's funeral. He called in her elder half-sister BERNIECE MIRACLE to help. Marilyn's business manager INEZ MELSON also assisted. Under DiMaggio's express instructions, none of Marilyn's Hollywood friends were invited—he held them responsible, morally if not actually, for her death. Journalists and news cameras were kept at a distance.

Marilyn Monroe's funeral took place at 1:00 P.M. on August 8, 1962, at the Westwood Village Mortuary Chapel on the grounds of the WESTWOOD MEMORIAL PARK CEMETERY. It was a very private service conducted by Reverend A. J. Soldan, a Lutheran minister from the Village Church of Westwood. Readings were made of Psalm 23, chapter 14 of the Book of John, and excerpts from Psalms 46 and 139. The Lord's Prayer was also read. The somber occasion began with the strains of Tchaikovsky's Sixth Symphony, and included, at Marilyn's request, JUDY GARLAND's "Over the Rainbow." LEE STRASBERG delivered the eulogy, though only after DiMaggio's first choice, CARL SANDBURG, was forced to decline due to ill-health.

During the service Marilyn's body lay in an open bronze casket lined with champagne-colored satin. Partially exposed, she was dressed in her green Pucci dress and a green chiffon scarf, a favorite which she had worn at a press conference in Mexico City earlier that year. For the last time, ALLAN "WHITEY" SNYDER did her makeup, a flask of gin fortifying him enough to carry out a promise he had made in jest many years earlier, and of which Marilyn had reminded him with an inscription on a gold money clip she gave him, saying "Whitey Dear, While I'm still warm, Marilyn."

Because of the damage done by the autopsy, AGNES FLANAGAN, who prepared her hair that day, had to use a wig similar to how Marilyn had been wearing her hair in her aborted last picture *SOMETHING'S GOT TO GIVE*. In her hands was a posy of pink teacup roses, a gift from DiMaggio, who had sat in vigil the night before.

Snyder was among her pallbearers, along with Allen Abbott, SIDNEY GUILAROFF, Ronald Hast, Leonard Krisminsky, and Clarence Pierce.

The solemn occasion was attended by just thirty-one mourners:

DiMaggio, JOE DIMAGGIO JR., Agnes Flanagan, Aaron Frosch, LOTTE GOSLAR, DR. RALPH GREENSON, his wife Hildi and children Dan and Joan, Sidney Guilaroff, Anne Karger, Mary Karger, Rudy Kautzsky, ENID and SAM KNEBELCAMP, Inez and Pat Melson, Berniece Miracle, EUNICE MURRAY, PAT NEWCOMB, PEARL PORTERFIELD, MAY REIS, RALPH ROBERTS, Milton Rudin, Allan "Whitey" Snyder, wife Berly and daughter Sherry, George Solotaire, Lee and Paula Strasberg, and Florence Thomas.

Marilyn's body was laid to rest in a marble crypt, not far from the last resting places of former guardian GRACE MCKEE GODDARD, and beloved "Aunt" ANA LOWER.

The bronze plaque on the marble wall crypt where Marilyn is buried reads simply:

MARILYN MONROE
1926–1962

BOOK:

*Marilyn: A Hollywood Farewell*, Leigh Weiner. Los Angeles: Leigh Weiner, 1990.

## FURNACE CREEK INN

THE FURNACE CREEK RESORT,
DEATH VALLEY, CALIFORNIA

Death Valley motel where Marilyn and photographer DAVID CONOVER stayed during a mid-forties photo shoot.

(SEE HOTELS)

"All the News That's Fit to Print"

The New York Times.

VOL. CXI . . No. 38,180. © 1962 by The New York Times Company. Times Square, New York 36, N. Y. NEW YORK, MONDAY, AUGUST 6, 1962. 10 cents beyond 50-mile zone from New York City except on Long Island. Higher in air delivery cities.

COMMON MARKET AND BRITISH VOICE HOPES IN IMPASSE

Both Sides Say Gains Were Made on Role for London Before Session Ended

OCTOBER MEETING SET

Failure to Settle Question of Commonwealth Exports Is Blow to Macmillan

By EDWIN L. DALE Jr.
Special to The New York Times.

BRUSSELS, Belgium, Aug. 5—Representatives of Britain and the European Economic Community expressed disappointment and some bitterness but no discouragement today over their failure to reach full agreement on the basis for British membership in the Community.

They stressed that substantial progress had been made on major issues.

The protracted negotiations, the present session of which lasted four days, will resume early in October.

After nearly twenty-two hours of continuous effort, the negotiators gave up this morning on the key matter still impeding agreement: Britain's effort to assure markets for the agricultural imports she receives from Canada, Australia and New Zealand.

New Tariff to Be Imposed

At the end, only a few points were still unsettled in a Common Market plan designed to give some assurance to the three Commonwealth countries. Their exports, now in large part duty-free in the British market, will be subject to a new common tariff and a variable levy system for farm products if Britain joins the six-nation Community.

The plan includes world commodity agreements, a pledge of a "reasonable" farm price policy aimed at preventing overproduction and a detailed arrangement to maintain preferential treatment for all British Commonwealth countries during a transition period up to 1970.

[The inconclusiveness of the negotiations was viewed in Britain as a setback for Prime Minister Macmillan. It is believed he will now find it more difficult to hold doubtful Conservatives in line and to get

Marilyn Monroe Dead, Pills Near

Star's Body Is Found in Bedroom of Her Home on Coast

Police Say She Left No Notes—Official Verdict Delayed

Special to The New York Times.

HOLLYWOOD, Calif., Aug. 5—Marilyn Monroe, one of the most famous stars in Hollywood's history, was found dead early today in the bedroom of her home in the Brentwood section of Los Angeles. She was 36 years old.

Beside the bed was an empty bottle that had contained sleeping pills. Fourteen other bottles of medicines and tablets were on the night stand.

The impact of Miss Monroe's death was international. Her fame was greater than her contributions as an actress.

As a woman she was considered a sex symbol. Her marriages to and divorces from Joe DiMaggio, the former Yankee baseball star, and Arthur Miller, the Pulitzer Prize playwright, were accepted by millions as the prerogatives of this contemporary Venus.

The events leading to her death were in tragic contrast to the comic talent and zest for life that had helped to make "Seven Year Itch" and "Some

Associated Press
Marilyn Monroe

Like It Hot" smash hits all over the world.

Miss Monroe's physician had prescribed sleeping pills for her for three days. Ordinarily the bottle would have contained forty to fifty pills.

The actress had also been under the care of a psychoanalyst for a year, and had called

him to her home last night. He had suggested she take a drive and relax. She remained home, however.

After an autopsy the Los Angeles coroner reported that Miss Monroe's "was not a natural death." He attributed it to a drug. He added that a toxicological study, to be completed within forty-eight hours, should yield more detailed information. He refused, until then, to list the death as a suicide.

PRESIDENT NAMES DEAN AT COLUMBIA TO POST ON A. E. C.

John G. Palfrey Is Second Lawyer Picked for Agency in Resolution of Dispute

Special to The New York Times.

HYANNIS PORT, Mass., Aug. 5 — President Kennedy announced today his intention to appoint John G. Palfrey, dean of Columbia College, New York,

N.A.A.C.P. to Ask Courts To End Union Racial Bars

By JOHN D. POMFRET
Special to The New York Times.

WASHINGTON, Aug. 5—The National Association for the Advancement of Colored People is planning a major legal assault on discrimination against Negroes by labor unions. The new effort is to begin in early fall. The aim will be to create a body of judge-made law equal to that now found in the field of public education.

The N. A. A. C. P. was instrumental in creating these laws following the 1954 Supreme Court decision outlawing segregation in public schools.

Much as the association attacked the doctrine of "separate but equal" in the school segregation case, its lawyers are preparing to make the doctrine of "voluntary association" a main target in the union field.

This doctrine holds that private voluntary groups have the right to decide whom they will admit. It has been advanced by some unions as a defense against legal efforts to compel them to take in Negroes.

Role of Unions Cited

CITY ACTS TO PAY ITS BILLS FASTER

Economies Are Expected—Tenney Says Poor Liaison Is a Cause of Delays

By PAUL CROWELL

Steps are being taken to have the city pay its bills more quickly, city Administrator Charles H. Tenney reported yesterday.

Mr. Tenney said that delays were a result, in part, of inadequate liaison between the office of the Controller and the management offices of other city agencies.

His report was based on a



Marilyn Monroe Dead, Pills Near

Star's Body Is Found in Bedroom of Her Home on Coast

Police Say She Left No Notes—Official Verdict Delayed

Special to The New York Times.

HOLLYWOOD, Calif., Aug. 5—Marilyn Monroe, one of the most famous stars in Hollywood's history, was found dead early today in the bedroom of her home in the Brentwood section of Los Angeles. She was 36 years old.

Beside the bed was an empty bottle that had contained sleeping pills. Fourteen other bottles of medicines and tablets were on the night stand.

The impact of Miss Monroe's death was international. Her fame was greater than her contributions as an actress.

As a woman she was considered a sex symbol. Her marriages to and divorces from Joe DiMaggio, the former Yankee baseball star, and Arthur Miller, the Pulitzer Prize playwright, were accepted by millions as the prerogatives of this contemporary Venus.

The events leading to her death were in tragic contrast to the comic talent and zest for life that had helped to make "Seven Year Itch" and "Some

Associated Press
Marilyn Monroe

Like It Hot" smash hits all over the world.

Miss Monroe's physician had prescribed sleeping pills for her for three days. Ordinarily the bottle would have contained forty to fifty pills.

The actress had also been under the care of a psychoanalyst for a year, and had called

him to her home last night. He had suggested she take a drive and relax. She remained home, however.

After an autopsy the Los Angeles coroner reported that Miss Monroe's "was not a natural death." He attributed it to a drug. He added that a toxicological study, to be completed within forty-eight hours, should yield more detailed information. He refused, until then, to list the death as a suicide.

Pending a more positive verdict by Dr. Theodore J. Curphey, the coroner, the Los Angeles police refused to call the death a suicide. They said they had no idea how many pills the actress might have taken, or whether any overdose might have been accidental. Miss Monroe left no notes, according to the police.

In addition to a physical autopsy, Los Angeles has a "psychological" autopsy. Two experts will look into the psychological history of Miss Monroe.

However, the non-physical

Continued on Page 13, Column 6

G

Marilyn and Clark Gable on the set of *The Misfits* (1961).

## GABLE, CLARK
(1901–1960, B. WILLIAM CLARK GABLE)

CLARK GABLE:
"I think she's something different to each man, blending somehow the things he seems to require most."

"She's a kind of ultimate, in her way, with a million sides to her, each one of them fascinating. . . completely feminine, and femininity without guile. . . . Everything Marilyn does is different from any other woman, strange and exciting, from the way she talks to the way she uses that magnificent torso."

Marilyn and Clark Gable on the set of *The Misfits* (1961).

For almost three decades Clark Gable was Hollywood's most popular male lead, starring in *Red Dust* (1932), *It Happened One Night* (1934), *Mutiny on the Bounty* (1935), *San Francisco* (1936), *Gone with the Wind* (1939), and *The Tall Men* (1955). As a young girl Norma Jeane loved seeing Gable in action at the Saturday matinees.

For Norma Jeane it was more than Gable's good looks and winning smile that made him special. He closely resembled the mustached man she had once seen in a photograph her mother, Gladys, had shown her and told her was her FATHER. To a fatherless little girl, Gable was the very embodiment of all paternal virtues. Norma Jeane cut out and treasured a photo of the actor and considered him to be her "secret" father.

In 1954, following her rise to prominence, rumors circulated to the effect that Gable and Marilyn were romantically involved. They did at least meet at the big Hollywood party thrown in Marilyn's honor at Romanoff's RESTAURANT, where they danced together twice. A few days later Gable sent an enormous bunch of red roses to Marilyn, who was recovering from an operation at the Cedars of Lebanon HOSPITAL.

When the chance came for Marilyn to work with Gable on *THE MISFITS* (1961), she was co-starring with a Hollywood leading man who had worked with every leading lady since the early thirties. Gable's fee for playing veteran cowboy Gay Langland was reputedly more than $800,000, almost a quarter of the entire budget, plus a $25,000 per-day fee for an overrun; like Marilyn, he was making up for the early part of his career when he had been a relatively low-paid contract actor. He also had script approval, which he exercised more than once as the plot changed daily with ARTHUR MILLER's rewrites.

Marilyn even had an opportunity to get physical, at least on screen, in a love scene sequence where she lay naked under a bed sheet. She later said to a friend, "I was so thrilled when he kissed me, we had to do the scene over several times. Then the sheet dropped and he put his hand on my breast. I got goose bumps all over." Plausible but dubious is Marilyn's supposed attempt to seduce the great actor on the set. In a book on the sex lives of Hollywood sirens, Marilyn is quoted as saying, "Whenever he was near me, I wanted him to kiss me and kiss me and kiss me. We did a lot of kissing, touching and feeling. I never tried harder to seduce a man." Gable, though, was deeply in love with his new wife Kay, who was pregnant at the time.

Life on location for *The Misfits* was not easy for any of the participants. Gable had to show great patience as Marilyn, under severe emotional pressure during the final throes of her break up with Arthur Miller, was even more temperamental, late, and difficult to work with. Gable's behavior was exemplary. Miller himself writes, "He behaved as though Marilyn was a woman in physical pain, despite his having to spend what might have been humiliating hours each day waiting for her to start working, no hint of affront ever showed on his face." Some biographers assert that his gentlemanly approach to a woman in distress survived the entire experience. Marilyn herself recalled, "The place was full of so-called men, but Clark was the one who brought a chair for me between the takes." However, stories circulated that his patience finally snapped one day, and he became so enraged at Marilyn's endemic LATENESS that he refused to continue shooting until she apologized, which she duly did, in private in his trailer. Marilyn publicly said, "He never got angry with me once for blowing a line or being late or anything—he was a gentleman. The best."

*The Misfits* was to be the last film either of these actors completed. Marilyn's next picture, *SOMETHING'S GOT TO GIVE*, was abandoned half-way through. As for Gable, on November 5, 1960, the day after completion of shooting at PARAMOUNT STUDIOS, he suffered a massive heart attack. A second fatal coronary followed eleven days later.

At the time it was rumored that Gable's heart attack had been brought on by the strains of working with a distraught and unreliable Marilyn. It is more likely that, if anything, it was provoked by the arduous stunts Gable insisted on doing himself, including being pulled along the ground by a wild mustang (in actual fact a truck pulled him over four hundred feet at thirty-five miles an hour). Despite his protective clothing he was cut and bruised. Gable told his wife that JOHN HUSTON's demands on his stuntmen were beyond the call of duty, and that he didn't seem to care if they lived or died. Gable's belief in the film, perhaps, was what pulled him through; after filming the final shot, Gable told Miller that from what he had seen in rushes, *The Misfits* was the best picture he had ever done, and that he was proud of having worked on the movie. Huston, however, still wanted to add scenes at that late stage.

Gable was buried at Forest Lawn, alongside Carole Lombard, the great love of his life. Marilyn was extremely upset by his death, and by the gossip column rumors that she had somehow been a contributing factor. Marilyn confessed her concern to friend SIDNEY SKOLSKY, "I kept him waiting—kept him waiting for hours and hours on that picture. Was I punishing my father? Getting even for all the years he's kept me waiting?"

## GABLE, KAY

CLARK GABLE's fifth and final wife was pregnant with Gable's son during shooting of *THE MISFITS* (1961). After her husband's death Kay publicly accused Marilyn that her antics during filming had contributed to his heart attack. Marilyn was devastated by this and went into deep depression. She replied publicly through George Carpozi's 1961 biography *Marilyn Monroe: Her Own Story*:

> "Clark Gable was one of the finest men I ever met. He was one of the most decent human beings anyone could have encountered anywhere. He was an excellent guy to work with. Knowing him and working with him was a great personal joy. I send all my love and deepest sympathy to his wife, Kay."

When Marilyn was invited to the May 1961 christening of John Clark Gable, it was a great relief to know that Kay harbored no ill feelings toward her.

## GABOR, ZSA ZSA
(B. 1919, SARI GABOR)

Not one of Marilyn's greatest fans, rival actress Gabor supposedly made arrangements to ensure that, on the set of the 1950 film *ALL ABOUT EVE*, Marilyn had no more than a professional liaison with fellow actor GEORGE SANDERS, to whom Zsa Zsa was married. Nevertheless, rumors were rife that Marilyn and Sanders evaded the Hungarian actress's spies and managed an affair. Zsa Zsa was right to be so suspicious: biographer FRED LAWRENCE GUILES recounts how a year or two earlier Sanders had met Marilyn at a party and within two minutes had proposed to her.

Years later the Hungarian actress said unflattering things about Marilyn: "She thought that if a man who takes her out for dinner doesn't sleep with her that night—something's wrong with her. When George was making *All About Eve* we had a suite and next to us Marilyn Monroe had a room. George made a thing out of it and said, 'Let's see how many men are going to go into her room tonight!' I'd seen about four."

Zsa Zsa actually shared the same screen with Marilyn in the movie *WE'RE NOT MARRIED* (1952)—though the two rivals were in separate episodes and did not necessarily have to meet on the set. They shared the publicity campaign for the movie as "America's Dream Girls."

## GAMBLING

One vice Marilyn did not appear to suffer from, perhaps because she was never awash in money, perhaps because she had grown up so poor she did not want to waste her own money. After her divorce from ARTHUR MILLER, Marilyn spent time with FRANK SINATRA and alleged MAFIA mobsters at the CAL-NEVA LODGE, built on the California/Nevada state border to exploit gambling possibilities.

JOHN HUSTON's legendary gambling was, according to some sources, one of the reasons why filming on *THE MISFITS* (1961) was so delayed—reputedly he used Marilyn's emotional problems as a cover while he scrambled to find money to pay off the massive gambling debts he was accumulating every night at the craps tables. Marilyn, Huston, and Arthur Miller were photographed around a craps table by EVE ARNOLD.

## GARBO, GRETA
(1905–1990, B. GRETA LOVISA GUSTAFSON)

The original screen goddess, the ethereal Garbo was brought to America by director and discoverer Mauritz Stiller and, from Hollywood, became the world's most famous screen actress of her day. She was the very embodiment of the unattainable star who somehow felt and suffered more than mere mortals. Norma Jeane spent many of her childhood matinee visits to the cinema entranced by Garbo's performance, the most famously in *The Flesh and the Devil* (1927), *Anna Christie* (1930), *Grand Hotel* (1932), *Queen Christina* (1933), *Anna Karenina* (1935), *Camille* (1936), *Ninotchka* (1939), and *Two Faced Woman* (1941). Garbo retired while still at the top, preserving the legend so carefully built by MGM. Although none of her four nominations for an ACADEMY AWARD resulted in an actual Oscar, in 1954 she received a special Academy Award in recognition of her "unforgettable screen performances."

Marilyn Monroe closely identified with Garbo as a child and in her adult life; they were both actresses who bewitched the camera with their sexuality, and they were both desperately lonely in life.

Marilyn chose a reading of *ANNA CHRISTIE*, Garbo's first "talkie," for her stage debut before the ACTORS STUDIO.

## GARDENING

MARILYN:
"Some day I want to have a house of my own with trees and grass and hedges all around, but never trim them at all—just let them grow any old way they want."

Marilyn's passion and empathy for all living creatures extended to plants. Living in ROXBURY, Connecticut with ARTHUR MILLER she dabbled in gardening. After she bought her house in Brentwood, she finally had her own green space to look after. Assisted by a gardener named Tataishi, she planted an herb garden and spent hours pottering around her flourishing creation; she was still buying plants for her garden in the week before her untimely death and the citrus trees and flowering plants she ordered from nearby Frank's Nursery were delivered to her home the day before she died.

In a 1960 interview with *Cosmopolitan* she revealed: "I have a green thumb. I can even plant things without roots. I just transplant them and they grow. I planted some seeds, nasturtiums, I think, when they come up, you're supposed to thin them out. What a pity, I thought, to throw out these little growing things, so I pulled them up and transplanted them very carefully; they had been so close together some didn't even have roots. Arthur said, 'That's impossible, they can't live.' But all of them did. And it says on the cover of the seed packages that you can't transplant them!"

John Huston and Marilyn at a craps table in Reno, Nevada, during filming of *The Misfits* (1961).

## GARLAND, JUDY
(1922–1969, B. FRANCES GUMM)

The two tragic actresses were friends. Garland said, "I knew Marilyn and loved her dearly. She asked me for help—ME! I didn't know what to tell her. One night at a party at Clifton Webb's house Marilyn followed me from room to room. 'I don't want to get too far away from you, I'm scared,' she said. I told her, 'We're all scared. I'm scared too.'" This was very much a case of the blind leading the blind. It was Garland who once said, "If I'm such a legend, why am I so lonely?" The last time they met was probably at MADISON SQUARE GARDEN the night that Marilyn congratulated President JOHN KENNEDY on his birthday.

Marilyn was a big fan of Garland's, attracted not just by her fine singing voice but by the tragedy and hurt that characterized her life. Garland had been born into a vaudeville family and began performing at the age of five. Her film debut came at fourteen, and by the time she was seventeen she had received a special ACADEMY AWARD for "her outstanding performance as a screen juvenile" in *The Wizard of Oz* (1939) and *Babes in Arms* (1939). Other memorable performances followed in *For Me and My Gal* (1942), *Meet Me in St. Louis* (1944), *The Clock* (1945), *Ziegfeld Follies* (1946), *Easter Parade* (1948), and *A Star Is Born* (1954), which earned her an Oscar nomination.

Marilyn liked to listen to Garland SONGS. "Who Cares?" was a particular favorite, and Garland's classic song "Over the Rainbow" was played at Marilyn's FUNERAL. Garland had her own special insight into Marilyn's death: "I don't think Marilyn really meant to harm herself. It was partly because she had too many pills available, then was deserted by her friends. You shouldn't be told you're completely irresponsible and be left alone with too much medication." In 1969 Garland herself died of a drug overdose.

## GARNETT, TAY (1894–1977)

Garnett, who co-wrote and directed *THE FIREBALL* (1950), the roller skating movie in which Marilyn has a small part, began his Hollywood career as a writer before landing his first movie as a director, *Celebrity* (1928). His most respected films were *One Way Passage* (1932), *Slave Ship* (1937), and *The Postman Always Rings Twice* (1946). He concluded his career working in television.

## GAYNOR, MITZI
(B. 1930, FRANCESCA MITZI VON GERBER)

Gaynor's career twice brought her into Marilyn productions, first in the compilation movie *WE'RE NOT MARRIED* (1952), and then in *THERE'S NO BUSINESS LIKE SHOW BUSINESS* (1954). Gaynor's singing and dancing talents ensured her some popularity during the fifties, in films such as *Golden Girl* (1951), *The Joker Is Wild* (1957), and *South Pacific* (1958).

## GENERAL BROCK HOTEL
5865 FALLS, NIAGARA FALLS

Marilyn stayed here during the location shooting of *NIAGARA* in 1952. It has since changed its name to the Sheraton Brock, and is now the Skyline Brock.

The nearby Niagara Casino has its very own "Marilyn's Penthouse Lounge and Bistro" hung with stills from the making of the film.

(*see* HOTELS)

## GENEROSITY

Few people in the cynical and unforgiving movie industry could have been as spontaneously and naturally generous as Marilyn. No sooner did she earn her first modest sums for walk-on roles than she began to make gifts to the people who mattered most to her. When her income increased, she extended her largesse to people in need, whether in the form of sponsoring charities or helping out crew members in financial difficulty.

Out of the $800 Marilyn earned in early 1949 for her brief cameo in the Marx brothers' movie, *LOVE HAPPY*, she bought a gold watch for former lover FRED KARGER and gifts for his mother and sister. She also sent a present to her former benefactors LUCILLE RYMAN and JOHN CARROLL.

Long-time hairdresser and friend AGNES FLANAGAN deliberately bit her lip before mentioning to Marilyn that there was some garment or household items she liked the look of; Marilyn would invariably make a few calls and the next day that item would be delivered direct to the Flanagan home.

On a December 1950 shopping trip to Tijuana, Marilyn spent most of the money she had brought to buy travel companion NATASHA LYTESS a gold-framed ivory cameo brooch. Two months later Marilyn came to Lytess's rescue when she heard her drama coach needed an extra $1000 to complete the purchase of a small house in Hollywood; the day after finding out about the problem, Marilyn arrived at Lytess's house with the money, which she raised by selling a gift JOHNNY HYDE had given her.

In 1952, the year her career really took off, Marilyn contacted Lucille Ryman and offered to pay her back the money Ryman and her husband had given her when she had been penniless. An amazed Ryman told her there was no need, but if she wanted she could pass it on to some other young actress struggling as Marilyn had done.

Yet Marilyn still felt the need to reciprocate to people who showed her kindness. This included the widow of drama teacher MICHAEL CHEKHOV. For years after Michael's death, Marilyn would stop in and visit Xenia when time allowed, and help out when money was tight. She was even named as a beneficiary in Marilyn's WILL. Weeks after filing for divorce from JOE DIMAGGIO, she gave him a gold watch to mark his fortieth birthday. Marilyn gave acting coach PAULA STRASBERG a string of pearls she had received from the emperor of Japan, after Paula admired it once too often. JOHN STRASBERG's best eighteenth birthday present was the keys to Marilyn's 1955 black Ford Thunderbird convertible.

Husband ARTHUR MILLER received a full *Encyclopaedia Britannica*, the Strasbergs were showered with books and records, while SUSAN STRASBERG was delighted to receive a Chagall sketch which Marilyn had picked out because "it looked like you."

On her 1962 trip to MEXICO to find furniture for her new Spanish-style home, Marilyn visited a local orphanage and made a $10,000 donation. This was just one of many occasions when she gave her time and money to worthy causes. Numerous friends of Marilyn's attest to the fact that she could not walk past a homeless person without slipping a dollar bill into his hand. During her many incognito forays along New York streets, she would stop and talk to down and outs who importuned her. She felt guilty if she had left her apartment without any money and therefore couldn't help out.

In her last interview, to *Life* journalist RICHARD MERYMAN, the one answer she asked him not to use in the article concerned a donation she had made; giving was a private gesture for Marilyn, her CHARITABLE WORKS were not something she wanted or needed to share with the public.

## *GENTLEMEN PREFER BLONDES* (1953)

As a twenty-sixth birthday present Marilyn learned she had landed the plum role of Lorelei Lee while celebrating at her then home, the BEL AIR HOTEL. Studio chief DARRYL ZANUCK preferred Marilyn to BETTY GRABLE, who had been slated for the role, after hearing an unreleased recording of Marilyn's voluptuous rendition of "Do It Again" for the marines at Camp Pendleton earlier that year. Another reason why Marilyn got the nod ahead of the vastly more experienced Grable was that she was locked into a studio contract and cost only one tenth of what Grable would have. And what Marilyn's free agent sidekick in this tale of gold-digging gals, JANE RUSSELL, obtained for her services.

*Gentlemen* had already had several incarnations before Marilyn made it indelibly hers. The original book, by ANITA LOOS, was reputedly based on the experiences of H. L. Mencken and was first published as six

Publicity photo for *Gentlemen Prefer Blondes* (1953) in which Marilyn is wearing the robe she wore in *Niagara* (1953).

monthly installments in *Harper's Bazaar* magazine, under the slightly different title *Gentlemen Always Prefer Blondes*. The book spawned a 1928 movie with Ruth Taylor and Alice White, and then a highly successful 1950 Broadway musical starring Carol Channing, who was briefly in the running for the movie version. TWENTIETH CENTURY-FOX had to fight off other studios and spent half a million dollars to secure the rights for what was to become one of the most popular musicals of the fifties, pitting the sensual Marilyn with the worldly Russell.

For the first time on film, Marilyn was all-singing and all-dancing. She sang a duet with Russell in "Two Little Girls from Little Rock" by JULE STYNE and Leo Robin, "When Love Goes Wrong" by Hoagy Carmichael and Harold Adamson, and "Bye Bye Baby" by Styne and Robin. Marilyn's high point, though, was her solo rendition of "Diamonds Are a Girl's Best Friend," another Styne and Robin number, in which Marilyn was originally set to wear an extremely revealing outfit before a change of heart and costume (and fear of the censor's scissors) made her a dazzling apparition in a pink strapless gown supported by a cast of fawning men in tuxedos. This number is the most famous of all Marilyn's musical pieces, and to this day is instantly recognizable. One song and dance number cut from the movie, known as the "Four French Dances," had Monroe and Russell cavorting in Eiffel Tower hats. Their costumes for these numbers can be briefly glimpsed during the movie when Gus first meets the girls.

Filming, as ever, was a trial. Co-star Jane Russell recalled how terrified her fellow actress was, but despite their on-screen rivalry, Russell and Monroe were very friendly throughout production. Musical director LIONEL NEWMAN later spoke of Marilyn's perfectionism during recording of the music: "She was damned sure of what she wanted. The men in the orchestra adored her. She was always congenial, courteous, not temperamental, and never forgot to thank everyone who worked with her." Director HOWARD HAWKS was less complimentary about Marilyn's insistence on multiple retakes even when he was happy with what she had already done. For instance, Hawks was perfectly satisfied with the very first take of "Bye Bye Baby" but Marilyn demanded another ten takes before she was happy.

It is rumored that Hawks did not shoot any of the musical numbers; that instead they were directed by seasoned choreographer JACK COLE.

One very apt dialogue exchange was added to the script by Marilyn herself. Her rich boyfriend's father says, "I thought you were dumb!" to which she retorts "I can be smart when it's important, but most men don't like it."

This movie brought Marilyn her first awards for performance (rather than for her pin-up looks). She won the *PHOTOPLAY* magazine Best Actress of 1953 award for her performance as Lorelei Lee, and the lesser known "The Best Friend a Diamond Ever Had" award from the Jewelry Academy.

MEMORABLE COSTUMES:

Tight red sequined "Little Rock" dress, slit to the thigh

Pink strapless "Diamonds Are A Girl's Best Friend" dress with big pink bow at the back

Gold lamé gown deemed too risqué for more than a brief appearance

Jane Russell, Charles Coburn and Marilyn in a publicity shot for *Gentlemen Prefer Blondes* (1953).

**Credits:**
Twentieth Century-Fox (Technicolor)
Length: 91 minutes
Release date: July 15, 1953

Directed by: Howard Hawks
Produced by: Sol C. Siegel
Written by: Charles Lederer, from a stage musical by Joseph Fields and Anita Loos; original serialized novel by Anita Loos
Cinematography by: Harry J. Wild
Music by: Lionel Newman, Leo Robin, Jule Styne
Costume Design by: Travilla
Film Editing by: Hugh S. Fowler

**Cast** (credits order):
Jane Russell . . . Dorothy Shaw
Marilyn Monroe . . . Lorelei Lee
Charles Coburn . . . Sir Francis Beekman
Elliott Reid . . . Detective Malone
Tommy Noonan . . . Gus Esmond
George Winslow . . . Henry Spofford III
Marcel Dalio . . . Magistrate
Taylor Holmes . . . Esmond Sr.
Norma Varden . . . Lady Beekman
Howard Wendell . . . Watson
Steven Geray . . . Hotel Manager
Henri Letondal . . . Grotier
Leo Mostovoy . . . Phillipe
Alex Frazer . . . Pritchard
Harry Carey Jr. . . . Winslow
William Cabanne . . . Sims
George Chakiris . . . Dancer
Jack Chete . . . Proprietor
John Close . . . Coach
George Davis . . . Cab Driver
Charles De Ravenne . . . Purser
Jean Del Val . . . Ship's Captain
Alphonse Martell . . . Headwaiter
Ray Montgomery . . . Peters
Alvy Moore . . . Anderson
Robert Nichols . . . Evans
Philip Sylvestre . . . Steward
Charles Tannen . . . Ed
Jimmy Young . . . Stevens
Matt Mattox . . . Featured Dancer (uncredited)
Lee Theodore . . . (uncredited)
Dick Wessel . . . (uncredited)

**Crew:**
Claude E. Carpenter . . . set decorator
Jack Cole . . . choreographer
Eliot Daniel . . . vocal director
Leonard Doss . . . color consultant
Earle H. Hagen . . . orchestration
Paul Helmick . . . assistant director

Publicity photo for *Gentlemen Prefer Blondes* (1953).

Marilyn as Lorelei Lee seduces Tommy Noonan as Gus Esmond in *Gentlemen Prefer Blondes* (1953).

Roger Heman . . . sound
Ray Kellogg . . . special effects
Charles Le Maire . . . wardrobe director
Bernard Mayers . . . orchestration
Ben Nye . . . makeup
Herbert W. Spencer . . . orchestration
E. Clayton Ward . . . sound
Lyle R. Wheeler . . . art director
Joseph C. Wright . . . art director

**Plot:**
Entertainers Lorelei Lee (Marilyn Monroe) and Dorothy Shaw (Jane Russell) board a ship bound for Paris, where Lorelei is due to marry her beau, the wealthy Gus Esmond (Tommy Noonan). Their capers on board are closely watched by a private detective called Malone (Elliott Reid), hired by Gus's father who is convinced that Lorelei is only interested in his son for the money. Things start to go awry when Dorothy falls for Malone, and then Malone photographs Lorelei in the arms of diamond merchant Sir Frances Beekman (Charles Coburn), who in fact was giving her a perfectly innocent demonstration of how a python wraps itself around a goat. Impervious to the attentions of a host of eligible and handsome young men, Dorothy and Lorelei scheme to get the photo back, which they succeed in doing by drugging the private eye. Sir Beekman is so relieved that this evidence cannot be used against anyone (including him) that he gives Lorelei his wife's diamond tiara as a mark of his appreciation.

By the time they get to Paris, however, Gus's father feels vindicated in his suspicions, and the girls suddenly find they are destitute, a situation they quickly remedy by landing jobs in a night club. In the meantime Lady Beekman (Norma Varden) has declared her tiara stolen, and Lorelei is the chief suspect. Dorothy helps out her friend by putting on a blonde wig and taking her place in court, so that Lorelei has one last chance to persuade Gus that she really does love him. Malone finds out that Beekman himself was the tiara thief, and solves the problem by presenting it to the court. Dorothy, dressed as Lorelei, rewards Malone with her affections, and because Lorelei has won over not just Gus but his doubting father, it all ends happily ever after in a spectacular double wedding.

**Reviews:**
*Los Angeles Examiner*
"And there is Marilyn Monroe! Zounds, boys, what a personality this one is! Send up a happy flare. At last, she is beautifully gowned, beautifully coiffed, and a wonderful crazy humor flashes from those sleepy eyes of hers."

*New York Herald Tribune*
"Putting these two buxom pin-up girls in the same movie is merely giving two-to-one odds on a sure thing, and the payoff is big in a rousing musical. . . . Singing, dancing or just staring at diamonds, these girls are irresistible and their musical is as lively as a string of firecrackers on the Fourth of July. . . . As usual, Miss Monroe looks as though she would glow in the dark, and her version of the baby-faced blonde whose eyes open for diamonds and close for kisses is always amusing as well as alluring."

*Los Angeles Citizen News*
"As Lorelei Lee, Marilyn looks as delectable as a ripe peach. She also surprises with a remarkably stylish voice piping 'Diamonds Are a Girl's Best Friend' in a lavish production number."

## GIANCANA, SAM

Chicago mobster Sam Giancana is the MAFIA connection most often associated with CONSPIRACY theory interpretations of Marilyn's death.

According to *Double Cross*, a biography of the Chicago mobster by his godson and younger brother, Giancana was at the CAL-NEVA LODGE, which he part-owned, with Marilyn the last weekend she was alive. She told him all about her troubles with ROBERT KENNEDY and how he had dumped her. Giancana responded by providing her with some sexual comfort. One week later a duo of mob killers called Needles and Mugsy tracked Robert Kennedy to outside Marilyn's house. They overheard him quarrel with her, and after Kennedy left, gave her the fatal barbiturate overdose by suppository. Their motive was to frame the attorney general for murder, and get him definitively off their Godfather's back. Biographer ANTHONY SUMMERS quotes an FBI memo from July 1961 in which Giancana threatens to "tell all" about the Kennedy brothers and their philandering, which he knew through his girlfriend Phyllis McGuire and PETER LAWFORD.

A variation on this theme appeared in the *National Enquirer* in March 1998, claiming that Giancana had been hired by the CIA to kill Marilyn in order to prevent her from revealing everything she knew about the organization. Giancana has, over the years, been linked to a number of other government organizations including the FBI.

BOOK:
*Double Cross*, Sam and Chuck Giancana. New York: Warner Books, 1992.

## GIELGUD, SIR JOHN (B. 1904)

Marilyn was an admirer of this great English actor, better known for his stagework than screen performances, though his first film was as early as 1924. At one time Marilyn was planning to do a movie version of *Rain* by Somerset Maugham, with her as streetwalker Sadie Thompson opposite Gielgud as the minister who is overwhelmed by passion.

(*see* FILMS MARILYN CONSIDERED OR WANTED)

## GIFFEN, HARVEY AND FAMILY

A FOSTER PARENT for Norma Jeane in 1935, Harvey Giffen and his wife took her into their home off Highland Avenue about a year after GLADYS BAKER was committed to NORWALK STATE HOSPITAL. The Giffens offered to adopt Norma Jeane as they were getting ready to move to Mississippi (or New Orleans in some accounts), but Gladys did not give her consent. After the Giffens, Norma Jeane briefly lived with another foster parent before taking up residence at the Los Angeles ORPHANAGE.

## GIFFORD, C. (CHARLES) STANLEY

Gifford was Marilyn's FATHER, the man with a mustache in the photograph her mother had shown her—or so Marilyn believed. In 1925 and 1926 C. Stanley Gifford was working at CONSOLIDATED FILM INDUSTRIES in Hollywood, either as a foreman of the day shift or as a salesman, depending on accounts. Under his charge was GLADYS BAKER. Gifford was known as something of a philanderer. His wife, Lillian Priester, had left him in late 1923, and in the divorce papers which came through in May 1925 he did not contest that he had "shamelessly boasted of his conquests with other women." One of his conquests was film-cutter Baker—who also happened to live in the same apartment block. The affair did not continue after she informed him she was pregnant. Biographer FRED LAWRENCE GUILES writes that Gifford offered Gladys

A publicity photo of Marilyn, 1953

some money and told her she should thank her lucky stars she was still married.

There is no evidence of any contact between father and daughter during Norma Jeane's childhood. But at the age of eighteen, when still married to JAMES DOUGHERTY, a family friend handed Norma Jeane his phone number. She called, only for Gifford to hang up as soon as she had announced herself as Gladys's daughter.

Several encounters between Marilyn and Gifford in later years may have taken place. After tracking Gifford down to the Red Rock Dairy cattle farm in the village of Hemet, near PALM SPRINGS, Marilyn made more than one drive down from Hollywood; in 1951, in the space of a couple of weeks, she first took drama coach NATASHA LYTESS, and then reporter SIDNEY SKOLSKY. More than ten years later, in 1961, Marilyn apparently made another two trips, once with her masseur RALPH ROBERTS, and then with her publicist PAT NEWCOMB. Biographer DONALD SPOTO questions whether these trips were real attempts to meet her putative father, or ruses to garner sympathy from people in her life. Sometimes she stopped and turned round halfway; on other occasions she parked off the property and walked up to a house hidden behind some trees, only to return soon after saying that he didn't want to see her.

It seems that Gifford had a change of heart not long before Marilyn died. He reportedly sent her a "get well" card after her 1961 stay in a New York psychiatric HOSPITAL. Then, in 1962, after suffering a heart attack, Gifford had a nurse contact Marilyn on his behalf. The nurse told Marilyn he wanted to talk to her before he died. Marilyn did not see why she should accede to his demands when he had rebuffed hers. In the end, Gifford outlived Marilyn by quite a few years.

## GLADSTONE HOTEL, THE
E. 52ND ST., NEAR LEXINGTON AVE., NEW YORK

Marilyn's first New York residence after walking out on TWENTIETH CENTURY-FOX and turning her back on Hollywood. Recently divorced ex-husband JOE DIMAGGIO helped her move in on January 19, 1955. A suite was rented for her by business partner MILTON GREENE, which she used until she moved into the WALDORF-ASTORIA that April.

(*see* HOTELS)

## *GLAMOUR PREFERRED*

Marilyn Monroe's first stage appearance before a paying audience was in this play, which ran at the Bliss-Hayden Miniature Theater in Beverly Hills from October 12 to November 2, 1947. It was common practice at this theater—part professional company, part acting school—for performers to play different parts or share roles. On the recommendation of benefactor LUCILLE RYMAN, soon after the disappointment of being released by TWENTIETH CENTURY-FOX, Marilyn auditioned for the second lead role. Marilyn alternated with fellow actress Jane Weeks in the part of a Hollywood starlet who unsuccessfully attempts to ensnare a glamorous Hollywood actor. Even at this early stage in her career, art imitated life: Marilyn reputedly tried to seduce Lucille Ryman's husband, handsome actor JOHN CARROLL. Written by Florence Ryerson and Colin Clements, the play had made its Broadway debut in 1940, but lasted only eleven performances. The cast included Lee Elson, Christine Larson, Nancy O'Neill, Bill McLean, Charlotte Payne, Trudy Leeds, Jack Hire, Don Hayden, and Owen Tyree. Actor Bill McLean said, "She was so very, very sweet and nice. Very inexperienced on stage. However, when she walked on stage, she stood out so much that nobody looked at anybody else."

## GODDARD, ELEANOR "BEEBE" (BEBE)

DOC GODDARD's daughter from a previous marriage, either two years or six months younger than Norma Jeane—reports vary—Beebe shared a room with Norma Jeane starting in 1938 or 1940, after Norma Jeane came out of the orphanage and went to live with her guardian GRACE MCKEE GODDARD. Beebe and Norma Jeane became great friends. They shared clothes, makeup, and a love of the movies. This friendship came to an end in 1942 when the Goddard family moved East, and Norma Jeane prepared to marry boy the next door, JAMES DOUGHERTY.

If Norma Jeane's childhood was troubled, Bebe's was truly tragic. Some biographers have claimed that many of Marilyn's stories about her terrible childhood were things she had heard from Beebe. Her parents divorced when she was a year and half old, her mother became mentally ill—in Beebe's words "a sociopath—no conscience, no knowledge of right and wrong," and then Beebe had to look after her younger brother and sister through a succession of foster homes across Texas. In later life Marilyn and her former foster sister stayed in touch sporadically until 1955, when Marilyn left California for New York.

## GODDARD, ERWIN "DOC"

Erwin (sometimes spelled "Ervin") was a research engineer at the Adel Precision Products Company when he met Grace McKee, who was guardian to Norma Jeane. Depending on accounts, Erwin's nickname "Doc" either derived from his skill as an inventor, or because his father had been a surgeon. He was a very imposing man, six feet five inches tall in his socks, and said to bear a passing resemblance to dashing actor Randolph Scott. Doc's dreams of a film career never progressed beyond stand-in and extras work, including a stint as a rosy-cheeked toy soldier with Laurel and Hardy in *Babes in Toyland*.

Doc first met Norma Jeane in 1935, the year he courted and married Grace, who had been the girl's legal guardian since GLADYS BAKER had been committed to a mental institution. Ten years younger than his new wife, he had three children from a previous marriage—Eleanor, Nona, and John—or Beebe, Josephine, and John according to FRED LAWRENCE GUILES. Josephine, the youngest daughter born in 1930, was to carve out an acting career under the name JODY LAWRANCE.

Times were tough for the newly married couple, and Norma Jeane, it seems, was one mouth too many to feed. Within months, she was taken to the Los Angeles ORPHANAGE. Almost two years later Norma Jeane left the orphanage and returned to live with Doc and Grace. Many Marilyn biographers relate an incident soon after her return when a very drunk Goddard grabbed at and kissed young Norma Jeane in an "intimate" manner. This event has been corroborated by Marilyn's first husband JAMES DOUGHERTY, whom she told about the ordeal.

After this incident, Norma Jeane only spent brief periods living under the same roof as Doc and Grace—some biographers point to the incident as the cause, though most agree that it was poverty that led to her departure. Most of the time, between her return from the orphanage and her 1942 marriage to Dougherty, Norma Jeane lived with Grace's aunt, ANA LOWER, just down the road on NEBRASKA AVENUE.

The precipitating factor in Norma Jeane's hastily-arranged marriage was a promotion. Doc was offered a job as Head of Sales in the Adel Precision Products' East Coast branch. He and his family, minus Norma Jeane, moved to Huntington, West Virginia in 1942.

Years later, after Norma Jeane had become Marilyn and was beginning to forge a career for herself, Doc Goddard offered to be her business manager. Marilyn turned him down. There is no evidence that Marilyn and Goddard ever met up after 1945. After Grace committed suicide in 1953, Goddard remarried twice: to Anna Alice Long, and then to Annie Rundle, with whom he died in a car crash in Ventura on December 4, 1972.

## GODDARD, GRACE MCKEE (1895–1953)

Grace McKee, as she was called when Norma Jeane came into the world, was born in Montana on January 1, 1895 and christened Clara Grace Atchinson. In 1923 Grace was working as a supervisor (or film librarian, according to some sources) at CONSOLIDATED FILM INDUSTRIES when she met GLADYS BAKER, who took a job there as a negative cutter. The two of them soon became great friends. Co-worker Olin G. Stanley remembered Grace as "freewheeling, hard-working and fast-living. Ambitious to succeed. A busybody. Whoever and whatever she wanted, she went and got. Partying and booze seemed the most important things in her life, and work was just means to that end." Gladys loved to party as well, and the two women often went out on the town together.

Norma Jeane was born in 1926 and very soon was placed with foster parents, the BOLENDERS. Grace and Gladys continued to live the high life. Grace often accompanied Gladys and her little girl on day trips. In 1933–34 Grace was a frequent visitor to Gladys's home on ARBOL STREET, the only place where Norma Jeane, then aged seven, ever lived as a child with her mother.

Best friend Grace played either a starring or supporting role in the committal of Norma Jeane's mother to a mental hospital. Biographers even disagree about the year she was taken away to hospital—either 1934 or 1935. In one version, Grace and Gladys had a fight, Gladys attacked Grace with a knife and the police were called, though the most oft-told story is that Gladys was taken away after a severe anxiety attack, the culmination of gradual deterioration in her mental health. Reports also differ regarding the immediate fate of little Norma Jeane. Either Grace looked after her at the Arbol Street house, or else Gladys's tenants, an English actor by the name of GEORGE ATKINSON and his family, took care of the girl before Grace stepped in to take charge. In any event, Grace commenced proceedings to become the legal guardian of her best friend's little girl when it became clear that Gladys was destined to stay in hospital for some time. What biographers do agree about is that Grace channeled her own thwarted ambitions to be a movie star into the little girl she officially became a ward to in mid-1935. Fellow worker Leila Fields went so far as to say, "If it weren't for Grace, there would be no Marilyn Monroe. . . . Grace raved about Norma Jeane like she was her own. Grace said Norma Jeane was going to be a movie star. She had this feeling. A conviction. 'Don't worry, Norma Jeane. You're going to be a beautiful girl when you get big—an important woman—a movie star.'" Another fellow worker, Mr. Stanley, remembered Grace bringing the little girl to work on Saturdays, and getting her to promenade up and down in front of her colleagues. Norma Jeane told anyone who would listen that when she grew up she was going to be a movie star.

After Gladys's home at Arbol Street was sold off to pay debts, Grace did not take Norma Jeane into her own home, but sent her to stay first with the Giffen family, and then with her own mother, Emma Willette Atchinson. At this time she was seeing ERWIN "DOC" GODDARD, a relationship that quickly became serious. By the summer of 1935, they were married. Here too, accounts diverge as to whether Norma Jeane moved in with the couple to the small bungalow they were renting at 6707 ODESSA AVENUE in Van Nuys, or whether she went straight from Atchinson's home on Lodi Place to the Los Angeles ORPHANAGE. Whatever the circumstances surrounding her placement in the orphanage, for Norma Jeane this was the biggest shock of her tumultuous childhood. When Grace took her to the orphanage, the girl pleaded that there must be some mistake, she wasn't an orphan, she had a mother. Grace too, it seemed, was deeply shaken, but either her finances or the arrival of love in her life meant that she was not prepared to take in her best friend's little girl. For almost two years, Grace paid for the girl's room and board ($15 per month), plus a similar amount on clothes and expenses. For a Saturday treat, she would take out Norma Jeane for lunch and a movie. On special occasions, the routine would change, and Grace would take the girl to a beauty parlor where the girl was given the whole works. Grace's step-daughter BEEBE GODDARD recalls that she was "something of a wizard with cosmetics, and she loved to sweep down on us with all kinds of advice about makeup."

One week after Norma Jeane's eleventh birthday on June 7, 1937, Grace finally took her out of the orphanage to live with her family in Van Nuys. Here again, biographers disagree about how long Norma Jeane lived with Grace before moving on to "Aunt" ANA LOWER. Marilyn later talked about her feelings at the time: "At first I was waking up in the mornings at the Goddards' and thinking I was still at the orphanage. Then, before I could get used to them, I was with another aunt and uncle, walking round thinking I was still at the Goddards'. It was all very confusing." However, the reason why she didn't stay was probably "Doc" Goddard's drunken attempt to molest her.

Over the next five years Norma Jeane lived less with Grace than with Lower, but she did go back to live with the Goddards at times when Ana Lower's heart condition prevented her from looking after the girl. On one such occasion, in 1940, while living with the Goddards at their apartment at 14743 ARCHWOOD STREET in Van Nuys, Norma Jeane struck up a firm friendship with Beebe.

The end of Norma Jeane's disjointed living arrangements under the legal guardianship of Grace came in early 1942 when Doc was offered a promotion that meant moving across country to West Virginia. Norma Jeane was not part of the plan. Instead, she faced the nightmare of returning to the orphanage until she reached adulthood. Grace's plan, one which she skillfully brought to fruition, was to marry off her young charge to JAMES DOUGHERTY, the boy next door and son of her good friend Ethel Dougherty. Many years later Marilyn bluntly recounted the background to this marriage: "Grace McKee Goddard arranged a marriage for me. I never had a choice. . . . They couldn't support me, and they had to work out something. And so I got married." Years later, Dougherty told an interviewer that when Norma Jeane found out that she would not be taken along with the Goddards to their new life, "her respect for Grace altered. . . . Grace had told Norma Jeane that she would never feel insecure again, and now the poor girl felt that Grace had gone back on her word."

While married to Jim, Norma Jeane remained in regular contact with Grace. She went to visit her in Chicago—her first trip outside the state of California—and even sent her some money from her job at the RADIO PLANE MUNITIONS FACTORY to help her out. At this time Grace was living alone, away from Doc, and was working once more at a film lab. According to Beebe, Grace had left their home in West Virginia because "she had developed a drinking problem. . . . All my father's wives had that, probably because one of his own chief occupations was whooping it up every day, and they joined him." On the trip Norma Jeane also stopped for a visit with Beebe and Doc.

In a letter sent to Grace on June 15, 1944, seven weeks after Dougherty was posted to active war duty in Asia, Norma Jeane seemed happy with her fate as a waiting war wife: "Of course I know that if it hadn't been for you we might not have never been married and I know I owe you a lot for that fact alone, besides countless others... I love Jimmie in a different way I suppose than anyone, and I know I shall never be happy with anyone else as long as I live, and I know he feels the same towards me. So you see we are really very happy together, that is of course, when we can be together. We both miss each other terribly."

Grace and family moved back to California and continued to invite Norma Jeane. By this time, Norma Jeane was launching into her MODELING career, and she did not always take up these invitations. Grace continued to drink heavily, and was not always the best of company. Then, in August 1946, on a proud and hopeful day for guardian and ward, Grace accompanied Norma Jeane to TWENTIETH CENTURY-FOX studios to apply her signature to Norma Jeane's first film contract. The signature was required because Norma Jeane was still under the age of twenty-one. After this, recorded contacts between Norma Jeane and Grace were few and far between. Marilyn visited Grace in 1949 and 1951, but was apparently extremely distressed at the ravages of alcoholism on her former guardian.

On September 28, 1953 Marilyn learned of Grace's death, by an overdose of barbiturates, after a number of years of chronic alcoholism and debilitating strokes. Marilyn did not attend her funeral at WESTWOOD MEMORIAL PARK three days later, though in some accounts it was Marilyn who took care of the arrangements.

Later on in life Marilyn did not seem to have a great deal of gratitude toward Grace. She resented her for putting her in the orphanage, she resented her for taking off to West Virginia and effectively abandoning her after promising she would never again be sent away, and she resented what she later saw as her arranged marriage to Jim Dougherty. However, in 1960 Leila Fields told biographer MAURICE ZOLOTOW, "She was one in a million. She was Gladys's best friend, and she loved and adored Norma Jeane. It if it weren't for Grace, there wouldn't be a Marilyn Monroe today."

## GOLDEN GLOBE AWARDS

Marilyn may never have won an ACADEMY AWARD, but she twice won the accolade of "World Film Favorite" from the Hollywood Foreign Press, first in 1954, then in 1961. In March 1960 she received the 1959 Best Actress in a Comedy or Musical Golden Globe for her performance in *SOME LIKE IT HOT*.

Marilyn arrived at the 1961 award presentation (on March 5, 1962) on the arm of JOSÉ BOLAÑOS, a young Mexican she had befriended the week before during a brief visit south of the border.

Marilyn was awarded the Golden Globe for Best Actress in a Comedy or Musical for her performance in *Some Like It Hot* (1959).

## GOODMAN, BENNY
(1909–1986, B. BENJAMIN DAVID GOODMAN)

Bandleader and clarinetist Benny Goodman, known as "the king of swing," was one of the most popular jazz men of his era.

In 1948, after COLUMBIA decided not to renew her contract— the second studio to do so in a short space of time—Marilyn Monroe unsuccessfully auditioned to be a singer in the Benny Goodman Band.

## GOSLAR, LOTTE

In 1953 Marilyn worked with drama coach MICHAEL CHEKHOV. To help her with her timing—crucial to making the most of the comic potential of Pola in *HOW TO MARRY A MILLIONAIRE* (1953)—he took her to Lotte Goslar, a mime artist who ran the Hollywood Turnabout Theater. With Goslar, Marilyn did a number of exercises and studied dance, mime, and movement. Goslar assisted Marilyn with her final dance number in *RIVER OF NO RETURN* (1954), and also helped her on the set of other films.

Goslar told biographer FRED LAWRENCE GUILES, "She wanted solo instruction in mime but she needed to be with other people. I placed her in a class with ten pupils.... I saw at once how very serious she was about her art.... She was exceptionally talented and one of the best pupils in the group."

Goslar was one of the select view who were invited to attend Marilyn's FUNERAL.

## GOULD, DEBORAH

Deborah Gould was briefly wife number three for PETER LAWFORD, who had previously been married to JOHN F. KENNEDY's sister, Patricia. According to Gould, Peter Lawford had told her that JFK was sexually very curious about Marilyn and keen to meet her. Lawford arranged an introduction some time before Kennedy became president, and their affair continued after he entered the White House.

Also according to Gould, Lawford played a murky part in the proceedings on Marilyn's last evening alive; not only did he receive a call from her in which she threatened to commit suicide, but he later went to her Brentwood home to "sanitize" the place before reporters arrived on the scene. Gould also stated that Lawford had destroyed a suicide note Marilyn had written.

## GRABLE, BETTY
(1916 1973, B. ELIZABETH RUTH GRABLE)

"It may sound peculiar to say so, because she is no longer with us, but we were very close. Once when we were doing that picture together, I got a call on the set: my younger daughter had had a fall [from a horse]. I ran home and the one person to call was Marilyn. She did an awful lot to boost things up for movies, when everything was at a low state; there'll never be anyone like her for looks, for attitude, for all of it."

Lauren Bacall, Betty Grable, and Marilyn in a break shooting *How to Marry a Millionaire* (1953).

Grable was Hollywood's biggest female star when Marilyn was first starting out in the movies, though it had taken her ten years to get to the top and become, with Rita Hayworth, the wartime pin-up darling of the nation's troops. Throughout the forties Grable was TWENTIETH CENTURY-FOX's number one female attraction, the highest paid actress of her day.

If, as some commentators suggest, Marilyn's first movie part was in *THE SHOCKING MISS PILGRIM* (1947), then the two actresses may have come face-to-face in 1946. By this time, Grable had cornered the market with her energetic but rather chaste appeal—not to mention her legs which had been insured for a million dollars—in movies such as *Tin Pan Alley* (1940), *Moon over Miami* (1941), *Pin-Up Girl* (1944), and then *Mother Wore Tights* (1947). Grable was well aware of the truth: "There are two reasons why I'm in show business, and I'm standing on both of them."

As Grable's long reign at the top came to an end, Marilyn was rising fast to take her place in the all-American male's imagination. The baton was handed from one actress to another over the space of two movies, *GENTLEMAN PREFER BLONDES* (1953) and *HOW TO MARRY A MILLIONAIRE* (1953).

In 1952 Marilyn was cast ahead of Grable for the role of Lorelei Lee in *Gentlemen Prefer Blondes*, despite Grable's keenness for the part. For her next movie, Marilyn was pitted opposite the outgoing Screen Queen. Far from showing any bitterness, Grable was graciousness personified. She sprang to her co-star's defense in the tumult surrounding Marilyn's "scandalous" attire at the *PHOTOPLAY* awards in March 1953, commenting, "Why, Marilyn's thc biggest thing that's happened in Hollywood in years. The movies were just sort of going along, and all of a sudden, Zowie, there was Marilyn. She's a shot in the arm for Hollywood."

The eagerly-awaited "Battle of the Blondes" the studio publicity department was so keen to promote, and the press hounds were so keen to cover, simply never materialized. Marilyn never forgot the way the studio had marched her into Betty Grable's dressing room and introduced the starlet to Hollywood's most popular female star of the time as if to serve notice on her. In 1960 Marilyn told journalist W. J. WEATHERBY that this was when she realized

Betty Grable and Marilyn arriving at Walter Winchell's birthday party at Ciro's restaurant, 1953.

just how ruthless, disloyal, and underhanded the studios were.

Grable wasn't jealous of Marilyn. "There's room for us all," was her attitude; if anything she was protective of her younger co-star, who during the final ascent to the heights of stardom was dogged by press revelations (the infamous new calendar, and then news that far from being an orphan her mother was still alive). Grable knew that her unprecedented run at the top—thirteen years running as a top ten box-office star—was coming to an end. One day she said to Marilyn, "Honey, I've had it. Go get yours. It's your turn now."

Though Betty Grable got on fine with Marilyn during shooting, she was not at all happy with the studio. By the end of filming, she had marched in to studio head DARRYL ZANUCK's office and ripped up her contract. The studio did not seem to be overly upset; Marilyn moved right into Grable's old dressing room, Dressing Room M, in time for shooting of *THERE'S NO BUSINESS LIKE SHOW BUSINESS* (1954).

The two actresses crossed paths once more two years later. After Marilyn had walked out on Fox, the studio tried to entice Grable back as her replacement in *How to Be Very, Very Popular*, a film specially crafted for Marilyn Monroe by NUNNALLY JOHNSON. Perhaps against her better judgment, Grable returned to take part in a film where she was not even Marilyn's replacement, but a supporting actress for SHEREE NORTH, the starlet Fox vainly hoped could replace Marilyn.

## GRAHAM, SHEILAH

Famous Hollywood columnist who was not always Marilyn's most trustworthy press ally. She believed that Marilyn "went to bed with half of Hollywood, including Brando, Sinatra and members of the Kennedy family—JFK and Bobby. But strangely she was a sex symbol who didn't care too much for sex."

Graham often enjoyed impeccable sources. In 1962 Graham was tipped off and published the news that Marilyn had been dismissed from *SOMETHING'S GOT TO GIVE* on the very same day as Marilyn's lawyer found out.

In 1963 Graham unsuccessfully lobbied the Motion Picture Academy to award Marilyn an honorary posthumous Oscar.

## GRANDISON, LIONEL

Deputy CORONER's aide who made some sensational claims to biographer MILO SPERIGLIO: that both a red DIARY and a suicide note mysteriously disappeared from Marilyn's Brentwood home, that bruises on Marilyn's body did not feature on the final autopsy report, and that necrophiliacs had abused her body.

He also stated that despite the fact he "personally felt there were circumstances surrounding her death that should have been investigated," he signed the death certificate as a "probable suicide."

## GRANDPARENTS AND GREAT-GRANDPARENTS

Norma Jeane's maternal grandparents were DELLA MAE HOGAN, who died a year after Norma Jeane was born, and OTIS ELMER MONROE, who died many years earlier. Who her paternal grandparents were depends on who her father was, and no biographer has yet indulged in such speculation.

Maternal great-grandfather Tilford Marion Hogan, born in 1851, was the son of Illinois farmers George Hogan and Sara Owens. He married Jennie Nance in Barry Country, Missouri, and they had three children. The marriage lasted about twenty years, during which time he supported the family working as a day laborer. Tilford remarried at the age of seventy-seven, and set up home with a widow named Emma Wyatt. His long life came to an end on May 29, 1933. Like so many thousands of people during the Depression, he was forced off his land. Receipt of the eviction notice was too much for him, and he hanged himself from the beams of his barn. Within months of his suicide, daughter GLADYS BAKER also succumbed to mental illness, leaving Norma Jeane effectively an orphan.

## GRANT, ALLAN

Probably the last PHOTOGRAPHER to do a still session with Marilyn, on July 9, 1962. These pictures accompanied RICHARD MERYMAN's interview in the August 3 issue of *Life* magazine.

## GRANT, CARY
(1904–1986, B. ARCHIBALD LEACH)

British-born Cary Grant was the thinking woman's leading man, the ultimate comic sophisticate whose talents graced seventy-two films. To some critics, he was quite simply the finest actor in Hollywood. Two-time Oscar nominee, he picked up a special Academy Award in 1969, in recognition of his performances in such classics as *She Done Him Wrong* (1933), *His Girl Friday* and *The Philadelphia Story* (both 1940), *Arsenic and Old Lace* (1944), *Mr Blandings Builds His Dream House* (1948), and the Hitchcock masterpiece *North by Northwest* (1959).

Grant's one film with Marilyn Monroe was HOWARD HAWKS's 1952 picture *MONKEY BUSINESS*. There is a singular lack of rumors regarding an on-set romance between Grant, famous for his sexual conquests, and Marilyn. He could not be enticed to star opposite her in *LET'S MAKE LOVE* (1960), a role that eventually went to YVES MONTAND. Grant is one of the improbable number of people said to have spoken with Marilyn by phone on the night of her death.

Publicity photo of Marilyn and Cary Grant for *Monkey Business* (1952).

## GRANT, STEFFI

"They were both like frightened puppies, both brighter than they knew, and of course Marilyn had a weakness for fatherly, intellectual Jewish men."

The daughter of columnist SIDNEY SKOLSKY listened in on an extension to some of Marilyn's calls to her father, because he wanted somebody else to listen to the things Marilyn would say to him "off the record." When Steffi Skolsky married Leonard J. Grant in 1960, Marilyn and ARTHUR MILLER gave the couple a sterling silver cigarette box bearing an engraved inscription in Marilyn's handwriting: "For this wonderful day—affectionately, Marilyn and Arthur."

## GRAUMAN'S CHINESE THEATER
6925 HOLLYWOOD BLVD., HOLLYWOOD
(NOW MANN'S CHINESE THEATER)

"When I was younger, I used to go to Grauman's Chinese Theater and try to fit my foot in the prints in the cement there. And I'd say, 'Oh, oh, my foot's too big, I guess that's out.' I did have a funny feeling later when I finally put my foot down into that wet cement. I sure knew what it really meant to me—anything's possible, almost."

Like most little girls Norma Jeane looked forward to the treat of a Saturday matinee. Before she was taken in to care, her mother GLADYS BAKER took her along. After that it was generally legal guardian GRACE MCKEE GODDARD who accompanied Norma Jeane. When she was older she went on her own, clutching the dime she needed to get in. Practically every weekend she went to one of the Grauman's theaters, either the Chinese or the Egyptian, both of which were on Hollywood Boulevard. This was where her dreams were forged.

On June 26, 1953, as part of the publicity campaign for *GENTLEMEN PREFER BLONDES*, the moment arrived for Marilyn and JANE RUSSELL to cast their own handprints and footprints in the celebrated movie house theater courtyard, following in a tradition that was accidentally created in the mid-twenties when Douglas Fairbanks and Mary Pickford stumbled into some cement freshly poured outside the movie theater.

That day the two stars made their appearance in matching white polka-dot dresses. The cement was poured, wet and waiting for their prints, when Marilyn suggested they make a more personal contribution to posterity. Jane Russell could leave an imprint of her bust, and she would do likewise with her posterior. When the suggestion was ignored, Marilyn proposed a diamond to dot the "i" in her name. The rhinestone used for the purpose did not take very long to catch the eye of a souvenir hunter. Marilyn's prints are not far from JEAN HARLOW's, left eighteen years earlier.

*The Seven Year Itch* (1955) at Grauman's Chinese Theater.

Marilyn and Jane Russell were immortalized at Grauman's Chinese Theater on June 26, 1953.

### GRAUMAN'S EGYPTIAN THEATER

As a girl Norma Jeane also went regularly to Grauman's Egyptian Theater (at 6708 Hollywood Boulevard instead of 6925 for the present-day Mann's Chinese Theater). She liked to look at the monkeys in a cage outside the theater. In June 1950 one of her early movies, *The Asphalt Jungle,* premiered here; Marilyn did not attend that showing, but ex-husband Jim Dougherty, by then a policeman, was on duty that night controlling the crowds.

## GREENE, AMY

A New York fashion model, married to photographer MILTON GREENE. According to almost all biographers, Amy and Marilyn became almost inseparable best friends when Milton and Marilyn set up as partners in MARILYN MONROE PRODUCTIONS.

From late 1954, when Marilyn turned her back on her straitjacket contract with Fox and effectively went into hiding from Hollywood and the PRESS, she holed up with the Greenes in their Weston, Connecticut, home, where for a couple of months she became one of the family. Marilyn was "Auntie" to the Milton's young son Joshua, whom she sometimes fed, bathed, and babysat, as well as buying him presents, including a huge stuffed bear.

During the year, as Milton arranged the details of Marilyn Monroe Productions, Marilyn and Amy went shopping together, did the New York social circuit, and spent time together both in town and at their country home: "She wanted to become an educated lady, but she also wanted to be a star. That was a conflict. But in the beginning she was very happy, functioning well, fighting Zanuck."

Amy was on camera beside Marilyn in her live TV appearance on "Person to Person" on April 8, 1955. Their friendship continued through 1956: Amy was by Marilyn's side as she flew into Los Angeles to work on *BUS STOP* (1956); she was a matron of honor in Marilyn's formal Jewish WEDDING ceremony to Arthur Miller; and along with Milton, she was in England during the late summer and fall of 1956 for work on the one film Marilyn Monroe Productions made, *THE PRINCE AND THE SHOWGIRL* (1957).

Of the tempestuous relations that developed between her husband and friend, Amy once said, "When they loved and hated, it was with all their being. When they drank and drugged, they did so with great passion." Amy always denied that this great passion overflowed into sexual relations.

Their friendship did not survive Marilyn's rather acrimonious disentanglement from business partner Milton. Amy told biographer ANTHONY SUMMERS, "Never forget that Marilyn wanted above all to become a *great* movie star. She would do anything, give up anyone, to move up."

Amy Greene features prominently in the Marilyn documentary "Marilyn: Life after Death."

## GREENE, MILTON HAWTHORNE
(1922–1985, B. GREENHOLTZ)

PHOTOGRAPHER Milton H. Greene was the man who between 1953 and 1957 gave Marilyn the belief to tough it out against the all-powerful Hollywood studios and set out on her own. Before taking a sabbatical from photography to promote MARILYN MONROE PRODUCTIONS full-time, Greene had quickly risen to great prominence as a leading fashion photographer who had a way with stars, including MARLENE DIETRICH, JUDY GARLAND, and AUDREY HEPBURN. He won plaudits from fellow photographers such as RICHARD AVEDON, who thought Greene "the greatest photographer of women." Many fans consider Greene's photographs of Marilyn, in both public and private, to have a unique quality, and of course he had unprecedented access to Marilyn.

The generally accepted story—confirmed by Milton's son Joshua in *Milton's Marilyn*—is that Marilyn and Milton hit it off the first time they met, in 1953 when Greene was in Hollywood to do a *Look* magazine cover story on Marilyn. In a 1956 interview with EDWARD R. MURROW on "Person to Person" Marilyn and Milton described this meeting. She saw him and exclaimed "Why, you're just a boy!" to which he replied "And you're just a girl."

It was Greene who had the foresight to turn Marilyn's discontent with TWENTIETH CENTURY-FOX into a carefully prepared exit strategy, and the alluring opportunity to control her own cinematic future. In late 1953 when he returned to Los Angeles with his new wife Amy, Milton encouraged her to actually do something about the insultingly low salary she was locked into and to rebel against the roles she felt demeaned her. Marilyn was keen to put into practice his suggestion that she form her own production company, and was not fazed that Milton had no background in film. It took a year of plan-

This stunning photograph of Marilyn was taken by Milton Greene on the Twentieth Century-Fox backlot, 1953.

Milton Greene took this photo of Marilyn in Richard Rodgers's swimming pool in Connecticut, 1953.

Marilyn speaks with the press at the Los Angeles airport after having flown in from New York with her business partner Milton Greene, February 25, 1956.

ning for Milton to set things up, during which time Marilyn married and divorced JOE DIMAGGIO. Then, just ten days after the big Romanoff's party consecrating Marilyn as a big time Hollywood star, Milton flew into town to lay the plans for Marilyn's getaway. In December 1954 she holed up in a New York hotel, and then moved in with Milton and AMY GREENE at their home in Weston, Connecticut.

Marilyn had told Greene that in Hollywood "they rushed me from one picture into another. It's no challenge to do the same thing over and over. I want to keep growing as a person and as an actress, and in Hollywood they never ask me my opinion. They just tell me what time to show up for work. In leaving Hollywood and coming to New York, I feel I can be more myself. After all, if I can't be myself, what's the good of being anything at all?"

The mad press scramble to "find Marilyn" ended when Milton and Marilyn held a press conference to take the wraps off Marilyn Monroe Productions, a company owned by the two founding shareholders on a 51/49 percent split. However, Fox was not going to give up on Marilyn's contract without a fight, and Marilyn's fledgling production company had its own struggles keeping Marilyn in true star style, despite the fact that they had no income, only potential projects. Marilyn's expenses included $250 per week for an apartment at the WALDORF-ASTORIA, $100 per week to pay for care of Marilyn's mother GLADYS BAKER, $125 per week for PSYCHOANALYSIS, and an entire new wardrobe (Marilyn arrived in New York with little more than the clothes on her back).

After it became apparent that Greene was not going to succeed in attracting a cash-rich sponsor for Marilyn Monroe Productions, he gave the go-ahead to his team of lawyers to renegotiate Marilyn's hopelessly outdated contract with Fox. Milton was by her side when she made her triumphant return to Hollywood in 1956 to star in *BUS STOP*. This must have been a proud moment for Marilyn, who through Greene seemed at last to have some control over her destiny. Greene scouted for deals, negotiated on Marilyn's behalf, filtered out unwanted complications and generally acted as a buffer between Marilyn and the world. One seasoned reporter unhappily noted, "No one gets to Marilyn without first clearing through him."

Greene also had creative input to contribute, beyond the photographs he took throughout his relationship with Marilyn. On *Bus Stop* he designed the look of the picture, supervised the lighting, and came up with Cherie's incredible wan makeup. Milton's design—specifically Marilyn's makeup—caused great concern among Fox management. Buddy Adler expressed his concern to Greene, but after seeing the rushes was very impressed—enough to offer Greene a producing job in Los Angeles.

Milton's status as "the genius" to whom Marilyn turned for all her professional needs was bound to be short-lived, as it was for so many others who filled that role, and the new people who entered her life throughout 1955 and 1956 helped ensure his fall from Marilyn's graces. In LEE STRASBERG she had found a man she could look up to, a dramatic guide who also recommended she start seeing a psychoanalyst; Milton recommended his former one, MARGARET HOHENBERG. Marilyn was also spending a lot of time with ARTHUR MILLER, whose faith in the Greene did not match hers.

Acclaimed by critics and the public, *Bus Stop* at last gave Marilyn a role offering the latitude for a fine dramatic performance. Marilyn Monroe Productions followed this success with its one and only production, *THE PRINCE AND THE SHOWGIRL* (1957), filmed in the UK with the finest British talent: leading actor LAURENCE OLIVIER, making his non-Shakespearean directorial debut, cinematographer JACK CARDIFF, and writer TERENCE RATTIGAN. During their time in ENGLAND, the Greenes stayed at Tibbs Farm in Ascot, where Arthur and Marilyn had originally intended to stay before the press got wind of their movements and they decided to move to the more secure Parkside House in EGHAM.

The England experience, soon after Marilyn married Arthur, proved to be the final chapter in the active collaboration of Marilyn and Greene. Miller told biographer FRED LAWRENCE GUILES that "Greene thought he would be this big-shot producer and she would be working for him. But she saw that he had ulterior aims." For Greene's part, he was not happy with the idea that Miller would be part of the team on future Marilyn Monroe Productions projects.

By the time filming was over in England, Marilyn was barely speaking with Greene. Things did not improve between them on their return to New York. Greene became increasingly resentful of Arthur Miller's influence over Marilyn. Meanwhile Miller, who by now displayed outright hostility towards Greene, was strongly advising Marilyn to take full control of the production company. By April 1957, Marilyn had broken with Milton Greene and begun court proceedings to oust him from the company.

Marilyn attempted to buy her former mentor out for $500,000 around the time they left England. He declined, asking instead for $100,000 and reimbursement for out-of-pocket expenses incurred.

Greene did not vent his spleen against Marilyn in public. At the time he stated, "I haven't seen her for a long time. It seems Marilyn doesn't want to go ahead with the program we planned... I don't want to do anything now to hurt her career. She seems to want to have a baby and not work for a while." In a 1982 interview he told a Los Angeles newspaper that he remembered her as "ultrasensitive, and very dedicated to her work, whether people realize this or not. She came through magnificently in *Prince* and she was great in *Bus Stop*. All I did was believe in her. She was a marvelous, loving, wonderful person I don't think many people understood."

He has also been quoted as saying, "I thought I'd seen them all; being in the business I'd seen so many models and actresses. But I'd never seen anyone with that tone of

Marilyn and Joshua Greene during filming of *Bus Stop* (1956).
Photograph by Milton Greene

voice, that kindness, that real softness. If she saw a dead dog in the road, she'd cry. She was so supersensitive you had to watch your tone of voice all the time. Later I was to find out that she was schizoid—that she could be absolutely brilliant or absolutely kind, then, the total opposite."

Over the years there have been many rumors that Marilyn and Greene were having an affair. Many of their friends believed this to be the case, and said so in print. Amy Greene always denied that anything took place between Milton and Marilyn.

In 1992 Amy Greene told DONALD SPOTO, "Everyone who knew [Milton's] work acknowledged that he had a streak of genius. But he was also a man of frightening excesses and eventually he destroyed himself, and almost his family, too." Marilyn was aware of this, and even once admitted to her that by driving a wedge between her and Milton, "Arthur was taking away the only person I ever trusted."

BOOKS:

*Milton's Marilyn*, Milton M. Greene, James Kotsilibas-Davis and Joshua Greene. Munich: Schirmer/Mosel Verlag Gmbh, 1995.

*Of Women and Their Elegance*, Norman Mailer text and Milton Greene photos. New York: Simon & Schuster, 1980.

*My Story*, Marilyn Monroe. New York: Stein and Day, 1974.

"Autobiography" ghost-written by BEN HECHT in the mid-fifties, and then reworked by Milton Greene before finally being published.

## GREENSON, DR. RALPH
(1910–1979, B. ROMEO SAMUEL GREENSCHPOON)

It would be fair to say that in the last year of Marilyn's life, nobody knew more about Marilyn's fragile state of mind than her psychiatrist. Stories conflict regarding how Marilyn first got in contact with Greenson. He either came recommended by Marilyn's LAWYER Milton Rudin (Greenson's brother-in-law), by ARTHUR MILLER's friend FRANK TAYLOR, or by Marilyn's New York psychoanalyst, DR. MARIANNE KRIS, in August 1960, when Marilyn was flown back to Los Angeles for hospital treatment during shooting on *THE MISFITS* (1961). By the time Marilyn was doing the last post-production work on *The Misfits* she was visiting Dr. Greenson at his Beverly Hills office (436 North Roxbury Drive) every day of the week.

Greenson was born and raised in Brooklyn. His twin sister, Juliet, grew up to become an accomplished concert pianist. Greenson went on to study at Columbia University and then in Switzerland at the University of Berne, where he met his future wife, Hildegarde (Hildi) Troesch. In 1938 he underwent Freudian analysis with Otto Fenichel in Europe. Greenson and Hildi returned to America and had two children, before he joined the army in the war, finishing as a captain in charge of the Army Air Force Convalescent Hospital in Colorado. After his discharge he set himself up in his own Los Angeles psychiatric practice. He was a founding member of the Los Angeles Psychoanalytic Society, connected to ANNA FREUD in London, and was a clinical professor of psychiatry at the UCLA Medical School.

Greenson specialized in treating Hollywood stars. He even made it onto the screen himself, in *Captain Newman M.D.* (1964), based on a novel to which Greenson had contributed his wartime reminiscences. GREGORY PECK played the part, and Greenson earned 12.5 percent of gross receipts.

Greenson has had mixed press. Though nobody doubts his commitment to Marilyn, his methods were decidedly unorthodox, and for some biographers his motives were downright spurious. He has been portrayed as an attention seeker who sought out famous people and produced "pop psychology" because he wanted to be liked and esteemed; he has been implicated in the cover-up of Marilyn's death, or even worse, has been accused of complicity in her murder.

After Marilyn had moved back to Los Angeles from New York, she went for counseling session with Dr. Greenson on a daily basis. Marilyn's friend, masseur, and driver RALPH ROBERTS, who took her everyday in the second half of 1961 for her four o'clock appointment, told biographer DONALD SPOTO, "At first she adored Greenson, but it did not seem to any of us that he was good for her. He began to exert more and more control over her life, dictating who she should have for friends, whom she might visit and so forth. But she felt it was necessary to obey."

Professionally, Greenson had both advocates and critics. He was prolific in writing papers and giving lectures, and esteemed by Anna Freud—at one stage he treated her brother, Ernst Freud. As was common at the time, he advocated psychotherapy in combination with drugs therapies, such as BARBITURATES or tranquilizers. Distinctly unorthodox, though, was the way he invited patients into his everyday life. Marilyn became a surrogate member of the family, in what may have been an ill-conceived attempt to develop a new approach to PSYCHOANALYSIS. In one public paper he gave, he exhorted his colleagues to "be willing to become emotionally involved with their patients if they hope to establish a reliable therapeutic relationship."

Greenson's thesis, as he apparently told his family, was that traditional Freudian therapy would not and had not worked for Marilyn; what she needed was to see and experience a normal stable family in order to be able to create one for herself. In doing this, he seems to have ignored the first rule of his profession: the preservation of critical distance. Not only was Greenson involved personally, but his family was too. By the end of 1961, Marilyn was dining with the family three or four times a week, calling at all hours for advice on even minor details of her life, and staying overnight. She also spent her last Christmas with "Romey," as she called him (Romeo was what he was known as at home) despite the fact that JOE DIMAGGIO had flown in to be with her.

Greenson began to exert an influence on all areas of Marilyn's life as she became increasingly dependent upon him. He suggested that Marilyn would do well to get back to work, and persuaded her to take on the ill-fated *SOMETHING'S GOT TO GIVE*, in which he obtained a role as special counselor to Marilyn Monroe. At his prompting, she hired his friend EUNICE MURRAY to be her own housekeeper, first at her DOHENY DRIVE apartment, and later at the FIFTH HELENA DRIVE home Murray found and Marilyn bought because it was so much like Dr. Greenson's own Mexican-style house. She and Eunice Murray even went to MEXICO together on a shopping trip for furniture. On her return from Mexico, Greenson invited Marilyn to stay at his house for the week until her own new place was ready. This was not the first or last time that Marilyn stayed overnight at her psychotherapist's home (902 Franklin Street, Brentwood).

With the pressures of working on *Something's Got to Give*, Marilyn began seeing Greenson as frequently as twice a day. His was the only appointment she did not cancel during a two-week hiatus from work when she was suffering acute sinusitis. Then, on May 10, Greenson and his wife left Los Angeles for a five-week trip to Israel and Switzerland. After almost complete dependency, Marilyn found herself suddenly alone, with only extra supplies of Dexamyl as comfort. This was precisely the moment when tensions at TWENTIETH CENTURY-FOX came to a head and Marilyn was suspended from the picture. Greenson was called back from vacation early, took the situation in hand, and issued orders to Murray not to say anything to Marilyn's agents or publicist. Marilyn did not show up to a crisis meeting with studio executives. Instead, Greenson issued a statement to Fox executives saying that Marilyn would be prepared to return to the studio to work. At least one biographer speculates that Greenson behaved in his autocratic fashion to cover up the fact that, while in his care, Marilyn had suffered a facial injury, as a result of which Greenson not only took her to a doctor, but kept her away from all the people who knew her, and more importantly, from the meeting at Fox that settled her fate on the film.

By this time Marilyn was apparently telling close friends that she was concerned about her level of dependence on Dr. Greenson, and expressing fears that the relationship was not doing her much good. She was also increasingly concerned that Greenson was cutting her off from all the relationships that mattered to her. Ralph Roberts, one of the friends Greenson had counseled Marilyn against, told Donald Spoto, "She'd deeply resented what she saw as his use of her... He had tried to get rid of almost everyone in her life, and she didn't have that many people to begin with. But when he tried it with Joe [DiMaggio]—I think that's when she began to reconsider the whole thing."

The events surrounding Marilyn's DEATH are nothing if not sketchy, contradictory, and controversial. Dr. Greenson's role is one of the aspects that varies greatly in conflicting accounts. On August 4, 1962, at her request, Dr. Greenson went to see Marilyn at her home, either in the early or late afternoon or both. He may have spent as many as seven hours with her, until 7:00 P.M., with a small break in the middle, or just been with her for a couple of hours until 7:00 P.M., by which time he had calmed her down. In his statement to the police, he said he then went home. The more extreme conspiracy theories question whether he went home at all. In the early evening he called to check that everything was okay with Marilyn, and was told by Eunice Murray that Marilyn was safe and sound in her room. In Dr. Greenson's version, the basis for the original official verdict on Marilyn's death, at some time around 3:00 or

3:30 A.M. the following morning he received a call from Mrs. Murray, who was alarmed that the light was still on in Marilyn's room and her door was locked. Dr. Greenson arrived, smashed the window to Marilyn's bedroom and found the star dead. Dr. Hyman Engelberg arrived to confirm that Marilyn was dead, and then at 4:25 A.M. they called the police.

Many biographers consider that Marilyn's time of death was nearer 10:00 or 11:00 P.M., and that the time discrepancy allowed Greenson to participate in or organize a COVER-UP to conceal the true circumstances of Marilyn's death. It has also been suggested that Greenson was unwittingly responsible for her death by prescribing sedatives which worked in combination with others Marilyn had taken without his supervision. Spoto hypothesizes that, "Out of patience, fearing the loss of his best beloved, enraged at himself and at what he considered her ill-advised dismissal of Eunice and of himself (which was imminent if not actual), Ralph Greenson ordered Marilyn Monroe sedated... so that the rupture of their relationship might not occur."

While he was still alive, Dr. Greenson was scrupulously and ethically correct in not revealing any of his famous patient's confidences during analysis. The only time he passed public comment was in 1973, to counter the version of events put forward by NORMAN MAILER in his biography of Marilyn. At the time, Greenson said, "It's wrong to connect her death with any sort of political intrigue. I want to discredit Mailer. He distorts, makes innuendoes about her sexual life and suggests that unethical things were done to her by doctors. They're a bunch of lies."

Since his death, however, a number of letters and papers have been brought to light by Marilyn biographers. In a letter he wrote to Dr. Marianne Kris, two weeks after Marilyn's tragic death, Greenson said, "I was her therapist, the good father who would not disappoint her and who would bring her insights, and if not insights, just kindness. I had become the most important person in her life. I also felt guilty that I put a burden on my own family. But there was something very lovable about this girl and we all cared about her and she could be delightful."

He has also been quoted as saying, "She was a poor creature I tried to help, and I ended up hurting her."

### THE GREENSON FAMILY

GREENSON, DAN
Son of Marilyn's Hollywood psychiatrist, he too grew up to become a psychiatrist.

GREENSON, JOAN
Ralph's daughter, in her late teens when Marilyn started attending her father's house for psychoanalysis sessions. Marilyn played big sister, giving her advice on boyfriends, makeup tips, and pointers on how to walk sexily. One month before she died, Marilyn threw a party at her Brentwood home to celebrate Joan's twentieth birthday—and taught her how to do the Twist. Joan sometimes drove Marilyn around town when Marilyn's usual driver Rudi Kautzky was off duty.

## GUILAROFF, SYDNEY (SIDNEY)
(1906–1997)

Hollywood's hairdresser to the stars, Sydney Guilaroff was the first hairdresser ever to receive a screen credit. During almost half a century working as chief hair stylist at MGM, he worked on more than a thousand films.

He began his hairdressing career in New York, where he found his first star client Claudette Colbert, and then Louise Brooks, for whom he created the boyish "shingle" style. Louis B. Mayer brought him to Hollywood in 1935, after the studio boss discovered that Guilaroff and his scissors were the reason why JOAN CRAWFORD insisted on traveling to New York before shooting began on any of her films. From that moment on, Guilaroff washed, brushed, and sculpted the hair of generations of Hollywood's hottest stars, including GRETA GARBO in *Camille* and VIVIEN LEIGH in *Gone With the Wind*.

Guilaroff styled Marilyn's hair for her last screen appearance in *THE MISFITS* (1961). He also frequently did her hair for off-screen occasions, such as her meeting with NIKITA KHRUSHCHEV. Marilyn also regarded him as a friend and confidant. He described Marilyn as "the sweetest, kindest person, the most underrated person. The saddest person aside from Garbo."

Reportedly Guilaroff was one of several people a very depressed Marilyn called on the night of her DEATH. Guilaroff wrote in his 1996 autobiography *Crowning Glory* that she was considering telling the world about her affair with ROBERT KENNEDY. In that same book Guilaroff claimed that he had affairs with several of his illustrious and devoted clients, including Greta Garbo and Ava Gardner.

Guilaroff was a pall-bearer at Marilyn's FUNERAL.

BOOK:
*Crowning Glory*, Sydney Guilaroff and Cathy Griffin. Los Angeles: General Publishing Group, 1996.

## GUILES, FRED LAWRENCE

Author of two long-respected Marilyn BIOGRAPHIES, the second of which adds fresh information on Marilyn's relationships with the KENNEDYS. Guiles has also written biographies of Tyrone Power, Stan Laurel, Marion Davies, Jane Fonda, ANDY WARHOL, and JOAN CRAWFORD.

BOOKS:
*Norma Jeane: The Life of Marilyn Monroe*, Fred Lawrence Guiles. New York: McGraw Hill, 1969.

*Legend: The Life and Death of Marilyn Monroe*, Fred Lawrence Guiles. New York: Stein and Day, 1984.

H

## HAIR

MARILYN:
"In Hollywood a girl's virtue is much less important than her hairdo."

In all her childhood pictures, Norma Jeane's hair is chestnut to reddish brown and straight. Then, around the age of puberty, her hair became wavy.

"I wouldn't ever want to be a bleached blonde," Norma Jeane Dougherty told EMMELINE SNIVELY who ran the BLUE BOOK MODELING AGENCY sometime in early 1946. But on the advice that with blonde hair she would photograph better, not to mention be in much greater demand for modeling work, within months Norma Jeane was dispatched to the FRANK AND JOSEPH SALON to have her naturally wavy hair cut, straightened, and bleached. They liked their work so much they used her to advertise the store. The actual before-and-after difference is plain to see in the photographs of JOSEPH JASGUR in his book *The Birth of Marilyn*. An alternative story runs that Marilyn went blonde in order to land a job ADVERTISING a hair product called Lustre-Creme Shampoo, after photographer Raphael Wolff persuaded her that it was worth the six hours at $10 per hour to go blonde.

Going blonde was just the start. Before she became a major star in 1953, Marilyn's hair went through just about every shade of blonde: from ash blonde in *THE ASPHALT JUNGLE* (1950), to golden blonde in *ALL ABOUT EVE* (1950), to silver blonde in *AS YOUNG AS YOU FEEL* (1951), to amber blonde in *LET'S MAKE IT LEGAL* (1951), to smoky blonde in *LOVE NEST* (1951), to honey blonde in *O. HENRY'S FULL HOUSE* (1952), to topaz blonde in *WE'RE NOT MARRIED* (1952), to unbleached dark blonde in *DON'T BOTHER TO KNOCK* (1952), and then, at last, to platinum blonde in *MONKEY BUSINESS* (1952).

Over the years, aside from at least a dozen studio hairstylists, Marilyn called on the services of KENNETH BATTELLE, AGNES FLANAGAN, SYDNEY GUILAROFF, PETER LEONARDI, GEORGE MASTERS, and Gladys Rasmussen. Naturally, these people were privy to many of Marilyn's secrets.

Masters in particular is an oft-quoted source. He summed up Marilyn's attitude to hair: "If I had done her hair in a way that would evoke the comment, 'Your hair looks fabulous!' I'm sure I would never have seen her again. She didn't want to hear, 'Your hair looks great,' or 'Your earrings are beautiful.' She only wanted to hear, 'You look fantastic!'" He also revealed: "She had one long blonde hair on her chest that she wouldn't let me cut off. She liked to play with and fondle it. It was her security blanket."

Gladys Rasmussen had this to say on the practicalities of getting Marilyn's hair just right: "There are several problems with doing Marilyn's hair. Her hair is very fine and therefore hard to manage. It gets oily if it isn't shampooed every day. And her hair is so curly naturally that to build a coiffure for her I have to first give her a straight permanent. . . . The way we got her shade of platinum is with my own secret blend of sparkling silver bleach plus twenty volume peroxide and a

A modeling shot of brown-haired Norma Jeane.

secret formula of silver platinum to take the yellow out."

In later years, every Saturday Marilyn would have her hair re-platinumed by a very old and ostensibly retired lady who came once a week from San Diego. Marilyn told SIMONE SIGNORET that this lady, PEARL PORTERFIELD, had worked for MGM where she had been responsible for Jean Harlow's platinum locks. Marilyn sent a car to the airport to pick her up every week, and take her to Signoret's bungalow next door to hers at the BEVERLY HILLS HOTEL. Then, after the old lady picked at a buffet Marilyn laid out, she set to work on the two actresses, regaling them with tales of her time with the original blonde bombshell.

The damage to Marilyn's hair from all those years of harsh treatments is evident in many of the last photographs taken of her in 1962.

Marilyn's classic hairdo in *How to Marry a Millionaire* (1953).

Marilyn with her hair cut short for *Clash by Night* (1952).

### HAIR FACTS

- Marilyn always wore her hair brushed toward the left.
- When Marilyn wanted to go out and about incognito, she resorted to a trusty black wig and big dark glasses.
- Marilyn had to work hard to live up to her desire—"to feel blonde all over"—and that included bleaching her pubic hair.
- According to Simone Signoret, Marilyn hated her widow's peak as if it were her personal enemy: it didn't take the platinum dye as well as the rest of her hair. To camouflage this, hairdressers brushed that lock of hair artfully over one eye.
- At its candy-floss whitest toward the end of her career—Marilyn referred to it as "pillowcase white"—she had to have her roots retouched every

Marilyn's hair in *Something's Got to Give*, 1962.

five days. The whiter and more artificial her hair color, the more vulnerable and fragile she looked.

On at least two movies Marilyn was unhappy that co-stars were trying to out-blonde her. As a result, Hope Lange had her hair darkened for *Bus Stop*. Marilyn was also convinced that Cyd Charisse was deliberately trying to lighten her hair to outshine Marilyn on screen in *Something's Got to Give*. Her assurance was apparently not enough for Marilyn, who grumbled, "Her unconscious wants it blonde."

## HALL, JERRY

Texan-born model and former wife of Mick Jagger, Hall once played the part of Cherie in a production of BUS STOP, and owns the *Old Black Magic* outfit from that film.

## HALSMAN, PHILIPPE

Halsman took photographs of Marilyn three times over the span of a decade. The first time he met her was in 1949, on a *Life* magazine photo feature on up-and-coming starlets, "Eight Girls Try Out Mixed Emotions," in which the girls were told to pose while thinking of four situations (a scary monster, a delicious drink, a funny joke, and a lover's embrace): "I remember that one of the girls was an artificial blonde by the name of Marilyn Monroe and that she was not one of the girls who impressed me the most." He was more impressed by Ricki Soma, JOHN HUSTON'S wife and mother of Anjelica. But it was Halsman who, three years later, photographed Marilyn for her first *Life* cover, oozing assured sensuality in a white off-the-shoulder gown.

It was only after several years of trying that Halsman managed to get Marilyn to indulge his pet project—photographs of people jumping, which he claimed told a great deal about their personalities. Marilyn obliged in 1959; the shots show her in mid-air, arms locked and fists clenched.

## HAMPSHIRE HOUSE HOTEL, THE
150 CENTRAL PARK SOUTH, NEW YORK

Where Marilyn and JOE DIMAGGIO stayed during location shooting for THE SEVEN YEAR ITCH in 1954.

(*see* HOTELS)

## HARLOW, JEAN
(1911–1937, B. HARLEAN CARPENTER)

AMY GREEN:
"She really wanted to be Jean Harlow. That was her goal. She always said she would probably die young, like Harlow; that the men in her life were disasters, like Harlow's; that her relationship with her mother was complicated, like Harlow's. It was as if she based her life on Harlow's—the instant flash, then over."

To Marilyn, Jean Harlow was more than a hero: Harlow's life was in many ways a blueprint for her own.

Born on March 3, 1911 in Kansas City, Jean Harlow was known simply as "The Baby" when growing up with her maternal grandparents. Like so many of Hollywood's most memorable sex symbols, Harlow often played the parts of dangerous, sexually charged women with flaws that mirrored her own nature and history.

Harlow's break into the movies came in 1928, when she began to pick up roles as an extra. Then in 1930, HOWARD HUGHES put her in *Hell's Angels*, in which Harlow stole the show with her sly and assured sexuality. Frank Capra made history with his lingering shots of her body in *Platinum Blonde* (1931). A year later she incurred the wrath of censors in *Red-Headed Woman*. During the brief period when young Norma Jeane lived with her mother, GLADYS BAKER and best friend GRACE MCKEE GODDARD often took her to see their screen idol Harlow in movies such as *Dinner at Eight* (1933), *Bombshell* (1933), and *The Girl from Missouri* (1934). Harlow's last movie, opposite CLARK GABLE, was *Saratoga* (1937). She died on June 7, 1937, aged just twenty-six, from complications of uremic poisoning (acute nephritis).

Grace would often tell Norma Jeane that when she grew up she would become a great screen siren, so it is little surprise that Harlow became the little girl's idol too. Grace's admiration for Harlow went as far as dying her HAIR the same shade of platinum blonde, and for a period she dressed exclusively in white, and bought only white clothes for Norma Jeane too. Grace is reported as telling her charge, "You're perfect except for this little bump"—referring to the tip of her nose—"But one day you'll be perfect—like Jean Harlow."

The parallels in the lives of Monroe and Harlow are overwhelming: both were brought up by strict Christian Scientists (in Norma Jeane's case, her beloved foster parent ANA LOWER); both were married three times; both left school at sixteen to marry their first husbands (Harlow eloped with a millionaire); both spent their lives seeking out their father; and both died in tragic and some say suspicious circumstances. They both acted opposite Clark Gable in the last film they ever made. Intriguingly, Gable once said of Harlow, "She didn't want to be famous, she wanted to be happy," a quote that could be equally applied to Marilyn.

They were both great lovers of ANIMALS and willing to provide a haven for strays. Both of them tested the morals of their days by posing nude, flaunting their bodies, and eschewing UNDERWEAR; both of them acted under their mothers' maiden names. Each lived on NORTH PALM DRIVE at one point in their lives. Marilyn, like Harlow, had to go on a one woman strike to improve her extremely unfavorable contract terms and payment rates at the height of her popularity. The parallels continue even at the end of their lives: both actresses were regularly prescribed sedatives by their doctors; just months before both actresses died, they went to a presidential birthday celebration (Harlow went to President Franklin Delano Roosevelt's birthday ball, Marilyn to President JOHN KENNEDY'S), for which they were reprimanded by their respective studios.

Marilyn certainly played her part in setting herself up on a parallel path to her hero. When she met influential Hollywood columnist SIDNEY SKOLSKY in 1950, she told him that for her whole life, Harlow had been her role model. Skolsky, who had known Harlow, agreed to help Marilyn achieve her aim, and for the next few years he placed tidbits in his column and used his influence with studio contacts. The two of them also plotted to make a Harlow movie.

Marilyn's first national press feature, in *Collier's* magazine, boldly said, "Like her famous predecessor, Jean Harlow, Marilyn's name is rapidly becoming the current Hollywood definition of sex appeal." This was echoed through the rest of 1951 in a host of other magazines. In 1954, *Life* magazine defined Marilyn as "the inheritor of a tradition founded by Jean Harlow." *Time* agreed that "she is the most talked about new star since Harlow."

After she had become a star, Marilyn became ruefully aware of the striking similarities in their lives. In 1957 she told MILTON GREENE: "I kept thinking of her, rolling over the facts of her life in my mind. It was kind of spooky, and sometimes I thought, am I making this happen? But I don't think so. We just seemed to have the same spirit or something, I don't know. I kept wondering if I would die young like her, too."

Although Marilyn never managed to fulfil her long-held dream of playing Harlow on screen, she did pose as her hero for photographer RICHARD AVEDON in 1958, as part of a screen goddesses series. In his commentary on the photographs, ARTHUR MILLER expressed his own personal preference for her homage to Harlow, which she portrayed "not so much by wit as by her deep sympathy for that actress's tragic life. . . . She has identified herself with what was naive, what was genuine lure and sexual truth."

Clark Gable, who had acted opposite Jean Harlow in five films, compared the two actresses after working with Marilyn on THE MISFITS (1961): "Harlow was always very relaxed, but this girl is high-strung, and she worries more—about her lines, her appearance, her performance. She is constantly trying to improve as an actress."

A month or so before she died, Marilyn went with Sidney Skolsky to visit Jean Harlow's mother, "Mama Jean" Bello, to ask her permission to press ahead with their planned film of Harlow's life. "Mama Jean" reputedly looked at Marilyn and exclaimed that her baby had come back to life. The next meeting for this project allegedly was scheduled for August 5, when Skolsky was due to go to Marilyn's house and work on a treatment for *The Jean Harlow Story* (*see* FILMS MARILYN CONSIDERED OR WANTED).

Even in death Marilyn emulated her heroine. The flowers delivered every few days to her grave in Los Angeles by JOE DIMAGGIO were the fulfillment of a promise he had made to Marilyn that he would be as devoted to Marilyn as William Powell had been to Harlow. Powell regularly sent flowers to his love's resting place in Forrest Lawn.

## HARPER AVENUE

Marilyn twice lived along this West Hollywood residential street, once in 1948 when she stayed with lover FRED KARGER at his mother Anne's house, and then sporadically in 1950 and 1951 when she lived with

NATASHA LYTESS, at 1309 North Harper Avenue.

## HASPIEL, JAMES

Self-proclaimed number-one FAN who fell under Marilyn's spell at the age of fourteen after seeing her in *CLASH BY NIGHT* (1952). Like the MARILYN SIX, Haspiel hung around the New York hotels where Marilyn stayed during the mid-fifties. Marilyn sometimes invited him to come along for rides in cabs and limousines as she went from one appointment to the next. Haspiel's memories and collection of Marilyn MEMORABILIA are featured in a number of articles and two books. He has also served as a consultant on Marilyn documentaries.

Haspiel's devotion to Marilyn is cast in stone—literally. One day in 1954, after meeting Marilyn outside her hotel, he carved the words "Marilyn Monroe was here" into wet cement on the street (155 West 23th Street, New York).

It is Haspiel's opinion that Marilyn was murdered as part of a CONSPIRACY reaching up to the highest echelons of government, an opinion based upon tapes reputedly recorded by wiretapper BERNIE SPINDEL.

BOOKS:
*Marilyn: The Ultimate Look at the Legend*, James Haspiel. New York: Henry Holt, 1991.
*Young Marilyn: Becoming the Legend*, James Haspiel. New York: Hyperion, 1994.

## HATHAWAY, HENRY
(1898–1985, B. HENRI LEOPOLD DE FIENNES)

Hathaway's long film career began as a child actor when he was just nine years old. In 1932 he moved into directing. Often described as a "dependable" director, Hathaway's best-known movies were the Oscar-nominated *Lives of a Bengal Lancer* (1935), *The House on 92nd Street* (1945), *Rommel, Desert Fox* (1951), and *North to Alaska* (1960). He developed a reputation principally for his Westerns, culminating in John Wayne's 1969 Oscar-winning performance in *True Grit*.

By the time Hathaway came to direct Marilyn in *NIAGARA* (1952), he was preceded by quite a reputation: "To be a good director," he once said, "you've got to be a bastard. I'm a bastard and I know it." Marilyn, with a swelling reputation of her own, had the constant support of drama coach NATASHA LYTESS. Hathaway banned Lytess from the set, so Marilyn worked with her back at the hotel. On-set fireworks were kept to a minimum, at least for a Marilyn movie, and the result was a huge success and *Niagara* confirmed that Marilyn was Hollywood's biggest rising star.

After working with Marilyn on *Niagara*, Hathaway told columnist SIDNEY SKOLSKY, "She's the best natural actress I've directed. And I go back. I worked with Barbara LaMar, Jean Harlow, Rene Adoree—right up to today. And she's the greatest natural talent. Wait 'til you see her in this picture." His appreciation was not enough for Marilyn to want to repeat the experience.

Henry Hathaway and Marilyn on the set of *Niagara* (1952).

They never worked together again, and his name was absent from her 1955 list of approved directors.

Hathaway later recalled Marilyn as "marvelous to work with, very easy to direct and terrifically ambitious to do better. And bright, really bright. She may not have had an education, but she was just naturally bright. But always being trampled on by bums. I don't think anyone ever treated her on her own level. To most men she was something that they were a little bit ashamed of—even Joe DiMaggio."

## HAVER, JUNE
(B. 1926, JUNE STOVENOUR)

Born the same year as Marilyn, Haver had a string of successes in the forties, mainly in musicals. When Marilyn was just starting out at TWENTIETH CENTURY-FOX, the studio was grooming Haver as a possible replacement for number-one blonde BETTY GRABLE—she picked up the nickname "The Pocket Grable"—but it was Marilyn who, years later, achieved that status.

In the two movies they did together, Haver had top billing and Marilyn walk on parts: *Scudda Hoo, Scudda Hay!* (1948), and then *Love Nest* (1951).

Haver's career included playing the role of the woman from whom Marilyn took her name, Marilyn Miller, in the 1949 hit *Look for the Silver Lining* (as the tagline says, "The sunshine story of Broadway's glory girl!").

*Love Nest* was actually Haver's penultimate film. She retired in 1953 to dedicate herself to life in a convent. Serious illness curtailed her monastic life, and she emerged to marry actor Fred MacMurray, with whom she had worked early in her career.

In a 1966 interview with *Coronet* magazine, Haver shared her recollections of working with Marilyn on *Love Nest*:

> "She was so young and pretty, so shy and nervous on that picture, but I remember the scene where she was supposed to be sunning in the backyard of the apartment house we all lived in. When Marilyn walked on the set in her bathing suit and walked to the beach chair, the whole crew gasped, gaped and seemed to turn to stone. They just stopped work and stared; Marilyn had that electric something—and mind you, movie crews are quite used to seeing us in brief costumes. They've worked on so many musicals and beach sequences. But they just gasped and gaped at Marilyn as though they were stunned. In all my years at the studio, I'd never seen that happen before. Sure, the crew gives you the kidding wolf-whistle routine, but this was sheer shock."

## HAWAII

In 1954 newlyweds Marilyn and JOE DIMAGGIO were on a plane that stopped in

Marilyn as a disruptive tenant in a house owned by June Haver in *Love Nest* (1951).

Hawaii for refueling en route to Tokyo. Six police officers encircled the illustrious guests to protect them from a frenzied crowd of well-wishers.

## HAWKS, HOWARD (1896–1977)

"Monroe's problem was that many directors handled her as if she were real. She wasn't. She was only comfortable in unreal roles."

Hawks began writing for the cinema during the silent era. As a director, beginning in 1926, he confounded genre boundaries, mixing comedy into his action pictures and drama into his comedies, to make a string of movies which many regard as among Hollywood's finest: *Scarface* (1932), *Twentieth Century* (1934), *Barbary Coast* (1935), *Bringing Up Baby* (1938), *His Girl Friday* (1940), *The Big Sleep* (1946), *Red River* (1948), and *Rio Bravo* (1958). Hawks worked with practically all the greatest actors over a thrity-year period, often coaxing intimacy between actors onto the screen, as with LAUREN BACALL and Humphrey Bogart in *The Big Sleep*. In 1974 he was awarded an honorary Oscar for his work as "a master American filmmaker."

Hawks twice directed Marilyn, in the CARY GRANT farce *MONKEY BUSINESS* (1952) and in the musical *GENTLEMEN PREFER BLONDES* (1953). On this second movie Hawks grew increasingly exasperated with Marilyn's endemic LATENESS, debilitating nerves, and what he saw as interference from Marilyn's drama coach NATASHA LYTESS. Hawks fought it out with Lytess, had her banned from the set, but had to recant when Marilyn's lateness became even more chronic. When the studio began to seriously worry about the overrun costs, Hawks suggested that the best way to speed things up was to "replace Marilyn, rewrite the script and make it shorter, and get a new director." He was only joking. He finished the movie and succeeded in extracting a surprisingly relaxed performance from his high-strung star. Perhaps part of the reason why is that he all but handed over direction of the film's musical numbers to choreographer JACK COLE, with whom Marilyn got along very well.

Legendary director Howard Hawks with Marilyn, ca. 1952.

## HECHT, BEN (1894–1964)

A seasoned Hollywood wordsmith who worked on over one hundred productions, enough to know that "a movie is never any better than the stupidest man connected with it."

Hecht scripted Oscar-winner *Underworld* (1929) and picked up nominations for *Wuthering Heights* (1939), *Angels over Broadway* (1940), and *Notorious* (1946). In 1954 he was contacted by Marilyn's agent, CHARLES K. FELDMAN, and commissioned to write Marilyn's first "autobiography."

Marilyn and Hecht had already crossed paths professionally at least two years earlier when Marilyn was working on *MONKEY BUSINESS* (1952); he had also written one of the segments for the compilation movie *O. HENRY'S FULL HOUSE* (1952), and may even have met Marilyn as early as 1949, when they both worked briefly on the Marx Brothers movie *LOVE HAPPY* (1950).

For a couple of months Marilyn and her ghost writer met on a regular basis, joined frequently by SIDNEY SKOLSKY, and in April Hecht showed Marilyn the result of his handiwork. Extracts of the manuscript, in a doctored form, were then sold by Hecht's agent Jacques Chambrun, without the knowledge of either Marilyn or Hecht, and serialized in the *Empire News* of London that summer. Hecht fired his agent in June and the whole project ground to a halt. The book did not see the light of day until twenty years later.

*MY STORY*, eventually published in 1974 by Stein and Day and presented as Marilyn's unfinished autobiography, is in fact a rather hybrid mixture of anecdotes about Marilyn's life as recounted by Marilyn and Sidney Skolsky, written up by Hecht, and later re-edited by MILTON GREENE.

Marilyn once told ARTHUR MILLER, "I never intended to make all that much about being an orphan. It's just that Ben Hecht was hired to write this story about me, and he said, 'Okay, sit down and try to think up something interesting about yourself.' Well, I was boring, and I thought maybe I'd tell him about them putting me in the orphanage, and he said that was great and wrote it, and that became the main thing suddenly."

## HEFNER, HUGH

The founder of *Playboy* MAGAZINE launched his empire with a shrewd business deal, snapping up the recently discovered nude photographs of Marilyn to be the cover girl and centerfold for issue one in December 1953. The magazine was a hit.

Hefner has purchased the crypt next to Marilyn's at the WESTWOOD MEMORIAL PARK CEMETARY.

## HEPBURN, AUDREY
(1929–1993, B. EDDA VAN HEEMSTRA HEPBURN-RUSTON)

Born in Belgium to Irish and Dutch parents, Hepburn served her movie apprenticeship in England before taking Hollywood by storm in 1953 and winning an Oscar for *Roman Holiday*. For the next ten years she was the embodiment of the classy and ethereal gamine—quite the other end of the scale from the bursting sensuousness of Marilyn's screen presence. Hepburn picked up several further Oscar nominations, including one for *Breakfast at Tiffany's* (1961), a role for which Marilyn was originally considered (see FILMS MARILYN CONSIDERED OR WANTED). Hepburn is also remembered for her performances in *Sabrina* (1954), *War and Peace* (1956), *Funny Face* (1957), *My Fair Lady* (1964), and *Wait until Dark* (1967).

## HERMITAGE STREET
NORTH HOLLYWOOD

After first husband JAMES DOUGHERTY was sent on active duty to Asia, Norma Jeane moved in with mother-in-law ETHEL MARY DOUGHERTY at number 5254. She lived there for part of 1944 and 1945, until her modeling career began to really take off.

(*see* HOMES)

## HEROES

Norma Jeane's childhood heroes were the stars she saw on the screen at Saturday matinees: JOAN CRAWFORD, BETTE DAVIS, JEAN HARLOW, Gloria Swanson, MARLENE DIETRICH, GRETA GARBO, and CLARK GABLE. Of these, Marilyn felt a lifelong attachment to Harlow and Garbo, actresses who, like herself, were as lonely and unhappy in their personal lives as they were celebrated on-screen. As for Gable, ever since she was a little girl Norma Jeane had dreamed that the handsome actor with the dashing mustache was her real father. Norma Jeane gave first husband JAMES DOUGHERTY a statue of General MacArthur, leading some biographers to speculate that he was an early hero of hers.

In 1954 she listed the men she thought were the most outstanding of the time: MARLON BRANDO, MICHAEL CHEKHOV, JOHN HUSTON, JERRY LEWIS, ARTHUR MILLER and Jawaharlal Nehru.

By the mid-fifties, when she was studying the art of acting with LEE STRASBERG, a man she admired for the last decade of her life, Marilyn's acting heroes were classic Italian stage actress ELEANORA DUSE, and character actors Will Rogers and MARIE DRESSLER, people who, as she said, "As soon as you looked at them, you paid attention because you knew: They've lived; they've learned."

Outside the entertainment world, Marilyn greatly admired men of genius and integrity: ALBERT EINSTEIN, ABRAHAM LINCOLN, CARL SANDBURG, and LINCOLN STEFFENS. Before his fall from grace, Arthur Miller was also in this category.

## HILLDALE AVENUE
WEST HOLLYWOOD

In 1952 Marilyn briefly lived in a small furnished house at number 1121 which friend DAVID MARCH found for her. She moved out not long afterward because she did not like living alone; her move was up-market, to a luxury suite at the secluded BEL AIR HOTEL.

(*see* HOMES)

## HITCHCOCK, SIR ALFRED (1899–1980)

Marilyn and Hitchcock shared a mutual admiration but never worked together. Marilyn included him on her 1955 list of DIRECTORS she would work with, and he once named her among the three actresses he believed were the only genuine female stars in the movie industry—the other two being ELIZABETH TAYLOR and Ingrid Bergman.

## HOFFA, JIMMY (1917–1975)

U.S. union leader Jimmy Hoffa led the powerful Teamsters union from 1957 to 1967, when he was imprisoned for conspiracy, pension fund fraud, and perversion of justice.

A number of CONSPIRACY theories pitch Hoffa's name among suspects who were involved in Marilyn's DEATH. Under government investigation from 1957 for dealings with organized crime, Hoffa allegedly employed wiretapper BERNIE SPINDEL to bug Marilyn's home and find incriminating material on the KENNEDYS. He is said to have obtained secret tapes of Marilyn and one of the Kennedys having sex, which he intended to use to blackmail the administration into dropping investigations into his own nefarious conduct. Indeed, Hoffa was indicted for extortion just one day before Marilyn sang "Happy Birthday" to President Kennedy.

Hoffa was officially declared dead in 1983, eight years after he disappeared. The last time he was seen alive was in a Michigan restaurant where he was due to meet two mobsters, both of whom denied having made such an arrangement.

## HOGAN, DELLA MAE (1876–1927)

Marilyn's grandmother (also referred to as Della Mae Monroe, Della May Graves, and Della May Grainger), born in Brunswick County, Missouri on July 1, 1876, was the second of three children. Her parents—Tilford Marion Hogan and Jennie Nance (see GRANDPARENTS)—separated when she was thirteen. She spent the following years traveling between her parents.

Della Mae married husband OTIS ELMER MONROE in late 1899. In 1901 they moved to MEXICO, where Otis began working for the Mexican railways. In 1902 Marilyn's mother Gladys (see GLADYS BAKER) was born. Otis Elmer found better paid work in Los Angeles, so he and Della Mae returned to the U.S., where in 1905 Della Mae gave birth to a son, MARION OTIS ELMER.

After the death of husband Otis in 1909, Della Mae returned to the free ways of her earlier life. Soon enough she found a new husband, Lyle Arthur Graves, a man originally from Green Bay, Wisconsin and six years younger than Della Mae. Their marriage was doomed from the start. Just eight months after their nuptials, celebrated on March 7, 1912, Della Mae moved herself and her two children out of Graves's home. Their divorce was finalized on January 17, 1914. Two years later Della set up home in one room of a boarding house in the newly developed beach district of Venice, California, just south of Santa Monica. Son Marion Monroe, aged eleven, was sent to live with cousins in San Diego, while fourteen-year-old daughter Gladys was just beginning to develop her own set of male admirers. One of these men, JOHN BAKER, aided by Della Mae who testified that her daughter was old enough to marry, became Gladys's husband. Around this time Della Mae met Charles Grainger, a man who had traveled the world working for oil companies. Della Mae took to calling herself "Mrs. Grainger," without bothering to go through the trouble of a ceremony. Though they did not live together, Grainger was the man in her life for a number of years, at least when he wasn't out of the country. Some biographers state that Della Mae spent some time with Grainger in India, where he was posted on a drilling project.

In 1921 Della Mae briefly took in her daughter after her marriage to Baker collapsed. Gladys remarried in 1924, but that marriage quickly turned sour too. A year later, Norma Jeane was born. Della Mae was a mixed presence in the life of her young granddaughter. Della Mae was by then living in Hawthorne, California, not far from IDA AND WAYNE BOLENDER, the couple who looked after Norma Jeane for the first seven years of her life. She had become a devout follower of SISTER AIMEE SEMPLE MCPHERSON, and insisted that Norma Jeane be baptized at Sister Aimee's Angelus Temple.

Perhaps the most horrific incident of Norma Jeane's infancy involved her grandmother. In July 1927 Della Mae reportedly attempted to smother Norma Jeane with a pillow. On August 4, 1927 she was committed to the NORWALK STATE HOSPITAL. She died nineteen days later from heart failure during a manic seizure, a victim of what Marilyn's mother Gladys, and Marilyn herself, came to regard as the curse of MENTAL ILLNESS in their family.

According to another version of events, espoused by biographer DONALD SPOTO, Della's wild behavior was not caused by mental illness, but by degenerative heart disease which caused acute depressions. This was compounded by a stroke just before the summer of 1927. Spoto concedes that Della Mae broke into the Bolender house, where baby Norma Jeane was living with foster parents, but did not do anything to the child.

## HOHENBERG, DR. MARGARET

Dr. Hohenberg was a Freudian psychoanalyst of Hungarian origin, trained in Vienna, Budapest, and Prague. In 1955 Marilyn began attending Dr. Hohenberg's consulting rooms (155 East 93rd Street, New York) on the recommendation of business partner MILTON GREENE, who was already a patient. Marilyn was keen to undergo PSYCHOANALYSIS, a practice that LEE STRASBERG considered a pre-requisite for actors to "free" themselves and be able to engage in THE METHOD.

Between 1955 and 1957 Dr. Hohenberg wielded a great deal of influence in Marilyn's life. At no little expense she was flown to England in the fall of 1956, to help a depressed Marilyn during production of *THE PRINCE AND THE SHOWGIRL* (1957).

Marilyn stopped seeing Dr. Hohenberg in early 1957, soon after the end of her association with Greene. It is hard to imagine how Hohenberg managed to maintain an objective approach to two patients whose lives were so entwined. Perhaps she failed. Biographer DONALD SPOTO writes that she later told Greene he had made a dreadful mistake in ever going into business with Marilyn.

## HOLGA STEEL COMPANY

Norma Jeane's first modeling assignment for the BLUE BOOK MODELING AGENCY was as a hostess for the Holga Steel Company at an industrial fair held at the Pan Pacific Auditorium (7600 Beverly Boulevard, Los Angeles) which was destroyed by fire in 1989. Because she was still employed at the RADIO PLANE MUNITIONS FACTORY, she had to call in sick in order to take the $10-a-day assignment.

## HOLIDAY, BILLIE (1915–1959)

Marilyn's appreciation for the singing talents of "Lady Day" was severely shaken in the early fifties, after an incident at the Los Angeles nightclub, Tiffany's. Marilyn went there with costume designer WILLIAM TRAVILLA, who years later told the story to biographer ANTHONY SUMMERS: Holiday was using the office as a dressing room, and in that office Travilla spied a copy of the Marilyn nude CALENDAR as he was on the way to the restrooms. He told Marilyn, and she was desperately keen to see it. But when Holiday realized that Marilyn had not stopped in to say hello but to admire her own nude likeness, she balled up the calendar, threw it in Marilyn's face, and called her a four-letter word.

## HOLIDAY HOTEL
111 MILL STREET, RENO, NEVADA

Arthur and Marilyn moved into suites 846, 848, and 850 at this HOTEL following a stay at the nearby Mapes Hotel, during location shooting for *THE MISFITS* in 1960.

882 Doheny Drive, Marilyn's home in 1953. (In the driveway is the black Cadillac convertible with red leather interior she was given in lieu of cash payment for her appearance on the Jack Benny show.)

Marilyn and Arthur Miller's house in Amagansett, Long Island.

A rear view of Marilyn's Mexican-style home at 12305 Fifth Helena Drive, Brentwood, California.

## HOLLOWAY DRIVE

In 1951 Marilyn is supposed to have shared an apartment at number 8573 with fellow actress SHELLEY WINTERS. It was during this spell that the two of them sat down and one evening wrote out lists of which MEN they thought were the world's most desirable. Marilyn's list included her future husband ARTHUR MILLER and later lover YVES MONTAND.

In 1976, at this same apartment complex, actor Sal Mineo was murdered in the garage.

(*see* HOMES)

## HOLLYWOOD ROOSEVELT HOTEL
7000 HOLLYWOOD BOULEVARD, HOLLYWOOD

Marilyn came to this HOTEL, just across the street from what was then GRAUMAN'S CHINESE THEATER, in 1951 for a poolside photo session. She also stayed in room 1200 some time during the mid-fifties. Nowadays the hotel is popular for its many Hollywood-themed rooms.

## HOLLYWOOD WALK OF FAME

Marilyn's star is located outside McDonald's at 6774 Hollywood Boulevard.

## HOLM, CELESTE (B. 1919)

"I never thought of Marilyn as being an actress. Even in the films she did later on. I mean—even a puppy dog will act cute and pretty, if you give it enough encouragement."

Originally a stage actress, Holm won an Oscar for her third movie, *Gentleman's Agreement* (1947). In 1950 she was hired at three times her standard salary to play Karen Richards in *ALL ABOUT EVE*, for which she was nominated once again for an Academy Award. Other films of note are *The Snake Pit* (1948) and *High Society* (1956).

## HOMES

Marilyn spent her first seven years living in one home with a foster family, and the last six months in the only home she ever owned. In the intervening three decades, Marilyn called a selection of fifty different places "home," many of them hotels.

Biographers do not always concur about when and where Marilyn lived in the first half of her life, particularly in the period before and after her spell at the Los Angeles ORPHANAGE. During the period from 1946 to 1952 Marilyn was almost constantly on the move, living just a few weeks or months in one place before moving on to a favorite hotel, hence the multiple entries for each year in the list below.

| | |
|---|---|
| 1926 | 5454 Wilshire Boulevard, Los Angeles |
| 1926–1933 | 459 East Rhode Island Street, Hawthorne |

| | |
|---|---|
| 1933 | 6012 Afton Place, Hollywood |
| 1933–34 or 35 | 6812 Arbol Street, Hollywood |
| 1935 | Lodi Place, Hollywood |
| 1935 | 6707 Odessa Avenue, Van Nuys |
| 1935–1937 | Los Angeles Orphans' Home, 815 North El Centro Avenue, Hollywood |
| 1937 | 6707 Odessa Avenue, Van Nuys |
| 1938–1940 | 11348 Nebraska Avenue, West Los Angeles |
| 1940–1941 | 14743 Archwood Street, Van Nuys |
| 1942 | 11348 Nebraska Avenue, West Los Angeles |
| 1942 | 4524 Vista Del Monte Street, Sherman Oaks |
| 1943 | 14747 Archwood Street, Van Nuys |
| 1943 | Bessemer Street, Van Nuys |
| 1943–1944 | Catalina Island |
| 1944–1945 | 5254 Hermitage Street, North Hollywood |
| 1945–1946 | 11348 Nebraska Avenue, West Los Angeles |
| 1946 | 604 South Third Street, Las Vegas |
| 1946–1947 | Hollywood Studio Club, 1215 North Lodi Place, Hollywood |
| 1947 | 131 South Avon Street, Burbank |
| 1947–1948 | El Palacio Apartments, 8491-8499 Fountain Avenue, West Hollywood |
| 1948 | Franklin Avenue, Hollywood |
| 1948 | Harper Avenue, West Hollywood |
| 1948–1949 | Hollywood Studio Club, 1215 North Lodi Place, Hollywood |
| 1949 | 141 South Carolwood Drive, Holmby Hills |
| 1949–1950 | Beverly Carlton Hotel, 9400 West Olympic Boulevard, Beverly Hills |
| 1949–1950 | 718 North Palm Drive, Beverly Hills |
| 1950–1951 | 1309 North Harper Avenue, West Hollywood |
| 1951 | Beverly Carlton Hotel, 9400 West Olympic Boulevard, Beverly Hills |
| 1951 | 8573 Holloway Drive, Hollywood |
| 1951–1952 | 611 North Crescent Drive, West Hollywood |
| 1952 | 1121 Hilldale Avenue, West Hollywood |
| 1952 | Beverly Carlton Hotel, 9400 West Olympic Boulevard, Beverly Hills |
| 1952 | Bel Air Hotel, 701 Stone Canyon Road, Bel Air |
| 1952 | 2393 Castilian Drive, Outpost Estates, Hollywood Hills |
| 1952–1954 | Beverly Hills Hotel, 9641 West Sunset Boulevard, Beverly Hills |
| 1953–1954 | 882 North Doheny Drive, Beverly Hills |
| 1954 | 2150 Beach Street, San Francisco |
| 1954 | 508 North Palm Drive, Beverly Hills |
| 1954 | 8336 Delongpre Avenue, Hollywood |
| 1954 | Voltaire Apartments, 1424 North Crescent Heights Boulevard, West Hollywood |
| 1954–1955 | Fanton Hill Road, Weston, Connecticut |
| 1955 | Gladstone Hotel, East 52nd Street, New York |
| 1955 | Waldorf-Astoria Hotel, 301 Park Avenue, New York |
| 1955–1956 | 2 Sutton Place, New York |
| 1956 | 595 North Beverly Glen Boulevard, West Los Angeles |
| 1956 | Sunset Boulevard, Beverly Hills |
| 1956–1960 | Roxbury, Connecticut |
| 1956 | Parkside House, Egham, England |
| 1957 | Amagansett, Long Island |
| 1957–1962 | 444 East 57th Street, New York |
| 1958–1960 | Beverly Hills Hotel, 9641 West Sunset Boulevard, Beverly Hills |
| 1961–1962 | 882 North Doheny Drive, Beverly Hills |
| 1962 | 12305 Fifth Helena Drive, Brentwood |

## *HOMETOWN STORY* (1951)

At a time when Marilyn was happy to pick up any roles at all, JOHNNY HYDE brokered her into this General Motors-financed propaganda film for American industry. In her final appearance for MGM, Marilyn played a secretary named Miss Iris Martin. In her role, Marilyn wore her own sweater-dress, a veteran of appearances in *THE FIREBALL* (1950) and *ALL ABOUT EVE* (1950). Arthur Pierson, who wrote, produced, and directed this movie, had previously directed Marilyn in *DANGEROUS YEARS* (1947), her first performance to be released.

Marilyn with Alan Hale Jr. in *Hometown Story* (1951).

**Credits:**
MGM, Black and White
Length: 61 minutes
Release date: May 1951

Directed by: Arthur Pierson
Produced by: Arthur Pierson
Written by: Arthur Pierson
Cinematography by: Lucien N. Andriot
Music by: Louis Forbes
Film Editing by: William F. Claxton
Art direction by: Hilyard M. Brown

**Cast (credits order):**
Jeffrey Lynn . . . Blake Washburn
Donald Crisp . . . John MacFarland
Marjorie Reynolds . . . Janice Hunt
Alan Hale Jr. . . . Slim Haskins
Marilyn Monroe . . . Iris Martin
Barbara Brown . . . Mrs. Washburn
Melinda Plowman . . . Katie Washburn
Griff Barnett . . . Uncle Cliff
Kenny McEvoy . . . Taxi Driver
Glenn Tryon . . . Kenlock
Byron Foulger . . . Berny Miles
Virginia Campbell . . . Phoebe Hartman
Harry Harvey . . . Andy Butterworth
Nelson Leigh . . . Dr. Johnson
Speck Noblitt . . . Motorcycle Officer
Joseph Crehan

**Plot:**
Blake Washburn, played by Jeffrey Lynn, returns to his home town after being defeated in his campaign for the state legislature by the son of a powerful businessman. Washburn takes over the local newspaper after his uncle retires; one of the assets he inherits is a very pretty secretary named Miss Martin (Marilyn Monroe). Washburn wages a bitter one-man campaign against the evils of big business, only to recant when machinery manufactured by big business saves the life of his kid sister after she is trapped in a mine shaft.

**Reviews:**
*Variety*
"Arthur Pierson wrote and directed, using a competent professional cast. . . . Marilyn Monroe, Barbara Brown and Griff Barnett are up to script demands."

## HONEYMOONS

JAMES DOUGHERTY
Sixteen-year-old Norma Jeane and Jim Dougherty did not have a honeymoon, just a weekend fishing trip to Sherwood Lake.

JOE DIMAGGIO
After a night at the budget CLIFTON INN motel in Paso Robles (and a meal in the restaurant of the Hot Springs Hotel, or at the Clifton Inn according to some versions), Joe and Marilyn drove in his dark blue Cadillac to a mountain lodge outside Idyllwild, near PALM SPRINGS, loaned to them for the occasion by Marilyn's attorney, Lloyd Wright. Here they had the uncommon luxury of two weeks alone together.

Two weeks later the newlyweds went on what was to be their international honeymoon in JAPAN. In actuality, the trip had been arranged some time earlier. Joe wanted to honor his previous commitment to accompany his friend Frank "Lefty" O'Doul for a series of exhibition balls games, so he took his new wife along. Marilyn also added a work component to the journey, with a side trip to KOREA where she wowed the U.S. troops stationed there.

ARTHUR MILLER
Instead of a classic honeymoon, Arthur and Marilyn went for an extended trip to London for the production of *THE PRINCE AND THE SHOWGIRL* (1957). Their delayed honeymoon came six months after their

Joe DiMaggio and Marilyn on their honeymoon in Japan, 1954.

wedding, on January 3, 1957 when they left for a sixteen-day stay in a seaside villa in JAMAICA.

## HOOVER, J. EDGAR (1895–1972)

Director of the FBI for forty-eight years, Hoover was responsible for turning the bureau into a major crime busting outfit and, during World War II, counter-espionage organization. After the war the bureau focused on anti-subversive actions, including combating organized crime.

As head of the FBI, Hoover ordered a file to be opened on Marilyn after she became involved with ARTHUR MILLER, a prime target of the HOUSE UN-AMERICAN ACTIVITIES COMMITTEE. The Marilyn file (see FBI) contained nothing about any liaison of a sexual nature between Marilyn and Hoover's enemy, attorney general ROBERT KENNEDY.

Hoover has been implicated in the events surrounding Marilyn's mysterious DEATH. According to biographers such as ANTHONY SUMMERS, Hoover was engaged in a battle with both JOHN F. KENNEDY and Bobby Kennedy, as well as conducting his more standard duties of warning the state about threats from the MAFIA and subversives. Summers also claims that Hoover issued orders to dispose of the telephone records of Marilyn's last evening alive.

Hoover has been accused of bugging Marilyn's FIFTH HELENA DRIVE home in an attempt to find information with which to blackmail the Kennedys, and has even been held responsible in some quarters for indirectly causing her death.

## HOPE, BOB
(B. 1903, LESLIE TOWNES HOPE)

English-born comedian Hope followed a vaudeville apprenticeship with a film career that took off in the early forties when he teamed up with BING CROSBY to make the "Road" films. The quintessentially gung-ho comic coward who muddles through in the end, Hope was awarded no less than three special Academy Awards between 1940 and 1952, as much in recognition of his work entertaining the troops and raising money for charity as for his screen prowess.

In 1955, months after Marilyn announced she was going independent with MARILYN MONROE PRODUCTIONS, and that she had long harbored the ambition to play Grushenka in the DOSTOEVSKY classic *The Brothers Karamazov*, Bob Hope did a little sketch routine at that year's Oscar ceremony, in which he asked THELMA RITTER, "Is Marilyn here?" "Yes," came the reply, "she just walked in with the Brothers Karamazov." This was apparently soon after Hope had unsuccessfully tried to track down Marilyn, then staying incognito in Connecticut, to ask her to entertain the troops in Alaska.

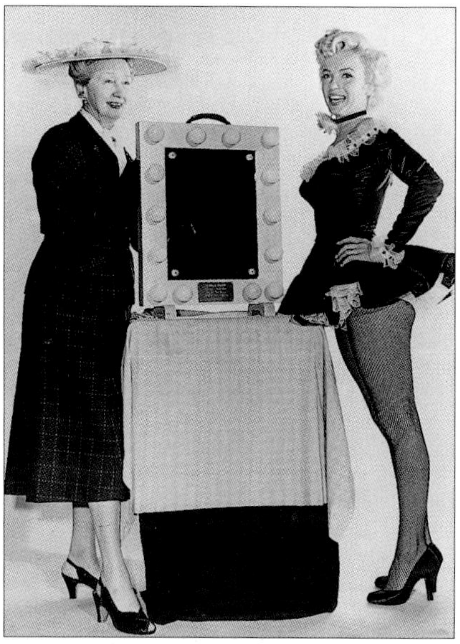

A publicity photo for *There's No Business Like Show Business* (1954) featured Marilyn being awarded *The Detroit Free Press's* "New Faces Award" by Hollywood gossip columnist Hedda Hopper.

## HOPPER, HEDDA
(1890–1966, B. ELDA FURRY)

An influential Hollywood gossip columnist, Hopper wrote a syndicated round-up of movie news. She had a wary eye on the future star even before Norma Jeane signed her first studio contract at TWENTIETH CENTURY-FOX. Indeed, her piece, printed on July 29, 1946, hastened the studio's decision by warning them they faced competition: "HOWARD HUGHES is on the mend. Picking up a magazine, he was attracted by the cover girl and promptly instructed an aide to sign her for pictures. She's Norma Jean [sic] Dougherty, a model." According to biographer FRED LAWRENCE GUILES, in actuality neither Hopper nor Hughes knew much about this item, as it was sent in directly by EMMELINE SNIVELY, the head of the BLUE BOOK MODELING AGENCY.

Hopper was still championing Marilyn in 1952: "Blowtorch Blondes are Hollywood's specialty, and Marilyn Monroe, who has zoomed to stardom after a three-year stretch as a cheesecake queen, is easily the most delectable dish of the day."

Later on, though, Hopper was not so popular with Marilyn. In 1960 she broke the story that Marilyn was having an affair with her then co-star YVES MONTAND, after obtaining this top secret information from the man himself over tea.

## HOSPITALS

During her lifetime Marilyn underwent at least twenty invasive surgical procedures. Marilyn's many hospital visits included a tonsillectomy as a child, minor cosmetic surgery on at least two occasions, an appendectomy at twenty-five, gallbladder removal not long before she died, a series of operations to combat the chronic endometriosis from which she suffered throughout her adult life, miscarriages, hospitalization for recurrent bronchitis and, in 1960 and 1961, three visits caused by nervous exhaustion.

Below is a list of Marilyn's recorded time in hospitals.

(*see* MEDICAL HISTORY *and* DOCTORS)

**Cedars of Lebanon Hospital**
8700 Beverly Boulevard, Los Angeles
(now Cedars-Sinai Medical Center)
Marilyn attended this hospital more frequently than any other.

1950: Marilyn was a regular visitor to benefactor JOHNNY HYDE, who died following a heart attack in December 1950.

1952: Tests in early March showed that Marilyn's severe stomach pains, which kept her away from TWENTIETH CENTURY-FOX where she was working on two movies, were due to appendicitis. She was not operated on until April 28, after she had fulfilled her filming commitments on

MONKEY BUSINESS. Dr. Marcus Rabwin, who performed the surgery, found a poignant note taped to Marilyn's abdomen, pleading with him not to do anything that might endanger her chances of having children.

1954: Bronchitis

1954: From November 6–12, Marilyn was in the hospital for an operation to correct her endometriosis. On discharge, despite her best attempts to slip out by the back door, Marilyn was waylaid by hundreds of press flashbulbs.

1961: In May, Marilyn returned either for further surgery on her endometriosis, or to remove part of her pancreas, depending on accounts.

1962: On July 20, Marilyn returned to the hospital once more for an operation on her chronic endometriosis. JOE DIMAGGIO took her home afterward. However, some biographers claim that on this visit she aborted a child fathered by one of the Kennedy brothers. This is not borne out by the notes of Marilyn's gynecologist, Dr. Leon Krohn.

**Columbia University Presbyterian Medical Center**
622 West 168th Street, New York

1961: Joe DiMaggio arranged for Marilyn to be moved from the locked psychiatric ward of Payne Whitney Clinic to this New York hospital. She stayed in room 719 from February 11 to March 5. According to her publicists she was "suffering from physical and emotional exhaustion." Every day of her stay, Joe DiMaggio was with her.

A few days before discharging herself, Marilyn wrote the following letter to her Los Angeles psychoanalyst DR. RALPH GREENSON:

> Dear Dr. Greenson,
> Just now when I looked out the hospital window where the snow had covered everything, suddenly everything is kind of a muted green. There are grass and shabby evergreen bushes, though the trees give me a little hope—and the desolate bare branches promise maybe there will be spring and maybe they promise hope. . . . As I started to write this letter about four quiet tears had fallen. I don't know quite why.
> Last night I was awake all night again. Sometimes I wonder what the night time is for. It almost doesn't exist for me.

When Marilyn left, a swarm of reporters was waiting to welcome her back to what, for her, was normal life.

**Doctor's Hospital, New York**
170 East End Avenue, New York

1957: Marilyn was rushed to this hospital on August 1 suffering from severe abdominal pains. ARTHUR MILLER was at her side. Her pregnancy had to be terminated after it was discovered to be ectopic.

**Las Vegas General Hospital**
201 North 8th Street, Las Vegas

1946: While waiting out the residency requirement in order to divorce first husband JAMES DOUGHERTY, Marilyn twice went to this hospital. Her first stay was after she developed an acute mouth infection—trenchmouth—the result of an operation to remove her wisdom teeth. Then, just one day after being discharged, she was hospitalized once more, this time with measles.

Marilyn confronted a swarm of reporters when she left Columbia University Presbyterian Medical Center after nearly a month of psychiatric treatment in 1961.

**Lenox Hill Hospital**
100 East 77th Street, New York

1959: On June 22 Marilyn entered this hospital for a further operation, by Dr. Mortimer Rodgers, to remedy her chronic endometriosis. Arthur Miller took her home again on June 26.

**Los Angeles General Hospital**
1200 North State Street, Los Angeles (now the Los Angeles County USC Medical Center)

1926: On June 1, at 9:30 A.M., Norma Jeane Mortensen was born here in the charity ward.

1934: In January Marilyn's mother GLADYS BAKER was brought to this hospital after her breakdown. She was later transferred to the NORWALK STATE HOSPITAL.

**Payne Whitney Psychiatric Hospital**
525 East 68th Street, New York (now Cornel Medical-Payne Whitney Clinic)

1961: On the advice of psychoanalyst MARIANNE KRIS, following a divorce and the unfavorable critical reception of *THE MISFITS*, on February 7 Marilyn checked in to the psychiatric ward of this New York hospital. To avoid publicity she signed the admission papers with the name Faye Miller. Far from finding an environment conducive to rest and recuperation, Marilyn was placed in a locked psychiatric ward. She broke down as the worst of her fears had come true: like her mother and grandmother before her, she too was incarcerated in a facility for the mentally ill. Three days later Joe DiMaggio, whom Marilyn had not seen in years but who dropped everything at her call, flew in and arranged for her to be transferred to the more congenial surroundings of the Columbia University Presbyterian Medical Center.

**Polyclinic Hospital**
West 50th Street, New York (since moved to 330 West 30th Street)

1958: In December a highly distraught Marilyn was brought into this hospital after a miscarriage during the third month of pregnancy.

1961: On June 28 she returned to the Polyclinic to have her gallbladder removed—the fifth time she had been in the hospital in just ten months. Joe DiMaggio kept her company throughout. When Marilyn was discharged on July 11 she was practically mobbed by well-wishers and photographers as she left. She later said, "It was scary. I felt for a few minutes as if they were just going to take pieces out of me. Actually it made me feel a little sick. I mean I appreciated the concern and their affection and all that, but—I don't know—it was a little like a nightmare. I wasn't sure I was going to get into the car safely and get away!"

**St. Vincent Hospital**
2131 West 3rd Street, Los Angeles (now St. Vincent Medical Center)

1956: In April Marilyn was forced to take a break from shooting on *BUS STOP* and check into this hospital for four days to recover from bronchitis.

**Westside Hospital**
La Cienega Boulevard, Los Angeles

1960: When the trials of filming *The Misfits* became too much for Marilyn in late August, she checked in to this private Los Angeles hospital. In his statement to the press, internist Dr. Hyman Engelberg said she was suffering from exhaustion. This did not prevent speculation that she was brought to the hospital after a suicide attempt. During her stay, she was visited by MARLON BRANDO, FRANK SINATRA and Joe DiMaggio.Ten days later she returned to RENO to continue filming.

## HOTEL DEL CORONADO
1500 ORANGE AVENUE, CORONADO, CALIFORNIA

Location shooting for *SOME LIKE IT HOT* (1959) took place here in 1958. Marilyn stayed at the Vista Mar cottage.

## HOTELS WHERE MARILYN STAYED

**California**
CLIFTON MOTEL, Paso Robles
FURNACE CREEK INN, Death Valley
HOTEL DEL CORONADO, Coronado

**Los Angeles**
BEL AIR HOTEL, Beverly Hills
BEVERLY CARLTON HOTEL, Beverly Hills
BEVERLY HILLS HOTEL, Beverly Hills
CHATEAU MARMONT, West Hollywood
HOLLYWOOD ROOSEVELT Hotel, Hollywood
KNICKERBOCKER HOTEL, Hollywood
LAFONDA MOTOR LODGE, Van Nuys

**New York City**
CARLYLE HOTEL
DRAKE HOTEL
GLADSTONE HOTEL
HAMPSHIRE HOUSE
ST. REGIS HOTEL
SHERRY NETHERLAND HOTEL
WALDORF-ASTORIA HOTEL

**Others**
BANFF SPRINGS HOTEL, Banff, Canada
CAL-NEVA LODGE, Lake Tahoe
CONTINENTAL HILTON HOTEL, Mexico City
Country Inn, Virginia City, Nevada
Fontainebleau Hotel, Miami
GENERAL BROCK HOTEL, Niagara Falls
Government Lodge, Mount Hood, Oregon
HOLIDAY HOTEL, Reno
IMPERIAL HOTEL, Tokyo
MAPES HOTEL, Reno
SAHARA MOTOR HOTEL, Phoenix

## HOUSE UN-AMERICAN ACTIVITIES COMMITTEE (HUAC)

Marilyn came under investigation by this House of Representatives body after then fiancé ARTHUR MILLER was subpoenaed to appear in Washington in 1956. Originally founded to monitor foreign agents during the war years, HUAC later became known for its dogged pursuit of reputed Communists, culminating in black listing and jail sentences for many well-known Hollywood actors and writers for their "dangerous political beliefs." Miller ultimately believed that HUAC was interested in him more for publicity than anything else.

Miller was called before the committee in June 1956. It quickly became apparent that, despite the best efforts of the FBI, there was no proof that Miller had been a member of the Communist Party. Miller admitted to the committee that he had attended Communist Party writers' meetings, but denied ever having been "under Communist discipline."

In his autobiography *Timebends*, Miller clarifies: "The simple truth was that I myself could barely recall a great many of the organizations or causes to which I had given my support. . . . I had indeed at times believed and with passionate moral certainty that in Marxism was the hope of mankind and of the survival of reason itself, only to come up against nagging demonstrations of human perversity, not least my own."

Miller refused to name names: "I'll tell you anything about myself, but my conscience will not permit me to use the name of another person." Even though it meant a trial for contempt, Marilyn greatly admired his principled stand that writers should be able to write what they wanted, and his refusal to implicate others in order to save his own skin.

The most widely reported incident during the courtroom hearing, however, had nothing to do with Communists. In support of his request to have his passport returned so he could go to ENGLAND, Miller stated that his reasons were to attend a production of one of his plays, and that he wanted "to be with the woman who will then be my wife." Under further questioning, he announced: "I will marry Marilyn Monroe before July 13. . . . When she goes to London she will go as Mrs. Miller." Some people, including Marilyn's publicist RUPERT ALLEN, have said that this was the first Marilyn knew of these firm wedding plans.

Marilyn too had been put under pressure to make Arthur capitulate. Fox heavyweight SPYROS SKOURAS visited Marilyn in New York to convince her to use her influence over Miller and end what he considered bad publicity for his star. Marilyn stood firm: "I said, 'I'm proud of my husband's position and I stand behind him all the way.'"

In May 1957 Miller appeared on trial for

Reporters kept an all-day vigil outside Marilyn's Sutton Place apartment to get her comment on the testimony of her fiancé Arthur Miller who testified before the House Un-American Activities Committee.

contempt for refusing to answer questions put forth by HUAC. He was found guilty and sentenced to a $500 fine as well as one month in jail, but then immediately launched an appeal. Marilyn dutifully went with him to Washington to lend her support, staying with JOSEPH RAUH and his wife Olie. To help her husband's case, she even held a press briefing. In the summer of 1958, on the grounds that Miller had not been adequately informed of the reasons why he was answering questions, the guilty verdict was overturned and Miller's name was cleared.

## *HOW TO MARRY A MILLIONAIRE* (1953)

TWENTIETH CENTURY-FOX brought out big guns BETTY GRABLE, Marilyn Monroe, and LAUREN BACALL in this story of gold diggers prospecting to catch a rich husband. The studio was keen to show off its top three stars, in the first wide-screen Cinemascope movie ever made (though it came out after the second, *The Robe*, a religious-themed movie starring Richard Burton and Jean Simmons). Writer NUNNALLY JOHNSON claimed that he adapted the characters to match the personalities of the three stars.

Although the studio tried to arouse press interest with stories about intense rivalry between chief blondes Grable and Monroe, the actresses got on well behind the scenes. By all accounts Grable graciously handed over her mantle after ten years as the nation's sweetheart. But by the time the movie came out, Grable had ripped up her Fox contract, which still had five years left to run, and as a result slipped from top billing.

Marilyn was originally drawn to Loco, the character Grable played, because she didn't like the idea of her character Pola wearing glasses. Director JEAN NEGULESCO persuaded her that this was the best part. He was right. The comic possibilities of severe myopia earned Marilyn a number of favorable notices about her comedic touch. Marilyn, though, did not regard this movie performance as one of her best. When she asked the director

Publicity photograph for *How to Marry a Millionaire* (1953).

David Wayne with Marilyn in *How to Marry A Millionaire* (1953).

what the motivation for her character was, he replied, "You're as blind as a bat without glasses. That is your motivation." This was not enough to satisfy Marilyn's ambition to throw her all into her work.

Marilyn knew she had made it to the very top of the trade with the movie's premiere on November 4, 1953. It took over six hours of hard work by WILLIAM TRAVILLA, ALAN "WHITEY" SNYDER, and Gladys Rasmussen to prepare her for her entrance, sewn into a dress borrowed from the studio wardrobe: a flesh-colored crépe de chine and shimmering sequins, long white evening gloves, and a white fox stole. At the pre-premiere drinks party, hosted by writer/producer Johnson, an evidently nervous Marilyn drank down several glasses of bourbon and soda, and was visibly tipsy by the time she walked past the clamoring crowds into the Fox-Wilshire Theater. Johnson was heard to say "women who have been sewn into their clothes should never drink to excess." For Marilyn, though, the night was a triumph, "just about the happiest night of my life." The *Hollywood Reporter* wrote, "Nothing like it since Gloria Swanson at her most glittering." Negulesco agreed. That evening, he said, she felt "she had proved to everyone (and herself) that she could stand any competition."

Within a few months of opening, the film had grossed five times its extravagant budget of $2.5 million.

The floor length cream-colored wool gown, used in the film's poster campaigns, sold at auction in June 1997 for $57,000, a world record for any film costume.

**Nominations:**
ACADEMY AWARD:
Best Costume Design (Color): Charles Le Maire, Travilla

BRITISH ACADEMY AWARDS:
Best Film from any Source

**Credits:**
Twentieth Century-Fox, (Cinemascope and Technicolor)
Length: 95 minutes
Release date: November 10, 1953

Directed by: Jean Negulesco
Produced by: Nunnally Johnson
Written by: Nunnally Johnson, Zoe Akins (writer of original play *The Greeks Had a Word for It*), Katherine Albert (writer of original play *Loco*), Dale Eunson (play) original story by Doris Lilly
Cinematography by: Joseph MacDonald
Music by: Cyril J. Mockridge (incidental music), Alfred Newman—musical direction
Costume Design by: Charles Le Maire, Travilla
Film Editing by: Louis R. Loeffler

**Cast (credits order):**
Marilyn Monroe . . . Pola Debevoise
Betty Grable . . . Loco Dempsey
Lauren Bacall . . . Schatze Page
David Wayne . . . Freddie Denmark
Rory Calhoun . . . Eben
Cameron Mitchell . . . Tom Brookman
Alexander D'Arcy . . . J. Stewart Merrill
Fred Clark . . . Waldo Brewster
William Powell . . . J. D. Hanley
George Dunn . . . Mike, Elevator Operator
Percy Helton . . . Benton
Robert Adler . . . Cab Driver
Harry Carter . . . Elevator Operator
Tudor Owen . . . Otis
Maurice Marsac . . . Antoine
Emmett Vogan . . . Man at Bridge
Hermine Sterler . . . Madame
Abney Mott . . . Secretary
Rankin Mansfield . . . Bennett
Jan Arvan . . . Tony
Ivan Triesault . . . Captain of Waiters
Van Des Autels (uncredited)

**Crew:**
Alfred Bruzlin . . . sound
Leonard Doss . . . color consultant
Leland Fuller . . . art director
Roger Heman . . . sound
F. E. "Johnny" Johnston . . . assistant director
Ray Kellogg . . . special effects
Charles Le Maire . . . wardrobe director
Cyril J. Mockridge . . . incidental music
Ben Nye . . . makeup
Edward B. Powell . . . orchestration
Stuart A. Reiss . . . set decorator
Walter M. Scott . . . set decorator
Lyle R. Wheeler . . . art director

**Plot:**
Three pretty models—Pola Debevoise (Marilyn Monroe), Loco Dempsey (Betty Grable), and Schatze Page (Lauren Bacall)—figure that they have more chance of reeling in a rich husband if they pool their resources and rent out a fancy New York penthouse apartment.

Each girl has her own adventures, the stories interweaving only briefly until the grand finale. Early contender Tom Brookman (Cameron Mitchell) who helps Loco carry her groceries and falls in love with Schatze, is ruled out because he is far too poor. Schatze is more interested in oil tycoon J. D. Hanley (William Powell). Meanwhile Loco is hoodwinked into going to a country lodge with married man Waldo Brewster. When she discovers the deception she immediately wants to return to the city, but is prevented by a bout of the measles, which fortunately allows her to meet and fall in love with handsome forest ranger Eben (RORY CALHOUN), who in the end admits that he is lord of the enormous forest he is ranging.

Meanwhile severely short-sighted Pola is convinced that boys don't make passes at girls who wear glasses. Unfortunately she sees very little without her spectacles, so when she heads off to meet her beau J. Stewart Merrill (ALEX D'ARCY) she gets on the wrong plane. This turns out to be the right move, as it enables her to bump into Freddie Denmark (DAVID WAYNE), her landlord, who is tracking down his unscrupulous tax accountant.

Back in the big city, penniless Schatze agrees to marry her wealthy suitor. Loco and Eben arrive on the wedding day, as do Pola and a rather worse-for-wear Freddie, who have married. Also at the wedding is the previously poor Tom Brookman—the gallant groom-to-be calls off the wedding because he sees that this is the man Schatze really loves. At a dinner for all three couples, Brookman reveals that he is a man of truly enormous means. All three gold-digging girls land their wealthy man—and love too.

**Reviews:**
*New York Daily News*
"Betty Grable, Lauren Bacall and Marilyn Monroe give off the quips and cracks, generously supplied by Nunnally Johnson, with a naturalness that adds to their strikingly humorous effect, making the film the funniest comedy of the year."

*New York Herald Tribune*
"The big question, 'How does Marilyn Monroe look stretched across a broad screen?' is easily answered. If you insisted on sitting in the front row, you would probably feel as though you were being smothered in baked Alaska. Her stint as a deadpan comedienne is as nifty as her looks. Playing a near-sighted charmer who won't wear her glasses when men are around, she bumps into the furniture and reads books upside down with a limpid guile that nearly melts the screen. . . . *How to Marry a Millionaire* is measured, not in square feet, but in the size of the Johnson-Negulesco comic invention and the shape of Marilyn Monroe—and that is about as sizable and shapely as you can get."

*New York Post*
"It is particularly noteworthy that Miss Monroe has developed more than a small amount of comedy polish of the foot-in-mouth type."

Rock Hudson presents Marilyn with "The World's Favorite Female Star" Golden Globe Award, 1962.

## HUDSON, ROCK
(1925–1985, B. ROY HAROLD SCHERER)

Larger-than-life male lead Rock Hudson started in Hollywood soon after returning from his navy war service in 1946. He served his movie apprenticeship in adventure and B-movie fare, in 1952 and 1953 churning out a diligent six pictures a year. He was nominated for an Oscar for his performance in *Giant* (1956), before easing into a series of comfortable comedies, often paired up with DORIS DAY. *Pillow Talk*, which the two made in 1959, was a movie Marilyn was interested in at one time. Hudson continued to work, often in television, until he contracted AIDS. His final notoriety in Hollywood was as the first high-profile actor to die of this disease.

Hudson and Marilyn nearly worked together on several occasions. In 1955 negotiations were advanced for him to star opposite Marilyn in *BUS STOP* (1956), until he changed his mind—according to some sources because Marilyn's business partner MILTON GREENE had once spurned Hudson's advances. Producer JERRY WALD also unsuccessfully attempted to cast Hudson as the lead in *LET'S MAKE LOVE* (1960).

The only Marilyn picture Rock Hudson worked on was after her death, when he hosted TWENTIETH CENTURY-FOX's tribute movie *Marilyn* (1963).

## HUETH, POTTER (ALSO SPELLED HEWETH)

PHOTOGRAPHER Hueth played a vital part in the chain of command that took Norma Jeane from a job in a factory to the cover of MAGAZINES as a popular model. This friend of photographer DAVID CONOVER was sufficiently impressed with the results of a photo session with Norma Jeane—posed in tight sweaters, variously with a dalmation and on a bale of hay—that he took them to show EMMELINE SNIVELY, who ran the BLUE BOOK MODELING AGENCY.

## HUGHES, HOWARD ROBARD
(1905–1976)

Before his years as a recluse, famous millionaire Howard Hughes had three consuming passions: aviation, cinema, and pretty women. Columnist HEDDA HOPPER reported that while lying in a hospital bed after crash landing a plane, he had been extremely taken by a young woman emblazoned on the covers of many of the magazines he read while confined to bed. The story goes that he issued orders to sign her up. . . . Too late, for one week earlier talent spotter BEN LYON had signed her to TWENTIETH CENTURY-FOX.

In fact, it didn't quite happen that way. Hughes, recovering from serious injuries, was apparently in no state to read anything. The Hopper column merely quoted a press release judiciously sent out by Emmeline Snively, anxious to drum up some competition for one of her girls at the BLUE BOOK MODELING AGENCY. Some biographers, though, maintain that Marilyn first had a screen test with Hughes's RKO studio before landing her contract at Twentieth Century-Fox.

A number of sources point to a liaison between Marilyn and Hughes during her starlet days, when he summoned her to a desert airfield and flew her off to Palm Springs for amorous pursuits. NATASHA LYTESS confirms that Hughes and Marilyn did have a fling; columnist EARL WILSON mentioned that Marilyn had once returned from a meeting with Hughes with red cheeks because he had been unshaven. They reportedly came face to face a couple of years later, while Marilyn was filming *CLASH BY NIGHT* (1952) on the RKO lot.

A brooch Marilyn was given by Hughes is cited as proof of an affair. She was apparently surprised to learn that the piece of jewelry given to her by one of the world's wealthiest men was only worth $500.

## HUNTER, ARLINE

The real star of an infamous early-fifties pornographic film called *APPLES, KNOCKERS AND COKE* wrongly attributed to a young and impoverished Marilyn Monroe. Hunter's body of work includes such titles as *A Virgin In Hollywood* (1948), *Sex Kittens Go to College* (1960), and *The Art of Burlesque* (1968). In August 1954 she was PLAYBOY Playmate of the Month.

## HUSBANDS

JAMES DOUGHERTY
Married June 1942—September 1946

JOE DIMAGGIO
Married January 1954—October 1954

ARTHUR MILLER
Married June 1956—January 1961

## HUSTON, JOHN (1906–1987)

MARILYN (working on *The Misfits*):
"Nobody would have heard of me if it hadn't been for John Huston. [He told me] if you're not nervous, you might as well give up. John has meant a great deal in my life. It's sort of a coincidence to be with him ten years later."

HUSTON:
"I was far more taken with her in the flesh than on the screen when we first worked together. I had no idea that she would go so far so fast."

"She went right down into her own personal experience for everything, reached down and pulled something out of herself that was unique and extraordinary. She had no techniques. It was all the truth, it was only Marilyn. But it was Marilyn, plus. She found things, found things about womankind in herself."

Son of actor Walter Huston, John wrote and directed a string of Academy Award-nominated films. His directorial debut, *The Maltese Falcon* (1941), brought immediate recognition and the start of a working relationship with Humphrey Bogart that was to continue with great success through *The Treasure of the Sierra Madre* (1947), *Key Largo* (1948), and *The African Queen* (1952). Other successes include *The Night of the Iguana* (1964), *The Man Who Would Be King* (1975), and his penultimate film, *Prizzi's Honor* (1985). A man of great charisma and occasional cruelty, the harder a film was to make, and the more rugged the shooting conditions, the happier he seemed to take on the project.

Huston also developed a very successful sideline as an actor, receiving an Oscar nomination for *The Cardinal* (1963), and featuring memorably in *Chinatown* (1974) and many other movies.

It was John Huston who gave Marilyn her first high-profile role in classic heist gone wrong movie *THE ASPHALT JUNGLE* (1950), though apparently a year earlier he had tried to land her for a part in *We Were Strangers*, only for his then studio, Columbia, to refuse the expense of screen testing her.

In his autobiography, *An Open Book*, Huston claims credit for casting Marilyn on the spot, after JOHNNY HYDE had suggested she audition for the part of Angela Phinlay. In fact it was a more tortuous process than that, judging by the number of versions of the story in circulation. Marilyn is said to have vamped it up so much at the first audition that the role was cast to rival blonde Lola Albright. Then, it seems, LUCILLE RYMAN intervened to champion Marilyn where Johnny Hyde had left off. First Ryman argued that Marilyn would be much more suited to the role's pay check than first choice Albright; then Ryman forced the issue by calling in the debt Huston had run up for stabling his horses at the Ryman/Carroll ranch. When threatened with the sale of his stallions to recoup the $18,000 he owed, or give Marilyn the part, Huston quickly buckled.

Although Huston is remembered as something of a "man's director," Marilyn's memories of working on *The Asphalt Jungle* were rosy, in contrast to practically every movie she did afterward. She considered Huston to be a genius, and was full of appreciation for the way he directed her: "Everything I did was important to the director, just as important as everything the stars of the picture did."

Marilyn put Huston on her 1955 list of approved directors, but it was not until 1960 that they worked together again. Huston noticed how far she had come, transforming in those ten years from "a simple little blonde who took direction rather well" into "an actress who acted from the inside out, someone who had to feel it in her insides before she could perform."

As well as being a notorious gambler,

John Huston, Marilyn, and Arthur Miller on the set of *The Misfits* (1961).

Huston himself was a keen horseman, hence his interest in directing *THE MISFITS* (1961). Before shooting commenced Huston had to convalesce from a broken leg sustained after a fall during a hunting session.

More has been written about shooting *The Misfits* than about the movie itself. The project was dogged by a slew of problems, any one of which would have been enough to ruin a production: Marilyn and ARTHUR MILLER's break-up, tensions between Miller and Huston, the ten days Marilyn spent in the hospital recovering from nervous exhaustion, large budget overruns, the combination of Huston and Marilyn ordering endless retakes, stifling desert heat on location, and dangerous scenes resulting in injury to stunt men and doubles (not to mention the toll it all took on CLARK GABLE, who did his own stunts and died of a heart attack less than two weeks after the end of shooting). As for the problem of drama coach PAULA STRASBERG second-guessing his direction, according to Arthur Miller, Huston earnestly listened to everything Paula had to say and then carried on regardless.

According to more than one Marilyn biographer, Huston's addictions to smoking, drinking, and GAMBLING were more of the threat to the production than Marilyn's dependence on sleeping pills. Huston regularly stayed out playing craps until five in the morning, losing as much as $20,000 in a single night. On one such evening Huston handed Marilyn the dice and told her to try her luck. Wondering what numbers she needed to throw to win, she asked him, "What should I ask for, John?" He replied, "Don't think, Honey, just throw. That's the story of your life. Don't think, do it."

Huston has also been accused of colluding with Marilyn's doctors to send her away for a week's convalescence in Los Angeles, and in her absence circulating rumors that she had had a breakdown to cover up the fact that shooting could not go on because of his enormous unpaid gambling debts.

Even after the harrowing experience of working on *The Misfits*, Huston thought of reuniting Marilyn with MONTGOMERY CLIFT in his film treatment of the father of psychoanalysis, *Freud* (1962). On the advice of her own analyst, Marilyn declined.

Huston provided the narrative for the 1966 documentary *The Legend of Marilyn Monroe*.

BOOK:
*An Open Book*, John Huston. New York: Alfred A. Knopf, 1980.

## HYDE, JOHNNY
(1896–1950, B. IVAN HAIDABURA)

MARILYN:
"Johnny was more than twice my age, a gentle, kind, brilliant man, and I had never known anyone like him. He had great charm and warmth. It was Johnny who inspired me to read good books and enjoy good music."

"He not only knew me, he knew Norma Jeane too. He knew all the pain and all the desperate things in me. When he put his arms around me and said he loved me, I knew it was true. Nobody had ever loved me like that. I wished with all my heart that I could love him back... it was like being with a whole family and belonging to a full set of relatives."

When he first met Norma Jeane, Hyde, fifty-three, was vice president of William Morris, one of the top AGENCIES in Hollywood; he was married with four sons, and he was seriously ill with a heart condition. Where they met is not clear. One version of how it happened was that JOHN CARROLL introduced Marilyn to him at a PALM SPRINGS Racquet Club party thrown by JOSEPH SCHENCK in January 1949. Another is that they met at a New Year's Eve party thrown by producer Sam Spiegel, after which Hyde invited her down to Palm Springs to discuss her career in a more private atmosphere.

Like so many of the people that mattered in Hollywood, Hyde had been born in Europe. Hyde spent the first ten years of his life in Russia, son of a family of acrobats who brought him to America in 1906. Since 1935 he had been building up quite a portfolio of top names: Betty Hutton, BOB HOPE, Rita Hayworth, and Lana Turner, whom he is credited with turning into a star. Over the course of 1949, during meetings and evenings spent together, Hyde fell head over heels in love with his final discovery. Marilyn found in Johnny the archetypal sugar daddy, a man with the best connections keen to give some much-needed direction to her fledgling career. They made quite a comic pair: Hyde was not only more than twice her age, he was close to a foot shorter than her.

Within a few months Hyde had left his wife, Mozelle Cravens Hyde, who later told biographer FRED LAWRENCE GUILES, "I tried to take it for a long time, but in the end, it was impossible. I'm a tolerant person, but there is always a limit."

Hyde took Marilyn to live in a rented house at 718 NORTH PALM DRIVE in Beverly Hills. To fend off prying eyes, Marilyn kept on a room at the BEVERLY CARLTON HOTEL on West Olympic Boulevard.

Hyde arranged COSMETIC SURGERY for final adjustments to her nose and chin—though in some accounts other would-be mentors had already undertaken this work. He had her hair dyed platinum blonde, her hairline raised, and a minor imperfection in her teeth fixed. He bought her a swank new wardrobe and she was seen on his arm in all the hottest spots.

On the business side, Hyde bought out Marilyn's contract from her first agent HARRY LIPTON, allowing him a small percentage retainer, and dedicated himself body and soul to making her the star she became. Most importantly, Hyde called in favors from long-time pals to get Marilyn the exposure she needed. He persuaded producer LESTER COWAN to add her to his Marx brothers movie *LOVE HAPPY* (though some biographers suggest that she had already done this part, and it was a sight of her in the rushes that first aroused Hyde's interest in her); he arranged a new audition at Fox that won her a chorus line part in musical Western *A TICKET TO*

William Morris agent Johnny Hyde and Marilyn, 1950.

*TOMAHAWK* (1950), and then he got what he wanted: a small but perfect part for Marilyn in JOHN HUSTON's high-profile *THE ASPHALT JUNGLE* (1950).

He did all of this for love. Yet no matter how many times he proposed to her, Marilyn said no. She didn't love him and she would not marry without love, even though saying yes would have made her an extremely wealthy woman. Marilyn was still lovelorn after FRED KARGER, the man she described as the first love of her life, had finished with her. She also told RUPERT ALLAN, "It would be ridiculous to pass myself off as Mrs. Johnny Hyde. I'd be taken less seriously than I am now."

Hyde continued to call in favors until his weak heart began to give out. He arranged a screen test at Fox for a movie called *Cold Shoulder*. He smoothed her path into minor exposure in *RIGHT CROSS* (1950) and *HOMETOWN STORY* (1951). He also guided her into a role in Academy Award-winning movie *ALL ABOUT EVE* (1950), opposite GEORGE SANDERS, and promise of that all-important seven year option at TWENTIETH CENTURY-FOX.

When Hyde had the first of the series of heart attacks, Marilyn was not with him. Depending on the source, she was nearby having a costume fitting for *AS YOUNG AS YOU FEEL* (1951), on which, incidentally, she first met ARTHUR MILLER, or on a trip to Tijuana with NATASHA LYTESS. Hyde died on December 18, 1950. Marilyn told ELIA KAZAN that she had been at the hospital when he died, outside his room; she could hear him calling her name but Hyde's family would not let her in.

Hyde's last words to secretary Dona Holloway were reputedly, "Be sure that Marilyn is treated as one of the family." Holloway did not have the power to carry out his wishes. After his death the family threw Marilyn out of the home where she had lived with Hyde, and repossessed all of the jewelry and clothes he had given her. Although Hyde had instructed his lawyers that he wished to leave a third of his estate to Marilyn, he had not actually revised his will, so Marilyn received nothing.

The family also forbade Marilyn from attending the funeral; Marilyn, however, veiled and dressed in black, went with Lytess to Forest Lawn Cemetery in Hollywood Hills at the appointed time. Even here, versions diverge: she either threw herself, sobbing, onto the coffin, or with more self-possession plucked a single white rose from the spray on the coffin, to preserve for years between the pages of a Bible.

After Hyde's death Marilyn was extremely upset. She was overcome by sudden bouts of tears, and for many months was withdrawn and reserved. She reputedly made a SUICIDE ATTEMPT at this time, but Lytess, with whom she was staying, discovered her in time.

## IMPERIAL HOTEL
1-1 SHINKAWA 1-CHOME, CHUO-KU, TOKYO

In February 1954 Marilyn and new husband JOE DIMAGGIO stayed at this hotel in Tokyo. Throughout their stay FANS kept up a vigil, after almost causing a riot on the first day.

## IMPERSONATORS

Scores of people around the world make a living as a Marilyn look-alike, sound-alike, and pout-alike. Practically every nation in the world has performers who act out famous Marilyn show numbers, who are hired as cabaret acts, or turn up as Marilyngrams in the most unlikely places. One look-alike took her resemblence a little too far by committing suicide when she was thirty-six years old.

The enduring symbol of sensuous, buxom womanhood is a great gay icon, and many a male impersonator has graced the stage in Marilyn's likeness. One of the most famous of these was Jimmy James, a man who looked and sounded so much like Marilyn that he was threatened with legal action if he continued. More recently, actor Christopher Morley has impersonated Marilyn on TV and the big screen in *Don't Tell Mom the Babysitter's Dead* (1991).

Even when first starting out in showbiz, Norma Jeane enjoyed going out to clubs on Sunset Strip where there were impersonators, for example a man called Ray Bourbon. During filming of *THE MISFITS* (1961) Marilyn went to watch herself being "done" at San Francisco club Finnocchio's—but apparently walked out before the act was finished.

BOOKS:
*How to Impersonate Famous People*, Christopher Fowler. New York: Crown Books, 1984.
*Dying to Be Marilyn*, Yvette Paris. Cheyenne, WY: Lagumo Corp., 1996.

(*see* ACTRESSES WHO HAVE PORTRAYED MARILYN OR MARILYN-BASED CHARACTERS)

## INGE, WILLIAM MOTTER (1913–1973)

U.S. playwright best known for his 1950s Broadway plays about life in small Midwest communities which were made into movies: *Come Back Little Sheba* (1952), *Picnic* (1956), *BUS STOP* (1956), and *The Dark at the Top of the Stairs* (1960). In 1961 Inge was awarded an Oscar for his screenplay, *Splendor in the Grass*.

Marilyn's performance in the screen version of Inge's *Bus Stop* is acclaimed by many as her finest. For a time she considered another Inge play, *A Loss of Roses*, before rejecting the role.

## *INSIGNIFICANCE* (1985)

Originally a stage play written by Terry Johnson which ran at the Royal Court Theatre in London in the summer of 1982, *Insignificance* brings together iconic characters Marilyn Monroe, ALBERT EINSTEIN, Senator Joseph McCarthy, and JOE DIMAGGIO, for a fantasy exchange of zeitgeist. Director Nicholas Roeg cast his wife Theresa Russell in the Marilyn role, alongside TONY CURTIS (the Senator), Michael Emil (the Professor), and Gary Busey (Ballplayer).

BOOK:
*Insignificance: The Book*, Terry Johnson. London: Sidgwick, 1985.

## INTERNET

The world's most popular woman has spawned thousands of tribute sites on the World Wide Web. Type in the words "Marilyn Monroe" on any of the major search engines and you get back a bewildering number of matches.

Entertainment sites often feature Marilyn-related news, auction sites sell MEMORABILIA, book and video sites allow easy browsing of Marilyn content, movie sites list Marilyn film details and often links to television showings in different parts of the world. An increasing number of Marilyn's photographers have Web sites, from which it is possible to view and purchase prints of Marilyn images. Magazines such as *Life* have excellent archives containing a wealth of Marilyn photographs.

FAN sites range from a few favorite photographs to complex and award-winning designs chock full of sound files, rare photographs, movie excerpts, and well-researched biographical material.

The best way to start researching Marilyn on the Web is to go to one of the web addresses listed under FAN CLUBS, all of which contain copious lists of other Marilyn sites.

The official Marilyn Monroe site, owned by CMG Worldwide Inc., is at http://www.marilynmonroe.com

There is also a Marilyn webring, to which many Marilyn sites are affiliated: http://www.webring.org/cgi-bin/webring?random&ring=marilynm

# J

## JACOBS, ARTHUR

Head of the New York-based Arthur P. Jacobs Company which handled Marilyn's publicity from 1955 until her death. With East and West Coast offices, the company—which he ran in partnership with John Springer, employing agents Lois Weber, RUPERT ALLAN, and PATRICIA NEWCOMB—was ideally placed to serve Marilyn in her new career as an independent filmmaker through newly-formed MARILYN MONROE PRODUCTIONS. The year after Marilyn hired Jacobs and Co., he was in London with Marilyn.

Marilyn strongly encouraged Jacobs to go into producing; before her death she was planning for him to produce a picture called *I Love Louisa*, which after her death became a SHIRLEY MACLAINE vehicle released in 1964 as *What a Way to Go*. Jacobs went on to produce ten movies, including the *Planet of the Apes* film series.

Jacobs was, according to ANTHONY SUMMERS, one of the very first to know of Marilyn's DEATH, when he and his wife Natalie (an actress who worked as Natalie Trundy) were informed during a concert at the Hollywood Bowl. She told Summers, "We got the news long before it broke, we left the concert at once and Arthur left me at our house. He went to Marilyn's house, and I don't think I saw him for two days. He had to fudge to the press."

## JAMAICA

Marilyn and ARTHUR MILLER took their delayed HONEYMOON in Jamaica after completing Marilyn's filming commitments for *THE PRINCE AND THE SHOWGIRL* (1957). From January 3–19, 1957, they vacationed on the north coast at Moon Point, in a villa belonging to Lady Pamela Bird.

## JAPAN

HONEYMOON spot for Marilyn and JOE DIMAGGIO, on a trip with Joe's friend and associate "Lefty" O'Doul and his wife, arranged by the Japanese newspaper *Yomiuri Shimbun* to commemorate the start of the Japanese baseball season. Joe had previously been to Japan in 1951, when he played in exhibition games.

The couple flew to Tokyo on Pan Am, with a stopover in Honolulu. They arrived at Tokyo's Haneda International Airport on February 2, 1954, to be greeted by ten thousand wild fans whose welcome was so enthusiastic—Marilyn had locks of hair pulled out—that they had to take refuge back in the plane. In the end they had to sneak out of the baggage hatch and hide in the customs office until things had quieted down enough.

At the IMPERIAL HOTEL the situation was no less chaotic. Two hundred fans refused to leave the hotel where their idol was staying. When the police began to insist, some of the fans threw themselves through plate glass doors. The fracas did not calm down until Marilyn was persuaded to make an appearance and give the fans a wave from her balcony.

The next day, at Joe's press conference, Marilyn was the focus of attention. Joe was apparently not so happy at being upstaged on what was meant to be his tour. Together with Lefty and Jean O'Doul, Marilyn and Joe also toured Fuji, Osaka, and Yokohama. Marilyn also went off with Jean on her memorable tour of the troops in KOREA. During her time in Japan, Marilyn was dubbed "Honorable Buttocks-Swinging Actress."

## JASGUR, JOSEPH

On the recommendation of EMMELINE SNIVELY (head of the BLUE BOOK MODELING AGENCY) noted celebrity photographer Jasgur agreed to take some test photos of Norma Jean in March 1946. He recalls that she arrived an hour late, "a shy girl, nothing like a typical model, all breathless and anxious."

The photographs he took mark the passage of the keen novice to the consummately skilled stills model. In some photos she could be any young girl horsing around on the beach, in others she plays the vamp.

In his book of Marilyn photos Jasgur makes a bizarre claim that Marilyn had six toes—an allegation dashed by all the photos in the book except one, in which there is a ridge of sand next to one of her feet. Jasgur also once claimed that Norma Jean asked him to marry her . . . and that he turned her down.

BOOK:
*The Birth of Marilyn: The Lost Photographs of Norma Jeane*, Joseph Jasgur. New York: St. Martins Press, 1991.

## JEAKINS, DOROTHY (1914–1995)

Marilyn twice worked with this Oscar-winning costume designer, on *NIAGARA* (1953) and *LET'S MAKE LOVE* (1960).

## JEAN-LOUIS (1907–1997)

Head of costume at COLUMBIA PICTURES from 1944 to 1958, Jean-Louis first met Marilyn at the very beginning of her career, when she was working on *LADIES OF THE CHORUS* (1948). He worked with Marilyn again on *THE MISFITS* (1961), and on the abandoned *SOMETHING'S GOT TO GIVE* project. During his long career, Jean-Louis dressed almost all of Hollywood's leading ladies.

Jean-Louis designed the dress Marilyn wore when she famously sang "Happy Birthday" to President John F. Kennedy in 1962.

This was the designer Marilyn turned to when she wanted to make a truly breathless entrance. He designed the sheer silk gown that made Marilyn look as if she was shimmeringly naked under the spotlights during her "Happy Birthday" performance for PRESIDENT KENNEDY.

In the days before her death Marilyn had been measuring up for a $1600 gown Jean-Louis was creating for her. Depending on accounts, this was either a white sequined evening gown, or the wedding dress in which she planned to re-marry JOE DIMAGGIO.

## JEFFRIES, NORMAN II

After more than thirty-three years of silence, Norman Jeffries, Marilyn's handyman and nephew of housekeeper EUNICE MURRAY, told biographer DONALD WOLFE that BOBBY KENNEDY twice visited Marilyn's house on August 4, 1962, once in the afternoon, and then later around 10 P.M. Jeffries claimed that Kennedy told him to leave, and when he returned "Marilyn was near death." In the book Jeffries's story is corroborated by a retired policeman who claims that Marilyn's previously missing police file contains a reference to Kennedy and Lawford being stopped that night for speeding as they drove away from Marilyn's house.

Jeffries, and his brother Keith, were employed to do the work remodeling Marilyn's home at FIFTH HELENA DRIVE. It has also been said that Jeffries repaired the broken window in Marilyn's bedroom on the night she died, before the police arrived.

## JEWELRY

Diamonds may have been a girl's best friend, but off screen Marilyn rarely wore jewelry. Hairdresser GEORGE MASTERS confirms, "Marilyn never wore jewelry of any kind because she wanted nothing to detract from her."

This is not to say that admirers failed to heap her with expensive baubles—JOE DIMAGGIO, for one, gave her a huge diamond ring.

Marilyn received a gift of a natural pearl necklace made by Mikymota from the Emperor of Japan during her 1954 trip. She wore this same string of pearls to the divorce hearing against DiMaggio, and later gave the necklace to PAULA STRASBERG. After her death the necklace passed to her daughter SUSAN STRASBERG, who sold it in early 1999.

According to some biographers, in the second half of her career Marilyn made dangling diamond (or paste) earrings a regular feature of her look. In 1960 she took to wearing a fine amber necklace around her neck or in her hair like a tiara.

## JOHN, ELTON
(B. 1947, REGINALD DWIGHT)

One of the most prolific and successful singer-songwriters in the world, Elton John (and lyricist Bernie Taupin) wrote the famous tribute to Marilyn, "Candle in the Wind" (1973).

Publicity photo for *There's No Business Like Show Business* (1954).

In 1997 Elton John rewrote the lyrics in tribute to PRINCESS DIANA, a woman who counted him among her favorite recording artists.

## JOHNSON, NUNNALLY (1897–1977)

"She was ten feet under water... a wall of thick cotton... you stick a pin in her and eight days later it says 'ouch.'"

Writer, producer, and sometimes director Johnson had an impressive list of credits behind him, including *Jesse James* (1939) and *The Grapes of Wrath* (1940), by the time TWENTIETH CENTURY-FOX cast Marilyn in Johnson's ensemble piece *WE'RE NOT MARRIED* (1952).

A year later he was working up a script from two separate plays for *HOW TO MARRY A MILLIONAIRE* (1953). For this picture he gave the three gold-digging stars (Marilyn, BETTY GRABLE, and LAUREN BACALL) traits from their past. Marilyn, in the role of Pola, also got (and ably exploited) the hilarious comic opportunities of being blind as a bat without glasses.

For Johnson, working with Marilyn was no picnic: "Marilyn made me lose all sympathy for actresses. In most of her takes she was either fluffing lines or freezing. I don't think she could act her way out of a paper script. She's just an arrogant little tail-twitcher who learned to throw sex in your face."

Johnson then wrote two Fox projects especially for Marilyn. Unhappily for Johnson, Marilyn had had enough of typecast sex-pot roles and was preparing to strike off on her own with business partner MILTON GREENE. *Heller In Pink Tights* was never made and *How to Be Very, Very Popular* (1955) was recast with SHEREE NORTH.

Despite this earlier antipathy, Johnson and Marilyn were reunited on the SOMETHING'S GOT TO GIVE project, after he was called in to replace a previous scriptwriter. After Johnson himself was replaced for refusing to work on set and do daily rewrites, he championed Marilyn's cause against director GEORGE CUKOR, until Marilyn herself was fired. Johnson stated that, as tensions rose on the production, "Marilyn kept retreating farther and farther from reality."

Johnson's originally scathing opinions of Marilyn softened in time: "[Marilyn] had such a right sense of knowing the character she was playing—the way to enter a scene, to hold singular attention as the scene developed, the way to end a scene."

## JORDAN, TED

Actor Ted Jordan made a number of claims in his book about Marilyn which have aroused a degree of skepticism, not the least of which being that Marilyn had a daughter by him in the late forties. He claimed he met her at the AMBASSADOR HOTEL where he was a lifeguard and Norma Jeane was on working for the BLUE BOOK MODELING AGENCY. By his account their relationship continued unabated until Marilyn's dying day, hence the information contained in the book: that Marilyn had a LESBIAN relationship with his then wife, stripper Lili St. Cyr, and that he had had in his possession Marilyn's infamous but never publicly retrieved red DIARY.

The 1996 TV movie *Norma Jean and Marilyn* starring Ashley Judd and Mira Sorvino was loosely adapted from his book.

*Norma Jean: My Secret Life with Marilyn Monroe* (William Morrow, New York,1989).

K

## KAEL, PAULINE

The enormously influential *New Yorker* film critic who did not subscribe to the Marilyn myth. In her review of NORMAN MAILER's *Marilyn*, she wrote, "She would bat her Bambi eyelashes, lick her messy suggestive open mouth, wiggle that pert and tempting bottom and use her hushed voice to caress us with dizzying innuendoes. Her extravagantly ripe body bulging and spilling out of her clothes, she threw herself at us with the off-color innocence of a baby whore."

## KANIN, GARSON (B. 1912)

Versatile writer of screenplays and plays, director of movies and stage productions, who has also written extensively about his experience in Hollywood.

Marilyn was screen tested but not selected for Kanin's 1950 movie *Born Yesterday*. His 1979 novel *Moviola*, which laid bare the workings of Hollywood and included a very Marilynesque protagonist, was also made into a series of television movies (*see* FICTION). His best remembered movie work includes *The True Glory* (1945), *Adam's Rib* (1949), and *The Girl Can't Help It* (1956).

## KARGER, FRED (1916–1979)

MARILYN:
"I know he liked me and was happy to be with me but his love didn't seem anything like mine. Most of his talk to me was a form of criticism. He criticized my mind. He kept pointing out how little I knew and how unaware of life I was."

Marilyn was sent to Fred Karger for VOICE coaching during her six-month spell at COLUMBIA PICTURES in 1948. Karger was director of music, recently separated from his wife, and living with his mother Anne and young daughter Terry in an extended family that included his divorced sister Mary and her children. Thirty-two and handsome—with more than a passing resemblance to the man in the famous photograph her mother GLADYS BAKER had told her was her father—Marilyn fell head over heels in love with him. Though their romance was fleeting, throughout her life Marilyn referred to Karger as her first true love.

There are at least two versions of their first evening together. In one, Fred brought Marilyn home to his mother's house, and introduced her as "a little girl who is very lonely and broke." In another version, after Marilyn was brought round to the Karger family home for a meal, Fred drove her home not to the STUDIO CLUB, where she was living at the time, but to a run-down Hollywood tenement she had borrowed from a starlet friend, to show her new beau how impecunious she was and to elicit his sympathy, precisely so she would be invited to stay.

Biographers agree: Marilyn was smitten. She confided to drama teacher NATASHA LYTESS that Freddy was the man of her dreams, the man she wanted to marry. Biographers don't agree whether she stayed with the Kargers for weeks or months.

Fred Karger and Jane Wyman, 1952.

Nevertheless, he not only acted as her voice coach but taught her wardrobe tips and etiquette, and introduced her to the pleasures of good music and books; he took her out on the town; and he arranged for her to see an orthodontist who corrected a slight overbite, bleached her teeth, and put her in corrective braces. For Christmas 1948 Marilyn bought a $500 watch for Fred, on a credit payment plan that meant two years of payments (in some versions the payments lasted poignantly until just before Karger married Jane Wyman).

Despite his mother and sister's fondness for his new girlfriend, and Marilyn's burning desire to marry Fred, he did not consider her to be proper wife material: "You cry too easily. That's because your mind isn't developed. Compared to your figure, it's embryonic." More damning, he did not feel that this twenty-one-year-old starlet was potential mother material for his daughter Terry.

It has been rumored for that Marilyn became pregnant by him on a number of occasions, each time having an abortion.

On an evening in November 1952, when Fred Karger married actress JANE WYMAN, Marilyn couldn't resist crashing their reception at Chasen's RESTAURANT to give bride and groom her personal congratulations. According to SIDNEY SKOLSKY, this was the one "bitchy thing" that Marilyn ever did.

Many years later, at the height of rumors about a romance between Marilyn and then presidential candidate JOHN F. KENNEDY, Fred Karger refused to take his band to a convention ball for Kennedy.

Karger died on the seventeenth anniversary of Marilyn's death, August 5, 1979.

### THE KARGER FAMILY

KARGER, ANNE (1886–1975)
Marilyn's relationship with the mother of her first great love Fred Karger lasted far longer than the love affair. Anne Karger took Marilyn under her wing the moment she walked into her home, and from then on Mrs. Karger was an important older female presence in her life, a mother figure. She was of great comfort to Marilyn that year, 1948, when beloved "Aunt" Ana Lower died. Mrs. Karger was somebody she could turn to for advice and coddling when she needed it. According to Fred Lawrence Guiles, when Marilyn learned that Columbia Studios was not renewing her contract, the first person she shared her dismay with was Anne Karger. In 1954, after her divorce from Joe DiMaggio and as she prepared to flee Hollywood for New York, Marilyn stayed at Anne's apartment on Sunset Boulevard. From there she gleefully read the barrage of headlines asking "Where's Marilyn?"

Marilyn remained in touch with "Nana" for the rest of her life. Not long after Marilyn's death, Anne said, "She was groping her last few years, she was so ill."

KARGER, MARY (also known as Mary Karger Short),
Fred's sister Mary, and Marilyn were of a similar age and soon became firm friends. Six years later Mary was supporting Marilyn through her unravelling marriage to Joe DiMaggio. Mary sat by Marilyn in court during the divorce proceedings.

After moving East herself in 1955, Marilyn often visited Mary, who had since remarried and was living in New Jersey.

Both Anne and Mary were mourners at Marilyn's funeral.

## KAZAN, ELIA
(B. 1909, B. ELIA KAZANJOGLOU)

This distinguished director for many decades a major figure in the drama world, directing many of the most successful Broadway plays of the forties and fifties. His movies, many of them adaptations of Broadway hits, include *A Tree Grows in Brooklyn* (1945), *Gentleman's Agreement* (1947), *A Streetcar Named Desire* (1951), *Viva Zapata* (1952), *On the Waterfront* (1954), EAST OF EDEN (1955), and *A Face in the Crowd* (1957). The Lifetime Achievement Award Kazan received at the 1999 Academy Awards refocused attention on Kazan's past as a left-wing turncoat whose 1952 testimony to the HOUSE UN-AMERICAN ACTIVITIES COMMITTEE led to the blacklisting of many of his associates and colleagues.

In early 1950, soon after JOHNNY HYDE died, "Gadge" (as he was known to his friends) met and seduced Marilyn on the set of the Fox movie AS YOUNG AS YOU FEEL (1951). Photographer SAM SHAW has confirmed: "Marilyn had a big romance with Kazan, and because she was idle much of that spring, she and I and Kazan often drove out to the Fox ranch."

Kazan and Marilyn met at her BEVERLY CARLTON HOTEL apartment, or at the home of Marilyn's agent (and Kazan's producer on *A Streetcar Named Desire*), CHARLES FELDMAN. Kazan's place was out: he shared his home with Molly Thatcher, his wife of eighteen years, and their four children. Depending on sources, the affair was brief, or else it continued until the summer of 1951 when, it is claimed, Marilyn had a pregnancy scare, told Kazan she thought he was the father, and watched him beat a hasty retreat.

Although in his autobiography, *A Life*, Kazan claims that he continued to have occasional sexual relations with Marilyn on and off for the next decade, his importance in Marilyn's life was for the significant introductions he made. On the set of *As Young As You Feel*, Kazan introduced starlet Marilyn to ARTHUR MILLER. This first encounter, and the times they saw each other over the following couple of days, lit the flame they were to rekindle five years later when Marilyn moved to New York.

Elia Kazan, 1957.

Kazan's next appearance in Marilyn's life was less constructive. As a result of his 1952 testimony to HUAC, in 1956 Marilyn's then fiancé Miller was hauled in for questioning. Miller's was just one of the names he named, along with PAULA STRASBERG, Morris Carnovsky and wife Phoebe Brand, CLIFFORD ODETS, and other colleagues of Kazan's from the New York Group Theater in the thirties.

Kazan's second introduction came in New York in 1955. Along with Cheryl Crawford, he set up a meeting between Marilyn and famed drama teacher LEE STRASBERG, head of the ACTORS STUDIO that Kazan had helped found in the late forties.

Although relations were frosty between Miller and Kazan, Marilyn turned out as an usher for an Actors Studio benefit for *East of Eden* on March 9, 1955; she was also in the audience for the premiere of the Kazan-directed Broadway production of Tennessee Williams's *Cat on a Hot Tin Roof*. Marilyn was upset at the feud between her husband and Kazan, and reportedly finessed some sort of reconciliation.

It was some years until Miller and Kazan renewed their earlier successful working relationship. After Marilyn's death, Kazan directed Miller's play *AFTER THE FALL*. Actress Barbara Loden, who played the character based on Marilyn, later married Kazan, who had a small role in the play too.

In a 1961 letter to psychoanalyst DR. RALPH GREENSON, Marilyn writes, "I know I will never be happy but I know I can be gay! Remember I told you Kazan said I was the gayest girl he ever knew and believe me, he has known many. But he *loved* me for one year and rocked me to sleep one night when I was in great anguish. He also suggested that I go into analysis and later wanted me to work with Lee Strasberg."

In retrospect, Kazan described Marilyn as "a simple, decent-hearted kid whom Hollywood brought down, legs parted."

## KELLEY, TOM (1914–1984)
STUDIO AT 736 NORTH SEWARD STREET, HOLLYWOOD

Photographer of Marilyn for beer ADVERTISEMENTS, MODELING, and then perhaps the most famous images of Marilyn—certainly the most scandalous—the infamous CALENDAR nudes. Kelley had formerly worked as an Associated Press cameramen and was well-regarded in his field.

Kelley apparently first bumped into Marilyn in 1948 on Sunset Boulevard, immediately after she had driven into the back of another car. Kelley pushed his way forward through the crowd of onlookers and slipped Marilyn a $5 bill (she had no money for a taxi to get to the meeting she was hurrying to) and his business card. However, some biographers say that Kelley was among the first photographers to use Norma Jeane as a model after she signed up with the BLUE BOOK MODELING AGENCY in 1945.

In 1949 Kelley was contacted by Chicago calendar manufacturer John Baumgarth, who was looking for a new model to grace his 1951 publications. Kelley contacted Marilyn and asked her to pose nude for him, as he had in the past. This time Marilyn said yes. No longer under contract and out of work, she was in need of the $50 he was offering to meet her financial commitments (a room at the BEVERLY CARLTON HOTEL, at the STUDIO CLUB, or repayments on her car, depending on reports, though by this time she was with super agent JOHNNY HYDE). Marilyn had already posed bare breasted for illustrator EARL MORAN, had had her fill of cheesecake work, but was reassured by the presence of Kelley's wife, Natalie.

Recently some of the long-lost transparencies from the shoot—Kelley took twenty-four nudes of Marilyn—have turned up and been offered for sale.

## KELLY, GENE
(1912–1996, B. EUGENE CURRAN KELLY)

Versatile good-guy star whose dancing skills made him one of Hollywood's biggest draws throughout the forties and fifties. In 1951 he received a special Academy Award "in appreciation of his versatility as an actor, singer, director, and dancer, and for his brilliant achievements in the art of choreography on film." Kelly is best remembered for his work in *For Me and My Gal* (1942), *The Three Musketeers* (1948), *On the Town* (1949), *An American in Paris* (1951), and *Singin' in the Rain* (1952).

Photographer Tom Kelley in front of one of his famous calendar shots of Marilyn.

Kelly made a cameo appearance in Marilyn's 1960 movie *LET'S MAKE LOVE*. At the time Marilyn died, he was discussing working with her on a project called *I Love Louisa*, which was released by TWENTIETH CENTURY-FOX in 1964 as *What a Way to Go*.

## KELLY, GRACE (1928–1982)

Grace Kelly was on the opposite end of the "blonde spectrum" from Marilyn: a woman from a rich family whose image was regal and pure. In a career lasting just five years, she shot to prominence in *High Noon* (1952), received an Oscar for *The Country Girl* (1954), starred in three Hitchcock movies, including *Rear Window* (1954), and then bid Hollywood adieu in *High Society* (1956).

There have been rumors that before Prince RAINIER OF MONACO alighted on Grace Kelly, Marilyn had been on the shortlist of movie stars to court.

In 1960, as work on *THE MISFITS* was drawing to a close, Marilyn's long-time press aide RUPERT ALLAN left her employment to go and work with Princess Grace in Monaco.

## KENNEDYS

GLORIA STEINEM:
"Partly because of them, there seems to be more interest in her death than in her life."

No aspect of Marilyn's life has aroused more long-lasting controversy than her relationship with the Kennedys. Over the years, every possible permutation of this relationship has been put forward: that Marilyn had a brief affair with one Kennedy, a long-lasting affair with one Kennedy, a fling with both Kennedys, or a passionate affair first with one then with the other—complete with a mistress's hopes that her paramour was preparing to leave his wife and make an honest woman of her.

Practically every one of the CONSPIRACY theories surrounding Marilyn's DEATH center on her relationship with the two most powerful men in the U.S., President JOHN F. KENNEDY and Attorney General ROBERT KENNEDY. A flood of biographies and TV documentary exposés have uncovered (or invented, as far as doubters are concerned) affairs, secret rendezvous, classified State information, promises of marriage, a threatened press conference to spill the beans, BUGGING, blackmail, COVER-UPS, mob dealings, and murder. The lineage goes back to right-wing activist FRANK A. CAPELL in the sixties, developing through ROBERT SLATZER and MILO SPERIGLIO in the seventies, moving on to ANTHONY SUMMERS in the eighties and DONALD WOLFE in the nineties, to name just some of the proponents of a Kennedy involvement in Marilyn's death. In many of these readings, the Kennedy boys are practically interchangeable—Marilyn was pregnant with the love child of JFK or RFK, she was expecting a proposal of marriage from Robert or John, she was a security threat to the president or to the attorney general, a potential weapon to be used by the Kennedys' sworn enemies. And not only had Marilyn kept records of all this in a red DIARY, she was on the brink of revealing all.

That's one view. The other, upheld by all biographers who believe that Marilyn took her own life, is that the Kennedy brothers' responsibility in Marilyn's death is no greater or no less than the responsibility of the other significant people in her life at that time. It has plausibly been argued that the Kennedys did not consider Marilyn to be a threat at all. For years JFK, and possibly Bobby, had carried on affairs with complete impunity. In addition, never in her life had Marilyn publicly attacked people whom she felt had wronged her, so the threat of a press conference "outing" Robert Kennedy's alleged mistreatment of her appears dubious.

Marilyn's last psychoanalyst, DR. RALPH GREENSON, adamantly denied that Marilyn had had an affair with either man. But his daughter Joan has been quoted as saying, "She told me that she was seeing somebody, but she didn't want to burden me with the responsibility of knowing who it was, because he was well-known," adding that she said she would refer to him as "the General." Anthony Summers quotes a colleague of Greenson's who says that he was aware of a close relationship with men "at the highest level."

Biographer FRED LAWRENCE GUILES, one of the first to hint at Marilyn's Kennedy romances, draws the following distinction between the high flying brothers: "Her affair with the attorney general would turn out to be much more serious then Marilyn's fling with the President. She was not drawn to Bobby physically, as he was to her. But he took a personal interest in her, while the President did not. This was far more dangerous to Marilyn than a strictly sexual attraction would have been."

## KENNEDY, JOHN FITZGERALD (1917–1963)

So much has been said about relations between Mr. President and Marilyn that the truth is well and truly buried beneath layers of speculation and supposition. The consensus view is that they had a weekend together in March 1962, though some people, such as Marilyn's friend and movie stand-in EVELYN MORIARTY, say they never saw any evidence of a relationship with either of the Kennedy brothers.

According to FRED LAWRENCE GUILES, Marilyn's affair with JFK continued through the last year of her life, especially when she went on trips to New York. Then again, there are those who discount anything more than a one night stand. DONALD SPOTO writes "no serious biographer can identify Monroe and Kennedy as partners in a love affair. All that can be known *for certain* is that on four occasions between October 1961 and August 1962, the president and the actress met, and that during *one* of those meetings they telephoned one of Marilyn's friends from a bedroom; soon after, Marilyn confided this one sexual encounter to her closest confidants, making clear that it was the extent of their involvement."

The first of the four occasions documented by Spoto was in October 1961, when Marilyn and fellow leading ladies were invited to PETER LAWFORD's beach house to attend a dinner in honor of Patricia Lawford's brother, President Kennedy. The second was in early 1962, a dinner party for the president in New York. Encounter number three took place on March 24, 1962. This was at BING CROSBY's home in PALM SPRINGS. This was where they shared a bedroom and Marilyn made a call to RALPH ROBERTS, who later said, "Marilyn told me that this night in March was the only time of her 'affair' with JFK. Of course she was titillated beyond belief, because for a year he had been trying, through Lawford, to have an evening with her. A great many people thought, after that weekend, that there was more to it. But Marilyn gave me the impression that it was not a major event for either of them: it happened once, that weekend, and that was that."

Two more of Marilyn's close friends agree. It is SUSAN STRASBERG's opinion that, "Not in her worst nightmare would Marilyn have wanted to be with JFK on any permanent basis. It was OK for one night to sleep with a charismatic president—and she loved the secrecy and drama of it. But he certainly wasn't the kind of man she wanted for life, and she was very clear to us about this." SIDNEY SKOLSKY has said, "For Marilyn, what counted was the idea of 'the little orphan waif indulging in free love with the leader of the free world.'"

It was during the Palm Springs weekend that Marilyn agreed to attend the Democratic Gala planned for May 1962 at MADISON SQUARE GARDEN, and promised to personally lead the "Happy Birthday" chorus. She did not know that fulfilling this promise would be seized on by TWENTIETH CENTURY-FOX as an excuse to close down production of *SOMETHING'S GOT TO GIVE*, the film she was working on at the time. This was the last documented occasion Marilyn and JFK met. Marilyn gave her inimitable breathy rendition of "Happy Birthday" before 17,000 Democrats and a huge assortment of stars who had gathered to fund JFK's successful presidential campaign. Marilyn also paid the $1,000 admission price. Hosting the evening's entertainment—which included ELLA FITZGERALD, Peggy Lee, Henry Fonda, Maria Callas, and Harry Belafonte—was entertainer JACK BENNY. Late as usual, and rather drunk, Marilyn was ushered on stage by Peter Lawford, who announced her as "the late Marilyn Monroe." In a dress that veteran diplomat Adlai Stevenson described as "skin and beads—only I didn't see the beads," Marilyn sang the first verse of "Happy Birthday" and then waved her arms to encourage the audience to sing along for a reprise as a six-foot cake with forty-five oversized candles was carried on stage by two chefs. Marilyn then sang (to the tune of "Thanks for the Memory"):

Thanks, Mr. President,
For everything you've done,
The battles that you've won—
The way you deal with US Steel
And our problems by the ton,
We thank you—so much.

At the end of the event, Kennedy thanked the evening's performers: "I can now retire after having had 'Happy Birthday' sung to me in such a sweet, wholesome way."

According to biographer DONALD WOLFE, a week after the birthday event Marilyn was informed by Lawford that JFK no longer wanted to have anything to do with her. Wolfe is one of many to assert that this was the end of an affair that had been going on for eight years or more. Marilyn and JFK are said to have met as early as 1951, though 1954 is more commonly cited, at a party thrown by CHARLES FELDMAN, Marilyn's agent at the time. Reportedly during a period of hospitalization in October 1954, Kennedy

Marilyn sings "Happy Birthday" at a fundraising event for the Democratic party in May of 1962 (JFK sits front row and center).

hung a poster of Marilyn wearing blue shorts, upside down opposite his bed—a story very similar to an apocryphal tale about HOWARD HUGHES. Under this scenario Marilyn was sneaking off to motels in Malibu with Kennedy during the last couple of months of her marriage to JOE DIMAGGIO. Allegedly throughout the course of Marilyn's marriage to ARTHUR MILLER, she continued to meet the future president for rendezvous at his habitual New York hotel, the CARLYLE, or at Lawford's Santa Monica beach home.

Marilyn was reputedly flown from New York to Los Angeles by Kennedy to provide him with a celebratory romantic interlude after his triumphant 1960 Democratic Convention. After delivering his "New Frontier" acceptance speech, he met up with Marilyn, who had been brought to the celebration party by SAMMY DAVIS JR. Part of the evening's entertainment for the future president, reportedly, was when he put his hand up Marilyn's dress under the table—and found out that she did not wear anything underneath. Later that night they went skinny dipping in the ocean. There have been allegations too that Kennedy asked Lawford to accompany Marilyn to the East Coast on Air Force One, and that once Jackie Kennedy was enraged to find blonde hairs in the presidential bed.

Rumors about a romance between JFK and Marilyn began to surface in the press during 1960. Late that year, influential columnist Art Buchwald penned a piece entitled "Let's Be Firm on Monroe Doctrine." The article read: "Who will be the next ambassador to Monroe? This is one of the many problems which president-elect Kennedy will have to work on in January. Obviously you can't leave Monroe adrift. There are too many greedy people eyeing her, and now that Ambassador Miller has left she could flounder around without any direction."

Kennedy aide Pete Summers told biographer ANTHONY SUMMERS (no relation) that Marilyn was a frequent visitor to the Lawford beach house during the presidential campaign: "They were very close friends. I would say she was a very special guest—the president was really very, very fond of Marilyn.... I did feel that she was so impressed by Kennedy's charm and charisma that she was almost starry-eyed.... But she was totally able to hold her own conversationally; she was very bright."

JFK's name has been often mentioned in connection with the last weeks of Marilyn's life too. Although nobody has yet leveled the accusation that they met up at this time, some biographers believe that Marilyn's trip to the Cedars of Lebanon HOSPITAL on July 20 (or the following weekend in some accounts) was to abort JFK's love child.

The most stalwart accusers of JFK claim that he was the man who decided that Marilyn had to be silenced. Stories have circulated that the president's sexual escapades with Marilyn at Lawford's home had been bugged—either by the FBI, MAFIA boss SAM GIANCANA, or even Teamsters' boss JIMMY HOFFA. CONSPIRACY theories of this type frame Lawford as the hit-man, in league with DR. RALPH GREENSON to prescribe Marilyn an unusually large quantity of Seconal and then force her to take an overdose.

## KENNEDY, ROBERT FRANCIS
(1925–1968)

The story of Robert Kennedy's involvement with Marilyn is almost a carbon copy of that of his big brother, the difference being that his liaison, if indeed it did take place, began after JFK had finished with Marilyn, reportedly soon after Marilyn's "Happy Birthday" performance.

Some biographers maintain that there was nothing more than a simple friendship between Robert Kennedy and Marilyn. There is a view that unlike John, Robert was not a philanderer but remained faithful to his wife Ethel. In 1960 he received the accolade of "Father of the Year." Robert Kennedy biographer Arthur Schlesinger believes otherwise: "Bobby was human. He liked a drink and he liked young women. He indulged that liking when he traveled—and he had to travel a great deal."

According to DONALD SPOTO, Marilyn and Robert only actually met four times, though they spoke on the phone with some regularity: "Their respective whereabouts during this time made anything else impossible—even had they both been inclined to a dalliance, which is itself far from the truth on both sides." Spoto traces the first meeting to early October 1961, when they met at the Lawford beach house. That night Marilyn got sufficiently drunk on champagne that Bobby and his assistant Edwin Guthman had to drive her home. The next time they met was on February 1, 1962, at another Lawford party. They met again in New York, on May 19, when Marilyn sang "Happy Birthday" to Bobby's big brother. Adlai Stevenson commented how, that night, Robert "was dodging around her like a moth around the flame."

Biographer ANTHONY SUMMERS feels this was enough for a flame of passion to kindle between them. As proof, he cites a note that Kennedy's sister, JEAN KENNEDY SMITH, wrote to Marilyn, in which she comments, "[I] understand that you and Bobby are the new item! We all think you should come with him when he comes back East!" This note, however, has never been positively identified as written by Smith.

In mid-June 1962, Marilyn was invited to visit Robert and Ethel Kennedy at their Virginia home, but was unable to attend. On June 26 or 27, depending on sources, the Lawfords and Robert Kennedy were invited to see Marilyn's new home before going on to the Lawford house for dinner. In another version Marilyn arrived two and a half hours late, and Kennedy visited Marilyn's home the next day. Proponents of Marilyn murder theories claim that Bobby's purpose on this trip to Los Angeles was to personally break things off with Marilyn.

Records do not indicate that they met in July, but Marilyn placed eight calls to the attorney general's office. Employees of Kennedy, and Marilyn's publicist PAT NEWCOMB, have said that these calls were short and friendly, not rambling chats between lovers. A rival interpretation is that Marilyn originally called Bobby on his private line; when he refused to answer, she called the general switchboard. This theory is somewhat undermined by the fact that Marilyn's address book did not contain the number for his private line.

Stories of a liaison between RFK and Marilyn first surfaced on the right-wing fringes of American politics, gaining a public voice in 1964 in a book published by FRANK A. CAPELL. Four years later, biographer FRED LAWRENCE GUILES made a reference to a romantic link between Marilyn and an unnamed "lawyer and public servant with an important political career," who was generally believed to be Kennedy. NORMAN MAILER took up the story in his 1973 biography of Marilyn; he named names. However, Mailer came to the conclusion that there was no more than a flirtation between Marilyn and Bobby Kennedy, whose "hard Irish nose for the real was going to keep him as celibate as the happiest priest of the county holding hands with five pretty widows." As evidence Mailer quoted a comment Marilyn made to her masseur RALPH ROBERTS: "I like him, but not physically." Marilyn's longtime friend SIDNEY SKOLSKY also believed there was nothing between them: Skolsky knew of her liaison with John, but "as for Robert Kennedy, she never mentioned him."

Not surprisingly, many people have asserted exactly the opposite. Schlesinger, once again, believes that there was something special between RFK and Marilyn: "Robert Kennedy, with his curiosity, his sympathy, his absolute directness of response to distress, in some way got through the glittering mist as few did." JEANNE CARMEN, Marilyn's neighbor at her DOHENY DRIVE apartment, recalled opening Marilyn's front door to Bobby Kennedy sometime in late 1961. She has also talked of going with Marilyn and the attorney general to a nude beach, with RFK disguised in a false beard (a story she has repeated about JACK BENNY too). ROBERT SLATZER has reported that Marilyn told him, "Bobby Kennedy promised to marry me." Slatzer and others are adamant that Marilyn was about to call a press conference and publicly reveal her affairs—before dying in mysterious circumstances. Confirmation of Marilyn's hopes for marriage has also come from Anne Karger, though via one of her daughters-in-law, not directly. New York maid LENA PEPITONE said, "I know Bobby used to phone her many times but they were very secretive. He would only say 'May I speak to Marilyn'; then she would close the bedroom door and speak for maybe one hour. I knew it was him because she told me once, and after that I knew the voice." Hairdresser SYDNEY GUILAROFF claims in his autobiography that Marilyn called him the day before she died and told him she was threatening to tell the world all about her and Bobby, "and he had threatened to shut her up."

Proponents of RFK's culpability seize upon the fact that he had the motive, and the means, to be on the site of the "crime" at the time Marilyn died. In the more outlandish scenarios, Marilyn was pregnant either by Robert or his brother John. Peter Lawford was charged with taking Marilyn to Lake Tahoe, where she was subjected, perhaps by force, to an abortion. There are also claims that RFK was either a participant in Marilyn's murder because she was not going along with his desire to end their affair, or alternatively, he had been dispatched by the president to pass on the message that JFK no longer wanted to continue their affair.

Robert Kennedy, his wife Ethel, and four of the children arrived in California on Friday August 3, 1962, the weekend of Marilyn's DEATH, to stay at a ranch belonging to friend JOHN BATES and his family, near Gilroy, eighty miles south of San Francisco. Kennedy's arrival was reported in the press; he was using the weekend with friends to prepare his opening address for an American Bar Association convention the following Monday. A large number of witnesses saw them at the ranch that weekend, and then in

San Francisco on Sunday afternoon, the day of Marilyn's death.

However, there are conflicting testimonies as to whether Kennedy was in L.A. at the actual time of Marilyn's death. According to former L.A. mayor Sam Yorty he was; Bates has always maintained that RFK was with him at his ranch in Gilroy throughout Saturday.

The next door neighbor to Marilyn on FIFTH HELENA DRIVE claimed to have seen Robert Kennedy arrive at Marilyn's home on the day she died. In 1985 housekeeper EUNICE MURRAY changed the story she had told ever since Marilyn's death, to say that Bobby had been at Marilyn's home on the afternoon of August 4. Recently, allegations have surfaced that Robert Kennedy and Peter Lawford were stopped for speeding by uniformed police officers in the early hours of August 5, 1962, but that the officers waved the car on when they realized who the occupants were.

Some proponents of the theory that Marilyn took her own life believe that Bobby was at Marilyn's house, where he was unwittingly caught up in the drama. His involvement, though, did not go beyond organizing a COVER-UP to allow incriminating evidence to be removed, and to give him enough time to get back to Peter Lawford's beach house, from where he took a helicopter to a local airport and was then flown back to San Francisco.

Further incriminating evidence to be cited is that after Marilyn's death, phone records were seized by the police, reputedly at the behest of Robert Kennedy. Although he did make a deposition to police, he was never publicly investigated. It has been alleged that L.A. police chief WILLIAM H. PARKER boasted that, because of his delicate handling of Marilyn's death, Bobby Kennedy was going to appoint him to lead the FBI.

Robert Kennedy was assassinated at the AMBASSADOR HOTEL, Los Angeles, in June 1968, after celebrating his victory in the California Democratic Party primary.

### KENNEDY, JACQUELINE

Speculation about a love triangle of Marilyn, Jackie, and John F. Kennedy surfaces periodically. To mark the thirty-sixth anniversary of Marilyn's death, an article appeared with photographs reportedly found by a bargain hunter who purchased a jewelry box at a Manhattan flea market, only to discover some negatives inside portraying Marilyn in a black wig. The article claimed that Marilyn was dressing up as her rival. It is more likely that the photographs were taken by Bert Stern in June 1962, during a fashion photo shoot he did for *Vogue* magazine. The black wig may even have belonged to Marilyn, as during her New York days she would don a black wig when she wanted to go incognito.

In an unauthorized biography of Jackie written by C. David Heymann, it is claimed that Marilyn called Jackie at the White House to discuss her future with JFK. The story runs that Jackie said she would divorce JFK if Marilyn was willing to take on the role of first lady and live in the White House.

## KHRUSCHEV, NIKITA (1894–1971)

Marilyn met the Soviet leader on September 19, 1959, when he visited TWENTIETH CENTURY-FOX studios as part of his tour of America. She was so keen to take part in the event that she flew in from New York, and despite the customary hours getting made up and coiffed for the luncheon, for once she arrived early at the studios, where the Soviet delegation and many other Hollywood luminaries dined on the set of *Can-Can*.

When they were introduced, Khruschev squeezed her hand and told her, through a translator, that she was a very lovely young lady. After greeting him in Russian—she had been coached by NATALIE WOOD—Marilyn expressed her wish for world peace and better relations between the superpowers. She also conveyed her husband ARTHUR MILLER's greetings. Reportedly Marilyn later told New York maid LENA PEPITONE that Khruschev was "fat and ugly and had warts on his face and growled."

During the meal, studio head SPYROS SKOURAS told Khruschev that America was a land where he had arrived with nothing and become chief of a powerful studio; Khruschev replied that he, the son of a poor coal miner, now ran the entire Soviet Union. Arthur Miller tells us in his autobiography, "Marilyn thought that a fantastic reply; like her, Khruschev was odd man out."

Khruschev reportedly once said that America could be summed up by baseball, Coca Cola, and Marilyn Monroe.

## KILGALLEN, DOROTHY

New York gossip columnist who wrote two pieces about Marilyn's love life that were either works of great insight or total fabrication, but have ever since taken on lives of their own. In 1952 she wrote that while Marilyn and JOE DIMAGGIO were romancing their way to marriage, another suitor, "dark horse" ROBERT SLATZER, was claiming a place in her affections. Ten years later, just two days before Marilyn's DEATH, Kilgallen noted that Marilyn was "vastly alluring to a handsome gentleman who is a bigger name than Joe DiMaggio," a story that was taken up by other journalists and has been used as proof of Marilyn's liaisons with JFK.

In 1953 studio boss DARRYL ZANUCK refuted a claim by Kilgallen that Marilyn had not sung her numbers in *GENTLEMEN PREFER BLONDES* (1953)by sending her a sworn affidavit that she had. From then on, Kilgallen was profuse in her praise of Marilyn's singing talents.

There was evidently little love lost between Marilyn and this journalist, if TRUMAN CAPOTE's book *Music for Chameleons* is to be believed. Marilyn told Capote that she didn't like going to a certain bar because it was "full of those advertising creeps. And that bitch Dorothy Kilgallen, she's always in there getting bombed. What is it with these micks? The way they booze, they're worse than Indians... she's written some bitchy stuff about me."

## KIRKLAND, DOUGLAS

One of the few good things to come out of the abandoned production of *SOMETHING'S GOT TO GIVE* was Marilyn's photo sessions with young photographer Douglas Kirkland, working for *Look*'s special twenty-fifth anniversary issue.

Kirkland, then twenty-six, and just a year into his career as a freelance photographer for glossy magazines, found Marilyn "very white, almost luminescent—this white vision drifted as if in slow motion into the studio. She seemed to give off a glow."

Halfway through the session, with Marilyn under silk sheets in a bed, Marilyn asked everybody in the room except the photographer to leave. "I think I should be alone with this boy. I find it works better that way." Her wishes catered to, Marilyn resumed her longest running affair—with the still camera—teasing and beckoning and giving Kirkland one of the great iconic Marilyn poses, shot from above, naked, wrapped up in silk, clutching a white pillow.

## KISSING MARILYN

At least two colleagues commented on their on-screen experiences kissing Marilyn: TOMMY NOONAN said, "It was like being sucked into a vacuum" and, famously, TONY CURTIS, frustrated after Marilyn's tardiness on *SOME LIKE IT HOT* (1959), said, "Kissing Marilyn was like kissing Hitler."

Marilyn and Tom Ewell fall for each other in *The Seven Year Itch* (1955).

Tony Curtis as Joe (posing as millionaire Osgood Fielding) ensnares Marilyn's Sugar Cane on Osgood's yacht in *Some Like It Hot* (1959).

## KNEBELCAMP, ENID AND SAM

FOSTER PARENTS to Norma Jeane for a short and under-reported period, when legal guardian GRACE MCKEE GODDARD had difficulties accommodating her ward in the late 1930s. DONALD SPOTO describes Enid as Goddard's sister. The Knebelcamps were Marilyn's only foster parents to attend her funeral.

## KNICKERBOCKER HOTEL

1714 NORTH IVAR, HOLLYWOOD

Where JOE DIMAGGIO usually stayed while in L.A., a popular celebrity destination until it closed down in 1972. Marilyn dropped off Joe here after their first date.

(*see* HOTELS)

## KOBAL, JOHN

"She stood for life. She radiated life. In her smile hope was always present. She glorified in life, and her death did not mar this final image. She had become a legend in her own time, and in her death, took her place among the myths of our century."

This well-known movie stills collector displayed many of his Marilyn shots in his 1974 book *Marilyn Monroe: A Life on Film* published by Hamlyn, London.

## KOREA

MARILYN:
"For the first time in my life, I had the feeling that the people seeing me were accepting and liking me."

Soon after arriving in Tokyo with JOE DIMAGGIO in February 1954, Marilyn received an invitation from General John E. Hull's Far East command to entertain the more than one hundred thousand U.S. troops still stationed in war-torn Korea. Although, technically, Marilyn was on an extension of her HONEYMOON with DiMaggio, who had traveled to JAPAN to open the 1954 baseball season, Marilyn said yes. She later told her friend AMY GREENE that the Korea tour was one of the highlights of her entire career.

Marilyn in Korea, 1954.

Marilyn, Jean O'Doul (the wife of DiMaggio's pal Frank "Lefty" O'Doul), and army entertainment officer Walter Bouillet went on a four day marathon tour. Marilyn performed ten shows in snow flurries and sub-zero temperatures, wowing the troops in a skin tight, low-cut purple sequined gown and no underwear—husband Joe was furious when he saw the newsreels. Marilyn's set included hit SONGS "Diamonds Are a Girl's Best Friend," "Bye Bye Baby," "Somebody Love Me," and "Do It Again," toned down to "Kiss Me Again" so as not to overexcite her rapturous audience. (Changing the words was not enough to prevent a rock fight at one of her concerts.) Everywhere she went, she was received with enormous warmth.

Marilyn recalled what it felt like: "There were 17,000 soldiers in front of me, and they were all yelling at me at the top of their lungs. I stood smiling at them. . . . Standing in the snowfall facing these yelling soldiers, I felt for the first time in my life no fear of anything. I felt only happy."

A measure of how much she enjoyed the rapturous reception of the U.S. troops in Korea was that leaving one of the sites by helicopter, she lay face down on the floor of the cargo bay, with two airmen anchoring her by her legs, and leaned right out to wave and blow upside-down kisses. One Army Corps of Engineers officer said, "Of all the performers who came to us in Korea—and there were a half dozen or so—she was the best.... It was bitter cold, but she was in no hurry to leave. Marilyn was a great entertainer. She made thousands of GIs feel she really cared."

Marilyn's pianist during her 1954 goodwill tour, Albert Guastafeste, was amazed at how modest and down to earth she had been: "Someone ought to go up and tell her she's Marilyn Monroe. She doesn't seem to realize it. When you make a goof, she tells you *she's* sorry. When she goofs, she apologizes to me!"

Not everyone was happy with the tour. *New York Times* journalist Hanson Baldwin was appalled that, "On two occasions during the visit of the motion picture actress, troops rioted widely and behaved like bobbysoxers in Times Square, not like soldiers proud of their uniform."

Footage of Marilyn's tour was put together in 1961 for a television special narrated by Marilyn herself. "USO Wherever They Go!" was broadcast that year on October 8 as the NBC "DuPont Show of the Week." Excerpts have also appeared in many Marilyn documentaries. Marilyn's Korea tour continues to provide a steady flow of never-before-seen photographs of her, snapped by her adoring military fans.

## KRASNA, NORMAN (1909–1984)

Playwright, screenwriter, producer and director, Norman Krasna's Academy Award-nominated and -winning productions—*The Richest Girl in the World* (1934), *Fury* (1936), *The Devil and Mrs. Jones* (1941), and *Princess O'Rourke* (1943)—were almost all adapted from his Broadway hits, and did not feature Marilyn. Instead, he produced her in *CLASH BY NIGHT* (1952), and scripted the rather unsuccessful comedy *LET'S MAKE LOVE* (1960), casting French lead YVES MONTAND as Marilyn's love interest.

## KRASNER, MILTON R. (1901–1988)

In a career spanning over 150 movies, Krasner was the cinematographer Marilyn worked with more than any other, on *ALL ABOUT EVE* (1950), *MONKEY BUSINESS* (1952), *THE SEVEN YEAR ITCH* (1955), and *BUS STOP* (1956). Not surprisingly, when Marilyn submitted to TWENTIETH CENTURY-FOX a list of cinematographers she would agree to work, Krasner was one of the four to make the grade.

Krasner received an Academy Award for *Three Coins in the Fountain* (1954).

## KRIS, DR. MARIANNE

Marilyn spent longer undergoing analysis with Dr. Marianne Kris than with either of her other two psychoanalysts, DR. MARGARET HOHENBERG and DR. RALPH GREENSON. It is commonly believed that Marilyn began seeing Dr. Kris in 1957, after she left Dr. Hohenberg, who was also analyst to business partner MILTON GREENE. This arrangement no longer suited Marilyn, who was in the process of distancing herself from Greene. However, some biographers also claim that Marilyn began analysis in 1955 directly with Dr. Kris.

Kris was recommended by an illustrious source: ANNA FREUD, daughter of Sigmund, whom Marilyn had asked for advice.

Born in Vienna, Marianne Rie had grown up in the inner sanctum of PSYCHOANALYSIS. Sigmund Freud not only supervised her training, he referred to her as his "adopted daughter." Marianne, her husband, artist Ernst Kris, and the Freuds together fled Austria and the Nazis in 1938. Travelling on to New York, Marianne and Ernst set up a private practice specialized in child psychoanalysis.

Marilyn visited Dr. Kris at her office at 135 Central Park West on a regular basis—as many as five sessions a week—right up until early 1961, though during the period that Marilyn was on the West Coast filming *THE MISFITS* (1961), she began to see Greenson, who was to be her last psychoanalyst.

Marilyn's trust in Dr. Kris were irrevocably damaged in February 1961 when, depending on sources, either at Marilyn's request because of the emotional strains of the preceding months, or because Dr. Kris was anxious over signs of suicidal behavior in her patient, Kris arranged for Marilyn to stay at the Payne-Whitney HOSPITAL. As soon as Marilyn realized that she was being put in a locked ward, she snapped—her worst nightmare of being locked away, like her mother and her grandmother before her, had come true. After a few days, Marilyn managed to get a message to JOE DIMAGGIO, who flew in from Florida and managed to transfer her to an environment more conducive to recovery. Soon after, Dr. Kris reputedly told Marilyn's friend and masseur RALPH ROBERTS, "I did a terrible thing, a terrible, terrible thing."

Most biographers agree that this was the last time Marilyn saw Kris. However, FRED LAWRENCE GUILES writes that when in New York, Marilyn continued to have sessions with Dr. Kris.

In any event, either because she had not had time to rewrite her January 1961 will, or because she had rebuilt some trust with her psychoanalyst, Kris was one of the main beneficiaries in Marilyn's WILL. When Kris died, she bequeathed this legacy to a child therapy center at the London Tavistock Center Clinic, originally founded by Anna Freud. This money has been used to fund the Monroe Young Family Centre.

## LADIES OF THE CHORUS (1948)

During her six month stint at COLUMBIA STUDIOS Marilyn worked in this one picture—shot in its entirety in ten days—and graduated from walk-on roles to a supporting character as Peggy Martin, a chorus girl desperate to marry her handsome socialite boyfriend.

For the first time, she had a chance to sing. VOICE coach FRED KARGER, with whom she fell head over heels in love, helped her give a solid rendition of the Allan Roberts and Lester Lee songs "Every Baby Needs a Da Da Daddy" (reprised in 1952 Columbia movie *Okinawa*) and "Anyone Can Tell I Love You." With this film Marilyn began her six-year working relationship with drama coach NATASHA LYTESS. She also worked for the first time with costume designer JEAN-LOUIS, with whom she was to work again on her last two films.

Although Marilyn received her first press write-up from Tibor Krekes in the *Motion Picture Herald*, her performance did not lead to further work with Columbia—studio chief HARRY COHN was not impressed—and as no other studio stepped in after Marilyn's contract lapsed, there followed two years of poverty and uncertainty.

The *Hollywood Reporter* summed up the one movie Marilyn was to do for Columbia as a film that "sets out to prove that burlesque queens are really quite proper wives for wealthy young members of socially prominent families and does a fairly competent job of making its audience like it." All ends happily ever after.

"I kept driving past the theater with my name on the marquee. Was I excited. I wished they were using 'Norma Jeane' so that all the kids at the home and schools who never noticed me could see it."

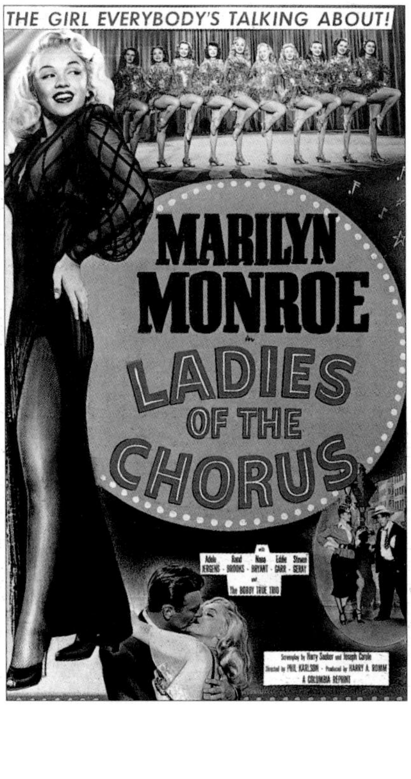

Publicity photo for *Ladies of the Chorus* (1948).

**Credits:**
Columbia Pictures, Black and White
Length: 61 minutes
Release date: October 22, 1948

Directed by: Phil Karlson
Produced by: Harry A. Romm
Written by: Joseph Carole, Harry Sauber (screenplay and story)
Cinematography by: Frank Redman
Music by: Mischa Bakaleinikoff
Film Editing by: Richard Fantl

**Cast (credits order):**
Adele Jergens . . . May Martin
Marilyn Monroe . . . Peggy Martin
Rand Brooks . . . Randy Carroll
Nana Bryant . . . Mrs. Carroll
Eddie Garr . . . Billy Mackay
Steven Geray . . . Salisbury
Bill Edwards . . . Alan Wakefield
Marjorie Hoshelle . . . Bubbles LaRue
Frank Scanell . . . Joe
Dave Barry . . . Ripple
Myron Healey . . . Ripple Jr.
Robert Clarke . . . Peter Winthrop
Gladys Blake . . . Flower Shop Girl
Emmett Vogan . . . Doctor
Dorothy Tuttle . . . (uncredited)

**Crew:**
Jack Boyle . . . production number staging
James A. Crowe . . . set decorator
Robert Peterson . . . art director

**Plot:**
A moral tale of the dangers of love across social class lines in which Marilyn plays burlesque star Peggy, daughter of another burlesque star May Martin. May fears for her daughter when she falls in love with rich socialite Randy Carroll—she too had been bitterly disappointed by a match with a man of far higher social standing. Peggy's humble origins are cruelly betrayed at an engagement party for the lovebirds held by Randy Carroll's mother, but all finishes well as love triumphs over class-based adversity.

**Reviews:**
*Motion Picture Herald*
"One of the bright spots is Miss Monroe's singing. She is pretty and, with her pleasing voice and style, she shows promise."

*Variety*
"Enough musical numbers are inserted, topped with the nifty warbling of Marilyn Monroe . . . Miss Monroe presents a nice personality in her portrayal of the burley singer."

## LAFONDA MOTOR LODGE
VENTURA BOULEVARD, SAN FERNANDO VALLEY

Norma Jeane spent a passionate weekend in this motel in 1945, when she was reunited with husband JAMES DOUGHERTY who was on leave from his military posting.

(*see* HOTELS)

## LANG, FRITZ (1890–1976)

Formidable German director of silent futurist classics *Metropolis* (1926) and M (1931), who moved to Hollywood in 1934. In 1952 he directed Marilyn Monroe in the RKO picture CLASH BY NIGHT. He had terrible problems directing the upcoming star. She was petrified, intimidated by co-star BARBARA STANWYCK, and was quickly convinced that co-star Paul Douglas hated her. Lang not only had to cope with Marilyn, he also had to handle Marilyn's total reliance on drama coach NATASHA LYTESS. Before long, Lang had had enough of being second-guessed and banned Lytess from the set. And like all other directors who took this course of action, he was forced to accept her return if he wanted Marilyn to continue.

Lang remembered Marilyn being "scared as hell to come to the studio, always late, couldn't remember her lines and was certainly responsible for slowing down the work."

In later years Lang reflected, "She was a very peculiar mixture of shyness and—I wouldn't say 'star allure'—but she knew, exactly, her impact on men."

Fritz Lang and Robert Ryan on the set of *Clash by Night* (1952).

## LANG, WALTER (1898–1972)

Walter Lang was calling the shots the first time that Norma Jeane ever left her image on film, shooting one hundred feet of silent footage at the request of TWENTIETH CENTURY-FOX colleague BEN LYON.

Eight years later Lang directed Marilyn in *THERE'S NO BUSINESS LIKE SHOW BUSINESS* (1954), though he wasn't happy about it: "Even with all those other people in it, that didn't seem to be enough without having Monroe's name in it too. She was the hottest thing in the business, so [the studio] put her in it. She fitted the part all right, and did several good numbers in it but just didn't seem to be able to work with the rest of us."

Lang's directorial career was spent mainly at Fox, where he specialized in big, brash musicals, many starring BETTY GRABLE. His best remembered movies are *The Bluebird* (1940), *Tin Pan Alley* (1940), *State Affair* (1945), *Mother Wore Tights* (1957), and *The King and I* (1956), for which he received an Oscar nomination.

## LANGE, HOPE (B. 1931)

Lange's break into the movies was in *BUS STOP* (1956) as the young traveler to whom Marilyn spills her heart.

In the run-up to shooting Marilyn reputedly insisted that Miss Lange's hair be dyed a darker shade so that it did not detract from her own luminous aura.

Lange reported that she had to do her close-ups with a male stand-in as Marilyn was not interested in waiting around on the set any longer than strictly necessary.

Oscar-nominated the following year for her role in *Peyton Place*, Lange has worked in movies and television ever since.

## LAS VEGAS

Officially, from May 14, 1946 Norma Jeane lived in Las Vegas, with Minnie Willette, the aunt of GRACE MCKEE GODDARD, at her home on 604 South Third Street. For four months she kept up the pretence of living here, until she had fulfilled the four-month residency requirement she needed to divorce first husband JAMES DOUGHERTY. In fact she spent much of that period either in Los Angeles or around California on photo shoots. She returned on September 13 to attend the divorce hearing.

During this time she twice went to the Las Vegas General HOSPITAL, once for trench mouth, once for measles.

Despite a number of offers over the years, the firmest of which came in 1955 and then again in the weeks before her death, Marilyn never performed in Las Vegas.

## LAST DAY ALIVE (AUGUST 4, 1962)

Surprisingly, there is general agreement about Marilyn's movements in the early evening of her last day alive. The one major discrepancy regards the length of time DR. RALPH GREENSON spent with Marilyn. The most widely-held belief is that he spent most of the day with her, though it has also been claimed that he spent just a couple of hours with her, in the late afternoon.

Throughout the day Marilyn made many calls. She received significantly fewer; housekeeper EUNICE MURRAY did not always put people through. The list of people Marilyn spoke to, though, is impressively long—some of the claimants may have insinuated their presence into Marilyn's final act, and the phone records of her last evening have not been made public. Similarly, the selection of things Marilyn had planned for the following day is remarkably broad: depending on source, golf; a business meeting with SIDNEY SKOLSKY; a press conference to expose the philandering Kennedy brothers. . . .

Those with whom she definitely spoke during the day include Skolsky, MARLON BRANDO, RALPH ROBERTS, JOE DIMAGGIO JR., and PETER LAWFORD.

PAT NEWCOMB slept over at Marilyn's house on August 3, 1962, the night before Marilyn died. Marilyn woke up early after a typically poor night's sleep.

Marilyn with Hope Lange in *Bus Stop* (1956).

8 A.M.: Housekeeper Eunice Murray reports for work.
9 A.M.: Marilyn breakfasts on a glass of grapefruit juice. During the morning she does a little gardening, and receives deliveries of new plants and a table she had ordered.
10 A.M.: Photographer Lawrence Schiller arrives to go through the photos he had taken of her on the set of *Something's Got to Give*—Marilyn approves a few. After this, Marilyn makes calls to friends.
Noon: Pat Newcomb gets up. Eunice Murray makes lunch.
1 P.M.: Ralph Greenson arrives. He is with Marilyn until after 7 P.M.
3 P.M.: Greenson asks Pat Newcomb to leave, and tells Eunice Murray to take Marilyn for a walk on the beach. A witness described Marilyn as "clearly under the influence, and she wasn't too steady in the sand."
4:30 P.M.: Marilyn returns home to continue therapy with Dr. Greenson.
Around 5 P.M.: Peter Lawford calls Marilyn to invite her to his house for dinner.
7:00 P.M.: Ralph Greenson leaves, asking Eunice Murray to stay overnight with Marilyn.
7:15 P.M.: Joe DiMaggio Jr. phones. Marilyn is apparently in good spirits.
7:45 P.M.: Peter Lawford calls again to check whether Marilyn is coming to dinner. Alarmed by her slurring, he begins a round of calls that concludes at 8:30 when Marilyn's lawyer Milton Rudin speaks to Murray and is assured that Marilyn is fine.

From here, the first sign of anything amiss:

10:00 P.M.: Publicist Arthur Jacobs is called out of a concert at the Hollywood Bowl with the news that Marilyn is dead—though at 11 P.M. Milton Rudin assures Peter Lawford's agent Joe Naar that Marilyn is fine, just sedated. Cover-up action ensues.

or

3 A.M. Eunice Murray awakens and calls Dr. Greenson because she is worried about the light under Marilyn's door.

*The Ultimate Marilyn* by Ernest W. Cunningham (1998) contains an excellent rundown of the various accounts of how Marilyn spent her final days.

## LATENESS

MARILYN:
"I've been on a calendar, but never on time."

BILLY WILDER:
"I don't think Marilyn is late on purpose. Her idea of time is different, that's all. I think maybe there's a little watchmaker in Zurich, Switzerland, he makes a living producing special watches only for Marilyn Monroe."

ERSKINE JOHNSON:
"Newsmen have waited for Marilyn to come out of airplanes. Airplanes have waited for Marilyn. Newsmen have waited for Marilyn to come out of trains. Trains have waited for Marilyn. Movie pro-

ducers, husband Arthur Miller, clothes designers have waited for Marilyn. Waiters have waited for Marilyn."

A legendary, lifelong trait, Marilyn's friends, colleagues, and husbands had to cope with her tardiness even at the very beginning of her career. She was late for photographer JOSEPH JASGUR, even though he was taking photographs for her portfolio as a favor. Her early roles may have been hard to come by, but that didn't stop her being late. Working on *A TICKET TO TOMAHAWK* (1950), she once turned up half an hour late for an exterior long shot, and was rebuked by the assistant director, who warned, "You know, you can be replaced." Marilyn retorted, "You can be replaced too, but they wouldn't have to reshoot you."

Marilyn was more than an hour late for an interview with journalist Robert Cahn, which appeared as the first ever national feature story in *Collier's* magazine in September 1951. In print he wryly concluded, "She is particularly concerned with looking her best and spends hours at the makeup table."

Reputedly while working on *NIAGARA* (1953), when berated for her constant lateness, Marilyn turned to the unit manager and said, "Am I making a picture or punching a time clock?" Photographer RICHARD AVEDON claimed that he booked Marilyn in for 9 A.M., then went about his day as normal and expected her to turn up in the evening.

ALLAN "WHITEY" SNYDER, who worked with Marilyn throughout her career, recalled that on *SOME LIKE IT HOT* (1959), "She picked up on anything. She'd say her eyebrows were wrong, or her lipstick—anything not to appear out there." Anxious that she didn't look quite like Marilyn, or could not perform as people expected either socially or on film, Marilyn would spend hours and hours preparing herself, being made up, shampooing her hair over and over again, calling friends to be reassured that she was planning to wear the right thing, even writing down notes for what she could say and topics for conversation.

LAUREN BACALL, co-starring in *HOW TO MARRY A MILLIONAIRE* (1953), hit the nail on the head: "She was always late, but I think it was in terror. She couldn't face doing what she was called upon to do; she couldn't cope."

In 1962, Marilyn teetered nervously onto the stage at MADISON SQUARE GARDEN, ready to wish President KENNEDY the sexiest happy birthday, announced by PETER LAWFORD as "the late Marilyn Monroe" (and she was).

Friends had to accept this feature of Marilyn's character. Many of them would simply bring forward arrangements and tell Marilyn that they were to meet an hour before the actual appointment. Friend NORMAN ROSTEN coined the expression "Marilyn time" to refer to her unique concept of punctuality.

In an interview a month before she died, lateness was one of the things she talked about: "I like the view from here. The future is here for me, and I have to make the most of it—as every woman must. So when you hear all this talk of how tardy I am, of how often it seems that I make people wait, remember—I'm waiting too. I've been waiting all my life."

Peter Lawford and Shelley Winters in an ABC Television special entitled "Marilyn Remembered," 1974.

## LAUGHTON, CHARLES (1899–1962)

SHELLEY WINTERS unsuccessfully tried to get Marilyn to join a drama study group held by English-born Charles Laughton in his Hollywood home in the late forties. Although Marilyn went twice, she was too nervous to participate. Perhaps her anxiety derived from his place on her list of most sexy MEN.

Only briefly did they work together, in an episode of *O. HENRY'S FULL HOUSE* (1952), when Laughton played a tramp to Marilyn's streetwalker.

In 1956 Marilyn listed Laughton as one of her favorite actors. Regarded as a serious artist, in his early performances Laughton left an indelible mark—an early Oscar for *The Private Life of Henry VIII* (1933), followed by *Les Miserables* (1935) and *Mutiny on the Bounty* (1935), before later suffering the kind of self-doubt that plagued Marilyn's career too. His sole directorial outing, *Night of the Hunter* (1955), is acclaimed as a masterpiece of American cinema.

## LAWFORD, PATRICIA

Marilyn's friendship with the Kennedy brothers was via PETER LAWFORD and his wife Patricia, née Kennedy. During 1962 Marilyn saw a lot of Patricia. She was a frequent house guest at their Santa Monica beach home, and reputedly they met up in New York during one of Marilyn's secret encounters with the president. In some accounts, Pat passed on the phone numbers for the Northern California ranch where BOBBY KENNEDY was staying on the last weekend Marilyn was alive.

Pat flew out from the East Coast to attend Marilyn's FUNERAL. JOE DIMAGGIO did not admit her or any of Marilyn's Hollywood friends, whom he blamed for her death.

Patricia Lawford divorced Peter not long after JFK was assassinated. Their son, Christopher Lawford, is also an actor.

## LAWFORD, PETER (1923–1984)

"Pat and I loved her dearly. She was probably one of the most marvelous and warm human beings I have ever met."

English-born former child actor who moved to Hollywood in 1938. Although he had (mostly minor) parts in close to fifty movies, Lawford is more famous as a (mostly minor) member of the RAT PACK, and for his links to the nation's number one family after marrying Patricia Kennedy. He played opposite FRANK SINATRA in *It Happened in Brooklyn* (1947), appeared in *Easter Parade* (1948) with JUDY GARLAND and Fred Astaire, and was a frequent guest star on TV.

When they were in Los Angeles, John and ROBERT KENNEDY often stayed with Pat and Peter at their Santa Monica beach house at 625 Palisades Beach Road. The overwhelming majority of Marilyn's documented meetings with JFK and RFK were at the Lawford beach house, painted as a den of iniquity by Jeanne Martin, then married to actor DEAN MARTIN: "The things that went on in that beach house were just mind boggling."

The only times that Marilyn and either Kennedy brother were seen in public together, Lawford was present: at Lawford's house during a party thrown for JFK to mark the end of the 1960 Democratic convention, and in May 1962 at MADISON SQUARE GARDEN where Lawford announced Marilyn as "the late Marilyn Monroe" before she took to the stage and sang "Happy Birthday" to the president.

Marilyn and Peter Lawford had known one another for some time. He was said to have had a long-standing crush on Marilyn, ever since 1950 when they met on the lot at MGM where starlet Marilyn was working on the low-profile *HOMETOWN STORY* (1951). Biographer ANTHONY SUMMERS quotes Lawford saying they had a couple of dates. However, in 1952 Marilyn took pains to publicly deny anything between them, telling a magazine, "I never have had a date with Peter. We were at the same table at a nightclub... and I may have danced with him, but that hardly constitutes a date, and certainly not a romance."

The CONSPIRACY theory version of events casts Lawford in the thick of things. He has been accused of pimping for his presidential brother-in-law; it has been rumored that he was in possession of photos of Marilyn performing fellatio on Kennedy; that his beach house was bugged; and that tapes of sex acts between Marilyn and the president had been recorded there by individuals wishing to discredit the Kennedys.

Peter Lawford's name crops up frequently in accounts of Marilyn's LAST DAY ALIVE. Most biographers agree that Marilyn visited the Lawford beach house on the day of her death, after housekeeper EUNICE MURRAY drove her out to the beach for a mid-afternoon walk. A little later, Lawford invited Marilyn to join him and some friends for dinner. He called once more a little before 8 P.M. to see if he could persuade Marilyn to come down to the house. Marilyn sounded severely drugged, and Lawford became concerned. At this point one of two things happened. According to DONALD SPOTO Lawford expressed his concern to friend Milton Ebbins, and then to Marilyn's lawyer Milton Rudin, and tried to get somebody to go to Marilyn's house to check what was happening. As the president's brother-in-law, if there was anything amiss his presence would have potentially caused a scandal. Alternatively, for conspiracy believers, Lawford went to Marilyn's home with Robert Kennedy, where he actively participated in Marilyn's murder and/or swept the place clean before the police were called.

## LAWRANCE, JODY

(B. 1930, JOSEPHINE LAWRANCE GODDARD)

A foster sister to Norma Jeane in 1935, soon after her father "DOC" GODDARD had married Norma Jeane's legal guardian GRACE MCKEE GODDARD. Recalling the short period they spent living together that year in a bungalow in the San Fernando Valley, she said, "Norma Jeane was a shy, introverted little girl... [we were] both neurotic children who clammed up and were very sensitive toward our surroundings."

Lawrance's film career spanned from 1951 to 1962, very similar in its dates to Marilyn's.

## LAWYERS

**Delaney, Frank**
Lawyer who encouraged Marilyn to quit TWENTIETH CENTURY-FOX and set up her own production company, MARILYN MONROE PRODUCTIONS. Marilyn announced the formation of this company from Delaney's Manhattan apartment—59 East 64th Street—in January 1955, and for the rest of the year Delaney spearheaded intense negotiations with Fox to rewrite Marilyn's contract. However, he left MMP before the year was out, revealing to MILTON GREENE that he felt Marilyn no longer had confidence in him.

**Frosch, Aaron**
In late 1960, as she was preparing to divorce ARTHUR MILLER, Marilyn found her own lawyer, Aaron Frosch, a well-known New York attorney who had a number of show business clients. Frosch handled her divorce from Miller, her final WILL, and negotiations regarding *SOMETHING'S GOT TO GIVE*. After her death he became executor of her estate. Mr. Frosch was himself on the receiving end of a lawsuit in 1981, when he was sued for illegally paying himself around $200,000 from the Marilyn Monroe estate, in a case initiated by the estate of DR. MARIANNE KRIS, Marilyn's New York analyst. An undisclosed out-of-court settlement was made.

**Giesler, Jerry**
In early October 1954 Marilyn hired this prominent Hollywood lawyer to handle her divorce from JOE DIMAGGIO. Giesler had a reputation for favorably resolving the problems of top stars. Not all, though—in 1949 he only managed to overturn ROBERT MITCHUM's conviction for conspiracy to possess marijuana after a spell in prison.

In his statement to the press about his client's grounds for divorce, Giesler cited a "conflict of careers" and said the divorce suit would be filed on the grounds of the usual mental cruelty, or, in legal parlance, "grievous mental suffering and anguish, all of which acts and conduct on the part of the defendant were without fault of the plaintiff." A funereal Marilyn leaned heavily on Giesler's arm as she left what had been her marital home with Joe DiMaggio. Before the court appearance on October 27, 1954, Giesler advised Marilyn on what she should say and wear.

**Montgomery, Robert**
In 1957 Marilyn conducted her strategic withdrawal from her partnership with Milton Greene through the offices of Arthur Miller's lawyer Robert Montgomery. Through Montgomery Marilyn issued a statement claiming that business partner Milton Greene had been mismanaging the company for personal gain, and entering into negotiations without either her knowledge or consent.

**Rudin, Milton ("Mickey")**
Marilyn's attorney at the end of her life, brother-in-law of Marilyn's psychoanalyst DR. RALPH GREENSON. Rudin handled the affairs of other showbiz clients, notably FRANK SINATRA.

There are conflicting reports as to exactly when Rudin took over Marilyn's affairs. Some biographers say he came into Marilyn's life through Greenson, that is, after Marilyn began entrusting her personal and professional life to her psychoanalyst; others contend that he had been introduced to Marilyn prior to this, probably by Sinatra.

Rudin drew up the documents required to buy her house on FIFTH HELENA DRIVE. Rudin was also involved in the business side of her life, notably when Twentieth Century-Fox suspended Marilyn from *Something's Got to Give*, and then the protracted negotiations to resuscitate the project. At the time of Marilyn's death, he was also reportedly in the process of putting together a heist movie project slated to star Marilyn and RAT PACK actors DEAN MARTIN, Sinatra, PETER LAWFORD, and SAMMY DAVIS JR.

Rudin was part of the shifting cast of characters involved in the night Marilyn died. In most accounts, around 8 p.m. Rudin received a call from a worried Peter Lawford who did not like the sound of Marilyn's slurring voice. Rudin then called Marilyn's housekeeper EUNICE MURRAY to see what was going on. Rudin told biographer DONALD SPOTO that Murray put the phone down to check, and then came back and told him that Marilyn was fine, but he had the impression she had not actually bothered to look.

As ever, what happened next depends on whether the teller of the tale believes Marilyn committed suicide or was murdered. In one version of events, Rudin and Dr. Greenson went to Marilyn's house and found her dead at midnight; in another, Rudin received a call earlier than that from his brother-in-law informing him that Marilyn was dead. In yet another version Rudin arrived on the scene for the first time soon after the police appeared. Later that morning he accompanied Marilyn's body to the Westwood Village Mortuary. It was Rudin who contacted Joe DiMaggio and asked him to look after FUNERAL arrangements.

**Stein, Irving**
A corporate lawyer brought in by colleague Frank Delaney in 1955 to work with Milton Greene and Marilyn on Marilyn Monroe Productions. Stein concentrated on renegotiating Marilyn's contract with Twentieth Century-Fox. He also arranged for Marilyn to transfer her residence to Connecticut to protect her from a potential Fox lawsuit. He was also the lawyer who handled her 1956 will. Stein parted company with Marilyn when she fell out with Greene in 1957.

**Wright, Lloyd**
Marilyn's attorney during 1954, taking her through her marriage to Joe DiMaggio (and quietly lending the honeymooners his secluded mountain retreat near Palm Springs). Wright also handled secret negotiations with Milton Greene and his attorney Frank Delaney aimed at giving Marilyn full control over her material and earnings by setting up Marilyn Monroe Productions.

**Other lawyers**

Raymond G. Stanbury: car accident (*see* CARS), 1955

W. Claude Fields Jr.: driving without a license (*see* CARS), 1956

Arturo Sosa Augilar and Aureliano Gonzalez: Mexican divorce from Arthur Miller, 1961

Elliot Lefkowitz: assisted Aaron Frosch

Martin Gang: concluding Marilyn's contract with agents at MCA, 1962

After Marilyn's death, her legal representation was taken on by CMG, the Curtis Management Group, on behalf of the ESTATE of Marilyn Monroe. From 1982 Estate affairs were handled by Roger Richman.

## LEAF, EARL

Hollywood celebrity PHOTOGRAPHER who had a number of sessions with Marilyn between 1950 and 1962.

BOOK:

*Marilyn Monroe, From Beginning to End*, text by Michael Ventura, photos by Earl Leaf. London: Blandford Press, 1997.

## LEAMING, BARBARA

Author of 1998 BIOGRAPHY *Marilyn Monroe*, published by Crown Books, including extensive material on Marilyn's long-running feud with TWENTIETH CENTURY-FOX and on Marilyn's years with ARTHUR MILLER. Leaming is a subscriber to the suicide theory. For Leaming, Marilyn stands as "the symbol of our secret desires."

## LEARY, DR. TIMOTHY

In 1962 Marilyn met Leary at a party. Intrigued by talk of his experiments into mind altering DRUGS, she asked him to introduce her to LSD. He obliged, and they went together to Venice Beach. Leary describe the event as "joyous."

## LEIGH, JANET
(B. 1927, JEANETTE HELEN MORRISON)

Janet Leigh broke into the movies at exactly the same time as Marilyn. The only time they ever shared a set was when Leigh visited then husband TONY CURTIS during production of *SOME LIKE IT HOT* (1959). Leigh heard more than most about how frustrating the experience was for Curtis: "She was there at the studio, but was hard put to muster the courage to appear. It was not malicious game playing or status tactics, but just plain terror that forced her to retreat."

Leigh's most famous role was as Marion Crane in Alfred Hitchcock's *Psycho* (1960). Other famous performances came in *The Naked Spur* (1953), and in Orson Welles's *Touch of Evil* (1958). Curtis and Leigh's daughter is actress Jamie Lee Curtis.

## LEIGH, VIVIEN
(1913–1967, B. VIVIEN HARTLEY)

Forever celebrated for Oscar-winning performances as Scarlett O'Hara in *Gone with the Wind* (1939) and Blanche DuBois in *A Streetcar Named Desire* (1951), Vivien Leigh had all the critical acclaim that Marilyn, in her insecurity, lacked.

The contrast must have been immense when, in 1956, Marilyn took on the role of Elsie that Leigh had famously performed in the original stage version of *THE PRINCE AND THE SHOWGIRL* (1957).

Though Marilyn and ARTHUR MILLER were nominally the guests of Leigh and her husband, LAURENCE OLIVIER, they met almost exclusively on formal occasions: at the airport, and at a party given by TERENCE RATTIGAN.

Marilyn and Leigh did not develop anything beyond a rivalry. Marilyn expressed displeasure when Leigh turned up at PINEWOOD STUDIOS to watch shooting. Meanwhile, Marilyn felt ill-treated and sneered at by director Olivier. SUSAN STRASBERG said, "Marilyn could play this role with her eyes closed, but Olivier seemed to feel that she should play it like Miss Leigh and he was infuriating her with his exacting and specific direction."

The two actresses did share some similarities. Throughout her life Leigh suffered ill-health and battled depression. She, like Marilyn, also suffered a miscarriage. In the first weeks of work on the movie, Leigh, then forty-two, told the press that she was expecting her first child with Olivier. Before the month was out, she lost the child.

Vivien Leigh and Laurence Olivier welcome the Millers to England in July of 1956. Filming for *The Prince and the Showgirl* would soon begin.

## LEMAIRE, CHARLES

As head of costume at TWENTIETH CENTURY-FOX between 1943 and 1960, LeMaire dressed Marilyn dozens of times, the first of which was in 1946 when she came to the studio for her very first SCREEN TEST. He also created the gown Marilyn wears in the party scene in *ALL ABOUT EVE* (1950).

## LEMMON, JACK
(B. 1925, JOHN UHLER LEMMON III)

Lemmon has been a leading actor since the early fifties, using his Broadway experience to good effect in *Mister Roberts* (1955), for which he won a Best Supporting Actor Oscar; and *SOME LIKE IT HOT* (1959), *The Apartment* (1960), and *Days of Wine and Roses* (1962), all of which were Oscar-nominated. His film credits also include *The Odd Couple* (1968), *The China Syndrome* (1979), and *Glengarry Glen Ross* (1992).

Over the years Lemmon has given some revealing insights into what it was like working with Marilyn on *Some Like It Hot*:

> "She had a built in kind of alarm clock that would go off when a scene wasn't right for her, which is very unusual as you don't normally have a stop unless a director says 'cut,' but Marilyn would just stop if it wasn't going right for her and it drove Tony absolutely fruit-cake!
>
> "Funnily enough that whole upper berth bed scene was done on the first take, it totally shocked me. It was the first take straight through, Billy Wilder said 'print' and she said 'I loved it too' and I thought 'what happened,' I was ready to go all day. It was lucky I got my words right because I had learned to pace myself with Marilyn. The day before we had gone 37 takes and she had exactly two lines to do, but the next morning we did the whole upper berth scene, before he goes down to get the booze, in one, she had it in the first take so you never knew!
>
> "I never heard such brilliant direction as Billy gave her, but nothing worked until she felt right about it. She simply said over and over, 'Sorry, I have to do it again.' And if Billy said, 'Well, I tell you, Marilyn, just possibly if you were to...'—then she replied, 'Just a moment, now, Billy, don't talk to me, I'll forget how I want to play it.' That took me over the edge more than once. Nobody could remind her that she had a professional commitment. She couldn't do it until she herself was ready."

Jack Lemmon, Tony Curtis and Marilyn in *Some Like It Hot* (1959).

## LEONARDI, PETER

Marilyn's factotum during her sojourn in New York during 1954-55, Peter Leonardi served as chauffeur, hairdresser, and assistant while MILTON GREENE and Marilyn planned the future of newly-formed MARILYN MONROE PRODUCTIONS. Leonardi told super-fan JAMES HASPIEL that during the summer of 1955 he would drive Marilyn down to the Bowery district of New York, where she would hand out money to homeless people.

Leonardi's working relationship with Marilyn ended abruptly. Leonardi claimed Marilyn had agreed and then failed to set him up with his own salon, and threatened legal proceedings to that effect.

## LESBIAN RUMORS

MARILYN:
"When I started reading books I ran into the words 'frigid,' 'rejected' and 'lesbian' and I wondered if I was all three of them. There was also the sinister fact that a well-made woman had always thrilled me to look at."

Marilyn's free approach to SEX, not surprisingly, has its feminine side. Rumors of lesbian relationships surfaced throughout her life and well after her death. Perhaps the first was in her starlet years, when according to biographer FRED LAWRENCE GUILES, JOAN CRAWFORD invited Marilyn back to her home and made a pass at her.

The intensity of Marilyn's relationship with drama coach NATASHA LYTESS was, most biographers agree, partly because of a sexual component. New York maid LENA PEPITONE quotes Marilyn about her affair with Natasha Lytess: "I let Natasha, but that was wrong. She wasn't like a guy. You know, just have a good time and that's that. She got really jealous about the men I saw, everything. She thought she was my husband. She was a great teacher, but that part of it ruined things for us. I got scared of her, had to get away."

According to ROBERT SLATZER, when jealous JOE DIMAGGIO broke into an apartment a week after Marilyn had begun divorce proceedings—the "WRONG DOOR RAID"—it was not to catch her with voice coach HAL SCHAEFER, but to surprise her in the act with a woman. Journalist WALTER WINCHELL reputedly believed that this lesbian relationship was the main reason for their divorce.

Rumors have also circulated that Marilyn had a night of passion with stripper Lily St. Cyr.

## *LET'S MAKE IT LEGAL* (1951)

Originally titled *Don't Call Me Mother*, this was one of the twelve movies Marilyn made in rapid succession in the early fifties, as TWENTIETH CENTURY-FOX slipped its hot new property into any movie it could find. Marilyn's supporting role in this movie did not require too much imagination for scriptwriter I. A. L. DIAMOND: Joyce Mannering is "the girl who won a beauty contest as Miss Cucamonga and has a contract to model. She's down here posing for cheesecake and trying to better her life."

Other episodes in the script that parallel Marilyn's own early Hollywood experiences are the pursuit of an influential man on a golf course (Marilyn had befriended JOHN CARROLL under just such circumstances) and a final scene in which she adorns a poker party for influential men, as she had done so many times at JOE SCHENCK's house.

Marilyn's LATENESS caused a showdown with director Richard Sale. When, in front of the entire crew, he demanded an apology, Marilyn stormed off the set, only to return soon afterward, full of contrition.

**Credits:**
Twentieth Century-Fox, Black and White
Length: 77 minutes
Release date: November 6, 1951

Directed by: Richard Sale
Produced by: Robert Bassler
Written by: I.A.L. Diamond, F. Hugh Herbert, Mortimer Braus (story)
Cinematography by: Lucien Ballard
Music by: Cyril J. Mockridge
Film Editing by: Robert Fritch
Costume Design by: Charles Le Maire, Renie

**Cast (credits order):**
Claudette Colbert . . . Miriam Halsworth
Macdonald Carey . . . Hugh Halsworth
Zachary Scott . . . Victor Macfarland
Barbara Bates . . . Barbara Denham
Robert Wagner . . . Jerry Denham
Marilyn Monroe . . . Joyce Mannering
Frank Cady . . . Ferguson
Jim Hayward . . . Pete the Gardener
Carol Savage . . . Miss Jessup
Paul Gerrits . . . Milkman
Betty Jane Bowen . . . Secretary
Vicki Raaf . . . Peggy, Hugh's Secretary
Ralph Sanford . . . Police Lieutenant
Harry Denny . . . Hotel Manager
Harry Harvey Sr . . . . Postman
Michael Ross . . . Policeman
Frank Sully . . . Laborer
Beverly Thompson . . . Reporter
Wilson Wood . . . Reporter
Abe Dinovitch . . . Laborer
Joan Fisher . . . Baby Annabella
Kathleen Freeman . . . Reporter
Harry Harvey . . . Postman
James Magill . . . Reporter
Jack Mather . . . Policeman
Rennie McEvoy . . . Reporter
Roger Moore . . . Reporter

**Crew:**
Paul S. Fox . . . set decorator
Albert Hogsett . . . art director
Harry M. Leonard . . . sound
Thomas Little . . . set decorator
Bernard Mayers . . . orchestration
Lionel Newman . . . musical director
Ben Nye . . . makeup
Edward B. Powell . . . orchestration
Fred Sersen . . . special photographic effects
E. Clayton Ward . . . sound
Lyle R. Wheeler . . . art director

**Plot:**
After twenty years of marriage, Miriam Halsworth (Claudette Colbert) obtains a divorce from husband Hugh (Macdonald Carey), publicity director for a fashionable hotel, after she can no longer abide his gambling.

Wealthy industrialist and former beau Victor Macfarland (Zachary Scott) comes to stay at the hotel. Hearing of the divorce, his interest in Miriam is rekindled; he had left town without any explanation twenty years earlier, just before Miriam married Hugh. Hugh, however, is still in love with Miriam; to make her jealous he starts seeing Joyce (Marilyn), who has designs on Macfarland's riches.

Victor and Miriam decide to wed; however, before he departs for a business trip to Washington, he admits that twenty years previously he and Hugh had rolled dice to see who would get to marry her. Miriam's anger is vented on Hugh; she threatens to wreak revenge on his prize rosebushes. To rescue them from her, Hugh attempts to smuggle them away at night, but he is arrested. The

MacDonald Carey, Marilyn, Zachary Scott, and Claudette Colbert in *Let's Make It Legal* (1951).

press gets hold of the story and writes that Miriam is engaged to Victor, who is none too happy to be associated with the palaver. Miriam tells Victor to go take a hike, and then Hugh shows her the dice he used to win her from Victor. She sees that the dice are loaded, that Hugh had cheated to make sure he would win her. For the second time in her life, Miriam is won over by Hugh.

**Reviews:**

*Hollywood Reporter*
"Marilyn Monroe is voluptuously amusing as a girl on a husband hunt."

*Los Angeles Times*
"Gorgeous Marilyn Monroe's in, flittingly. First time I've noticed her diction. It's execrable."

*New York Daily News*
"An inconsistent farce that luckily has sufficient saving graces, the predominating benefit being performances and comedy-wise co-stars, Claudette Colbert and Macdonald Carey. Their presences and a satisfactory amount of bright dialogue counteract strained farcical situations and the indifferent story... Marilyn Monroe is amusing in a brief role as a beautiful shapely blonde who has her eye on Zachary Scott and his millions."

*New York Daily Mirror*
"Claudette Colbert is a capable farceur, but she cannot make 'Let's Make It Legal' as merry as it was hoped. . . . It suffers from a weak script and incredible characterizations by Macdonald Carey and Zachary Scott... Marilyn Monroe parades her shapely chassis for incidental excitement."

## *LET'S MAKE LOVE* (1960)

This CinemaScope musical comedy scripted by NORMAN KRASNA as *The Billionaire* was brought to Marilyn by producer JERRY WALD, as TWENTIETH CENTURY-FOX stepped up the pressure for her to honor her studio commitments. In 1955 she had agreed to do four films for Fox, but before *Let's Make Love* went into production she had only done *BUS STOP* (1956).

Initially BILLY WILDER was a front runner for the director's chair. Apparently he was willing to try again after the harrowing experience of working together on *SOME LIKE IT HOT*, but he already was contracted to do *The Apartment*. GEORGE CUKOR was summoned as his replacement. He too had difficulties with Marilyn, and reputedly did a great deal of his communication through choreographer JACK COLE.

Marilyn's reputation made it next to impossible to find a male lead for this movie, a character rumored to be closely modeled after HOWARD HUGHES. Before YVES MONTAND was offered the role, it was turned down by a "who's who" of Hollywood's headliners: Yul Brynner, CARY GRANT, ROCK HUDSON, Charlton Heston, William Holden, GREGORY PECK, and James Stewart. It was Marilyn who suggested Montand; the studio was not happy, but she insisted, and Marilyn got her man, in more ways than one. Their very public love affair spelled the beginning of the end of Marilyn's marriage to ARTHUR MILLER, and came close to unraveling Montand's union with SIMONE SIGNORET.

There were script troubles too. Miller returned from Ireland, where he had been working with JOHN HUSTON on the script for *THE MISFITS* (1961), to do some emergency work on *Let's Make Love*: "Before production, I did some rewriting of a couple of scenes. I tried to give some point between these two featureless figures. When they talked, there was no character, no motivation, and so I stepped in and did what I could for the script. But we were beating a dead horse."

The biggest delays during filming were not due to Marilyn's LATENESS or illness, they were because of a strike by actors to preserve resid-

Choreographer Jack Cole rehearses a dance number with Marilyn for *Let's Make Love* (1960).

Marilyn in *Let's Make Love* (1960).

Yves Montand, Marilyn, and Gene Kelly on the set of *Let's Make Love* (1960).

Marilyn and fellow cast members in *Let's Make Love* (1960).

ual payments. The Writers Guild came out in support too, though this was precisely at the time when Arthur was doing the rewrites.

Marilyn sang four songs for the film: "My Heart Belongs to Daddy" by Cole Porter, and "Let's Make Love," "Incurably Romantic," and "Specialization" by Sammy Cahn and James Van Heusen. Marilyn's rendition of "My Heart Belongs to Daddy" is remarkable for the effortlessness of her performance, the result of at least two weeks of rehearsal.

Rather ominously, the planned premiere in RENO had to be cancelled because of a power black out. The movie bombed. Critical write-ups were almost all scathing, and the public stayed away. Inside Hollywood, gossip circulated that Marilyn's star was on the wane. Outside America, the film was renamed *The Millionaire*.

MEMORABLE COSTUME:
Sheer black leotard over slip and brazier

**Nominations:**
ACADEMY AWARDS:
Best music and scoring of a musical picture: Earle H. Hagen, Lionel Newman

BRITISH ACADEMY AWARDS:
Best film from any source: George Cukor
Best foreign actor: Yves Montand

**Credits:**
Twentieth Century-Fox, CinemaScope & Color (DeLuxe)
Length: 105 minutes
Release date: September 8, 1960

Directed by: George Cukor
Produced by: Jerry Wald
Written by: Norman Krasna, Hal Kanter, Arthur Miller (uncredited)
Cinematography by: Daniel L. Fapp
Music by: Earle H. Hagen, Lionel Newman
Costume Design by: Dorothy Jeakins
Film Editing by: David Bretherton

**Cast (credits order):**
Marilyn Monroe . . . Amanda Dell
Yves Montand . . . Jean-Marc Clement
Tony Randall . . . Howard Coffman
Frankie Vaughan . . . Tony Danton
Wilfrid Hyde-White . . . John Wales
David Burns . . . Oliver Burton
Michael David . . . Dave Kerry
Mara Lynn . . . Lily Nyles
Joe Besser . . . Lamont
Milton Berle . . . Himself (uncredited)
Harry Cheshire . . . Minister (uncredited)
John Craven . . . Comstock (uncredited)
Bing Crosby . . . Himself (uncredited)
Ray Foster . . . Jimmy (uncredited)
Gene Kelly . . . Himself (uncredited)
Madge Kennedy . . . Miss Manners (uncredited)
Dennis King Jr . . . Abe Miller (uncredited)
Mike Mason . . . Yale (uncredited)

**Crew:**
Gene Allen . . . art director
Jack Cole . . . staging of musical numbers
David Hall . . . assistant director
Lyle R. Wheeler . . . art director

**Plot:**
Yves Montand plays Jean-Marc Clement, a billionaire who is shocked to find out from his lawyer Wales (Wilfrid Hyde White) and his public relations manager Alex Coffman (Tony Randall) that he is to be spoofed in a planned off-Broadway play. When he goes to the theater to check these reports, he is smitten with Amanda Dell (Marilyn Monroe), and is then hired by the director, to play... himself.

Clement is too interested in Amanda to tell the director he is not an actor. During rehearsals he finds out not only that he has a rival, singer Tony Danton (Frankie Vaughan), but that Amanda is singularly unimpressed by men of wealth. Clement thwarts his own aides as they try to close the theater down. He gets three well-known entertainers (cameos by Bing Crosby, Gene Kelly, and Milton Berle) to train him for his role, and Wales comes up with much needed funding for the show.

Clement finally comes clean about who he really is, but Amanda refuses to believe him. The only way he can prove it is to get an injunction to stop the show, and then take her along to meet the theater owner—himself once again. He lands her a kiss, and she realizes that in spite of his money and his deceit, she is in love with him.

**Reviews:**
*The New York Times*
"The old Monroe dynamism is lacking in the things she is given to do by the cliché-clogged script of Norman Krasna and by George Cukor, who directed the film. It doesn't seem very important that she is finally brought together with Mr. Montand."

*Hollywood Citizen News*
"In the acting department, Miss Monroe is not impressive as in comedy-type roles. She plays a straight part here and does little that is effective. Visually? Marilyn offers her famous curves, not a little on the fleshy side. Diet, anyone?"

*New York World-Telegram and Sun*
"Marilyn Monroe is geared for some of the loudest laughter of her life in *Let's Make Love*...It is a gay, preposterous and completely delightful romp... Marilyn actually dares comparison with Mary Martin by singing 'My Heart Belongs to Daddy' in her first scene. The night I saw it, the audience broke into the picture with applause."

*New York Daily Mirror*
"Miss Monroe, basically a first-rate comedienne, doesn't have a single bright line. Of course, the famous charms are in evidence."

## LEVATHES, PETER

Levathes, trained as a lawyer and with a background in advertising, was appointed to the top job at TWENTIETH CENTURY-FOX in 1960, to reverse the studio's slow but alarming slump. Director JEAN NEGULESCO described him as "a tall, dark man, with manners and the faraway look of a man with responsibilities beyond his understanding or ability."

Levathes was personally involved with the convoluted process of getting Marilyn's final production, *SOMETHING'S GOT TO GIVE*, off the ground as directors and screenwriters were attached and then quickly detached from the project. He tried to stop Marilyn going to New York to sing "Happy Birthday" to JOHN F. KENNEDY, but Marilyn went all the same. In early June 1960 he made the decision to fire Marilyn. In his statement to the press, he cited "Miss Monroe's repeated willful breaches of her contract. No justification was given for a failure to report for photography on many occasions. The studio has suffered losses through these absences. We've let the inmates run the asylum."

However, after DEAN MARTIN invoked a clause in his contract allowing him refusal of any other actress in the female lead, and yet more changes in studio management, by mid-July Fox had had a change of heart. On July 25 Peter Levathes personally went to Marilyn's home. As he says, "I was the one responsible for firing her, so I wanted to be the one to personally rehire her."

Marilyn was very keen to resume work. They looked at the revised script, and Marilyn made a number of suggestions which Levathes received enthusiastically: "She was very happy and creative and glad to have a say in the revised script. She was in fine spirits and looking forward to getting back to work."

Dean Martin and Jerry Lewis with Marilyn at *Redbook* magazine's party to celebrate Marilyn's "Best Young Star of the Year" award, 1953.

## LEWIS, JERRY (B. 1926, JOSEPH LEVITCH)

Lewis is noted for getting up on his table and whistling at the sight of Marilyn in her gold lamé dress from *GENTLEMAN PREFER BLONDES* (1953), as she claimed her 1952 PHOTOPLAY award for Fastest Rising Star.

Lewis began his career with a string of films with comic partner DEAN MARTIN, before striking off on his own. Lewis turned director in the early sixties, but more recently has become a familiar face once a year on the Labor Day telethon for children suffering from muscular dystrophy.

## LINCOLN, ABRAHAM (1809–1865)

MARILYN:
"My father is Abraham Lincoln—I mean I think of Lincoln as my father. He was wise and kind and good."

The sixteenth president of the United States, the man who led to the Union to victory in the American Civil War and abolished slavery, was a HERO to Marilyn ever since she wrote an essay on him in junior high school.

Soon after meeting ARTHUR MILLER in 1950, Marilyn wrote a letter in which she confessed, "Most people can admire their fathers, but I never had one. I need someone to admire." Miller wrote back, "If you want someone to admire, why not Abraham Lincoln?" Marilyn went out and bought a large framed portrait and a biography written by CARL SANDBURG, with whom she later became friends. She reputedly also kept a copy of Lincoln's Gettysburg Address for inspiration. On screen in *BUS STOP* (1956), DON MURRAY, playing country boy Bo Decker, tries to get Marilyn to become "attracted to his mind" by reciting her the Gettysburg address.

For years Marilyn gave her framed photo of Lincoln pride of place in her homes at DOHENY DRIVE in Beverly Hills, at the WALDORF-ASTORIA suite in New York, and later in a smaller version on her nightstand at the East FIFTY-SEVENTH STREET apartment she shared with Arthur Miller.

More than one biographer has asserted that until the relationships soured, Marilyn identified Arthur with Lincoln. She saw both of them as honorable men, committed to their principles, erudite, and cultured.

In 1955, accompanied by photographer EVE ARNOLD, Marilyn was invited to officially open a Lincoln museum in the town of BEMENT, ILLINOIS.

## LIPTON, HARRY

Harry Lipton of the National Artists Corporation was Marilyn's first movie AGENT. In one of the conflicting stories about the way Marilyn arrived at her very first SCREEN TEST, Lipton orchestrated a kind of bidding war between HOWARD HUGHES and BEN LYON, head of talent at Fox, who in Lipton's words "nearly tripped over my feet, his eyes were so glued on her." Lipton takes joint credit for giving Norma Jeane her new movie moniker too. Biographer FRED LAWRENCE GUILES is skeptical about the chronology of these events, and prefers the version in which EMMELINE SNIVELY, head of the BLUE BOOK MODELING AGENCY, called Lipton's boss at the agency, and the starlet client was passed on to Lipton. In any event, on July 23, 1946 Marilyn Monroe signed her first ever movie contract, verified by Lipton.

In his time representing her, Marilyn spent a year with Fox, six months at COLUMBIA STUDIOS, and then a lean year or two before lover JOHNNY HYDE took over, in 1949, and pushed her career in a more effective direction.

Marilyn reputedly told ROBERT SLATZER how important Harry Lipton had been: "I never showed him any real appreciation for what he did for me at the beginning... I really owe him so much, and I feel guilty that I didn't give him more credit. He was wonderful. I can't imagine how he put up with me in those days."

## LLOYD, HAROLD (1893–1971)

A star of gravity-defying silent slapstick, one of the most famous comedians of the silent age, Lloyd had become a PHOTOGRAPHER by the time Marilyn became a big star. He was snapping away in 1952 during the photo shoot for Marilyn's first *Life* cover, and he arranged several more sessions over the following year. His photographic specialty was color stereo pictures. Seven pictures of Marilyn appeared in a 1992 book of his 3-D photographs, with text by Lloyd's granddaughter Suzanne Lloyd Hayes.

## LOGAN, JOSHUA (1908–1988)

"Monroe is as near genius as any actress I ever knew... She is the most completely realized actress since Garbo. Watch her work. In any film. How rarely she has to use words. How much she does with her eyes, her lips, with slight, almost accidental gestures... Monroe is pure cinema."

Top Broadway stage director, best known for his productions of *South Pacific* and *Mister Roberts*, Logan had recently directed SUSAN STRASBERG in the film version of *Picnic* (1956) when he was approached by Marilyn's agent LEW WASSERMAN to direct Marilyn in *BUS STOP* (1956), her first movie after walking out on TWENTIETH CENTURY-FOX. Logan initially protested that she had no acting talent. His friend LEE STRASBERG reassured him: "I have worked with hundreds and hundreds of actors and actresses, both in class and in the Studio, and there are only two that stand out way above the rest. Number one is Marlon Brando, and the second is Marilyn Monroe."

Logan, who had a reputation as a talented director of "sensitive" actors—and something of a personal history of depression—certainly did his homework on Marilyn. For a start, he was well-versed in STANISLAVSKY and THE METHOD, so from a theoretical point of view, he and his star were on the same wavelength. And knowing about her famed LATENESS he had a second morning schedule set up for practically every day of shooting, ready for the inevitable occasions when Marilyn turned up too late. Only once, when Logan wanted a particular type of light, did he lose

Director Joshua Logan and Marilyn on the set of *Bus Stop* (1956).

patience and personally go and haul Marilyn out of her hotel, where she had been sitting for makeup for hours.

This uncommonly strife-free relationship between director and actress continued throughout filming. Then, the day that Marilyn saw the final cut of the movie, she flew into a rage because, she felt, Logan had cut the best parts of her performance, including much of her monologue in the presence of actress HOPE LANGE. She later confided that she blamed this for compromising her otherwise good chances of an Oscar nomination.

More than any other director, Logan sang Marilyn's praises to the world. She was "one of the most unappreciated people in the world" and "one of the great talents of all time, and the most talented motion picture actress of her day—warm, witty, extremely bright and totally involved in her work. I'd say she was the greatest artist I ever worked with in my entire career."

When LAURENCE OLIVIER was weighing Marilyn's offer to direct *THE PRINCE AND THE SHOWGIRL* (1957), he asked Logan what it was like to direct her. His reply: "She's worth all the trouble."

## LOLLOBRIGIDA, GINA (B. 1927)

"Italy's Marilyn Monroe," as she had been billed, was in New York in 1954 when Marilyn was in town shooting on location for *THE SEVEN YEAR ITCH* (1955). The two met at the Trans Lux Theater on Lexington Avenue and Fifty-second Street hours before the filming of the infamous billowing skirt scene. They also met at a party thrown in honor of "La Lollo" by press agent RUPERT ALLAN.

Lollobrigida's film career spanned many international productions. Among her best-known English-language works are *Bread, Love and Dreams* (1953) and *Beat the Devil* (1954). In the eighties she was a regular on TV soap *Falcon Crest*.

## LONELINESS

MARILYN:
"It's better to be unhappy alone than unhappy with someone."

"A woman can't be alone. She needs a man. A man and a woman support and strengthen each other. She just can't do it by herself."

JOSEPH MANKIEWICZ:
"She was not a loner, she was just plain alone."

Marilyn feared the consequences of abandonment, but it was something she had to contend with more and more in the later stages of her life.

After finally buying a HOME of her own in 1962, Marilyn said, "I could never imagine buying a home alone. But I've always been alone, so why couldn't I imagine it?"

A few weeks before her death, radio DJ Tom Clay pressed Marilyn about her loneliness. Marilyn replied, "Have you ever been in a house with 40 rooms? Well, multiply my loneliness by 40."

## LOOS, ANITA (1891–1981)

Actress turned writer who wrote the original novel for the film *GENTLEMAN PREFER BLONDES* (1953), inspired by writer H. L. Mencken's fling with a blonde bombshell. Loos, who had written a number of scripts for JEAN HARLOW, saw much in Marilyn that reminded her of the first platinum blonde actress.

At the time of Marilyn's DEATH, a note was found among her possessions in which Loos inquired if Marilyn was interested in starring in an adaptation of a French play called *Gogo*.

## LOREN, SOPHIA
(B. 1934, SOFIA SCICOLONE)

Renowned international actress whose poor beginnings mirrored Marilyn's: "We both rose from the same place... and she is like a sister to me. And of course I feel like I could've [saved her] if I tried. But it's a full-time job to save someone like that. Maybe if I met her I could have..."

An Academy Award winner for *Two Women* (1961), Loren's memorable performances also include *Heller In Pink Tights* (1960), *Yesterday, Today, and Tomorrow* (1964), *Marriage Italian Style* (1964), and a spate of more recent appearances.

In 1964 first husband producer Carlo Ponti was in the bidding for film rights to ARTHUR MILLER's play *AFTER THE FALL*, in which Loren was slated to star opposite Paul Newman. The film was made ten years later, with FAYE DUNAWAY in the Marilynesque role of Maggie.

## LOS ANGELES

Marilyn was born and bred in Los Angeles. Apart from the period 1955 –1960, when she was based in NEW YORK with husband ARTHUR MILLER, Marilyn always had a HOME in L.A.

## LOS ANGELES DISTRICT ATTORNEY

Prompted among other things by published allegations in ROBERT SLATZER and MILO SPERIGLIO's books, in 1982 District Attorney John Van de Kamp ordered a preliminary investigation to see whether there was reasonable cause for a murder inquiry on the Marilyn case. The verdict of the inquiry was that the facts "do not support a finding of foul play." Mr. Van de Kamp added, "Permit me to express a faint hope that Marilyn Monroe be allowed to rest in peace."

## LOVE

Marilyn believed in love and she felt the pain of its absence. She was a romantic, and romantics marry for love.

In her unfinished autobiography, she reveals, "I never dreamed of anyone loving me as I saw other children loved. That was too big a stretch for my imagination. I compromised by dreaming of my attracting someone's attention (besides God), of having people look at me and say my name."

The first person from whom she received the love she missed as a child was "Aunt" ANA LOWER, whom she later described as "the greatest influence on my whole life. She was the only person I have ever loved with such a deep love that one can only have for someone so good, so kind, and so full of love for me."

In one of her last interviews, Marilyn said, "My father never married my mother. I guess that's what broke her heart... When you love a man and tell him you are going to have his child and he runs out on you, it is something a woman never gets over. I don't think my mother ever did."

However, in 1962, the year of her death, she was still feeling the pain of its absence: "All I ever wanted out of life is to be nice to people and have them be nice to me. It's a fair exchange. And I'm a woman. I want to be loved by a man, from his heart, as I would love him from mine. I've tried, but it hasn't happened yet."

## LOVE HAPPY (1950)

As with so much surrounding Marilyn's faltering start in Hollywood, the truth about how Marilyn met the Marx brothers is lost in conflicting accounts. Biographers are split down the line even on the year this movie came out. Most say 1950, but a thriving minority state the year of release as 1949. The anomaly seems to be because the movie was filmed in early 1949, the production ran into finance problems, and release was put back to the following year.

In order of probability, Marilyn arrived at her audition with producer LESTER COWAN either through agent and boyfriend JOHNNY HYDE, first agent HARRY LIPTON, agent Louis Shurr, benefactor JOHN CARROLL, or under her own steam. All biographies agree that Lester Cowan left the casting decision to GROUCHO MARX.

Marilyn recalled, "There were three girls there and Groucho had us each walk away from him. I was the only one he asked to do

Marilyn and Groucho Marx in *Love Happy* (1950).

it twice. Then he whispered in my ear, 'You have the prettiest ass in the business.' I'm sure he meant it in the nicest way." Another Marilyn memory of the event: "I had to wiggle across a room. I practiced jiggling my backside for a week. Groucho loved it." The week's work on her WALK landed her the role and, for the first time, a chance to sashay on film.

In what was the last Marx brothers movie and Marilyn's fourth, she merited an "Introducing Marilyn Monroe" credit in the opening titles, despite only having one scene in the movie. Marilyn enters the office of private detective Groucho, wearing a revealing strapless gown. In four speaking lines Marilyn asks him for help because "men are following me." Groucho quips "Really? I can't understand why."

For her role Marilyn was paid $500 plus a further $300 for promotional still photographs. When she was dispatched on the publicity tour she picked up a further $100 per week, plus an allowance for a new wardrobe. On the advice of her two mentors Hyde and NATASHA LYTESS, she bought a demure set of outfits, wool suits and sweaters, high-necked blouses and a jacket, but found Chicago and New York to be so hot and humid she had to buy a whole new set of summer clothes. She lasted through Detroit, Cleveland, and Milwaukee, before quitting the tour and returning to LOS ANGELES after over a month away.

This movie is regarded by many Marx brothers fans as their worst; the reason the movie was made in the first place is that Chico Marx needed to raise money to pay back debts. Harpo, not known for his way with words, came up with the story. The brothers rarely appear in the same scene together.

**Credits:**
United Artists, a Mary Pickford Presentation
Length: 85 minutes
Release date: April 7, 1950

Directed by: David Miller
Produced by: Lester Cowan, Mary Pickford
Written by: Mac Benoff, Ben Hecht (uncredited), Harpo Marx (story), Frank Tashlin
Cinematography by: William C. Mellor
Music by: Ann Bonnell
Production Design by: Gabriel Scognamillo
Costume Design by: Grace Houston, Norma
Film Editing by: Albrecht Joseph, Basil Wrangell

**Cast** (credits order):
Harpo Marx . . . Harpo
Chico Marx . . . Faustino
Groucho Marx . . . Sam Grunion
Ilona Massey . . . Madame Egelichi
Vera-Ellen . . . Maggie Phillips
Marion Hutton . . . Bunny Dolan
Raymond Burr . . . Alphonse Zoto
Melville Cooper . . . Lefty Throckmorton
Paul Valentine . . . Mike Johnson
Leon Belasco . . . Mr. Lyons
Eric Blore . . . Mackinaw
Bruce Gordon . . . Hannibal Zoto
Marilyn Monroe . . . Grunion's Client
Lois Hall

**Crew:**
Howard A. Anderson . . . photographic effects
Richard Bachler . . . men's wardrobe
Billy Daniel . . . production number stager
Harry Geller . . . orchestration
Ray Heinze . . . production manager
Fred B. Phillips . . . makeup
Scotty Rackin . . . hair styles
Casey Roberts . . . set decorator
Paul J. Smith . . . orchestra conductor, musical director

**Plot:**
Groucho Marx plays detective Sam Grunion, who tells the tale of how he cracked the missing Romanoff diamond case. Hi-jinks ensue as an impoverished group of actors rehearsing in an empty theater become embroiled in the plot to smuggle the booty into the United States in a tin of sardines, which kleptomaniac Harpo steals to help feed his fellow theatricals. The evil mastermind of the heist, Madame Egilichi, tracks the can to the theater, where it is found on opening night. Quick as a flash, Harpo scoops it up and is pursued to the roof, where he eludes their clutches by dashing in and out of huge flashing neon signs. As Grunion arrives at the theater, he is importuned by Marilyn in her brief walk-on role as a beautiful nonsequitur who asks detective Grunion (played by Groucho) to help her as "men keep following her." Grunion solves the crazy caper not by getting hold of the diamonds, but by getting hold of the heistress, who became his wife.

**Reviews:**
*New York Herald Tribune*
"Thank goodness there's a little normality in a dizzy world. The Marx Brothers, in slightly amended form, are back in the cinema world and the event is an occasion for celebration... Marx fans will get their money's worth. An aficionado asks only for certain time-tested maneuvers from the comedians. They will get them at the Criterion."

*New York Post*
"The picture is both ingenious and lively, within the pattern previously set by the Marxes. Whether it will bring new joys to a generation that has not known them before, or recover hysterical merriment for oldsters who once split their sides over these antics are questions that experience alone can answer."

*The New York Times*
"The Marx brothers are loose again and have turned the Criterion's screen into a comic shambles. *Love Happy* is a helter-skelter entertainment . . . a see-saw affair; sometimes the antics are incredibly funny, and pianissimo, please—sometimes the gags fall with a flat thud."

## LOVE NEST (1951)

With Marilyn signed to a new contract, TWENTIETH CENTURY-FOX was intent on fitting her into any film requiring a sexy blonde. She was shoe-horned into this light comedy, the eleventh movie in her short and hitherto low-key career.

Though not much more than an embellishment in this movie, Marilyn's part caused quite a stir. Columnist SIDNEY SKOLSKY wrote that when Marilyn undressed for her shower scene the crowded set was so quiet "you could hear the electricity."

**Credits:**
Twentieth Century-Fox, Black and White
Length: 84 minutes
Release date: October 10, 1951

Directed by: Joseph M. Newman
Produced by: Jules Buck
Written by: I. A. L. Diamond, Scott Corbett (novel)
Cinematography by: Lloyd Ahern
Music by: Cyril J. Mockridge
Film Editing by: J. Watson Webb Jr.
Art direction by: George Patrick, Lyle R. Wheeler

**Cast (credits order):**
June Haver . . . Connie Scott
William Lundigan . . . Jim Scott
Frank Fay . . . Charley Patterson
Marilyn Monroe . . . Roberta "Bobby" Stevens
Jack Paar . . . Ed Forbes
Leatrice Joy . . . Eadie Gaynor
Henry Kulky . . . George Thompson
Marie Blake . . . Mrs. Quigg
Patricia Miller . . . Florence
Maude Wallace . . . Mrs. Arnold
Joe Ploski . . . Mr. Hansen
Martha Wentworth . . . Mrs. Thompson
Faire Binney . . . Mrs. Frazier
Caryl Lincoln . . . Mrs. McNab
Michael Ross . . . Mr. McNab
Bob Jellison . . . Mr. Fain
John Costello . . . Postman
Charles Calvert . . . Mr. Knowland
Leo Clary . . . Detective Donovan
Jack Daly . . . Mr. Clark
Ray Montgomery . . . Mr. Gray
Florence Auer . . . Mrs. Braddock
Edna Holland . . . Mrs. Engstrand
Liz Slifer . . . Mrs. Healy
Alvin Hammer . . . Glazier

**Plot:**
After the war Jim Scott (William Lundigan) returns to New York with wife Connie (June Haver) and moves into an old building she has bought. The building provides them rental income, and an endless succession of problems that thwart his intentions as a writer.

June Haver, William Lundigan, and Marilyn in a publicity shot for *Love Nest* (1951).

Marilyn plays Roberta Stevens, an ex-WAC and wartime friend of Jim's, who moves into the building, arousing the suspicions of Connie. Most of the film's plot revolves around two other tenants, Charley Patterson (Frank Fay) and Eadie Gaynor (Leatrice Joy), who marry. After loaning some money to the needy Jim, Charley is unmasked as a no-good cheat who has taken money from rich widows. Eadie stands up for her husband, and the one who goes to jail, for taking the money earlier, is Jim Scott, who finally has time to get down to writing his memoirs. On his release the memoirs are published and make enough money to renovate the building. By the time Charley comes out, he is a man reformed by the love of a good woman (Eadie) and in due course becomes the father of twins.

**Reviews:**
*Film Daily*
"Lightly skipping about in its treatment of a GI's postwar investment, engineered by his wife while he was overseas, in a rundown house in the Gramercy Park section of Manhattan, 'Love Nest' is a mild variety of comedy which gets a considerable boost from the expert talents—in that line—of Frank Fay. Rarely seen, he registers here as a smoothie, glib and ultra sophisticated, handy with the correct word on the correct occasion. Leatrice Joy is also present in this number. She gives mature warmth to the proceedings. Marilyn Monroe has that other quality, while William Lundigan, an author, and June Haver play at being married and troubled with their creaky domicile."

*Variety*
"There are only a few fresh lines and situations in the script, and they are not enough to add any punch to a rather 'dated' theme, no matter how hard the cast toppers try to keep the laughs going... Marilyn Monroe is tossed in to cause jealousy between the landlords."

## LOVERS

MARILYN:
"There were times when I'd be with one of my husbands and I'd run into one of these Hollywood heels at a party and they'd paw me cheaply in front of everybody as if they were saying, "Oh, we had her." I guess it's the classic situation of an ex-whore, though I was never a whore in that sense. I was never kept; I always kept myself."

Marilyn has been hailed as a forerunner of free love. She has been accused of using sex to get to the top. She has been pitied for falling foul of the unwritten rule of male-run Hollywood, where pretty young girls service powerful old men. And claims have been made by dozens of men (and some women—see LESBIAN RUMORS) that they had their night or two of passion with the biggest sex symbol of her day.

The following is a compilation of lists of the people who went to bed with Marilyn. Some of them did. Some of them didn't—they merely expressed their desire to do so loudly enough to be picked up by the rumor mill.

(*see* SEX APPEAL)

James Bacon
Milton Berle
José Bolaños
Marlon Brando
Yul Brynner
Oleg Cassini
Paddy Chayefsky
John Carroll
Charlie Chaplin Jr.
Harry P. Cohn
David Conover
Tony Curtis
Sammy Davis Jr.
André de Dienes
Joe DiMaggio
Jim Dougherty
Blake Edwards
Albert Einstein
Charles Feldman
Milton Greene
Howard Hughes
Johnny Hyde
Ted Jordan
Elia Kazan
Fred Karger
John F. Kennedy
Robert Kennedy
Anton LaVey
Hans Jorgen Lembourn
Ben Lyon
Natasha Lytess
Dean Martin
Arthur Miller
Robert Mitchum
Yves Montand
Edward G. Robinson Jr.
Mickey Rooney
Henry Rosenfeld
Porfirio Rubirosa
George Sanders
Hal Schaefer
Joseph M. Schenck
Bugsy Seigel
Frank Sinatra
Spyros Skouras
Robert Slatzer
Mel Tormé
William Travilla
Orson Welles
Tommy Zahn
Darryl F. Zanuck

## LOWER, ANA (1880–1948)

MARILYN:
"She changed my whole life. She was the first person in the world I ever really loved and she loved me. She was a wonderful human being. I once wrote a poem about her and I showed it to somebody and they cried... It was called 'I Love Her.' She was the only one who loved and understood me.... She never hurt me, not once. She couldn't. She was all kindness and all love."

Of all her succession of foster mothers, Marilyn retained the greatest affection for Edith Ana Atchinson Lower. For a ten year period, "Auntie" Ana—in actual fact the aunt of Norma Jeane's legal guardian GRACE MCKEE GODDARD—was the closest thing Norma Jeane had to a solid, dependable maternal presence.

Born on January 17, 1880, Ana Lower was

Marilyn with Ana Lower (far right), ca. 1939.

fifty-eight years old when Norma Jeane went to live with her at 11348 NEBRASKA AVENUE, in West Los Angeles. Ana Lower had divorced her husband Will in 1933; he died in 1935, but she had some income from renting out several bungalows and cottages they had bought during the 1920s, as well as small change she received from her counseling as a CHRISTIAN SCIENCE advisor. ELEANOR GODDARD said she was not fanatical, though, "In fact she was very sensible, compassionate and accepting of others. She looked severe and stern and had an imposing carriage, but she was putty inside, not the dominating matron she was often made out to be." Physically, she has been described as a picture-book white-haired grandma figure.

Between leaving the Los Angeles ORPHANAGE in 1937 and marrying JAMES DOUGHERTY on June 19, 1942, Norma Jeane spent more time living with Lower than with anyone else. It has been said that this arrangement began soon after an incident when "DOC" GODDARD molested the girl. The only time Norma Jeane lived with the Goddards or other foster families was when Lower's health was very poor.

Aunt Ana gave Norma Jeane LOVE and self-confidence. She taught Norma Jeane that "it's what you are that really counts. Just keep being yourself, honey, that's all that matters." She gave the guidance Norma Jeane needed at puberty, brought her into contact with the precepts of Christian Science, and may have been the first person to tell her something about sex. One of Aunt Ana's strongest precepts was that the mind could achieve anything it wished to achieve.

Ana made and designed Norma Jeane's wedding gown. She gave the bride away to Jim Dougherty. Later, as the marriage was failing and Norma Jeane needed a place to stay, she found a haven with Lower, who had an empty apartment below hers. On this occasion Norma Jeane was joined for a few weeks (months in some accounts) by her mother GLADYS BAKER, on one of her brief spells away from the hospital.

Lower's failing heart finally gave out on March 14, 1948, too early to see Marilyn realize her dreams. Marilyn told ARTHUR MILLER, "I went and lay down in her bed the day after she died... just lay there for a couple of hours on her pillow. Then I went to the cemetery and these men were digging a grave and they had a ladder into it, and I asked if I could get down there and they said sure, and I went down and lay on the ground and looked up at the sky from there. It's quite a view, and the ground is cold under your back."

Marilyn was buried in the same cemetery as her beloved Aunt Ana.

## LYON, BEN (1901–1971)

Ben Lyon's career in show business spanned genres and continents. A leading man in the twenties and thirties, including a blockbuster performance opposite JEAN HARLOW in *Hell's Angels* (1930), he and his wife moved to England where they became famous radio personalities on the BBC, in *Life with the Lyons*. During the war years he flew missions for the Royal Air Force, and then he returned to Los Angeles to take up a job variously described as a casting director or head of talent at TWENTIETH CENTURY-FOX. On July 17, 1946, twenty-year-old Norma Jeane Dougherty walked into Lyon's office at the studios. It is generally assumed that HELEN AINSWORTH had pestered Lyon into giving Norma Jeane a look over, though Lyon has said that she simply turned up out of the blue, no appointment arranged.

Lyon asked Norma Jeane to read a few lines from the studio's 1944 wartime melodrama *Winged Victory*, from a part played by Judy Holliday. Legend has it that after meeting her he told a colleague, "It's Jean Harlow all over again." Such was his enthusiasm that two days later he assembled four of the studio's top crew members for an extravagant (Technicolor) SCREEN TEST on the set of the latest BETTY GRABLE vehicle *Mother Wore Tights*. It has been rumored that Lyon's keen support was at least partly in exchange for sexual favors received from the aspiring actress.

Lyon's boss at Fox, DARRYL F. ZANUCK, was not as convinced with the screen test results, but at a cost of $75 per week, it was not a great expense for the studio to bow to the head of talent's instincts. When Lyon told Norma Jeane that she was going to be signed to a seven-year contract, she reputedly burst into tears. Before the contract was signed, Norma Jeane met with Lyon to discuss a rather important detail: her screen NAME. From a number of possibilities, they finally settled on Marilyn Monroe.

Lyons' faith was repaid. "She was the most conscientious youngster signed by the company. She devoted all her time to study, training, and exercising so that when an opportunity came she would be prepared."

In thanks years later, Marilyn sent an autographed photo to Lyon, bearing the inscription, "You found me, named me and believed in me when no one else did. My love and thanks forever."

## LYTESS, NATASHA (1915–1964)

"Marilyn needed me like a dead man needs a coffin."

Marilyn was sent to COLUMBIA's drama coach Natasha Lytess in April 1948. Lytess, whose theater and cinema background was in Europe, had been working as a drama coach in Hollywood for seven years. Her initial assignment with Marilyn was to prepare her for her first supporting role, in *LADIES OF THE CHORUS* (1948). She continued to tutor Marilyn in her performances for the next six years and twenty movies, right up to *THE*

Natasha Lytess and Marilyn during filming of *Love Happy* (1950).

SEVEN YEAR ITCH in 1955. Lytess was an important mother figure, a sometime lover, an island of stability in the young actress's life; she was prepared to believe and invest in Marilyn at a time when nobody else would. She helped Marilyn to develop and express her talents and curiosity for the world of drama and culture. Lytess is also, in many biographies, painted as a bitter and resentful woman—when the contorted mistress/pupil relationship ended, it was abrupt and, for the older woman, painful.

Lytess wrote that when Marilyn first came to her her acting was "inhibited and cramped, and she could not say a word freely. Her habit of barely moving her lips when she spoke was unnatural. . . . All this I tried to teach Marilyn. But she knew her SEX APPEAL was infallible, that it was the one thing on which she could depend."

In dramatic terms, Lytess exerted a discipline on Marilyn's style by promoting understated movement, diction and recitation. Many of the mannerisms in Marilyn's speaking VOICE were elicited by Lytess, for whom "the keyboard of the human voice is the gamut of emotion, and each emotion has its corresponding shade of tone."

After their initial experience working together, Lytess gave Marilyn intensive coaching prior to all her auditions. For example, they worked three days and nights rehearsing for Marilyn's second audition for THE ASPHALT JUNGLE (1950). When Marilyn got the part, Lytess gave up her job at Columbia to coach Marilyn full-time. JOHN HUSTON became the first director to have to cope with Marilyn's near-total reliance on her drama coach; after every take Marilyn looked to her coach for approval or disapproval. This glance is visible in Marilyn's first scene in the movie.

Much has been written about the physical aspect of the relationship. Whether or not Lytess's love was requited is a matter of conjecture. Marilyn was later non-committal: "She was in love with me and she wanted me to love her." Among others, Marilyn's New York maid LENA PEPITONE, columnist Florabel Muir, and reporter SIDNEY SKOLSKY are all of the opinion that there had been a sexual relationship. In her memoirs, Lytess is candid about her desire: "I took her in my arms one day, and I told her 'I want to love you.' I remember she looked at me and said, 'You don't have to love me, Natasha—just as long as you work with me.'"

When Marilyn finally achieved her goal of a long-term contract with TWENTIETH CENTURY-FOX, the one major change she made to the standard terms was to have Lytess added to the payroll as her private drama coach. Lytess was on a retainer of $500 per week; Marilyn paid her an additional $250 per week for private tutorials, which meant that in Marilyn's first year on contract, her drama coach earned more than she did.

Lytess's sideline direction made her extremely unpopular with directors. Tutor and pupil devised a set of hand signals, so that Marilyn could see from Lytess if she was doing anything different to how they had rehearsed her scenes: "I signaled to her if she turned too soon, or if a turn had been 'empty' because it hadn't been motivated by proper thought about herself and the character."

In the fall of 1950 Marilyn moved in to Natasha's home, at HARPER AVENUE in West Hollywood; she slept on a living room sofa, studied and read, and looked after both Natasha's daughter and the chihuahua that JOSEPH SCHENCK had given Marilyn as a twenty-fourth birthday present. It has been written that the dog's lack of house training soon became a major cause of friction between houseguest and host.

The two went away to Tijuana together in December 1950, at the time that JOHNNY HYDE had his fatal heart attack. Soon afterwards Natasha discovered Marilyn comatose, with a dribble of white spittle issuing from her mouth and a bottle of pills from Schwab's at her bedside. Marilyn subsequently told business partner MILTON GREENE that Lytess found her with a melted sleeping pill in her mouth and then blew up the incident into a SUICIDE ATTEMPT to emphasize her heroic actions as a savior.

When Lytess moved home in early 1951 she was $1000 short on her mortgage (though in some accounts, Lytess required the money for a surgical procedure). Marilyn, who had moved back to her room at the BEVERLY CARLTON HOTEL, immediately took steps to remedy the situation. She raised the money by selling the mink stole Hyde had given her, possibly her most valuable possession. Lytess acknowledged, "She treasured nothing more than that stole. Yet she went out, sold it and came back and put $1,000 in my hand—to help me out of my difficulties."

Not long after this Lytess accompanied Marilyn on a trip to see her long-lost FATHER. This was neither the first nor last time that Marilyn sought (and won) sympathy from a person who filled an almost parental role in her life, by driving down to PALM SPRINGS in an unsuccessful attempt to make contact with C. STANLEY GIFFORD.

Marilyn briefly moved back in with Lytess in late 1951, sharing her Beverly Hills home at 611 NORTH CRESCENT DRIVE during the making of DON'T BOTHER TO KNOCK. They worked together intensely to prepare her for Marilyn's first starring role, as a psychotic babysitter. Director ROY BAKER was thankful, as budget constraints during filming meant he for many scenes he had to make do with first-take material.

In 1952, when Marilyn began dating JOE DIMAGGIO, Natasha, who according to Marilyn had always been jealous of the men she saw, saw the ball player as an enemy: "I disliked him at once. He is a man with a closed, vapid look. Marilyn introduced us and said I was her coach, which made no impression on him. A week later I telephoned her and Joe answered: 'I think if you want to talk to Miss Monroe'—Miss Monroe!—'you'd better call her agent.'" Joe disliked Lytess just as much. Marilyn attempted to make peace between the two people closest to her, but it was to no avail. Lytess apparently warned Marilyn, "This man is the punishment of God in your life."

In their working relationship, a pattern was developing as directors rebelled against Lytess's presence during shooting. Lytess was banned from the set by FRITZ LANG (director of CLASH BY NIGHT, 1952) and HOWARD HAWKS (director of GENTLEMEN PREFER BLONDES, 1953), only to return within a short space of time, to coax her frightened charge before the cameras. Lytess wrote, "Her habit of looking at me the second she finished a scene was to become a joke in projection rooms... The film of the daily rushes was filled with scenes of Marilyn, finishing her dialogue and immediately shading her eyes to find me, to see if she had done well." The only director who regarded Lytess as an ally was BILLY WILDER: "Without Natasha, there would be nothing."

By 1953, after Marilyn's work on HOW TO MARRY A MILLIONAIRE, the relationship seemed to some to be more vital to the coach than to the pupil. Co-star ALEX D'ARCY said, "Natasha was really advising her badly, justifying her own presence on the set by requiring take after take and simply feeding on Marilyn's insecurity. 'Well, that was all right, dear,' she often said to Marilyn, 'but maybe we should do it one more time.'" As with her previous pictures at Fox, the moment came when the director lost his patience with the countless retakes required until Natasha gave her approval, and the drama coach was banned from the set. The next day Marilyn failed to show, claiming an attack of bronchitis. Marilyn's agent CHARLES FELDMAN told the studio point blank, "Monroe cannot do a picture without her," and Lytess was rehired and given a bonus package.

Similar problems recurred with OTTO PREMINGER on RIVER OF NO RETURN (1954); to his intense irritation, the director found that Marilyn would only listen to her drama coach, who forced her to speak her lines with, as he said, "grave ar-tic-yew-lay-shun."

By the time Marilyn married DiMaggio she saw very little of Lytess outside of work. Still, in mid-1954, she had Lytess by her side during shooting of THERE'S NO BUSINESS LIKE SHOW BUSINESS (1954). Lytess was on hand to comfort Marilyn when Joe became violent after suspecting she was having an affair with voice coach HAL SCHAEFER. Marilyn sought to repay this support by getting Natasha a further salary hike, which the studio turned down but, as before, recanted.

In late 1954 Marilyn's plans for the new year were out with the old and in with the new. She moved to New York to rebuild her life after Joe; her new life included a new drama guru, LEE STRASBERG, at the ACTORS STUDIO. In her haste to turn over a new leaf, she failed to say anything to Natasha. In February 1956 Lytess learned that Marilyn had flown back into town to start shooting on BUS STOP. Lytess had been replaced by PAULA STRASBERG as Marilyn's on-set mentor; no longer protected by Marilyn, Twentieth Century-Fox was preparing to dump her. Lytess made a number of desperate attempts to get in touch with her former pupil—in the first week alone, more than a dozen phone calls and hand-delivered letters. Marilyn had her LAWYER Irving Stein call Natasha to tell her to stop bothering his client. Natasha told Stein, "My only protection in the world is Marilyn Monroe. I created this girl—I fought for her... I am her private property, she knows that. Her faith and security are mine." Marilyn was not moved, not even when two days later Natasha turned up at Marilyn's rented home. Agent LEW WASSERMAN answered the door and prevented her from entering. Natasha saw Marilyn looking down impassively from a second floor window.

Not long before she died from cancer in 1964, Lytess gave her final view on their relationship: "I wish I had one-tenth of Marilyn's cleverness. The truth is, my life and my feelings were very much in her hands. I was the older one, the teacher, but she knew the depth of my attachment to her, and she exploited those feelings as only a beautiful younger person can. She said she was the needy one. Alas, it was the reverse. My life with her was a constant denial of myself."

M

## MacLaine, Shirley
(b. 1934, Shirley MacLean Beatty)

Plucked from a career as a dancer on Broadway, MacLaine's career as an actress began in 1955, when she took on the first of her impish girl roles.

A number of memorable MacLaine roles were originally offered to Marilyn—*Some Came Running* (1958), *Can-Can* (1959), MacLaine's Oscar-nominated performance in the Billy Wilder movie *Irma La Douce* (1963), and *What a Way to Go* (1964), which Marilyn had been planning to do after *Something's Got to Give*. Incidentally, MacLaine was one of the actresses Twentieth Century-Fox bosses unsuccessfully tried to interest in replacing Marilyn after she was fired from the production.

## Madison Square Garden
4 Penn Plaza, New York

Marilyn twice stole the show at this famous New York venue.

Her Madison Square Garden debut, on March 30, 1955, could not have been more dramatic. As part of an evening's benefit for the Arthritis and Rheumatism Foundation arranged by Mike Todd and his circus, Marilyn made a breathtaking entrance on a pink elephant named Karnaudi. Just before she was due to go on, last-minute adjustments needed to be made to Marilyn's costume after part of it came undone and jabbed her in the bottom.

Milton Berle emceed the evening's proceedings. As Marilyn rode into the ring, he announced, "Here comes the only girl in the world who makes Jane Russell look like a boy!" The crowd of 18,000 roared in delight. A week later Marilyn commented on the experience to TV presenter Edward R. Murrow: "It meant a lot to me because I'd never been to the circus as a kid."

The second time Marilyn performed at the Garden was on May 19, 1962, when she sang "Happy Birthday" to John F. Kennedy at a gala fund-raising evening attended by 17,000 Democratic supporters and a star-studded cast, all of whom, including Marilyn, had paid $1,000 to attend.

Marilyn makes her entrance in Madison Square Garden riding an elephant named Karnaudi, 1955.

Marilyn with Maf Honey, 1961.

This trip to New York had a number of unforeseen repercussions for Marilyn. Twentieth Century-Fox chiefs back in Los Angeles were outraged that she had appeared in New York after missing a week's shooting on *Something's Got to Give* by claiming illness. Within days they informed her that she had been fired.

Another consequence was decades of speculation that this occasion was chosen by JFK to end their alleged long-term relationship, and step aside for younger brother Bobby.

## Maf Honey

White poodle given to Marilyn by either Frank Sinatra, publicist Pat Newcomb, or by an unnamed friend who wanted her to have some loving company after she was released from a psychiatric hospital in 1961.

In the Sinatra version, Marilyn named the dog in honor of Sinatra's Mafia connections. Newcomb proponents suggest that she obtained the dog from a client of hers, Natalie Wood, whose mother was a poodle breeder.

After Marilyn died the dog went to live with Sinatra's secretary Gloria Lovell. This would seem to support the Sinatra version, though it is also said that Lovell had been a neighbor of Marilyn's in 1961 when she lived at Doheny Drive, so they may have made the arrangement independently of him.

## Mafia

One strand of speculation in Marilyn's death involves Frank Sinatra, Sam Giancana, and an assorted cast of wiretappers and heavies. It has also been claimed that Marilyn had links, through Frank Sinatra, with gangster Bugsy Seigel.

(*see* Conspiracy)

## Magazines

Marilyn's first step in her show business career was as a model. Hostess jobs led to magazine work, and magazine work brought covers. Norma Jeane's first cover was a David Conover photograph which appeared in *Yank* magazine in 1945—or in some accounts, in *Douglas Air Review* in January 1946. Her first national cover was an André De Dienes photograph published in the April 26, 1946 issue of *Family Circle*. This opened the floodgates, and that year she appeared on anywhere up to thirty-six covers in the U.S.—depending on who is telling the story—including *Peek*, *See*, *U.S. Camera*, *Parade*, *Glamorous Models*, *Personal Romances*, *Pageant*, *Salute*, and *Laff*. It took hundreds of cheesecake photographs to become a favorite pin-up, but Marilyn stayed the course until her film career took off.

Throughout her life and beyond, Marilyn has continued to be featured on magazine covers. New sex symbols have come and gone, but Marilyn is still to be found peering at her fans from magazine racks around the globe.

**American Weekly, The**
Magazine to which Marilyn twice gave long and revealing interviews. On November 16, 1952, under her own byline, Marilyn placed an article entitled "The Truth about Me." Three years later, in late September 1955, Maurice Zolotow wrote a series of articles which he later expanded into his 1960 biography *Marilyn Monroe*.

**Collier's**
The first national U.S. magazine to publish a feature on Marilyn, in its September 8, 1951 issue. In his introduction to "Hollywood's 1951 Model Blonde," journalist Robert Cahn writes, "She's filmdom's Marilyn Monroe; Miss Cheesecake to GIs, whistlebait in the studios—and an actress on her way up. . . . Marilyn Monroe is not a girl anyone quickly forgets."

**Cosmopolitan**
Marilyn made the cover in May 1953. She also gave interviews which have been widely quoted over the years, particularly the 1960 article "Marilyn Monroe: The Sex Symbol vs. The Good Wife."

**Eros**
A short-lived adult magazine which launched in late 1962 with photographs of Marilyn, in an unsuccessful attempt to mimic the success of *Playboy*, another magazine that led its first issue with the nation's hottest sex symbols.

**Esquire**
In life and death Marilyn frequently featured in this magazine. Arthur Miller's original short story, which he developed into *The Misfits* (1961), was first published here.

**Family Circle**
This wholesome magazine gave budding model Norma Jeane one of her first (some biographers say her very first) magazine covers. On its April 26, 1946 issue she poses in a long old-fashioned country dress, clasping a newborn lamb in her hands.

**Focus**
A cover for Marilyn in December 1951, and an article correctly prophesizing that "she bids fair to outstrip Betty Grable, June Haver, and Rita Hayworth as the most sexciting glamour girl on the 20th Century lot."

***Life***
Marilyn's first appearance in *Life* was on October 10, 1949, as one of Hollywood's aspiring stars photographed by PHILIPPE HALSMAN.

Marilyn knew she had hit the big time when she featured on the *Life* cover on April 7, 1952, clad in an off-the-shoulder white gown. The caption ran "Marilyn Monroe: The Talk of Hollywood," and inside she was described as "naïve and guileless but smart enough to have known how to make a success in the cutthroat world of glamour." The photo feature, by Halsman, showed Marilyn at work (vamping it up for the camera) and at rest in her own apartment.

Marilyn's last major interview was with RICHARD MERYMAN for *Life* in 1962. Quotes from this article feature prominently in the vast majority of Marilyn biographies, as if it were her last testament.

Two weeks after her death, *Life* ran a tribute to Marilyn: "Her death has diminished the loveliness of the world in which we live."

The only actress to rack up more *Life* covers than Marilyn was AUDREY HEPBURN, who made nine. For the duration of Marilyn's career, *Life* ran two or three features a year on her.

### MARILYN'S *LIFE* COVERS

April 7, 1952, photographed by Philippe Halsman

Marilyn covered only by her first four national magazine covers in 1946. This Blue Book Modeling publicity stunt inspired a fury of photographs that appeared all over the world.

July, 1953.

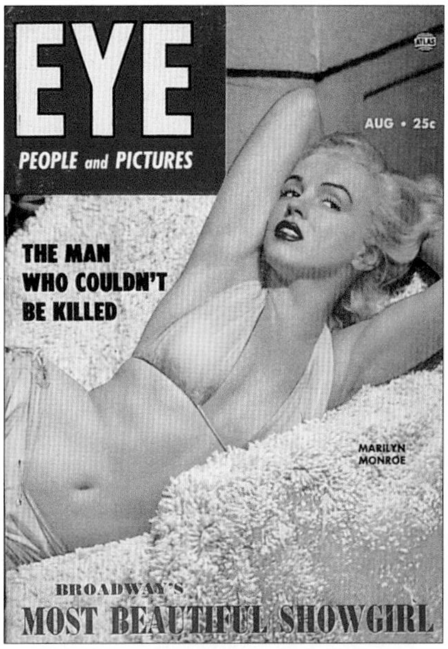


August, 1953.

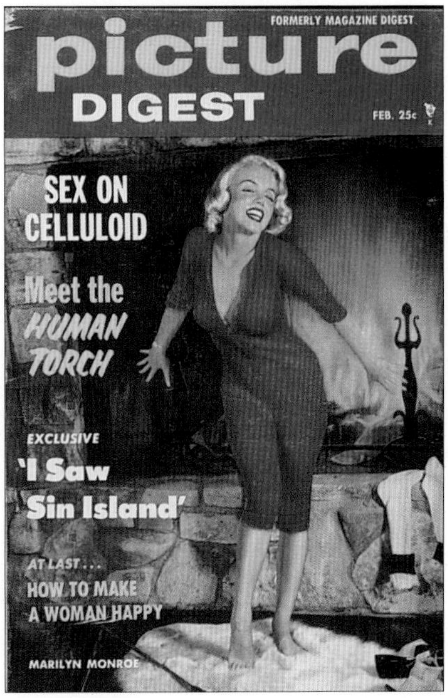


February, 1956.

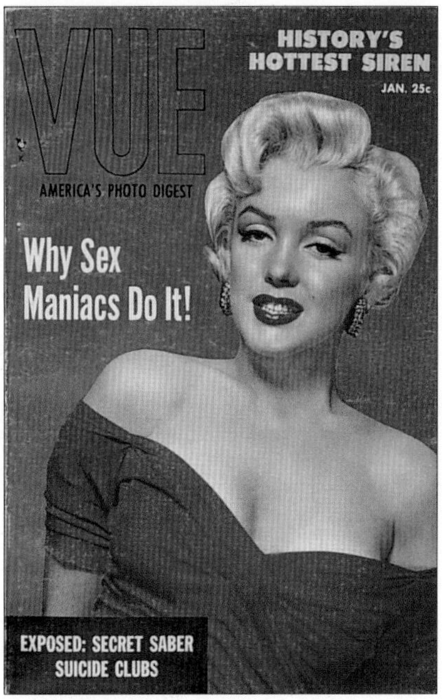


January, 1957.

Note that Marilyn is wearing the same yellow bathing suit on the *Eye* and *Photo* magazine covers from 1953. At that time, models had to supply their own outfits and Marilyn was fond of her yellow bikini.

May 25, 1953, (with Jane Russell) photographed by Edward Clark
April 20, 1959, photographed by Richard Avedon
November 9, 1959, photographed by Philippe Halsman
August 15, 1960, (with Yves Montand) photographed by John Bryson
June 22, 1962, photographed by Lawrence Schiller and William Read Woodfield
August 7, 1964, photographed by Milton H. Greene
September 8, 1972, photographed by Eve Arnold

See Marilyn's *Life* covers at:
http://pathfinder.com/@@ssOmgAYAt0HIlDGX/Life/covers

***Look***
Marilyn was a favorite in this widely read magazine starting in 1950. Her appearances brought her more than FAME. Two important business relationships developed with people who were sent to cover her. RUPERT ALLAN, who wrote the first piece on her, later became her publicist. And in 1953 the magazine sent a young photographer named MILTON H. GREENE. Two years later, Greene held a 49 percent stake in MARILYN MONROE PRODUCTIONS, her independent film company.

### MARILYN'S *LOOK* COVERS

October 23, 1951
June 3, 1952
September 9, 1952
June 30, 1953
November 17, 1953
July 5, 1960

***Newsweek***
Unlike *Time* magazine, *Newsweek* never featured Marilyn on its cover during her lifetime. The magazine made up for this ten years after her death.

***Paris-Match***
Head of the New York bureau of this magazine, MARA SCHERBATOFF, died in a car accident while tracking Marilyn and Arthur Miller on their WEDDING day. When Marilyn died, the magazine published a thirty-six-page tribute to her.

***Photoplay***
On her promotional tour for *LOVE HAPPY* (1950), Marilyn did some publicity shots for *Photoplay*'s "Dream House" feature. She was photographed improbably wielding a vacuum cleaner.

Marilyn featured in a Fredda Dudley article called "How a Star is Born," the first of the magazine's numerous articles about Hollywood's most popular star of the fifties. In March 1953 the magazine also featured an article entitled "Marilyn Monroe Was My Wife," written by former husband JAMES DOUGHERTY.

At the start of her career the magazine effectively championed her cause by twice giving her prestigious film awards (see also individual entry).

***Playboy***
Marilyn's infamous "Golden Dreams" calendar shots were published as the men's magazine's first "Sweetheart of the Month" centerfold in its inaugural December 1953 issue. HUGH HEFNER, who paid $500 for the privilege, must have looked on in amazement as, rather than Marilyn's career being destroyed because she had posed nude, she was celebrated for her honesty and held up as an example of how hard work could lead to success despite adversity.

The magazine paid fifty times the original price in 1962 for LAWRENCE SCHILLER's nude photographs of Marilyn, taken on the pool set of *SOMETHING'S GOT TO GIVE*. Marilyn initially agreed to pose in nothing but a white stole for the front cover of the issue these pictures were scheduled to run in, but then, in her last week alive, she changed her mind. The magazine ran the nudes in January 1964.

As an homage to Marilyn after her death, in October 1962 the magazine introduced a buxom blonde cartoon character, "Little Annie Fanny," created by artists Harvey Kurtzman and Wil Elder. In 1987 the magazine published previously unseen nudes taken by illustrator EARL MORAN in 1946.

*Playboy* continues to feature Marilyn articles and photographs in the U.S. and around the world, and Marilyn's popularity as a sex symbol still refuses to wane. In late 1998 Marilyn beat the stiffest competition (Sophia Loren, Elizabeth Taylor, Madonna, Jean Harlow, Pamela Anderson) to be crowned the sexist female star of the twentieth century, topping a list of one hundred sensuous women.

***Redbook***
In July 1952 Marilyn had a letter to the editor published in this women's magazine. Less than a year later she picked up the magazine's award for "Best Young Box Office Personality."

***Stars and Stripes***
During her MODELING days and into her movie career, Marilyn was a regular in this magazine for US servicemen, particularly in the early 1950s. So popular was she that she featured on the front cover on every single issue of 1952. Not surprisingly, when it came to the magazine's annual awards for the best cheesecake around, Marilyn was a repeated winner.

***Time***
Marilyn had one cover in her lifetime (May 14, 1956) and dozens of articles since mid-1952 in this news magazine.

***Variety***
Marilyn's first mention in the movie trade magazine was on September 5, 1946, when still as Norma Jeane Dougherty she appeared under the "New Contracts" column.

***Vogue***
In its tribute following Marilyn's death, *Vogue* noted, "She has given a warm delight to millions of people, made them smile affectionately, laugh uproariously, love her to the point of caring deeply—often aggressively—about her personal happiness."

BOOKS:

*Marilyn Monroe unCovers*, Clark Kidder and Madison Daniels. Alberta, Canada: Quon Editions, 1994.
An anthology of vintage Marilyn Monroe covers.

*Marilyn Monroe: The Life, The Myth*, Giovanni Brambilla Battista. New York: Rizzoli International, 1996.
Contains many photos of Marilyn-cover magazines.

## MAGNUM GROUP

The Magnum Group had an exclusive contract to shoot stills during the making of *THE MISFITS* (1960). EVE ARNOLD worked throughout the two month shoot, and was joined on a revolving basis by HENRI CARTIER-BRESSON, BRUCE DAVIDSON, ELLIOT ERWITT, Ernest Haas, PHILIPPE HALSMAN, Erich Hartmann, Bob Henriques, INGE MORATH, and Dennis Stock.

BOOK:

*Magnum Cinema, Photographs from Fifty Years of Moviemaking*, Alain Bergala. London, England: Phaidon, 1995.
Contains twenty-six pictures from *The Misfits*.

## MAIDS/HOUSEKEEPERS

For the first half of her career Marilyn lived most of the time in HOTELS.

In New York, the first time she had a home for more than a year was the Fifty-seventh Street apartment she shared with husband ARTHUR MILLER. Fanny Harris and LENA PEPITONE and, in some reports, a woman named Hazel Washington, all served as maids and cleaners—Washington was hired by TWENTIETH CENTURY-FOX as part of Marilyn's contract. Other names of maids noted in passing are Hattie Stevenson and Florence Thomas.

In Marilyn's final home, FIFTH HELENA DRIVE in Brentwood, Los Angeles, EUNICE MURRAY was hired on the recommendation of DR. RALPH GREENSON to organize Marilyn's home affairs.

## MAILER, NORMAN (B. 1923)

MARILYN:
"He's too impressed by power, in my opinion."

MAILER ON MARILYN:
"[She] was blonde and beautiful and had a sweet little rinky-dink of a voice and all the cleanliness of all clean American backyards. She was our angel, the sweet angel of sex."

Mailer's first novel, *The Naked and the Dead* (1948) drew on his World War II experiences and made him one of the leading writers of his generation. When Marilyn moved to the East Coast in 1955, Mailer's curiosity led him to seek a meeting.

Although he had lived in the same brownstone in BROOKLYN as ARTHUR MILLER, and owned a house not far from Miller's country retreat in ROXBURY, Connecticut, and although he tried hard to meet Marilyn, she was evidently not interested. Miller reports that the one time Marilyn agreed to invite Mailer to a party, it was on an occasion that she knew he would be unable to attend.

Drawing on his innovative way of blending fact and fiction that had brought him the Pulitzer Prize for *Armies of the Night* (1968), in 1973 Mailer published a fictionalized biography of Marilyn. This project was commissioned originally by photographer LAWRENCE SCHILLER to run alongside his anthology of Marilyn photos. The book was an enormous success—but not with Miller, who regarded the Marilyn depicted by Mailer as actually being a version of Mailer in drag, a young whore who came out with great one-liners. Miller writes this is exactly how Marilyn would have hated to appear, "as a kind of joke taking herself seriously."

Mailer's Marilyn infatuation continued, unabated, for the next decade and a half. As he writes (the third person refers to himself), "The secret ambition, after all, had been to steal Marilyn; in all his vanity he thought no one was so well suited to bring out the best in her as himself, a conceit which fifty million other men may also have held."

In 1980 he published *Of Women and Their Elegance*, an "imaginary diary" of Marilyn's time staying with MILTON and AMY GREENE. Then in 1985 he cast his own daughter Kate as the lead in his Marilynesque play *Strawhead*, which ran for two weeks at the ACTORS STUDIO.

BOOKS:

*Marilyn*, photobook ed. Lawrence Schiller, biography by Norman Mailer. New York: Grosset and Dunlap, 1973.

*Of Women and Their Elegance*, Norman Mailer text and Milton Greene photos New York: Simon & Schuster, 1980.

## MANKIEWICZ, JOSEPH L. (1909–1993)

"Marilyn was the most frightened little girl. And yet scared as she was, she had this strange effect when she was photographed. . . . In fact, the camera loved her."

Joseph L. Mankiewicz and Marilyn between takes of *All About Eve* (1950).

Mankiewicz worked his way through every job in the industry before, at the age of thirty-five, finally being allowed to direct. His movies often focused on a strong and ironic central character, as in ALL ABOUT EVE (1950), a double Oscar winner (script and direction), in which Marilyn had a small but strategically important part as Miss Caswell, "a graduate of the Copacabana school of acting."

JOHNNY HYDE's ceaseless promotion of starlet Marilyn prompted him to knock on Mankiewicz's door before he had even finished writing *All About Eve* (1950). The writer/director was won over when he auditioned Marilyn. He took her on, he later wrote, because she "had done a good job for John Huston [and had a] breathlessness and sort of glued-on innocence right for the part."

On the set, Mankiewicz found that Marilyn required an inordinate number of takes—up to twenty-five for one particular scene. He also recalled Marilyn the starlet as being incredibly solitary and lonely. Even when the cast and crew invited her to join them for a drink or a meal, she kept her own timid company.

Other notable Mankiewicz movies are *A Letter for Three Wives* (1949), *Five Fingers* (1952), *The Barefoot Contessa* (1954), and *Cleopatra* (1963), the movie whose cost overruns threatened to sink Fox at the time that Marilyn was fired from her final movie.

Before walking out on Fox in late 1954, Marilyn unsuccessfully tried for a role in *Guys and Dolls* (1955). But, Mankiewicz wanted to retain Vivian Blaine as Adelaide—the role Marilyn was interested in—after her Broadway triumph in the original stage play.

## MANSFIELD, JAYNE
(1932–1967, B. VERA JAYNE PALMER)

Marilyn RIVAL Jayne Mansfield was heavily promoted by TWENTIETH CENTURY-FOX as "Marilyn Monroe King-Size" as the studio tried to fill the hole left by Marilyn walking out on her contract in 1955. Former beauty queen Mansfield had scored success on Broadway in *Will Success Spoil Rock Hunter?*, playing a character who was Marilyn in all details but name, before Fox signed her up. This was the culmination of Mansfield's master plan, to retrace Marilyn's footsteps from poor beginnings, to the BLUE BOOK MODELING AGENCY, SCREEN TESTS, nude photographs and, according to some sources, a similar experience to Marilyn's with the Lawford and Kennedy crowd.

By 1957 Mansfield was up there, big on screen all over the country in *The Girl Can't Help It* and a film version of *Will Success Spoil Rock Hunter?*

Fox's publicity department worked overtime to convey Mansfield's Marilyn-beating credentials (apart from 40-24-36 measurements). She appeared on film in the gold lamé dress Marilyn had worn to such devastating effect in *GENTLEMAN PREFER BLONDES* (1953), and she featured on the JACK BENNY show, just like Marilyn had done, to perform the exact same sketch.

The Hollywood blondes met up on at least one occasion. Both were at the post-premiere party for *The Rose Tattoo* (for which Anna Magnani won an Oscar), held at the Astor Hotel, New York on December 2, 1955. Photographs from this event show Marilyn giving Mansfield a frosty look.

After Marilyn's death, Mansfield was quoted as saying, "They probably expect me to do that someday, but they don't know me well enough to know it couldn't happen." By the time of her death, in a car accident on June 29, 1967, Mansfield's star was on the wane.

## MAPES HOTEL, THE
30 NORTH VIRGINIA STREET, RENO, NEVADA

RENO hotel where the company of *THE MISFITS* (1961) was billeted for several months, taking up more than half of the hotel's rooms. Marilyn joined ARTHUR MILLER in room 614 on July 20, 1960. By the time they moved out to the nearby Holiday Hotel in town, it was to separate rooms as their marriage unraveled.

## MARCH, DAVID

A friend of Marilyn's who in 1952 not only found her temporary accommodation in a house on Hilldale Avenue, West Hollywood, but is generally credited for acting as go-between with an interested party named JOE DIMAGGIO. In some accounts March was trying to land Marilyn as a client (he was a business manager) so when he ran into Joe, who was trying to woo Marilyn, he set up a date at the Villa Nova RESTAURANT.

Jayne Mansfield and Marilyn Monroe at the premiere for *The Rose Tattoo*, 1955.

However, in alternative versions of how Marilyn met Joe, it was an unnamed studio friend of Marilyn's who invited both of them to join a party of people at the Villa Nova.

## MARCH, FREDERIC
(1897–1975, B. FREDERICK MCINTYRE BICKEL)

Reputedly, the original owner of a WHITE PIANO that GLADYS BAKER bought her daughter Norma Jeane during the all too brief period, from 1933 to 1934, when mother and child lived together on ARBOL STREET in Hollywood.

March's acting career ran from 1929 to 1973, including two Oscars for *Dr. Jekyll and Mr. Hyde* (1952) and *The Best Years of our Lives* (1946). He also starred in the original version of *A Star Is Born* (1937).

March acted in *Middle of the Night* (1959), a film Marilyn discussed doing, and was one of the actors being lined up for an abandoned project to remake Somerset Maugham's *Rain*.

## MARILYNISMS

Q: Do you wear underwear?
Marilyn: "I'm buying a kimono tomorrow."
Q: Is your walk natural?
Marilyn: "I've been walking since I was six months old."
Q: "What kind of fur are you wearing?
Marilyn: "Fox, and not the 20th Century kind."
"Lee [Strasberg] says I have to start with myself, and I say, 'With *me*?' Well, I'm not so important! Who does he think I am, Marilyn Monroe or something?"

Despite Marilyn's anxiety before an audience and her unease at press conferences, she had a sharp way with words and a real knack for disarming hostile questions. Though some of her responses were undoubtedly scripted or suggested, either by studio publicists such as HARRY BRAND, or friends (SIDNEY SKOLSKY drafted more than one of Marilyn's written replies to hostile accusations), the vast number of Marilynisms scattered through these pages are ample proof of what ARTHUR MILLER described as her "insouciance and wit."

(*see* QUOTES)

## MARILYN MONROE PRODUCTIONS

In 1954 Marilyn finally had enough of mediocre sex-role typecasting and a salary pegged to just $1500 per week, many times lower than the vast majority of her colleagues. In November she divorced JOE DIMAGGIO, and in December, after months of planning with MILTON GREENE, she left for New York and put the finishing touches to her brainchild, Marilyn Monroe Productions.

The world learned of the formation of Marilyn Monroe Productions on January 7, 1955, when a public statement was read out to eighty journalists and friends at the East Sixty-fourth Street home of LAWYER Frank Delaney—the only notable PRESS absentees were "hostile" columnists DOROTHY KILGALLEN and WALTER WINCHELL. Marilyn was appointed company president, with Greene named vice president; 51 percent belonged to Marilyn, the remaining 49 percent to Greene.

To celebrate the launch, Marilyn took the Greenes and their pals to see FRANK SINATRA's show at the Copacabana night club. The fact that it had been sold out for weeks was no problem, the management fitted in an extra table by the stage. In some reports, the party continued at MARLENE DIETRICH's apartment.

A few months later Marilyn explained on live national TV—EDWARD R. MURROW's "Person to Person" show—exactly why she had taken this step: "It's not that I object to doing musicals and comedies—in fact, I rather enjoy them—but I'd like to do dramatic parts too."

In going it alone, Marilyn was single-handedly taking on the all-powerful studio system. The immediate reaction at TWENTIETH CENTURY-FOX was outrage. She was sued by the studio, mocked by colleagues, and vilified by the press.

Meanwhile, Marilyn began what would turn out to be a sabbatical year. She stayed with the Greenes, lived in the WALDORF ASTORIA when in New York City, began studying with LEE STRASBERG, and went into PSYCHOANALYSIS. Greene dedicated himself to personally bankrolling the company's asset (Marilyn), generating movie projects, and working with the team of lawyers led by Delaney, who were renegotiating Marilyn's contract with Fox.

It took a full year of negotiations before the fledgling company was in a position to announce that it had struck a revised nonexclusive deal with the studio. The huge success of *THE SEVEN YEAR ITCH* (1955) the previous summer considerably strengthened Marilyn Monroe Productions' hand, and Marilyn beat the Fox into submission. Her new deal brought a check for past earnings, a new salary of $100,000 for four movies over a seven year period, and approval over all major aspects of her productions. Her victory created one of the first breaches in the Hollywood studio system.

Marilyn Monroe Productions pressed ahead with two projects, *BUS STOP* (1956) for Fox, and its first (and only) independent production, *THE PRINCE AND THE SHOWGIRL* (1957).

Undoubtedly the fact that she was president of her own production company gave Marilyn far more power than most actresses at the time. For a start, in her new Fox contract she had script, director, and cinematographer approval. Less positive was an occasional attitude of superiority, now that she was the boss. During filming on *Bus Stop* Marilyn was less than friendly to her fellow actors, and some of her behavior was report-

A 1956 issue of *Screen Stories* magazine announces Marilyn's "come-back" in the first film from Marilyn Monroe Productions, *Bus Stop*.

Photograph by Milton Greene, 1953.

edly close to paranoia—she was convinced that male lead DON MURRAY would make her look stupid, or that young co-star HOPE LANGE would make her look old and dowdy.

Through 1956 relations between the company's two shareholders slowly but surely deteriorated. Marilyn's new husband ARTHUR MILLER wanted to make his own contribution to his wife's future business plans, and Marilyn began to feel that Greene was not worth his share of her earnings.

Before the release of *The Prince and the Showgirl* in April 1957, Marilyn issued a statement claiming that Greene had been mismanaging the company and conducting secret negotiations without her knowledge. Marilyn proposed to bring in a new Board of Directors. Five days later Marilyn replaced the company lawyers with Arthur Miller's own legal advisor Robert H. Montgomery, his brother-in-law George Kupchik, and friend George Levine.

Milton Greene publically responded in the *Los Angeles Times*: "It seems that Marilyn doesn't want to go ahead with the program we planned. I'm getting lawyers to represent me, I don't want to do anything now to hurt her career."

Marilyn's counterstatement was far less conciliatory, accusing Greene of giving himself false credits: "My company was not formed merely to parcel out 49.6 percent of all my earnings to Mr Green, but to make better pictures, improve my work, and secure my income."

Marilyn Monroe Productions made no more movies, though it continued to exist for tax purposes to handle Marilyn's earnings. This ultimately led to problems with the tax authorities, which had, from the company's foundation, suspected that Marilyn had created the company purely for purposes of creative accounting.

Dean Martin and Marilyn on the set of *Something's Got to Give*, 1962.

## MARILYN MONROE THEATER
7932 SANTA MONICA BLVD,
WEST HOLLYWOOD, CALIFORNIA

West Coast branch of the LEE STRASBERG Theater Institute.

## MARILYN SIX, THE
(ALSO KNOWN AS THE MONROE SIX)

A group of avid New York-based Monroe FANS who would congregate around Marilyn's hotel every time she was in town. John Reilly, Gloria Milone, Eileen and Jimmy Collins, Edith Pitts, and Frieda Hull would tip each other off about her arrival, and they were always present whenever she was scheduled to make an appearance. Among themselves they referred to her as "Mazzie." During the years Marilyn lived in New York, they shadowed her like guardian angels. Marilyn once invited these number one fans of hers to her country house at ROXBURY for a picnic.

## MARRIAGE

Marilyn's models for marriage were all wholly unsuccessful. Growing up she had seen failed marriages, DIVORCES, unhappy marriages, marriages where the man had simply disappeared, sham marriages, and marriages of great emotional dishonesty. Her grandmother DELLA MAE HOGAN, her mother GLADYS BAKER, legal guardian GRACE MCKEE GODDARD, foster parent ANA LOWER, and great aunt IDA MARTIN were all women whose husbands either left them or died.

Marilyn once summed up her marriage to JOE DIMAGGIO as "a sort of crazy, difficult friendship with sexual privileges. Later I learned that's what marriages often are."

(*see* WEDDINGS *and husbands* JAMES DOUGHERTY, JOE DIMAGGIO, and ARTHUR MILLER.)

## MARTIN, DEAN
(1917–1995, B. DINO PAUL CROCETTI)

Crooning lead Martin made his name in the fifties in a double act with JERRY LEWIS, before going on to a solo career in the sixties that ranked him with fellow RAT PACK member FRANK SINATRA. These films included *The Stooge* (1952), *Pardners* (1956), *Rio Bravo* (1959), *Kiss Me Stupid* (1964), and many more.

Marilyn and Martin almost worked together on *Some Came Running* (1958). After Marilyn moved back to Los Angeles in 1961, she saw a lot of Martin and his wife Jeanne.

Martin became involved in *SOMETHING'S GOT TO GIVE* after Marilyn picked him; in some reports he had invested a personal stake in the production. Martin gallantly stood up for his friend after she was dismissed by TWENTIETH CENTURY-FOX. The studio hired LEE REMICK as Marilyn's replacement, but Martin invoked a clause in his contract allowing him approval of his opposite number, and informed the studio that he would not work with anyone except Marilyn on this picture. Fox sued Martin, Martin sued Fox, and then the picture was put back on track, to no small degree because of Martin's intransigence and support for Marilyn.

After Marilyn was reinstated on the picture, Martin and Marilyn discussed at least two future projects, a comedy called *I Love Louisa*, and an unnamed heist movie to involve the Rat Pack crew.

## MARTIN, IDA

In his biography, DONALD SPOTO writes that after Norma Jeane was taken out of the ORPHANAGE, legal guardian GRACE MCKEE GODDARD placed the girl with distant relative Ida Martin, who lived in Compton, between November 1937 and August 1938.

Martin was the mother of Olive Brunings, who had married Norma Jeane's uncle (Gladys's brother MARION MONROE). Marion and Ida had three children: Jack in 1925; Ida Mae in 1927; and Olive in 1929. Months after the youngest was born, MARION MONROE told his wife he was going out to buy a newspaper, and that was the last his family saw of him. He was officially pronounced dead ten years later.

At the time Norma Jeane lived with her great-aunt by marriage, Ida was also looking after her three grandchildren, all around Norma Jeane's age, while their mother Olive was working as a migrant farmhand. Ida Mae recalled Norma Jeane often said she was never going to marry: "She said she was going to be a school teacher and have lots of dogs."

During her stay with Ida Martin, an older cousin is said to have sexually assaulted Marilyn (so she told friends BEBE GODDARD and NORMAN ROSTEN, among others). Ida Mae reported that for days afterward Norma Jeane bathed obsessively. Grace Goddard took Norma Jeane back to Los Angeles, this time placing her with her aunt, ANA LOWER.

## MARX, GROUCHO
(1890–1977, B. JULIUS HENRY MARX)

A vaudeville clan under their mother's guidance, the Marx brothers were the kings of zany comedy from *Animal Crackers* (1930), *Horse Feathers* (1932), and *Duck Soup* (1932). When producer LESTER COWAN was casting for the last of the Marx brother's films, *LOVE HAPPY* (1950), Groucho was in on the auditions. The man of a thousand ripostes (such as "They say a man is as old as the woman he feels"), Groucho told the three hopeful actresses that he was looking for "a young lady who can walk by me in such a manner as to arouse my elderly libido,

Marilyn and Groucho Marx during filming of *Love Happy* (1950).

and cause smoke to issue from my ears." In Marilyn, he found her. His considered verdict? "Mae West, Theda Bara and Bo Peep rolled into one!"

Marx is quoted by biographer Richard Anobile as saying, "Boy, did I want to fuck her. She wore this dress with bare tits. . . . She was goddam beautiful. I may have tried to lay her once but I didn't get anywhere with her. . . . She was the most beautiful girl I ever saw in my life."

## MASTERS, GEORGE (1936–1998)

"My first meeting with Marilyn Monroe is etched in my memory. She was a mess. She was waiting for me in her suite at the Beverly Hills Hotel, the world's greatest sex symbol, in a terry cloth robe, one shoulder torn, her yellow hair hanging down around her neck, no makeup, and champagne and caviar everywhere."

"It took me hours to get her all pulled together. But eventually, when she was set to go—pow!""

One of Marilyn's favorite HAIR stylists in her last years, George Masters had styled and made up many of Hollywood's leading ladies.

His frank comments on what Marilyn was like when she was not "doing a Marilyn," and of the work it took to get her into her public persona, reveal a side of Marilyn her fans never suspected.

Masters accompanied Marilyn on her 1962 furniture buying (and conference giving) trip to MEXICO.

## MCKNIGHT, MARIAN

JOE DIMAGGIO never remarried after his DIVORCE from Marilyn, but apparently he came close in 1957 with Marian McKnight, a woman who bore a passing resemblance to Marilyn. McKnight capitalized on this resemblance in the talent competition of the MISS AMERICA pageant of that year, when she imitated Marilyn for the judges. Unbeknownst to her, DiMaggio was in the audience.

## MCPHERSON, AIMEE SEMPLE

Charismatic and dynamic American evangelist who founded the International Church of the Foursquare Gospel, where Marilyn was baptized on December 6, 1926.

After being converted by her first husband, Robert Semple, Aimee Semple became a Pentecostal evangelist and went on missionary work in Asia. She returned to the United States a widow, married Harold McPherson, settled in Los Angeles, and began to hold rallies which attracted a mass following. Among them was Marilyn's mother GLADYS BAKER, grandmother DELLA MAE HOGAN, and the BOLENDER FAMILY, who fostered young Norma Jeane until the age of seven. In 1923 Aimee opened her Angelus Temple, a 5,300-seat auditorium costing an enormous $1.5 million, funded by donations of her faithful. There she propagated the beliefs of her "foursquare movement,"

Joe DiMaggio's girlfriend after his divorce from Marilyn was Marian McKnight, winner of the Miss America pageant in 1957.

founded on her understanding of the four roles of Jesus Christ as "Redeemer, Great Physician, Baptizer with the Holy Spirit and Soon-Coming King."

McPherson's popularity was at one stage national, before scandal (including a rumored affair with Charlie Chaplin) reversed the church's expansion. She died in 1944, aged fifty-three, of an overdose of barbiturates.

## MEASUREMENTS

Marilyn's "vital statistics" as they were once called, naturally varied over the years. They also changed depending on who was giving out the numbers.

In 1945, when she signed up to the BLUE BOOK MODELING AGENCY, Norma Jeane declared:

height: 5' 5"
weight: 118 pounds
measurements: 36-24-34, size 12
hair color: medium blonde, "too curly to manage, recommend bleach and permanent"
eyes: blue and "perfect teeth"

In her first national feature in a 1951 issue of *Collier's* magazine, starlet Marilyn was billed as 37-23-34.

In her earliest STUDIO BIOGRAPHIES Marilyn's height is up by half an inch to 5' 5½", and, inexplicably, her date of birth was brought forwards to 1928. TWENTIETH CENTURY-FOX initially quoted her measurements at 36½-23-34, but by 1955 she was advertised as 38-23-36, a set of measurements corroborated by Marilyn's costume designer, WILLIAM TRAVILLA.

When filming *LET'S MAKE LOVE* (1960), Marilyn was a voluptuous size 16, and weighed around 140 lbs. Much has been written on the difference between the curvy Marilyn and today's waif models, but it should be remembered that because of changes to the way clothing sizes are calculated, a 16 in the fifties is equivalent to a size 12 (sometimes said to be 8) today. Marilyn took a U.S. size 7AA in shoes.

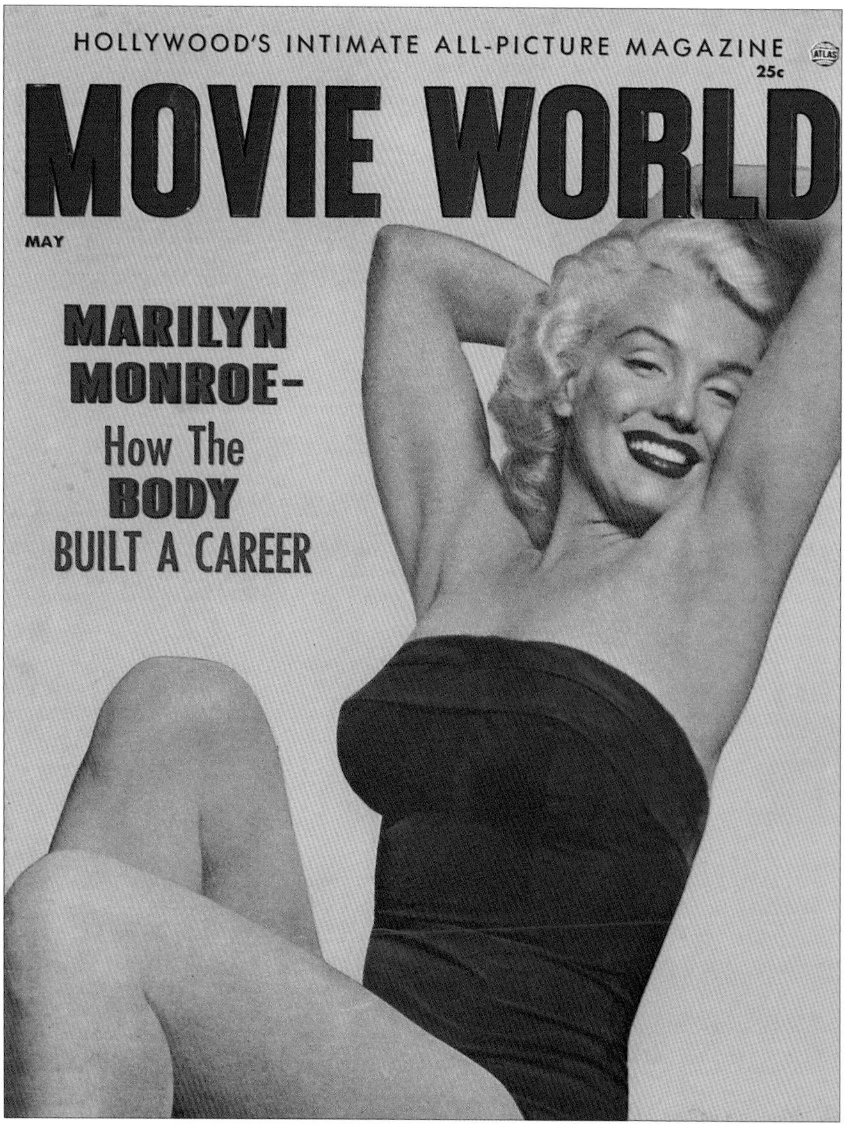


As the title of this article in the May, 1953 issue of *Movie World Magazine* notes, many moviegoers felt that Monroe's rise to stardom had everything to do with her extremely impressive measurements.

Even Marilyn's famous quip about using her measurements as her epitaph comes in different versions: it's either "Here lies Marilyn Monroe, 37-22-35" or "Here lies Marilyn Monroe, 38-23-36."

## MEDICAL HISTORY

Throughout her life Marilyn suffered recurring bronchial problems, and her gynecological troubles caused her pain and mental anguish as she found she was unable to conceive. She was in and out of HOSPITALS as many as five times a year towards the end of her life.

Little is recorded of Norma Jeane's childhood maladies, beyond a bout of whooping cough she had (at age five or seven, depending on accounts) when living with the BOLENDER FAMILY. This was serious enough for her mother to move in and care for her. Some biographers record she had a tonsillectomy.

Norma Jeane started menstruating in September 1938, at the age of twelve. Throughout her life Marilyn suffered debilitating menstrual pains and cramps. At the worst of times friends recall her sobbing in pain, writhing on the floor, and being incapacitated. Many years later, Marilyn inserted a clause into her contracts with TWENTIETH CENTURY-FOX excusing her from work during her periods. Gynecological problems dogged her life, including chronic endometriosis.

In 1946, while living temporarily in LAS VEGAS, Norma Jeane had her wisdom teeth removed, an operation that was followed by a mouth infection (trench mouth). Shortly afterward she contracted measles.

In some reports, in 1949 Marilyn contracted a condition of the inner ear called Ménière's disease, which results in nausea, dizziness, and irreversible partial hearing loss.

Marilyn was particularly susceptible to heavy colds which turned into bronchitis and, once, after entertaining the troops in sub-zero temperatures in KOREA, full-fledged pneumonia. Bronchitis or flu forced her to take time off filming many of her movies, including *A TICKET TO TOMAHAWK* (1950), *GENTLEMEN PREFER BLONDES* (1953), and *BUS STOP* (1956). Not surprisingly, she caught a chill during three hours standing bare-legged over an updraft for the skirt scene in *THE SEVEN YEAR ITCH* (1955). More often than not, film studio bosses believed she was malingering, using "convenient" illnesses like bronchitis to cover up for her failures to arrive at work.

Suspicious studio bosses were not always wrong. Marilyn was not averse to feigning illness or incapacity when she did not feel like doing something, or to elicit sympathy from people around her. One example was her "broken" ankle during filming of *RIVER OF NO RETURN* (1954), which halted filming though doctors could find nothing seriously wrong. On Marilyn's last film she took time off with laryngitis, only to be caught chatting with a friend.

In 1952 Marilyn visited surgeon Dr. Marcus Rabwin, who was to perform an appendectomy. Before being wheeled down to the operating theater, Marilyn had taped a note to her abdomen:

> "Dr Rabwin—most important to Read Before operation!
> Dear Dr. Rabwin,
> Cut as little as possible. I know it seems vain but that doesn't really enter into it. The fact that I'm a woman is important and means much to me.
> Save please (I can't ask you enough) what you can—I'm in your hands. You have children and you must know what it means—please Dr. Rabwin—I know somehow you will!
> Thank you—thank you—thank you. For Gods sake Dear Doctor No ovaries removed—please again do whatever you can to prevent large scars.
> Thanking you with all my heart
> Marilyn Monroe"

Marilyn already knew that her troublesome menstrual cycle may have indicated fertility problems. In 1954 she was told that a hysterectomy would provide relief from the severe pains. Marilyn refused point blank. According to AMY GREENE, "Marilyn was emphatic. She said, 'I can't do that. I want to have a child. I'm going to have a son.'"

On November 7, 1954 Marilyn checked in to Cedars of Lebanon Hospital in Los Angeles under surgeon Leon Krohn, "for correction of a female disorder she has suffered for years." The operation was to correct chronic endometriosis. Krohn operated on Marilyn seven years later for this same painful condition, and she underwent a third intervention just two weeks before she died.

From the early fifties, Marilyn's increasing use of DRUGS to combat anxiety and insomnia had repercussions on her general health, and on her ability to work. She suffered grogginess in the mornings, lack of focus, inability to learn and deliver lines, lateness, and a constant need for reassurance. The ravages of drug and alcohol abuse became apparent in later life: when she didn't have any engagements, she could reputedly go days without washing or changing her clothes.

Marilyn's flight from Hollywood in 1955 could have eased some of the pressure that had been contributing to poor mental and physical health, but in New York she continued to find it hard to sleep and relax. During this period she began intensive PSYCHOANALYSIS, which she was to continue until her death.

On June 23, 1959 Marilyn was admitted to Lenox Hill Hospital where her New York gynecologist Dr. Mortimer Rodgers operated on her once more for chronic endometriosis. Marilyn's Los Angeles gynecological specialist Dr. Krohn operated on her once more for endometriosis in 1961, and then again just two weeks before she died (though CONSPIRACY theorists claim this was for an abortion).

There is no proof that Marilyn ever had any abortions. Dr. Leon Krohn, who was Marilyn's gynecologist from 1952, stated that she didn't have a single one. Nevertheless, biographers including NORMAN MAILER and ANTHONY SUMMERS say that, like many young Hollywood hopefuls, she underwent numerous—as many as twelve in some reports—abortions, many of the back street variety during her penniless starlet years, and it was this that permanently ruined her chances of conceiving. Marilyn reputedly told some friends that she had indeed had abortions.

In the mid-1950s Marilyn told a hairdresser that she had been sterilized through tube-tying to make sure she did not become pregnant; she also said that later she had this operation reversed. If this was the case, it may have been JOHNNY HYDE, whose helping hand was vital to Marilyn's fledgling career, who advised her to have the tubal ligation. However, some biographers say that although she initially agreed, she changed her mind before going through with the operation.

Depending on sources, Marilyn had two or three miscarriages during her marriage to ARTHUR MILLER, one induced because it was an ectopic pregnancy. In some biographies Marilyn is said to have had a miscarriage less than two months after marrying Miller, in the summer of 1956, while in England filming *THE PRINCE AND THE SHOWGIRL* (1957). The two documented miscarriages were on August 1, 1957, when Marilyn was rushed to the hospital in great pain and had her ectopic pregnancy terminated. In December 1958, after taking it as easy as filming commitments on *SOME LIKE IT HOT* (1959) allowed, Marilyn had a miscarriage when she was two months pregnant. Marilyn was severely shaken by these experiences. Between 1957 and 1959 Marilyn is said to have put on as much as fifteen pounds, for what are termed "false pregnancies."

Between May 1960 and May 1961 Marilyn was in the hospital no less than five times, culminating in a pancreas operation and gallbladder removal at the Polyclinic Hospital in New York. Removal of her gallbladder finally freed her from the digestive problems that had troubled her at night for many years.

Marilyn began work on her final film *SOMETHING'S GOT TO GIVE* a week late because of an acute sinus infection and fever. She managed just one day on set before her general doctor, Dr. Hyman Engelberg, advised her that she needed bed rest for at least a week more. She was suspended from production after one too many absences for a viral infection—or so said TWENTIETH CENTURY-FOX, which, according to some sources, was seeking excuses to close down a production for its own reasons. Marilyn publically exclaimed her frustration with this situation: "Executives can get a cold and stay home and phone in—but the actor? How dare you get a cold or a virus! I wish they had to act a comedy with a temperature and a virus infection!"

Marilyn's final hospital stay was just two weeks before she died, when Dr. Krohn operated on her once again for endometriosis. Speculation that this hospitalization episode was for an abortion (after becoming pregnant by either JOHN or BOBBY KENNEDY) seems unlikely, in view of her enormous desire to have children.

(*see* HOSPITALS *and* DOCTORS.)

## MELSON, INEZ

Inez Melson became Marilyn's business manager in the early fifties (either 1951 or 1952 depending on accounts) just as major fame began to arrive. Biographer FRED LAWRENCE GUILES describes her as "a tower of reserve" who protected Marilyn's interests and privacy. In 1952 Melson was appointed legal guardian ("conservator") to GLADYS BAKER, who was still in a state asylum. Melson went regularly to visit Marilyn's mother on her employer's behalf, and looked after financial arrangements for her care. This included protecting Gladys in 1952 when the press got wind that Marilyn's mother was alive and reasonably well and living in a mental institution, and not, as the studio had claimed, long dead.

Melson took the witness stand in October 1954 to testify that JOE DIMAGGIO "was very indifferent and not concerned with Mrs. DiMaggio's happiness."

Biographies contain few reports of Melson's involvement in Marilyn's business affairs during Marilyn's NEW YORK period (1955–1960), but she remained in touch for consultation, if not for managing all of her client's affairs.

On the morning of August 5, 1962 Melson was one of the first people to be called to Marilyn's home after her DEATH. In some reports, it was Melson who went to the Los Angeles morgue to complete formalities for Marilyn's body to be taken for FUNERAL preparation. Melson was one of the select few at the ceremony.

Melson continued to visit Gladys Baker after Marilyn died. Melson died in 1986, after which her personal papers—including documents taken from Marilyn's home the day after she died—were acquired by biographer DONALD SPOTO.

## MEMORABILIA

With such a huge, loyal fan base over the last forty years, it is little wonder that there is a thriving market among Marilyn FANS for anything to do with Hollywood's greatest siren—from scripts bearing notes in her handwriting, to the checks she wrote out on the last day she was alive, to the furniture she had specially made in MEXICO for her Brentwood home, to contracts with movie studios and model agencies, to official legal documents, and any of the "vintage" Marilyn memorabilia from when she was alive.

Fans who don't have thousand dollar budgets collect MAGAZINES, stills, press kits from the original films, and books (which can cost hundreds of dollars) on Marilyn published during her lifetime. Marilyn memorabilia is a staple commodity on the many INTERNET auction sites. Many Los Angeles film merchandise emporia do a thriving trade in Marilyn items, everything from postcards to plates and posters, not to mention phone cards, stamps, dolls, lighters, key rings, refrigerator magnets, jigsaws . . . anything large enough to bear a likeness (one of Norma Jeane's actual childhood dolls was recently restored, while Marilyn's costumes from *THE SEVEN YEAR ITCH* (1955), and *GENTLEMEN PREFER BLONDES* (1953) have appeared on Barbie).

Covers from Norma Jeane's early modeling career, such as in *Family Circle*, fetch up to $500, but magazines in which she features are more reasonable priced at around $50. Competition is fierce among collectors to pick up Marilyn magazines from yard sales and clear outs. At the other end of the scale, first issue *Playboy* covers with Marilyn Monroe, and rare original Golden Dreams CALENDAR shots, change hands for thousands of dollars.

Marilyn's costumes consistently outsell all other film memorabilia at auction. For example, the floor-length, cream-colored wool gown Marilyn wore in *HOW TO MARRY A MILLIONAIRE* (1953), used in the poster campaigns, sold at auction in June 1997 for $57,000, almost three times its expected price.

At the lower end of the market, printed "copies" of Marilyn's driving license go for $3. Mock-ups with wrong information, these are a typical specimen of the huge Marilyn novelty industry; the photo is a wardrobe still from *NIAGARA* (1952), her birth date is wrong, and the expiration date is listed as the day she actually died.

Among the more ghoulish and questionable items that have been sold are an ornate douche bag holder claimed to have been Marilyn's, and even purported pap smears (hawked for six figure sums, despite the fact that the practice only became common in the seventies). A lock of Marilyn's HAIR, originally kept as a memento by her mother, went for auction (by Early American History auctions) in September 1997.

The Marilyn Monroe name as a brand logo has, not surprisingly, been in great demand. As well as the products Marilyn advertised during her life, the Marilyn Monroe ESTATE has licensed dozens of Marilyn lines: Bloomingdale's, one her favorite SHOPPING haunts, purchased licensing rights from the Marilyn Monroe estate to open and run Marilyn Monroe Clothing Boutiques; the Thom McAn shoe chain brought out a line of Marilyn Monroe leather goods and accessories; the estate has licensed the sale of Marilyn jeans, bathing suits, perfumes, and many more articles. Recent Marilyn Monroe merchandise includes lingerie in the U.K. Freeman's catalog, and a line of Marilyn bras by Warner's. Marilyn has her own wines (Marilyn Merlot, bottled in Nappa Valley) and her own computer games, while the entertainment industry continues to churn out books and documentaries to celebrate her life and legend.

Perhaps the most significant piece of Marilyn memorabilia is her home at 12305 FIFTH HELENA DRIVE, the place where she died. Marilyn originally paid $90,000, but the last time it changed hands it was reportedly for $1.3 million.

The contents of a trunk packed by Marilyn herself when she moved out of the Connecticut home she shared with Arthur Miller.

### SOME RECENT AUCTION PPRICES

A 1943 letter from Norma Jeane to guardian Grace McKee Goddard sold for $43,125 at auction in late 1998.

An autographed 1957 portrait fetched $8,270 in London in 1998.

An early 1947 agreement between Monroe and Twentieth Century-Fox—a contender for the first document she ever signed under her professional name—sold at auction for $4,140.

A check signed on the last day Marilyn was alive, made out to handyman Norman Jeffries, was auctioned in 1998 for $9000.

Autographed photos, including a junior high school picture, fetched up to $10,000.

Program for John Kennedy's birthday salute at Madison Square Garden held May 19, 1962, signed by Marilyn Monroe, was sold in May 1998 for $6,500.

On October 27–28, 1999, Christie's in New York City auctioned off over 1,500 items of Marilyn memorabilia. Bequeathed to the auction house by ANNA STRASBERG, part of the proceeds were to be donated to two different charities, the World Wildlife Fund and New York City's Litreracy Partners. In fitting Marilyn fashion, it was one of the most publicized auctions of recent memory.

BOOKS:

*Marilyn Monroe: The Collector's & Dealer's Price & Identification Guide*, Dennis C. Jackson. USA: Illustrator Collector's News, 1996.

*The Price and Identification Guide to Marilyn Monroe*, Dennis C. Jackson. USA: Illustrator Collector's News, 1996.

*Marilyn Monroe Collectibles: A Comprehensive Guide to the Memorabilia of an American Legend*, Clark Kidder. New York: Avon Books, 1999.

## MEN

MARILYN:
"You don't look for someone like yourself. You look for someone different, with different qualities. Nobody could be more unlike the men I've been friendly with—Arthur and Joe and Frank and... and, and, and. So many, yet here I am alone. I don't like being alone."

ARTHUR MILLER:
"Most men become more of what they are around her: a phoney becomes more phoney, a confused man becomes more confused, a retiring man more retiring. She's kind of a lodestone that draws out of the male animal his essential qualities."

WILLIAM TRAVILLA:
"She was the one woman I've known who could make a man feel tall, handsome, fascinating, with that unblinking look of hers, dead in the eyes. You were the king of the evening, if she so decided. She made you feel like the only one, even when you were not."

GLORIA STEINEM:
"Marilyn kept hoping that a relationship with a man would give her the identity she lacked, and that her appearance would give her the man. This impossible search was rewarded and exaggerated by a society that encourages women to get their identity from men—and encourages men to value women for appearance, not mind or heart."

Norma Jeane was such a quiet and unassuming little girl that she was known as "The Mouse." When she reached puberty men began to take an interest. Norma Jeane reveled in the attention, even though, at that time, "The truth was that with all my lipstick and mascara and precocious curves I was as unresponsive as a fossil. . . . I used to lie awake at night wondering why the boys came after me."

The effect she had on men undoubtedly smoothed her path to FAME. Whether she slept with one or dozens of influential men in positions of power, she used what she had. Marilyn had a way of looking at people, especially men, with great seductive intensity. ARTHUR MILLER writes, "Aged men often evoked in her so intense an awareness of her own power over them that it turned to pity within her and sometimes even love. Her nearness could make such men actually tremble, and in this was more security for her than in a vault full of money or a theater echoing with applause." A constant of many of Marilyn's relationships with men, particularly in her early years, was that they belittled her and criticized her for being gauche and uneducated.

Many of the male PHOTOGRAPHERS granted a private shoot found that Marilyn was seducing them (or rather, their camera). According to PHILIPPE HALSMAN, the only way Marilyn seemed to relate to men was by provoking their desire: "Her talent in this respect was very great. I remember my experience in her tiny apartment with my assistant and the *Life* researcher. Each of us felt that if the other two would leave, something incredible would happen."

Marilyn knew very well that, as she once said, "my popularity seemed almost entirely a masculine phenomenon." She also believed that "Men like happy girls"—one thing no biographer accuses her of being.

The kind of man Marilyn was looking for was someone she could admire; generally a man of accomplishments, often an intellectual. It is generally reported that looks were not so important to her—she said she often fell for men with glasses—but she was also strongly attracted to the handsome hunks of her day, such as MARLON BRANDO and YVES MONTAND.

It has been said that Marilyn sought out a knight in shining armor who could make all her troubles disappear. She idealized MILTON GREENE for his ability to handle finances, LAURENCE OLIVIER for his acting skills and standing, and Miller for his erudition.

It is common for children who grow up with an absent or neglectful mother to seek out as adults the tenderness of maternal LOVE, rather than sexuality. Marilyn may well have fallen into this category, as she fell head over heels in love only to become disappointed as the relationship developed. The longer her long-term relationships continued, the greater the burden on the partner. Miller, at four years, was with her the longest of any man.

Most studies of the Marilyn phenomenon comment on her own peculiar blend of innocence and carnality. If she was the nation's sweetheart, it was strictly for a bit on the side, not for long-term romancing. GLORIA STEINEM's interpretation is that, "A compliant child-woman like Monroe solves this dilemma by offering sex *without* the power of an adult

It was rumored that Marilyn cast an interested eye at co-star Clark Gable on the set of *The Misfits* (1961).

woman, much less of an equal." And yet Marilyn's vulnerability, the desire she arouses in men to protect her, continues to win her fans to this day, legions of men who believe that if only they had been around, they would have been able to shield her from her fate.

At the end of her life, according to FRED VANDERBILT FIELD, Marilyn "said she wanted to quit Hollywood and find some guy—a combination of Miller and Joe DiMaggio . . . who would be decent to her but also her intellectual leader and stimulant."

During her starlet years, according to SHELLEY WINTERS, as a game the two young actresses drew up a list of their "Most Wanted" Men. Marilyn's list was:

### MARILYN'S MOST WANTED

Harry Belafonte
Charles Bickford
Charles Boyer
Albert Einstein
Ernest Hemingway
John Houston
Dean Jagger
Elia Kazan
Charles Laughton
Arthur Miller
Yves Montand
Zero Mostel
Clifford Odets
Nick Ray
Jean Renoir
Lee Strasberg
Eli Wallach

Marilyn had a romantic attachment to at least three, and possibly more, of this illustrious group.

Marilyn's charms were not infallible. A number of studio chiefs appeared to be immune to her appeal, though in some biographies they are cited as lovers. DARRYL ZANUCK, whose tenure at TWENTIETH CENTURY-FOX took in Marilyn's rise to fame and reign as box office champion, was apparently unimpressed by her charms on- and off-screen. Marilyn reportedly said, "I would have done anything he wanted. I tried but he wasn't interested. He was the only guy who wasn't and I never knew why."

There were others. DORE SCHARY of MGM did not think she was talented or attractive enough to justify a contract, despite her solid performance in *THE ASPHALT JUNGLE* (1950).

Marilyn reputedly came on strong to JOHN CARROLL, and even announced to his wife LUCILLE RYMAN that Carroll was going to run off with her, but a majority of biographers write that he spurned her advances.

FRED KARGER, the first—and some say greatest—love of Marilyn's life certainly did not return her affections, though whether or not that meant he kept their relationship platonic is another question.

According to LENA PEPITONE, a couple of years before they worked together on *THE MISFITS* (1961), Marilyn unsuccessfully tried to seduce MONTGOMERY CLIFT, whose sexual preferences lay elsewhere. Marilyn also reputedly attempted to seduce CLARK GABLE, as her marriage to Arthur Miller was unraveling. Gable was not interested; he was newly married, and his wife Kay was just months away from giving birth to their first child.

## MENTAL ILLNESS

Marilyn's mother and both of her maternal GRANDPARENTS suffered from mental illness, and Marilyn lived in fear of a preordained destiny to follow them to incarceration in an institution. Norma Jeane was just eight years old when she watched her mother GLADYS BAKER forcibly being taken to a mental hospital; Gladys spent almost all the rest of her long life in an institution. Biographer DONALD SPOTO, however, claims that at least in the case of Marilyn's grandparents, their symptoms of mental illness were in fact merely the side-effects of other diseases—syphilis in the case of grandfather OTIS MONROE, heart disease in the case of grandmother DELLA MAE HOGAN.

Marilyn battled with her demons. She resorted to DRUGS to help her get through the day and rest at night, and for the last seven years of her life she underwent intense psychotherapy.

Much has been written about a kind of schizophrenia that split Marilyn in two—the public persona of Marilyn on the outside, a frightened and abandoned little girl on the inside. Hairdresser GEORGE MASTERS said, "She was two personalities inhabiting the same body." LAURENCE OLIVIER, who had a disastrous time directing her in *THE PRINCE AND THE SHOWGIRL* (1957) decided that she was "schizoid; the two people that she was could hardly have been more different."

Marilyn's last psychotherapist, DR. RALPH GREENSON is said to have told colleagues that Marilyn was, in his view, a schizophrenic.

GLORIA STEINEM's perspective is that the legend of Marilyn has endured because many women identify with her as a victim of childhood abuse, over-medication, and a prevailing attitude that her underlying problems were "all in the mind." In her 1986 biography of Marilyn, Steinem quotes extensively from *Your Inner Child of the Past*, a 1963 book by psychiatrist Dr W. Hugh Missildine, in which he outlines behavioral patterns of adults who were neglected in childhood by one or both parents: a constant craving of love, skills in obtaining at least fleeting recognition from peers, a propensity to go into the theater or movies where they are able to build on a fantasy life, an inability to be happy with partners who would be perfectly good for them, and a ceaseless search for the maternal love they lacked in their earliest years.

A number of modern-day psychiatrists believe that Marilyn actually suffered from something called Borderline Personality Disorder, a condition often found in adults who suffered abuse as children. It is believed that children who suffer abandonment during their first three years, or are fostered for long periods of time, do not develop their personalities fully, but rather shut down their development in important areas in an attempt to protect themselves. In adult life, this manifests itself in a number of ways: a strong desire to latch on to a parent figure in a dependent relationship; viewing people as either wholly good or wholly evil; diminished feelings of self-worth, which can lead to depression; and impulsiveness.

Diagnostic symptoms of Borderline Personality Disorder range through: Avoidance of real/imagined abandonment as a priority; sequential intense and unstable relationships, swerving between extremes of idealization and devaluation; identity issues (unstable sense of self); impulsive and potentially self-damaging addictive behavior (spending, sex, substance abuse, recklessness); recurrent suicidal behavior, gestures, threats, or self-mutilation; wild mood swings (intense sadness, irritability, anxiety); chronic feelings of emptiness; rage, temper tantrums; periodical paranoid thoughts during times of stress.

### MARILYN'S TIME IN A MENTAL WARD

Marilyn managed to stave off her worst nightmare—being locked up in a psychiatric ward—until the very last years of her life. In February 1961 Marilyn's then-psychotherapist Dr. Marianne Kris advised her that the best way to recuperate from the angst of separating from Arthur Miller, and from the enormous strains of filming *The Misfits*, was to check in to the Payne-Whitney Hospital. Kris did not, it seems, tell her that she was going into a locked psychiatric ward.

Marilyn screamed and shouted but nobody listened. She later wrote to her California psychotherapist, Dr. Ralph Greenson, about what she did to attract attention: "I got the idea from a movie I made once called *Don't Bother to Knock*. I picked up a lightweight chair and slammed it against the glass, intentionally—and it was hard to do because I had never broken anything in my life. It took a lot of banging to get even a small piece of glass, so I went over with the glass concealed in my hand and sat quietly on the bed waiting for them to come in. They did, and I said to them, 'If you are going to treat me like a nut, I'll act like a nut.' I admit the next thing is corny, but I really did it in the movie except it was with a razor blade. I indicated if they didn't let me out I would harm myself—the farthest thing from my mind at the moment, since you know, Dr. Greenson, I'm an actress and would never intentionally mark or mar myself, I'm just that vain."

They didn't let her out. Two days after being locked up, she managed to get a note delivered to Lee and Paula Strasberg:

> "Dr. Kris has put me in the hospital under the care of two idiot doctors. They both should not be my doctors. I'm locked up with these poor nutty people. I'm sure to end up a nut too if I stay in this nightmare. Please help me. This is the last place I should be. I love you both.
> Marilyn
> PS: I'm on the dangerous floor. It's like a cell. They had my bathroom door locked and I couldn't get the key to get into it, so I broke the glass. But outside of that I haven't done anything that is un-cooperative."

The Strasbergs were unable to persuade the doctors to let Marilyn out. It was then that Marilyn contacted Joe DiMaggio. Ever-faithful, Joe came to Marilyn's rescue. When the hospital said it would require Dr. Kris's approval for Marilyn's release, Joe is said to have threatened Dr. Kris that if Marilyn wasn't out of hospital by the end of the next day, he would "take the hospital apart brick by brick."

A couple of weeks later, from the much more comfortable Colombia University hospital room Joe had organized for her, Marilyn described her experience to Dr. Ralph Greenson:

> "There was no empathy at Payne Whitney—it had a very bad effect on me. They put me in a cell (I mean cement blocks and all) for *very disturbed*, depressed patients, except I felt I was in some kind of prison for a crime I hadn't committed. The inhumanity there I found archaic. They asked me why I wasn't happy there (everything was under lock and key, things like electric lights, dresser drawers, bathrooms, closets, bars concealed on the windows—and the doors have windows so patients can be visible all the time. Also, the violence and markings still remain on the walls from former patients). I answered: 'Well, I'd have to be nuts if I like it here!' "

## MERYMAN, RICHARD

MARILYN:
"I really resent the way the press has been saying I'm depressed and in a slump, as if I'm finished. Nothing is going to sink me, although it might be a kind of relief to be finished with movie making."

The *Life* journalist to whom Marilyn gave her last-ever interview, a carefully prepared rebuttal—Marilyn asked for the questions in advance—of the claims circulating that Marilyn was finished after being fired from SOMETHING'S GOT TO GIVE. The article appeared on August 3, 1962, the day before she died. It was titled "Marilyn Lets Her Hair Down about Being Famous."

Meryman later said, "I was very impressed by her, she was much smarter than I had expected. . . . I've often thought what a sad person Marilyn Monroe would be if she were alive today. I also privately believed that she only intended to scare people with the pills. There was no sign to me that this woman was on the way to suicide."

In *The Ultimate Marilyn*, Ernest W. Cunningham describes this interview as Marilyn's "Gettysburg Address." Cunningham says the best thing Marilyn said during this interview, and indeed ever, was, "It was the creative part that kept me going—trying to be an actress. . . . And I guess I've always had too much fantasy to be only a housewife."

## THE METHOD

LEE STRASBERG built upon KONSTANTIN STANISLAVSKY's drama teachings to create The Method, an approach to acting which he taught at the ACTORS STUDIO. After Marilyn moved to New York in 1955, she began working with Strasberg and soon became one of the most prominent "Methodists."

In Strasberg's words, The Method is "The sum total of the experience of the great actors throughout all ages and countries. The best things in it come from Stanislavsky. The rest comes from me. It sets no rules. It points a path that leads to control rather than hit-or-miss inspiration. It fosters fusion of the actor with the character."

Under The Method, actors are encouraged to go beyond merely imitating reality, but rather to reproduce it by using their own personal emotional recall or "affective memory." Actors are encouraged to focus on the sensory objects that make up their memory, and work from these to summon up affective memories that can be used in performance as a "Golden Key." For Method practitioners, the process of acting is a means to revealing truth in an actor's individual personality. Actors draw upon themselves for raw material, hence Strasberg's emphasis on self-learning and introspection through Freudian PSYCHOANALYSIS. Strasberg agreed to give Marilyn private tuition in The Method on the condition that she went into psychoanalysis to deal with her repressed past and tap into her hidden energy.

Marilyn's first application of The Method was in *BUS STOP* (1956), which brought her the first substantial critical acclaim for a dramatic performance. But the man Marilyn was to work with next, in the only movie made by her own production company MARILYN MONROE PRODUCTIONS, was one of the most bitter critics of The Method. LAURENCE OLIVIER firmly believed that acting was an amalgam of technique and the accumulation of external details: "What they call 'The Method' is not generally advantageous to the actor at all. Instead of doing a scene over again that's giving them trouble, they want to discuss, discuss, discuss. I'd rather run through a scene eight times than waste time chattering away about abstractions. An actor gets a thing right by doing it over and over. Arguing about motivations and so forth is a lot of rot."

On *THE MISFITS* (1960) Marilyn followed The Method almost verbatim, changing lines and paraphrasing speeches because, as she said, what really counted were the emotions, not the words. ARTHUR MILLER, who was a critic of the often slavish devotion of actors who subscribed to The Method, wrote, "With the encouragement of her mentors she was losing her way in an improvisational approach that might belong in acting class but not in actual performance."

## MEXICO

Marilyn's association with Mexico ran in the family. Her mother GLADYS BAKER was born in Piedras Negras, Mexico in 1902.

ROBERT SLATZER has said that Marilyn and he went to Mexico to get married in 1954, though much skepticism surrounds this claim.

A less than felicitous trip to Mexico for Marilyn was in January 1961, when she traveled to Juarez to obtain her divorce from ARTHUR MILLER. Under happier circumstances she returned in 1962, together with housekeeper EUNICE MURRAY, publicist PAT NEWCOMB, and hairdresser GEORGE MASTERS, on a shopping trip to furnish her brand-new home in Los Angeles. Marilyn stayed at the CONTINENTAL HILTON, where she also gave two press conferences. Then friends FRED AND NIEVES VANDERBILT FIELD took her on a tour of Cuernavaca, Toluca, Taxco, and Acapulco.

During this trip Marilyn apparently found some gentlemanly companionship with a man named JOSÉ BOLAÑOS . He was seen with her several times around Mexico City and then was flown back to Los Angeles to escort Marilyn to the GOLDEN GLOBE AWARDS.

## MGM

10202 WASHINGTON BOULEVARD, CULVER CITY

JOHN HUSTON's classic heist movie *THE ASPHALT JUNGLE* (1950), in which Marilyn had a breakthrough role, was made at MGM Studios, after JOHNNY HYDE persuaded Huston and studio chiefs to give his starlet girlfriend the part. His hope that she would be officially signed to the studio, the most prestigious at the time, was never realized. She made two more minor appearances, in *RIGHT CROSS* (1950) and *HOMETOWN STORY* (1951), but head of production DORE SCHARY let her go because he didn't feel she had sufficient star potential.

## MILLER, ARTHUR (B. 1915)

MARILYN:
"When we were first married, he saw me as so beautiful and innocent among the Hollywood wolves that I tried to be like that. I almost became his student in life and literature. . . . But when the monster showed, Arthur couldn't believe it. I disappointed him when that happened. But I felt he knew and loved all of me. I wasn't sweet all through. He should love the monster too. But maybe I'm too demanding. Maybe there's no man who could put up with all of me."

"He's a brilliant man and a wonderful writer, but I think he is a better writer than a husband."

ARTHUR MILLER:
"She has more guts than a slaughterhouse. Being

George Barris took this famous photograph of Marilyn in the cardigan sweater she purchased on a trip to Mexico, 1962.

with her, people want not to die. She's all woman, the most womanly woman in the world."

"The terrible irony was that I had reinforced the idea of the innocent victimization because I could not bear to accept her life as it was, because I had wanted to heal the wound rather than acknowledge it as hers. . . . All that was left was for her to go on defending her innocence, in which, at the bottom of her heart, she did not believe. Innocence kills."

Marilyn and Arthur first met in early 1951 (late 1950 in some accounts) on the set of AS YOUNG AS YOU FEEL (1951). Miller writes that they were introduced by his friend ELIA KAZAN, who has said he was having an affair with her at the time. Other accounts state that Miller and Kazan came across Marilyn alone in an empty studio building, weeping uncontrollably about the death of benefactor JOHNNY HYDE. Alternatively it is said that actor CAMERON MITCHELL introduced Marilyn to Kazan and Miller as they bumped into one another outside the TWENTIETH CENTURY-FOX commissary.

Miller writes in his autobiography *Timebends* that when they shook hands "the shock of her body's motion sped through me, a sensation at odds with her sadness amid all this glamour and technology and the busy confusion of a new shot being set up."

The next day Miller, Kazan, and Marilyn went to see HARRY COHN, head of COLUMBIA STUDIOS, to talk about a screenplay Miller had written and Kazan wanted to direct, for a movie called *The Hook*. This script, which told the story of Brooklyn longshoremen who fight against exploitative racketeers, was dropped by the studio after union complaints that it was full of anti-American sentiment. They also met up later that week at a party thrown by agent CHARLES FELDMAN, and spent time together around town as a threesome.

At the time they first met Marilyn was still a struggling starlet whose career had twice been launched but had yet to really take off. Miller, thirty-five, was ten years older than her, the son of a coat manufacturer ruined during the Depression, who first rose to prominence as a playwright while still at college. Since then he had married his college sweetheart Mary Grace Slattery, with whom he had had two children, and become one of the most celebrated playwrights of the time. The realist style of his Broadway successes *All My Sons* (1947), which was the New York Drama Critics' Circle best play of the year, and *Death of a Salesman* (1948), which won the Pulitzer Prize for drama, had propelled him to the forefront of the dramatic arts. He was an influential social commentator, a man who, in Marilyn's eyes, was worthy of admiration for the way he championed the downtrodden.

It was five years before they had the opportunity to build on the initial spark they both felt. At the time, Marilyn told NATASHA LYTESS that the experience was "like a cool drink when you've got a fever."

Miller recounts that he felt the stirrings of a passion so strong that he resolved to cut short his trip to Los Angeles and return home to New York, rather than risk being unfaithful to his wife:

> "She was in a beige skirt and a white satin blouse, and her hair hung down to her shoulders, parted on the right side, and the sight of her was something like pain, and I knew that I must flee or walk into a doom beyond all knowing. With all her radiance she was surrounded by a darkness that perplexed me. I could not yet imagine that in my very shyness she saw some safety, released from the detached and centerless and invaded life she had been given; instead, I hated my lifelong timidity, but there was no changing it now. When we parted I kissed her cheek and she sucked in a surprised breath... I had to escape her childish voracity, something like my own unruly appetite for self-gratification, which had both created what art I had managed to make and disgusted me with its stain of irresponsibility."

Arthur Miller and Marilyn announced their wedding plans at a press conference in front of Miller's house in White Plains, New York, on June 29, 1956. Later that day they were married at the court house in White Plains.

After he departed for New York, Marilyn had a photo of him framed and hung up on her wall. She wrote to him too, explaining the lack in her life of a man to admire, a FATHER FIGURE. Miller suggested that rather than him, she should admire somebody like ABRAHAM LINCOLN, and suggested she buy the recent CARL SANDBURG biography. This she duly did, along with a large framed portrait, both of which remained treasured possessions. Miller added, "Bewitch them with this image they ask for, but I hope and almost pray you won't be hurt in this game, nor ever change."

Little has been written about contacts between 1951 and 1955, when Marilyn moved to NEW YORK. Miller most certainly featured on Marilyn's list of sexy MEN, and then in 1954, just two months after marrying JOE DIMAGGIO, Marilyn was having a nightcap with confidante SIDNEY SKOLSKY when, out of the blue, she told him that she was going to marry Arthur Miller. Skolsky reacted in disbelief, but Marilyn was insistent: "You wait. You'll see."

Marilyn and Arthur rekindled the initial flame in early 1955, after Marilyn moved to New York from Hollywood. Once again, there are conflicting accounts of who acted as go-between. It was either common friends NORMAN AND HEDDA ROSTEN, or PAULA STRASBERG. In the meantime, Miller had continued to write seminal plays, such as *The Crucible*. As he began seeing Marilyn, he was just putting the finishing touches to *A View from the Bridge*—the world premiere of which Marilyn attended on September 29, 1955 at New York's Coronet Theater.

Biographers almost unanimously report that Miller's marriage to Mary Grace Slattery was already in trouble before he was bowled

Miller and Marilyn at the London premiere of *A View From the Bridge*, 1956.

over by Marilyn: "She was endlessly fascinating, full of original observations, there wasn't a conventional bone in her body. . . . She was a whirling light to me then, all paradox and enticing mystery, street-tough one moment, then lifted by a lyrical and poetic sensitivity that few retain past early adolescence." During Marilyn's first year in New York the couple spent increasing amounts of private and public time together. When the press got wind of this seemingly unlikely friendship, they both denied any involvement beyond friendship.

Friends knew better. Jim Proctor, a friend of Arthur's, said, "I don't think I ever saw two people so dizzy with love for each other. Having known Arthur a long time as an introspective guy, it was, well, like a miracle to see him so outgoing." As Marilyn said around the time they decided to get married, "We're so congenial. This is the first time I've been really in love. Arthur is a serious man, but he has a wonderful sense of humor. We laugh and joke a lot. I'm mad about him." Arthur mirrored her sentiments, announcing, "This is the first time I think I've really been in love."

When, in early 1956, Marilyn had to return to the West Coast to start work on *BUS STOP* (1956), Miller called every day. To keep things under wraps, Marilyn referred to him as "Mr. A." During the course of their relationship, Marilyn most often referred to him as "Daddy," "Papa," or "Pa," though she had other pet names too: "Art," "Poppy," and "Arturo." He called her Penny Dreadful, Sugar Finney, and Gramercy 5.

Miller went to obtain his divorce in RENO, Nevada. Miller began his two-month residence in April 1956 that year, and moved into a cottage at Pyramid Lake. That very day Marilyn was admitted to St. Vincent's HOSPITAL in Los Angeles, after picking up a virus during mountain exterior shooting for *Bus Stop*. It was at this time, he says in his autobiography, that "she was dancing on the edge and the drop down was forever. . . . She had concealed her dependency before, and I saw suddenly that I was all she had." Despite the residency requirements, Miller took the risk of regular weekend visits to Marilyn in Los Angeles. They spoke all the time; in one call Marilyn told him, "I don't want this any more, Papa, I can't fight them alone, I want to live with you in the country and be a good wife." The day after Miller's divorce came through, June 11, 1956, he was back in New York with Marilyn, who had since finished filming.

It is generally believed that the first public announcement of Arthur and Marilyn's wedding plans occurred before the HOUSE UN-AMERICAN ACTIVITIES COMMITTEE—when asked why he had applied for a passport, he answered to go to England, "to be with the woman who will then be my wife." Several conflicting versions of this episode exist. Apparently Marilyn, completely unaware of her impending nuptials, was watching Arthur on television as he made his stand, only to learn of the wedding at the same time as the committee. Long-time friend RUPERT ALLAN said that Marilyn, "Admired him from that day, although his tactic for the wedding announcement greatly distressed her. . . . I'm sorry to say that at that moment I think he used her." Miller himself makes it clear in his autobiography that the wedding had been planned well in advance of his appearance before the committee; this version seems to

Miller and Marilyn in Roxbury, Connecticut, 1956.

be borne out by an article that appeared a day before he took the stand, in which *The New York Post* broke the news about the planned wedding. In whatever way the news came out, the press had a field day. One witty title-writer came up with the snappy headline: "Egghead Weds Hourglass."

Whatever the timing of the announcement, many commentators assert that Marilyn's support for Arthur saved him from the worst excesses of the HUAC investigations into his political affiliations—more precisely whether or not he had ever been a paid-up member of the Communist Party. Miller had long been under surveillance by the authorities. Ever since his college days the FBI had been building up an enormous file on him and closely monitoring his activities. Marilyn's liaison with the playwright, whose works had been condemned by the FBI as "a negative delineation of American life," earned her her very own file. During the committee proceedings Marilyn flew down to Washington to be by Miller's side. She publicly declared her love for him and her unswerving belief in his innocence, despite the fact that SPYROS SKOURAS, the head of Fox, had flown out to New York specifically to persuade her to get her fiancé to supply the names the committee wanted from him. Marilyn put her convictions above her career, brushing aside Skouras's reputed threats to destroy her if she persisted in her headstrong pro-Miller publicity. Miller stood up for the causes he believed in, which he later defined as "my fear of a looming victory of fascism and my alienation from the waste of potential in America while knowing nothing about life under any socialist regime."

Marilyn and Arthur were married in two different private ceremonies. The first was a brief, secret civil WEDDING in White Plains, New York, on June 29, 1956, held after Marilyn and Arthur gave a press conference officially announcing their plans to be wed. Two days later they were joined in matrimony in a Jewish ceremony officiated by Rabbi Robert Goldberg at the home of Kay Brown (Arthur's agent) not far from Katonah, New York. On what should have been one of the happiest days of her life, Marilyn was highly distressed when journalist MARA SCHERBATOFF was killed in a road accident while following Marilyn and Arthur along the country roads near their Connecticut house. Marilyn took this as the worst of omens for their marriage.

Miller later said he had no idea what he was letting himself in for by marrying the nation's favorite film star: "My only excuse as I looked back is that I had probably seen a half-dozen television programs in my life. . . . It was a painful business, but for more than the obvious intrusion; I quickly realized that something in me was proud of identification with Marilyn—and aware, too, that our seeming so ill suited was part of what made us such news."

Miller was granted his passport and visa to accompany his wife to ENGLAND, where, in a blaze of press interest, they arrived two weeks later. Arthur had the premiere of *A View from the Bridge* to occupy him, while Marilyn began working with LAURENCE OLIVIER on *THE PRINCE AND THE SHOWGIRL* (1957). They settled in to a beautiful house at EGHAM, not far from London, and at first things went well. Miller writes, "My vision had been of each of us doing our own work side by side, drawing strength from one another, and it

Marilyn poses with her new husband and in-laws at the Roxbury, Connecticut, house on the weekend of her wedding.

seemed to be coming true."

Biographers generally agree that the honeymoon period in their marriage came to an end very quickly indeed, just a few weeks after the wedding. On August 29, 1956 Miller rushed back to New York—unconfirmed rumors are that frightened by one or a number of journalists, Miller's daughter Jane had crashed through a plate glass door and cut herself badly. However, the more common version of how the first cracks appeared in their relationship was that during Arthur's absence Marilyn discovered a diary belonging to him—in some accounts he deliberately left it open for her to find—in which she read that he had grave doubts about the marriage, the burden he had taken on, and the dangers it posed to his own creativity. Soon after Marilyn was quoted as saying, "He thought I was some kind of angel but now he guessed he was wrong—that his first wife had let him down, but I had done something worse." Miller told biographer FRED LAWRENCE GUILES that he believes this version of events was transposed from an incident in his play *AFTER THE FALL*.

In England, Miller became increasingly drawn into Marilyn's orbit. His own writing took a back seat to her commitments, not least the torment of Marilyn working with Laurence Olivier, whom she felt was denigrating her as a person and an actress, and then her growing dissatisfaction with business partner MILTON GREENE. At the London premiere of *A View from Bridge* on October 12, 1956 at the Comedy Theatre, Marilyn turned up in one of her hallmark low-cut gowns and stole the show, at least in the eyes of the paparazzi and lead writers. Miller supported his wife as far as he felt he could in her increasingly bitter battles with Olivier, but, he writes, "Inevitably, the time soon came when in order to keep reality from slipping away occasionally I had to defend Olivier or else reinforce the naïveté of her illusions; the result was that she began to question the absoluteness of my partisanship on her side of the deepening struggle." He had begun to feel that she was "all need and all wound."

After the ordeal of London, with all its unrest and turmoil, Marilyn and Arthur recouped on a delayed HONEYMOON to JAMAICA in January 1957. On their return they moved in to a rented apartment at 444 East FIFTY-SEVENTH STREET, not far from where Marilyn had been living before going to London. However inauspicious the beginnings of their married life, Marilyn gave it a heartfelt try. On the back of a wedding photograph, she had written, "Hope, Hope, Hope." Her hope was founded on the intense love she and Arthur had for one another. Paula Strasberg once said, "I have never seen such tenderness and love as Arthur and Marilyn feel for each other. How he values her. I don't think any woman I've ever known has been so valued by a man." For the next three years Marilyn and Arthur moved between their New York apartment and a country house they bought in ROXBURY, Connecticut not far from Arthur's old house. While remodeling work was being done on the country house in the summer of 1957, they rented a home at AMAGANSETT, Long Island.

Marilyn tried her best to be the housewife she said she wanted to be. She got on well with Arthur's parents Augusta and Isidore, and, as with the children of previous husband Joe DiMaggio, she established a long-lasting relationship with her step-children Jane and Robert.

She strove not to let her career get in the way of her marriage. But this was not without cost to herself: "If she loved to fool in a flower garden and endlessly move furniture around the house and buy a lamp or a coffee pot, these were pleasing preparations for a life she could not live for long without a new flight to the moon in a new part and a new film."

Things may have gone differently if Marilyn had not been cruelly thwarted in her attempts to start a family (see MEDICAL HISTORY). When she did become pregnant in the summer of 1957, it was an ectopic pregnancy which could not continue. Through 1958 it was becoming apparent to friends that something was seriously amiss in the Millers' relationship. Sometimes in company Marilyn would get into a rage at her husband, whose response was simply to leave the room. Norman Rosten recalled that Miller would seek refuge in his study, "more unraveled than ever." According to maid LENA PEPITONE, towards the end of their marriage they practically lived in different time zones. They hardly ever ate together, and Arthur spent as much time as he could in his study. Marilyn, meanwhile, had her routine of lessons with LEE STRASBERG, and almost daily outings to her psychiatrist. Miller rationalizes that after Marilyn's admiration of him had been shattered, what was left was "no recognizable image at all."

Marilyn was by turns upset and angry at Arthur because she feared that he judged her harshly, regarded her as unprofessional and self-absorbed. When Miller came to join Marilyn on the set *of SOME LIKE IT HOT* (1959), the tension between them was obvious. BILLY WILDER noted, "I remember saying at the time that in meeting Miller at last I met someone who resented her more than I did." Marilyn became pregnant again during work on this movie, but miscarried once more as the pregnancy entered the third month. She was devastated, and reputedly made one, if not two, SUICIDE ATTEMPTS. Miller rescued her and helped to nurse her back to health.

Meanwhile Arthur Miller was struggling with his writing, going through lean years after a decade of success. The project he spent most time on was the film he was writing for Marilyn, suggested to him by photographer SAM SHAW—*THE MISFITS* (1961). It took him at least two years to get the script into shape. By the time Marilyn was working on *LET'S MAKE LOVE* (1960) with YVES MONTAND in Los Angeles, he had reached a stage where he could travel to Ireland and work with director JOHN HUSTON on final touches. However, he was called back to Los Angeles in March 1960 to salvage the script for *Let's Make Love*. This was during a period when the Writers Guild was on strike; in his autobiography Sidney Skolsky questions this move on Miller's part: "Arthur Miller, the big Liberal, the man who always stood up for

Arthur Miller and Marilyn at the preview showing of *Some Like it Hot* (1959).

Arthur Miller and Marilyn on Hampton Beach, 1958.
Photograph by Sam Shaw.

the underdog, ignored the Writers Guild strike and rewrote. . . . his wife no longer looked up to him. . . . Any resemblance he had once possessed, in Marilyn's eyes, to a president assassinated nearly a century ago [Lincoln] had vanished."

Biographer DONALD SPOTO pinpoints this as the moment when Marilyn knew their marriage was over. Miller's recollection of this incident is quite different. In his autobiography he claims that he practically gave up his own work to try to show Marilyn that they had a life together, that he was there for her, even "slumming it" by doing rewrites on her film *Let's Make Love*. He concludes: "If it was plain that her inner desperation was not going to let up, it was equally clear that literally nothing I knew to do could slow its destructive progress." Marilyn may have been angry with Miller for abandoning his ideals, but he had plenty of reason to be angry with her too—most importantly, for having an affair with co-star Montand. One thing was certain: the months they spent together during work on *Let's Make Love* were months of high tension.

The death knell for the marriage came with the shooting of *The Misfits*. According to ANGELA ALLEN, Marilyn's "antagonism towards Arthur could be noticed by everyone." Halfway through shooting Arthur and Marilyn moved into separate rooms. The process of making the movie took a lot out of Miller. He even began to doubt his talents. At that time he told journalist W. J. WEATHERBY: "I feel a failure with all my writing. I never seem to get down on paper the effect it has had on me. That's why in this film it's been very difficult when John [Huston] or the actors have come and questioned a line, not to think they are bound to be right. I've had to learn that maybe I'm right and they're blaming my lines for something they should do themselves." Miller spent practically every night brushing up the dialogue for the following day. Through most of the shooting process he wavered between alternative endings—which cowboy would get the girl in the end?

One day during soundstage work, HENRY HATHAWAY, who had directed Marilyn years earlier in *NIAGARA* (1952), came across the star in tears. She confided in him,

> "All my life I've played Marilyn Monroe, Marilyn Monroe, Marilyn Monroe. I've tried to do a little better and find myself doing an imitation of myself. I so want to do something different. That was one of the things that attracted me to Arthur when he said he was attracted to me. When I married him, one of the fantasies in my mind was that I could get away from Marilyn Monroe through him, and here I find myself back doing the same thing, and I just couldn't take it, I have to get out of there. I just couldn't face having to do another scene with Marilyn Monroe."

Miller and Marilyn left the studio in separate cars after the last day of filming. Marilyn told friends, at the end of October 1960, that she had requested Miller move out of their bungalow at the BEVERLY HILLS HOTEL. Their DIVORCE was announced on November 11 when Marilyn was back in New York and living alone in the East Fifty-seventh Street apartment (Arthur was staying at the Chelsea Hotel). Reportedly Marilyn once called Miller at the Chelsea and asked him whether he was coming home. Under the terms of their agreement, Arthur retained the house in Roxbury (which had been funded from the sale of his previous house nearby), beyond which there were no financial arrangements. Marilyn obtained the divorce for "incompatibility of character" in Juarez, MEXICO, on January 20, 1961, a day chosen by Marilyn because PRESIDENT KENNEDY was being inaugurated and press attention was otherwise occupied.

By the time their marriage failed completely, Miller was, according to Marilyn's psychoanalyst DR. RALPH GREENSON (who interviewed him at the start of his professional relationship with Marilyn) a man with "the attitude of a father who had done more than most fathers would do, and is rapidly coming to the end of his rope."

Miller was deeply affected when he heard of Marilyn's breakdown soon after they split up. He reportedly even considered going to help her in the hospital, before being persuaded at the last minute by friends that he could do her no good now that he was out of her life.

For a time after her death he was assailed by guilty thoughts that their divorce had hastened her suicide. Partly to allay these feelings, he sat down to write *After the Fall* (1964), a play about a doomed Marilynesque character named Maggie. Although many biographers comment on how poorly this play was received, and question the ethics of laying bare the soul of his former wife in such a public fashion, the play contains a great deal of insight into Marilyn's character. Many commentators have noted that taken together, *The Misfits* and *After the Fall* paint the two conflicting sides of Marilyn's character—her vitality and luminescence, and the darkness of her despair.

Marilyn was with Miller for longer than anyone else in her life. Miller has sometimes been criticized and even blamed for Marilyn's gradual loss of control over her fears and anxieties, and consequent spiral into drug dependency. Donald Spoto, for example, asserts that "his tendency to lecture her and to be the wisdom-figure fed her sense of inferiority. Try though he might, and love her though he surely did at the outset, many who knew them realized that Arthur Miller was soon wandering into the dangerous territory of suppressed disdain, effected (however subtly) by his assumption of moral and intellectual superiority."

There is no denying his devotion to her through long years of crisis. In the end, though, devotion wasn't enough. He writes that by the end of *The Misfits*, "I was worse than useless to her now, a bag of nails thrown in her face, a reminder of the failure to pull herself out of her old life even when she had at last truly loved someone."

In 1961 Miller married photographer INGE MORATH, whom he had met while she was working for the MAGNUM photo agency taking stills on *The Misfits*. They had a daughter the following year, and have been together ever since. Miller has continued to write plays, screenplays and, in 1987, his autobiography, *Timebends*.

BOOKS:

*The Misfits* (screenplay written as a novel, with photos). New York: Viking, 1961; reprinted by Viking, 1981.

*After the Fall*, Arthur Miller. New York: Viking, 1964.

Note: Both of these works are published together in "Arthur Miller's Collected Plays", Volume II, New York: Viking, 1981.

*Timebends: A Life*, Arthur Miller. New York: Grove, 1987.

"My Wife Marilyn" *Life* magazine, December 22, 1958 (with Richard Avedon's "Fabled Enchantresses" photo feature).

## THE MILLER FAMILY

**MILLER, AUGUSTA**
Arthur Miller's mother taught Marilyn the rudiments of Jewish cooking, including borscht, chicken soup with matzoh balls, and chopped liver. Despite having since divorced Arthur, and only out of the hospital three days earlier, Marilyn attended Augusta's funeral on March 8, 1961.

**MILLER, ISIDORE**
Marilyn was introduced by Arthur to his parents one day in the fall of 1955, at their modest apartment in Flatbush, as "the girl I'm going to marry." For the occasion, Marilyn dressed demurely in a plain gray skirt, a high-collar black blouse, and she wore no makeup. They hit it off right away. Arthur's sister Joan said, "She adored my father. She was comfortable with my father and he adored her. . . . She felt she could tell him anything and if she said, 'I'd like this to be between you and me ' it would only be between her and him."

On many occasions Isidore and Augusta visited Marilyn and Arthur at their Fifty-seventh Street apartment, where Marilyn would cook food for Isidore, and dote on him if he was unwell—a luxury she had never had with her own father.

Isidore was proud of his friendship with Marilyn. Marilyn kept in regular touch with him, writing him long letters which began "Dear Dad." In February 1962 she visited him in Florida, concerned that he was lonely after his wife had died. For three days she took him out and about. After she left, Isidore found $200 stuffed into an overcoat pocket. "You see, Marilyn wanted me to protect her, but she also protected me."

Three months later he was thrilled when Marilyn invited him to be her escort as she went to Madison Square Garden to sing the breathiest and most famous rendition of "Happy Birthday" ever sung. That evening she proudly introduced Isidore to the president as "my former father-in-law," and brought him along as an escort to the party afterward.

**MILLER, JANE**
Arthur Miller's daughter, age eleven when Marilyn became her step-mother, spent time with Marilyn and Arthur at their country house in Roxbury, along with brother Robert. Marilyn reputedly had a hard time winning over Jane, who was distraught about her parents' divorce, but eventualy Marilyn's winning ways with children prevailed.

**MILLER, KERMIT**
Arthur's brother, who came to the intimate family wedding.

**SLATTERY MILLER, MARY**
Arthur Miller's first wife, whom he left when he fell in love with Marilyn. It has been said that Marilyn bore a striking resemblance to Mary Slattery.

The fifteen years of their marriage, before divorce in 1956, coincided with Miller's most prolific writing period. In the early years she supported her husband's writing by working as a waitress. Some believe that the experiences of her father's life as an insurance salesman provided the inspiration for Miller's *Death of a Salesman*. Arthur and Mary had two children, Jane and Robert, born in 1945 and 1947, respectively.

**MILLER, MORTON**
Arthur Miller's cousin, who had a home near Miller's country retreat at Roxbury, Connecticut. Morton played a supporting role in and around Arthur and Marilyn's marriage; not only did he

take their blood to the State Bureau of Laboratories for the standard pre-marriage tests, he and his wife Florence drove Marilyn and Arthur to White Plains, New York, for their secret wedding ceremony on June 29, 1956, where he served as a witness.

MILLER, ROBERT
Arthur Miller's son, aged nine when Marilyn became his step-mother. Marilyn stayed in touch after divorcing Arthur. The day after meeting Robert Kennedy at a dinner, Marilyn wrote to Bobby Miller, telling him how impressed she was at the senator's intention to tackle civil rights issues. After moving back to Los Angeles, Marilyn invited Bobby and his sister Jane to visit with her in Los Angeles, offering to pay for their tickets. She wrote, "You and Janie are always welcome. I guess we are all a little sloppy about writing, but I think we all know what we mean to each other, don't we? At least I know I love you kids and I want to be your friend and stay in touch. I love and miss you both."

## MILLER, MARILYN
(1898–1936, B. MARY ELLEN REYNOLDS)

The original owner of the Marilyn name was a famed Broadway singing and dancing star during the twenties, who trod the boards in many musicals including *Ziegfeld Follies* and *As Thousands Cheer*.

BEN LYON, the man who suggested Norma Jeane Dougherty change her name to Marilyn, had been engaged to the blonde Marilyn Miller many years previously. Miller had a brief film career, reprising roles she had played on stage, and fitted in three marriages before dying at the age of thirty-seven. Hollywood did not forget her in death, casting JUDY GARLAND and JUNE HAVER to play her in, respectively, *Till the Clouds Roll By* (1946) and *Look for the Silver Lining* (1949).

## MIRACLE, BERNIECE (B. 1919)

Norma Jeane's half-sister, born Berniece (sometimes spelled Bernice) Inez Gladys Baker in Venice, California to Jack and GLADYS BAKER on July 30, 1919, making her seven years older than her famous sibling.

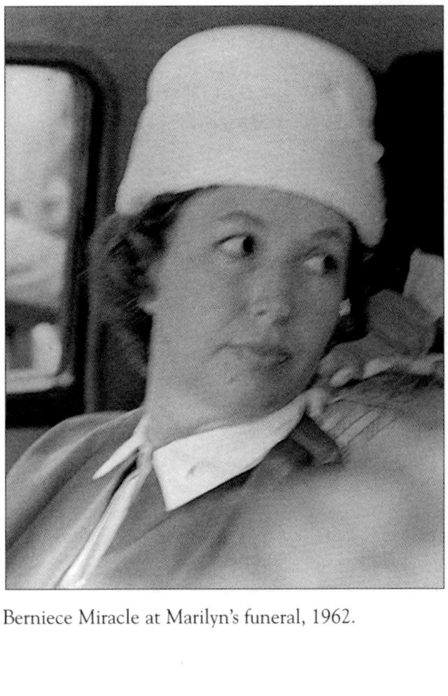

Berniece Miracle at Marilyn's funeral, 1962.

Father JACK BAKER took Berniece and her brother Jack to Kentucky with him in 1923, after divorcing Marilyn's mother.

Accounts conflict about how much contact there was between the half-sisters over the years. During Norma Jeane's upbringing, Berniece lived with her father in Kentucky. Marilyn told early biographer MAURICE ZOLOTOW, "I have never seen my half-sister. We have nothing in common. She is married to an airplane engineer. I am not sure where he lives. It's in Florida, Clearwater or St. Petersburg." More recent biographer DONALD SPOTO mentions Norma Jeane briefly visiting her half-sister in Tennessee in the summer of 1944. FRED LAWRENCE GUILES writes that the half-sisters met up several times during the fifties, and Marilyn had occasion to introduce Mrs. Miracle to JOE DIMAGGIO.

In 1961 Berniece accompanied Marilyn to ARTHUR MILLER's country home in ROXBURY, where Marilyn had lived, to pick up the last of her things. They were in touch with some regularity in the last years of Marilyn's life, and Marilyn visited her sister, then living in Gainesville, during her 1961 trip to Florida.

Berniece was contacted immediately following Marilyn's DEATH, and with Joe DiMaggio she helped arrange the FUNERAL. Marilyn left $10,000 to her half-sister in her final WILL. In 1967 Berniece took over the care of their mother, Gladys Baker, who went to live with her.

Berniece's 1994 book sheds light on Marilyn's early life and last years. It includes rare family photographs and a number of never previously published letters.

BOOK:
*My Sister Marilyn*, Berniece Baker Miracle. NC: Algonquin Books, 1994.

## MIRRORS

NATASHA LYTESS:
"If she caught sight of herself in a full-length mirror, she'd sit down—or just stand there—with her lips hanging slack and eyes droopily half shut like a cat being tickled, absorbed in the mirror's reflection of herself."

Marilyn's obsession with mirrors began in CHILDHOOD, when she would be found mesmerized in front of her image. In adult life friends and colleagues often found her gazing critically at herself in a three-leaf mirror, or studying herself in a wall-length mirror, adjusting the angle of an eyebrow or the hang of a dress.

It was practically impossible for Marilyn to walk past a mirror without stopping and taking a critical look at her reflection. TRUMAN CAPOTE wrote that he once observed Marilyn sitting for ages and staring into a mirror. He asked her what she was doing. Without turning, Marilyn replied, "Looking at her."

Before moving to the apartment she lived in with Arthur Miller on East FIFTY-SEVENTH STREET, Marilyn had several walls redone in floor-to-ceiling mirrors.

It shouts and sings
with life...
explodes with love!
Seven Arts Productions presents
CLARK Gable MARILYN Monroe MONTGOMERY Clift
in the John Huston production of the Misfits
Co-starring
Thelma Ritter Eli Wallach
Screenplay by Arthur Miller
Produced by Frank E. Taylor
Directed by John Huston
United Artists


## *MISFITS, THE* (1961)

Marilyn's twenty-ninth and final picture, barring the abandoned *SOMETHING'S GOT TO GIVE*, began as a short story that ARTHUR MILLER wrote for *Esquire* MAGAZINE in 1957. During his stay in RENO awaiting a divorce so that he could marry Marilyn, Miller met men who, like the CLARK GABLE and MONTGOMERY CLIFT characters in the finished movie, captured wild horses to sell them as pet food. Miller began to adapt the short story after SAM SHAW suggested it would make an excellent movie for Marilyn; this involved fleshing out the Marilyn character (Roslyn) from the minimalist sketch in the original work. Right up until the end of shooting, Miller continued to rework the script, changing his mind about the ending and which of the cowboys would ride off into the sunset with the girl. Clift was not alone in thinking that the final ending, with the aging Gable getting the girl, was wishful thinking on the author's part.

In early 1958 Miller brought close friend and editor FRANK TAYLOR on board as producer, and it was he, reputedly, who suggested sending the script to director JOHN HUSTON. When Huston first read Miller's script, "I read it like a boxer with my guard up, and suddenly I received a punch in the pit of my stomach."

A very promising cast was assembled, including Marilyn's friends Clift and ELI WALLACH. The biggest coup, though, was Gable, to whom Miller described the project as "sort of an Eastern Western—it's about our lives' meaninglessness and maybe how we got to where we are."

Initially Marilyn referred to this project as Miller's "Valentine" to her. But by the time the movie went into production in early 1960, relations between Arthur and Marilyn were strained to breaking point. As Arthur says in his autobiography, "By the start of *The Misfits* it was no longer possible to deny to myself that if there was a key to Marilyn's despair I did not possess it."

Strikes by actors and writers in early 1960 pushed back the finish date on Marilyn's

In 1955 Marilyn invited Eve Arnold to photograph her during a trip to the town of Bement, Illinois, where she was to inaugurate a museum in honor of Abraham Lincoln. Here she is captured primping in the ladies room of Chicago's O'Hare airport before their flight.

Arthur Miller and Marilyn on the set of *The Misfits* (1961).

previous movie *LET'S MAKE LOVE* (1960), and delayed the start of *The Misfits* location shooting in the Nevada desert to mid-July, when daytime temperatures soared well past 100°F.

This movie is perhaps unjustly remembered more for the on-set tensions than the finished work, or the remarkable dramatic performances. The atmosphere was riven by Marilyn's hostility toward her soon-to-be ex-husband, battles between director Huston and Marilyn's drama coach PAULA STRASBERG, and various other permutations of anger and resentment. Marilyn and Arthur fought viciously in public and private, until halfway through filming, as things deteriorated beyond repair, Marilyn took the drastic step of moving out of their shared apartment in the hotel and into Paula's apartment. One bone of contention between Marilyn and Arthur was Marilyn's opinion that Miller had failed to ask for enough MONEY—against Gable's $750,000, Mr. and Mrs. Miller shared $500,000. Marilyn eventually lost faith in Huston, too: "Arthur's been complaining to Huston about me, and that's why Huston treats me like an idiot with his 'dear this' and 'dear that.'"

According to one journalist, "Producer Frank Taylor played peacemaker among the warring personalities on set, as well as minimizing friction between the talent and the studio executives worried about their money. And worry they did, with the many rumors of in-fighting emanating from location, not to mention Huston's decision to aid his actors in their intense characterization by shooting the film in continuity, from first scene to last."

Miller was constantly rewriting the dialogue, staying up deep into the night and then trying out the revisions with Huston the following morning as they drove from the hotel to the location. Marilyn found it hard to memorize her lines at the best of times, so these rewrites were an additional challenge to her. No longer was this a Valentine for Marilyn: "He could have written me anything, and he comes up with this. If that's what he thinks of me, well, then I'm not for him and he's not for me."

Marilyn's LATENESS, illnesses, grogginess from a gargantuan intake of BARBITURATES to help her sleep—not to mention the bitter feud with Arthur—made for slow and tortuous progress. As filming proceeded, she began to appear for work later and later, and when she did turn up she would only listen to Strasberg, not Miller or Huston. In late August, Huston sent Marilyn back to Los Angeles for ten days, to be detoxed from barbiturates, or to recover from a breakdown, depending on accounts. It has also been claimed that this episode was a clever ruse designed by Huston to cover up for his severe GAMBLING debts, which were crippling the production as much as the war between Miller and Marilyn and the desert heat.

Publicity photo for *The Misfits* (1961).

MAGNUM photographer Ernest Haas, who worked on set, commented, "All the people who were on the film were misfits—Marilyn, Monty, John Huston, all a little connected to catastrophe, Gable not saying much, just himself being Gable."

Back in Los Angeles for soundstage work at PARAMOUNT, uncertainty over the exact shape of the film continued when UNITED ARTISTS executives ordered a reshoot of several scenes because they did not like the rough cut they saw at an early screening. Plans were made to reunite cast and crew, until Clark Gable, who had a script approval clause written into his contract, vetoed the idea.

Post-production work was sped up to bring the film out in time to qualify for the 1960 Oscar nominations—in the end, none were forthcoming, not even a posthumous nomination for Gable. The movie ended up costing almost $4 million, making it—in 1961—the most expensive black and white movie ever made.

When filming was finished, Marilyn announced to the press that her four year marriage to Arthur Miller was over. Many years later, Miller said, "The film seemed purely a torture for her. . . . I now marvel at how she managed, under the circumstances, to do what she did." Arthur Miller subsequently married Magnum still photographer INGE MORATH, whom he had met during location shooting.

The gala premiere was held on January 31, 1961, in honor of Clark Gable, who died less than two weeks after filming wrapped. Just eleven days after obtaining her DIVORCE from Arthur Miller, Marilyn's escort to the Capitol Theater (on Broadway and Fifty-first Street) was Montgomery Clift.

Like so many of Marilyn's films, the plot mirrors her own life story in significant ways. It has been speculated that by casting Clark Gable opposite his wife, Arthur Miller was perhaps trying to take her cathartically through her lifelong fears and to the other side, when she would be able to live her life without constant reminders of her loveless upbringing. To young Norma Jeane, the dashing figure of Clark Gable she had seen on the screen became, in her imagination, her real FATHER. RUPERT ALLAN, Marilyn's long-time publicist who left her employ after this movie, has said that Marilyn was "desperately unhappy at having to read lines written by Miller that were so obviously documenting the real-life Marilyn. . . . She felt lonely, isolated, abandoned, worthless, that she had nothing more to offer but this naked, wounded self. And all of us who were her 'family,'—well, we did what a family tried to do."

Portentously, Marilyn first appears in the film standing on a bridge in Reno over the Truckee, a river where newly divorced women customarily toss their wedding bands. Her own suggestion about the troublesome matter of how *The Misfits* should end was that the characters should split up.

With hindsight, Marilyn said of her performance, "Maybe I didn't have enough... distance from the character. . . . Maybe I was really playing me, and Arthur was writing how he saw me instead of a character—or how he saw me before we broke up. Roslyn now might be more of a bitch."

In her last ever interview, Marilyn told *Life* journalist RICHARD MERYMAN about the trials of working on *The Misfits*: "I had to use my wits, or else I'd have been sunk—and nothing is going to sink me. . . . Everyone was always pulling at me, tugging at me, as if they wanted a piece of me. It was always, 'Do this, do that,' and not just on the job but off, too. . . . God, I've tried to stay intact, whole."

BOOK:

*The Story of the Misfits*, James Goode. Indianapolis: Bobbs-Merrill, 1963. (Reprinted 1986 as *The Making of the Misfits*.)
Day-by day-breakdown of how Marilyn's last completed movie was filmed.

MEMORABLE LINES:

"Maybe you're not supposed to believe what people say, maybe it's not even fair to them?"

"How do you find your way back in the dark?" (Marilyn's final words ever in a completed film.)

MEMORABLE COSTUME:

Low-cut white dress with red cherry decoration.

**Tagline:**

"It shouts and sings with life . . . explodes with love!"

**Credits:**

United Artists / Seven Arts Production, Black and White
Length: 124 minutes
Release date: February 1, 1961

Directed by: John Huston
Produced by: Frank E. Taylor
Written by: Arthur Miller
Cinematography by: Russell Metty
Music by: Alex North
Production Design by: Frank R. McKelvy
Film Editing by: George Tomasini

**Cast (credits order):**

Clark Gable . . . Gay Langland
Marilyn Monroe . . . Roslyn Taber
Montgomery Clift . . . Perce Howland
Thelma Ritter . . . Isabelle Steers
Eli Wallach . . . Guido
James Barton . . . Old Man
Estelle Winwood . . . Church Lady
Kevin McCarthy . . . Raymond Taber
Dennis Shaw . . . Young Boy
Philip Mitchell . . . Charles Steers
Walter Ramage . . . Old Groom
J. Lewis Smith . . . Cowboy
Marietta Tree . . . Susan
Bobby LaSalle . . . Bartender
Ryall Bowker . . . Man in Bar
Ralph Roberts . . . Ambulance Driver
Peggy Barton . . . Young Bride

**Crew:**

Stephen B. Grimes . . . art director
William Newberry . . . art director
Lew Smith . . . dialogue coach
Allan "Whitey" Snyder . . . makeup
Agnes Flanagan . . . hair stylist
Sydney Guilaroff . . . hair stylist
Frank La Rue . . . makeup
Frank Prehoda . . . makeup
Frank McKelvy . . . set decoration
C.O. Erickson . . . production manager
Carl Beringer . . . assistant director
Charles Grenzbach . . . sound recordist
Philip Mitchell . . . sound recordist
Chuck Roberson . . . stunts (uncredited)
Angela Allen . . . script supervisor
Billy Jones . . . wrangler
Jean Louis . . . wardrobe: Ms. Monroe
Edward Parone . . . assistant to producer
Tom Shaw . . . second unit director
Lew Smith . . . dialogue coach (uncredited)
Paula Strasberg . . . coach: Ms. Monroe (uncredited)
Rex Wimpy . . . photographer

**Plot:**

Roslyn Tabor (Marilyn Monroe) is in Reno to get a divorce from husband Raymond (Kevin McCarthy). Her landlady Isabelle Steers (Thelma Ritter) introduces her to Guido, played by Eli Wallach, who has been desperately unhappy since his wife died. Guido introduces Roslyn to cowboy Gay Langland (Clark Gable), and love strikes.

Langland is planning a sortie into the hills to round up some horses that live wild in the area. To help he enlists the services of Guido and Perce Howland (Montgomery Clift), a battered rodeo rider.

Roslyn goes along with the three men, only to learn that Langland's intention is to sell the wild animals for dog meat. He is impervious to her protests, but she manages to convince Perce to release the creatures after their capture. A furious Langland immediately sets off to recapture the lead horse, at great physical cost to himself. But as soon as he has achieved this, he frees the horse.

The three horsemen decide to go their separate ways after the abortive roundup. Langland and Roslyn drive off into the distance, the implication being that they are setting off on a life together.

**Reviews:**

*The Hollywood Reporter*
"Miss Monroe has seldom looked worse; the camera is unfailingly unflattering. But there is a delicacy about her playing, and a tenderness that is affecting."

*Life*
"Marilyn plays a role into which are written bits and pieces reminiscent of her own life. The wrangler is all uncomplicated masculinity, virile, violent and, in spirit, the perfect part for Clark Gable. . . . Gable especially was enthusiastic about it. If he judged right—and he was ever slow to praise his own movies—his last film will be one of his best."

*New York Daily News*
"Gable has never done anything better on screen, nor has Miss Monroe. Gable's acting is vibrant and lusty, hers true to the character as written by Miller. . . . The screen vibrates with emotion during the latter part of the film, as Marilyn and Gable engage in one of those battles of the sexes that seem eternal in their constant eruption. It is a poignant conflict between a man and a woman in love, with each trying to maintain individual characteristics and preserve a fundamental way of life."

*New York Herald Tribune*
"After the long drought of vital American pictures, one can now cheer, for *The Misfits* is so distinctly American nobody but an American could have made it.

In this era when sex and violence are so exploited that our sensibilities are in danger of being dulled, here is a film in which both elements are as forceful as in life but never exploited for themselves. Here Miss Monroe is magic but not a living pin-up dangled in skin-tight satin before our eyes. . . . And can anyone deny that in this film these performers are at their best? You forget they are performing and feel that they 'are.'"

## MISS AMERICA

On September 2, 1952, Marilyn took part in her one and only Miss America beauty pageant, as "Grand Marshal," the first woman to fulfill this honorary role. The event was held at the Atlantic City Convention Hall (2300 Boardwalk) in Atlantic City, New Jersey, and Marilyn's presence was arranged as part of the TWENTIETH CENTURY-FOX publicity drive for the launch of her latest film, *MONKEY BUSINESS* (1952).

Marilyn was driven through town in an open-top Nash car, in a low-cut dress that was far more revealing than the outfits worn by the competitors; she also posed with each of the forty-eight candidates for that year's Miss America crown. The press had a field day with the shots their photographers obtained from above. In her inimitable faux-coy style, Marilyn commented a few days later, "People were staring down at me all day long, but I thought they were admiring my grand marshal's badge."

In 1952 Marilyn played Annabel Norris, winner of the Miss Mississippi beauty competition in the ensemble movie *WE'RE NOT MARRIED* (1952).

Marilyn served as Grand Marshall at the Miss America Pageant in 1952.

## MITCHELL, CAMERON
(1918–1994, B. CAMERON MIZELL)

In some accounts, it was Mitchell who in early 1951 made the fateful introduction between starlet Marilyn Monroe and Pulitzer Prize-winning playwright ARTHUR MILLER. Mitchell, who was also a radio commentator and theater actor, starred in both the 1948 stage version and 1952 film version of Miller's seminal work *Death of a Salesman*.

Mitchell's film and television career spanned almost fifty years, and included an appearance opposite Marilyn in *HOW TO MARRY A MILLIONAIRE* (1953).

## MITCHELL, JIMMY

As staff photographer at TWENTIETH CENTURY-FOX, Mitchell was clicking away on the set of *SOMETHING'S GOT TO GIVE* when Marilyn discarded her flesh-colored swimsuit and posed nude. The only other two photographers present were William Woodfield and LAWRENCE SCHILLER, who cannily purchased the rights to Mitchell's photographs for a reputed $10,000.

## MITCHUM, ROBERT (1917–1997)

Cool, self-deprecating, sleepy-eyed Hollywood lead who starred opposite Marilyn in *RIVER OF NO RETURN* (1954).

Mitchum had first encountered Marilyn many years earlier as Norma Jeane, when she was just seventeen and married to JAMES DOUGHERTY, then a colleague of his at the Lockheed factory in Van Nuys. Dougherty is said to have proudly showed a snapshot of his wife to Mitchum; in some versions it was a nude photograph.

Norma Jeane and Mitchum met once or twice at the time, and Mitchum reportedly thought she was "very shy and sweet, but not very comfortable around people."

After working together on *River of No Return*, Mitchum and Marilyn remained friends. On their return to Hollywood, he helped to protect her from a jostling throng of over a hundred newsmen and photographers. Mitchum recalls that "she thought they were cheering for someone else."

Marilyn and Robert Mitchum in a publicity photo for *River of No Return* (1954).

In 1947 Marilyn posed for a series of publicity photos as if skiing on sand dunes for studio-planted newspaper and magazine pieces detailing the young starlet's rise to fame.

In the early 1990s Mitchum penned an introduction to a book by Matthew Smith called *The Men Who Murdered Marilyn*, in which he recounted an incident that took place on the evening when Marilyn was scheduled to serenade PRESIDENT KENNEDY with "Happy Birthday." Such were her nerves that Marilyn steered herself away from MADISON SQUARE GARDEN and into Mitchum's nearby hotel room. He persuaded her to go as planned, and delivered her into a "swarm of Secret Service agents."

Mitchum appeared in over a hundred movies, including *The Sundowners* (1960), *Cape Fear* (1962), *Ryan's Daughter* (1971), and *Farewell My Lovely* (1975).

## MMMMM GIRL

Marilyn Monroe, MM, the "Mmmmm girl." As with so much of the Marilyn myth, competing stories abound.

Supposedly the first time she picked up this sobriquet was as a term of abuse at school, where shy Norma Jeane had a stutter and was known, teasingly, as the Mmmmm Girl.

Fate had it that BEN LYON chose names starting with the letter she had most trouble saying; reputedly the very first time she tried to pronounce her new name, she stuttered "Mmmmmm," and thus became the Mmmmm Girl.

During her tour to promote the Marx brothers movie *LOVE HAPPY* (1950), columnist EARL WILSON further muddied the Mmmmm waters:

> "She has a nice flat waist that rises to an (MMMMM!) 36" bra line. She also has long pretty legs. 'But, why do they call you the Mmmmmmm Girl?' I asked her. 'Well,' she said, 'it seems it started in Detroit where they were having a sneak preview of my picture.' 'But why?' 'Well,' she said, doubtless remembering it just as the press agent told her to, 'it seems some people couldn't whistle so they went Mmmmmmmmm.'"

In her 1955 TV interview with EDWARD R. MURROW, Marilyn stated that her first ever lines on celluloid were "Mmmmm" in *SCUDDA HOO! SCUDDA HAY!* (1948), but this contribution was cut. In the movie, she makes a fleeting (and mute) background appearance.

## MODELING

MARILYN:
"I think cheesecake helps call attention to you. Then you can follow through and prove yourself."

Marilyn's first attempt to break into the world of show business was as a young model. She learned the rudiments of posing before a camera from EMMELINE SNIVELY, at the BLUE BOOK MODELING AGENCY.

Marilyn's first modeling job was an unglamorous assignment being a hostess for the HOLGA STEEL COMPANY at a trade show. On her second assignment, on location at Malibu beach with a group of models for the Montgomery Ward store catalogue, she was sent home on the second day. A devastated Norma Jeane learned from Miss Snively that she was dismissed because she was just "too sexy" and it was felt nobody would bother looking at the clothes.

As her film career slowly got into gear, Marilyn modeled swimsuits and did cheesecake shots right through until the early fifties.

Her considered opinion on modeling:

> "It's kind of funny. You smile for the camera, you hold very still, you act as if you're having a good time—but it's a day when you're really having terrible cramps. I guess I shouldn't say this, but sometimes modeling seemed so phony and fake I just had to laugh. They thought that was great, they had a great smile from you, and they just snapped away, thinking that, well, I was having a good time. Sure, sometimes it was fun. But modeling can also be a little crazy. I once asked why I had to wear a bathing suit for a toothpaste ad. He looked at me as if I was some kind of crazy!"

## MONEY

MARILYN:
"I'm not interested in money. I just want to be wonderful."

The accumulation of wealth was never a priority in Marilyn's life. She grew up through the Depression, raised in hard-working but poor families. Biographers generally agree that Norma Jeane did not suffer the worst hardships of the time, but life with some of her foster parents and in the Los Angeles ORPHANAGE was basic to say the least.

A wartime factory job at the RADIO PLANE MUNITIONS FACTORY brought her her first income. Her first modeling assignment paid for the signing-on fee to her MODELING agency, at the rate of $10 per day. Some of those early modeling jobs were paid for in kind. For example she walked away from advertising Tar-Tan Sun Lotion with the swim costume she had posed in.

After her initial year's contract with TWENTIETH CENTURY-FOX, starting on $75 per week, she spent four years in and out of work, one of many starlets trying to break into the Hollywood big time. Financially these were hard times, with money scarce, the need for BENEFACTORS—rumors of PROSTITUTION date from this period—and days when she had to make do with only thirty cents a day for food.

Marilyn wrote that when she first was brought along to glamorous Hollywood parties she couldn't help remembering,

> "How much twenty-five cents and even nickels meant to the people I had known, how happy ten dollars would have made them, how a hundred dollars would have changed their whole lives. I remembered my Aunt Grace and me waiting in line at the Homes Bakery to buy a sackful of bread. . . . And I remembered how she had gone with one of her lenses missing from her glasses for three months because she couldn't afford the fifty cents to buy its replacement."

When stardom came, Marilyn unenviably became one of the lowest paid topliners in Hollywood. After so many years struggling to land a long-term studio contract, the seven year deal she signed with Fox in 1951 bound her to a pay scale that lagged woefully behind her burgeoning status. In 1952, the year that she became an established star, she was making just $750 a week, minus tax and 10 percent to her agents, not nearly enough to cover her outgoings which included up to $200 per week on the various drama and singing lessons, on employing business manager INEZ MELSON, paying for her mother's care and keeping up a room in the prestigious BEL AIR HOTEL—fortunately she had a little extra money coming in from *DON'T BOTHER TO KNOCK* (1952), which she made for RKO studios. For smash hit *Gentleman Prefer Blondes* (1953) Marilyn earned $18,000, just one-tenth of what co-star JANE RUSSELL made.

If she still didn't care too much about money, Marilyn did mind about the injustice of her remuneration. In 1954, she dug in her heels and refused to work on the next Fox project, *The Girl in Pink Tights*, on which FRANK SINATRA was to have made more than three times her $1,500 weekly fee. The first day of principal photography came and went and days later Marilyn was tracked by the studio to SAN FRANCISCO, where soon after she married JOE DIMAGGIO. Marilyn and DiMaggio stood up to the studio's bullying tactics and managed to win a renegotiated contract, the promise of a $100,000 bonus, and at last a degree of approval over the projects she took.

A year later Marilyn walked out on the studio again, this time to strike off on her own under the umbrella of MARILYN MONROE PRODUCTIONS, owned 51 percent by Marilyn Monroe, 49 percent by partner MILTON GREENE. From this point on, Marilyn (or at least her various financial advisors) exerted greater control on her livelihood. Greene and his team of LAWYERS renegotiated a much more favorable contract with Fox, while the production company's sole movie, *THE PRINCE AND THE SHOWGIRL* (1956), saw Marilyn beginning to work on a profit share basis, earning a very healthy 10 percent for both *The Prince and the Showgirl* and later *SOME LIKE IT HOT* (1959).

By 1960, Marilyn was earning enough to put her in the top 90 percent tax bracket, with an income of $300,000 for *THE MISFITS* (1961) and a further $50,000 as her share of *Some Like It Hot* profits.

Many of Marilyn's friends, and many of the people she worked with, have had occasion to note that Marilyn's attitude toward money meant frequent and unbidden acts of GENEROSITY. GEORGE MASTERS, Marilyn's preferred hairstylist in the last years of her life, writes, "In her own peculiar way, Marilyn was very outgoing and generous. There was never any haggle about fees or tips. . . . I once flew to New York, at her request and expense, to do her for an important event. . . . she greeted me at the door of her suite with, 'Oh, George, I don't feel like it now. Come back next week.' And she put a crumpled two thousand dollar check in my shirt pocket."

Evidently, Marilyn has generated much more money dead than alive. Her initially insolvent ESTATE was bailed out by her percentage film deals. In the last decade the Estate has been cleverly managed into an enormous revenue-generating business, though the vast majority of its profits go to a woman who never met Marilyn, ANNA STRASBERG, second wife of LEE STRASBERG. Marilyn as an industry of content and MEMORABILIA continues to grow, and is now so large and diffuse that nobody dares put an estimate on its total size.

### SALARIES

Starting salary at the Radio Plane Company, circa 1943–44: $20 a week
Ending salary at Radio Plane, 1945: $50 a week
First modeling assignments, 1945: $5 an hour
As a hostess/model for the Holga Steel Company, 1945: $10 a day
Posing for illustrator Earl Moran, 1946–1950: $10 an hour
First contract with Twentieth Century-Fox, 1946: $75 a week
Fox contract renewal, 1947: $150 a week
Columbia contract, 1948: $125 a week
Promoting *Love Happy* (1949): $100 a week
For *The Asphalt Jungle* (1950): $350 a week (a total of $1,050)
Second Fox contract, 1951: $500 a week
*Clash by Night* (1952): $500 a week
*We're Not Married* (1952): $750 a week
*Gentlemen Prefer Blondes* (1953): $1,250 a week
May 11, 1953: $1,500 a week (contractual ceiling limit)
*River of No Return* (1954), *There's No Business Like Show Business* (1954), and *The Seven Year Itch* (1955): $1,500 a week
New Fox contract, 1956: $100,000 per film flat fee, plus $500 a week for expenses
*Some Like It Hot* (1959): $100,000 flat fee, plus 10 per cent of the profits
*The Misfits* (1961): $300,000 flat fee, plus 10 percent of the profits
What Marilyn would have received for *Something's Got to Give* (1962): $100,000 flat fee, later renegotiated to $500,000

## MONKEY BUSINESS (1952)

After the her first lead in *DON'T BOTHER TO KNOCK* (1952), Marilyn was demoted to a decorative secretary role in this CARY GRANT comedy-by-numbers involving a chimpanzee and a magical elixir of youth. TWENTIETH CENTURY-FOX tried to squeeze the most mileage possible out of their rising young star. After this, there were no more secretary roles for Marilyn.

Marilyn's dimwit secretary character cannot type and is described in the movie as "cute... but half infant."

According to biographer FRED LAWRENCE GUILES, "It was [writers] Lederer and Diamond's idea to have the girl whom Zanuck had already dubbed as 'empty-headed' to turn out to be the only sane character on the premises" in this screwball comedy.

Grant, who played opposite practically all of Hollywood's leading ladies, did not particularly spark in his single on-screen hook up with Marilyn.

As part of the publicity tour for this film, which premiered in Atlantic City, New

Jersey, the studio arranged for Marilyn to be the first ever woman Grand Marshal of the MISS AMERICA Pageant.

When the movie came out, and did reasonably well, the theaters where it was shown put Marilyn's name, rather than those of her much more famous colleagues Grant and GINGER ROGERS, on their billboards.

**Credits:**
Twentieth Century-Fox, Black and White
Length: 97 minutes
Release date: September 5, 1952

Directed by: Howard Hawks
Produced by: Sol C. Siegel
Written by: I. A. L. Diamond, Ben Hecht, Charles Lederer, Harry Segall (original story)
Cinematography by: Milton R. Krasner
Music by: Leigh Harline
Production Design by: George Patrick, Lyle R. Wheeler
Costume Design by: Travilla
Film Editing by: William B. Murphy

**Cast (credits order):**
Cary Grant . . . Barnaby Fulton
Ginger Rogers . . . Edwina Fulton
Charles Coburn . . . Mr. Oliver Oxley
Marilyn Monroe . . . Lois Laurel
Hugh Marlowe . . . Hank Entwhistle
Henri Letondal . . . Siegfried Kitzel
Robert Cornthwaite . . . Dr. Zoldeck
Larry Keating . . . G. J. Culverly
Douglas Spencer . . . Dr. Brunner
Esther Dale . . . Mrs. Rhinelander
George Winslow . . . Little Indian
Emmett Lynn . . . Jimmy
Joseph Mell . . . Barber
George Eldredge . . . Auto Salesman
Heinie Conklin . . . Painter
Kathleen Freeman . . . Nurse
Olan Soule . . . Hotel Clerk
Harry Carey Jr. . . . Reporter
John R. McKee . . . Photographer
Faire Binney . . . Dowager
Bill McLean . . . Bellboy
Paul Maxey . . . Dignitary
Mack Williams . . . Dignitary
Gil Stratton . . . Yale Man
Forbes Murray . . . Man
Marjorie Holiday . . . Receptionist
Harry Carter . . . Scientist
Harry Seymour . . . Clothing Store Salesman
Harry Bartell . . . Scientist
Jerry Paris . . . Scientist
Roger Moore . . . Bit Man
Ruth Warren . . . Laundress
Isabel Withers . . . Laundress
Olive Carey . . . Laundress
Dabbs Greer . . . Cab Driver
Russ Clark . . . Policeman
Ray Montgomery . . . Policeman
Melinda Plowman . . . Girl
Terry Goodman . . . Boy
Ronnie Clark . . . Boy
Rudy Lee . . . Boy
Mickey Little . . . Boy
Brad Mora . . . Boy
Jimmy Roebuck . . . Boy
Louis Lettieri . . . Boy
Robert Nichols . . . Garage Man
Mary Field . . . Clerk
Jerry Sheldon . . . Guard

**Crew:**
W. D. Flick . . . sound
Earle H. Hagen . . . orchestration
Paul Helmick . . . assistant director
Roger Heman . . . sound
Ray Kellogg . . . special effects
Charles Le Maire . . . wardrobe director
Thomas Little . . . set decorator
Lionel Newman . . . musical director
Ben Nye . . . makeup
George Patrick . . . art director
Walter M. Scott . . . set decorator
Helen Turpin . . . hair styles
Lyle R. Wheeler . . . art director

**Plot:**
Scientist Dr. Barnaby Fulton (Cary Grant) is trying to discover the elixir of youth, but his work is foiled by one of his tested chimpanzees, which escapes from his cage and miraculously creates the magic mixture. Some of the sauce gets into the water cooler, and Fulton takes a long draught. He immediately reverts to college age. When Fulton's boss sends his secretary Lois Laurel (Marilyn) to track down the now missing Fulton, the rejuvenated scientist whisks her off swimming, roller skating, and then for a hi-speed tour in a fast car. Fortunately the effects of the potion wear off, but then Fulton's wife Edwina (Ginger Rodgers) unwittingly drinks the elixir and her adolescent behavior almost provokes a scandal. Then things go from bad to worse after husband and wife drink coffee brewed with water from the contaminated cooler, this time regressing to unruly kids. The water does the rounds of all the main characters except for Marilyn, whose job is to provoke the most ardent of youthful desires in the many rejuvenated men around her. Everybody finally reverts to their actual age, and because the formula was concocted willy-nilly by the chimp, there is no chance for the elixir to be recreated.

**Reviews:**
*New York Post*
"Marilyn Monroe, described by Grant as 'half child' and counter-described by Rogers with 'not the visible half,' poses and walks in a manner that must be called suggestive. What she suggests is something that this picture seems to have on its mind much of the time, with or without the rejuvenation."

*New York Herald Tribune*
"Not having seen Miss Monroe before, I know now what that's all about, and I've no dissenting opinions to offer. She disproves more than adequately the efficacy of the old stage rule about not turning one's back to the audience."

*Photoplay*
"Marilyn Monroe garners laughs and whistles, bouncing in and out as a secretary who can't type. Typing skill, however, is the only attribute which the lady appears to be lacking in."

*New York Daily News*
"Marilyn Monroe can look and act dumber than any of the screen's current blondes."

Marilyn and Cary Grant in *Monkey Business* (1952).

## MONROE, MARION (1905–1929?)

Norma Jeane's uncle, who by some reports died after suffering from paranoid schizophrenia, disappeared one fine day, saying he was going out to get a newspaper, and never coming back.

(*see* DELLA MAE HOGAN *and* IDA MARTIN)

## MONROE, OTIS ELMER (1866–1909)

Norma Jeane's grandfather, Otis Elmer Monroe, is the shadowiest figure of her close maternal relatives.

He is generally believed to have been born in Scotland. By trade a house painter, he was ten years older than his wife DELLA MAE HOGAN, whom he married in late 1899. Soon afterward, Otis took a job working for the Mexican National Railway, just over the border in Porfirio Diaz, a town named in honor of Mexico's president at the time (today the town is called Piedras Negras).

Norma Jeane's mother, Gladys Pearl Monroe (*see* GLADYS BAKER), was born on May 27, 1902 in MEXICO. The family moved back north to the U.S., following the jobs, and led an itinerant existence up and down the West Coast, mainly in the expanding Los Angeles area.

Otis Monroe's health began deteriorating while his daughter was still young. He drank heavily, his memory became erratic, he suffered headaches, developed violent trembling in his hands and feet, and became emotionally unstable, before in 1908 being admitted to the Southern California State Hospital, Patton (San Bernardino County). He died in that hospital nine months later, on July 22, 1909.

According to biographer DONALD SPOTO, Marilyn's grandfather was diagnosed with general paresis, the terminal stage of syphilis of the brain. This would mean that, in contradiction to the stories put forward by many biographers, his mental problems were the result of a disease, and not some kind of inherited condition. Marilyn, and her mother before her, lived in fear that they had a genetic predisposition toward MENTAL ILLNESS.

## MONTAND, YVES
(1921–1991, B. IVO LIVI)

RUPERT ALLAN:
"It was true that sex was a pretty big part of it but Yves offered her something more. They were both from unhappy childhoods. He often didn't have enough food when he was a kid in Italy. Marilyn thought she was in love with the guy."

Marilyn's most public affair was with Yves Montand, a Frenchman who was actually born to a peasant family in Italy. After traveling to Marseilles, he was "discovered" as an eighteen-year-old by Edith Piaf. A singing career and an affair with France's premier songstress brought film work in France, and international cinema success. By 1960 he was ready to try his hand at Hollywood.

Yves Montand celebrates Marilyn's birthday with her during filming of *Let's Make Love* (1960).

When Montand and his wife SIMONE SIGNORET arrived in Hollywood to work with Marilyn on *LET'S MAKE LOVE* (1960), they were already personal friends of Marilyn and ARTHUR MILLER, and Yves shared Miller's public commitment to leftist causes. In late 1956 Miller had met them in Paris to finalize plans about a production of his play *The Crucible*, in which they both performed. In September 1959 the Montands were in New York while Yves was touring his successful one-man show on Broadway. The Millers and Montands hit it off and saw one another often. This was at a moment when TWENTIETH CENTURY-FOX was having a devil of a time finding a male lead willing to work with Marilyn after *SOME LIKE IT HOT* (1959). When Marilyn put Montand's name forward to play opposite her in *Let's Make Love* (1960), the studio said yes, and Montand thought he at last had his big Hollywood break. It is also said that it was Miller who told the studio that he thought Montand would be perfect in the role.

Marilyn told the world what she thought of her co-star's looks in a toast on the first day of shooting: "Next to my husband and Marlon Brando," she said, raising a toast, "I think Yves Montand is the most attractive man I've ever met."

Marilyn, Arthur, Yves, and Simone moved into neighboring bungalows at the BEVERLY HILLS HOTEL. Gossip-hounds were on the lookout for any sign of shenanigans, and it didn't take them long to dig something up. In late April 1960, as fate would have it both Arthur and Simone were called away on business. What happened next varies depending on the account. Either Marilyn turned up at his bungalow wearing a mink coat and nothing else; or in Montand's memoirs, one evening he looked in on Marilyn, who had been suffering in bed with a cold all day, to see if she wanted anything to eat or drink. "I bent over to kiss her goodnight, but suddenly it was a wild kiss, a fire, a hurricane I couldn't stop."

On shoot days Fox sent a limousine to pick up Marilyn and Montand every morning. Signoret, who retained her sang-froid throughout, tells the story in her autobiography of what happened one morning when Marilyn had one of her days when she just didn't feel like going to work. After steadfastly ignoring phone calls and then Signoret pounding on her bungalow door, Montand wrote a little note and slipped it under Marilyn's door:

> "You can do whatever you like to Spyros Skouras and the Fox studio and all the producers in town, if that's what you want. But next time you decide to hang around too late listening to my wife tell you stories instead of going to bed, because you've already decided not to get up the next morning and go to the studio, please tell me! Don't leave me to work for hours on end on a scene you've already decided not to do the next day. I'm not the enemy, I'm your pal. And capricious little girls never amused me. Best, Yves."

The story runs that Marilyn was so mortified she did not dare apologize in person; she got Miller to call the Montands from Ireland, where he was working with JOHN HUSTON on the script for *THE MISFITS* (1961), and explain that they should go over to Marilyn's room; they knocked, entered, and then Marilyn burst out in tears saying "I'm bad, I'm bad, I'm bad. I won't do it again, I promise."

Montand and Marilyn met up when Marilyn was in Los Angeles during filming of *The Misfits* in Nevada. But it is unlikely that she wanted to have much to do with him after September 1, 1960, the day that an exclusive interview Montand had given columnist HEDDA HOPPER hit the newsstands. Among the things he said about Marilyn that she found hurtful was: "I think she's an enchanting child, a simple girl without any guile." This article was regarded by many as ungallant to say the least, though it seems that the words printed in the article were a rather free interpretation of his less than perfect English. Marilyn's press aide RUPERT ALLAN said as much: "Maybe he didn't understand enough English to know what she was putting into his mouth, but [Hopper] quoted him as saying Marilyn had a 'schoolgirl crush' on him. To give him the benefit, he might have said Marilyn was like a girl or something like that. The next day, Hedda brought out the story and Marilyn was very upset."

Montand's movie career did not flourish in the States, but he continued to put together a good body of work with Europe's most talented directors, including Costa-Gavras, Alain Resnais, and Vincent Minnelli, and in 1986 starred in Berri's *Jean de Florette* and *Manon des Sources*.

BOOK:
*You See, I Haven't Forgotten*, Yves Montand with Herve Hamon and Patrick Rotman, New York: Knopf, 1992.

## MOORE, JOHN

When she lived in New York, John Moore was one of Marilyn's favorite designers. He came round to her East FIFTY-SEVENTH STREET apartment to measure her for new creations, and he also visitedb as a friend.

He was at Marilyn's wedding to ARTHUR MILLER; he gave Marilyn help redesigning their New York apartment; and he was the man who made the dress with a shoulder strap so thin that it snapped, right on cue, at the press conference Marilyn called to announce the formation of MARILYN MONROE PRODUCTIONS.

At the New York press conference announcing production of *The Prince and the Showgirl* (1957) the tiny strap of Marilyn's John Moore dress snapped right on cue.

Marilyn poses for a Moran drawing in 1946. The finished drawing would be titled "Bus Stop" and would be accompanied by the following poem: Little Boy Blue/Come blow your horn./She wants a ride,/This maid, forlorn/But she's prepared/If you run out of gas./So, save your tricks/For some other lass.

## MORAN, EARL

One of Norma Jeane's earliest regular MODELING assignments, to help pay the rent while she fought for an entree into the movie business, was for illustrator Earl Moran, one of America's most renowned cheesecake artists. He paid her ten dollars an hour to photograph her in various costumes and states of toplessness from 1946 to 1949, and then used these photographs to make his very popular charcoal and chalk drawings. Moran's Marilyn work was used, among others, by major CALENDAR company Brown & Bigelow.

## MORATH, INGE (B. 1923)

Inge Morath was one of the photographers sent by photo agency MAGNUM to cover shooting on *THE MISFITS* (1961). Just days after Marilyn's lawyers announced she was to divorce ARTHUR MILLER, he was back in New York where he bumped into Austrian-born Morath on Fifth Avenue. They fell in love, she moved to America, and on February 7, 1962 became Miller's third wife. Morath, then thirty-nine, gave birth to a daughter, Rebecca, five weeks after Marilyn's death.

According to Miller, Marilyn had very much liked the pictures she took on the set of *The Misfits*, appreciating the warmth and kindness she showed.

## MORIARTY, EVELYN

The same height and coloring as Marilyn, Moriarty was spotted by director GEORGE CUKOR in a line of showgirls at Earl Carroll's nightclub and picked to be Marilyn's stand-in for *LETS MAKE LOVE* (1960). She kept the job on *THE MISFITS* (1961) and the unfinished *SOMETHING'S GOT TO GIVE*. A reporter who interviewed her in 1987, twenty-five years after Marilyn's death, noticed her "slip into Marilyn's mannerisms that she learned first hand—pursing her lips, batting her lashes or whispering in Marilyn's silky voice."

Moriarty unfailingly recalls Marilyn as a kind, generous, and loyal person, who loved and took care of animals. She also helped people, such as during production of *Let's Make Love* when she made (an anonymous) donation of $1,000 to pay for the funeral expenses of the wife of a crew member.

The last time Moriarty saw Marilyn was on the star's thirty-sixth birthday, on what turned out to be the last day of shooting on *Something's Got to Give* before the studio closed the picture down. Moriarty had gone round the set and collected fifty cents from all the crew to buy a surprise cake. When an executive said he would cover the costs she returned the money and was driven by studio car to Humphries bakery at the Farmer's Market. Marilyn was said to be delighted by the impromptu celebration.

Ever since Marilyn's death, Moriarty has faithfully paid her respects on the star's birthday at the WESTWOOD MEMORIAL PARK CEMETARY. Moriarty has featured in many Marilyn DOCUMENTARIES and has always been the voice of unending praise. Of the flood of books that have come out about Marilyn, Moriarty says "they are writing fiction and saying it is true, it's mind boggling."

## MORTENSEN, MARTIN EDWARD (1897–1929?)

Not only is Martin Edward Mortensen (sometimes spelled Mortenson) the name of one of the several men who could have been Norma Jeane's FATHER, it is a name shared by two individuals, one of whom died in 1929, the other who lived until 1981.

Hence there are two parallel tracks to his upbringing. The Norwegian Mortensen was born at a town called Haugesund, became a baker, married young, and had three children before moving alone to the United States in 1923; the Californian Mortensen had also married but divorced.

By the time he met GLADYS BAKER in 1924, he was a devout Lutheran. He thought that as a church-going Christian Scientist she would make a good wife—though it has been said that Gladys's fervor only came about because best friend and roommate GRACE MCKEE GODDARD had a boyfriend who was a devout church member.

Gladys married her second husband, Mr. Mortensen, on October 11, 1924. Four months later she was back living with Goddard, apparently unable to adjust to the boredom of wedded bliss after her carefree pre-marriage existence—though in some accounts it was he who left her.

In his petition for divorce, filed with the courts on May 26, 1925, Mortensen claimed that Gladys "willfully and without cause deserted [him] and ever since has and now continues to . . . desert and abandon [him]."

Just over a year later, Baker gave birth to Norma Jeane at 9:30 A.M. on June 1, 1926 in the maternity ward of the Los Angeles General HOSPITAL. On the birth certificate the father is entered as Edward Mortensen, of unknown residence.

It seems that Mortensen tried, unsuccessfully, to win back Gladys's affections, before the final divorce was granted on August 15, 1928.

At this point, Mortensen resumes his double life. The majority of biographers subscribe to the theory that Martin Edward Mortensen perished in a motorcycle accident in Ohio on

Inge Morath took this photograph of Marilyn during filming of *The Misfits* (1961).

June 18, 1929. However, on February 10, 1981 at the age of eighty-three a second Martin Edward Mortensen died of a heart attack in Riverside, California. In life he had claimed to be the father of Marilyn Monroe, and among his possessions was found a copy of Norma Jeane's birth certificate.

On her marriage certificates to both JOE DIMAGGIO and ARTHUR MILLER, Marilyn herself listed her father as Edward Mortensen, though there is evidence that she did not think he was her father. He was not the man she made a number of abortive attempts to visit.

Don Murray and Marilyn in *Bus Stop* (1956).

## MOTHER AND MOTHER FIGURES

MAUREEN STAPLETON:
"She brought out the mother in everybody. She was a very appealing woman and a very strong woman. A bright woman."

Marilyn only lived with her mother GLADYS BAKER for a little over a year, when she was seven. Otherwise, she grew up with a number of mother figures and foster mothers, the most important of whom were IDA BOLENDER, GRACE MCKEE GODDARD, and ANA LOWER. It has been written that along with imaginary FATHER Clark Gable, she dreamed that actress/ singer Jeanette MacDonald was her mother.

The greatest figure of maternal LOVE in her girlhood was beloved "Aunt" Ana Lower. Marilyn recalled, "She became a true mother to me—the only touch of mother love I had ever known. . . . When Aunt Ana died, I felt the first poignant grief I had ever known."

Long-time drama teacher NATASHA LYTESS was a complex presence in Marilyn's life for the first half of her film career. At times, this included playing the tough mother figure. Lytess writes in her autobiography, "She had no discipline, and she was lazy, but I pounded at her. When she came unprepared for a lesson, I was furious. I berated her as I would my own daughter. And always Marilyn would look at me as though I were betraying her."

GLORIA STEINEM notes that Marilyn's lifelong difficulties in making friends with women stemmed from the ambiguity of her relationship with her own mother, and the fact that so many women came and went in her young life, none of whom could unreservedly give her the love and attention most children get. The few women who showed her some kindness as a child were remembered with enormous fondness, especially "Aunt" Ana Lower, and even the woman who ran the ORPHANAGE, whom Marilyn recalled allowing her the treat of putting on makeup, and then complimented her on her beautiful soft skin.

In contrast to her rather few friendships with women her own age, Marilyn kept up friendships with a number of older women such as Anne Karger (mother of early beau FRED KARGER), XENIA CHEKHOV (widow of drama teacher Michael), and mothers-in-law Rosalie DiMaggio and Augusta Miller.

Perhaps the greatest personal regret of Marilyn's life was her inability to have her own CHILDREN. She miscarried twice and had one ectopic pregnancy which had to be terminated. In 1958, not long after her second miscarriage, she shared with friend NORMAN ROSTEN the quandary she was in: "Should I do my next picture or stay home and try to have a baby again? That's what I want most of all, the baby, I guess, but maybe God is trying to tell me something, I mean with all my pregnancy problems. I'd probably make a kooky mother, I'd love my child to death. I want it, yet I'm scared."

In just two of her thirty on-screen roles was Marilyn cast as a mother: *WE'RE NOT MARRIED* (1952), and her final, unfinished movie *SOMETHING'S GOT TO GIVE*.

## MURRAY, DON (B. 1929)

Marilyn's co-star in *BUS STOP* (1956) was plucked from relative obscurity for this, his first screen role, after seven years making a name for himself in the theater. Director JOSHUA LOGAN cast Murray after being impressed with his performance in *The Skin of Our Teeth*. Logan's faith paid off in an Oscar nomination for Murray's portrayal of abrasive country boy Beauregard "Beau" Decker.

Despite his devout beliefs, it was not always an easy task for Murray to work with Marilyn. Not only was she a vastly more famous and established star than he, but she came into *Bus Stop* after walking out on TWENTIETH CENTURY-FOX and renegotiating her straitjacket contract to give her wide-ranging powers on her movies.

Murray has told of one incident: "When she thought I'd ruined a scene of hers, she continued the action as rehearsed, taking her costume and hitting me across the face with it. Some of the sequins scratched the corner of my eye and she ran off. But she wasn't deliberately mean."

During filming Murray shared with a *New York Times* journalist his personal impressions of Marilyn, circa 1956: "Here she is, one of the country's most important personalities. Suddenly she discovers that, well, something is missing. So right now she is going through what most of us experience in our teens, trying to get inside her own personality through philosophy and psychology."

Still, life on the set was not without its interest for Murray. He became very close to fellow actress HOPE LANGE, and soon afterward they married.

Murray has worked a great deal in television, including a role as ROBERT KENNEDY in the 1974 TV movie *The Sex Symbol*. His best-remembered film performances, apart from *Bus Stop*, came in *The Bachelor Party* (1957), *The Hoodlum Priest* (1961), and *Advise and Consent* (1962).

## MURRAY, EUNICE

In the last nine months of Marilyn's life, Eunice Murray was a constant presence in her life as housekeeper and general factotum, on the recommendation of psychoanalyst DR. RALPH GREENSON.

Murray was born Eunice Joerndt in March 1902, in Chicago. Her parents, devout Jehovah's Witnesses, moved to Ohio, where she attended a junior college run by the Swedenborgian sect. In 1921 Eunice married carpenter John Murray, the son of a Swedenborgian minister. They had three daughters, Jacquelyn, Patricia, and Marilyn.

In Los Angeles, with her husband John, Eunice Murray built a Mexican-colonial style house at 902 Franklin Street. Just four months after moving in, the couple fell behind with their mortgage payments and had to sell. Greenson, who purchased the house from them in 1947 for $16,500, was later to become Marilyn's psychoanalyst.

Eunice separated from her husband soon afterward. Greenson hired her to work in the homes of his important clients. In her autobiography, Murray writes that Greenson sent her to work with clients who were "seriously ill with depression or schizophrenia, [or with] others, like Marilyn Monroe, [who] was simply recovering from stressful experiences and needed supportive aid." The most commonly held view is that Murray's role was to be the doctor's eyes and ears, reporting back on what his patients said and did. According to Murray's son-in-law Philip Laclair, "She did it for the money. Her husband left her badly, she had no formal training as a nurse—not even a high school education—but she was a kind woman and became a valuable asset to Greenson. She always followed his orders very closely."

In November 1961, on Greenson's recommendation, Marilyn hired Eunice as her companion, driver, nurse and housekeeper. Murray was initially taken on at a weekly salary of $60 (or $100, depending on sources). Murray accompanied Marilyn on her furniture-buying spree to MEXICO in February 1962, taking the opportunity to visit her brother-in-law Churchill Murray, who lived in Mexico City. Hairdresser GEORGE MASTERS, who also went along on the trip, found her very bizarre indeed: "She was—how can I put it?—a very weird woman, like a witch. Terrifying, I remember thinking. She was terrifically jealous of Marilyn, separating her from her friends—just a divisive person."

PAT NEWCOMB recalled, "At first Marilyn sought her advice because she was supposed to be this wonderful housekeeper Greenson had found for her. But from day one, I did not trust Eunice Murray, who seemed to be always snooping around. I tried to stay out of her way because I just didn't like her. She was sort of a spook, always hovering, always on the fringes of things." Other members of Marilyn's entourage, such as ALLAN "WHITEY" SNYDER, remembered her as "a very strange lady. . . . she was always whispering—whispering and listening. She was this constant presence, reporting everything back to Greenson, and Marilyn quickly realized this."

Members of the entourage were pleased to learn in May 1962, soon after Greenson had left on a five-week holiday, that Marilyn had handed Murray a check and told her that her services were no longer required. However, on Marilyn's return from New York, where she had regaled President KENNEDY with his fondest "Happy Birthday" of the year, Murray was still there, claiming that she had understood the dismissal to be only a temporary lay-off, and had returned.

It has been reported that Murray was planning to accompany her sister and brother-in-law on a trip to Europe starting August 6, but she didn't tell Marilyn until August 1. Marilyn wrote her a check and told her not to bother coming back in September. According to more than one biographer, Marilyn had already contacted a former MAID (Hattie Stevenson or Florence Thomas, depending on who is telling the story) to see if she could come as a replacement. Marilyn's friends viewed the removal of Murray as a positive step by Marilyn in reclaiming her life, and a sign that she was coming out from under the thrall of Dr. Greenson.

Marilyn's housekeeper Eunice Murray.

On August 4, 1962, the last day that Marilyn was seen alive, Eunice Murray reported for duty at 8 A.M. One of the few undisputed facts about what happened that day was that Mrs. Murray was there the entire time—and, oddly enough, she stayed overnight; she did not return to her Santa Monica home.

During the day Murray answered Marilyn's phone calls while Dr. Greenson saw Marilyn at her home. Murray drove Marilyn to the beach in mid-afternoon, and then back home for continuation of her day-long therapy session (though in some versions, Greenson only attended to Marilyn for a couple of hours in the late afternoon). Murray continued to screen Marilyn's incoming calls, including reputed calls from concerned friends that Marilyn was in some kind of trouble. More often than not, Murray gave out excuses as to why Marilyn could not come to the phone.

In her account of Marilyn's DEATH, the one she gave to the police in her official statement, Eunice said she woke at 3 A.M. and noticed a light on under Marilyn's bedroom door, and that, oddly, the door was locked. Concerned, she called Dr. Greenson who told her to check from outside if she could see anything through the curtains. She reported back that Marilyn was lying on the bed, nude, in an "unnatural position." She then called Greenson who came over, broke into the bedroom through the window, and found Marilyn dead.

A number of discrepancies have been identified in her testimony. To start with, the brand-new deep pile carpeting was too thick to allow light to be seen under the door; in later testimonies, Eunice said she was alerted by the telephone call. A bigger doubt regards the locked door. Some biographers claim that there was no working lock on the door, and Marilyn had always slept with her bedroom door open. Indeed, she abhorred the idea of locks altogether after her brief and distressing enforced stay in a psychiatric ward at the Payne-Whitney HOSPITAL.

Murray has also not been consistent regarding the timing of the discovery, and hence the time, of Marilyn's death. She is said to have told the first policeman to arrive on the scene, Sergeant JACK CLEMMONS, that she first alerted Dr Greenson at midnight, not 3 A.M. as she later told officials. Clemmons said that when he arrived at the house at 4:40 A.M., Mrs. Murray was busy running the washing machine and cleaning up. Detective Sergeant Robert E. Byron, who took over from Clemmons, wrote in his official POLICE REPORT, "It is officer's opinion that Mrs. Murray was vague and possibly evasive in answering questions pertaining to the activities of Miss Monroe during this time."

Since Marilyn's death, and the emergence of rumors surrounding one or both Kennedy brothers, a great deal of scrutiny has fallen on Mrs. Murray. In 1985 she told BBC documentary makers that ROBERT KENNEDY had indeed been at Marilyn's home on the afternoon of Marilyn's last day alive. However, she later retracted this admission, claiming, "I'm in my eighty-second year. Once in a while, everything becomes confused."

Edward R. Murrow lights Marilyn's cigarette, 1955.

BOOK:

*Marilyn: the Last Months*, Eunice Murray and Rose Shade. New York: Pyramid Books, 1975.

Murray tries to set the record straight.

## MURROW, EDWARD R.

In 1955 Marilyn made an appearance on Murrow's CBS TV show "Person to Person." The show was broadcast on April 8, from the Connecticut home of MILTON and AMY GREENE.

Not long before the live show was due to go on air, Marilyn was in a state of high anxiety. First, she thought that her rather simple makeup and clothing put her in a bad light compared to Amy Greene. She was calmed when one of the crew told her, "Just look at the camera, dear. It's just you and the camera—just you two."

Marilyn's nerves continued through filming, and she was not pleased with her performance.

## MUSIC

Marilyn's own musical career began when she was five years old, when mother GLADYS BAKER found the extra money to pay for piano lessons with a teacher named MARION MILLER. Norma Jeane never became very proficient—though her one on-screen performance, the chopsticks number in *THE SEVEN YEAR ITCH* (1955), was the only scene in the entire film to be filmed in a single take—but the piano remained a potent symbol for Marilyn throughout her life. During the brief time she lived with her mother as a child, a WHITE PIANO had pride of place in the house on ARBOL STREET. That piano, or one very like it, accompanied Marilyn through many of her moves in later life.

Marilyn found music stirring. The first

love of her life is generally reported to be voice coach FRED KARGER, and an affair with a later coach, HAL SCHAEFER, led to the "WRONG DOOR RAID," a jealous outburst from her almost-divorced husband JOE DIMAGGIO.

Marilyn's singing VOICE won plaudits early in her career. Over the years her breathlessly flirtatious ballads sent shivers up and down the spines of many male admirers. From *LADIES OF THE CHORUS* (1948) to *LET'S MAKE LOVE* (1960), she sang in no less than ten musicals, as well as a number of live performances entertaining American troops.

Marilyn was friends with many singers whose work she admired, including DEAN MARTIN, ELLA FITZGERALD, JUDY GARLAND, FRANK SINATRA, and MEL TORMÉ. Marilyn's connection with music continues to this day in the many SONGS (and performer names) she has inspired.

### WHAT MARILYN LISTENED TO

In 1939, on a wind-up portable Victrola gramophone given to her as a Christmas present by Grace McKee Goddard, Norma Jeane played her favorite Glenn Miller records.

In 1949, as Marilyn lounged on a piece of red velvet and Tom Kelley took nude photographs for a calendar, the background music was Artie Shaw's "Begin the Beguine."

A 1952 *Life* cover feature on Marilyn described her musical tastes as "distinctly highbrow."

In 1955 Earl Wilson wrote that Marilyn's favorites were Louis Armstrong, Earl Bostick, Mozart, and Beethoven.

In 1955 Lee Strasberg took it upon himself to broaden Marilyn's musical horizons by lending her recordings of several Russian greats—Tchaikovsky, Scriabin, and Prokofiev. In October that year she went to a Carnegie Hall concert by Russian pianist Emil Gilels.

In 1956, when asked what kind of music she liked, Marilyn replied, "I like, well, jazz, like Louis Armstrong, and Beethoven."

In 1958, maid Lena Pepitone says she loved to listen to Sinatra's "All of Me," as well as "Every Day I Have the Blues," and "The Man I Love."

In 1962, in her final home, Marilyn's record collection included works by Bach, Beethoven, Vivaldi, and Jelly Roll Morton. On her last night alive, Marilyn was listening to Frank Sinatra records.

## MY STORY

"Marilyn's Autobiography," as it was presented on publication in 1974 by Stein and Day, was actually written by screenwriter, film critic, and journalist BEN HECHT in 1954. Hired to ghost write an "autobiography" of Hollywood's newest star, Hecht spent five days listening to Marilyn. Two months later he had whipped up a 106 page manuscript which Marilyn, according to Hecht's wife Rose, had said "captured every phase of her life," spanning from Norma Jeane's orphan upbringing to her triumphant tour raising morale among the U.S. servicemen in KOREA.

This rather saccharine book took two decades to appear because, after Hecht's agent had serialized the book in the British magazine *Empire News*—apparently without his client's permission—Hecht and the agent parted company. Then JOE DIMAGGIO told Marilyn point blank that as she had never actually signed a final contract, the book shouldn't be published at all.

In the early seventies, former business partner MILTON GREENE presented the book to publishers Stein and Day, and the book was published with his name as copyright holder. Biographer DONALD SPOTO compared Hecht's original manuscript with the version published in 1974 and found that the first sixty-six pages of the book were by a hand other than Hecht's.

N

## NAMES

The legend runs that Norma Jeane was named by her mother after silent screen siren NORMA TALMADGE and platinum bombshell JEAN HARLOW. As appealing as this may sound, Jean Harlow did not change her name from Harlean Carpenter until 1928, two years after young Norma Jeane was born.

A number of people over the years have claimed responsibility for the naming of Hollywood's greatest sex symbol. The man who actually did the naming was BEN LYON, head of talent at TWENTIETH CENTURY-FOX. There was at least one false start, when the studio flirted with the idea of "Carole Lind." Not long after Norma Jeane's first movie studio contract was finalized, she went to see Lyon and his wife Bebe Daniels at their Malibu beach house. They ran through some possible first names. Norma Jeane suggested keeping the Jean part, in homage to her childhood idol Harlow—whom incidentally Lyon had helped to groom twenty years earlier. In the absence of a better suggestion than Jean, they went on to the last name. Norma Jeane was quick to propose her mother's maiden name, Monroe. Jean Monroe. Then Lyon suggested the name Marilyn. Marilyn was a name that meant a great deal to Lyon; years earlier he had been engaged to stage actress MARILYN MILLER. Norma Jeane actually became Marilyn Miller years later, after marrying ARTHUR MILLER.

Soon after Norma Jeane was renamed by the studio, the publicity department sent her out to a parade. Her name was so new that when she was asked for an autograph, she had to check with someone how to spell it.

Norma Jeane took a long time to get used to the name. In 1952 she revealed, "I've never liked the name Marilyn. I've often wished that I had held out that day for Jean Monroe. But I guess it's too late to do anything about it now."

It wasn't until March 12, 1956 that her name was legally changed from Norma Jeane Mortensen to Marilyn Monroe.

### OFFICIAL NAMES

Born: Norma Jeane Mortensen
Baptized: Norma Jeane Baker
School names: Norma Jeane Baker, Norma Jean Baker, Norma Baker
Name on marriage certificate, 1942: Norma Jeane Mortenson
Married name, 1942–6: Norma Jeane Dougherty
Modeling names: Norma Dougherty, Norma Jeane Dougherty, Jean Norman
First mention in the press (Hedda Hopper), 1946: Norma Jean Dougherty
First studio name: Carole Lind
Name on first contract with Twentieth Century-Fox, September 1946: Norma Jeane Dougherty
Name on renewed contract with Twentieth Century-Fox, February 1947: Marilyn Monroe
Other possible studio names: Clare Norman, Marilyn Miller, Jean Monroe
Name on management contract with John Carroll, 1947: Journey Evers
Name on register when marrying Joe DiMaggio: Norma Jeane Mortenson Dougherty
Married name, 1954: Marilyn DiMaggio
Married name, 1956: Marilyn Miller
Name on death certificate: Marilyn Monroe

### UNOFFICIAL NAMES

At school: Norma Jeane, The Human Bean, String Bean, The Mouse
At school after her figure filled out: The Oomph girl, The Mmmmm Girl (an unkind reference to her stammer)
What Grace McKee Goddard called her: The Mouse
Nickname to Fred Karger and family: Maril
Names used when allegedly working at a strip joint: Marilyn Monroe, Marilyn Marlowe, Mona Monroe
Name used for nude calendar release form: Mona Monroe
A press agent on *Love Happy* called her: The Woo Woo Girl
Soldiers knew her as: Miss Flamethrower, Miss Cheesecake of 1951, Miss Morale, The Girl We'd Rather Have Come Between Us and Our Wives, The Atomic Blonde, Miss Bountiful, The Nation's #1 Sex Thrill
Sidney Skolsky dubbed her: The Girl with the Horizontal Walk
Name used when publicly paging Sidney Skolsky: Miss Caswell
Hedda Hopper anointed her: The Blowtorch Blonde
Louella Parsons called her: Movie Glamour Girl
Jane Russell called her: Baby Doll, The Round One
Name used checking in to a Westwood motel, 1954: Norma Baker
Name used to leave Hollywood, incognito, for New York, 1954: Zelda Zonk
The "Marilyn Six" New York fans referred to her as: Mazzie
Name used when calling Arthur Miller (before he divorced his current wife): Mrs. Leslie
Arthur Miller called her: Penny Dreadful, Sugar Finney, Gramercy 5—and Maggie in *After the Fall*
Simone Signoret: The Milkmaid
Name registered when admitted to the Payne-Whitney clinic: Miss Faye Miller
Alias used traveling to Palm Springs, 1962: Tony Roberts

### MARILYN NAME FACTS

The source name of Marilyn is Mary, which means, paradoxically in Norma Jeane's case, "wished-for-child."

A bright star recently discovered by a Japanese astronomer has been named after Hollywood's most luminous actress.

In the 1990 U.S. census, "Marilyn" was the eightieth most popular name for females.

## NEBRASKA AVENUE

Between 1938 and 1946 Norma Jeane lived with beloved "Aunt" ANA LOWER at her home on 11348 Nebraska Avenue, West Los Angeles. In 1945, as Norma Jeane first began to model, she moved out of her disapproving mother-in-law's house, back to Nebraska Avenue and the apartment below Aunt Ana. During this stay, her mother GLADYS BAKER came to visit for a few months, on a brief release from the mental institution in northern California where she had been living.

(*see* HOMES)

## NEGULESCO, JEAN (1900–1993)

A Romanian-born director who emigrated to the U.S. in 1927 and worked his way through the ranks from stage painter to director. After a spell at Warners, during which time he made *The Mask of Dimitrios* (1944) and *Humoresque* (1947), he moved to TWENTIETH CENTURY-FOX, where his most successful

Director Jean Negulesco.

films were *Roadhouse* (1948), *Johnny Belinda* (1948), *Three Coins in the Fountain* (1954), *Woman's World* (1954), and *Daddy Longlegs* (1955).

In 1952 Fox chose Negulesco to direct their first ever Cinemascope feature, *HOW TO MARRY A MILLIONAIRE* (1953), showcasing the brand-new technology it was hoped would fight off the rival of television. The studio threw three of its leading ladies into the fray—queen BETTY GRABLE, crown princess Marilyn Monroe, and the sultry LAUREN BACALL.

Negulesco is one of the small club of directors who refrained from publicly rehashing the troubles he had while working with Marilyn. But like so many colleagues, he clashed with NATASHA LYTESS, whose presence by his side infuriated him enough to order her temporarily off the set.

Despite the huge box office success of *How to Marry a Millionaire*, Negulesco and Marilyn did not repeat their experience together. If Marilyn had lived, however, they would have met up on the set of *SOMETHING'S GOT TO GIVE*, after Negulesco had been hired to replace GEORGE CUKOR on the planned resurrection of the project.

BOOK:

*Things I Did…and Things I Think I Did*, Jean Negulesco. New York: Simon & Schuster, 1984.

Contains a chapter on Marilyn.

## NEW YORK

During her starlet years Marilyn studied at the ACTORS LAB in Los Angeles, an outpost of East Coast theatrical folk in the heart of film industry territory. At that time she thought of New York as a "far, far away place . . . where actors and directors did very different things than stand around all day arguing about a close-up or a camera angle. . . . It seemed so exciting to me, and I wanted to be part of that life."

In 1954 she decided to make it happen. In the Big Apple she holed up with business partner MILTON GREENE to plan her life as an independent producer; she began working with LEE

Miller and Marilyn in New York, ca. 1956.

STRASBERG, the ultimate drama coach; she renegotiated her contract with Fox; she plunged into the world of PSYCHOANALYSIS; and she fell in love with ARTHUR MILLER. Love prompted her to eulogize about BROOKLYN, where Miller was living at that time: "I've fallen in love with Brooklyn," she cryptically told a journalist. "I'm going to buy a little house in Brooklyn and live there. I'll go to the coast only when I have to make a picture."

Marilyn had a number of HOMES in New York City from 1955 until her death. For most of that time, she had an apartment on East FIFTY-SEVENTH STREET. Her last visit to New York was in May 1962, when she sang "Happy Birthday" to President KENNEDY at MADISON SQUARE GARDEN.

When taking a cab in town, Marilyn would not say whether she was going uptown or downtown, she'd say "I'm going that way," pointing in the direction she wanted to go.

(*see* HOMES, RESTAURANTS, and HOTELS)

## NEWCOMB, PAT
(B. 1930, MARGOT PATRICIA)

In 1956 Pat Newcomb, a publicist working for the New York-based ARTHUR JACOBS Public Relations agency, was assigned to travel with Marilyn to Los Angeles, and handle her press arrangements during filming on *BUS STOP* (1956). At first Marilyn and Newcomb got on like old friends. Then, during location shooting in Phoenix, it all fell apart. Biographer FRED LAWRENCE GUILES tells the story:

> An attractive man in his thirties got interested in Marilyn and was courageous enough to ask for a date. When he came up to Marilyn's suite to pick her up, Pat Newcomb was in the sitting-room, not quite dressed—the two women often wandered between their suites with little on—and the man was visibly shocked to see Marilyn's press agent when he expected to find Marilyn. Marilyn was furious at what she saw as Pat's competitiveness for this man, and the camaraderie between the women was shattered. Pat Newcomb was soon replaced.

In November 1960, Marilyn's longtime publicist RUPERT ALLAN quit at the end of shooting on *THE MISFITS* (1961). Arthur Jacobs suggested replacing him with Newcomb, with JOHN SPRINGER continuing to handle affairs at the New York office. Marilyn agreed and Newcomb returned. Her first job was the daunting task of handling fallout from Marilyn's divorce from ARTHUR MILLER, including accompanying Marilyn and LAWYER Aaron Frosch to MEXICO for the divorce proceedings. In the next year and a half, Newcomb became an essential member of Marilyn's entourage, and by all accounts a friend as well as an employee. According to Guiles, her loyalty to Marilyn sometimes made her over-protective.

In 1962 Marilyn had a second line installed at Newcomb's home, so that she could get through to her at any time of day or night. Marilyn bought her a new car after her old one broke down. As well as strictly work-related duties, Newcomb ran errands for Marilyn, helped in the search for a home to buy, and went with her to Mexico in early 1962 to buy furniture for the FIFTH HELENA DRIVE house Marilyn eventually bought. She also arranged the intense schedule of interviews and photo sessions Marilyn conducted in the final months of her life, as she strove to resurrect her career after Fox dismissed her from *SOMETHING'S GOT TO GIVE*.

Newcomb woke up at Marilyn's home on August 4, 1962, the last day of Marilyn's life. She had stayed overnight, after an evening out to dinner with PETER LAWFORD—and in some accounts ROBERT KENNEDY—at the La Scala RESTAURANT. Newcomb slept right through to midday, which reportedly infuriated the insomniac Marilyn. Accounts differ as to how long Newcomb remained at Marilyn's home that day, sunning herself by the pool, depending on the version of what time DR. RALPH GREENSON began his session with Marilyn. Biographer ANTHONY SUMMERS claims that Marilyn was unhappy with Newcomb not just because of her ability to sleep, but because of a perceived rivalry for the affections of Robert Kennedy.

In Newcomb's words, she heard about Marilyn's death after being "awakened at four in the morning by the lawyer Mickey Rudin. He told me Marilyn was dead—an overdose. I rushed to Marilyn's house. It has been printed that I saw her body, but I never did. The press was there, and I did become overwrought and yell at them, calling them 'vultures.' Then I went home, knowing no more about how Marilyn had died than anyone else." She later said that Marilyn "seemed normal that last day I saw her," but was severely critical of the lack of coordination between Marilyn's doctors, the result of which was that Marilyn had access to large numbers of sedatives and barbiturates.

For the next two days Newcomb fielded two hundred and fifty calls from journalists the world over. It is her opinion—and she was in a better position than most to know—that Marilyn died of an accidental overdose. Newcomb was one of the select few mourners to attend Marilyn's FUNERAL.

CONSPIRACY theorists have seized upon Newcomb's movements in the years after Marilyn's death as a sign of complicity in a

COVER-UP. It has been reported that immediately after the funeral Newcomb was flown to the Kennedy estate at Hyannisport. In a 1963 article, WALTER WINCHELL claimed that she was working in Washington D.C., in a job obtained for her by Robert Kennedy. Stories of Kennedy's gratitude have often been repeated over the years, despite vehement public denials by Newcomb. She continued to pursue her career in public relations and then transferred into the movie business, where for some years she was a vice president at MGM studios.

## NEWMAN, ALFRED (1901–1970) AND LIONEL (1916–1989)

Between them, the musical Newman brothers worked with Marilyn either as songwriters or musical directors on almost all of her movies—on many occasions as a team.

Alfred Newman composed the musical scores for more than two hundred and fifty films during his long Hollywood career, in the process winning no less than seven Academy Awards. Newman was responsible for the scores or musical direction on six Marilyn films: *ALL ABOUT EVE* (1950), *O'HENRY'S FULL HOUSE* (1952), *HOW TO MARRY A MILLIONAIRE* (1953), *THERE'S NO BUSINESS LIKE SHOW BUSINESS* (1954), *THE SEVEN YEAR ITCH* (1955), and *BUS STOP* (1956).

Alfred's younger brother Lionel worked with Marilyn on her first ever film, *SCUDDA HOO! SCUDDA HAY!* (1948), and went on to repeat the experience in *AS YOUNG AS YOU FEEL* (1951), *WE'RE NOT MARRIED* (1952), *DON'T BOTHER TO KNOCK* (1952), *NIAGARA* (1953), *GENTLEMAN PREFER BLONDES* (1953), *RIVER OF NO RETURN* (1954), *THERE'S NO BUSINESS LIKE SHOW BUSINESS* (1954), and again on Marilyn's final musical, *LET'S MAKE LOVE* (1960).

## NIAGARA (1953)

TWENTIETH CENTURY-FOX knew they were on to something big with Marilyn, but the studio was obviously still unsure how to exploit Marilyn's incredible sexual charge to best effect. For her second leading role, Marilyn played a woman within whom evil and sexual temptation co-exist, until the evil triumphs and she plans to murder her husband. This time she shared top billing not with any of her fellow actors, but with another phenomenon of nature, Niagara Falls.

In the run-up to production, ANNE BAXTER pulled out of the Polly Cutler role after the part was downscaled so as not to upstage the main characters in the movie—Marilyn and Niagara Falls—though in some versions of the story the rewriting took place after Baxter's withdrawal. JEAN PETERS stepped in to the breach.

Her sultry sexuality is proclaimed early on, when in a red dress she lies back and hums along to the song she has requested, "Kiss" (written by LIONEL NEWMAN and Haven Gillespie): "Kiss me / thrill me / Hold me in your arms / This is the moment..." The conclusion to the "Kiss" scene, in which onscreen husband George Loomis smashes the record to smithereens, was reputedly added at the last minute to placate an outraged visiting representative of the Woman's Clubs of

Marilyn and Richard Allan in an illicit embrace in *Niagara* (1953).

America, who was shocked at the sexual charge of the scene.

In *Niagara* Marilyn performed what was credited at the time as the longest WALK in film history. Measured at 116 feet, "The Girl with the Horizontal Walk" swiveled purposefully away from the camera, clad in a tight-fitting black skirt. At the time Marilyn told *Life* magazine, "I use walking just to get me around."

Many fans consider *Niagara* to showcase Marilyn at her sultriest and most seductive. On its release, this was certainly the majority view among cinemagoers. The movie earned five times what it cost to make, despite threatened boycotts by groups protesting the film's indecency, and it established Marilyn as one of the nation's biggest draws. However, *Niagara* has also been criticized for its unbalanced feel; Marilyn looms so much larger than any of the other characters, especially her lackluster older husband played by JOSEPH COTTON.

BOOKS:

*Falling for Marilyn: The Lost Niagara Collection*, photographs by Jock Carroll. New York: Michael Friedman publishing, 1996.

*Marilyn Monroe and the Making of Niagara*, George Bailey. Published locally in Niagara.

MEMORABLE COSTUME:

Magenta low-cut dress tied at the bust—the dress, in the words of Jean Peters, that you have to make plans for when you are sixteen.

**Tag line:**
"Marilyn Monroe and *Niagara*—a raging torrent of emotion that even nature can't control!"

**Credits:**
Twentieth Century-Fox, Technicolor
Length: 89 minutes
Release date: January 21, 1953

Directed by: Henry Hathaway
Produced by: Charles Brackett
Written by: Charles Brackett, Richard L. Breen, Walter Reisch
Cinematography by: Joseph MacDonald
Music by: Sol Kaplan
Costume Design by: Dorothy Jeakins
Film Editing by: Barbara McLean

**Cast** (credits order):
Marilyn Monroe . . . Rose Loomis
Joseph Cotten . . . George Loomis
Jean Peters . . . Polly Cutler
Casey Adams . . . Ray Cutler
Denis O'Dea . . . Inspector Starkey
Richard Allan . . . Patrick
Don Wilson . . . Mr. Kettering
Lurene Tuttle . . . Mrs. Kettering
Russell Collins . . . Mr. Qua
Will Wright . . . Boatman
Lester Matthews . . . Doctor
Carleton Young . . . Policeman
Sean McClory . . . Sam
Minerva Urecal . . . Landlady

Marilyn as Rose Loomis in *Niagara* (1953).

Nina Varela . . . Wife
Tom Reynolds . . . Husbands
Winifield Hoeny . . . Straw Boss
Neil Fitzgerald . . . Customs Officer
Norman McKay . . . Morris
Gene Wesson . . . Guide
George Ives . . . Carillon Tower Guide
Patrick O'Moore . . . Detective
Arch Johnson . . . Taxi Driver
Harry Carey Jr. . . . Taxi Driver
Henry Beckman . . . Motorcycle Cop
Willard Sage . . . Motorcycle Cop
Bill Foster . . . Young Man
Robert Ellis . . . Young Man
Gloria Gordon . . . Dancer
Marjorie Rambeau . . . Bit part

**Crew:**
Leonard Doss . . . color consultant
W.D. Flick . . . sound
Roger Heman . . . sound
Ray Kellogg . . . special effects
Charles Le Maire . . . wardrobe director
Lionel Newman . . . musical director
Ben Nye . . . makeup
Gerd Oswald . . . assistant director
Edward B. Powell . . . orchestration
Maurice Ransford . . . art director
Stuart A. Reiss . . . set decorator
Lyle R. Wheeler . . . art director

**Plot:**
As in DON'T BOTHER TO KNOCK (1952), the action revolves around a hotel where two couples are staying, honeymooners Ray Cutler (Casey Adams) and Polly (Jean Peters), and grizzled war veteran George Loomis (Joseph Cotten) and Rose (Marilyn Monroe), all against the spectacular backdrop of Niagara Falls. Polly catches sight of Rose kissing Ted Patrick (played by Richard Allan), a man who is not her husband, but says nothing even when George Loomis says he suspects Rose of having an affair. Loomis disappears soon after Rose and Ted plot to do him in. Rose plays her part well in front of the police, until she discovers that the body found by the police is not that of her husband, but of her lover. It turns out that Loomis has killed in self-defense the man who was going to kill him. Meanwhile, Rose manages to escape from the hospital where she has been under sedation. Her husband spots her and gives chase, right up into the belfry of Carillon Tower, and strangles her there. Now he has to get out of Niagara; his plan is to get away by boat, but he bumps into Polly, who still has not given him away to the police. Polly refuses to get off the boat as Loomis requests, so he starts the engine and they speed inexorably toward the thundering falls. Just before the boat, out of fuel, is pulled over the edge of the raging torrent, Loomis puts Polly off on a rocky ledge, from where Polly is plucked to safety by helicopter in the final scene.

Moviegoers and critics were struck by Marilyn's magnetism before the camera in *Niagara* (1953).

A publicity photo for *Niagara* of Joseph Cotten and Marilyn as the unhappily married Rose and George Loomis.

**Reviews:**
*The New Yorker*
"Marilyn Monroe, whom Hollywood has been ballyhooing as a new-day Lillian Russell, takes a fling at big-league melodrama in *Niagara* and demonstrates a wide assortment of curves and a tendency to read her lines as if they were in a tongue she is not entirely familiar with. . . . however admirably constructed Miss Monroe may be, she is hardly up to competing with one of the wonders of this continent."

*The New York Times*
"Obviously ignoring the idea that there are Seven Wonders of the World, Twentieth Century-Fox has discovered two more and enhanced them with Technicolor in 'Niagara'. . . . For the producers are making full use of both the grandeur of the Falls and its adjacent areas as well as the grandeur that is Marilyn Monroe. The scenic effects in both cases are superb."

*Los Angeles Examiner*
"Two of nature's greatest phenomena, Niagara Falls and Marilyn Monroe, get together in *Niagara* and the result is the sexiest, tingling-est, suspenseful-est film in lo, these many months. . . . Here is the greatest natural star since Jean Harlow. She has more intelligence than Harlow. She out-lures Lana. She makes any other glamour girl you care to name look house-wifely."

*New York Herald Tribune*
"Director Henry Hathaway has put on quite a show in this 'Niagara,' with Marilyn Monroe, Joseph Cotten, and Jean Peters sharing the billing with the natural splendors. Miss Monroe plays the kind of wife whose dress, in the words of the script, 'is cut so low you can see her knees.' The dress is red; the actress has very nice knees, and under Hathaway's direction she gives the kind of serpentine performance that makes the audience hate her while admiring her, which is proper for the story."

*Time*
"What lifts the film above the commonplace is its star, Marilyn Monroe."

*Newsweek*
"All the performances are competent, but Marilyn Monroe—hitherto typed as a glamour girl—easily comes off best with a surprisingly effective impersonation of a mousy maniac."

## NOGUCHI, DR. THOMAS

The deputy CORONER on duty at the Los Angeles City Morgue when Marilyn's body arrived on the morning of Sunday August 5, 1962 also conducted many other high-profile autopsies on stars and politicians who died in Los Angeles, including ROBERT KENNEDY, Sharon Tate, NATALIE WOOD, and John Belushi.

Noguchi's opinion, after filing his CORONER'S REPORT, was that the most probable cause of Marilyn's death was suicide. However, his findings show that the DRUGS which killed Marilyn were not ingested orally—there was no pill residue in her stomach. For proponents of murder theories, Noguchi did not satisfactorily explain the higher concentrations of Nembutal in Marilyn's liver than in her bloodstream, which indicate that she had consumed this drug many hours earlier and was well on her way to metabolization. An injection would have left a mark and bruising, and resulted in sudden death and far higher levels of barbiturates in her blood. It has been speculated that the most likely administration of the fatal dose was by enema; the autopsy showed that Marilyn's colon had "marked congestion and purplish discoloration."

Noguchi has been criticized for failing to analyze Marilyn's intestine for drug residue, though in ANTHONY SUMMERS' biography he states that he asked head toxicologist R. J. Abernethy to carry out just such an examination, only to be told that the specimens had already been destroyed. Noguchi is quoted by Summers as saying, "It seemed to me, from all I observed, that it's very likely the Police Department did close things down. I've encountered this often in my experience, in deaths involving important people." In 1985, Noguchi voiced suspicions about a bruise Marilyn had low down on her back, which in his words, "has never been fully explained."

## NOONAN, TOMMY
(1921–1968, B. THOMAS NOON)

Marilyn's co-star in *GENTLEMEN PREFER BLONDES* (1953) made his film debut in *Boys Town* (1938). Not only did he star as Marilyn's love interest in this popular comedy, he was also in *How To Be Very, Very Popular* (1955), a movie originally developed as a Marilyn star vehicle until she walked out on TWENTIETH CENTURY-FOX. Noonan's other movies include *A Star Is Born* (1954), *The Ambassador's Daughter* (1956), and *Promises, Promises* (1963), opposite JAYNE MANSFIELD.

Out-gunning TONY CURTIS and his more famous kissing Hitler comment, Noonan described his on-screen experience as "like being sucked into a vacuum."

(*see* KISSING MARILYN)

## NORELL, NORMAN

On AMY GREENE'S advice, fashion designer Norman Norell was hired in 1955 to provide Marilyn with a new wardrobe with which to wow her new hometown of NEW YORK.

## NORTH BEVERLY GLEN BOULEVARD,
WEST LOS ANGELES

Marilyn's return to Los Angeles after her 1955 hiatus in New York was to a nine room house at no. 595 North Beverly Glen, rented from a Mr. and Mrs. Sidney Lushing for $995 per month. Marilyn shared the premises with business partner MILTON GREENE, his wife Amy, and their two-year-old son, Joshua. Although Marilyn was intending to stay in the house throughout the shooting for *BUS STOP* (1956), she reputedly moved out to a two bedroom apartment on Sunset Boulevard after a couple of months. This was because Milton and Amy made too much noise at night during the parties they threw, which prevented Marilyn from getting to sleep.

(*see* HOMES)

## NORTH CRESCENT DRIVE
BEVERLY HILLS , CALIFORNIA

During filming of *DON'T BOTHER TO KNOCK* (1952), her first starring role, Marilyn moved in with drama coach NATASHA LYTESS, at no. 611, in order to spend as much time as possible preparing for her role. After she moved out, Marilyn was sued by the telephone company for unpaid bills at this address.

(*see* HOMES)

## NORTH PALM DRIVE, BEVERLY HILLS

The two occasions when Marilyn lived along this swank residential street ended badly. In 1949 she was installed at no. 718 by Hollywood agent JOHNNY HYDE, who had left his wife to live with the starlet. Head over heels in love, Hyde masterminded Marilyn's all-important early high-profile roles in *THE ASPHALT JUNGLE* and *ALL ABOUT EVE* (both 1950). Hyde had their dining room decorated with leather booths and a dance floor to resemble Romanoff's, his favorite RESTAURANT. Hyde's weak heart finally gave out in December 1950, and immediately after his death his family requested that Marilyn leave the premises.

In early 1954 the mock-Tudor style house at 508 North Palm Drive became one of the nation's most photographed addresses, thanks to its new residents, the DIMAGGIOS. The newlyweds took out a six-month lease on the eight bedroom luxury residence, paying what, for the time, was a very high rent of $700 per month.

To begin with, Marilyn and Joe stayed in SAN FRANCISCO, where he felt much more at home. They moved in properly when Marilyn had to return to Los Angeles to work on *THERE'S NO BUSINESS LIKE SHOW BUSINESS* (1954), and later *THE SEVEN YEAR ITCH* (1955). Joe was unhappy that Marilyn continued to dedicate herself wholly to her film career, and he was jealous of the way this exposed her to the gaze of others.

On October 4, 1954, outside 508 North Palm Drive, America's most famous couple announced their plans to DIVORCE. For the next two days the house was besieged by pressmen, photographers, and fans. Helped by a pal, Joe moved out on October 6. When Marilyn emerged from the house that day she was mobbed by the press and had to be led away in tears.

Decades earlier Marilyn's childhood idol JEAN HARLOW had lived for a spell at the house next door, no. 512.

(*see* HOMES)

## NORTH, SHEREE
(B. 1933, DAWN BETHEL)

MARILYN:
"Sometimes I kid the fans. They say, 'Oh, you're Marilyn Monroe! I say, 'Oh, no, I'm Mamie Van Doren' or 'Sheree North'—if I'm in a real hurry."

TWENTIETH CENTURY-FOX'S publicity department pulled out all the stops to promote Sheree North as the new Marilyn Monroe around the time that Marilyn began to cause trouble and refuse the projects the studio put her away.

With only a few minor roles behind her, North was very much a young hopeful—ideally pliable material for the studio to use to browbeat Marilyn into accepting *THERE'S NO BUSINESS LIKE SHOW BUSINESS* (1954), a movie she had been stalling on. When Marilyn turned down *How to Be Very Very Popular* (1955) and *The Girl in Pink Tights*,

Sheree North

the studio very publicly proclaimed that their sex-siren in waiting was the new "in" thing. However, *How to Be Very Very Popular*, in which North starred opposite BETTY GRABLE, acting in her last movie, opened to indifferent reviews, and *The Girl in Pink Tights* was never made. North's next movie, *The Lieutenant Wore Skirts* (1956), was yet another project Marilyn had reputedly declined.

Since her beginnings in the film industry, North has worked in over fifty film and television movies, as well as appearing in many popular TV series from the fifties to the nineties.

North played Marilyn's mother GLADYS BAKER in the TV movie *Marilyn: The Untold Story* (1980).

## NORWALK STATE HOSPITAL

(LATER METROPOLITAN STATE HOSPITAL AT NORWALK) 11400 S. NORWALK BOULEVARD, NORWALK

When Norma Jeane was just one year old, Her grandmother DELLA MAE HOGAN was brought to this mental HOSPITAL after a breakdown. She died of a heart failure less than three weeks later, on August 23, 1927.

In early 1934, Norma Jeane's mother GLADYS BAKER was brought to this hospital after her own breakdown. Apart from a brief period in 1945 when she went to stay with her daughter, Gladys Baker lived at this institution until 1953. After this time she moved on to the ROCKHAVEN SANITARIUM.

## NOVAK, KIM

(B. 1933, MARILYN PAULINE NOVAK)

Kim Novak took the traditional route to Hollywood: moving out of low-paid jobs into modeling, winning a beauty title (Miss Deepfreeze), and then catching the eye of a studio executive. Her timing was impeccable, as HARRY COHN, head of COLUMBIA STUDIOS, had ordered talent chief Max Arnow to find him "another Monroe." The aptly named Marilyn Novak was who he came up with. A series of acting lessons and a name change later—first Kit Marlowe, then Kim Novak after the actress insisted on retaining at least her family name—and she was ready for action.

Novak made her screen debut as an uncredited extra in *The French Line* (1953), and was then promoted to major roles in *Pushover* and *Phffft* (1954), before making a real name for herself in *Picnic* (1956). She scored opposite FRANK SINATRA in *Pal Joey* (1958), and then took a leaf out of Marilyn's book by going on a one woman strike to improve her salary of $1250 a week.

Novak is perhaps best remembered as the scheming suicide in Hitchcock's *Vertigo* (1958), a role she got only after actress Vera Miles dropped out because she was pregnant. The following year she beat Marilyn to the lead in *Middle of the Night*, a part that Marilyn had sought. In 1962, after firing Marilyn from *SOMETHING'S GOT TO GIVE*, Twentieth Century-Fox unsuccessfully tried to entice Novak as Marilyn's replacement.

The end of the star system in the sixties brought fewer roles for Novak, though she continued to appear in films until the early nineties.

## NUDITY

MARILYN:
"My impulse to appear naked and my dreams about it had no shame or sense of sin in them. Dreaming of people looking at me made me feel less lonely."

"I'm only comfortable when I'm naked."

Marilyn had no shame about her BODY. For her, nudity was natural. As a little girl, she had a recurring DREAM that took place in church: "No sooner was I in the pew with the organ playing and everybody singing a hymn than the impulse would come to me to take off all my clothes. I wanted desperately to stand up naked for God and for everyone else to see me. I had to clench my teeth and sit on my hands to keep myself from undressing."

In 1947, after being taken in by actor JOHN CARROLL and his wife LUCILLE RYMAN, Marilyn regularly slept nude with her door open, and dressed scantily around the house. There was nothing affected or calculated about this behavior, it was just the way she liked to be when she was "off duty." A few years later, at the NORTH PALM DRIVE home she shared with agent JOHNNY HYDE, she tended to walk around the place in the nude. Throughout her life, when at home, or even in her bungalow on set, Marilyn would walk around the place naked, unconcerned about roommates, husbands, makeup women, wardrobe girls, or hairdressers. She even conducted a number of interviews either naked in bed, or at least revealingly attired.

When, in early 1949, photographer TOM KELLEY offered Marilyn $50 for a two hour nude photo shoot, she accepted because she needed the money and this was the easiest way to earn it. In so doing, she was following in the footsteps of her childhood idol JEAN HARLOW, who had posed in see-through chiffon and in a fishnet. When the press got wind of the Marilyn CALENDAR, the scandal briefly threatened to cut short her career, just as she had finally made it to top billing. Marilyn is generally credited with persuading the TWENTIETH CENTURY-FOX publicity department that honesty was the best policy. In so doing, Marilyn won fans for her honesty, millions of buyers for her calendar, and a place in posterity, with her "Golden Dreams" nude epitomizing the voluptuous female body in modern times.

NATASHA LYTESS, with whom Marilyn lived on a number of occasions, recounts: "She'd come wandering naked from her bedroom and into the bathroom at 11 A.M. and mid-day. It took her at least an hour to bathe. Then—still without a stitch on—Marilyn would drift in a sort of dreamy, sleep-walking daze into the kitchen and fix her own breakfast."

CASEY ADAMS and ROBERT SLATZER have both said that at Niagara Falls during location work Marilyn appeared naked at her hotel window, giggling and enjoying the crowd that quickly formed below.

According to JEANNE CARMEN, on two occasions Marilyn reputedly put on a black wig and went to a local nudist beach, once with JACK BENNY, and once with no less than U.S. Attorney General ROBERT KENNEDY.

Marilyn famously eschewed UNDERWEAR. On shopping trips she frequently elicited gasps from shop assistants, as they saw her slip out of her clothes—all her clothes—before trying garments on. Housekeeper EUNICE MURRAY says that Marilyn was still sleeping in the nude at the end of her life. XENIA CHEKHOV, wife of Marilyn's acting coach Michael, apparently used to send Marilyn nightgowns because she was worried that sleeping in the nude was bad for her health.

In the last years of her life, Marilyn returned to public displays of nudity. According to photographer EVE ARNOLD, there was a degree of desperation about this decision: "She had lost the contours of a young woman by then, but she refused to acknowledge her body was becoming mature. She insisted that she could measure up to the kind of nudity or semi-nudity that was being printed in *Playboy* and similar magazines. Her blindness to her physical change was almost tragic."

On a number of occasions, Marilyn gave a nude calendar signed with a witty personal dedication, as a gift to people she wanted to thank for something—often members of the PRESS who consistently provided her with positive publicity .

### MARILYN NUDE ON STILLS AND MOVIES

NUDE PHOTOS:
Marilyn's nude photographs shocked and delighted in equal measure over the years. But many Marilyn nudes have gone missing too. Photographers Tom Kelley and Eve Arnold, to name but two, have discovered that negatives of Marilyn nudes have "disappeared" from their files. Reportedly, first husband Jim Dougherty had a nude picture of his wife that he showed off to colleagues at work, which has never been produced.

1946: Marilyn posed topless and nude for illustrator Earl Moran. These photographs were published in a 1987 *Playboy* tribute to Marilyn.

Photograph by Bert Stern, 1962.

1949: Marilyn famously posed nude against a backdrop of red velvet for Tom Kelley. Only in 1998 did some of the missing photographs from that session turn up.
1960/61: Marilyn posed nude for Eve Arnold.
1962: Marilyn approved for publication fifty-two nude photographs taken on the set of *Something's Got to Give*.
1962: Bert Stern photographed Marilyn in varying states of undress and nudity. His assistant Leif-Erik Nygards took a photograph in which a reclining Marilyn has her pubic hair visible, published by *Playboy* in 1984.

In the fifties, nudity was more a question of not wearing clothes while being covered up, usually by a sheet, or the frosted glass of a shower door. In her movies, Marilyn's instinct when filming was to see how far she could go.

***Niagara*** (1953)
In the movie that made her name, Marilyn lies nude under the sheets in bed, and appears naked through a frosted glass shower door.

***Bus Stop*** (1956)
As suitor Beauregard tries to summon up some interest in her, a sleepy and hungover Marilyn lies beneath the sheets.

***The Misfits*** (1961)
Marilyn famously let the sheets slip from her breast as she lay in bed, on the seventh take of a scene with CLARK GABLE. JOHN HUSTON was not impressed, though Marilyn is said to have wanted this take to be used.

***Something's Got to Give***
On May 28, 1962, during shooting of *Something's Got to Give*, Marilyn pulled off her flesh-colored swimsuit and posed in and out of the pool. One story runs that director GEORGE CUKOR thought that Marilyn's idea to invite three photographers (William Woodfield, LAWRENCE SCHILLER, and Fox stills photographer JIMMY MITCHELL) to take photos of Marilyn nude in the same pool they had used for shooting that day would make an ideal piece of pre-production publicity. However, Marilyn's quote, "We did some test scenes of me in a pool, sort of nude. I hope they give me some good nude lines to go with it," would seem to indicate that the idea came from the studio, not from the star. This opinion was shared by ARTHUR MILLER, who wrote that for Marilyn these nudes were a defeat, a return to being a body, not an actress, after all her struggles to be taken seriously.

Over the years, a number of stag films have surfaced in which starlet Marilyn is said to have "acted." *APPLES, KNOCKERS AND COKES* starred an actress called ARLINE HUNTER; in 1980, *Penthouse* magazine published photographs allegedly of Marilyn performing in a similar movie; more recently a Spanish magazine claimed to have unearthed a similar artifact.

## NUMBERS

Registration number at Los Angeles ORPHANAGE: 3463
Social Security Number: 563-32-0764
USO Entertainer Serial Number: 129278
Phone numbers at last home: 476-1890/472-4830

## NYE, BEN (1907–1986)

The head of makeup at TWENTIETH CENTURY-FOX throughout Marilyn's career, Ben Nye is credited on almost all of the movies Marilyn made for the studio.

It is likely that Marilyn's personal makeup man ALLAN "WHITEY" SNYDER looked after Marilyn's makeup from her first screen test to her final movie, despite some accounts in which Nye is credited with doing her makeup for that all-important 1946 test. Snyder has gone on record to say that Ben Nye "never once touched her face."

*Previous page*: Photograph by Bert Stern, 1962.

## O'CONNOR, DONALD
(B. 1925, DAVID DIXON O'CONNOR)

Born to the world of show business, O'Connor made his stage debut at three days old, sitting on his mother's lap as she played the piano to a full house.

O'Connor profited from this early start and became, during the forties and fifties, a perennial teenager. By the time he was cast opposite Marilyn in *THERE'S NO BUSINESS LIKE SHOW BUSINESS* (1954) he was thirty years old, but his youthful looks made him a rather unlikely love interest for Marilyn. Bringing together actors assembled more because they were under contract to TWENTIETH CENTURY-FOX than because of any potential chemistry, Marilyn is said to have pleaded with the writers not to cast her as O'Connor's girl.

The best remembered of O'Connor's movies are *Sing You Sinners* (1938), *Patrick the Great* (1945), *Francis* (1949), *Singin' in the Rain* (1952) (in which he somersaults off the walls), *Call Me Madam* (1953), and *The Buster Keaton Story* (1957). He also had his own TV show in the fifties.

A poster for *O'Henry's Full House* (1952) pictured Marilyn and Charles Laughton in a scene from the film.

## ODESSA AVENUE, VAN NUYS

Norma Jeane twice lived along this residential street, with the GODDARD family at number 6707, both before and after her time in the Los Angeles ORPHANAGE.

(*see* HOMES)

## ODETS, CLIFFORD (1903–1963)

The original "Angry Young Man," Clifford Odets was regarded as the most gifted American social-protest playwright of the 1930s, paving the way for the more lauded ARTHUR MILLER and TENNESSEE WILLIAMS. Marilyn herself once referred to him as "sort of the Arthur of the thirties."

Odets is best known for his plays *Awake and Sing* (1935), *Waiting for Lefty* (1935), and *Golden Boy* (1937). His later plays include *The Country Girl* (1950), and *CLASH BY NIGHT* (1952) in which Marilyn had an important supporting role. Odets's associations with Hollywood were sporadic, but like so many other writers, he sometimes succumbed to the lure of the screen dollar.

Clifford Odets

Marilyn first came across Odets's work in 1947 when studying at the ACTORS LAB in Los Angeles, which was an offshoot of the Group Theater. Odets had co-founded the Group Theater in 1931 with LEE STRASBERG and ELIA KAZAN.

What struck Marilyn was the way Odets championed the downtrodden, and his portrayal of the loneliness afflicting people within family settings.

Odets' name cropped up in the theater circles Marilyn frequented during her time with Lee Strasberg, and she met with him socially during her marriage to Arthur Miller. Like Miller, Odets had fallen foul of the HOUSE UN-AMERICAN ACTIVITIES COMMITTEE and been called to testify. Under oath, he admitted that he had been a member of the Communist Party, but said he had left the party when he was told he had to tow the party line in his writing.

Odets was reputedly originally offered the job of writing *THE MISFITS* (1961).

## *O. HENRY'S FULL HOUSE* (1952)

TWENTIETH CENTURY-FOX heavily promoted Marilyn in this anthology movie based on five stories by O. Henry (pseudonym of William Sidney Porter). Marilyn received top billing despite the fact that she only appeared on-screen for one minute.

Much to the chagrin of boyfriend JOE DIMAGGIO, Marilyn played a streetwalker in the first of the five tales, entitled "The Cop and the Anthem." She co-starred in the piece with idol CHARLES LAUGHTON. John Steinbeck provided the narration.

**Credits:**
Twentieth Century-Fox, Black and White
Length: 117 minutes
Release date: October 16, 1952

Directed by: Henry Hathaway ("The Clarion Call"), Howard Hawks ("The Ransom of Red Chief"), Henry King ("The Gift of the Magi"), Henry Koster ("The Cop and the Anthem"), Jean Negulesco ("The Last Leaf")
Produced by: André Hakim
Written by: Richard L. Breen ("The Clarion Call"), Walter Bullock ("The Gift of the Magi"), Ivan Goff ("The Last Leaf"), Nunnally Johnson ("The Ransom of Red Chief"), Ben Roberts ("The Last Leaf"), Lamar Trotti ("The Cop and the Anthem")
Cinematography by: Lloyd Ahern, Lucien Ballard, Milton R. Krasner, Joseph MacDonald
Music by: Alfred Newman
Film Editing by: Nick DeMaggio, Barbara McLean, William B. Murphy

**Cast (credits order):**
John Steinbeck . . . Narrator
Charles Laughton . . . Soapy ("The Cop and the Anthem")
Marilyn Monroe . . . Streetwalker ("The Cop and the Anthem")
David Wayne . . . Horace ("The Cop and the Anthem")
Dale Robertson . . . Barney Woods ("The Clarion Call")
Thomas Browne Henry . . . Manager
Richard Widmark . . . Johnny Kernan ("The Clarion Call")
Anne Baxter . . . Joanna ("The Last Leaf")
Jean Peters . . . Susan ("The Last Leaf")
Gregory Ratoff . . . Behrman ("The Last Leaf")
Fred Allen . . . Sam ("The Ransom of the Red Chief")
Oscar Levant . . . Bill ("The Ransom of the Red Chief")

Marilyn backstage at a New York theater visiting Broadway star Carol Haney, 1954

Jeanne Crain . . . Della ("The Gift of the Magi")
Farley Granger . . . Jim ("The Gift of the Magi")
Joyce Mackenzie . . . Hazel
Lee Aaker . . . J. B.
Richard Rober . . . Chief of Detectives ("The Clarion Call")
Fred Kelsey . . . Santa Claus ("The Gift of the Magi")
Richard Garrick . . . Doctor ("The Last Leaf")

**Rest of cast:**
Irving Bacon . . . Mr. Dorset
Carl Betz . . . Jimmy Valentine
Frank Cusack . . . Waiter
Abe Dinovitch . . . Bartender
Fritz Feld . . . Maurice
Kathleen Freeman . . . Mrs. Dorset
Steven Geray . . . Randolf
Harry Hayden . . . Mr. Crump
Bert Hicks . . . Sheldon Sidney
Frank Jaquet . . . Butcher
Richard Karlan . . . Headwaiter
Nico Lek . . . Owner
Tyler McVey . . . O. Henry
Alfred Mizner . . . Storekeeper
House Peters . . . Bascom
Stuart Randall . . . Detective
Hal J. Smith . . . Dandy
Phil Tully . . . Guard
William Vedder . . . Judge
Ernö Verebes . . . Waiter
Herburt Vigran . . . Poker player
Ruth Warren . . . Neighbor
Billy Wayne . . . Bystander
Martha Wentworth . . . Mrs. O'Brien
Will Wright . . . Manager

**Plot:**
In Marilyn's segment, *The Cop and the Anthem*, a gentlemanly tramp by the name of Soapy (Charles Laughton) tells fellow wayfarer Horace (David Wayne) he intends to commit some minor crime so that he can spend the winter months nice and warm in jail. Unfortunately the scheme is foiled by his singular lack of success in the crime department. One of his attempts is to accost a woman (Marilyn Monroe) in the hope that she attracts the police by screaming; the only problem is that she is in fact a streetwalker. Being a gentleman, he offers her his only possession, an umbrella, which he presents "for a charming and delightful young lady." On the verge of tears, Marilyn exclaims, "He called me a lady!"

Soapy and his pal Horace regroup in a nice warm church, and Soapy suddenly realizes that he could do something about his predicament—get a job and live a warm life that way. But then the two down and outs are spotted by a policeman. Horace shows a clean pair of heels, but poor old Soapy is taken in for vagrancy and sentenced to a jackpot ninety days in jail.

**Reviews:**
*New York Post*
"By a process of elimination one comes back to Charles Laughton in 'The Cop and the Anthem' as best of the lot. His performance, though pitched to his standard of arch comedy, is clearly underlined for laughs. . . . Marilyn Monroe, again as sleek as she was in 'The Asphalt Jungle,' is a streetwalker of stunning proportions."

Laurence Olivier and Marilyn meet the press during filming of *The Prince and the Showgirl* (1957).

## OLIVIER, LAURENCE
(1907–1989, B. LAURENCE KERR OLIVIER, LATER LORD OLIVIER)

MARILYN:
"He gave me the dirtiest looks, even when he was smiling."

OLIVIER:
"You know, I actually fancied her when I first met her. She's a freak of nature, not a genius. A beautiful freak."

Laurence Olivier is often regarded as the most accomplished theater and cinema actor of the twentieth century. His portrayal of Shakespearean leads in *Henry V* (1945) and *Hamlet* (1948) brought him Oscars; for Hamlet he also picked up Oscars for best director and producer. Olivier's Oscar-nominated *Richard III* (1956) and *Othello* (1965) continued to set the standard for film adaptations of the Bard. Further Oscars and nominations came for *Wuthering Heights* (1939), *Rebecca* (1940), *The Entertainer* (1960), *Sleuth* (1972), *Marathon Man* (1976), and *The Boys from Brazil* (1978). Olivier was also celebrated for his movie direction, and for his memorable stage performances on both sides of the Atlantic. He was also a great public figure, a champion of the theater, and in his private life married to three actresses: Jill Esmond, VIVIEN LEIGH, and Joan Plowright. Civil honors brought a knighthood in 1947 and ennoblement in 1970, when he became the first Baron Olivier of Brighton.

The first movie lined up by business partner MILTON GREENE to be made by Marilyn's own production company, MARILYN MONROE PRODUCTIONS, was *THE PRINCE AND THE SHOWGIRL* (1957)—on paper an enticing combination of world-renowned Olivier and the world's most popular sex symbol. It was also a bold move in the process of Marilyn's reinvention as a "serious" actress capable of working with and matching the most accomplished talent in the business. JOSHUA LOGAN, who had directed Marilyn the previous year in *BUS STOP* (1956), remarked, "It's the best combination since black and white." According to biographer FRED LAWRENCE GUILES, Olivier was initially approached only to act, but insisted on making the screen adaptation of TERENCE RATTIGAN's *The Sleeping Prince* his non-Shakespeare directorial debut.

Olivier and his wife Vivien Leigh flew to New York to conclude negotiations. When he arrived at Marilyn's SUTTON PLACE apartment on February 7, 1956, Marilyn kept him, his agent Cecil Tennant, and playwright Rattigan waiting for an hour and a half, but Olivier was bowled over anyway: "One thing was clear to me. I was going to fall most shatteringly in love with Marilyn. She was so adorable, so witty, and more physically attractive than anyone I could imagine." This is generally held to be the first meeting between Marilyn and Olivier, though it is sometimes said that they had previously come across one another in 1950, at a dinner dance to which JOHNNY HYDE escorted a petrified Marilyn.

The press conference held two days later at the PLAZA HOTEL saw the two actors trading compliments. When asked what he thought of Marilyn as an actress, Olivier replied, "She is a brilliant comedienne, and therefore an extremely good actress. She has the cunning gift of being able to suggest one minute that she is the naughtiest little thing, and the next minute that she is beautifully dumb and innocent." Marilyn summed up her enormous respect for Olivier in a simple sentence: "He has always been my idol." On this occasion, however, Marilyn stole the show thanks to the spaghetti-thin strap of her dress snapping in mid-conference.

Another press conference, on July 15 at the Savoy Hotel in London, was held to announce production of *The Prince and the Showgirl* soon after Marilyn's arrival in England, accompanied by new husband ARTHUR MILLER. However, the fine words and compliments ceased almost as soon as production began. Observers at the time were not surprised to learn that Marilyn's devotion to METHOD acting clashed titanically with Olivier's laissez-faire attitude. Against the agonized introspection, the trawling of sense memories which Marilyn brought to the interpretation of her character, Olivier just told her, "All you have to do is be sexy, dear Marilyn."

This comment acted as a red flag to the bull. Marilyn took refuge in the LATENESS and grudging cooperation for which she was famed. Soon enough Olivier had cause to believe her to be petulant, unreliable, and in his words "a professional amateur." Miller, who found himself increasingly called upon to mediate in this battle of wills, observes that at the heart of the ill-feeling, "There was a genuine conflict...between two different styles not merely of acting but of life."

As Miller himself later had occasion to find out, when Marilyn lost faith in people, it was total and forever: "As she had done with so many people, she had idealized Olivier, who as the great and serious artist must be above mortal considerations of the kind so common among the Hollywood fleshmongers she thought she had escaped." Once she felt betrayed, nothing would convince her that Olivier was not an enemy. Despite—perhaps because of—his mediation, Marilyn accused Miller of not backing her up enough against Olivier, and even, out of some kind of cultural affinity, taking Olivier's side.

In his autobiography Miller ventures that as filming continued, Marilyn began to believe that in some way, like a rival actress, Olivier was competing with her for the limelight. Olivier, in the meantime, had to contend with the presence of PAULA STRASBERG, to whose advice and indications Marilyn paid far more attention than his own direction. Marilyn began to have doubts about Olivier's motivation for doing the picture at all, and started to think that he was only there for the money. Sarcastically, she referred to him as "Mister Sir."

Years later Olivier still recalled Marilyn as a "thoroughly ill-mannered and rude girl. . . . I was never so glad to have a film over and done." But with the advantage of time, he acknowledged that, "She gave a star performance. Maybe I was tetchy with Marilyn and with myself, because I felt my career was in a rut. . . . I was as good as could be, and, Marilyn! Marilyn was quite wonderful, the best of all. What do you know?"

Although Marilyn turned in what is recognized as one of her finest comedic performances, *The Prince and the Showgirl* was only a qualified critical success. Sixteen years elapsed before Olivier next stepped into the breach as a director. In his later years he was far more focused on setting up the National Theatre in London, and he took up film roles more or less when financial requirements required him to do so.

BOOK:
*Confessions of an Actor*, Laurence Olivier. New York: Simon and Schuster, 1982.

## ORPHANAGE
LOS ANGELES COUNTY ORPHANAGE / LOS ANGELES ORPHANS HOME SOCIETY—LOCATED AT 815 NORTH EL CENTRO, HOLLYWOOD, (REBUILT AS HOLLYGROVE IN 1956)

MARILYN:
"I was never used to being happy during those years."

"I may have been only nine years old, but something like this, you never forget. The whole world around me just crumbled. . . . When a little girl feels lost and lonely and that nobody wants her, it's something she never can forget as long as she lives."

Norma Jeane was brought to the Los Angeles Orphanage on September 13, 1935, after legal guardian GRACE MCKEE GODDARD told her they were going out for a ride. When they pulled up outside the red brick building, Norma Jeane read the words "Orphans' Home" and understood what was happening. She broke down in tears and screamed that she wasn't an orphan. Years later Marilyn told husband ARTHUR MILLER that they had to pry her hands open from the car door to get her inside.

The general consensus among biographers is that Norma Jeane spent the next twenty-one months in the orphanage, until Goddard reclaimed her on June 26, 1937. However, some biographers state that in actuality Norma Jeane's stay was only nine months.

Different sources (not least Marilyn herself) have furnished widely varying descriptions of the orphanage, ranging from a Dickensian house of childhood horror to a well-run institution for its day. The building itself, described as an airy red brick colonial mansion, accommodated up to 60 or 250 children, depending on accounts. Some of these children, like Norma Jeane, were there on a short-term basis because their parents were unable to look after them. In separate wings, boys and girls slept in dormitories of six, or as many as twenty-five, depending on reports. Reputedly Norma Jeane's bedroom window looked out toward the water tower at RKO studios, where she would she later make *CLASH BY NIGHT* (1952).

The daily routine began at 6 A.M., when the orphan children tidied their rooms before sitting down to breakfast. The boys and girls earned pocket money for doing other chores, which were distributed according to the children's age. During her time at the orphanage Norma Jeane attended the nearby Vine Street School, which she had previously attended when living with the BOLENDER family. Fellow pupils at the school referred to Norma Jeane and the other kids as "the ones from the home." During her time at the orphanage she learned to swim, and was an enthusiastic member of the softball team.

One of the first entries in Norma Jeane's file at the orphanage states she was "a normal, healthy girl who eats and sleeps well, seems content and uncomplaining and also says she likes her classes." But to a girl who had already passed through a number of homes, and seen her mother taken away to a mental institution, months in the orphanage could only heighten her feelings of insecurity. By early 1937, the orphanage administrator, Mrs. Dewey noted in her file, "If she is not treated with much reassurance and patience . . . she appears frightened. I recommend her to be put with a good family."

Biographers report that Mrs. Dewey subtly bent the rules for the little girl on more than one occasion, allowing her to put makeup on in her office—a kindness which Marilyn remembered fondly in later life—and not berating her on a late return from a Saturday outing with Goddard, completely plastered in cosmetics.

Marilyn later said that during her time at the orphanage she took refuge in a fantasy life: "I sometimes told the other orphans I had real wonderful parents who were away on a long trip and would come for me any time, and once I wrote a postcard to myself and signed it from Mother and Daddy. Of course nobody believed it. But I didn't care. I wanted to think it was true. And maybe if I thought it was true it would come true."

Ten years after Norma Jeane left the orphanage, Mrs. Dewey added the final entry in her file: "Norma Jeane Baker has great success in pictures and promises to be a star. She is a very beautiful woman and is now acting as Marilyn Monroe."

In the early years of her career, the publicity department at TWENTIETH CENTURY-FOX seized upon Marilyn's stay at the orphanage as an excellent angle to promote their promising starlet, and wrote in her studio biographies that she was indeed an orphan. In consequence, a scandal erupted in 1952 when a journalist discovered that Marilyn's mother GLADYS BAKER was alive, if not particularly well, in a northern California mental institution.

Arthur Miller writes that Marilyn never got over the sense of abandonment she felt at being placed at the orphanage. Ever after she could "walk into a crowded room and spot anyone there who had lost parents as a child or have spent time in orphanages. . . . There is a 'do you like me?' in an orphan's eyes, an appeal out of bottomless loneliness that no parented person can really know."

## ORRY-KELLY
(1897–1964, B. JOHN ORRY KELLY)

Australian-born fashion designer whose costumes in *SOME LIKE IT HOT* (1959) won him one of the three Oscars he was awarded during his long career in film, which began after friend CARY GRANT found him a job at Warner Brothers.

## OSCARS

(*see* ACADEMY AWARDS)

## OTASH, FRED

ANTHONY SUMMERS writes in his biography of Marilyn that in 1954 Hollywood private detective Otash helped to extricate FRANK SINATRA from accusations that he was involved in the "WRONG DOOR RAID," as well as the BUGGING of Marilyn's home in 1961. In the stories surrounding the latter, Sinatra was in the pay of either the MAFIA, JIMMY HOFFA, or JOE DIMAGGIO.

P/Q

Jack Paar and Marilyn in *Love Nest* (1951).

## PAAR, JACK (B. 1918)

TV host Jack Paar, who had his own network show between the mid-fifties and mid-sixties, worked with Marilyn in LOVE NEST (1951).

## PALANCE, JACK
(B.1919, WALTER PALANUIK)

Best known for his work in Westerns, in 1950 Jack Palance met Marilyn at TWENTIETH CENTURY-FOX while she was working on *ALL ABOUT EVE* (1950). They talked earnestly about the craft of acting, and Palance put her in touch with drama coach MICHAEL CHEKHOV, who became a lasting influence in her life.

Palance won an Academy Award for *City Slickers* (1991) and was twice nominated, for *Sudden Fear* (1952) and *Shane* (1953).

## PALM SPRINGS

The desert resort of Palm Springs has a decades-long history of being a popular getaway spot for Hollywood's movers and shakers.

It was at the Palm Springs Racquet Club Resort Hotel (2743 North Indian Canyon Drive) in 1949 that agent JOHNNY HYDE first set eyes on Marilyn, swimming in the pool—according to one version of how they met. Hyde did more than any other single person to turn the struggling starlet into the household name she is today. At the same hotel, on December 17, 1950, Hyde suffered a fatal heart attack.

In January 1954 newlyweds Marilyn and JOE DIMAGGIO spent two weeks in a secret HONEYMOON location not far from the town, in a cabin lent to them by Marilyn's lawyer.

Several times during her life Marilyn drove out toward Palm Springs, with different passengers in the car, reputedly on a trip to track down her long-lost FATHER.

In the last year of her life Marilyn Monroe and JOHN F. KENNEDY are said to have spent a weekend together at BING CROSBY's home in the desert town.

## PARAMOUNT STUDIOS
5555 MELROSE AVENUE, HOLLYWOOD

Although none of Marilyn's movies were made for Paramount, between October 24 and November 4, 1960 she did the soundstage shooting for *THE MISFITS* (1961) here.

## PARKER, WILLIAM H.

Chief of the Los Angeles POLICE Department in 1962, and ultimately the man in charge of investigations into Marilyn's DEATH. Allegations have been made that Parker, who had contacts with the KENNEDYS, in some way made sure that a COVER-UP was successfully implemented. Parker died four years after Marilyn, in 1966.

## PARISIAN FLORISTS
7528 SUNSET BOULEVARD, LOS ANGELES

For twenty years, from August 1962 to September 1982, this flower store filled the order placed by JOE DIMAGGIO to deliver red roses to Marilyn's final resting place, twice a week (three times in some accounts). When DiMaggio's order expired, ROBERT SLATZER arranged for the florists to continue a weekly delivery—an order that was soon stopped due to nonpayment of bills.

In August 1962 the store did the floral arrangements for Marilyn's casket. Every year this florist sends out wreaths and sprays for the Marilyn Memorial Service held at the WESTWOOD MEMORIAL PARK CEMETERY.

## PARSONS, LOUELLA
(1881–1972, B. LOUELLA OETTINGER)

A powerful voice in Hollywood from the pulpit of her column in the *Herald Examiner*, and one of Marilyn's greatest allies. Parsons was arguably the most influential columnist in the industry—though rival HEDDA HOPPER would have disputed this.

Columnist Louella Parsons and Marilyn at a party at composer Jimmy McHugh's home, 1958.

By early 1953 Parsons was championing Marilyn as "the number one movie glamour girl" in Hollywood, and Marilyn could count on Parsons to draw a veil over rumors and generally give a positive spin to otherwise unflattering events. Marilyn chose to respond to JOAN CRAWFORD's 1953 outburst at the suggestive attire Marilyn wore to the *PHOTOPLAY* Awards through Parsons's column. She used this pulpit once more to explain to her public why she walked away from Fox at the end of 1954.

In 1956 Louella Parsons followed Marilyn to London, where she attended the party thrown in Marilyn's honor by TERENCE RATTIGAN.

Marilyn once told Parsons, "You and Mr. Schenck were my first friends in Hollywood, and I've never forgotten."

Parsons also made occasional appearances as herself on film, in *Hollywood Hotel* (1937) and *Starlift* (1951).

BOOK:
*Tell It to Louella*, Louella Parsons. New York: The Putnam Berkley Group, 1962.

Marilyn and agent Johnny Hyde poolside at the Palm Springs Resort Hotel, ca. 1949.

## PECK, GREGORY (B. 1916)

Long-time Hollywood favorite Gregory Peck almost worked with Marilyn on *LET'S MAKE LOVE* (1960). He pulled out of the project reputedly after ARTHUR MILLER's script revisions had taken away from his character and given more emphasis to Marilyn. His parting shot was that the script was now "about as funny as pushing grandma down the stairs in a wheelchair."

Peck's filmography includes *The Keys of the Kingdom* (1944), *The Yearling* (1946), *Gentleman's Agreement* (1947), *Roman Holiday* (1953), *The Man in the Gray Flannel Suit* (1956), and *To Kill a Mockingbird* (1963), for which he won an Oscar.

## PEPITONE, LENA (B. 1928)

Marilyn's MAID at her East FIFTY-SEVENTH STREET apartment in New York from late 1957 to the time of her death, came into the public limelight in 1979 when she published an account of her time with Marilyn. Mainly containing "as told to" recollections of Marilyn, her book has been criticized in some quarters for its scurrilous approach, including details about some rather unsavory hygiene habits ascribed to her employer.

Despite these criticisms, a number of Marilyn BIOGRAPHIES published since 1979 have quoted heavily from Pepitone's book, particularly regarding Marilyn's reactions to crises in her life—information which could only possibly be relayed by somebody who was on the spot as events unfolded.

BOOK:
*Marilyn Monroe Confidential*, Lena Pepitone and William Stadiem. New York: Simon & Schuster, 1979.

## PERFECTIONISM

MARILYN:
"My one desire is to do my best, the best that I can from the moment the camera starts until it stops. That moment I want to be perfect, as perfect as I can make it."

The flip side of her incredible stage fright and nerves, either when ACTING before the camera or appearing before an adoring public. Marjorie Plecher, who worked as wardrobe mistress on the 1952 movie *CLASH BY NIGHT*, recalled, "Every element had to be just so—not only in her performance, but also in wardrobe and props."

## PERFUME

Marilyn's passion for Chanel No. 5 is well documented; she was rumored to have twenty-six bottles of it in her possession at one time. She also liked to take long baths infused with Chanel.

When asked if it was true she wore only Chanel No. 5 to bed, she replied, "I like to wear something different once in a while. Now and then I switch to Arpège."

She also sometimes used Joy.

(*see* BEAUTY)

## PETERS, JEAN (B. 1926)

A popular leading lady during the early fifties, Peters played opposite Marilyn in *NIAGARA* (1953) in the role of Polly Cutler, the innocent woman taken hostage by JOSEPH COTTEN in the finale. In some accounts, Marilyn's femme fatale in *Niagara* was originally written for Peters; the more popular version, however, is that Peters stepped in to replace ANNE BAXTER, who pulled out of the project after the Polly Cutler character diminished in importance. Peters and Marilyn had previously worked together on *AS YOUNG AS YOU FEEL* (1951), and featured in different segments of ensemble piece *O. HENRY'S FULL HOUSE* (1952).

During production for *LET'S MAKE LOVE* (1960), when Marilyn, husband ARTHUR MILLER, co-star YVES MONTAND, and his wife SIMONE SIGNORET were staying at the BEVERLY HILLS HOTEL, Peters and HOWARD HUGHES were occupying the downstairs apartment.

Peters' other movie outings included *Viva Zapata* (1952), *Three Coins in the Fountain* (1954), and *A Man Called Peter* (1955). She retired from the movies to marry Howard Hughes in 1957, a marriage which lasted until 1971, after which she returned to star in a few TV movies.

## PETS

MARILYN:
"Dogs never bite me. Just humans."

During her long stay with foster parents IDA AND ALBERT BOLENDER, Norma Jeane had her very own pet, a little black and white dog—a stray in some accounts, a gift from Albert Bolender in others—which she named Tippy. The little dog faithfully followed Norma Jeane to school and waited patiently for her to emerge at the end of the day. In early 1933, a neighbor shot Tippy dead, either because he was kept up one night by the dog's barking, or because he was angry at damage done to his garden, depending on accounts. Norma Jeane was almost inconsolable. Her mother GLADYS BAKER came to help her bury the pet; she paid the last installment on her daughter's room and board, and took her little girl away to live with her. Marilyn remembered that dog to the end of her life; she named the cocker spaniel brought in for some scenes of *SOMETHING'S GOT TO GIVE* Tippy.

Soon after marrying JAMES DOUGHERTY, Norma Jeane got a new pet, a collie called Muggsy. Accounts differ as to whether she found it as a stray or was given it by her new husband to keep her company while he was with the Merchant Marine. Muggsy diednot long after Norma Jeane began her MODELING career, and had no time to visit the dog, who was living with her mother-in-law at the Dougherty family home.

For her twenty-fourth birthday, studio chief JOSEPH SCHENCK gave Marilyn a female chihuahua called Josefa, which Marilyn pampered and fed calf's liver. The dog, however, was never house-trained, and caused quite a lot of friction with NATASHA LYTESS, with whom she stayed at the time. Josefa

Miller and Marilyn with their basset hound Hugo in Roxbury, Connecticut, 1956.

was less trouble at the Palm Drive home Marilyn shared with JOHNNY HYDE. The dog died within a year. Also, Marilyn reportedly had a Persian cat called Mitsou when she first lived in New York in 1955.

A basset hound called Hugo lived with Marilyn and husband ARTHUR MILLER in the late fifties, at their New York apartment and at their country house at ROXBURY, Connecticut. After they divorced, Marilyn thought it was best for the animal to stay in the country. In 1958 Marilyn and Arthur bought a horse called Ebony from Miller's close friend FRANK TAYLOR. Marilyn rode Ebony around their extensive grounds only a few times. A Siamese cat called Serafina joined the Miller household in 1959.

Marilyn's last pet was MAF, a small white poodle she was given in early 1961 to keep her company after her brief sojourn to a psychiatric HOSPITAL. Maf, like other dogs Marilyn owned, was not properly house-trained. Maf moved with Marilyn back to Los Angeles. At her final home, on FIFTH HELENA DRIVE, Maf slept in its own room on an old beaver coat of Marilyn's, said to have been a gift from Miller. After Marilyn died, Maf was taken in by Gloria Lovell, FRANK SINATRA's secretary.

## PHOENIX, ARIZONA

The rodeo scenes in *BUS STOP* were shot in Phoenix, Arizona during March 1956. Marilyn stayed in town during the filming.

## PHOTOGRAPHERS AND PHOTOGRAPHY

BILLY WILDER:
"God gave her everything. The first day a photographer took a picture of her she was a genius."

DAVID THOMSON:
"She gave great still. She is funnier in stills, sexier, more mysterious, and protected against being."

RICHARD AVEDON:
"She understood photography and she also understood what makes a great photograph. Not the technique, but the content."

PHILIPPE HALSMAN:
"While the movie studios had yet refused to make this girl their star, the still photographers had made her theirs. Through them she had become better known than many actresses who had been on the screen for ten years or more. Here was a girl nobody could remember having seen in a movie, but men from one end of the country to the other whistled when you mentioned her name."

LASZLO WILLINGER:
"When she saw a camera—any camera, she lit up and was totally different. The moment the shot was over, she fell back into her not very interesting position."

Photographs were Marilyn's first entertainment love, and even after she had achieved fame on the big screen she adored the intimacy of photography—not to mention the control, something she could not experience in the collaborative and very hierarchical world of the movies. As soon as she had the power to do so, she demanded approval on all photo shoots, and her keen eye made sure that the photos used for publicity purposes or in magazine features portrayed the Marilyn she wanted the world to see.

JOHN SPRINGER, one of Marilyn's press agents in the later part of her career, remarked that Marilyn was "pleased if you liked her most recent motion picture but if you talked about her recent magazine cover or photo layout, she really came alive with pleasure."

Marilyn learned at the very start of her career the poses to strike, the angles that best suited her, the kind of light that would flatter. Practically all of the vast number of photographers who got close to her concur that she had an incredible gift for "turning it on" for the camera. Marilyn's natural gift—refined by the briefest stint at the BLUE BOOK MODELING AGENCY and then honed on the cheesecake photography circuit—was apparent to the first professional photographer for whom she posed, DAVID CONOVER. Many photographers, even in the early days, were surprised at how easily she flirted with the camera, and how self-critical she was in order to find out what she could improve.

EVE ARNOLD has said Marilyn was unique; unlike most people, for whom the camera usually adds a sensation of weight, she photographed ten pounds lighter. Arnold noted that Marilyn had a sixth sense that told her when a camera lens was on her—she would swivel, push out her breasts, suck in her tummy, and her face would light up: "The truth is that she was not only a natural to the camera but that she had a sure knowledge of how to use that affinity. It was to her what water is to a fish—it was her element and she exulted in it."

If the photographer was male, Marilyn often flirted outrageously during the shoot. Many photographers, especially during her starlet days, claimed to have had a sexual relationship with her. Not just men were entranced by Marilyn's seduction technique for the camera. INGE MORATH said, "You could not photograph her badly if you tried. When she was ready she would surpass the expectations of the lens. She had a shimmering quality like an emanation of water, and she moved lyrically."

Marilyn's preferred side to be photographed was her right (not the trademark mole side). Many semi-candid shots of her show her from behind, looking round and back, mock-coy, over her shoulder. The fine down on her face gave her a kind of halo, heightening the almost ethereal candid white of her skin.

In the last year of Marilyn's life, at least one photographer noted that Marilyn's body had become "mature," but she did not seem to notice the fact—she embarked on more than one nude and semi-nude session, as if to let the world know that she was not afraid of time. Prior to this, Marilyn had been the most critical judge of how she photographed. As she told editor Stanley Kauffman when he was collating a SAM SHAW book, "When people look at me, they want to see a star."

BERT STERN, who photographed Marilyn a month before she died, found her "very natural, without the affectation of a star complex. There was a rare quality that I haven't seen before or since—as if there were no other person in the world while you were there. Marilyn devoted herself single-mindedly to the task.... She did not seem depressed or anxious about anything: she sipped her Dom Perignon and was delighted to be doing what she most enjoyed."

After Marilyn's death, many photographers went through negatives of Marilyn that she had rejected and printed them in books. These are pictures Marilyn would have rigorously prevented from being published. Bert Stern's last sitting photos are almost all negatives that he failed to send to Marilyn after their three day photo shoot.

### MARILYN'S PRINCIPAL PHOTOGRAPHERS

Slim Aarons
Eve Arnold
Zinn Arthur
Richard Avedon
Ernest Bachrach
Ed Baird
Baron
George Barris
Cecil Beaton
Anthony Beauchamp
Hal Berg
Bernard of Hollywood
John Bryson
Bill Burnside
Tom Caffrey
Lee Caloia
Cornell Capa
Jack Cardiff
Jock Carroll
William Carroll
Henri Cartier-Bresson
Edward Clark
David Conover
Ed Coonenwerth
Henri Dauman
Bruce Davidson
André De Dienes
Nat Dillinger
Alfred Eisenstaedt
Glenn Embree
John Engstead
Elliott Erwitt
Ed Feingersh
John Florea
Len Globus
Allan Grant
Milton Greene
Ernst Haas
Philippe Halsman
Bob Henriques
Potter Hueth
George Hurrell
Joseph Jasgur
Tom Kelley
Douglas Kirkland
Gene Kornman
Hans Knopf
Earl Leaf
Lee Lockwood
Joshua Logan
Harold Lloyd
George Miller
Richard Miller
Jimmy Mitchell
Earl Moran
Inge Morath
Nikolas Muray
Arnold Newman
Leif-Erik Nygards
Paul Parry
Frank Powolny
Willy Rizzo
Lawrence Schiller
Sam Shaw
George Silk
Bert Stern
Phil Stern
Dennis Stock
Earl Theisen
John Vachon
Seymour Wally
Weegee
Leigh Winer
Laszlo Willinger
Bob Willoughby
Gary Winogrand
Raphael Wolff
William Read Woodfield

Thousands more photographed Marilyn over the years. For example, over 200 photographers were said to be present at the infamous New York shoot for the skirt scene in *THE SEVEN YEAR ITCH* (1955). Marilyn was always ready to pose for a fan's camera, and it is a sure bet that "undiscovered" photographs of Marilyn will continue to appear for decades to come.

*The Ultimate Marilyn*, by Ernest W. Cunningham, contains an extensive biographical dictionary of Marilyn photographers, including listings of where their work appears.

### SOME CLASSIC MARILYN PHOTOS

Red velvet calendar nudes: Tom Kelley, 1949
Jones Beach / Tobey Beach series: André De Dienes, 1949
Burlap Idaho potato sack: Earl Theisen, 1952 (*see* CLOTHES)
*The Seven Year Itch* skirt scene: Sam Shaw, 1954 (see film entry)
The chinchilla wrap and straw boater: Milton H. Greene, 1953 (*see* Greene entry)
Lying in bed with a flower: Cecil Beaton, 1956
In jeans and pigtails on the set of *The Misfits*: Eve Arnold, 1961 (see letter "O")
Marilyn in Mexican cardigan: George Barris, 1962 (see MEXICO)
The head and shoulders shot (with white eyeshadow): Bert Stern, 1962 (see Stern entry)

BOOKS:
*Marilyn*, Lawrence Schiller, ed., text by Norman Mailer. New York: Grosset & Dunlap, 1973.

Twenty-four of Marilyn's finest photographers together in one book. Often referred to as the definitive collection.

This famous photograph of a relaxed Marilyn was taken by Milton Greene in 1957.

*Marilyn by Moonlight*, ed. Jack Allen. New York: Barclay House, 1996.
One hundred and twenty mainly rare photographs.

*Marilyn, Her Life and Legend*, Susan Doll. New York: Beekman House, 1990.

Four hundred and fifty photos, almost half in color, tracing Marilyn's modeling and film career.

*Marilyn Monroe, A Life on Film*, John Kobal. New York: Exeter Books, 1984.
Two hundred and fifty black-and-white photos plus sixteen pages in color.

*Marilyn Monroe, A Never-Ending Dream*, Guus Luijters, ed. New York: St. Martins Press, 1987.
Over four hundred and fifty black-and-white photos.

*Marilyn Monroe and the Camera*, Lothar Schirmer. Boston: Little, Brown and Co., 1989.
Marilyn's most famous shots spanning her entire career, almost fifty color and over one hundred black-and-white photographs.

*Monroe: Her Life in Pictures*, James Spada and George Zeno. New York: Bantam Doubleday Dell, 1982.
Over two hundred and thirty mainly rare photographs.

*The Marilyn Album*, Nicki Giles. New York: Henry Books, 1991.
More than six hundred photos documenting Marilyn's life.

These are just a selection of Marilyn photo anthologies. Published works on Marilyn by individual photographers are featured under that photographer's entry.

Marilyn presents a key to the winner of *Photoplay* magazine's "Dream Home Contest," a Mrs. Virginia McAllister of Warrenburg, New York, in 1949.

A January 1953 issue of *Photoplay* magazine featuring Marilyn on the cover.

## *PHOTOPLAY*

Marilyn featured regularly in this film industry MAGAZINE beginning in 1949 when she posed for publicity shots on a promotional tour for LOVE HAPPY (1950). From then on, the magazine generally portrayed her in a positive light.

Marilyn's full-tilt rush to stardom received recognition in the magazine's annual movie AWARDS. The magazine gave Marilyn its award for "Fastest Rising Star of 1952," which she received at the March 9, 1953 awards ceremony literally sewn into the gold lamé dress she had worn in *GENTLEMEN PREFER BLONDES*.

Jealous JOE DIMAGGIO had perhaps wisely refused to accompany Marilyn to the event when he learned that she intended to wear the eye-popping dress deemed too risqué to feature more than fleetingly in the movie. Columnist and friend SIDNEY SKOLSKY, always ready to oblige, escorted her to the awards ceremony, where she arrived a typical two hours late. Marilyn's trademark sashay to and from the stage to pick up her award had men in the audience howling. Columnist SHEILAH GRAHAM commented, "How Marilyn flaunted her rear end. You could see every crevice." Another columnist described it as "a burlesque show. The audience yelled and shouted, and Jerry Lewis got up on the table and whistled." Hollywood leading ladies such as Lana Turner and JOAN CRAWFORD simply blended into the background, and for days the press reveled in the scandal of the dress, including Crawford's rather hypocritical denouncement of Marilyn's exploitation of sex.

A year later Marilyn picked up the magazine's 1953 Best Actress Award, in honor of her performances in *Gentlemen Prefer Blondes* and *HOW TO MARRY A MILLIONAIRE*. In a repeat performance, Marilyn was escorted to the event at the BEVERLY HILLS HOTEL by Skolsky, once more stealing the show—this year in a low-cut white satin sheath chosen specifically to set off her platinum hair.

## PINEWOOD STUDIOS
PINEWOOD ROAD, IVER, ENGLAND

Established in the 1930s in Buckinghamshire, England, by builder Charles Boot and millionaire J. Arthur Rank, Pinewood is one of

Marilyn at the *Photoplay* Gold Medal Awards Dinner, 1953.

the U.K.'s most prestigious film studios. It was here that in 1956 Marilyn Monroe and LAURENCE OLIVIER did the shooting for *THE PRINCE AND THE SHOWGIRL* (1957). Marilyn commuted to work everyday from her home at nearby EGHAM.

## PLAZA HOTEL

768 FIFTH AVENUE, NEW YORK

The location Marilyn chose for a press conference to announce production of *THE PRINCE AND THE SHOWGIRL* (1957), alongside LAURENCE OLIVIER. Apart from successfully fielding some rather hostile questions from the hundred-plus journalists, the most notable event was when the strap on Marilyn's dress snapped.

## PLECHER, MARJORIE (MARGE)

Longtime wardrobe supervisor and costumer, who worked with Marilyn on a number of films. Ms. Plecher married Marilyn's makeup man and friend ALLAN "WHITEY" SNYDER. It was Marge who dressed Marilyn's body for her FUNERAL.

## POETRY

MARILYN:
"I used to write poetry sometimes but usually I was depressed those times. The few I showed it to (in fact two people) said that it depressed them. One of them cried, but it was an old friend I'd known for a long time."

Marilyn not only enjoyed reading poetry, she wrote quite a lot of poems herself. Ever fearful of harsh judgement, Marilyn showed her poetry to a select few people, including MILTON GREENE, NORMAN ROSTEN, and CARL SANDBURG.

Rosten writes:

> She would often hand me a scrap of paper with something written on it and ask, "Do you think this is poetry? Keep it and let me know." Or she'd send a scribbled sheet in the mail asking for criticism. I would always encourage her. The poems were, in the best sense, those of an amateur; that is, they pretended to be nothing more than an outburst of feeling, with little or no knowledge of craft. But the poet within her—and one existed—found a form for her purpose.

Whether or not she would have risked letting husband ARTHUR MILLER see them is another question. Poems were transcribed from Marilyn's notebooks by different people; as a result, competing versions are in circulation.

### A SELECTION OF MARILYN'S POETRY

A reputed early poem/note to photographer Bill Burnside in early 1946:

In this publicity photo for *Love Nest* (1951) Marilyn reads Whitman's *Leaves of Grass.*

I could have loved you once, and even said it
But you went away,
A long way away.
When you came back it was too late
And love was a forgotten word.
Remember?

---

Night of the Nile—soothing—
darkness—refreshes—Air
Seems different—Night has
No eyes nor no one—silence—
except to the Night itself

### POETRY COLLECTIONS ABOUT MARILYN

*Marilyn Monroe and Other Poems*, Ernesto Cardena. London: Search Press, 1975.
*Anyone Can See I Love You*, Marilyn Bowering. Ontario, Canada: The Porcupine's Quill, 1987.
*The Faber Book of Movie Verse*, Philip French and Ken Wlaschin, eds. London: Faber and Faber, 1993.
*Marilyn Monroe*, Lyn Lifshin. Portland, OR: Quiet Lion Press, 1994.
*My Sex is Ice Cream – The Marilyn Monroe Poems*, Nellie McClung. Victoria, British Columbia: Ekstasis Editions, 1996.

## POLICE

ANTHONY SUMMERS's 1985 biography of Marilyn cast an accusatory finger at the way the Los Angeles Police Department handled the investigation of Marilyn's DEATH.

Generally well-respected Chief of Police WILLIAM H. PARKER has been implicated in helping to organize a COVER-UP surrounding Marilyn's death: allegations include confiscation of Marilyn's telephone records, (either to protect ROBERT KENNEDY or to be used for potential future blackmail), secrecy surrounding a deposition made to police by the Attorney General, and the disappearance of the Marilyn investigation file.

Police personnel involved in investigations:

Chief of Police: William H. Parker
Intelligence Division officer in charge of case: James Hamilton
Chief of Detectives: Thad Brown
First officer on the scene: Sergeant JACK CLEMMONS
Police report filed by: R. E. Byron

### DEATH REPORT OF MARILYN MONROE

Death was pronounced on 8/5/62 at 3:45 A.M., possible accidental, having taken place between the time of 8/4 and 8/5/62, 3:35 A.M., at residence located at 12305 Fifth Helena Drive, Brentwood, in Rptg. Dist. 814, Report # 62-509-463.

Marilyn Monroe on August 4, 1962 retired to her bedroom at about eight o'clock in the evening; Mrs. Eunice Murray of 933 Ocean Ave., Santa Monica, Calif., 395-7752, CR 61890, noted a light in Miss Monroe's bedroom. Mrs. Murray was not able to arouse Miss Monroe when she went to the door, and when she tried the door again at 3:30 A.M., when she noted the light still on, she found it to be locked. Thereupon Mrs. Murray observed Miss Monroe through the bedroom window and found her lying on her stomach in the bed and the appearance seemed unnatural. Mrs. Murray then called Miss Monroe's psychiatrist Dr. Ralph Greenson of 436 North Roxbury Drive, Beverly Hills, Calif., CR 14050. Upon entering after breaking the bedroom window, he found Miss Monroe, possibly dead.

Then he telephoned Dr. Hyman Engelberg of 9730 Wilshire Boulevard, also of Beverly Hills, CR 54366, who came over and then pronounced Miss Monroe dead at 3:35 A.M. Miss Monroe was seen by Dr. Greenson on August 4, 1962 at 5:15 P.M., at her request, because she was not able to sleep. She was being treated by him for about a year. She was nude when Dr. Greenson found her dead with the telephone receiver in one hand and lying on her stomach. The Police Department was called and when they arrived they found Miss Monroe in the condition described above, except for the telephone which was removed by Dr. Greenson. There were found to be 15 bottles of medication on the night table and some were prescription. A bottle marked 1 1/2 grains Nembutal, prescription #20853 and prescribed by Dr. Engelberg, and referring to this particular bottle, Dr. Engelberg made the statement that he prescribed a refill for this about two days ago and he further stated there probably should have been about 50 capsules at the time this was refilled by the pharmacist.

Description of deceased: Female Caucasian, age 36, height 5'4", weight 115 pounds, blonde hair, blue eyes, and slender, medium build.

Occupation: Actress. Probable cause of death: overdose of Nembutal, body discovered 8/5/62 at 3:25 A.M. Taken to County Morgue from there to Westwood Mortuary.

Report made by Sgt. R. E. Byron, #2730, W.L.A. Detective Division. Next of kin Gladys Baker (Mother).

Coroner's office notified. The body was removed from premises by Westwood Village Mortuary. (8/5/62 11:00 A.M., W.L.A. hf – J. R. Brukles 5829)

Follow-Up

Upon reinterviewing both Dr. Ralph Greenson (Wit #l) and Dr. Hyman Engelberg (Wit #2) they both agree to the following time sequence of their actions. Dr. Greenson received a phone call from Mrs. Murray (reporting person) at 3:30 A.M., 8-5-62 stating that she was unable to get into Miss Monroe's bedroom and the light was on. He told her to pound on the door and look in the window and call him back. At 3:35 A.M., Mrs. Murray called back and stated Miss Monroe was laying on the bed with the phone in her hand and looked strange. Dr. Greenson was dressed by this time, left for deceased residence which is about one mile away. He also told Mrs. Murray to call Dr. Engelberg.

Dr. Greenson arrived at deceased home at about 3:40 A.M. He broke the window pane and entered through the window and removed the phone from her hand.

Rigor Mortis had set in. At 3:50A.M., Dr. Engelberg arrived and pronounced Miss Monroe dead. The two doctors talked for a few moments. They both believe that it was about 4:00 A.M. when Dr. Engelberg called the Police Department.

A check with the Complaint Board and WLA Desk indicates that the call was received at 4:25 A.M. Miss Monroe's phone GR 61890 has been checked and no toll calls were made during the hours of this occurrence. Phone number 472-4830 is being checked at the present time. R E Byron 2730, 8-6-62

## POLITICS

MARILYN:
"I don't know much about politics. I'm just past the goodies and baddies stage. The politicians get away with murder because most Americans don't know any more about it than I do. Less even."

ARTHUR MILLER:
"Wherever she turned she saw what she called 'lallygagging,' temporizing, the absence of strong and even miraculous liberating blows."

Marilyn may not have read the newspapers every day, she may not have been sophisticated in the way she expressed her beliefs, but her strong opinions on politics earned her her very own FBI file. Biographers agree that Marilyn empathized with and on occasion actively helped the poor, the weak, and the abandoned. Marilyn's political views were formed through her personal experience growing up during the Depression years, and as a young adult when she studied agit-prop plays by left-wing playwrights such as CLIFFORD ODETS at the ACTORS LAB in the late forties. Mentor and lover JOHNNY HYDE shared with her his political beliefs that the future of democracy lay in what Marx had written, and NATASHA LYTESS, her drama coach of seven years, had lived in RUSSIA, a country whose theatrical and literary traditions Marilyn long admired.

Marilyn was always attracted to men who had sympathies with the poor and the downtrodden, whose views were liberal, and who sympathized with the underlying tenets (if not the actual practice) of Communism. As the leading social commentator of his generation, Marilyn's third husband ARTHUR MILLER embodied all these ideals. Despite threats from studio bosses, she backed Miller personally and financially in his fight to counter allegations made by the HOUSE UN-AMERICAN ACTIVITIES COMMITTEE.

Marilyn had courage in her convictions. Her beliefs in equality spurred her to action in late 1954, when she called up the owner of the Mocambo nightclub and told him that he had to book ELLA FITZGERALD, and not perpetuate the racism of hiring only white performers. Marilyn was one of the few white Hollywood actresses to be appreciated by the black community; the fact that she had suffered in life, had to overcome the adversity of her birth and upbringing, struck a chord. Marilyn once told a reporter that she had had an affair with a black man, but because of social expectations they could only meet in private. Publicist PAT NEWCOMB recalls the last declaration Marilyn ever gave to a journalist, RICHARD MERYMAN of *Life* magazine: "What I really want to say: that what the world really needs is a real feeling of kinship. Everybody: stars, laborers, Negroes, Jews, Arabs. We are all brothers. Please don't make me a joke. End the interview with what I believe." In 1959, when Marilyn met Soviet leader NIKITA KHRUSHCHEV, she expressed her wish that world peace would be achieved.

Marilyn became more active and outspoken as years went by. She joined both the Democrat party and S.A.N.E., an organization dedicated to the elimination of nuclear weapons. In 1960 she even campaigned during the presidential elections in the honorary capacity of Alternate Delegate to the Fifth Congressional District of Connecticut.

At the time, Marilyn said, "Some of those bastards in Hollywood wanted me to drop Arthur, said it would ruin my career. They're born cowards and want you to be like them. One reason I want to see Kennedy win is that Nixon's associated with that whole scene." She also wrote to *New York Times* editor Lester Markle, giving her interpretation of the political situation: "There hasn't been anyone like Nixon before, because the rest of them at least had souls!" Her view on Cuba was that the U.S. had not supported the Cubans in their battle against Battista for democracy, so the U.S. did not necessarily have the right to treat Castro the way they were.

Arthur Miller recounts that after their divorce, Marilyn joined a campaign to free Nigerian writer Wole Soyinka from jail. She asked Miller to intercede on behalf of Soyinka, and when he did so, General Gowon, chief of the Nigerian army, freed the writer, who went on to win the Nobel Prize in 1986.

In 1962 Marilyn expressed her continuing support for the Democrats in the form of her sexy rendition of "Happy Birthday" to PRESIDENT KENNEDY. The occasion was a Democrat fund-raising gala, held to cover costs incurred during the 1960 presidential campaign. As well as performing, Marilyn paid the $1000 entrance ticket.

FRED VANDERBILT FIELD, who met Marilyn on her 1962 visit to MEXICO, recalls her "strong feelings about civil rights, for black equality, as well as her admiration for what was being done in China, her anger at red-baiting and McCarthyism, and her hatred of J. Edgar Hoover."

CONSPIRACY theorists would have it that Marilyn's interest in the Kennedys was anything but political. However, on the occasion that Marilyn met ROBERT KENNEDY for dinner at PETER LAWFORD'S house, according to Pat Newcomb, "She had a list of questions prepared. When the press reported that Bobby was talking to her more than anyone else, that's what they meant. I saw the questions and I knew what they were talking about. She identified with all the people who were denied civil rights."

## PORTERFIELD, PEARL

A venerable hairdresser who had styled them all, including the original platinum blonde bombshell JEAN HARLOW, Pearl Porterfield colored Marilyn's hair before she began working on *SOMETHING'S GOT TO GIVE*. Porterfield, affectionately known as "Porter," was one of the few invited to Marilyn's FUNERAL service.

## POSTERITY

On reading a script about a former famous actress (JEAN HARLOW) with a view to playing the part, Marilyn exclaimed, "I hope they don't do that to me when I'm gone."

(*see* FAME)

## POWOLNY, FRANK

A staff stills photographer at TWENTIETH CENTURY-FOX for over four decades, Frank Powolny took many of the best-known movie stills of Marilyn, working with her from *THE ASPHALT JUNGLE* (1950) to her last uncompleted movie *SOMETHING'S GOT TO GIVE*.

## PREMINGER, OTTO (1906–1986)

"The studio first pampered her—she was pampered when we made *River*—to the point where she lost her perspective about what she could and what she could not do, and when it seemed she didn't have the drawing power which she used to have, they expected her to act like an ordinary actress."

"Directing her was like directing Lassie. You needed 14 takes to get each one of them right." (Note: Preminger has denied ever saying this).

Austrian-born director who before becoming a filmmaker studied to be a lawyer and an actor. Among others, he directed *Laura* (1944), *The*

Director Otto Preminger helps Marilyn walk on the set of *River of No Return* (1954). Marilyn suffered a serious sprain after falling off of a raft into the Athabasca River in the Canadian Rockies while shooting a scene for the film.

*Moon is Blue* (1953), *The Man with the Golden Arm* (1956), *Anatomy of a Murder* (1959), and *Advise and Consent* (1961).

Preminger was notorious for running a very tight set. He was given RIVER OF NO RETURN (1953) to direct as part of his contract commitment to TWENTIETH CENTURY-FOX, and it has been said that his lack of enthusiasm for anything but the location landscape shows in the finished movie.

Getting the movie made was a trial for all concerned. Preminger reputedly teased Marilyn about not being able to learn her lines, made her do her own stunts, and questioned her sexual virtue. Marilyn fought back the only way she knew how: by being late and by being difficult.

Needless to say, Preminger also clashed with NATASHA LYTESS, to whom Marilyn paid far more heed. He later said, "I pleaded with [Marilyn] to relax and speak naturally, but she paid no attention. She listened only to Natasha… and rehearsed her lines with such grave artic-yew-lay-shun that her violent lip movements made it impossible to photograph her." Preminger succeeded in having Lytess suspended from the picture, but had to recant when Marilyn dug in her heels. Producer STANLEY RUBIN later acknowledged the friction: "Preminger was a talented man. But he was the wrong director for that picture."

Marilyn afterwards referred to Preminger as "a pompous ass." In 1960 Preminger was asked if he would consider working with Marilyn again. He replied: "Not for a million dollars."

## PRESS

MARILYN:
"I've sometimes tried to charm critics, give them the impression I'm really attracted to them, and it works. With journalists and photographers generally. Experienced as they are, they're not beyond being wooed."

ARTHUR MILLER:
"To paraphrase Winston Churchill's characterization of the Germans, the press with Marilyn Monroe was either at her feet or at her throat."

Although we tend to think of press intrusion in the lives of the famous as a modern-day phenomenon, Marilyn was one of a long line of huge stars whose every move was stalked by men with cameras. Pieces in the press were important to make her a star, but once she was there, the paparazzi became an intrusion. Nevertheless, on many occasions Marilyn used her newsworthiness to push her own agenda.

Marilyn's first press exposure came in 1946, in the form of a judiciously planted item that appeared in HEDDA HOPPER's syndicated column. Mentions outside of trade publications and cheesecake MAGAZINES were few and far between for the next three years, though Marilyn did curry some favor with local Hollywood journalists, winning the 1948 "Miss Press Club" title at the Los Angeles Press Club.

On June 27, 1949 the story that started the avalanche of press coverage appeared in the *New York Daily Mirror* when Sidney Fields wrote, "Marilyn is a very lovely and relatively unknown movie actress. But give her time; you will hear from her." A month later Marilyn gave her first interview to EARL WILSON.

At the outset, Marilyn's contacts with the press were rigorously developed and massaged by the studio publicity department at TWENTIETH CENTURY-FOX, led by publicist-in-chief HARRY BRAND. When Marilyn won a degree of independence from the studios in the mid-fifties, she had her own publicists to arrange and vet interviews. But Marilyn quickly developed the skills required to turn the press to her best advantage. She found and cultivated press allies, and became a recognized master in the art of "the plant." Her main confederate in these endeavors was columnist SIDNEY SKOLSKY, whom she first met in the late forties. Skolsky not only gave Marilyn favorable coverage in his own column, he helped her draft articles that were published under her name (such as a 1952 series of articles entitled "Wolves I Have Known," as told to columnist Florabel Muir), advised her on how to combat negatives publicity, and became the second person to pub-

Marilyn at a press conference in Tokyo during her honeymoon with Joe DiMaggio, 1954.

lish a Marilyn BIOGRAPHY. Another reliable ally was columnist LOUELLA PARSONS, who came to Marilyn's assistance in 1953 when she was attacked by JOAN CRAWFORD for her display at the *PHOTOPLAY* awards.

By this time the Fox publicity department had finessed the more "uncomfortable" aspects of Marilyn's past. Hence in her official, STUDIO BIOGRAPHIES Marilyn became an orphan (eliciting greater sympathy than a mother in a mental institution), and the number of FOSTER PARENTS increased at every telling—at one point reaching fourteen.

To give an idea of how famous Marilyn was at her most famous: in 1952 Marilyn merited as many column inches (including photos) as the coronation of Queen ELIZABETH II in London, or the engagement of high society political couple Senator JOHN F. KENNEDY and Jacqueline Bouvier.

The flip side to all this media attention was the almost total absence of PRIVACY. Marilyn's romance with JOE DIMAGGIO was often a slalom between copy-hungry hacks. In November 1954 it was impossible for Marilyn to emerge from the Cedars of Lebanon HOSPITAL, where she had had surgery, because the press besieged the building.

Marilyn's secret flight to New York in late 1954 set off a frenzied press hunt to track her down. Life on the East Coast brought at least partial respite from presshounds, and Marilyn even managed to get to know future husband ARTHUR MILLER away from prying lenses and columnist sources. But when she returned to Hollywood in early 1956 to shoot *BUS STOP*, despite the best intentions of business partner MILTON GREENE to keep all press and newsmen off the set, he couldn't prevent photographers from using the longest lenses they could muster.

When, in her private life, Marilyn did make concessions to the press, it didn't always work to her benefit. Press conferences she held to announce the formation of her own company, MARILYN MONROE PRODUCTIONS, and official press notification about the company's first movie, *THE PRINCE AND THE SHOWGIRL* (1957), brought a barrage of unfriendly fire from journalists who belittled what they regarded as her pretensions.

As press speculation reached a fevered pitch regarding the impending marriage between Marilyn and Arthur Miller, the couple arranged a press conference at their ROXBURY home, attended by up to 400 journalists. Earlier that day *Paris-Match* reporter MARA SCHERBATOFF was killed in a car accident as she pursued Miller's car down narrow country lanes—an incident that left Marilyn shocked on her wedding day.

Press interest in Marilyn during her time in ENGLAND that year also was frenzied. If she and Arthur went out to the theater, which they did on numerous occasions, they were blocked by crowds of pressmen until police could clear a path. Miller writes that most of what was printed in British papers during their stay was fictitious, conversations invented by editors. One day, however, a conversation they had had in the privacy of their own home was repeated almost verbatim in a daily newspaper. The leak was traced back to the Hungarian servants; they were reprimanded by a British security operative, ex-policeman Roger Hunt, who acted as Marilyn's bodyguard in England, and threatened the servants with immediate repatriation to Budapest if it ever happened again.

Journalists and photographers lay in wait every morning from 8 A.M. outside the Millers' SUTTON PLACE apartment. One morning when Marilyn attempted to leave home incognito, the press pursued her out of the service entrance and took photos of her among the garbage cans.

Biographers unfailingly note that Marilyn never used the press to air personal grievances. She was always polite about her ex-husbands, and refused to be drawn into manufactured studio rivalries with other stars.

Particularly in the later part of her career, when she was not protected by a studio publicity department, sections of the press ran barbed snipes at Marilyn for alleged errors she had made. SIMONE SIGNORET writes that during the time they lived next door to one another at the BEVERLY HILLS HOTEL in 1960, snide pieces documented alleged gaffes at fancy restaurants, despite the fact that Marilyn seldom went out to eat, and when she did, she was in her Marilyn mode and would play the role that was expected of her.

For the reporter, the Marilyn beat was not the easiest. Columnist Erskine Johnson revealed his own experience in print:

> "Waiting for Marilyn" I'll never forget, and I doubt if Hollywood ever will. People may admire Marilyn Monroe, envy Marilyn Monroe, dislike Marilyn Monroe but, most of all, people wait for Marilyn Monroe.
>
> Once I waited for Marilyn in Phoenix. A visit to the set and a chat with her on location for *Bus Stop* had been arranged. I waited all day and Marilyn never came out of her dressing room. Another newsman, who had more time, waited in Phoenix for Marilyn for five days and she never came out of her hotel room. Or invited him in.

MARILYN'S PUBLICISTS
(through the Arthur P. Jacobs Agency):

Rupert Allan
Frank Goodman
Patricia Newcomb
John Springer
Lois Weber

## *PRINCE AND THE SHOWGIRL, THE* (1957)

High meets low both on screen and off, in this British-made movie, the first and only film made by MARILYN MONROE PRODUCTIONS.

LAURENCE OLIVIER and his wife VIVIEN LEIGH had starred in the 1953 stage version of TERENCE RATTIGAN's *The Sleeping Princess*, to which Marilyn's business partner MILTON GREENE had purchased the rights. Marilyn supposedly tracked down Rattigan (during a stopover at New York's Idlewild Airport and won him over to the project). Olivier, Leigh, and Rattigan arrived in New York with Olivier's agent Cecil Tennant to discuss terms in February 1956. Marilyn had been eyeing this property since 1954, when her then agent Hugh French suggested it to her. Olivier only agreed to reprise his stage role on the condition that he direct and have a credit as a co-producer.

A press conference was arranged at the PLAZA HOTEL to tell the world of this momentous screen pairing—England's finest classical actor and Hollywood's top screen siren. Although there have been denials of pre-meditation, the evidence is that Marilyn stage-managed the event to perfection, stealing the show from the world's greatest living actor when she leaned forward and one of her ultra-thin shoulder straps snapped—a trick Marilyn was apparently taught by publicists during her early days at Fox. The photographers went mad. A safety pin was hurriedly found, but the strap broke another two times before the pressmen and snap-happy photographers left the Plaza Terrace room. Marilyn's careful planning merited front page coverage, though the conference itself was a less than friendly affair as journalists ridiculed her "pretensions."

Marilyn and ARTHUR MILLER arrived in ENGLAND just weeks after their WEDDING, in a blaze of publicity. Shot at PINEWOOD STUDIOS (though Miller writes that filming was at Shepperton) filming began on August 7, 1956, after a week's rehearsal. The production wrapped on November 17, 1956.

Originally, musical numbers were planned for Marilyn, who plays chorus girl Elsie Marina. This idea was reputedly vetoed by Miller.

Shooting couldn't have got off to a worse start. Marilyn, at last breaking out of the straitjacket of typeset sex roles, and eagerly applying the introspection and search for motivation demanded by THE METHOD, was given the direction by Olivier "to be sexy." In retaliation for what she took to be condescension at the very least, Marilyn resorted to her tried and tested tactics of LATENESS and absence. LENA PEPITONE reports that Marilyn later told her, "He looked at me like he had just smelled a pile of dead fish. He'd say something like, 'Oh, how simply ravishing, my dear.' But really he wanted to throw up. I just felt like a little fool the whole time."

According to cinematographer JACK CARDIFF, the problems between Olivier and Marilyn arose because of different approaches to acting. Olivier would tell her how he wanted her to perform a scene, then Marilyn's drama coach PAULA STRASBERG would tell her, "Think of Frank Sinatra and Coca Cola," and she'd forget her lines and go to pieces. Half-way through filming Marilyn's psychoanalyst DR. MARGARET HOHENBERG was flown out to London to help her patient.

Tensions threatened to engulf the film. Marilyn was reportedly suspicious of everybody; Olivier thought Marilyn was petulant, and he couldn't stand what he saw as Paula Strasberg's meddling; Strasberg was often in the middle between Marilyn and Olivier, ferrying information between the movie's two principals who were not on speaking terms. Miller reputedly was unhappy with Milton Greene; Milton Greene distrusted Miller; and Marilyn was said to have started the movie under a cloud, after reading an entry in her husband's diary which shattered her belief that he loved her. Despite the friction and rumor, the movie came in under budget, and only required two days of reshooting.

At the end of shooting, Marilyn told the assembled cast and crew, "I hope you will all forgive me. It wasn't my fault. I've been sick all through the picture. Please, please, don't hold it against me."

Even after shooting, the wrangles continued. By this time Marilyn had fallen out with business partner Greene, convinced that against her will he had recut the film. She wrote a long letter to Jack Warner telling him as much, and she tried hard to prevent Greene from being credited as executive producer, something they had agreed upon at the outset.

The film premiered at RADIO CITY MUSIC HALL on June 13, 1957. Critical reception was mixed at the time, but Marilyn's performance has been acknowledged as among her finest, and she easily steals the movie from Olivier. This was also the first movie on which Marilyn's new standing as an independent contractor made her eligible for a percentage of profits, a highly unusual form of remuneration at the time of the studio system. Marilyn received 10 percent of profits, which worked out to $160,000 (since the picture made $1,600,000).

BOOK:

*The Prince, The Showgirl and Me*, Colin Clark. London: HarperCollins, 1995.

Day-by-day diary of what it was like to work as a humble gofer on this most eventful of sets.

MEMORABLE COSTUME:

Floor-length white dress with low square neckline and mermaid flare hem.

**Tagline:**

"Some countries have a medal for everything."

**Awards:**

Crystal Star (France): "Best Foreign Actress of 1958," Marilyn Monroe

David di Donatello (Italy): "Best Foreign Actress," Marilyn Monroe

**Nominations:**

BRITISH ACADEMY AWARDS:

Best Foreign Actress: Marilyn Monroe

Best British Actor: Laurence Olivier

Best British Film

Best British Screenplay: Terence Rattigan

Best Film from any source

**Credits:**

Laurence Olivier and Marilyn Monroe Productions, distributed by Warner Brothers, Technicolor

Length: 117 minutes

Release date: June 13, 1957

Directed by: Laurence Olivier

Produced by: Laurence Olivier

Written by: Terence Rattigan (also original play "The Sleeping Prince")

Executive producer: Milton Greene

Cinematography by: Jack Cardiff

Music by: Richard Addinsell

Film Editing by: Jack Harris

A publicity photo for *The Prince and the Showgirl*, 1957.

**Cast (credits order):**

Laurence Olivier . . . Grand Duke Charles

Marilyn Monroe . . . Elsie Marina

Sybil Thorndike . . . Queen Dowager

Jeremy Spenser . . . King Nicholas

Richard Wattis . . . Northbrooke

Jean Kent . . . Masie Springfield

Esmond Knight . . . Colonel Hoffman

Daphne Anderson . . . Fanny

Vera Day . . . Betty

Paul Hardwick . . . Major Domo

Andrea Malandrinos . . . Valet with Violin

Margot Lister . . . Lottie

Rosamund Greenwood . . . Maud

Aubrey Dexter . . . The Ambassador

Maxine Audley . . . Lady Sunningdale

Harold Goodwin . . . Call Boy

Gillian Owen . . . Maggie

Charles Victor

David Horne

Dennis Edwards

Gladys Henson

**Crew:**

Beatrice "Bumble" Dawson.... Costume design

William Chappell . . . choreographer

Carmen Dillon . . . art director

Gordon K. McCallum . . . sound mixer

**Plot:**

London, 1911, and the Prince Regent of Carpathia, Grand Duke Charles (Laurence Olivier) arrives in town for the coronation of George V, along with his young son King Nicholas (Jeremy Spenser) and mother-in-law Queen Dowager (Sybil Thorndike).

After seeing American showgirl Elsie Marina (Marilyn Monroe) perform in a show, the Prince Regent invites her back to the opulent Carpathian Embassy for dinner and, he hopes, a little amour. Down-to-earth Elsie manages to preserve her virtue, despite becoming quite drunk and eventually falling asleep. Throughout the evening a political crisis unfolds as Nicholas is locked into his room by his father when he plots to take power now rather than in eighteen months when he comes of age.

Despite her lowly standing, Elsie wins the approval of the austere Queen Dowager, who makes her a lady-in-waiting for the coronation. This is an ideal position for Elsie to resolve the conflict brewing between royal father and son. Ultimately, she persuades young Nicholas to wait his allotted moment. The Prince Regent, now in love with Elsie, plans to return and claim her as his bride.

**Reviews:**

*The New York Times*

"We are bound to tell you Miss Monroe never gets out of that dress and Mr. Rattigan never swings out of the circle in which he has permitted his thin plot to get stuck... He has not let his story do much more than go around and around, and then come to a sad end."

*New York Herald Tribune*

"*The Prince and the Showgirl* is great fun if you don't take it seriously. Certainly its author doesn't. Terence Rattigan is just playing a game, amusing us for two hours, and the actors enjoy the charade immensely. They try to look earnest but a twinkle in the eye betrays them.

In the case of Olivier, the twinkle must

fight its way through a thick monocle to reach the outside world and it does. This is a performance of rich, subtle humor... Marilyn's role has no such fine shadings. This is a dumb, affable showgirl and nothing more, and Miss Monroe goes through the motions with mirth, childish innocence, squeals of pleasure, pouts of annoyance, eyes big as golf balls, and many a delighted toss of her rounded surfaces."

*New York World-Telegram and Sun*
"The unpredictable waverings of Marilyn Monroe's acting promise soar to a triumphant peak in *The Prince and the Showgirl*... The movie is also a comic delight, matching the surprise bestowed upon us by Marilyn. As her co-star and director, Laurence Olivier brings out qualities none of her films ever summoned. She is captivatingly kittenish in her infectious mirth. Her love scenes are played as a girlish game. She romps through slapstick and turns solemn moments into part of her fun."

*The Los Angeles Times*
"This, I am sure, is Miss Monroe's best cinema effort. Under Olivier's direction, she reveals a real sense of comedy. Miss Monroe also proves that she can command attention now by other means than her famous hip-swinging walk."

*New York Post*
"Marilyn Monroe... has never seemed more in command of herself as a person and comedienne. She manages to make her laughs without sacrificing the real Marilyn to play-acting. This, of course, is something one can expect from great, talented and practiced performers. It comes as a most pleasant surprise from Marilyn Monroe, who has been half-actress, half-sensation."

*The New Yorker*
"Apart from the whimsicality of teaming up England's leading actor with a young lass whose dramatic experience has been largely confined to wiggling about in Technicolor pastries cooked up in Hollywood, it offers little in the way of diversion."

Laurence Olivier and Marilyn in *The Prince and the Showgirl* (1957).

## PRIVACY

Lack of privacy is the price stars pay for FAME. Over the years, Marilyn took a number of steps to preserve hers. If she wanted to go around town incognito, her favorite DISGUISE was black wig and sunglasses.

In her last home, to prevent people finding out her telephone number, she put a false one on the dial. When dialed, it reached the city morgue.

### PRODUCERS

| | |
|---|---|
| Buddy Adler | *Bus Stop* (1956) |
| Robert Bassler | *A Ticket to Tomahawk* (1950), *Let's Make It Legal* (1951) |
| Julian Blaustein | *Don't Bother to Knock* (1952) |
| Charles Brackett | *Niagara* (1953) |
| Jules Buck | *Love Nest* (1951) |
| Lester Cowan | *Love Happy* (1950) |
| Armand Deutsch | *Right Cross* (1950) |
| Charles K. Feldman | *The Seven Year Itch* (1955) |
| Bert Friedlob | *The Fireball* (1950) |
| Andre Hakim | *0. Henry's Full House* (1952) |
| Arthur Hornblow Jr. | *The Asphalt Jungle* (1950) |
| Nunnally Johnson | *We're Not Married* (1952), *How to Marry a Millionaire* (1953) |
| Walter Morosco | *Scudda Hoo! Scudda Hay!* (1948) |
| Laurence Olivier | *The Prince and the Showgirl* (1957) |
| Harriet Parsons | *Clash by Night* (1952) |
| Arthur Pierson | *Hometown Story* (1951) |
| Harry A. Romm | *Ladies of the Chorus* (1948) |
| Stanley Rubin | *River of No Return* (1954) |
| Sol C. Siegel | *Monkey Business* (1952), *Gentlemen Prefer Blondes* (1953), *There's No Business Like Show Business* (1954) |
| Frank E. Taylor | *The Misfits* (1961) |
| Lamar Trotti | *As Young as You Feel* (1951) |
| Jerry Wald | *Let's Make Love* (1960) |
| Henry Weinstein | *Something's Got to Give* (1962, unfinished) |
| Billy Wilder | *The Seven Year Itch* (1955), *Some Like It Hot* (1959) |
| Sol W. Wurtzel | *Dangerous Years* (1947) |
| Darryl F. Zanuck | *All About Eve* (1950) |

## PROSTITUTION

MARILYN:
"Men who tried to buy me with money made me sick. There were plenty of them. The mere fact that I turned down offers ran my price up . . . I didn't take their money, and they couldn't get by my front door, but I kept riding in their limousines and sitting beside them in swanky places. There was always a chance of a job and another wolf might spot you."

Short of cash and out of contract in the late 1940s, Marilyn picked up MONEY to live however she could. It has been said she worked as a stripper in a seedy Sunset Boulevard joint, and even engaged in casual prostitution. According to benefactor LUCILLE RYMAN, Marilyn supplemented her income by offering herself to men who cruised the Hollywood streets looking for paid sex. Ryman said: "It wasn't for cash. She told us without pride or shame that she made a deal—she did what she did, and her customers bought her breakfast or lunch."

It has also been claimed that Marilyn worked as a stripper at the seedy Mayan Theater, (1044 South Hill Street, Los Angeles), not long after her contract with COLUMBIA PICTURES was allowed to lapse.

Marilyn allegedly told her New York maid LENA PEPITONE that when she was splitting up from first husband JAMES DOUGHERTY she made fifteen dollars having sex with a man she met in a bar.

LEE STRASBERG once told an interviewer that Marilyn was mentally scarred by some of the things that befell her during her starlet years, particularly when working as a "hostess" at a convention center: "Marilyn was a call girl... and her call girl background worked against her."

Not long before she died, Marilyn told GEORGE BARRIS, "If there's only one thing in my life I was to be proud of, it's that I've never been a kept woman." Despite his pleading and insistence, Marilyn would not marry early agent and fixer JOHNNY HYDE—a man who was crazy about her, was suffering a very serious heart condition and had millions in the bank—because she did not love him.

In the mid-fifties, Marilyn turned down a string movies Fox wanted her to do, playing roles of barely disguised prostitutes, though one of the roles she wanted but didn't land was Sadie Thompson in *Rain*.

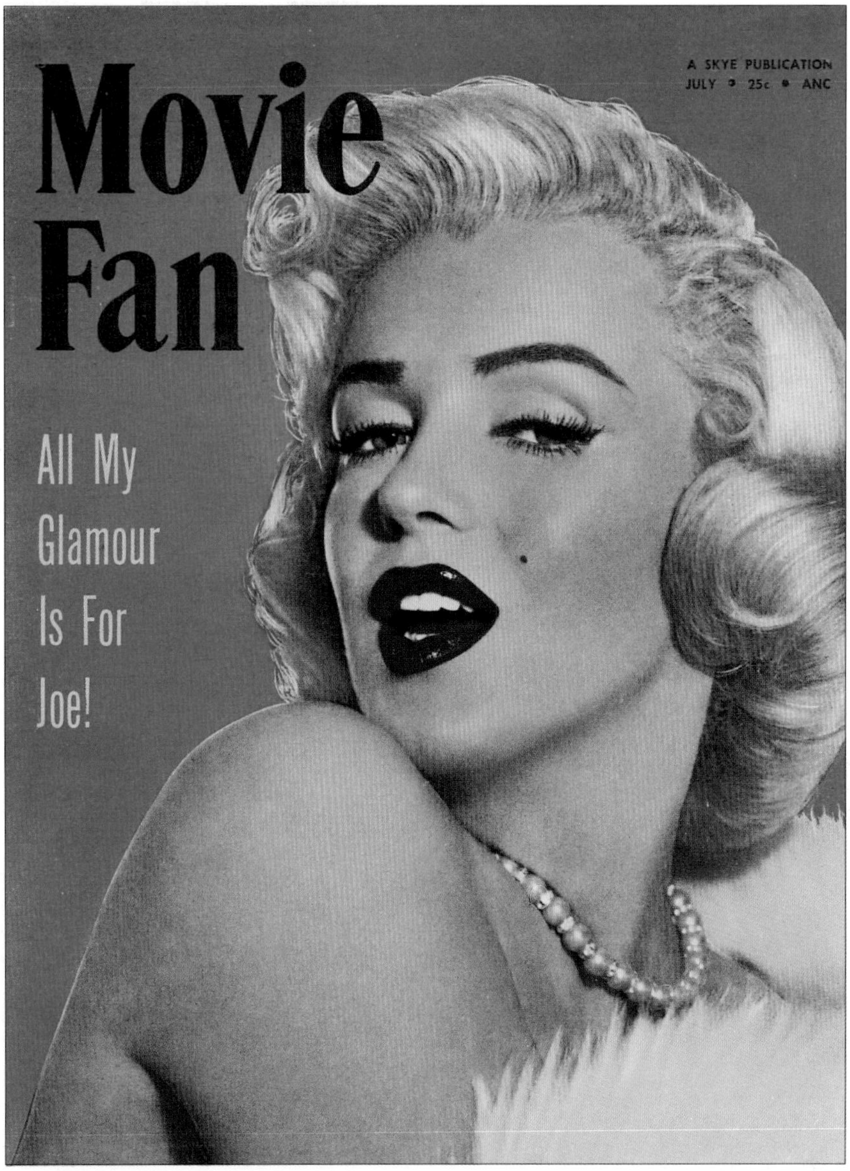

A July 1954 issue of *Movie Fan* magazine "quotes" Marilyn on her relationship to Joe DiMaggio.

## PSYCHOANALYSIS

MARILYN:
"Why haven't I the right to grow and expand like everybody else?"
"My problem is that I drive myself... I'm trying to become an artist, and to be true, and sometimes feel I'm on the verge of craziness. I'm just trying to get the truest part of myself out, and it's very hard. There are times when I think, 'All I have to be is true.' But sometimes it doesn't come out so easily. I always have this secret feeling that I'm really a fake or something, a phony."

BILLY WILDER:
"There are certain wonderful rascals in this world, like Monroe, and one day they lie down on an analyst's couch and out comes a clenched, dreary thing. It is better for Monroe not to be straightened out. The charm of her is her two left feet."

Marilyn began psychoanalysis, the branch of psychotherapy developed by SIGMUND FREUD, on the recommendation of LEE STRASBERG, who believed it imperative for his pupils to delve into their past to access the experiences they needed to perform: "As for the actor's training, I would say that the essential element is to train the inner faculties of the artist."

Marilyn's first psychoanalyst was recommended to her by business partner MILTON GREENE, and in February 1955 she began to have between three and five weekly sessions with DR. MARGARET HOHENBERG at her consulting room at 155 East Ninety-third Street. During these sessions Marilyn attempted to come to terms with her CHILDHOOD traumas, her lack of self-esteem, her obsessive seeking of approval from others, her inability to sustain friendships, and her fear of abandonment.

In 1957 Marilyn ceased seeing Dr. Hohenberg and began therapy with DR. MARIANNE KRIS, whom she saw for the next four years, as often as five times a week. In 1960 she began seeing her last psychoanalyst, DR. RALPH GREENSON.

Understandably, Marilyn was loath to answer public questions about her psychoanalysis. To one reporter who questioned her, she said she would not reply, "Except to say that I believe in the Freudian interpretation. I hope at some future time to make a glowing report on the wonders that psychiatrists can do for you."

In private, though, Marilyn avidly read BOOKS on the topic, and often talked to friends about her experience. Husband ARTHUR MILLER writes that for Marilyn, "There were no accidents of speech, no innocent slips: every word or gesture signaled an inner intention, whether conscious or not, and the most innocuous-seeming remark could conceal some sinister threat."

Some biographers are scathing about the effects of psychoanalysis on Marilyn; a few have gone so far as to accuse Marilyn's psychoanalysts of bad faith and ill-conceived clinical judgment. Arthur Miller, though, who had occasion to meet Marilyn's therapists, writes that Marianne Kris and Ralph Greenson were both "physicians of integrity and unquestionably devoted to her."

Marilyn once admitted to friend SUSAN STRASBERG that if she didn't understand a question put to her by has psychoanalyst, rather than give no answer she would make something up.

After years of psychoanalysis, Marilyn reputedly complained that it was "as if I were going round in circles." She was apparently referring to the focus of psychoanalysis on the past, which in her case was made up of almost unalloyed bad memories and lacking affection.

# Q

## QUOTES

PAT NEWCOMB:
"Marilyn Monroe never told anybody everything."

Many of the quotes both attributed to Marilyn and about her have been reported again and again, altering subtly at each retelling. Usually, Marilyn BIOGRAPHIES contain large blocks of text in which she recounts her story, feelings, and emotions. The sources for these quotes are in most cases a number of "Marilyn in her own words" books which have appeared over the years.

The main source is MY STORY, Marilyn's "unfinished autobiography," a book ghost-written by BEN HECHT in the mid-fifties, reworked by MILTON GREENE, and finally published in 1974. Other personal Marilyn quotes are drawn from the many interviews she gave during her life, or from encounters with journalists written down after the event, such as *Conversations with Marilyn* by British journalist W. J. WEATHERBY.

Marilyn's earliest published interviews tended to be scripted affairs, prepared either by the TWENTIETH CENTURY-FOX publicity department or by Marilyn's PRESS allies. Quotes taken from later, more intimate interviews, often vary from one source to the next, depending on whether the quotes have been extracted from interview notes or from the final published texts.

Alongside this rich vein of "direct" quotes, the Marilyn industry has flourished on sources held by some biographers to be suspect. As is so often the case, once a quote or rumor does the rounds and is picked up and reprinted, it takes on a sheen of truth. Biographer DONALD SPOTO casts doubt on the veracity of statements made over the years by several people, most notably ROBERT SLATZER, and what he describes as the "Kennedy conspiracy cottage industry," which refer back, according to Spoto, to statements that first appeared in Slatzer's own books. Spoto also describes as questionable testimonies given by policeman JACK CLEMMONS, coroner's aide LIONEL GRANDISON (the contention that Marilyn's autopsy was falsified by police), private detective MILO SPERIGLIO who further developed Slatzer's allegations, and JEANNE CARMEN, who claims to have been one of Marilyn's closest friends during the last two years of her life.

"As told to" reconstructions in the many memoirs published by people who knew Marilyn also muddy the waters—it is common for biographers and ghost writers to liven up accounts with reconstructed dialogue. For instance, New York maid LENA PEPITONE's insights into Marilyn's character and thoughts have been widely requoted, but are not universally regarded as reliable.

However, many of the quotes attributed to Marilyn, including most of her witty MARILYNISMS, were indeed things she actually said. Even if not everything Marilyn "said" was actually said, what emerges remains an intriguing composite portrait.

Marilyn on Tobey Beach. Photograph by André de Dienes, 1949.

R

Marilyn on NBC Radio's "Hollywood Star Playhouse," 1952.

## RADIO

Marilyn's first radio experience predated her first film, in 1946, when she was one of several hopeful starlets interviewed on KFI radio station in Los Angeles.

She made her dramatic radio debut on August 31, 1952, when she played a murderess in a segment called "Statement in Full" on NBC Radio's "Hollywood Star Playhouse"—she could have claimed typecasting, since she had just played a sadistic, homicidal babysitter in *DON'T BOTHER TO KNOCK* (1952). This recording had been made ten days earlier at the NBC Studios, 1500 Vine Street in Hollywood. Later that year, on October 26, Marilyn also guest-starred on the EDGAR BERGEN–Charlie McCarthy show.

## RADIO CITY MUSIC HALL
1260 AVENUE AND 50TH STREET, NEW YORK

Venue for the premiere of *THE PRINCE AND THE SHOWGIRL* on June 13, 1957.

## RADIO PLANE MUNITIONS FACTORY
METROPOLITAN AIRPORT (NOW BURBANK-GLENDALE-PASADENA AIRPORT),
2627 NORTH HOLLYWOOD WAY, BURBANK

The Radio Plane Company, owned by British-born actor REGINALD DENNY, principally manufactured radio-controlled aircraft for anti-aircraft training exercises. Norma Jeane's mother-in-law, Ethel Mary Dougherty who worked as a nurse at the factory, found Norma Jeane a job in early 1944, after husband JAMES DOUGHERTY had departed for Southeast Asia with the Merchant Marine. In the two years she worked there, she held two positions, one in the "dope room," coating the fabric fuselages of the aircraft in varnish, the other inspecting parachutes, for which she earned twenty dollars working a sixty-hour week. Marilyn told one columnist that initially she started work at the company as a typist, but because she wasn't fast enough she was transferred to the parachute inspection line. During her time at the factory her hard work was recognized with an "E for excellence" certificate.

Years later Marilyn described the experience:

> I first had a job inspecting parachutes —not the kind of parachutes a life depends on, the little parachutes they use to float down the targets after the gunners are through with them. That was before I worked in the 'dope' room, the hardest work I've ever done. The fuselage and various parts of the ship were made of cloth at that time—they use metal now—and we used to paint the cloth with a stiffening preparation. It wasn't sprayed on; it was worked in with brushes, and it was very tiring and difficult. We used a quick-drying preparation—a type of lacquer, I guess, but heavier—the smell was overpowering, very hard to take for eight hours a day. It was actually a twelve-hour day for other workers, but I only did eight because I was underage. After the cloth dried, we sanded it down to glossy smoothness.

In a letter to guardian GRACE MCKEE GODDARD, Norma Jeane explained just why she had decided to stick at this job despite the availability of lighter work elsewhere:

> I am working 10 hrs. a day at Radio Plane Co, at Metropolitan Airport. I am saving almost everything I earn (to help pay for our future home after the war). The work isn't easy at all for I am on my feet all day and walking quite a bit. I was all set to get a Civil Service Job with the army, all my papers filled out and everything set to go, and then I found out I would be working with all army fellows. I was over there one day, there are just too many wolves to be working with, there are enough of those at Radio Plane Co. with out a whole army full of them. The Personal [sic] officer said that he would hire me but that he wouldn't advise it for my own sake, so I am back at Radio Plane Co. and pretty contented.

It was just as well that Norma Jeane stayed put. It was at Radio Plane that she was first

While working at the Radio Plane Munitions Factory, army photographer Corporal David Conover spotted Marilyn's potential. Here she is in one of her first modeling assignments, a 1946 advertisement for Douglas DC-6 Luxury Airlines.

Marilyn sat next to Ronald Reagan at Charlton Heston's birthday party in 1953.

spotted by army photographer Corporal DAVID CONOVER, who came to the factory with colleagues to shoot footage of women working on the assembly line to boost the morale of the men on the front. Norma Jeane was prominently featured in this, her first ever appearance on film, and Conover was so taken with the girl's fresh beauty that for the next couple of weeks he drove out to Burbank to take color shots of her. Conover suggested she had a bright career in modeling, and that was all Norma Jeane needed to hear. She left Radio Plane in late 1945 after joining the BLUE BOOK MODELING AGENCY.

## RAINIER, PRINCE OF MONACO
(B. 1923, RAINIER LOUIS HENRI MAXENCE BERTRAND DE GRIMALDI)

In 1953, Aristotle Onassis bought into the casino in the principality of Monaco at a time when the French Riviera enclave was suffering a downturn. The story runs that either Onassis himself, or Gardner Cowles, publisher of *Look* magazine, came up with a plan to restore the luster to the famous playboy resort by arranging a marriage between Prince Rainier III and a major Hollywood movie star, and then watching as rich Americans poured in on the back of the free publicity. Cowles' first discreet approach was to Marilyn, whose response was all positive: "Give me two days alone with him and of course he'll want to marry me."

Marilyn never had a chance to unleash her charms on the prince, as he already had his sights set on GRACE KELLY. Still, Marilyn was tickled by the idea, and thereafter referred to the prince jokingly as "Prince Reindeer."

## RAT PACK

FRED LAWRENCE GUILES:
"The Rat Pack adopted her as a kind of special mascot."

Marilyn was personal friends with Rat Pack members FRANK SINATRA, DEAN MARTIN, PETER LAWFORD, and SAMMY DAVIS JR. in the last two years of her life, after moving back to Los Angeles. She spent the most time with Sinatra. Marilyn's final uncompleted movie, *SOMETHING'S GOT TO GIVE*, had her starring opposite Rat Pack founder Martin.

## RATTIGAN, SIR TERENCE MERVYN
(1911–1977)

Distinguished British playwright Terence Rattigan wrote a string of successful plays from the mid-thirties, many of which were turned into feature films. Rattigan also wrote a number of original screenplays, including Oscar-nominated *The Sound Barrier* (1952).

In 1955, Marilyn's business partner MILTON GREENE succeeded in landing the rights to Rattigan's 1953 play *The Sleeping Prince*. Rattigan agreed to write a screenplay, and came over to New York with LAURENCE OLIVIER and VIVIEN LEIGH in early 1956 to finalize details.

Not long after arriving in England for filming, Marilyn went to a party held by Rattigan at his home in Sunningdale, thrown in her and Arthur's honor. Apparently security was so strict that a policeman refused to let Marilyn's limousine pass until he was shown a proper invitation. At this party Marilyn met the elite of British theater.

Rattigan was reputedly asked by Queen ELIZABETH II what Marilyn was like. His opinion: "a shy exhibitionist."

## RAUH, OLIE AND JOSEPH

Joseph Rauh was ARTHUR MILLER's lawyer in his trial for contempt brought by the HOUSE UN-AMERICAN ACTIVITIES COMMITTEE. In May 1957 Arthur and Marilyn stayed at the Rauh home in Washington during Arthur's trial. Rauh's successful defense of Miller hinged upon the fact that because the questions Miller was accused of not answering were irrelevant, he could not be held in contempt.

## REAGAN, RONALD (B. 1911)

The fortieth U.S. president played a bit part in DISCOVERY of Marilyn Monroe. During the Second World War, Reagan was commanding officer of the Army 1st Motion Picture Unit, based at Fort Roach (the former Hal Roach Studios). It was Reagan who sent photographer DAVID CONOVER to take pictures of women helping the war effort at the RADIO PLANE MUNTIONS FACTORY, where Norma Jeane was working at the time.

Reagan's movie career, mainly as a B-movie lead, spanned over seventy-five movies, the best of which, in his opinion, was *King Row* (1951).

Marilyn's first love FRED KARGER later married Ronald Reagan's first wife, JANE WYMAN.

## REDMOND, CHERIE

Marilyn's last SECRETARY, from January 1962, who attended to Marilyn's appointments, mail, and phone calls, was recommended to Marilyn by her LAWYER Milton Rudin.

## REINHARDT, MAX (1873–1943)

A renowned theater producer and teacher, whose troupe had included Marilyn's drama coach NATASHA LYTESS, and whose theater workshop schooled fellow Hollywood star JANE RUSSELL. In December 1952 Marilyn and Natasha went to the Roy Goldenburg Auction Galleries in Beverly Hills, where the day's lots included 178 of Reinhardt's *Regiebücher*, or production notebooks containing his thoughts on direction and scenery. Marilyn began bidding from the start; she was competing against a rare book dealer named Jake Zeitlin, who was acting on the instruction of the University of Southern California. The bidding soon moved up from a few hundred dollars to over $1300. Zeitlin's last bid was $1320. Marilyn took the collection with her bid of $1335.

May Reis and Marilyn in Brooklyn, New York, for Augusta Miller's funeral on March 8, 1961.

The following week comments began to appear in the press that Marilyn was depriving the nation of something that could benefit many drama students, not just the one who had won the day at the auction house. Marilyn told reporters that she was indeed considering donating the notebooks to a university, perhaps Harvard or Stanford rather than USC's Doheny Library. Before Christmas Marilyn was contacted by Reinhardt's son Gottfried, who claimed that by rights the books should be his. He settled the bill at the auction house, and then sold the collection to a university, reputedly for a handsome profit.

## REIS, MAY

May Reis began working for Marilyn in 1955 (sometimes cited as 1957) as her private SECRETARY. From handling the scripts that came in, business inquiries, and personal errands, Reis gradually became a pivotal member of Marilyn's entourage as a friend, confidante, and, some biographers note, a MOTHER FIGURE. Reis, described as a petite and mild-mannered woman, came well recommended, having previously worked for ARTHUR MILLER and ELIA KAZAN.

May's sister Vanessa told biographer DONALD SPOTO that "because May was alone in the world and had no family. . . . Marilyn became her existence, her profession, her commitment."

FRED LAWRENCE GUILES writes that May Reis "rarely had to ask Marilyn what was to be done; she simply *knew*. She was always *there*, from early morning to night; not intrusive, but somehow always aware of who was in and who was out in her employer's life."

Reis was in the thick of the emotional

battles between Marilyn and Arthur on the set of *THE MISFITS* (1961), in the unenviable position of trying to prevent two people from destroying one another. In early 1961 she brought Marilyn out of the Columbia Presbyterian HOSPITAL following her breakdown. Biographers disagree whether Reis was still working for Marilyn at this time, or was helping her out of friendship and concern.

Marilyn recognized Reis's loyalty in her WILL, though Reis had to wait nearly ten years to receive her $10,000 bequest. By this time Reis was working as secretary to Barbra Streisand.

## RELIGION

Norma Jeane was baptized at the Foursquare Gospel Church, the center of an evangelical movement founded by Sister AIMEE SEMPLE MCPHERSON. Foster parent "Aunt" ANA LOWER, however, schooled Marilyn in CHRISTIAN SCIENCE from the period 1938 to 1946, and as she took her first steps into the movie business, Marilyn was sometimes seen with Christian Science religious books.

When she was with FRED KARGER, she was taken to Victor's Catholic Church, where according to some biographers she first met JOAN CRAWFORD.

During filming of *GENTLEMEN PREFER BLONDES* (1953), JANE RUSSELL invited Marilyn to her home to attend sessions of the Hollywood Christian Group. Most biographers record that Marilyn only went once.

Marilyn converted to the Jewish faith just before marrying third husband ARTHUR MILLER. Miller writes that it was Marilyn's desire to go through with a religious wedding ceremony and conversion to Judaism: "I'm not religious, but she wanted to be one of us. . . . I don't think you could say she became a Jewess, but still she took it all very seriously. I would say she wanted to join me and become part of my life."

Marilyn converted to Judaism on July 1, 1956 (the 22nd of Tammuz, 5716, in the Jewish calendar). Her certificate of conversion was signed by MILTON H. GREENE, Arthur Miller, and Rabbi E. Goldberg, who also presided over the Jewish WEDDING ceremony uniting Arthur and Marilyn.

## REMICK, LEE (1935–1991)

"I don't know whether to feel sorry for her or not. I feel she should have been replaced. The movie business is crumbling down around our ears because of that kind of behavior. Actors shouldn't be allowed to get away with that kind of thing."

Remick made her film debut in the 1957 ELIA KAZAN movie *A Face in the Crowd*. In 1962 TWENTIETH CENTURY-FOX lined her up to replace Marilyn after she was fired from *SOMETHING'S GOT TO GIVE*. In their hurry, the studio forgot that DEAN MARTIN had approval of his leading lady written into his contract, and he subsequently refused to work with anyone but Marilyn. Remick picked up one Oscar nomination, for *Days of Wine and Roses* (1963). Most of her later appearances were in TV movies.

## RENNA'S SALON

Beverly Hills beauty salon on Sunset Boulevard. Dr. G. W. Campbell, who gave Marilyn special facial treatments, introduced her to many BOOKS on metaphysics and philosophy. Marilyn was a regular when she lived in LOS ANGELES.

## RENO, NEVADA

Reno was the undisputed U.S. quickie DIVORCE capital, thanks to its lenient two month residency requirement, and, unlike New York, with no need to cite adultery as a motive for divorce. In early 1956 ARTHUR MILLER holed up at Pyramid Lake, forty miles from Reno, for his statutory residency requirement to divorce his first wife Mary Grace Slattery. Miller took a cottage next to one occupied by writer Saul Bellow, who was there for the same reason, while he worked on his novel *Henderson the Rain King*.

During his stay, Miller met the men who inspired the characters in *THE MISFITS* (1961). Four years later, when Miller and *The Misfits* troupe returned for location shots, the old place had changed and become a watersports area, complete with fast food stands. The bridge over the Truckee River is where Marilyn threw away her wedding band in the film; the cast stayed at MAPES HOTEL; and Harrah's is the casino where the Gay and Roslyn characters first meet.

## RESTAURANTS AND BARS

Below is a list of places where over the years Marilyn wined and dined and went for after-dinner fun:

LOS ANGELES

**Barney's Beanery**
8447 Santa Monica Boulevard, Hollywood
Marilyn often ate here in her starlet days after classes at the ACTOR'S LAB. It was here that she warmed up with a bowl of chili after posing for the famous nude CALENDAR photos, in 1949. This L.A. landmark was also a favorite of JEAN HARLOW's.

**Bruce Wongs**
La Cienega Boulevard, Hollywood
Marilyn and JOE DIMAGGIO's favorite Chinese haunt.

**Chasen's**
9039 Beverly Boulevard., Hollywood
JOHNNY HYDE first took Marilyn to this, one of Hollywood's most "in" places, and she soon became a regular.

On June 26, 1953 Marilyn chose Chasen's as a place to finish off a day's work promoting *GENTLEMAN PREFER BLONDES* (1953), during which she left her handprints on the sidewalk outside GRAUMAN'S CHINESE THEATER. Her companions for steak and fried potatoes that day were co-star JANE RUSSELL and columnist SIDNEY SKOLSKY. Marilyn also said that Chasen's was where she went for her first date with Joe DiMaggio, though most biographers say this historic meeting took place at the Villa Nova.

**Ciro's**
8433 Sunset Boulevard, Hollywood
A restaurant where Marilyn went with *HOW TO MARRY A MILLIONAIRE* (1953) co-star BETTY GRABLE to a party in honor of WALTER WINCHELL. She also visited this restaurant with friend Sidney Skolsky. Nowadays Ciro's is the Comedy Store.

**Florentine Gardens**
5951 Hollywood Boulevard
Italian restaurant/dance club where JAMES DOUGHERTY and bride Norma Jeane celebrated their 1942 WEDDING.

**Formosa Café**
7156 Santa Monica Boulevard,
West Hollywood
On the corner of the WARNER STUDIOS lot, formerly the MGM Studios, for decades the Formosa Café has been a favorite spot for a quick drink and snack for stars. Marilyn used to stop in during shooting on interiors for *SOME LIKE IT HOT* (1959). The Formosa featured recently in *L.A. Confidential* (1997).

**Greenblatt's Deli**
8017 Sunset Boulevard, Hollywood
A renowned Sunset Strip eatery in West Hollywood where Marilyn was known to go for hot pastrami with mustard on rye.

**La Scala**
9455 Santa Monica Boulevard, Beverly Hills, now 40 North Canon Drive, Beverly Hills
An Italian restaurant where Marilyn was a regular, particularly during the last year of her life. On August 3, 1962 this was the last place she dined out, with PETER LAWFORD, PATRICIA NEWCOMB, and, it has been rumored, ROBERT KENNEDY.

**Lucey's**
5444 Melrose Avenue, Hollywood, replaced by Walter's Plant Rentals
A meeting at this restaurant arranged by Sidney Skolsky reputedly led to Marilyn impressing producer JERRY WALD enough to land her a part in *CLASH BY NIGHT* (1952).

**Mocambo**
8588 Sunset Boulevard, Hollywood
A popular L.A. nightclub where in 1954 Marilyn went every day for two weeks to watch her favorite female singer ELLA FITZGERALD. The club closed down in 1958.

**Musso and Frank Grill**
6667 Hollywood Boulevard, Hollywood
Hollywood's self-proclaimed oldest restaurant, famous for its vodka gimlets and well-known patrons, where Marilyn first came looking to impress as a starlet, and continued to come for the rest of her career.

**The Retake Room Bar**
Washington Boulevard, Los Angeles
Marilyn came here with Johnny Hyde to celebrate her important break when she landed a role in *THE ASPHALT JUNGLE* (1950).

**Romanoff's**
326 North Rodeo Drive, Beverly Hills
An exclusive Hollywood restaurant for movie

Marilyn and Joe at the Stork Club, 1954.

business movers and shakers, run by Gloria and Mike Romanoff—the latter a self-appointed "Russian Prince" actually born in America, who featured in a number of movies. Marilyn was a regular there from the late 1940s, taken by Johnny Hyde, who had fallen desperately in love with her. Hyde had four leather booths installed in the NORTH PALM DRIVE home where he went to live with Marilyn; the dining room also had its own dance floor, and Marilyn referred to this room as her own private Romanoff's.

In 1954, Romanoff's was the restaurant chosen by Marilyn's then agent CHARLES FELDMAN for a dinner party for eighty guests, entirely in her honor. The roll call was a "Who's Who" of Hollywood: studio powerhouses DARRYL ZANUCK, Samuel Goldwyn and Jack Warner; stars such as Humphrey Bogart, CLARK GABLE, Claudette Colbert, Gary Cooper, Susan Hayward, and Loretta Young; director BILLY WILDER and a full complement of the columnists who counted. After Marilyn arrived she declared, "I feel like Cinderella!"

For Marilyn one high point of the evening was meeting and dancing with Gable, her long-time idol and father figure. They complimented one another on their work and said they wanted to do a picture together. Soon after, there were rumors of a romantic liaison between them.

**Schwab's Drugstore**
8024 Sunset Boulevard, Hollywood
The legendary Hollywood drugstore where eager young talent came for a milkshake in the hope that it was their lucky day and they would be spotted by a passing studio producer or top Hollywood agent. Marilyn was a regular during her early days in the business. Supposedly she was at Schwab's when she heard that the Marx Brothers were on the lookout for a sexy blonde.

Syndicated Hollywood reporter Sidney Skolsky practically used Schwab's as his office; his first meeting with Marilyn occurred here in late 1950, and they soon began a long-lasting professional and amicable relationship.

In *Conversations with Marilyn* W. J. WEATHERBY reveals:

> "It was the most depressing sight in Marilyn's Hollywood, the daily gathering of young hopefuls at Schwab's drugstore. Perched like starlings over their Coca-Colas and hamburgers, they chattered their mock tales of woe about producers ('Wouldn't even see me'), about agents ('He can't be trying'), about their awful, incredibly bad luck so far. They consoled themselves and each other with endless repetition of the legends of how stars were made overnight. Surely it might happen to them."

After Marilyn starred in her first movie, she dropped back in to Schwab's: "I had the idea it would help their confidence to see someone who had gotten a break. But no one recognized me and I was too shy to tell anyone. I was a misfit there." Schwab's was demolished in 1989.

**Trader Vic's**
The Beverly Hilton Hotel, 9876 Wilshire Boulevard, Beverly Hills
High class L.A. restaurant where Marilyn often dined over the years.

**Villa Capri**
6735 Yucca Street, Hollywood
Noted celebrity watering hole, one of Joe DiMaggio's favorites, and consequently a place where Marilyn dined a number of times between 1952 and 1954. The restaurant closed down in 1982.

**The Villa Nova**
(now the Rainbow Grill)
9015 Sunset Boulevard, Hollywood
The most popular account of Marilyn and Joe's first date puts them at this popular Italian restaurant in March 1952, in most versions on a double date with mutual friend David March and his girl Peggy Rabe. Reports vary wildly from stilted conversation over dinner followed by a drive around town, to them hitting it off immediately and driving to a secluded lover's lane. What all biographers to agree on is that Marilyn arrived up to two hours late.

### NEW YORK

**Copacabana**
10 East 60th Street
One of New York's glamour hotspots in the fifties, to which Marilyn took her entourage to see FRANK SINATRA after the press conference announcing the formation of MARILYN MONROE PRODUCTIONS. Although the place had been sold out for ages, such was Marilyn's cachet that she had an extra table brought out and set up by the stage.

In *ALL ABOUT EVE* (1950), Marilyn's character is introduced by theater critic Addison De Witt (George Saunders) as "a graduate of the Copacabana school of acting."

**El Morocco**
154 East 54th Street (since moved to 307)
This fashionable restaurant was one of Marilyn's first tastes of New York glitz when she visited in 1949, on a publicity tour for *LOVE HAPPY* (1950). It was also one of the last places she was seen out in public as Mrs. DiMaggio, during location shooting of *THE SEVEN YEAR ITCH* (1955).

**Four Seasons**
99 East 52nd Street
One of Marilyn's regular New York restaurants, as prestigious now as ever.

**Howard Johnson's**
46th Street and Broadway
Marilyn occasionally grabbed a quick bite here.

**Jim Downey's**
705 8th Avenue
Popular New York theater restaurant whose walls were adorned with photos of Broadway stars. Marilyn's photo was added after she stepped onto the stage for a curtain call at the Martin Beck THEATER, where her friend ELI WALLACH was starring in *Teahouse of the August Moon*.

**Manny Wolf's Chophouse**
Third Avenue and 50th Street
A restaurant Marilyn frequented when living in New York, according to maid LENA PEPITONE.

**Sardi's**
234 West 44th Street
Well-known New York restaurant, a favorite with celebrities including Marilyn.

Joe, Marilyn, and Toots Shor at his restaurant, ca. 1953.

**The Stork Club**
3 East 53rd Street
Joe and Marilyn often dined here in 1954, when Marilyn was in town to shoot *The Seven Year Itch*.

**Toots Shor's**
51st Street between 5th and 6th Avenues, then 52nd street, then 33 West 33rd Street
Joe DiMaggio's home away from home, and the New York restaurant where he would go on a regular basis before he met Marilyn, to enjoy the clubby male atmosphere described as "a gymnasium with room service."

When they were in New York together, Joe often took Marilyn along to Toots Shor's. On June 1, 1955, six months after they split up, Joe threw a surprise birthday party for Marilyn after the screening of *The Seven Year Itch*—his way of making up with her after their DIVORCE. But his well laid plans went badly wrong; Marilyn walked out on him after a screaming fight.

**Twenty One Club**
21 West 52nd Street
Another renowned New York address Marilyn often patronized.

### OTHER LOCATIONS

**Bucket of Blood Saloon**
3 South C Street, Virginia City, Nevada
A bar where Marilyn and FRED KARGER went for drinks in 1948. In 1960, Clark Gable, MONTGOMERY CLIFT, and Marilyn took time off at this bar during shooting of *THE MISFITS* (1961).

**Christmas Tree Inn**
23900 Mount Rose Highway, Reno, Nevada
*The Misfits* company threw a joint birthday party there for ARTHUR MILLER and Montgomery Clift on October 17, 1960. EVE ARNOLD photographed the event, just before the final day of location shooting.

**Club Gigi**
Fountainebleau Hilton,
4441 Collins Avenue, Miami, Florida
Marilyn took Arthur's Miller's widower father Isidore for a meal at this restaurant during her 1962 trip to Florida.

**Country Inn Restaurant**
South B Street, Virginia City, Nevada
A favorite place for Marilyn to eat during shooting of *The Misfits* in 1960. Edith Palmer, in charge of the restaurant, told biographer FRED LAWRENCE GUILES, "Marilyn Monroe loved the food I prepared so much. She was a gourmet, you know. . . . 'My oasis in the desert,' she called our place." According to owner Norm Brown, Marilyn once stayed at the Inn, hence the naming of a "Marilyn Monroe Suite" in her honor.

**DiMaggio's**
245 Jefferson Street, Fisherman's Wharf, San Francisco, California
Joe and Dominic DiMaggio owned and ran the DiMaggio's restaurant in San Francisco's popular Fisherman's Wharf district. Marilyn was regularly seen here during her courtship and marriage to Joe. In 1985 the DiMaggios passed the lease to another restaurant owner.

**Finnochio's**
506 Broadway, North Beach, San Francisco, California
A San Francisco nightclub Marilyn visited during a break from shooting *The Misfits* in 1960, to see a drag artist doing a Marilyn show. Marilyn and friends did not stay until the end of the performance. If Marilyn had learned Italian from former husband Joe DiMaggio, she may have realized what kind of a floor show she was in for: "Finnocchio" is Italian slang for homosexual.

**Hot Springs Hotel**
13th and Spring Street, Paso Robles, California
In some versions of events, Marilyn and Joe dined here on their wedding night, before returning to the CLIFTON MOTEL for their first night as man and wife.

**Last Frontier Hotel**
3120 South Las Vegas Boulevard, Las Vegas, Nevada
In 1946 while waiting out her time in LAS VEGAS to divorce first husband Jim Dougherty, Marilyn dined at this hotel with ROY ROGERS, who was in town making a movie.

## RETTIG, TOMMY (1941–1996)

Actor Tommy Rettig was one of the few CHILDREN that Marilyn had a hard time befriending. For the first three days of shooting on *RIVER OF NO RETURN* (1954) Rettig studiously avoided Marilyn. Upset, Marilyn asked him why. The boy explained that his priest had told him he was allowed to work with a woman "like Marilyn" but not have any more contract than necessary. At the time Marilyn was very upset by this, but things went better between the movie's stars when JOE DIMAGGIO arrived, and they went off fishing together.

Director OTTO PREMINGER recounts an incident during filming where Marilyn's drama coach NATASHA LYTESS severely hampered the otherwise reliable young actor: "He knew his lines and sometimes we had to do eighteen or more takes, but he did the right thing every time, no variation or loss in quality. One day, I did a scene with him and Marilyn, and he just couldn't remember his lines and he cried. 'What's the matter?' I asked. His mother said that Miss Lytess talked to Tommy and told him that at the age of fourteen all child actors lose their

Marilyn accompanied child actor Tommy Rettig to the premiere of his film *The 5,000 Fingers of Dr. T* in 1953.

talent unless they take lessons and learn to use their instrument."

For this piece of advice, Lytess was temporarily banned from the set.

Rettig's movie career did not flourish in adulthood. He is remembered mostly as Lassie's best friend in the 1950s television series.

## REYNOLDS, DEBBIE
(B. 1932, MARY FRANCES REYNOLDS)

Debbie Reynolds began her film career around the same time as Marilyn. She made a name for herself in musicals, including *Singin' in the Rain* (1952) and *Susan Slept Here* (1954). Her one Oscar nomination was for *The Unsinkable Molly Brown* (1964).

Marilyn and Reynolds never worked together, but in 1964 Reynolds starred in *Goodbye Charlie*, a TWENTIETH CENTURY-FOX movie that Marilyn had previously turned down.

Reynolds ploughed much of her earnings into the LAS VEGAS Debbie Reynolds Hotel, housing a Hollywood museum containing over 3000 costumes, including the famous pleated white halter dress from *THE SEVEN YEAR ITCH* (1955). After the hotel was sold in 1998, this and other Hollywood memorabilia has gone into storage.

## RHODE ISLAND STREET
HAWTHORNE, CALIFORNIA

Number 459 East Rhode Island Street was home to the BOLENDER family, Norma Jeane's FOSTER PARENTS, for the first seven years of her life.

(*see* HOMES)

## RIESE, RANDALL AND NEAL HITCHENS

Authors of the 1987 reference book *The Unabridged Marilyn, Her Life from A-Z*, a compendium of Marilyn information long esteemed by serious Marilyn fans.

## *RIGHT CROSS* (1950)

After her highly promising start in *THE ASPHALT JUNGLE* (1950), MGM shoehorned Marilyn into two more movies, neither of which did much to showcase her. In this tale of love and boxing, Marilyn is picked up by the Dick Powell character, but doesn't even make the credits.

**Credits:**
MGM, Black and White
Length: 90 minutes
Release date: November 15, 1950

Directed by: John Sturges
Produced by: Armand Deutsch
Written by: Charles Schnee
Cinematography by: Norbert Brodine
Music by: David Raksin

**Cast (credits order):**
June Allyson . . . Pat O'Malley
Dick Powell . . . Rick Garvey
Ricardo Montalban . . . Johnny Monterez
Lionel Barrymore . . . Sean O'Malley
Barry Kelley . . . Allan Goff
Teresa Celli . . . Marina Monterez
Mimi Aguglia . . . Mom Monterez
Marianne Stewart . . . Audrey
John Gallaudet . . . Phil Tripp
Wally Maher . . . First Reporter
Larry Keating . . . Second Reporter
Kenneth Tobey . . . Third Reporter
Bert Davidson . . . Fourth Reporter
Marilyn Monroe . . . Dusky Ledoux (uncredited)

**Crew:**
Cedric Gibbons . . . art director
James Scognamillo . . . art director

**Plot:**
Ricardo Montalban plays champion prizefighter Johnny Monterez, a man who is discriminated against because of his Mexican origins. Out of love for his traniner's daughter, Pat (June Allyson). Johnny turns down a top bout from promoter Allan Goff (Barry Kelly). Johnny's best friend is sports reporter Rick Gavery (Dick Powell), who takes to drink and women when he realizes that the love of his life is in love with the boxer, not the boxing hack. Enter Marilyn, who joins in his evening out on the town.

Fearing that his fighting days are numbered due to an injury to his right hand, Johnny realizes that the best way to take care of Pat and her father, O'Malley (Lionel Barrymore), is to accept that fight with Goff and make a big purse. Unfortunately, on learning of Johnny's desertion, old O'Malley dies of a heart attack. Oblivious to his true motives, Pat blames Johnny. Johnny then has his final fight for the O'Malley stable... and loses. Back in the dressing room he fights with Rick, and lands him such a terrific punch that he permanently damages his right hand. When it seems that Johnny has lost everything, Pat realizes that everything he has done has been for her, and Rick shows he has no hard feelings.

**Reviews:**
*New York Daily News*
"The movies are overdue with a picture like *Right Cross*. It's long past time Hollywood took up the cudgels in defense of the plain old American majority, and it's good to have

Dick Powell and Marilyn in *Right Cross* (1950).

the shoe on the other foot for a change. . . . Outstanding dialogue, a wonderful sense of humor and a talented cast would make it exceptional film fare, with or without the lesson in sociology."

*New York Daily Mirror*:
"John Sturges directed with neat balance between love-making and leather-pushing, for smooth continuity. The characters come alive. A thin thread of racial conflict seems superfluous. . . . *Right Cross* doesn't let down in action or heart appeal. It depicts some backstage skullduggery with realism. The fight sequences are thrilling and convincing."

*New York Post*
"*Right Cross*... is a boxing story with a romance sidelighted by Mexican racial feeling. It doesn't come out of the grinder a great picture, but it does offer a few pleasures of its own."

## Ritter, Thelma (1905–1969)

Well-respected character actress, six times nominated for a Best Supporting Actress Oscar, who made her film debut in *Miracle on 34th Street* (1947). Her Oscar-nominated performances were in *All About Eve* (1950), *The Mating Season* (1951), *With a Song in My Heart* (1952), *Pickup on South Street* (1953), *Pillow Talk* (1959), and *Birdman of Alcatraz* (1962).

Ritter worked in three movies with Marilyn: *All About Eve* (1950), *As Young As You Feel* (1951), and *The Misfits* (1961).

## Rivals

Marilyn began her movie career as a bottle blonde, aspiring to follow in the footsteps of her hero Jean Harlow, the original platinum blonde, and Betty Grable, then the reigning queen of the blondes.

Many have tried to emulate Marilyn's success. In the first half of the fifties, the other Hollywood studios tried to produce their own versions of Fox's biggest female box-office draw. After Marilyn so dramatically turned her back on Fox in the mid-fifties, the studio chiefs began a desperate search for somebody to match her in the hearts of the movie-going public. Standard schooling for most of these Marilyn hopefuls consisted of repeated viewings of her finest moments.

Just in case the public did not get the idea, the studio clothed these "New Marilyns" in hand-me-down dresses which Marilyn had previously worn on screen. Jayne Mansfield made an outing in the sheer gold lamé dress from *Gentlemen Prefer Blondes* (1953); the white pleated dress from *The Seven Year Itch* (1955) was plundered for Roseanne Arlen; and the corset from *River of No Return* (1954) lived on again with Corinne Calvet.

The following is a small selection of the innumerable actresses who aspired to rival Marilyn for box-office blonde honors in her day. It does not include the many actresses who, in later decades, have laid claim to Marilyn's heritage:

Jayne Mansfield

Lola Albright
Roseanne Arlen
Caroll Baker
Brigitte Bardot
Corinne Calvet
Angie Dickenson
Diana Dors
Anita Ekberg
Zsa Zsa Gabor
Joy Harmon
Arline Hunter
Adele Jergens
Hope Lange
Joi Lansing
Jayne Mansfield
Beverley Michaels
Marion Michaels
Cleo Moore
Terry Moore
Barbara Nichols
Sheree North
Kim Novak
Roxanne Rosedale
Stella Stevens
Greta Thyssen
Barbara Valentin
Mamie Van Doren
Yvette Vickers

## *River of No Return* (1954)

Marilyn plays a saloon singer in this Western, shot against the dramatic backdrop of the Canadian Rockies. Amazingly, this was Marilyn's twenty-second film in just six years.

Producer Stanley Rubin originally intended the movie to be an American version of the Italian neo-realist classic *The Bicycle Thief*, transposed to the Wild West, where instead of a bicycle, the lead character's vital horse and gun are stolen. Location shooting took place in Canada, at the Banff National Park and Jasper in Alberta, and in the Canadian Rockies. Marilyn stayed at the Banff Springs Hotel.

Antagonism reigned on set as director Otto Preminger and Marilyn dug in for a war of attrition. Preminger made it clear that he was working on this movie only because he owed Twentieth Century-Fox a picture under his contract; Darryl Zanuck offered him the carrot of the new Cinemascope technology, and some critics have noted that Preminger was more interested in filming the dramatic scenery than extracting a dramatic performance from his actors.

Preminger, like many of his colleagues, had drama coach Natasha Lytess banned from the set, only to be forced to allow her back after the head office called in a favor.

Physically this was a very demanding role for Marilyn, with much of the action involving the protagonists' flight down the river, with its dangerous rapids. For these scenes Marilyn had to be doused with gallons of water for continuity's sake. Fox's special effects man Paul Wurtzel testified to her dedication: "We put her through a lot on that film, and there was never one complaint. She knew what the picture required, and once we got her on her marks she was a pro. The whole crew adored her." Preminger's insistence that his stars do their own stunts was

Marilyn as Kay Weston in *River of No Return* (1954).

not without consequence. Marilyn and co-star ROBERT MITCHUM's raft got stuck in the rapids and they had to be rescued.

Marilyn sings four KEN DARBY/LIONEL NEWMAN songs in this movie, rehearsing "One Silver Dollar," "I'm Gonna File My Claim," "Down in the Meadow," and the title song, "River of No Return," tirelessly until she got as close to perfection as she could. During the summer when the movie was released, RCA sold over 75,000 copies of "I'm Gonna File My Claim" in just three weeks.

For the last two weeks of shooting, JOE DIMAGGIO joined Marilyn on location. Part of the reason for his coming was an accident Marilyn sustained, after falling into the Athabasca River from the raft during filming. A local doctor diagnosed a possible sprain; the studio doctors could find nothing serious, but Marilyn insisted on being fitted with a plaster cast and for a few days she hobbled around on crutches, posing for pictures in the press. Marilyn's slow convalescence, however, may have been a ruse to get back at Preminger.

Back in Los Angeles for soundstage work, Marilyn deployed her full range of delaying tactics, often refusing to come out of her dressing-room for hours on end. DAVID CONOVER writes that out of revenge, Marilyn wanted to mess up the picture so much that Preminger would never work again at Fox. She succeeded in so far as this is one of her least popular movies.

Two years after working on the movie, Marilyn said, "I wouldn't accept *River of No Return* today. I think I deserve a better deal than a grade-Z cowboy movie in which the acting finished second to the scenery and the Cinemascope process. The studio was [backing] the scenery instead of actors and actresses."

MEMORABLE COSTUMES:
Deep red dress with off-the-shoulder spaghetti straps, slit to the thigh.

**Credits:**
Twentieth Century-Fox, Cinemascope and Technicolor
Length: 91 minutes
Release date: April 30, 1954

Directed by: Otto Preminger
Produced by: Stanley Rubin
Written by: Frank Fenton, Louis Lantz (story)
Cinematography by: Joseph LaShelle
Film Editing by: Louis R. Loeffler
Music by: Cyril J. Mockridge, Lionel Newman (songs)
Costume Design by: Charles LeMaire and William Travilla

**Cast (credits order):**
Robert Mitchum . . . Matt Calder
Marilyn Monroe . . . Kay Weston
Rory Calhoun . . . Harry Weston
Tommy Rettig . . . Mark Calder
Murvyn Vye . . . Colby
Douglas Spencer . . . Benson

**Uncredited:**
Ed Hinton . . . Gambler
Don Beddoe . . . Ben
Claire Andre . . . Surrey Driver
Jack Mather . . . Dealer at Card Table
Edmund Cobb . . . Barber
Will Wright . . . Trader
Jarma Lewis . . . Dancer
Hal Baylor . . . Young Punk

**Crew:**
Chester L. Bayhi . . . set decorator
Jack Cole . . . choreographer
Ken Darby . . . vocal direction, lyrics
Bernard Freericks . . . sound
Addison Hehr . . . art director
Paul Helmick . . . assistant director
Roger Heman . . . sound
Ray Kellogg . . . special photographic effects
Charles Le Maire . . . wardrobe director
Lionel Newman . . . musical director
Ben Nye . . . makeup
Edward B. Powell . . . orchestration
Walter M. Scott . . . set decorator
Lyle R. Wheeler . . . art director

**Plot:**
In her first Western, Marilyn plays Kay Weston, a saloon singer in a makeshift goldrush town somewhere in the American Northwest. Her admirers include ten-year-old Mark Calder (Tommy Rettig), whose father Matt (Robert Mitchum) returns to pick up his boy after serving a prison sentence for shooting a man in the back (a crime against honor we later find out was to save the life of a friend). Matt rescues Kay and gambler boyfriend Harry Weston (Rory Calhoun) from a raft near his new home, a farm he has bought to live on with his son. By way of thanks Weston runs off with Matt's only horse, in a mad dash to get to town and file a gold claim. Unfortunately for all concerned, the isolated farm is soon besieged by an Indian war party, and the only escape is by river.

Matt, Kay, and Mark have to take their chances with the raging river, hostile Indians, and outlaws. Matt is not happy that he is stuck with a woman while he is fighting for his and his son's life, not least because it was her friend who put them in this predicament.

Robert Mitchum and Marilyn in *River of No Return* (1954).

Kay, however, cares for the boy, but lets slip that his father was in jail for shooting a man in the back—something which the boy cannot come to terms with.

By the time the three of them make it to town, Kay is deeply in love with Matt. She desperately tries to stop Weston from fighting Matt, but Weston shoots at him, despite the fact that Matt is unarmed. Kay throws herself at Weston, but he throws her aside, and it is only the quick-thinking boy Mark who saves his dad by shooting Weston in the back.

All is still not well between Kay and Matt. She goes off to take up a job singing in a saloon again, but Matt manfully slings her over his shoulder and carries her off to a life with him and his boy.

Marilyn on the set of *River of No Return* (1954).

**Reviews:**

*Los Angeles Examiner*

"There's no doubt that Miss Monroe means every bit of business that she's required to do in the adventure yarn, but the heavily dramatic elements of the film are just a little too much for her at this point in her acting career."

*New York Post*

"Speaking generally, the scenery is beyond reproach, and CinemaScope here finds something to get its broad span of teeth into. The outdoor action on the river is dramatically very powerful. Mr. Mitchum and the other males seem at home among the mountains and trees, and that leaves only Miss Monroe as the picture's vibrant question mark. There is something at once incongruous and strangely stimulating in Miss Monroe's dazzled and dazzling antics in the surroundings of nature. She herself is a leading representative of the natural instinct mentioned previously, and she is also, by reason of the artificial aspect of her coloring and makeup, in opposition to nature. This creates a kind of tension, not too easily defined, but very easily translated into publicity, popularity, and public interest."

*The New York Times*

"It is a toss-up whether the scenery or the adornment of Marilyn Monroe is the feature of greater attraction in 'River of No Return'. . . . The mountainous scenery is spectacular, but so, in her own way, is Miss Monroe..."

## RKO

718 GOWER STREET, HOLLYWOOD

From her bedroom window in the orphanage Norma Jeane could gaze out on the letters "RKO" on the water tower in the RKO Radio Pictures STUDIOS, just one block away from the Los Angeles ORPHANAGE where she lived for almost two years in the mid-1930s. Just before Christmas 1936, Norma Jeane was one of the little orphan children to go on an outing to the studios. RKO ran a movie and then gave out gifts—a toy string of pearls for little Norma Jeane. Many years earlier, Marilyn's mother GLADYS BAKER had worked at RKO as a negative cutter.

Things came full circle in 1949, when Marilyn spent a day filming in the Marx Brothers film *LOVE HAPPY* (1950). She was to return to the studios for a more substantial role in late 1951, a film star on the cusp of super-stardom, after SIDNEY SKOLSKY persuaded producer JERRY WALD to give her a role in *CLASH BY NIGHT* (1952). Around the time of this movie's release, RKO had to deal with the crisis of Marilyn's nude CALENDAR shots surfacing. The original fears—revelations that the young star had posed nude would cause untold damage to the release of *Clash by Night*—were not only unfounded,

From the window of her room in the Los Angeles Orphan's Home Marilyn could see the RKO water tower.

but Marilyn's cool admission of why she had done it provided a huge amount of free publicity. However, one version of events has it that RKO deliberately played up the scandal of this star they had borrowed on loan from TWENTIETH CENTURY-FOX, precisely for the extra publicity it would garner for their film.

RKO, for decades one of the five major production companies in Hollywood, ceased production in 1953, five years after HOWARD HUGHES took control of the studio. The former RKO premises were taken over subsequently by PARAMOUNT.

## ROBERTS, RALPH (1922–1999)

Marilyn's personal masseur has been described as a gentle giant and a Southern gentleman. They first met in 1955 at LEE STRASBERG's home. Like Marilyn, Roberts was a student of THE METHOD who had become a friend of the family, and masseur to SUSAN STRASBERG. He took up massage to make ends meet between acting jobs, and quickly built up an appreciative clientele including MILTON BERLE, Ellen Burstyn, Judy Holliday, and Walter Matthau. Roberts also provided the inspiration (and behind-the scenes training) for the masseur character in the Broadway hit *Will Success Spoil Rock Hunter?*

Biographer DONALD SPOTO says that after Marilyn hired him to help her through filming of *LET'S MAKE LOVE* (1960), "he quickly became her closest friend and most intimate confidant for the rest of her life."

Roberts played a minor part as an ambulance driver in *THE MISFITS* (1961), as well as massaging the tired and aching limbs of actors in the production. He was in the thick of the battles between Marilyn and ARTHUR MILLER in the final months of their married life and he helped Marilyn through the loneliness she felt after the split. Roberts drove her home after her horrific experience in the psychiatric ward of the Payne Whitney HOSPITAL; later in 1961 he took Marilyn and her half sister BERNIECE MIRACLE to what had been Miller's and Marilyn's country home in ROXBURY to pick up some of Marilyn's things: her books, some sculptures, bone china, cocktail glasses, and a big TV set she had been given by RCA.

When Marilyn moved back to Los Angeles in August 1961, Roberts flew West with her. Marilyn rented a room for him at the CHATEAU MARMONT hotel, ten minutes from her DOHENY DRIVE apartment. Marilyn felt so close to him she nicknamed him "the Brother." However, some time in late November, Marilyn told Roberts that her psychoanalyst DR. RALPH GREENSON thought it would be better if Ralph went back to New York. He obeyed her wishes, but they stayed in touch, and Ralph was back in Los Angeles in March 1962 to help Marilyn with the many errands she had after moving into her new home in Brentwood. He stayed on, continuing to spend time with her and relieve her tensions with his massage skills.

On the day Marilyn died, Roberts called her home before 6 P.M. to double check what food to buy for the barbecue they had planned for the following evening. Dr. Greenson picked up the phone and told Roberts that Marilyn was not home. It has been said that later that evening a very groggy Marilyn left an incomprehensible message on Roberts's answering machine.

## ROBINSON, EDWARD G., JR.

Marilyn reputedly had a brief affair with Edward G. Robinson's then nineteen-year-old son, as well as a tryst with his friend Andrew James, not long before marrying JOE DIMAGGIO.

Edward G. Robinson Jr. had a small role in Marilyn's film *SOME LIKE IT HOT* (1959).

(*see* LOVERS)

## ROCKHAVEN SANITARIUM
2713 HONOLULU AVENUE, VERDUGO DISTRICT OF GLENDALE, CALIFORNIA

Marilyn's mother, GLADYS BAKER, was transferred to this private sanitarium in 1953. Marilyn took care of the monthly payments of $300 ($250 in some accounts). In 1963, Gladys apparently escaped for a day by climbing through a window.

Marilyn made provisions in her WILL to ensure that payments were made for Gladys's upkeep, until Baker went to live with her other daughter, BERNIECE MIRACLE, in 1967.

## ROGERS, GINGER
(1911–1995, B. VIRGINIA MCMATH)

Rogers followed the tried and tested showbiz path to discovery: vaudeville, roles on Broadway, and then the call from Hollywood, in her case from PARAMOUNT. Rogers was one of Norma Jeane's favorite actresses when she was growing up. Marilyn saw her in the succession of musicals she made that decade: *42nd Street* (1933), and then, in her legendary partnership with Fred Astaire, *Flying Down to Rio* (1933), *The Gay Divorcee* (1934), *Top Hat* (1935), *Follow the Fleet* (1936), and *Stage Door* (1937). In 1940 Rogers won her only Oscar, for *Kitty Foyle* (1940).

By the fifties, when Marilyn was on the way up, Rogers was just edging into the twilight of her career. They crossed paths twice on celluloid in 1952, in *WE'RE NOT MARRIED* and *MONKEY BUSINESS*, both films in which Marilyn, though only in supporting roles, received top billing.

## ROGERS, ROY
(1912–1998, B. LEONARD SLYE)

In 1946 Norma Jeane met singing cowboy Roy Rogers in LAS VEGAS, when she was living out the residency requirement for a DIVORCE from first husband JAMES DOUGHERTY, and he was working on his latest feature. Norma Jeane wrote to EMMELINE SNIVELY, the head of her modeling agency, that she rode Rogers's famous horse Trigger (1932-1965), went to dinner with Rogers and other members of the cast at the Last Frontier Hotel (*see* RESTAURANTS), and was then taken out to a rodeo.

## ROLES

MARILYN:
"Personally, I think the best performance I ever gave was in *The Asphalt Jungle*. The worst part I had to play was *Let's Make Love*. I didn't even have a part... it was part of an old contract; I had nothing to say."

Marilyn's roles may be broadly divided into three phases: decorative bit-part typecasting, typecasting as a woman of easy sexual mores, and, after she broke out of the mold created for her by TWENTIETH CENTURY-FOX, dramatic roles in which she could explore and develop her ACTING skills.

Yet Marilyn's greatest role was perhaps herself. Out of the public eye, she was still Norma Jeane; give her the lights and the crowds and she switched on her radiant, enticing, sexy persona to "do a Marilyn."

### MARILYN'S MOVIE CHARACTERS

Eve, waitress
*Dangerous Years* (1947)
Boat rower
*Scudda Hoo! Scudda Hay!* (1948)
Peggy Martin, burlesque star
*Ladies of the Chorus* (1948)
Grunion's client, a pretty girl
*Love Happy* (1950)
Clara, chorus girl
*A Ticket to Tomahawk* (1950)
Angela Phinlay, mistress
*The Asphalt Jungle* (1950)
Miss Caswell, aspiring actress
*All About Eve* (1950)
Polly, rollerskate groupie
*The Fireball* (1950)
Dusky Ledoux (uncredited)
*Right Cross* (1950)
Miss Martin, secretary
*Hometown Story* (1951)
Harriet, secretary
*As Young As You Feel* (1951)
Roberta Stevens, ex-WAC
*Love Nest* (1951)
Joyce, the "other woman"
*Let's Make It Legal* (1951)
Peggy, fish cannery worker
*Clash by Night* (1952)
Annabel Norris, beauty queen
*We're Not Married* (1952)
Nell, psychotic babysitter
*Don't Bother to Knock* (1952)
Lois Laurel, secretary
*Monkey Business* (1952)
Streetwalker
*O. Henry's Full House* (1952)
Rose Loomis, homicidal adultress
*Niagara* (1953)
Lorelei Lee, gold-digging miss
*Gentlemen Prefer Blondes* (1953)
Pola Debevoise, myopic gold digger
*How to Marry a Millionaire* (1953)
Kay Weston, saloon singer
*River of No Return* (1954)
Vicky, nightclub singer
*There's No Business Like Show Business* (1954)
The Girl, upstairs neighbor
*The Seven Year Itch* (1955)
Cherie, chanteuse
*Bus Stop* (1956)
Elsie Marina, American showgirl in London
*The Prince and the Showgirl* (1957)
Sugar Kane, ukulele player
*Some Like It Hot* (1959)
Amanda Dell, Broadway actress
*Let's Make Love* (1960)
Roslyn Tabor, animal-loving divorcee
*The Misfits* (1960)

(*see* FILMS MARILYN CONSIDERED OR WANTED *and* THEATER)

## ROONEY, MICKEY (B. 1920, JOE YULE JR.)

Two honorary Oscars have been awarded to Mickey Rooney, the first in 1938 "for bringing to the screen the spirit and personification of youth," the second in 1982 to mark sixty years as a performer. Rooney captured the market in young heroes, becoming the most popular Hollywood star by the late thirties and early forties. His signature movies are *Boys' Town* (1938), *Babes in Arms* (1939), *The Human Comedy* (1943), *The Bold and The Brave* (1956), and *Breakfast at Tiffany's* (1961).

In 1950 Rooney starred as a rollerskate champ in *THE FIREBALL*, a movie in which Marilyn had a small part. As a Hollywood veteran, Rooney has often appeared in DOCUMENTARIES about Marilyn, and he mentions her a number of times in his autobiography *Life Is Too Short*. On the whole he has been less than complimentary, and in the opinion of some, economical with the truth: He claims that he introduced Marilyn to JOHNNY HYDE, the William Morris agent who orchestrated Marilyn's break into the Hollywood big-time, and personally gave her a part in *The Fireball*.

A further Rooney claim is perhaps the most colorful explanation for how Norma Jeane got the NAME Marilyn Monroe. According to this story, one day while he was telling her that she looked much more like a Marilyn than anything else, an agent called Monroe called him on the phone. He told the agent he couldn't speak, because "I'm talking with Marilyn, Monroe," and the name stuck. On a less flattering note, Rooney has also commented that Marilyn was "one of the best cocksuckers in Hollywood."

## ROSE, HELEN (1904–1985)

This multi-Academy Award-winning COSTUME DESIGNER made the costumes for Marilyn in her three MGM movies, *THE ASPHALT JUNGLE* (1950), *RIGHT CROSS* (1950), and *HOMETOWN STORY* (1951).

Marilyn on the set of *Some Like It Hot* in Coronado Beach, California, 1954.

## ROSENFELD, HENRY

A wealthy dress manufacturer, dubbed "the Bronx Christian Dior," whom Marilyn often saw when she was in New York. They first met at the El Morocco nightclub in 1949, when she was in town promoting LOVE HAPPY.

In some quarters it is said that Marilyn and Rosenfeld had an affair; they certainly remained lifelong friends. According to NORMAN ROSTEN, Rosenfeld wanted to marry Marilyn. It was Rosenfeld who paid for Marilyn's suite at the WALDORF-ASTORIA Hotel in 1955, as MARILYN MONROE PRODUCTIONS got off the ground. He gave her financial advice and loaned her money to tide her over while she and business partner MILTON GREENE were renegotiating her contract with TWENTIETH CENTURY-FOX. Greene also tried, unsuccessfully, to get Rosenfeld to bankroll future productions.

FRED LAWRENCE GUILES writes that it may have been Rosenfeld who first introduced Marilyn to JOHN KENNEDY.

## ROSSON, HAROLD (1895–1988)

Cinematographer on *THE ASPHALT JUNGLE* (1950), briefly married to Marilyn's childhood idol JEAN HARLOW, and 1936 Academy Award winner for *The Garden of Allah*. He also shot on the *The Wizard of Oz* (1939) and *Singin' in the Rain* (1952). Rosson featured on Marilyn's list of "approved" cinematographers.

## ROSTEN, HEDDA

"[Marilyn was] the quintessential victim of the male and also of her own self-destroying perversities."

Marilyn became friends with Hedda and her husband Norman in 1955, and from then on she spent a great deal of time with them either in NEW YORK or at their country home on Long Island. The most commonly told story of how Marilyn and ARTHUR MILLER renewed their acquaintance in New York has the Rostens as matchmakers. Hedda was a supportive friend throughout Marilyn's courtship with Miller, and she was present at their wedding in 1956. Soon afterward she traveled with Marilyn to ENGLAND for the making of *THE PRINCE AND THE SHOWGIRL* (1957), on a retainer of $200 per week, for her companionship and role as personal secretary.

According to Miller, Hedda, an old college friend of his, was their salvation during their time in England. As Marilyn's SECRETARY, she was completely supportive. With past experience as a psychiatric social worker, Hedda believed that Marilyn's main problem was her need to "constantly . . . test what she hasn't been able to put together yet." Rosten continued to handle Marilyn's affairs in New York after Marilyn moved back to LOS ANGELES in 1961.

Marilyn with Norman and Patricia Rosten at the premiere of *The Rose Tattoo*, 1955.

## ROSTEN, NORMAN

"She was a difficult woman, you know. We liked her and we said the nicest things about her and she deserved them; but, she was trouble and she brought that whole baggage of emotional difficulties of her childhood with her."

Poet and novelist Rosten and his wife Hedda were introduced to Marilyn one evening in early 1955, not long after Marilyn moved to NEW YORK. They remained friends until Marilyn's death.

That first evening in 1955 mutual friend SAM SHAW brought her to their BROOKLYN home. Shaw, who wanted them "to meet her as a young woman, not a movie star," introduced Marilyn to them simply as "a friend of my camera." Neither Norman nor Hedda realized who she was until she told them her acting name.

Born to Russian immigrant parents, Rosten was principally known for his poetry, though he also wrote two novels and the screenplay for the screen version of ARTHUR MILLER's *A View from the Bridge* (1961).

Marilyn nicknamed Norman Rosten "Claude" because of his passing resemblance to actor Claude Rains. Initially, when Marilyn and Arthur 's relationship was still a secret to the outside world, the courting couple often met at the Rosten home, or at their country place on Long Island. Marilyn chose Rosten as one of the few people to whom she showed her own POETRY, and he was highly encouraging. According to Rosten, on one occasion he saved Marilyn's life when she was pushed into the sea by a melee of adoring FANS, though some doubt has been cast on this story.

The Rostens were one of the few who attended Marilyn's FUNERAL. Marilyn showed her appreciation for their friendship by leaving $5000 for the education of their daughter Patricia, though owing to legal wrangles this money was not released until 1975, many years after she had graduated from college.

Rosten's acute observations of Marilyn in his two books have added depth and candor to the enormous body of literature about her.

BOOKS:

*Marilyn: An Untold Story*, Norman Rosten. New York: Signet Books, 1973.

*Marilyn Among Friends*, Sam Shaw and Norman Rosten. New York: Henry Holt, 1987.

## ROSTEN, PATRICIA

Marilyn made friends with young Patricia Rosten and was happy to play with her whenever they were together in the country. She gave the girl a little dog as a birthday present one year.

## ROXBURY, CONNECTICUT

ARTHUR MILLER owned two properties near Roxbury. The original property, which he had before marrying Marilyn, was on Old Tophet Road. It was in this house, on June 29, 1956, that Marilyn and Miller arranged to give a press conference about their upcoming WEDDING, which they celebrated later that day. There was a shadow over the whole day's proceedings: a few hours earlier *Paris-Match* journalist MARA SCHERBATOFF had been killed in a car accident while pursuing the couple. After the last reporters had started the drive back to New York, they left with Miller's cousin Morton for Westchester County Court House for the most private of wedding ceremonies.

Immediately after their marriage Arthur put this house on the market for $29,500, or $38,500 to include 26 acres of land. The proceeds from this sale were put into a new property just a half mile away, a two-story country retreat originally built in 1783, with 325 acres of land, later increased to 400, planted with fruit trees. Marilyn enthusiastically oversaw the remodeling and DECORATING. Originally, she and Arthur had grand plans to shift their new residence to a more favorable location on the land. She even contacted architect FRANK LLOYD WRIGHT, then aged ninety, to draw up a blueprint for a new house on a wooded crest nearby. His plan featured a circular living-room with a sunken center, beneath a sixty-foot diameter domed ceiling, looking out over a swimming pool, plus one master bedroom, one guest room and a conference room. But as Marilyn told columnist Radie Harris:

> "All our friends agreed the land was beautiful, but they said the house was just uninhabitable. I looked at it and thought how it had been standing there, weathering everything for more than 180 years. And I just hated the idea of its being torn down or even left unoccupied. So Arthur and I ignored everybody's advice and got to work. We modernized the back part, put in sliding glass doors, built a garage and a separate one-room studio for Arthur. But in the house itself, we left all the old beams and ceilings intact."

Between 1957 and 1960, the year they split up, Marilyn and Arthur spent a great

The house that Arthur Miller and Marilyn bought together in Roxbury, Connecticut.

deal of time in this house. After they parted Miller made it his permanent residence.

(*see* HOMES)

## RUBIN, STANLEY

Producer of *RIVER OF NO RETURN* (1954), Rubin turned Marilyn down two years previously for a TV film he was making because he thought she was too inexperienced.

## RUDITSKY, BARNEY

Private detective hired either directly by JOE DIMAGGIO or by friend FRANK SINATRA in November 1954 to find evidence of Marilyn's adulterous behavior. Ruditsky's legwork led to the embarrassing WRONG DOOR RAID as Sinatra, DiMaggio, and a few well-built pals burst into the wrong apartment.

## RUSSELL, JANE
(B. 1921, ERNESTINE JANE RUSSELL)

"Marilyn is a dreamy girl. She's the kind who's liable to show up with one red shoe and one black shoe."

The PRESS was thrilled at the prospect of on-set fireworks when it was announced that Jane Russell, known for her titanic bust, and Marilyn Monroe, said to have the best bottom in the business, were to star in *GENTLEMEN PREFER BLONDES* (1953). Despite columnists hailing it as the "bout for the glamour championship of the world" and the "battle of the bulges," Marilyn and Jane soon struck up a friendship. Russell went into the picture the bigger star, but when the movie came out people only talked about Marilyn.

Russell admired Marilyn's dedication to her job (on most days Marilyn stayed behind to rehearse long after Russell had gone home), and did her best to help her younger colleague overcome her paralyzing nerves. She considered her co-star to be "far more intelligent than people gave her credit for." Their friendship blossomed off-set too. Jane helped Marilyn to decorate her apartment on DOHENY DRIVE, and she invited Marilyn to join her at the Hollywood Christian Group. As Marilyn later said, "Jane, who is deeply religious, tried to convert me to her religion and I tried to introduce her to Freud. Neither of us won." In June 1953, blonde and brunette went together to add their handprints and footprints to the sidewalk outside GRAUMAN'S CHINESE THEATER.

Five years older than Marilyn, Russell had grown up in the same part of town as Norma Jeane. During her high school days at Van Nuys High, Jane was in the same class as JAMES DOUGHERTY, who was later to marry sixteen-year-old Norma Jeane. Jane and Jim not only knew each other, they both performed in the local youth drama outfit, the Van Nuys Maskers Drama Group. She played Jim's daughter in a production of *Shirtsleeves*.

Russell's film career followed a path similar to Marilyn's: first modeling, then a spell studying her craft—in Russell's case at the Max Reinhardt Theatrical Workshop. Like all legends, the genesis of Russell's leap to movie fame is contested. She was "discovered" by HOWARD HUGHES after her agent sent him her photograph, or after he

Marilyn and Jane Russell put their hand prints in the sidewalk in front of Grauman's Chinese Theater on June 26, 1953.

spotted her himself, or while she worked as a nurse to his regular dentist.

Hughes reputedly indulged his engineering talents by inventing a special cantilevered bra for Russell, and then pitched her into a Western, *The Outlaw* (1943), which spent three years in limbo while the censors sulked over the suggestive display of Russell's breasts. When the film was released, the poster campaign featured Russell holding a pistol under the caption, "Mean... Moody... Magnificent." Russell remained under contract to Hughes for the best part of three decades. Apart from *Gentlemen Prefer Blondes*, her most critically-acclaimed performances were in *The Paleface* (1948), *Gentlemen Marry Brunettes* (1955), and the *Revolt of Mamie Stover* (1957), a movie which Marilyn turned down.

## RUSSIA

From her earliest experiences as a drama student, Marilyn had a lifelong curiosity and respect for Russian culture. All of her drama coaches, from Morris Carnovsky at the ACTORS LAB to NATASHA LYTESS, MICHAEL CHEKHOV and LEE STRASBERG, in one way or another, carried the torch of the Russian-based theatrical research originated by KONSTANTIN STANISLAVSKY. Many of Marilyn's favorite BOOKS and pieces of MUSIC were by Russian authors and composers.

Besides these professional influences, in her personal life Russian-born mentor/lover JOHNNY HYDE shared with Marilyn his interest in Russian culture and history.

In 1955 Marilyn accepted an invitation by Carleton Smith of the National Arts Foundation to lead a delegation of American artists on a trip to Moscow. She got as far as applying for a visa, but, in conflicting versions of the story, it either never came through, or Marilyn turned her attention to other priorities.

Marilyn was immensely popular in Russia. Around the time when NIKITA KHRUSHCHEV visited America, *SOME LIKE IT HOT* (1959) was attracting over 40,000 Soviet viewers each day.

## RYAN, ROBERT (1909–1973)

"I got the feeling she was a frightened lonely little girl who was trying awfully hard. She always seemed to be so mournful-looking around the set, and I always tried to cheer her up."

Robert Ryan co-starred with Marilyn in *CLASH BY NIGHT* (1952), one of her early forays into above-the-title billing.

Ryan's long career included performances in *Gangway for Tomorrow* (1943), *Crossfire* (1947), *God's Little Acre* (1958), *Odds Against Tomorrow* (1959), and *The Wild Bunch* (1969).

## RYMAN, LUCILLE

"Under Marilyn's baby-doll, kitten exterior, she's tough and shrewd and calculating."

This early benefactor of Marilyn's first met her in the summer of 1947, after Ryman's, husband, actor JOHN CARROLL, was assigned Marilyn as a starlet caddy in a celebrity golf tournament at Cheviot Hills Country Club. However, it has also been reported that Ryman engineered a meeting after seeing Marilyn's 1946 SCREEN TEST for TWENTIETH CENTURY-FOX. In her own words, when the talent spotter first saw Marilyn, "I remember thinking, 'Oh, this poor little child, this stray kitten.'"

Head of talent at MGM at the time, Ryman's intuition served her well and her track record must have impressed Marilyn. She had fulfilled a similar mentoring role with Lana Turner and JANET LEIGH. Ryman and Carroll took in the penniless starlet, gave her a weekly $25 allowance, and set about improving her skills, furthering her career, and keeping her off the streets of Hollywood.

In September 1947 Ryman put Marilyn in touch with the proprietors of the Bliss-Hayden Miniature Theater, which led to a stage part in *GLAMOUR PREFERRED*. Marilyn played a Hollywood starlet whose plan to seduce a glamorous leading man was, as in real life, thwarted by his smart and honest wife—Marilyn reputedly propositioned Carroll more than once. Ryman and her husband also paid for Marilyn's ongoing studies at the ACTORS LAB. Most biographers report that Marilyn made more and more demands on the couple, turning the arrangement into a relationship of parental surrogacy. By 1948, in Ryman's words, "Marilyn had become a problem. . . . She called me at my office, and John at the studio, as often as four times a day, even though we repeatedly asked her not to. We were in a trap we had unwittingly stepped into. Finally, we had no control over her: she controlled us."

Even after Marilyn had moved on to another benefactor (movie agent JOHNNY HYDE), Ryman continued to help advance her career. She was instrumental in persuading JOHN HUSTON to cast Marilyn in the role of Angela Phinlay in *THE ASPHALT JUNGLE* (1950), in one version of events sweeping away his reticence by threatening to call in a large debt he had run up as a result of stabling his stallions at the ranch run by Ryman and Carroll.

Some years later Marilyn got back in touch with Lucille to thank her, and even offered to repay her generosity. HEDDA HOPPER quoted Ryman's reaction in her May 4, 1952 column: "I was stunned. It was the first time anyone had ever offered to pay me back. I told her to forget it, and to pass the money along to some other kid someday—some kid who needed a helping hand."

The two were in touch again in early 1954, when Marilyn called her and asked Ryman to give full cooperation to BEN HECHT, who was ghostwriting an autobiography for her.

S

## SAHARA MOTOR HOTEL
401 NORTH FIRST STREET, PHOENIX, ARIZONA

Marilyn stayed here during location shooting on *BUS STOP* (1956).

(*see* HOTELS)

## ST. REGIS HOTEL
2 EAST FIFTY-FIFTH STREET, NEW YORK

Marilyn and husband JOE DIMAGGIO stayed at this New York HOTEL during location shooting for *THE SEVEN YEAR ITCH* (1955). They were in suite 1105-6. It was here they fought after Joe saw Marilyn being ogled by at least a thousand onlookers during shooting of the famous skirt scene. The following day Joe stormed off. Their marriage never recovered.

## SALE, RICHARD (1911–1993)

Two-time DIRECTOR of Marilyn, in early movies *A TICKET TO TOMAHAWK* (1950), which he also co-wrote, and *LET'S MAKE IT LEGAL* (1951).

## SAMUEL GOLDWYN STUDIOS
1041 NORTH FORMOSA AVENUE,
HOLLYWOOD
LATER WARNER HOLLYWOOD STUDIOS

This was where Marilyn did soundstage work for *SOME LIKE IT HOT* in 1958.

## SAN FRANCISCO

JOE DIMAGGIO's family lived in San Francisco. His brothers ran a RESTAURANT on Fisherman's Wharf, and between 1952 and 1954 Marilyn made regular visits up the California coast. In January 1954 Joe and Marilyn became man and wife at the San Francisco City Hall. After their HONEYMOON, they moved in to the BEACH STREET home, but only for a couple of months, until Marilyn returned to Los Angeles to work on her next film, *THERE'S NO BUSINESS LIKE SHOW BUSINESS* (1954).

## SANDBURG, CARL (1878–1967)

"She was not the usual movie idol. There was something democratic about her. She was the type who would join in and wash up the supper dishes even if you didn't ask her."

"She was a good talker. There were realms of science, politics and economics in which she wasn't at home, but she spoke well on the national scene, the Hollywood scene, and on people who are good to know and people who ain't. We agreed on a number of things. She sometimes threw her arms around me like people do who like each other very much. Too bad I was forty-eight years older—I couldn't play her leading man."

Poet and Pulitzer Prize-winning biographer Sandburg, author of the definitive six-volume biography of ABRAHAM LINCOLN, met Marilyn during shooting of *SOME LIKE IT HOT* (1959). Marilyn had been keen to meet him ever since she read the Lincoln biography, which was recommended to her by ARTHUR MILLER when they first met in the early fifties. Back in NEW YORK she and Sandburg met a few times, and continued their friendship by phone. Marilyn owned a bust of Sandburg, which she took with her after splitting up with Miller.

Carl Sandburg was the first person JOE DIMAGGIO approached to give the eulogy at Marilyn's FUNERAL. Sandburg declined because he was too ill, though it has also been said that he did not accept this appointment because he felt he did not know her sufficiently well. The honor then passed to LEE STRASBERG.

## SANDERS, GEORGE (1906–1972)

English-educated screen sophisticate George Sanders had a long and glorious Hollywood career, mainly as a succession of gentlemanly villains and cads, after playing The Saint in a series of films in the late thirties. Sanders' sole Oscar was for his performance as critic Addison De Witt in *ALL ABOUT EVE* (1950), the film that featured Marilyn in her first influential role, as his young protégé Miss Caswell. Other memorable Sanders performances came in *Lancer Spy* (1937), *Rebecca* (1940), *The Picture of Dorian Gray* (1944), *A Scandal in Paris* (1946), *Forever Amber* (1947), and *Village of the Damned* (1960).

By all accounts, Sanders was severely smitten with Marilyn on the set of *All About Eve*, an infatuation which had begun years earlier when he met her on the Hollywood party circuit. His ultra-jealous wife at the time, ZSA ZSA GABOR, got wind of his keenness and forbade him any contact with Marilyn outside the studio. Her insistence did nothing to stop rumors that they had an affair. Sanders later married Zsa Zsa's sister, Magda, his fourth and final wife.

Sanders recalled Marilyn as being "very inquiring and unsure—humble, punctual and untemperamental. She wanted people to like her, her conversation had unexpected depths. She showed an interest in intellectual subjects which was, to say the least, disconcerting. In her presence it was hard to concentrate."

## SANTA MONICA HOSPITAL
1225 FIFTEENTH STREET, SANTA MONICA, CALIFORNIA

Although there are no records that Marilyn was at this hospital the night she died, some CONSPIRACY theorists believe she was rushed by AMBULANCE to the emergency room in the early hours of August 5, 1962, only to be pronounced dead on arrival. Under this scenario, her body was then returned to her home, and the POLICE were finally called.

## SARTRE, JEAN-PAUL (1905–1980)

The famous French philosopher, a leading proponent of the theory of existentialism, who in 1964 rejected the Nobel Prize for literature because he didn't want to compromise his integrity, considered Marilyn to be the finest actress alive. He was keen to interest her in taking the female lead in *Freud*, for which he wrote the first (unfilmed) screenplay. With respect like this, it was little wonder that ARTHUR MILLER claimed that only the French really appreciated his wife.

## SCADUTO, ANTHONY,
ALIAS TONY SCIACCA

Expanding on a 1975 article in adult magazine *Oui*, Scaduto wrote a book in which he alleged the existence of a red DIARY in which Marilyn wrote down government secrets she had obtained from ROBERT KENNEDY during their affair. Scaduto also said that tapes had been made by wiretapper BERNIE SPINDEL of Marilyn in conversation with both Kennedy brothers (see BUGGING). The source for this information was ROBERT SLATZER.

BOOK:
*Who Killed Marilyn*, Tony Sciacca. New York: Manor Books, 1976.

## SCHAEFER, HAL

"I always felt she never really achieved her potential as a singer—I felt she could have been a really good singer. I gave her Ella Fitzgerald albums to listen to for homework, and she fell in love with Ella. She had great potential and never realized it."

Marilyn began working with voice coach Hal Schaefer at Fox in 1952, in the build-up to filming *GENTLEMEN PREFER BLONDES* (1953). They worked together on *RIVER OF NO RETURN* (1954), and at Marilyn's insistence, Schaefer coached her through her singing numbers in *THERE'S NO BUSINESS LIKE SHOW BUSINESS* (1954). They often worked into the night at the studio, much to the annoyance of jealous new husband JOE DIMAGGIO.

Rumors began of an affair between Marilyn and Schaefer—Marilyn had once before fallen for a vocal coach, FRED KARGER, in 1948. These rumors gained strength in July 1954 after Marilyn rushed to Schaefer's bedside at Santa Monica Hospital, where he was brought after being discovered unconscious in his bungalow on the Fox lot. He had swallowed a potentially lethal combination of Benzedrine, Nembutal, and typewriter cleaning fluid. Although Schaefer never commented publicly on this incident, biographers have speculated that he may have tried to take his life because Marilyn was forced by DiMaggio to cut their romance short, or because he had been given some sort of strong warning to stay away.

Marilyn and voice coach Hal Schaefer, ca. 1953.

At the time there was speculation that Marilyn's separation a few months later from DiMaggio was precipitated by this dalliance. In the infamous "WRONG DOOR RAID" when an irate DiMaggio and FRANK SINATRA burst into an apartment in an attempt to catch an adulterous Marilyn, Schaefer was the man they expected to find. But years later, Schaefer told biographer ANTHONY SUMMERS, "I was not the cause of the break-up [between Marilyn and Joe DiMaggio]. . . . She would have left him no matter what . . . but DiMaggio couldn't believe that."

## SCHARY, DORE (1905–1980)

"I did not recognize her star potential. . . . Darryl Zanuck signed Miss Monroe, she became an extraordinary figure in movie history and for years I blushed with embarrassment every time her name was mentioned."

Schary worked his way to the top of MGM after amassing a quantity of writing and producing credits, including an Oscar for *Boys' Town* (1938). In 1948 he took over as head of production at the studio, reigning over the lion's lot until 1956, during which time he took over from founder Louis B. Mayer.

In 1950, Marilyn made her first notable movie incursion in MGM's *THE ASPHALT JUNGLE*. JOHNNY HYDE persuaded Schary to put Marilyn in future films, but all that came her way were minor roles in *RIGHT CROSS* (1950) and industrial movie *HOMETOWN STORY* (1951), after which Schary declined to sign her to a long-term contract, despite Hyde's advocate, executive Ben Thau, fighting in Marilyn's corner. She was apparently told that because the studio already had Lana Turner to cater to their blonde ambitions, they had no further need for her services; Schary told Hyde that in his opinion Marilyn neither had the looks nor the talent to be a top notch movie-star.

## SCHENCK, JOSEPH M. (1878–1961)

MARILYN:
"Mr. Schenck and I were good friends. I know the word around Hollywood was I was Joe Schenck's girlfriend, but that's a lie."

SAM SHAW:
"Long before she was a major star, Joe Schenck was her benefactor. If she was hungry and wanted a good meal, or sad and wanted a good cry, she called him."

The most commonly told story of how Marilyn met the Russian-born co-founder of TWENTIETH CENTURY-FOX, some time in late 1947 or early 1948, is that Schenck was being driven through the studio lot in his limousine when he spotted her, told the chauffeur to stop, and invited her over to dinner at his Holmby Hills home. A competing version is that an acquaintance of Marilyn's, ice cream magnate Pat De Cicco, took her along to one of Schenck's infamous Saturday night poker parties, and she caught the eye of her host. Yet another claim is that Marilyn was invited initially to an open Sunday lunch Schenck regularly threw.

Marilyn soon became a fixture, one of what columnist SHEILAH GRAHAM described as his "Gin Rummy Girls" who served cigars and drinks and looked pretty while Schenck, DARRYL ZANUCK, and other movie moguls played cards. Marilyn later confirmed, "I was invited as an ornament, just someone to brighten the party."

Schenck, then sixty-nine years old, had enjoyed a long career as one of Hollywood's top moguls. Along with his brother he built a successful amusement park business in New Jersey, before joining up with Marcus Loew to diversify into movies and nickelodeons. From 1917 to 1935 he was married to silent movie siren NORMA TALMADGE. In 1933 he co-founded Twentieth Century Productions with Zanuck, spent a brief spell in jail for perjury after being found guilty of bribing a labor racketeer in the early forties, and then in 1943 returned as head of production at Twentieth Century-Fox.

Although Marilyn always publicly denied any sexual component to this "friendship," over a period of eighteen months she was a frequent guest, and in some accounts moved in to a cottage in the grounds of Schenck's mansion, located on CAROLWOOD DRIVE. Marilyn's contract at Fox had not been renewed, and this was a period when she needed all the influential friends she could muster.

Many biographers contend that it was unlikely Schenck enjoyed Marilyn's company because, as she later said, he valued her solely for her "offbeat personality." According to DONALD SPOTO, one evening Marilyn called LUCILLE RYMAN for advice about what to do when Schenck made his desires abundantly clear. Ryman reputedly suggested that she say she was saving her virginity for Mr. Right; then, much later that evening, Marilyn woke Ryman with a call to tell her that Schenck knew she had already been married. Marilyn's friend AMY GREENE told an interviewer, "Marilyn spoke quite openly of her affair with Schenck. He helped her career and she provided what she was asked to provide."

Schenck pulled strings to get Marilyn's career back on the rails. He contacted poker pal HARRY COHN, head of COLUMBIA STUDIOS, and persuaded him to hire her on a six-month contract, which resulted in an appearance in *LADIES OF THE CHORUS* (1948). He continued to keep a friendly eye on her career progression through 1950. Schenck gave her a PET chihuahua for her twenty-fourth birthday, which she named Josefa in his honor. He was in touch with her very soon after her agent JOHNNY HYDE died of a heart attack, offering her a place to stay. When

Joseph M. Schenck and Marilyn at Walter Winchell's birthday party, 1953.

Marilyn re-signed with Fox in early 1951, Schenck kept a watchful eye over her progress. Schenck had a debilitating stroke in 1957, and died four years later. Marilyn stayed in contact with him, and went to visit him not long before he died.

## SCHERBATOFF, MARA

This forty-eight year-old *Paris-Match* New York bureau chief, a Russian princess, was killed in a car accident on a country road near ARTHUR MILLER's Connecticut home on June 29, 1956, the day that Marilyn and Arthur held a press conference to announce their marriage. In fact they wed secretly later the same day.

The generally accepted story is that Scherbatoff and her driver, eighteen-year-old Ira Slade, got wind that before arriving at Miller's home the couple had stopped off to visit Miller's cousin Morton, a few miles away. Scherbatoff then tailed Miller and Marilyn, who were being driven by Morton in a green Oldsmobile, back to their own home. On a sharp corner on Goldmine Road the journalist's car left the road and ploughed into a tree. Miller stopped his car when he heard the smash, and went back to see what had happened. Scherbatoff had gone through the windshield and was horrifically injured; accounts differ as to whether Miller managed to prevent Marilyn from seeing the fatally injured journalist, but she was extremely distraught nonetheless. Nothing could be done for Scherbatoff, and she died three hours later at New Milford Hospital. Understandably, Marilyn took this as a very ill omen on the day of her marriage.

In his autobiography, Miller has a slightly different account of the circumstances, claiming that the accident happened later that day, after their marriage, when Scherbatoff's driver mistook a passing car for his, spun around in the road, and smashed into a tree.

Emerson Jr. High School, 1941.

## SCHILLER, LAWRENCE (LARRY)

"She loved it, when I photographed her nude. She wasn't that busty and she had a little heavy hips. And she had freckles all over. And there were some little varicose veins in there. She was just like the girl next door."

Three months before her death, PHOTOGRAPHER Lawrence Schiller and colleague William Woodfield were sent by *Paris-Match* to cover Marilyn at work on the set of *SOMETHING'S GOT TO GIVE*. On May 28, 1962 they were on the TWENTIETH CENTURY-FOX lot when Marilyn shot a pool scene. At a certain point, either at the behest of director GEORGE CUKOR or of her own volition, Marilyn slipped out of her flesh-tone costume and for almost an hour posed nude for the photographers in and out of the pool.

Marilyn, usually so attentive to which pictures of her were released and which were not, apparently gave Schiller the go-ahead to market these photos. He knew exactly what he had, and persuaded fellow photographer Jimmy Mitchell to part with his negatives (in some accounts destroy them) for a fee of $10,000. Thus, Schiller and his colleague Woodfield exclusively owned Marilyn's last nudes, the first she had posed for in thirteen years.

Schiller sold the photographs to MAGAZINES in thirty-two countries. In the U.S. they were bought by *Playboy*, and he initially persuaded Marilyn to sit for further photographs to adorn the magazine's front and back covers. Marilyn later pulled out of this commitment. Schiller nonetheless visited Marilyn at her home on her last day alive to discuss which photographs Marilyn would approve. Four days later, he was at her FUNERAL, one of the very few photographers to get close enough to take photos.

To mark the tenth anniversary of Marilyn's death, Schiller curated a touring exhibition of Marilyn photographs taken by fifteen top photographers. At one location, a gold-framed TOM KELLEY nude and a half dozen other original Marilyn photographs were stolen.

A book accompanied the exhibition, and Schiller asked NORMAN MAILER to provide the text for an anthology of Marilyn photos. The combined result—some of the finest Marilyn photographs and Mailer's semi-fictionalized biography—was an enormous success. In 1980 Schiller produced a TV movie *Marilyn: The Untold Story*, adapted from Mailer's 1973 biography.

Schiller's other high-profile exploits include the last interview with Jack Ruby, an exclusive interview with a member of the Charles Manson family, and, more recently, co-authorship of O. J. Simpson's memoirs.

BOOK:

*Marilyn*, Lawrence Schiller, ed., text by Norman Mailer. New York: Grosset and Dunlap, 1973.

## SCHOOLS

During a childhood in which she was bounced from one home to another, it is no surprise that Norma Jeane hardly spent two years at the same school. Note that these dates are best guesses: biographers tend to give different years and grades.

**Hawthorne Community Sunday School**
1929–1930
Norma Jeane attended this school before starting kindergarten.

**Ballona Elementary and Kindergarten**
*(Renamed the Washington Elementary School)*
4339 West 129th Street, Hawthorne
Sept. 1931–June 1932
Norma Jeane's first ever day at school was on September 14, 1931. At that time she was living with the foster family the BOLENDERS.

**Vine Street School**
*(Renamed the Vine Street Elementary School)*
955 North Vine Street, Hollywood
Sept. 1932–June 1934
(1st, 2nd Grade)
Living with the Bolender family

**Selma Street School**
*(Renamed Selma Ave Elementary School)*
6611 Selma Avenue, Hollywood
Sept. 1934–June 1935
(3rd Grade)
During the only year she lived with her mother, Norma Jeane attended this local school.

**Vine Street School**
Sept. 1935–June 1937
(4th, 5th Grade)

**Lankershim School**
*(Renamed Lankershim Elementary)*
5250 Bakman Ave, North Hollywood
Sept. 1937–June 1938
(6th Grade)
Eleven-year-old Norma Jeane scored two gold medals in jumping and running, as she attended this school near the Goddard home.

**Sawtelle Blvd School**
*(Renamed the Nora Sterry School)*
1713 Corinth Ave, West Los Angeles
Sept. 1938–June 1939
(7th Grade)
Living with Ana Lower, Norma Jeane went to this local school. She was a member of the School Safety Committee.

**Emerson Jr. High School**
1650 Selby Ave, West Los Angeles
Sept. 1939–June 1941
(8th, 9th Grade)

**Van Nuys High School**
*(Renamed Van Nuys Senior High School)*
6535 Cedros Avenue, Van Nuys
Sept. 1941–Feb. 1942
(10th Grade)

**University High School**
11800 Texas Ave, West Los Angeles
Feb. 1942–June 1942
(10th Grade)
Norma Jeane Baker dropped out of school before completing tenth grade to marry first husband JAMES DOUGHERTY.

Although Marilyn Monroe did not go to college to study for a degree, in either the fall of 1950 or February 1951 she attended art appreciation and literature classes at UCLA.

## SCOTLAND YARD

Scotland Yard provided six officers to handle Marilyn and ARTHUR MILLER's security during their 1956 stay in ENGLAND. They were led by a detective named Roger Hunt, who acted as her personal bodyguard.

## SCREEN TESTS

Marilyn landed a contract with TWENTIETH CENTURY-FOX on the strength of her first screen test, arranged by casting director BEN LYON on July 19, 1946. At 5:30 A.M. Lyon assembled a top team on the set of the BETTY GRABLE picture *Mother Wore Tights* (1947): cinematographer LEON SHAMROY, makeup man ALLAN "WHITEY" SNYDER (who did her makeup from then onward), director WALTER LANG, and wardrobe chief CHARLES LEMAIRE, who selected a crinoline gown; Florence Bush, it is thought, did her hair. The screen test was shot in color, something not unusally done. At the last minute, Lyon changed his mind about recording sound on the test—Norma Jeane had been scheduled to read from the 1944 movie *Winged Victory*, a script that Judy Holliday had used for her audition. Norma Jeane followed these instructions: walk across the set a couple of times, perch on a high stool, light a cigarette, put it out, then walk back toward a stage window. Five years later, cinematographer Leon Shamroy recalled, "When I first watched her, I thought, 'This girl will be another Harlow!' Her natural beauty plus her inferiority complex gave her a look of mystery. . . . I got a cold chill. This girl had something I hadn't seen since silent pictures. She had a kind of fantastic beauty like Gloria Swanson . . . and she got sex on a piece of film like Jean Harlow. Every frame of the test radiated sex. She didn't need a sound track—she was creating effects visually. She was showing us she could sell emotions in pictures."

In the last year of her life, Marilyn remembered that on that occasion, "For some strange reason, instead of being nervous and scared, I just tried very hard because I knew Mr. Lyon and Mr. Shamroy were taking an awful chance. If it didn't work out well, they might get in trouble."

It has been reported that in 1948, while under contract to COLUMBIA, Marilyn tried out for the lead in *Born Yesterday*. Marilyn's test was not even viewed by studio boss HARRY COHN, who had already decided not to renew her six-month contract, and the role went to Judy Holliday, who put in an Oscar-winning performance.

On December 10, 1950, after incessant lobbying by JOHNNY HYDE, Marilyn was finally granted a second screen test by Fox, ostensibly for a role in a movie called *Cold Shoulder*. Unlike her first test for the studio four years previously, this time there was sound too. Wearing the flattering, good luck sweater-dress which she used to good effect in no less than three movie roles, Marilyn acted the part of a gangster's moll, opposite Richard Conte. Drama coach NATASHA LYTESS came along to offer moral and technical support to Marilyn as she delivered her lines:

> "I came to tell you that you can't stay here, Benny. If these gorillas find you here, what happens? You can't take such a chance!"
> *[Benny raises his hand, preparing to strike]*
> "Go ahead! It won't be the first time I've been worked over today. I'm getting used to it." *[Tears well in Marilyn's eyes as the camera fades.]*

There was no part for Marilyn in *Cold Shoulder* because the movie was scrapped, but studio chief DARRYL ZANUCK was sufficiently impressed to re-sign her to Fox—and give her yet another secretary role in AS YOUNG AS YOU FEEL (1951).

Marilyn's last recorded screen test at Fox came less than six months later, on June 14, 1951. Hot on the heels of her work in LOVE NEST (1951), she acted out a love scene with debutant actor ROBERT WAGNER, for LET'S MAKE IT LEGAL (1951), which was more to put the untried actor through his paces than to test her.

There have also been reports that in late 1951 or early 1952, Zanuck arranged a private test before finally assigning Marilyn her first lead, in DON'T BOTHER TO KNOCK (1952).

Marilyn's first screen test for Twentieth Century-Fox was taken on the set of the film *Mother Wore Tights* starring Betty Grable, 1947.

Marilyn in one of the discarded scenes from *Scudda Hoo! Scudda Hay!* (1948). In the final version Marilyn appears only for a moment.

## SCREENWRITERS

| | |
|---|---|
| George Axelrod | *The Seven Year Itch* (1955), *Bus Stop* (1956) |
| Arnold Belgard | *Dangerous Years* (1948) |
| Mac Benoff | *Love Happy* (1950) |
| Charles Brackett | *Niagara* (1953) |
| Richard Breen | *Niagara* (1953) |
| Joseph Carole | *Ladies of the Chorus* (1948) |
| I. A. L. Diamond | *Love Nest* (1951), *Let's Make It Legal* (1951), *Monkey Business* (1952), *Some Like It Hot* (1959) |
| Henry Ephron | *There's No Business Like Show Business* (1954) |
| Phoebe Ephron | *There's No Business Like Show Business* (1954) |
| Frank Fenton | *River of No Return* (1954) |
| Tay Garnett | *The Fireball* (1950) |
| Alfred Hayes | *Clash by Night* (1952) |
| Ben Hecht | *Love Happy* (1950), *Monkey Business* (1952) |
| F. Hugh Herbert | *Scudda Hoo! Scudda Hay!* (1948), *Let's Make It Legal* (1951) |
| John Huston | *The Asphalt Jungle* (1950) |
| Nunnally Johnson | *We're Not Married* (1952), *How to Marry a Millionaire* (1953) |
| Hal Kanter | *Let's Make Love* (1960) |
| Norman Krasna | *Let's Make Love* (1960) |
| Charles Lederer | *Monkey Business* (1952), *Gentlemen Prefer Blondes* (1953) |
| Mary Loos | *A Ticket to Tomahawk* (1950) |
| Ben Maddow | *The Asphalt Jungle* (1950) |
| Joseph Mankiewicz | *All About Eve* (1950) |
| Horace McCoy | *The Fireball* (1950) |
| Arthur Miller | *The Misfits* (1961) |
| Arthur Pierson | *Hometown Story* (1951) |
| Terence Rattigan | *The Prince and the Showgirl* (1957) |
| Walter Reisch | *Niagara* (1953) |
| Richard Sale | *A Ticket to Tomahawk* (1950) |
| Harry Sauber | *Ladies of the Chorus* (1948) |
| Charles Schnee | *Right Cross* (1950) |
| Daniel Taradash | *Don't Bother to Knock* (1952) |
| Frank Tashlin | *Love Happy* (1950) |
| Lamar Trotti | *As Young as You Feel* (1951), *O. Henry's Full House* (1952) |
| Billy Wilder | *The Seven Year Itch* (1955), *Some Like It Hot* (1959) |

## *SCUDDA HOO! SCUDDA HAY!* (1948)

Marilyn's first (uncredited) film role was in this Technicolor feature about a family of farmers feuding over how best to handle mules. (The film's title refers to the traditional call used to goad mule teams.) Two scenes were filmed with Marilyn. In one she and another starlet were in a rowboat; in the other, which did not survive the cutting room, she stood in the background and called out a hello to leading lady June Haver. Marilyn was relieved, after almost six months under contract to TWENTIETH CENTURY-FOX, to get a role at last—though in this time she may have had walk-on parts in other films.

Although this was the first film on which Marilyn worked, it was not the first to be released—*DANGEROUS YEARS* (1947) actually came out four months earlier.

In the U.K., the film was helpfully retitled *Summer Lightning*.

**Credits:**
Twentieth Century-Fox, Technicolor
Length: 95 minutes
Release date: April 14, 1948

Directed by: F. Hugh Herbert
Produced by: Walter Morosco
Written by: F. Hugh Herbert, George Agnew Chamberlain (story)
Cinematography by: Ernest Palmer
Film editing by: Harmon Jones
Music by: Cyril J. Mockridge

**Cast (credits order):**
June Haver . . . Rad McGill
Lon McCallister . . . Snug Dominy
Walter Brennan . . . Tony Maule
Anne Revere . . . Judith Dominy
Natalie Wood . . . Bean McGill
Robert Karnes . . . Stretch Dominy
Henry Hull . . . Milt Dominy
Tom Tully . . . Roarer McGill

**Uncredited:**
Les MacGregor . . . Ches
Geraldine Wall . . . Mrs. McGill
Ken Christy . . . Sheriff Bursom
Tom Moore . . . Judge Stillwell
Matt McHugh . . . Jim
Herbert Heywood . . . Dugan
Edward Gargan . . . Ted
Guy Beach . . . Elmer
G. Pat Collins . . . Malone
Charles Woolf . . . Jeff
Eugene Jackson . . . Stable Hand
Colleen Townsend . . . Girl Friend 1
Marilyn Monroe . . . Girl in rowboat
Charles Wagenheim . . . Barber

**Crew:**
Bonnie Cashin . . . costume design
Stanley Detlie . . . set decoration
Eugene Grossman . . . sound
Earle Hagen . . . orchestra arranger
Roger Heman Sr. . . . sound
Albert Hogsett . . . art director
Charles LeMaire . . . wardrobe
Thomas Little . . . set decoration
Lionel Newman . . . music conductor
Ben Nye . . . makeup
Fred Sersen . . . special effects photography
Herbert Spencer . . . orchestra arranger
Lyle R. Wheeler . . . art director

**Plot:**
Farm hand Snug Dominy (Lon McCallister) purchases a pair of mules from his boss, and then receives conflicting advice about how to train them. Equally stubborn appears to be the girl of his dreams, Rad McGill (June Haver), who keeps him guessing until the end, by which time he has also broken in his troublesome mules. Marilyn's fleeting appearance is as an uncredited girl rowing in a canoe while various other young farm folk are swimming.

## SECRETARIES

Marilyn's personal secretaries over the years—not to be confused with her MAIDS or publicists (see PRESS)—were HEDDA ROSTEN, MAY REIS, MARJORIE STENGEL, and CHERIE REDMOND.

## *SEVEN YEAR ITCH, THE* (1955)

*The Seven Year Itch* was the last film Marilyn did for TWENTIETH CENTURY-FOX under the old regime of a straitjacket contract and pitiable (by Hollywood standards) MONEY. She had long had her eye on this property, ever since the original stage play did so well on Broadway. Marilyn even agreed to star in a less desirable film, *THERE'S NO BUSINESS LIKE SHOW BUSINESS* (1954), on condition that Fox go ahead with purchasing the rights to GEORGE AXELROD's play, for a figure reputed to be $500,000. Delays to shooting *Show Business* meant that she went straight into filming *The Seven Year Itch* on August 10, 1954.

By this time BILLY WILDER and Axelrod had completely rewritten the script, including changing the ending. In the stage version

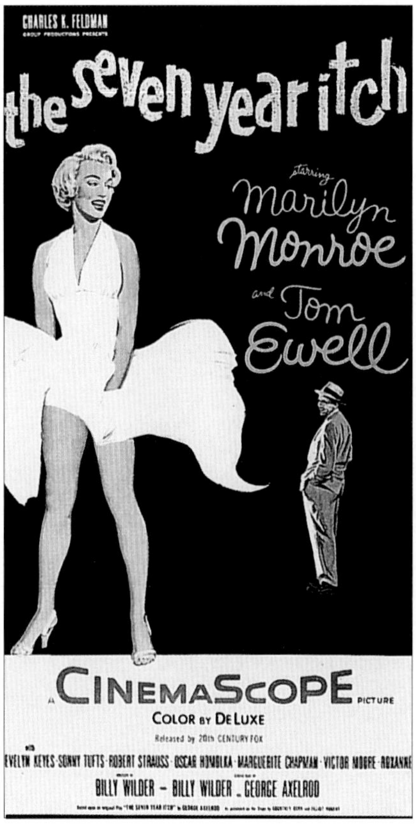


the characters go to bed with one another, but in the film virtue wins the day.

TOM EWELL, who had played the original Broadway role, is a New Yorker whose imagination runs rife during a long hot summer when his wife and kid are away. The arrival of a curvaceous blonde as his upstairs neighbor turns his world upside down. Monroe's character is the ultimate ingenue: she keeps her panties in the fridge, recognizes classical music because "there isn't a vocal," and manages to emit pure kittenish sexiness without ever realizing the effect she is having.

The Marilyn character in the movie curiously has no name. In the credits she is listed simply as "The Girl." When asked if there was any significance to this, Axelrod replied, "The truth of the matter is that I could never think of a name for her that seemed exactly right, that really fit the girl I had in mind."

In this movie Marilyn sported ten different outfits. Designer WILLIAM TRAVILLA completed all of his preliminary sketches in a single weekend, including the aerodynamically-designed outfit which is most closely associated with Marilyn: a simple pleated écru summer dress with a halter front. As with many costumes, more than one example of this dress was made—one was, until recently, on display at the DEBBIE REYNOLDS museum in Las Vegas; another is part of the legacy which passed to ANNA STRASBERG and was put up for auction in October 1999.

Production of the film was on a very tight schedule, but because of the long hours Marilyn spent on Lexington Avenue in the chill of early morning, she caught a serious lung infection that landed her in bed and prolonged the thirty-five-day schedule to forty-eight and a November 5 wrap date. The production came in 10 percent over budget, at a little under two million dollars, but made at least four times that figure on its initial run, beating all other movies that summer.

The location shooting in New York was as much about publicizing the movie as filming it. Marilyn's arrival in the Big Apple was a huge media event, complete with press conferences and a tight schedule of interviews. The publicity department leaked the shooting plans to the press, and on September 15, 1954 erected crowd barriers outside the Trans-Lux Theater on the corner of Lexington Avenue and Fifty-second Street. By 1:00 A.M., when shooting was due to start, several hundred photographers were jostling for position, among a crowd of as many as five thousand onlookers (Billy Wilder's estimate, though one newspaper put the figure at around a thousand) who cheered on each of the fifteen occasions that Marilyn's skirt flew upward in the draft of a huge fan installed below a street-level grate, revealing her legs and white panties (two pairs to be exact). Apparently the technicians who were operating the fans beneath Marilyn took bribes to let certain onlookers get a revealing view from below.

The shooting of Marilyn's iconic scene had a number of consequences. First, the material was nowhere near good enough to be used in the movie: there was too much noise, not enough freedom of movement because of the baying crowd, and the fan they were using did not produce the right kind of effect. Marilyn was overheard commenting to Wilder, "I hope this isn't for your private collection, to be shown in stag shows." In the finished scene used in the movie, shot on a Fox sound stage, Marilyn steps over a grating, her skirt levitates to just over knee level, and there is a cut to her face registering the pleasure of the cooling breeze on the hot summer's night. This is a chaste shadow of the revealing stills captured by the hordes of photographers that night on Lexington Avenue, and even then, one of the three shots in the original cut had to be removed to pass the Hays Code of what was suitable on the screen. Perhaps the best-known of all Marilyn moments, the billowing skirt scene is a short-cut symbol of fifties glamour, which is why it has appeared in one form or another in many movies over the years, including *Tommy* (1975), INSIGNIFICANCE (1985), and *Pulp Fiction* (1994).

But the biggest repercussion for Marilyn at the time was that JOE DIMAGGIO's jealous temperament boiled over. Perhaps against his better judgement, he had allowed his pal, columnist WALTER WINCHELL, to bring him along to the shoot. The sight of thousands of people ogling his wife for hours on end was too much. Back at the ST. REGIS HOTEL they had a vicious fight, and Joe reportedly became violent. The next day he flew back to California on his own. Three weeks later Fox issued a press release announcing that Marilyn and Joe were to separate.

Despite the difficulties of working with Marilyn—namely the incessant retakes—Billy Wilder recognized her special talents: "She's a kind of real image, beyond mere photography. But there's something else, too. She had a natural instinct for how to read a comic line and how to give it something extra, something special. She was never vulgar in a role that could have become vulgar, and somehow you felt good when you saw her on the screen."

Marilyn filmed the final retakes for the film on January 9, 1955, while officially suspended by Fox for having walked out on the studio and setting up her own production company. That day Billy Wilder greeted her, saying, "You're looking good." Marilyn's reply was, "Why shouldn't I, I'm incorporated!"

After seven years together, this was the final movie on which NATASHA LYTESS coached Marilyn. In some reports, PAULA STRASBERG took over from her halfway through shooting. However, in many accounts Marilyn did not meet Paula until the following year, when Marilyn was living in New York.

The film's premiere on June 1, 1955 was a star-studded gala. To mark the event the Loew's State Theater in Times Square received a 52-foot high poster of Marilyn in billowing skirts, at a cost of around $1,500. The original had to be replaced with a less revealing image after complaints were reported. Marilyn was escorted by DiMaggio (she told reporters, "We're just good friends," but that didn't stop a frenzy of press speculation that a reconciliation was taking place) into the theater, where the screening was attended, by among others, GRACE KELLY,

Top, Marilyn captivates Tom Ewell as Richard Sherman in *The Seven Year Itch* (1955). Below, in this never-used scene Marilyn did an imitation of Mae West.

Above, a pocket novelization of *The Seven Year Itch*, 1955. Below, Billy Wilder and Marilyn on the set of *The Seven Year Itch* (1955).

Henry Fonda, Margaret Truman, Eddie Fisher, Judy Holliday, and Richard Rodgers. The movie was the biggest hit of the summer, grossing almost $5 million, and going on to top anywhere between $6 and $15 million by the end of its initial run, depending on who is providing the figures. As ever, Marilyn had to wait for her $100,000 bonus from Fox, despite the fact that the studio and co-producers Wilder and CHARLES FELDMAN (who until then had been Marilyn's agent) made much more money.

MEMORABLE COSTUMES:
White halter "Billowing Skirt Scene" full pleated dress
Low-cut, tight white dress with crossing neck straps

**Awards:**
Golden Globes: Best Motion Picture Actor—Musical/Comedy: Tom Ewell

**Nominations:**
British Academy Awards: Best Foreign Actress: Marilyn Monroe

**Credits:**
Twentieth Century-Fox, CinemaScope and Color (DeLuxe)
Length: 105 minutes
Release date: June 3, 1955

Directed by: Billy Wilder
Produced by: Charles K. Feldman, Billy Wilder
Written by: Billy Wilder and George Axelrod, George Axelrod (original play)
Cinematography by: Milton R. Krasner
Music by: Alfred Newman, Sergei Rachmaninov ("Second piano concerto")
Costume Design by: Travilla
Film Editing by: Hugh S. Fowler

**Cast (credits order):**
Marilyn Monroe . . . The Girl
Tom Ewell . . . Richard Sherman
Evelyn Keyes . . . Helen Sherman
Sonny Tufts . . . Tom MacKenzie
Robert Strauss . . . Mr. Kruhulik the janitor
Oskar Homolka . . . Dr. Brubaker
Marguerite Chapman . . . Miss Morris, secretary
Victor Moore . . . Plumber
Roxanne . . . Elaine
Donald MacBride . . . Mr. Brady
Carolyn Jones . . . Miss Finch
Butch Bernard . . . Ricky Sherman
Doro Merande . . . Waitress
Dorothy Ford . . . Indian Girl
Uncredited:
Ron Nyman . . . Indian
Ralph Sanford . . . Train station gatekeeper
Mary Young . . . Woman in train station

**Crew:**
Saul Bass . . . title design
George W. Davis . . . art director
Leonard Doss . . . color consultant
Doane Harrison . . . associate producer
Ray Kellogg . . . special photographic effects
Charles Le Maire . . . wardrobe director
Harry M. Leonard . . . sound
Ben Nye . . . makeup
Edward B. Powell . . . orchestration
Stuart A. Reiss . . . set decorator
Joseph E. Richards . . . assistant director
Walter M. Scott . . . set decorator
Allan "Whitey" Snyder . . . makeup for Marilyn Monroe, uncredited
Helen Turpin . . . hairstyles
E. Clayton Ward . . . sound
Lyle R. Wheeler . . . art director
Saul Wurtzel . . . subway effects

**Plot:**
After seven years of marriage, New Yorker Richard Sherman (Tom Ewell) packs his wife Helen (Evelyn Keyes) and their boy Ricky (Butch Bernard) off for a cool summer vacation.

Things heat up considerably for him when he finds that the apartment upstairs has been let out to Marilyn Monroe in the shape of The Girl, a TV toothpaste model whose naivete is matched only by her sexiness. There seems to be no avoiding her: Sherman lets The Girl in to the building after she is locked out; when she accidentally knocks a tomato plant onto his balcony, almost killing him, Sherman's only thought is to invite her down for a drink. His fantasy takes over as he conjures up ways to woo and win her. Not long after The Girl confides that she feels safe with married men, he makes a pass at her when they play a duet of "Chopsticks," only to end up tumbling off the piano bench.

Despite his mortification, he cannot help thinking about her. He imagines the consequences of her telling people of his failed pass, and then sets his fantasy to his wife paying him back by having a fling with his worst enemy, a man named Tom MacKenzie (Sonny Tufts).

Sherman builds up the courage to ask The Girl to dinner and a movie—leading to the moment when she cools off by standing over the grille in a joyous updraft. This time, Sherman has no need of schemes to get that kiss: she shows how fresh her breath is by giving him a real smacker. Back at his place, she is so happy to find his air conditioning that she invites herself to stay the night. Sherman takes the couch and his mind runs riot—perhaps this is all a plot by The Girl and the janitor Kruhulik (Robert Strauss) to blackmail him.

The following morning, with Sherman now prey to doubts that any woman would find him attractive, there is a surprise visitor: Helen has asked Tom MacKenzie to bring a toy back for young Ricky. Sherman's jealous fantasy gets the better of him, so he unceremoniously punches MacKenzie out cold. At last, Sherman realizes that he had better get to his rightful place, with his wife and kid, but not before offering The Girl his air-conditioned apartment in his absence.

**Reviews:**

*The New York Times*

"Miss Monroe brings a special personality and a certain physical something or other to the film. . . . From the moment she steps into the picture, in a garment that drapes her shapely form as though she had been skillfully poured into it, the famous screen star with the silver-blonde tresses and the ingenuously wide-eyed stare emanates one suggestion. And that suggestion rather dominates the film. It is—well, why define it? Miss Monroe clearly plays the title role."

*The New Yorker*

"[It] offered stimulating views of Marilyn Monroe as a substitute for the comedy George Axelrod got into the original version of this trifle. There are occasions when Tom Ewell evokes a laugh or two, but when Miss Monroe turns up as a young lady too substantial for dreams, the picture is reduced to the level of a burlesque show."

*Hollywood Reporter*

"Marilyn is just about perfect in the role of the pleasantly vacuous and even more pleasantly curved heroine."

*New York Daily Mirror*

"This is the picture every red-blooded American male has been awaiting ever since the publication of the tease photos showing the wind lifting Marilyn Monroe's skirt above her shapely gams.

It was worth waiting for. 'The Seven Year Itch' is another example of cinema ingenuity in transplanting a stage success to celluloid. . . . Tom Ewell, who reaped critical acclaim in the legit show and won over other contenders for the role in the movie and La Monroe deserve most of the credit for carrying off the comedy coup. . . . [Monroe's] pouting delivery, puckered lips—the personification of this decade's glamour—make her one of Hollywood's top attractions, which she again proves here as the not too bright model."

*Time*

"Marilyn Monroe's eye-catching gait is more tortile and wambling than ever. She also displays a nice comedy touch, reminiscent of a baby-talk Judy Holliday."

Marilyn sizzles in a publicity still for *The Prince and the Showgirl* (1957).

## SEX APPEAL

MARILYN:

"It's easier to look sexy when you are thinking of one man in particular."

"I've given pure sex appeal very little thought. If I had to think about it, I'm sure it would frighten me."

"I never quite understood it—this sex symbol. I always thought symbols were those things you clash together. That's the trouble, a sex symbol is a thing. But if I'm going to be the symbol of something, I'd rather have it sex than some other things they've got symbols of!"

JERRY WALD:

"Her sexuality, well, it's something she has corked up in a bottle. She opens the bottle and uses some when she needs it for a scene and then she puts the cork back in the bottle and puts the bottle away until she needs it again."

Marilyn's unique combination of innocence and availability has become a universal sign of sexiness. Much as she may have striven to be respected as a serious actor, Marilyn is remembered first as the world's most recognizable sex symbol. Her sex appeal has struck a chord that spans the decades. Many biographers stress in the strongest of terms how much Marilyn single-handedly pushed back the barriers of what was acceptable behavior, both on screen and in the lives of a public figure. Almost half a century after her heyday, she still regularly tops surveys of the world's sexiest woman. In November 1998 *Playboy* magazine ranked Marilyn number one in its list of the hundred Sexiest Stars of the Century, and she was also E! Online's number one sex symbol of the century. Marilyn's FACE, or trademark costumes, or breathy VOICE, or typical pout, or inimitable gait, have been picked up by thousands of entertainment industry performers. One of Madonna's early "incarnations," assuring her a long-term place in the entertainment business, was her video for "Material Girl," filmed as an homage to Marilyn's "Diamonds Are a Girl's Best Friend" number.

This intimate photo of Marilyn accompanied Hollywood journalist Sidney Skolsky's 1954 piece for *Modern Screen* magazine titled "I Love Marilyn."

When she came onto the scene, Marilyn was more brazen and had a much higher public profile than the women who had preceded her. Although it is perhaps an exaggeration to say that Marilyn single-handedly pushed back the barriers of prudish fifties America, she certainly had a leading role in the process.

The image of voluptuous womanhood and childish innocence which she embodied was unique. Despite the outrage of puritanical groups and self-appointed upholders of public decency, Marilyn survived the kind of scandal which could quite easily have made her box office poison. She not only survived the scandal of posing nude, but somehow turned it into a publicity coup as she let the world know she was just a poor girl trying to get ahead, in the best tradition of the American Dream.

Biographer DONALD SPOTO puts it very well when he describes Marilyn as "the postwar ideal of the American girl, soft, transparently needy, worshipful of men, naïve, offering sex without demands. . . . But there was also something quietly aggressive in her self-presentation as a frankly carnal creature."

She was the most popular female actress

of her day, vastly eclipsing AUDREY HEPBURN and GRACE KELLY. She was also the last in a line of voluptuous woman ideals. After Marilyn came the sixties, the age of the waif and Twiggy, paving the way for much thinner ideals of female beauty.

## SEX LIFE

MARILYN:
"You can't sleep your way into being a star, though. It takes much, much more. But it helps. A lot of actresses get their first chance that way."

"No sex is wrong if there is love in it. But too often people act like it's gymnasium work, mechanical."

"I'm a failure as a woman. My men expect so much of me because of the image they've made of me and that I've made of myself, as a sex symbol. Men expect so much, and I can't live up to it. They expect bells to ring and whistles to whistle, but my anatomy is the same as any other woman's. I can't live up to it."

"The most unsatisfactory men are those who pride themselves on their virility and regard sex as if it were some form of athletics at which you win cups. It is a woman's spirit and mood a man has to stimulate in order to make sex interesting. The real lover is the man who can thrill you just by touching your head or smiling into your eyes or by just staring into space."

JEAN NEGULESCO, directing Marilyn in *How to Marry a Millionaire*:
"Marilyn, don't try to sell this sex thing, you are sex. . . . You are the institution of sex. The only motivation you need for this part is the fact that in the movie you are as blind as a bat without glasses."

NORMAN ROSTEN:
"With Marilyn, you're not talking about going to bed with a woman; you're talking about going to bed with an institution. Who can handle that? And how awful to be one!"

NUNNALLY JOHNSON:
"Copulation was, I'm sure, Marilyn's uncomplicated way of saying 'Thank You.'"

HENRY ROSENFELD:
"Marilyn thought sex got you closer. She told me that she hardly ever had an orgasm, but she was very unselfish. She tried above all to please the opposite sex."

PAULINE KAEL:
"Her mixture of wide-eyed wonder and cuddly drugged sexiness seemed to get to just about every male; she turned on even homosexual men."

One of the many ways in which Marilyn was ahead of her time, pushing back the boundaries of what was acceptable, was her frank acceptance of her BODY and of the pleasures of sex. "Sex is a part of nature," she said, "and I go along with nature." Aside from a few rare exceptions (*see* MEN), if she wanted to go to bed with a man, she went to bed with him. And of course, many men in positions of power made it quite clear what was required of her.

The whys and wherefores of Marilyn's sexual initiation most probably lie obscured in a number of accounts of early abuse. Many biographers have cast doubt on whether some, or perhaps any, of these incidents actually took place. There were times in Marilyn's life when she invented or embroidered stories to elicit sympathy from people important to her, but that doesn't necessarily mean that she did not suffer some kind of sexual abuse as a child. Indeed, some commentators claim that her adult patterns of behavior, particularly her craving for affection and inability to remain in long-term relationships, in some ways reflected early abuse.

The three most commonly reported incidents of abuse took place when Norma Jeane was eight and eleven (*The Unabridged Marilyn*, by Riese and Hitchens, however, lists no less than nine claimed incidents before the age of twelve). When she was eight, a boarder at an unnamed foster home beckoned her into his room where he kissed and molested her. When she ran out to tell her foster mother what had happened, she received a slap on the cheek and was admonished not to make up stories. When she was eleven, ERWIN "DOC" GODDARD drunkenly fondled her; also when she was eleven, a cousin molested her (*see* IDA MARTIN). In some tellings, these incidents are described as rape, and in the most extreme versions, resulted in her giving birth to a child.

Marilyn told photographer PHILIPPE HALSMAN that she first had sex at the age of seven. To his follow up question of how old the man was, she joked "younger." She also told at least one person that her first sexual experience was a brutal rape when she was nine, and that she had sex every day from the age of eleven. Marilyn later admitted inventing this story to elicit sympathy from MGM head of talent LUCILLE RYMAN. Whether true or not, the story did its job, as for the next year Ryman and husband JOHN CARROLL looked after her.

Norma Jeane first married at sixteen. Husband JAMES DOUGHERTY has stated that she was a virgin when they married, and respected biographers write that before her marriage she was extremely naïve about the mechanics of sex. DONALD SPOTO writes that her knowledge was circumscribed to schoolyard hearsay and a book that foster mother ANA LOWER loaned her, *What Every Young Lady Should Know About Marriage*—a chaste tome that managed to avoid completely topics involving bodily functions. Apparently just weeks before her marriage to Dougherty, Norma Jeane asked her legal guardian GRACE McKEE GODDARD and her mother-in-law-to-be Ethel Dougherty if she could marry the boy but not have sex.

Many of the PHOTOGRAPHERS with whom she went off on extended shoots in her early years later claimed that they had sex with Marilyn. Some of them undoubtedly did: ANDRÉ DE DIENES described her lovemaking as "playful and provocative, energetic and eager."

In her early MODELING days, Norma Jeane led a busy social life. Many of the assignments required her to be decorative and, perhaps, sexually available. It has been reported that she admitted, "When I started modeling, it was like part of the job... and if you didn't go along, there were twenty-five girls who would." Accounts of how Marilyn achieved her initial break into movies, her "discovery" by TWENTIETH CENTURY-FOX talent scout BEN LYON, include suggestions that sexual favors played a part.

Another disputed incident of molestation took place in early 1947, when Marilyn was house-sitting a property on SOUTH AVON STREET in Burbank. As Marilyn told the story, she awoke one night to discover a man climbing in through the bedroom window. She fled to a neighbor's house, called the police, and the intruder was either caught or slipped away in time, depending on which biographer is recounting the story. According to Marilyn, the intruder was an off-duty policeman whom earlier that day she had asked to help her cash her final paycheck from Fox. He had asked for her name and telephone number, cashed the check, and brought her the money. However, some biographers consider this to be another fictional incident Marilyn used to earn sympathy.

Many biographers assert that in the spell after her initial year-long contract with Fox, Marilyn supplemented her meager income with PROSTITUTION. It has also been claimed that at that time she worked as a stripper in Sunset Strip parlors, under the name "Mona Monroe."

What is certain is that like thousands of actresses past and present, Marilyn had to contend with the notorious casting couch. Some biographies quote her as saying, "They weren't shooting all those sexy movies just to sell peanut butter. They wanted to sample the merchandise. If you didn't go along, there were twenty-five girls who would." This quote has also appeared in relation to modeling (see above). She also is quoted as telling friend AMY GREENE, "I spent a great deal of time on my knees."

Biographer ANTHONY SUMMERS writes that Marilyn told journalist Jaik Rosenstein:

> "You know that when a producer calls an actress into his office to discuss a script that isn't all he has in mind. And a part in a picture, or any kind of a little stock contract is the most important thing in the world to the girl, more than eating. She can go hungry, and she might have to sleep in her car, but she doesn't mind that a bit—if she can only get the part. I know, because I've done both, lots of times. And I slept with producers. I'd be a liar if I said I didn't."

Many, many men, and a few women, have publicly added themselves to the list of Marilyn's LOVERS. Marilyn reputedly told maid LENA PEPITONE, "I'd let any guy, or girl, do what they wanted if I thought they were my friend." Even by today's standards, Marilyn would be regarded as sexually promiscuous. If all the allegations were to be believed, she would have had as many as a dozen abortions (*see* MEDICAL HISTORY) and hundreds of lovers. She also had affairs when she was married to JOE DIMAGGIO and ARTHUR MILLER. Perhaps, as one of Marilyn's psychiatrists postulated, she "found it difficult to sustain a series of orgasms with the same individual," hence the affairs she had even when she was in a positive, supportive relationship.

Marilyn apparently told a number of men that they had been the first to give her real sexual pleasure—a sign that she really liked them. It has been said that she considered DiMaggio her greatest lover.

### HOMOSEXUALITY

During her lifetime Marillyn had many gay friends: She felt a sense of protection and affinity for Montgomery Clift, admiration for Truman Capote,

*Previous page*: Eve Arnold took this photograph of Marilyn in the marshlands of Mount Sinai, Long Island in 1952.

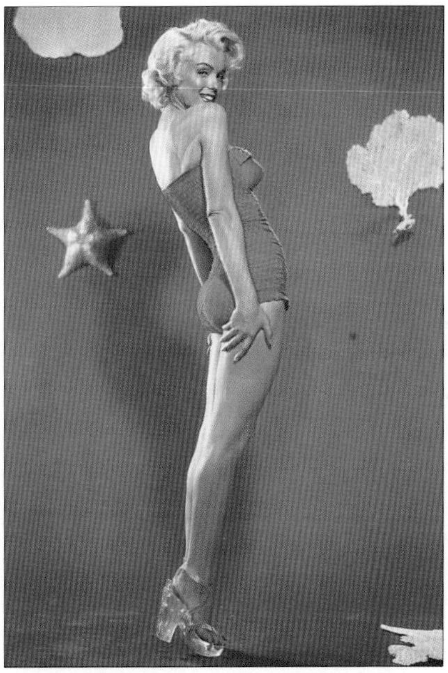

The famous clear plastic platform sandals Marilyn was fond of wearing with different colored ribbons.

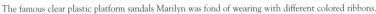

Marilyn's "strappy" sandals in *Niagara* (1953).

and friendship with and trust in her personal masseur Ralph Roberts. Gay director George Cukor, known for his sympathetic portrayal of women, featured on her 1955 approved list of directors.

Not long before her death Marilyn talked to reporter W. J. Weatherby about the lesbian rumors surrounding her: "People tried to make me into a lesbian. I laughed. No sex is wrong if there's love in it." Rumors abounded that Marilyn had a sexual relationship with her drama coach Natasha Lytess—and so she may have done, seeking some warmth from a woman after so many disappointments with men. In some quarters it was claimed that these rumors were initially seeded by Joe DiMaggio, in an attempt to persuade Marilyn not to institute divorce proceedings against him.

In that same interview with Weatherby, Marilyn admitted that she felt different from other women: "They could feel things I couldn't. And when I started reading books I ran into the words "frigid," "rejected," and "lesbian." I wondered if I was all three of them. . . . There were times when I didn't feel human and times when all I could think of was dying. There was also the sinister fact that a well-made woman had always thrilled me to look at."

Biographer Fred Lawrence Guiles writes that Marilyn "always felt especially close to gays of either sex, and they to her. One's sexuality was God-given, she felt; she expressed this to many people and numerous times in her life."

And yet biographer Anthony Summers says that Marilyn's psychoanalyst, Dr. Ralph Greenson, once wrote that Marilyn "had an outright phobia of homosexuality, and yet unwittingly fell into situations which had homosexual coloring."

## SHAMROY, LEON (1901–1974)

A distinguished Hollywood CINEMATOGRAPHER who won four Academy Awards for *The Black Swan* (1942), *Wilson* (1944), *Leave Her to Heaven* (1946), and *Cleopatra* (1963), plus seventeen nominations.

Norma Jeane was recorded on film, in Technicolor, by Shamroy on the occasion of her first ever SCREEN TEST on July 19, 1946. Shamroy was there as a favor to BEN LYON, who was doing the test as a favor to HELEN AINSWORTH, who in turn was doing a favor for MODELING agent EMMELINE SNIVELY—though Norma Jeane's agent at the time, HARRY LIPTON, claims that is was he who set up this screen test. Shamroy immediately spotted Norma Jeane's great innate ability in front of the camera: "I got a cold chill. This girl had something I hadn't seen since silent pictures. She had a kind of fantastic beauty like Gloria Swanson, when a movie star had to look beautiful, and she's got sex on a piece of film like Jean Harlow." His rave review did much to convince TWENTIETH CENTURY-FOX to offer this unknown hopeful her first studio contract.

Shamroy and Marilyn worked together eight years later, in the film version of the musical *THERE'S NO BUSINESS LIKE SHOW BUSINESS* (1954).

## SHAW, SAM

PHOTOGRAPHER and friend of Marilyn's from 1951. In 1954 he was hired by Marilyn's agent and producer CHARLES FELDMAN to work for TWENTIETH CENTURY-FOX and document the making of *THE SEVEN YEAR ITCH* (1955). He is generally credited with the idea of an open shoot on location in New York for the famous billowing skirt scene.

When she moved to New York in the mid-fifties, Marilyn often socialized with Shaw and his wife. Shaw introduced Marilyn to NORMAN and HEDDA ROSTEN, who became lifelong friends.

It was Shaw who, after visiting Marilyn in the hospital in late summer 1957, advised ARTHUR MILLER to convert a short story *THE MISFITS* into a full-length film specifically for Marilyn. He convinced Miller that this would be an ideal vehicle to showcase Marilyn's talent as a serious dramatic actress. Before this, he had turned down all offers to write screenplays.

BOOKS:

*Marilyn Monroe As the Girl: The Making of the Seven Year Itch*, Sam Shaw. New York: Ballantine, 1955.

*The Joy of Marilyn in the Camera Eye*, Sam Shaw. City: Exeter Books, 1979.

*Marilyn Among Friends*, Sam Shaw and Norman Rosten. New York: Henry Holt, 1987.

## SHERRY-NETHERLAND HOTEL

781 FIFTH AVENUE, NEW YORK

Marilyn stayed at this HOTEL on a stopover during her summer 1949 publicity tour for her film *LOVE HAPPY* (1950). This was Marilyn's first experience with the media circus accompanying the promotion of a movie. She stayed on the fifteenth floor, and reputedly delighted in watching the crowds milling below.

She returned to the Sherry-Netherland three years later for another publicity tour, this time to coincide with the release of *MONKEY BUSINESS* (1952).

## *THE SHOCKING MISS PILGRIM* (1947)

Some biographers list this as Marilyn's first screen appearance, with a walk-on part as a switchboard operator; however, there is no evidence that this is the case.

*The Shocking Miss Pilgrim* was a TWENTIETH CENTURY-FOX comedy, with songs by George and Ira Gershwin, about a nineteenth-century Boston stenographer, played by BETTY GRABLE, who makes a stand for women's rights.

(*see* FILMS)

## SHOES

Trademark Marilyn footwear was high-heeled clear plastic platform sandals which she would tie with different colored ribbons to match her outfits. There were red ribbons for publicity stills, white ones for her two-piece swimsuit at home, and red on screen in the 1953 movie *HOW TO MARRY A MILLIONAIRE*.

Arthur Miller and Marilyn photographed by Sam Shaw
in Amagansett, Long Island, 1958.

Another firm dress favorite was simple leather sandals, the more straps the better, so that her feet looked as bare as possible. When she felt like going casual, Marilyn often went for flats.

Ferragamo was her favorite shoemaker; over the years she commissioned him to make her dozens of pairs.

## SHOPPING

Growing up in the poverty years of the Depression did not make Marilyn a frugal spender. As soon as she began to earn MONEY from MODELING, she spent what she had left after paying rent on clothes; then, when she began to land a regular salary through film contracts, first with TWENTIETH CENTURY-FOX, then with COLUMBIA STUDIOS, she splurged on a Ford convertible, a professional hair dryer, BOOKS, a phonograph and records, plus plenty of cosmetics. She also indulged her GENEROSITY on people who had helped her or were important in her life.

Once she became famous, Marilyn's patronage was a source of pride to stores, though she did occasionally upset other shoppers and staff with her lack of UNDERWEAR, which became apparent when she tried on garments.

### MARILYN'S FAVORITE STORES

ELIZABETH ARDEN
691 5th Avenue, New York
Marilyn frequented this beauty shop in 1955; photographs by Ed Feingersh document her visit.

BLOOMINGDALE'S
1000 Third Avenue, New York
A favorite New York store for Marilyn. In 1983 the department store brought out their own line of "Marilyn" label garments.

BONWIT TELLER
4-10 East 57th Street, New York
A convenient place for Marilyn to buy clothes, not far from her New York apartment. Since converted to Galleries Lafayette.

BULLOCK'S
Beverly Hills
Teenage housewife Norma Jeane Dougherty went on shopping sprees at Bullock's department store.

FARMER'S MARKET
6333 West Third Street, Hollywood
Marilyn was photographed here as the newly elected "Miss Cheesecake" by *Stars and Stripes* magazine. The birthday cake for Marilyn's last birthday was ordered from here by fellow workers on *Something's Got to Give*.

HARROD'S
Knightsbridge, London
While in London, working on *The Prince and the Showgirl*, Marilyn went to Harrod's to buy gifts for her stepchildren. Such was the crush of admiring fans around her that the police had to be called to restore order.

I MAGNIN
9634 Rodeo Drive, Beverly Hills, and
3050 Wilshire Blvd, Los Angeles
Starlet Monroe spent some of her first earnings on clothes at this store. She came here many times over the years.

JAX
Wilshire Boulevard, Los Angeles,
now at 324 North Rodeo Drive, Beverly Hills, and
West 57th Street, New York
A favorite clothing store for Marilyn; slacks she bought there in 1962 appear in the Bert Stern photo session.

MARIAN HUNTER'S BOOKSHOP
352 North Camden Drive, Beverly Hills
The first charge account Marilyn ever opened was at this bookshop.

MARKS & SPENCER
Marble Arch, London
Marilyn shopped here in 1956—in private, after other customers had left.

MARTHA
475 Park Avenue, New York
Fashionable clothing shop favored by Marilyn.

MAY COMPANY
620 Seventh Street, Los Angeles
Armed with $75, Marilyn purchased some new outfits for her 1950 trip to New York. Unfortunately the three wool suits she bought were unwearable in the East Coast heatwave.

SAK'S FIFTH AVENUE
9600 Rodeo Drive, Beverly Hills, and
611 5th Avenue, New York
Benefactor Johnny Hyde introduced Marilyn to this store. Marilyn was a regular customer in both Los Angeles and New York.

TIFFANY AND COMPANY
727 5th Avenue, New York
Perhaps the world's most famous jewelry store inevitably attracted the world's most famousstar. Sam Shaw photographed Marilyn outside the store.

In her last home, Marilyn bought her food either at the Brentwood Mart on San Vicente Boulevard or at Jurgensen's in Beverly Hills. She also ordered food from Briggs delicatessen on San Vicente Boulevard, where she had a charge account. She filled her prescriptions, including the one for the pharmaceuticals which killed her, at the local Vicente Pharmacy (12025 San Vicente Boulevard).

## SIEGEL, SOL C. (1903–1982)

TWENTIETH CENTURY-FOX producer who worked with Marilyn on three of her hits, *MONKEY BUSINESS* (1952), *GENTLEMEN PREFER BLONDES* (1953) and *THERE'S NO BUSINESS LIKE SHOW BUSINESS* (1954).

## SIGNORET, SIMONE
(1921–1985, B. SIMONE KAMINKER)

MARILYN:
"Simone's too old for him. She's Arthur's type."

SIMONE SIGNORET:
"If Marilyn is in love with my husband, it proves she has good taste. I am in love with him too."

For four months during shooting of *LET'S MAKE LOVE* (1960), two married couples occupied adjacent bungalows at the BEVERLY HILLS HOTEL: Simone and YVES MONTAND, and Marilyn and ARTHUR MILLER.

Though Signoret and Montand were actually born respectively in Germany and Italy, they were France's highest profile acting couple, the French equivalent of England's LAURENCE OLIVIER and VIVIEN LEIGH. Her pedigree was impeccable, having started her film career in France during the war years, when she was forced to work illegally because her father was Jewish, before progressing to lead roles in the early fifties. Quite a beauty in her youth, many film critics note that she did nothing to fight the aging process. Her most acclaimed performances were in *Dédée d'Anvers* (1948), *Les Diaboliques* (1954), *Room at the Top* (1958), for which she won an Oscar, *Ship of Fools* (1965) and *Madame Rosa* (1978). She was also a staunch supporter of human rights issues and left-wing

Simone Signoret, Marilyn, and Yves Montand at the Twentieth Century-Fox cocktail party to introduce Marilyn's new leading man in *Let's Make Love*, 1960.

political causes, which was why the U.S. authorities originally refused her and her husband's visa applications in the mid-fifties.

Marilyn biographers are interested in Signoret for the way she reacted to the very public affair between her husband and her friend Marilyn. In her autobiography Signoret writes diplomatically of the good times they had together, not of the love affair between her husband and his leading lady.

Signoret states they were "two women who lived together as neighbors, as one does in any apartment house anywhere." She recalls how pleased Marilyn was to hear that Signoret's performance in *Room at the Top* had won an Oscar nomination, and records how Marilyn would eagerly bring her press clippings from the Hollywood press. Signoret and Marilyn spent hours chatting every evening, comparing stories about films they had done. Only once in four months did the foursome ever go out to a restaurant.

Whenever she publicly mentioned the affair between her husband and Marilyn, Signoret always rose above the level of scandal the press so gleefully maintained. She refused to judge "what may have happened during my weeks in Rome and Miller's weeks in New York between a man, my husband, and a woman, my pal, who were working together, living under the same roof, and consequently sharing their solitudes, their fears, their moods and their recollections of childhood poverty."

Signoret is categorical in her dismissal of much of the press hyperbole around the whole episode, questioning many of the quotes attributed to her husband. She says that Montand would never have said that Marilyn had a "schoolgirl crush" on him, for the simple reason that his English wasn't good enough.

In the end, for Signoret, her husband's dalliance was no reason "to confuse an affair with eternal love and make it a crisis in marriage." Many biographers comment that Montand had quite a reputation as a womanizer, and that Signoret never felt threatened by this.

For years Signoret treasured a champagne-colored silk scarf that Marilyn lent her one day when photographers were taking pictures of her; the accessory went so well with her outfit that in a characteristically spontaneous gesture of GENEROSITY Marilyn made a gift of it.

Montand and Signoret remained married until her death in 1985.

BOOK:

*Nostalgia Isn't What It Used to Be*, Simone Signoret. New York: Harper and Row, 1978.

## SINATRA, FRANK (1915–1998)

Frank Sinatra, considered by many to be the greatest all-round American entertainer of the century, made well over sixty movies, but "The Voice" was an even bigger singing star. His film performances include an Oscar for *From Here to Eternity* (1953), and critically acclaimed outings in many more such as *The Man with The Golden Arm* (1956), *Guys and Dolls* (1956), *High Society* (1956), *Pal Joey* (1957), *The Manchurian Candidate* (1962), and *The Detective* (1968). Throughout this time he was one of the most successful recording artists—he was Marilyn's FAVORITE—and a frequent recipient of Grammy Awards.

Marilyn and Sinatra probably met in the early fifties through JOE DIMAGGIO, a great friend of Sinatra's, though many biographers state that they first met through TWENTIETH CENTURY-FOX in late 1953, when the studio was trying to persuade Marilyn to star opposite Sinatra in the *The Girl in Pink Tights*. This project, and the many subsequent movies Marilyn, Sinatra, and their representatives discussed, fell prey to bad timing. On this occasion, Marilyn was beginning to flex her independent muscles and turn down projects she felt were unsuitable.

Rumors of a romance between the two date back to late 1954, immediately after Marilyn decided to divorce DiMaggio. This was when Sinatra helped DiMaggio try to catch Marilyn with another man in the infamous "WRONG DOOR RAID" fiasco; not only did they fail to ambush Marilyn, but both men wound up in court being sued for damages. (DiMaggio and Sinatra had a falling out soon afterwards.) More rumors circulated in 1955, a year when both Marilyn and Sinatra were between long-term relationships.

After moving to New York in 1955, Marilyn celebrated the official announcement of her own production company, MARILYN MONROE PRODUCTIONS, by taking friends to watch Sinatra doing a set at the Copacabana Club.

After Marilyn had married ARTHUR MILLER and renegotiated with Fox, she was approached to work with Sinatra on a number of film projects, including *Some Came Running* (1958) and *Can-Can* (1960). These did not come to fruition, either because of poor timing or Marilyn's lack of interest in the subject matter. Sinatra cut short the next collaboration after failing to agree on terms with BILLY WILDER to play one of the male leads in *SOME LIKE IT HOT* (1959).

In 1961, when Marilyn moved back to Los Angeles from New York, she stayed briefly at Sinatra's home while he was away on tour in Europe. Once more, the word got out that they were more than just friends. Sinatra gave her a couple of gifts that year: a pair of emerald earrings which she wore to the GOLDEN GLOBE AWARDS, and then passed on to New York maid LENA PEPITONE, and, by most accounts, Marilyn's last PET, a poodle she named MAF.

Back in Los Angeles, Marilyn saw a lot of Sinatra and his pals, particularly PETER LAWFORD and his wife Patricia. On a number of occasions she traveled to LAS VEGAS to see Sinatra or DEAN MARTIN perform. They also discussed yet more possible film projects: a RAT PACK movie and a musical remake of the 1945 movie *A Tree Grows in Brooklyn*.

Many biographers, particularly those with a special interest in the circumstances of Marilyn's DEATH, have much to say about Sinatra's MAFIA connections and how, during the last years of Marilyn's life, he provided a conduit for gangsters keen on settling scores with the KENNEDYS. On one of her last weekends alive, it has been widely written that

Marilyn, Elizabeth Taylor, and Dean Martin attending a performance by Frank Sinatra at The Sands Hotel in Las Vegas, 1961.

Marilyn was with Sinatra at the CAL-NEVA LODGE, a gambling establishment half in California, half in Nevada, in which Sinatra reputedly had a stake. In the more scurrilous accounts, Sinatra kept her supplied with pills, prevented a SUICIDE ATTEMPT, or shared her with his mob pals.

Sinatra biographer J. Randy Taraborrelli repeats claims that Sinatra was considering marrying Monroe shortly before her death so that people would "back off and give her some space" to pull herself back together. This was also the opinion of Pepitone, who says that in mid-1961 Marilyn told her of her hopes of marrying Sinatra.

One friend of Sinatra's, producer Milton Ebbins, believed that he was far more serious about Marilyn then she was about him. However, at this time Sinatra was seeing actress Juliet Prowse, to whom he later became engaged. Conjecture about wedding plans appears to clash with claims made by other biographers that Marilyn was indeed planning a marriage, but to Joe DiMaggio for a second time, not Sinatra.

When Marilyn's body was discovered, Sinatra records were on her record turntable. Like all her Hollywood friends, Sinatra was barred from Marilyn's FUNERAL by DiMaggio.

## SISTERS

Marilyn had a half-sister, BERNIECE MIRACLE, who was seven years older than her, and with whom she became quite close in the last years of her life. Though they only met up on a few occasions, they were in contact by telephone relatively frequently.

Norma Jeane had something of a sisterly relationship with BEBE GODDARD and JODY LAWRANCE, step-daughters of her legal guardian GRACE MCKEE GODDARD.

Through marriage she acquired a number of sisters-in-law: Billie Dougherty Campbell, Joan Miller Copeland, Frances DiMaggio, Mamie DiMaggio, Marie DiMaggio, and Nellie DiMaggio.

Perhaps because she had no sisters of her own, Marilyn developed "older sister" relationships with Patricia Rosten, the daughter of friends NORMA AND HEDDA ROSTEN—and JOAN GREENSON, daughter of her psychiatrist Ralph.

## SITWELL, EDITH DAME (1887–1964)

"She knows the world, but this knowledge has not lowered her great and benevolent dignity, its darkness has not dimmed her goodness."

Marilyn met English poet, critic, and biographer Edith Sitwell in late 1954 at a Hollywood tea. Sitwell, one of Britain's best known poets and something of an eccentric, came from what is often referred to as the most famous literary family of her day.

The poet commented that with her blonde hair and her green dress, Marilyn looked like a daffodil, and there was instant friendship between the two women. Marilyn told Sitwell of her personal interest in POETRY, and they discussed Rudolph Steiner's *The Course of Life*, the BOOK Marilyn was reading at the time.

Sitwell invited Marilyn to visit if she should ever be in ENGLAND. Two years later she was, and Marilyn went to sip gin and grapefruit juice, and chat about poetry.

## SKOLSKY, SIDNEY (1905–1983)

"She was always seeking advice, Marilyn was wiser than she pretended to be. She was not the ordinary blond actress-starlet you could find at any major studio. . . . She appeared kind and soft and helpless. Almost everybody wanted to help her. Marilyn's supposed helplessness was her greatest strength."

For half a century the energetic Sidney Skolsky was one of Hollywood's leading reporters, writing syndicated columns and features for papers on the East and West Coasts and keeping his finger on Hollywood's pulse. His particular specialty was discovering young hopefuls, and there was a steady parade of unknown actors and actresses who tried to catch his attention at Schwab's Drugstore (see RESTAURANTS), where Skolsky maintained an office on the mezzanine. Marilyn was just one such actress; in the late forties she caught his eye, made friends, and was, for a spell, one of the eager people who drove Skolsky around town, as many years before MARLENE DIETRICH had done.

Marilyn couldn't have chosen a more shrewd ally. He became one of her staunchest supporters and most reliable PRESS confederates, and she often called him up for advice, not only about publicity but even clothes and the image she should strive for. Skolsky, who had known JEAN HARLOW, saw enough resemblance between Marilyn and her childhood

Sidney Skolsky interviewing Marilyn in her apartment in 1954 for a piece for *Modern Screen* magazine titled "I Love Marilyn."

HERO to declare as early as 1952, "I think she's going to be one of the most popular actresses the movies have ever known."

Not only did Skolsky help to talk up her career when she was just starting out, he is generally credited with persuading producer JERRY WALD to give Marilyn a role in CLASH BY NIGHT (1952). On numerous occasions he ghost-wrote press releases to help her out of sticky situations, like the nude CALENDAR scandal and the discovery that her mother was alive, when her studio had always claimed she was an orphan. In 1954 he wrote the second biography ever published about Marilyn. As he had done for Lana Turner, whom he dubbed "The Sweater Girl," he came up with a sobriquet for Marilyn, "The Girl with the Horizontal Walk" (though some sources attribute this nickname to EARL WILSON). From 1952 to 1954, the years she was with JOE DIMAGGIO, Skolsky often escorted Marilyn to glitzy showbiz events—DiMaggio notoriously loathed being publicly reminded that his future wife was the country's leading sex symbol. These events included the 1952 PHOTOPLAY magazine awards, when Marilyn's attire caused such scandal; SHEILAH GRAHAM's wedding; and the party thrown for the visiting King and Queen of Greece.

Marilyn confided her innermost secrets to Skolsky, certain that he would not abuse her trust. Almost immediately after returning to Los Angeles from her HONEYMOON with DiMaggio, she cryptically told him that one day she would marry ARTHUR MILLER. Years later, she told Skolsky of her affair with President KENNEDY (but not, it seems, with the Attorney General ROBERT KENNEDY).

There was, however, a less salubrious side to Skolsky. Like Marilyn, he periodically suffered depression. According to DONALD SPOTO, they were confederates in pill abuse, and Skolsky, who worked out of a drugstore, had almost unlimited access to supplies.

As well as his day job as a reporter, Skolsky also produced two bio-pic movies—*The Jolson Story* (1946) and *The Eddie Cantor Story* (1953). For over a decade he and Marilyn had plans for another picture called *The Jean Harlow Story*, which was to star Marilyn herself. Indeed, the day Marilyn was found dead, Skolsky had an appointment to meet her for advanced-stage discussions. One month earlier the two of them had visited Harlow's mother, and, importantly, obtained her blessing to make the movie.

BOOKS:

*Marilyn*, Sidney Skolsky. New York: Dell Publishing, 1954.

*Don't Get Me Wrong—I Love Hollywood*, Sidney Skolsky. New York: Putnam, 1975.

## SKOURAS, SPYROS (1893–1971)

ARTHUR MILLER:
"By turns she resented him, hated him, and spoke of him warmly as a friend of last resort at the studio . . . she could still be moved by his repeated reassurances, often accompanied by actual tears, that she was closer to him than even his own adored daughter. At the same time she was sure it was his obduracy that denied her recognition as the number one Fox draw."

For the entire length of Marilyn's career, Spyros Skouras was president of TWENTIETH CENTURY-FOX. When Marilyn first arrived at the studio, it was not so much Skouras as DARRYL F. ZANUCK whom she had to impress. When Zanuck wanted to show Skouras an early Marilyn performance, Skouras waved him away, saying he was too busy with money to worry about bit players.

By 1951, when the studio had re-signed her, Skouras still couldn't tell Marilyn apart from the many starlets the studio had on its roster. This all changed at the studio exhibitors' party early that year. Skouras noticed the buzz around Marilyn and invited her to sit with him at the top table. Immediately afterward, Marilyn's six-month contract was converted into a seven-year deal, and the studio, keen to please the exhibitors, found parts for her in every possible movie.

Once famously described as a man who "always meant what he said while he was saying it," it was Skouras's job to protect the studio's image when he felt it was under threat. One such occasion arose in 1956, as Marilyn's partner ARTHUR MILLER was being called to testify before the HOUSE UN-AMERICAN ACTIVITIES COMMITTEE. The day before the hearing, Skouras flew to New York in an attempt to persuade Miller to cooperate with the committee. The deal he attempted to broker was that Miller name names in exchange for a closed session hearing, Skouras firmly believed that Marilyn's career would be finished if Miller was branded a communist. Marilyn's response was pride in Miller's integrity, and they married a few weeks later.

Skouras's lengthy tenure at the head of Fox came to an end within a month of the studio decision to dismiss Marilyn from her last, uncompleted movie, SOMETHING'S GOT TO GIVE—due mostly to the crippling cost overruns on the ELIZABETH TAYLOR vehicle *Cleopatra* (1963) and the studio's generally poor performance in the preceding years.

BOOK:

*Skouras, King of Fox Studios*, Carlo Curti. Los Angeles: Holloway House, 1967.

One-third of this book is a rather salacious biography of Marilyn.

## SLATZER, ROBERT (B. 1927)

"There was something magic about her, different from the other girls the talent men at the studios would fix you up with. I think I can say I loved her from the first time I saw her."

There is no middle ground for Robert Slatzer: he is either Marilyn's most stalwart defender and indefatigable seeker of the truth, or he is one of the most successful proponents of CONSPIRACY theories and unsubstantiated claims.

In his 1974 book *The Life and Curious Death of Marilyn Monroe*, Slatzer describes how, as a young reporter, he first met model and aspiring starlet Norma Jeane in the lobby of TWENTIETH CENTURY-FOX. He was reading a poetry book, waiting to be called to conduct an interview, when Marilyn came in carrying her portfolio: "She caught her heel or something and the pictures fell all over the floor. I went to her rescue, and I'm glad to say there was only one place for her to sit down and wait—next to me. She said she was really interested in poetry, and I said I might be able to write a story about her." They went out on a date that very evening, to Malibu. After dinner they walked on the beach, and ended up skinny dipping. "I was embarrassed, yet we made love on the beach that first night." Slatzer says that their romance continued for the next six years, and that until her dying day he was in close contact with Marilyn, and party to her innermost secrets.

Biographer ANTHONY SUMMERS, who has stated his beliefs in Slatzer's claim of a relationship with Marilyn, cites the first public reference to Slatzer in DOROTHY KILGALLEN's column in the *New York Journal-American* on August 28, 1952: "A dark horse in the Marilyn Monroe romance derby is Bob Slatzer, former Columbus, Ohio literary critic. He's been wooing her by phone and mail, and improving Her Mind with gifts of the world's greatest books."

This was during the first flush of Marilyn's romance with JOE DIMAGGIO. Slatzer recounts one evening when both he and DiMaggio turned up outside her house—she wasn't in, so they both waited. She let them in, DiMaggio told Slatzer to leave, but then Marilyn threw both of them out. Slatzer later said she called to apologize, explaining that she had "got her schedules mixed up."

Slatzer says that he wooed Marilyn with companionship, drinking binges, and even Arab POETRY, giving her a copy of *The Rubaiat of Omar Khayyam*. It paid off, according to Slatzer, when on a drunken spree they sped off to Tijuana for the weekend October 3–6, 1952, and got married. They then danced the night away at the Foreign Club, a nightspot on Fourth and Constitution. In the sober light of day the next morning at the Rosarita Beach Hotel, Marilyn realized she had made a huge mistake when she heard DiMaggio's voice on the radio, commentating on the World Series. On their return to Los Angeles, Fox chief DARRYL ZANUCK summoned them both. In no uncertain terms he laid down the law: the studio had $2 million invested in Marilyn, and they weren't going to throw it all away on a reckless drunken marriage to a lowly scriptwriter. The next day, the newlyweds returned to Tijuana and bribed the lawyer who had married them to burn the marriage certificate.

Slatzer's critics, and they are many, say that Slatzer is simply a world-class fantasist, who turned a passing acquaintance with Marilyn during the shoot on NIAGARA (1953) into a lifetime career. The sole piece of hard evidence that Slatzer offers in *The Life and Curious Death of Marilyn Monroe* is a photograph of him and Marilyn against the backdrop of Niagara Falls, on which Marilyn's signature appears with an inscription, "To Bob, Luck & Love, Marilyn." DONALD SPOTO, who has provided the most compelling debunking of Slatzer's claims so far, notes that Marilyn wrote far more personal dedications to people who were important to her. It would have been quite possible for Slatzer to have taken the photographs and then sent them to her, care of the studio, requesting her to autograph them.

Slatzer's has claimed that throughout Marilyn's life he was party to her most intimate secrets. However, none of Marilyn's

Marilyn's smile radiated at a party to announce production of the film *Some Like It Hot*, 1958.

In 1955 Marilyn invited Eve Arnold to photograph her during her trip to the town of Bement, Illinois, where she was to inaugurate a museum in honor of Abraham Lincoln. Arnold was fascinated by the furor that surrounded Marilyn in the small town. Here she captured Marilyn in a short break from the festivities.

entourage—except ALLAN "WHITEY" SNYDER, who contributed a rather ambiguous quote to Slatzer's book that, "Bob and Marilyn's long relationship was an unusual one, a good one, one that I feel was good for both of them,"—has ever acknowledged that they knew him, and Slatzer's name did not appear in any of Marilyn's personal address books. Many of the insights given by Slatzer into Marilyn's CHARACTER could have been gleaned elsewhere, from people who knew Marilyn closely and published accounts of their time with her, such as NATASHA LYTESS and WILLIAM TRAVILLA. Though he became the most vociferous proponent of the Kennedy theory, Slatzer's claims about the involvement of the brothers in Marilyn's death had already appeared in NORMAN MAILER's fictionalized biography of Marilyn, been alluded to by biographer FRED LAWRENCE GUILES, and first surfaced in a 1964 pamphlet published by right-wing activist FRANK A. CAPELL.

Since the publication of his first book in 1974, Slatzer has remained at the forefront of the Marilyn inquest industry. He brought others in to help him with his "crusade," including private detective MILO SPERIGLIO, who has also written two books on the conspiracy surrounding Marilyn's death. Slatzer has also been involved in two television productions about Marilyn, both based on his books, as well as appearing frequently in Marilyn DOCUMENTARIES. In 1996 Slatzer and Speriglio held a press conference to explain a further reason why Marilyn had to be silenced: she was going to explain what the government knew about alien landings at Roswell.

BOOKS:

*The Life and Curious Death of Marilyn Monroe*, Robert F. Slatzer. New York: Pinnacle House, 1974.

*The Marilyn Files*, Robert Slatzer. New York: Shapolsky Books, 1992.

These books have spawned television programs. The first provided the background for 1991 TV movie *Marilyn and Me*, in which Slatzer makes a cameo appearance, and then the 1992 documentary *The Marilyn Files*.

## SLEEP

MARILYN:
"Nobody's really ever been able to tell me why I sleep so badly, but I know once I begin thinking, it's goodbye sleep. I used to think exercise helped—being in the country, fresh air, being with a man, sharing—but sometimes I can't sleep whatever I'm doing, unless I take some pills. And then it's only a drugged sleep. It's not the same as really sleeping."

Insomnia was the bane of Marilyn's life. According to DONALD SPOTO, her sleeping problems escalated in 1954, when she was not only following a heavy filming schedule but was in conflict with her studio, battling with new husband JOE DIMAGGIO, and secretly planning to quit the Hollywood system altogether and set up her own production company. Her habitual use of BARBITURATES began at this stage—though she had been taking DRUGS to counter her anxiety and fear of performance since at least 1950—and continued even when she had eliminated some of the pressure and moved to New York. From this point on, it was rare indeed for Marilyn to get to sleep without chemical help. The grogginess she felt the morning after was one of the reasons for her notorious LATENESS.

GLORIA STEINEM speculates that Marilyn's lifelong insomnia was perhaps in some way caused by the incident when her grandmother DELLA MAE HOGAN allegedly tried to smother her with a pillow when she was an infant.

In order to make sure that no light disturbed her troubled sleep, Marilyn hung heavy black felt or serge material over her bedroom windows. She did this in all her HOMES from the mid-fifties onward, at least as early as the house she shared with MILTON and AMY GREENE in Los Angeles during shooting of *BUS STOP* (1956). This heavy black material was one of the first things to go up in the FIFTH HELENA DRIVE home she bought for herself in 1962.

Marilyn slept very badly on her last night alive. She awoke in a bad mood the next day, and was a little sharp with publicist PAT NEWCOMB, who had stayed over at her house and slept soundly right through until midday.

## SMILE

Marilyn's trademark quivering smile was the product of EMMELINE SNIVELY's comment that Norma Jeane did not have "enough upper lip between the end of your nose and your mouth." The head of the BLUE BOOK MODELING AGENCY suggested that she "try smiling with your upper lip drawn down," advice Marilyn put to good use for the rest of her life.

## SMITH, JEAN KENNEDY

Found among Marilyn's papers after her DEATH was a thank-you note from Jean Smith, probably written after Joe Kennedy suffered a stroke in December 1961:

> Dear Marilyn—Mother asked me to write and thank you for your sweet note to Daddy—He really enjoyed it and you were very cute to send it—Understand that you and Bobby are the new item! We all think you should come with him when he comes back East! Again, thanks for the note—Love, Jean Smith.

This note has often been cited as proof of a romance between Marilyn and ROBERT KENNEDY, though the handwriting has never positively been identified as that of Jean Kennedy Smith.

## SMOKING

Marilyn was, it seems, an occasional smoker, despite the strict urgings of her FOSTER PARENTS, the BOLENDERS, who taught young Norma Jeane to say in her nightly prayers that she would never touch tobacco or alcohol.

The first time Marilyn was seen sporting a cigarette on screen was in *RIGHT CROSS* (1950), though in her very first SCREEN TEST she lit and put out a cigarette. She appeared on at least one magazine cover smoking a cigarette, and she is smoking in bed in the opening scene of *NIAGARA* (1953).

Very few of the thousands of photographs taken of Marilyn show her smoking; however, she appears with a cigarette in one of the stills from the shooting of *THE MISFITS* in 1960.

## SNIVELY, EMMELINE

"She looked a fright at first, but my, how she worked!"

"Girls ask me all the time how they can be like Marilyn Monroe, and I tell them, if they had one-tenth of the hard work and gumption that girl had, they'd be on their way."

English-born Emmeline Snively was the prim owner/manager of the BLUE BOOK MODELING AGENCY. Snively was in her late forties in 1945, the year that the agency took on a young hopeful named Norma Jeane after photographer DAVID CONOVER suggested she go for an interview.

Miss Snively immediately recognized the potential of this new arrival:

> She was a clean-cut, American, wholesome girl—too plump, but beautiful in a way. We tried to teach her how to pose, how to handle her body. She always tried to lower her smile because she smiled too high, and it made her nose look a little long. At first she knew nothing about carriage, posture, walking, sitting or posing. She started out with less than any girl I ever knew, but she worked the hardest. . . . She wanted to learn, wanted to be somebody, more than anybody I ever saw before in my life.

Snively was sufficiently impressed to sign Norma Jeane up for a course and start sending her out on jobs. She also persuaded Norma Jeane to have her HAIR dyed blonde to increase her work opportunities. Before too long, it became apparent that Norma Jeane was not prime fashion model material: "Her size twelve fitted the manufacturer's garments just fine, except in one place. They were always too tight across the front of the blouse. We advised her to give up fashion work and concentrate on photo modeling." This switch paid dividends, with dozens of MAGAZINE covers through 1946. That year, Snively put Norma Jeane in touch with her friend HELEN AINSWORTH, who ran the West Coast office of talent AGENTS National Concert Artists Corporation. Ainsworth is generally credited with obtaining for Norma Jeane her first SCREEN TEST at TWENTIETH CENTURY-FOX. In some accounts of how Norma Jeane landed her first studio contract, Snively plays a part by circulating a false story that a convalescent HOWARD HUGHES was interested in signing "Jean Norman," as Norma Jeane was known at the time.

Emmeline Snively caught up with her most famous alumnus in 1954, when Marilyn invited her to visit the set of *THERE'S NO BUSINESS LIKE SHOW BUSINESS*.

Very few of the many photographs taken of Marilyn show her smoking as does this image by Ted Baron, 1954.

## SNYDER, ALLAN "WHITEY"

"This is a little kid who wants to be with the other little kids sucking lollipops and watching the roller coaster, but she can't because they won't let her. She's frightened to death of the public who think she is so sexy. My God, if they only knew."

"She had the greatest inferiority complex of any person I ever knew."

As MARLENE DIETRICH once commented, "The relationship between the makeup man and the film actor is like accomplices in crime."

One of TWENTIETH CENTURY-FOX's top makeup artists, Whitey Snyder made up Marilyn the first time she ever stood before a proper film camera, for her SCREEN TEST in July 1946. Snyder immediately took her under his wing, initiating her in the techniques and secrets of movie makeup and BEAUTY tips: "I could see at once that she was terribly insecure, that despite her modeling she didn't think she was pretty. It took a lot of convincing for her to see the natural freshness and beauty she had, and how well she could be used in pictures."

Snyder worked as Marilyn's personal makeup man on the vast majority of her movies, though he was actually credited on very few. In the last years of her life, after Marilyn moved back to Los Angeles, he was on almost personal call to make her up for any public engagements she had. His wife, costumier MARJORIE PLECHER, was also part of Marilyn's close-knit entourage.

Early in their long friendship on and off the set, Marilyn jokingly asked Snyder to look after her makeup needs even after her death. To remind him, she gave him a gold Tiffany's money clip bearing the inscription, "Whitey Dear, While I'm still warm, Marilyn." Whitey carried out her request to the letter, but it took the best part of a bottle of gin for him to do so. He was later one of Marilyn's pallbearers at her FUNERAL.

## *SOME LIKE IT HOT* (1959)

(WORKING TITLE: *Not Tonight, Josephine!*)

Marilyn's most successful film was based on the German film *Fanfaren das Liebe* (1951) in which two musicians dress in drag to get work. BILLY WILDER and I. A. L. DIAMOND transposed the action to 1929 Chicago, and made jazz musicians Joe (TONY CURTIS) and Jerry (JACK LEMMON) unwitting witnesses to the Valentine's Day Massacre. The two men run for their lives by dressing up as "Josephine" and "Daphne," members of an all-female band heading for Florida. They befriend Sugar Kane, the band's singer, and for Joe it means love. The result is a fast-paced cross-dressing comedy, where parody and slapstick traverse gender lines.

Wilder sent a short synopsis of this movie to Marilyn in late 1957. Having broken off her collaboration with MILTON GREENE in MARILYN MONROE PRODUCTIONS, she was looking for something to do, and the script piqued her interest. Wilder was reputedly surprised that Marilyn wanted to play a role which was only peripheral to the main action; it has been said that Marilyn did indeed have reservations about playing another dumb blonde, and a supporting one at that, but ARTHUR MILLER persuaded her that this was a sure-fire winner, and she needed a success after the less than warm critical reception of *THE PRINCE AND THE SHOWGIRL* (1957).

Initially, Marilyn was expecting to work with FRANK SINATRA, whom Wilder had contacted about playing the Curtis role. Apparently Wilder had a change of heart after Sinatra failed to turn up for a lunch date. With Marilyn on board, there was no need for such a high-profile (and expensive) name. As Wilder said about Marilyn's role, "It's the weakest part, so the trick was to give it the strongest casting." Marilyn was to be paid $100,000 plus 10 percent of profits—though in some reports her initial fee was as high as $300,000.

Marilyn reported for her first day of work on August 4, 1958, accompanied by Miller, PAULA STRASBERG, and her personal makeup man and hairdresser. She was surprised and dismayed to learn that the film was not going to be made in Technicolor, as written into her contract with Fox. The reason, Billy Wilder explained, was that the makeup of the male stars would look clownish. Color costume tests were shown to Marilyn, proving that Curtis and Lemmon's faces under their thick makeup took on a greenish tinge.

The signs were not good from the start. In one version of events, Marilyn saw the rushes and refused to do any more work until they sorted things out: "I'm not going back into that film until Wilder reshoots my opening. When Marilyn Monroe comes into a room, nobody's going to be looking at Tony Curtis playing Joan Crawford. They're going to be looking at Marilyn Monroe." Her suggestion, the train sending out a puff of steam as she clips along a railway platform on high heels, was one of her most impressive entrances. However, in Wilder's recollections it was he and co-writer Diamond who came up with this new opening.

Wilder's experience of working with Marilyn surpassed his worst nightmares. He later commented, "I knew we were in mid-flight, and there was a nut on the plane." Marilyn was hours late, constantly forgetting her lines, and practically every scene required multiple retakes—either because of some missed word, or because, perfectionist that she was, she thought she could do the scene better. Then, if she became upset after what she thought

A publicity shot of make-up man Whitey Snyder doing Marilyn's face for *River of No Return*, 1953.

was a poor performance, she would cry and her makeup had to be redone. Marilyn was apparently so engrossed in how she wanted to play each scene, so focused on the metaphors Strasberg supplied her with to help her understand the underlying feelings, that she undermined Wilder's authority on set.

Sometimes Marilyn arrived without knowing her lines, or, because of the drugs she had taken to get some SLEEP, unable to remember them. The words had to be taped on props or written on cue cards. Later, Wilder recalled, "This stretched out to three days something we could have completed in an hour." Examples were forty-seven takes for Marilyn to correctly say "It's me, Sugar," and fifty-nine takes for her to say "Where's the bourbon?" despite Wilder pasting the words into every one of the drawers she was looking through in the scene (the number of takes does vary in different tellings). Marilyn fortified herself between takes by drinking from a thermos an assistant kept filled for her. Sometimes it contained coffee; sometimes it had vermouth; sometimes it was filled with a mixture of the two.

Tony Curtis became famously exasperated by Marilyn's antics. He made his "Kissing Marilyn Monroe was like kissing Hitler" comment after multiple takes of his kissing scene with Marilyn.

With a month of shooting still to go, Marilyn found out that at last, she had become pregnant again. The black dress Marilyn wore in the movie in the "Are my seams straight?" scene—on display at the Museum of the Moving Image in London—had to be specially altered to accommodate the beginnings of a pregnant bulge. Marilyn lost the baby a month after the wrap date of November 6, 1958. She was devastated. In the meantime, Wilder had said some very unkind things about Marilyn. Arthur Miller and Wilder exchanged angry telegrams: Miller accused Wilder of overworking his wife even though he knew she was pregnant; Wilder listed the insults and humiliations he felt he had suffered from Marilyn on set, while expressing his sorrow at Marilyn's loss.

The movie premiered at Lowe's Capitol Theater, New York, on March 29, 1959. The Strasbergs held the premiere party at their own apartment; Marilyn was described as "like cotton candy," an ephemeral vision in white. Wilder had not invited Marilyn to the wrap party on completion of shooting.

Whether or not this was Marilyn's best movie—many Marilyn fans believe it is—it was certainly her most successful, and continues to be shown regularly more than four decades after it was made. *Some Like It Hot* outgrossed all other films in the first six months of 1959, and for many years established the box-office record for any comedy.

Halfway through shooting, Marilyn confided in a friend that the role of Sugar Kane was, she feared, exactly the sort of thing that had persuaded her to turn her back on Hollywood in 1954. In a note to another friend, she wrote, "I have a feeling this ship is never going to dock. We are going through the Straits of Dire, it's rough and choppy." She herself felt that her latitude was severely limited in the role, as her task was principally to play the "straight man" for her cross-dressing co-stars. This was not the view of the Hollywood foreign press, who awarded her a GOLDEN GLOBE.

In 1974 a stage musical version was produced, called *Sugar* starring Robert Morse and Ruddy Vallee.

A French poster for *Some Like It Hot* (1959).

MEMORABLE LINES:
Sugar Kane: "It's the story of my life. I always get the fuzzy end of the lollipop."

However, this cannot compete with the finest line in the whole movie, the last, after Jerry/Daphne finally tells suitor Osgood that he's a man—OSGOOD: "Well, nobody's perfect."

MEMORABLE COSTUME:
Feather fringed black dress with deep-V décolleté.

**Tagline:**
"The movie too HOT for words!"

**Awards:**
ACADEMY AWARDS:
Best Costume Design, Black and White: Orry-Kelly

GOLDEN GLOBES:
Best Motion Picture—Comedy
Best Motion Picture Actor—Musical/Comedy: Jack Lemmon
Best Motion Picture Actress—Musical/Comedy: Marilyn Monroe

BRITISH ACADEMY AWARDS:
Best Foreign Actor: Jack Lemmon

**Nominations:**
ACADEMY AWARDS
Best Actor: Jack Lemmon
Best Art Direction-Set Decoration, Black and White: Edward G. Boyle, Ted Haworth
Best Cinematography, Black and White: Charles Lang
Best Director: Billy Wilder
Best Writing, Adapted Screenplay: I. A. L. Diamond, Billy Wilder

BRITISH ACADEMY AWARDS
Best Film from any Source: Billy Wilder

**Credits:**
United Artists, Mirisch Company and Ashton Productions, Black and White
Length: 122 minutes
Release date: March 29, 1959
Directed by: Billy Wilder
Produced by: Billy Wilder, I. A. L. Diamond (associate), Doane Harrison (associate)
Written by: I. A. L. Diamond, Billy Wilder, M. Logan (story), Robert Thoeren (story)
Cinematography by: Charles Lang
Music by: Adolph Deutsch
Production Design by: Ted Haworth
Costume Design by: Orry-Kelly
Film Editing by: Arthur P. Schmidt

**Cast (credits order):**
Marilyn Monroe . . . Sugar Kane
Tony Curtis . . . Joe / Josephine
Jack Lemmon . . . Jerry / Daphne
George Raft . . . Spats Colombo
Pat O'Brien . . . Mulligan
Joe E. Brown . . . Osgood Fielding III
Nehemiah Persoff . . . Bonaparte
Joan Shawlee . . . Sweet Sue
Billy Gray . . . Sig Poliakoff
George E. Stone . . . Toothpick
Dave Barry . . . Beinstock
Mike Mazurki . . . Henchman
Harry Wilson . . . Henchman
Beverly Wills . . . Dolores
Barbara Drew . . . Nellie
Edward G. Robinson Jr. . . . Paradise
Marian Collier . . . Olga
Helen Perry . . . Rosella

**Crew:**
Edward G. Boyle . . . set decorator
Agnes Flanagan . . . hairstyles
John Franco . . . script supervisor
Ted Haworth . . . art director
Bert Henrikson . . . wardrobe
Emile LaVigne . . . makeup
Fred Lau . . . sound
Matty Malneck . . . song supervisor
Alice Monte . . . hair styles
Sam Nelson . . . assistant director
Eve Newman . . . music editor
Tom Plews . . . property
Milt Rice . . . special effects
Allen K. Wood . . . production manager

**Plot:**
Two musicians, Joe (Tony Curtis) and Jerry (Jack Lemmon) are unfortunate enough to be in a garage in 1929 Chicago just as Spats Colombo (George Raft) massacres a rival gang on Valentine's Day. The arrival of the police allows them to escape, and from that

Marilyn sings "Running Wild" as she does a Pullman-aisle "Charleston and Shimmy" in *Some Like It Hot* (1959).

moment they are on the run. The only way they can save their skins is to dress up in women's clothes and land a job in Florida as part of an all-girl orchestra. Joe is transformed into Josephine, and Jerry becomes Daphne.

The train trip down to Florida is just one temptation after another for the boys, especially for Joe, who falls in love with ukulele-strumming singer Sugar (Marilyn Monroe), who has a soft spot for saxophone players and gin.

In sunny Florida Jerry/Daphne catches the eye of millionaire Osgood Fielding (Joe E. Brown). This provides the perfect cover for Joe: while Jerry keeps Osgood occupied on shore, Joe can impress Sugar with Osgood's yacht, moored in the harbor. He becomes an oil baron, complete with Cary Grant accent, and tempts Sugar back to the waiting yacht by claiming he has a condition that prevents him from getting excited about women. This, for Sugar, is a challenge to which she cannot fail to rise.

Disaster strikes when Spats and his gang arrive in Florida for their annual gangster's convention. Joe and Jerry's hard-won cover is blown, and once again they find they are in the wrong place at the wrong time: under a table as a huge cake reveals not dancing girls at a gunman who sprays Spats and his henchmen with machine-gun fire. The police arrive on the scene too late, and Joe, Sugar, Jerry, and Osgood make for the yacht. Sugar does not mind that Joe is not rich; more surprisingly, Osgood does not bat an eyelid when Jerry pulls off his Daphne wig and confesses he is not a girl.

**Reviews:**

*Variety*

"*Some Like It Hot*, directed in masterly style by Billy Wilder, is probably the funniest picture of recent memory. It's a wacky, clever, farcical comedy that starts off like a firecracker and keeps on throwing off lively sparks till the very end. . . .

To coin a phrase, Marilyn has never looked better. Her performance as 'Sugar', the fuzzy blonde who likes saxophone players and men with glasses has a deliciously naïve quality. She's a comedienne with that combination of sex appeal and timing that just can't be beat."

*The New York Times*

"Mr. Wilder, abetted by such equally proficient operatives as Marilyn Monroe, Jack Lemmon and Tony Curtis, surprisingly has developed a completely unbelievable plot into a broad farce in which authentically comic action vies with snappy and sophisticated dialogue. . . . As the band's somewhat simple singer-ukulele player, Miss Monroe, whose figure simply cannot be overlooked, contributes more assets than the obvious ones to this madcap romp. As a pushover for gin and the tonic effect of saxophone players, she sings a couple of whispery old numbers ('Running Wild' and 'I Wanna Be Loved by You') and also proves to be the epitome of a dumb blonde and a talented comedienne."

*New York Post*

"To get down to cases, Marilyn does herself proud, giving a performance of such intrinsic quality that you begin to believe she's only being herself and it is herself who fits into that distant period and this picture so well."

## SOMETHING'S GOT TO GIVE

*Something's Got to Give* would have been Marilyn's thirtieth movie. The fact that no more than a third of the film was shot before it was abandoned has not prevented many biographers from writing more on the movie she didn't finish than any of the twenty-nine films she did.

*Something's Got to Give* was conceived as a remake of *My Favorite Wife*, a very popular 1940 CARY GRANT and Irene Dunne comedy about a shipwrecked wife, believed dead, who returns years later to find that her husband has remarried. The original script, written by Sam and Bella Spewack, was inspired by "Enoch Arden," a poem by Alfred Lord Tennyson, which in turn was perhaps modeled on a story by American writer David R. Locke.

Marilyn was offered this movie as one of the two pictures she still owed TWENTIETH CENTURY-FOX under the contract she signed in 1956. It has often been said that Marilyn's instinct was not to do this picture, but she was persuaded, among others, by her psychoanalyst DR. RALPH GREENSON, who believed that returning to work would only do her good after the emotional upheavals of 1961. One reason why the movie appealed to her was that her friend DEAN MARTIN's production company was involved in the project. From a dramatic point of view, the role was different from previous characters she had played.

Marilyn as Sugar Cane confides in Josephine . . . and gets intimate with Mr. Shell, the young oil magnate.

Above and right, Marilyn as Ellen Arden in the never-released *Something's Got to Give*, 1962.

She was a mother and a wife, and in the footage that has survived, she speaks her lines in her natural voice, not the breathless tones her fans were used to. In terms of her career, this was an important project. Her previous two movies, *LET'S MAKE LOVE* (1960) and *THE MISFITS* (1961), had failed to achieve the success she was used to, and Marilyn desperately wanted to silence the critics who claimed that she was finished. Once more, for this picture she was earning far less MONEY than her colleagues—$100,000, plus $500 per week during shooting—while co-star Martin and director GEORGE CUKOR were reportedly earning $300,000 each.

Cukor, who also owed the studio a movie under a long-term contract, was brought in by original producer David Brown. As many as seven SCREENWRITERS, according to biographer FRED LAWRENCE GUILES, had a hand in what was universally regarded as a troublesome script. Marilyn's greatest enthusiasm was for the version written by NUNALLY JOHNSON, with whom Marilyn had worked on *HOW TO MARRY A MILLIONAIRE* (1953). However, Johnson pulled out in March 1962, a month before shooting was scheduled to start. At the time he wrote to his friend JEAN NEGULESCO, "I don't know whether it will ever be made or not."

Original screenwriter Arnold Shulman was handed back the script, only to conclude that "the studio simply wanted to forget about the picture." He was then replaced by WALTER BERNSTEIN, taking script costs alone beyond $300,000. Rewrites continued all the way through shooting, some incorporating suggestions from Marilyn, and all but four pages of the original shooting script were altered in some way. At one point the studio tried to fool Marilyn that the script had not been changed—she was unhappy that alterations were detracting from the version she liked best—by giving her the rewritten pages on white paper, rather than the customary blue revision pages.

Mainly because of script problems, the principal shooting date was put back from February to April 23. By this time, PETER LEVATHES, vice president in charge of studio operations, had replaced the original producer David Brown with HENRY WEINSTEIN, a friend of Ralph Greenson, who it appears persuaded Levathes that Marilyn would work better with somebody who understood her. Greenson himself came on board as a special consultant to Marilyn.

April 23 came and went without Marilyn arriving for work because she was ill, but then Martin also failed to show as he was still working on another movie. Marilyn reported to the studio a week later, but only managed one day's work before her fever returned and sinusitis flared up. Marilyn's personal physician Dr. Hyman Engelberg and studio DOCTOR Lee Seigel agreed that she needed rest. At home, Marilyn continued to work with PAULA STRASBERG on the script, in an attempt to cope with the wholesale changes and rewrites which arrived at her home on an almost daily basis. Meanwhile, Cukor switched to filming scenes with the other actors and Marilyn's point of view shots.

Marilyn reported to work for a few days running through mid-May, but on May 17, she boarded a plane for New York. The studio immediately issued a warning that her trip was in breach of her contract, though it has also been said that the studio bosses had tacitly given her approval. On May 19, Marilyn sang "Happy Birthday" to JOHN F. KENNEDY at MADISON SQUARE GARDEN. On her return, Marilyn continued to work, including the pool sequence when she spontaneously removed her flesh-colored bikini for the last ever nude shots, but the decision had already been made to close down production.

Marilyn learned that she was going to be dismissed from the movie the day after the crew members threw a party to celebrate her thirty-sixth birthday. The production was not actually closed down until the end of the following week. Under threat of dismissal, Marilyn refused to continue until she worked out her position with her advisers. Meanwhile, the studio told Marilyn that they were preparing to sue her for breach of contract. Ralph Greenson took negotiations in hand, after being summoned back from a trip to Europe.

The circumstances of Marilyn's dismissal should be viewed in the light of the severe difficulties Fox, and indeed the whole film industry, was experiencing at the time. Fox was in a financially precarious position due to massive overruns on ELIZABETH TAYLOR's *Cleopatra* (1963), which came in at over $30 million (of which Taylor earned a cool million). Added to this was the competition all the Hollywood studios were experiencing from television, by that time in many American homes, and the increasing power of stars—a shift in power that Marilyn herself had helped to promote by walking out on the studio in the mid-fifties and renegotiating a more favorable contract.

One point of view is that Fox was looking for an excuse to close the film down. Many biographers have ventured to say that the studio wanted to recoup money by cashing in on insurance, and so deliberately played up Marilyn's health and reliability problems in order to justify her expulsion. At the time that all this was taking place, the old guard at Fox was being replaced by new managers, as the studio owners panicked at the company's loss of influence.

On June 7, 1962 Marilyn was officially dismissed from the movie for "breach of contract," after Levathes pulled the plug. Henry Weinstein told columnist SHEILAH GRAHAM, "I have had no official notification of her illness. All I get from her is she will not be reporting. Out of thirty-three days of shooting Marilyn has come to the set only twelve times and will only do one page a day, which adds to a total of four days of work only. . . . the fact is that the studios cannot operate with stars who do not report for work. If this sort of thing continues, there will be no movie industry at all."

The studio filed a suit against Marilyn claiming $500,000 in damages, a figure they later upped to $750,000. Between the suspension of production and Marilyn's official dismissal, the studio cast around for a replacement. After first choices KIM NOVAK and SHIRLEY MACLAINE had said no, Fox settled on LEE REMICK. In the end, it made little difference who Fox chose because Martin had a clause in his contract giving him approval of his leading lady, and he refused to work with anyone except Marilyn. In retaliation, the studio then sued Dean Martin's production company for the entire cost of the movie, over $3 million.

After the movie was cancelled, crew members got together to take out an ad in *Variety* sarcastically thanking Marilyn for getting them fired. Marilyn was very hurt by this public criticism.

Marilyn campaigned to be reinstated. As she wrote in a telegram to ROBERT KENNEDY and his wife, who had invited her to visit them in Virginia, "I would have been delighted to have accepted your invitation honoring Pat and Peter Lawford. Unfortunately, I am involved in a freedom ride protesting the loss of the minority rights belonging to the few remaining housebound stars. After all, all we demanded was our right to twinkle."

A couple of weeks after Marilyn was fired, long time Fox president SPYROS SKOURAS stepped down from the helm. However, in a secret move, scriptwriter Hal Kanter was brought in to revise the screenplay, and plans were afoot to reinstate Marilyn. On July 25, 1962, Peter Levathes personally went to Marilyn's home to tell her that Twentieth Century-Fox wanted her back: not only was the lawsuit against her going to be dropped, but she was going to be re-hired at a higher salary.

Marilyn's LAWYER Milton Rudin set to work on the contractual details of her return to the set. At Marilyn's suggestion, Jean Negulesco was sounded out to see if he would take on the director's role. On August 1, 1962, four days before her death, Fox re-signed Marilyn on a renewed salary of $250,000 (in some accounts the figure is put at $500,000).

The studio eventually revised the script and recast the project. It appeared in 1963 retitled *Move Over Darling*, starring James Garner and the number one box-office blonde of the day, DORIS DAY.

### WHAT WAS FILMED

Brief excerpts from shooting appeared in the 1963 Twentieth Century-Fox documentary *Marilyn*.

In 1992 Fox Video released a limited edition tape containing forty-five minutes of shots from this movie, along with outtakes, wardrobe and makeup tests. Other versions of footage from the film—there are five hours of material, rushes, and multiple takes of shooting—are in circulation among collectors. This vast bulk of material was discovered in a salt mine, where it had been stored for thirty years. It is said that Fox shot a total of eight hours of material, but at the time of Marilyn's dismissal the studio claimed that only seven minutes of usable material was ever completed.

The unanimous opinion of Marilyn fans who have seen her performance is that she is masterful and mature as an actress, and as radiant and resplendent as ever. Marilyn's stand-in on the movie, Evelyn Moriarty, has claimed that there was sufficient footage for a finished film to be made, though the story line would have had to be altered, and some technique such as flashbacks used.

This unfinished movie is regarded as a prime candidate for computer-generated compilation when technology comes of age to reproduce actors on-screen.

**Credits:**
Twentieth Century-Fox

Directed by: George Cukor
Produced by: Henry Weinstein
Written by: Nunnally Johnson, Walter Bernstein (adapted from screenplay by Samuel and Bella Spewack)

**Cast:**
Marilyn Monroe . . . Ellen Arden
Dean Martin . . . Nick Arden
Cyd Charisse . . . Bianca
Phil Silvers . . . Insurance Man
Wally Cox . . . Shoe Clerk
Tom Tryon . . . Steven Burkett
Steve Allen . . . Dr. Herman Schlick

## SONGS

LIONEL NEWMAN:
"I think she was a better singer than most people who were professional singers. She worked hard and was always on time."

Marilyn was as serious about her singing as she was about her ACTING. She studied diligently under a number of VOICE COACHES and singing tutors, and had two songs in her first role larger than a bit part, in *LADIES OF THE CHORUS* (1948). As with her normal speaking VOICE, she developed an inimitable style of delivery laden with sexual overtones.

Coach HAL SCHAEFER, who started worked with Marilyn on *GENTLEMEN PREFER BLONDES* (1953) said, "She loved to sing, she sang well, and she just adored her idol, Ella. The most important influence on Marilyn's vocal art was in fact a recording I gave her called 'Ella Sings Gershwin…'"

There were, however, people who refused to believe that Marilyn's movie singing voice was actually her own. New York columnist DOROTHY KILGALLEN made allegations that her numbers in *Gentlemen Prefer Blondes* had been dubbed by another singer, only to be refuted by an affidavit sent by Fox studio chief DARRYL ZANUCK. Kilgallen responded, "It just floors me that a girl who can sing as well as Marilyn does on the *Gentlemen Prefer Blondes* soundtrack (okay, it's not Dinah Shore, but it's a competent professional job) just happened to pick up the talent recently."

In October 1953 Marilyn signed a record deal with RCA, though this only led to three singles from *THERE'S NO BUSINESS LIKE SHOW BUSINESS* (1954). An exclusivity clause in Marilyn's contract resulted in Broadway star Dolores Gray being hired for the official soundtrack album. RCA also recorded

Marilyn listens to recordings of herself singing, 1951.

Marilyn singing "A Fine Romance," regarded by some as her finest singing performance, but not released until long after her death. Apart from this contract, Marilyn's songs from her movies were released on soundtrack albums published by the respective studios.

Many Marilyn compilation albums have come out over the years, using a combination of material from the soundtrack cuts and original recordings produced for release. In 1991 Legend Records brought out a double CD entitled "Marilyn Monroe: The Complete Recordings," featuring all of the songs she sang in her films, plus excerpts from radio programs, interviews and press conferences.

### MARILYN'S SONGS

SONGS PERFORMED IN MOVIES:
*Ladies of the Chorus* (1948)—"Anyone Can See I Love You," "Every Baby Needs a Da-Da-Daddy"
*A Ticket to Tomahawk* (1950)—"Oh, What a Forward Young Man You Are"
*Niagara* (1953)—"Kiss"
*Gentlemen Prefer Blondes* (1953)—"We're Just Two Little Girls from Little Rock," "When Love Goes Wrong," "Bye Bye Baby," "Diamonds Are a Girl's Best Friend" —Songs cut from the movie "Four French Dances" medley ("Sur le balcon," "La tentateur," "Sol taire," "Parle d'affair"), "Down Boy," "When the Wild Wild Women Go Swimmin' Down in the Bimini Bay," aka "When the Wild Wild Women Go Swimmin' Down in the Swimmin' Hole".
*River of No Return* (1953)—"River of No Return," "I'm Going to File My Claim," "One Silver Dollar," "Down in the Meadow"
*There's No Business Like Show Business* (1954)—"After You Get What You Want You Don't Want It," "Heatwave," "Lazy," "There's No Business Like Show Business," "A Man Chases a Girl," "You'd Be Surprised"
*Bus Stop* (1956)—"That Old Black Magic"
*The Prince and the Showgirl* (1957)—"I Found a Dream"
*Some Like It Hot* (1959)—"I'm Through with Love," "I Wanna Be Loved by You," "Running Wild"
*Let's Make Love* (1960)—"Let's Make Love," "Incurably Romantic," "Specialization," "My Heart Belongs to Daddy"

SONGS PERFORMED LIVE:
1948—at home of director Richard Quine: "Baby Won't You Please Come Home"
1952—Camp Pendleton: "Somebody Loves You," "Do It Again"
1953—The Jack Benny Show: "Bye Bye Baby"
1954—Korea Tour: "Do It Again" (toned down to "Kiss Me Again"), "Diamonds Are a Girl's Best Friend," "Somebody Love Me," "Bye Bye Baby"
1954—Romanoff's Party: "Do It Again"
1955—*The Seven Year Itch* wrap party: "Let's Do It"
1962—Kennedy Birthday, Madison Square Garden: "Happy Birthday, Mr. President," "Thanks, Mr. President" (to the tune of "Thanks for the Memories")

SONGS PERFORMED FOR AUDITIONS:
For *Ladies of the Chorus* (1948): "Love Me or Leave Me"
"How Wrong Could I Be".

SONG PLAYED AT HER FUNERAL:
"Over the Rainbow" by Judy Garland

SONGS ABOUT MARILYN (a selection from hundreds):
"Marilyn," written by Ervin Drake and Jimmy Shirl, performed Ray Anthony
"Candle in the Wind," by Elton John and Bernie Taupin
"Marilyn," by Martin Mull
"Norma Jean Wants to Be a Movie Star," by J. Cunningham
"Elvis and Marilyn," by Leon Russell
"Who Killed Marilyn," by Glen Danzia
"Marilyn Monroe," by Willy Russell, part of Blood Brothers soundtrack
"Marilyn Monroe/Neon and Waltzes," by Nanci Griffith
"Life Sized Marilyn Monroe," by Wild Strawberries "Marilyn Monroe," by Dave Frishberg
"Marilyn Monroe," Ana Belen, Miguel Rios, Victor Manuel, Joan Manuel Serrat
"Marilyn Monroe Had Six Toes," by The Refreshments
"Marilyn Monroe," by Piet Botha
"Marilyn Monroe," by Suckerpunch
"Marilyn Dean and James Monroe," John Kilzer,
"Marilyn Monroe," Blood Brothers International Cast Recording
"Do You Remember Marilyn?" John Kinkade
"Marilyn Monroe," Ian Campbell
"Marilyn Says," Thomas Anderson
"Claiming Marilyn," Acid House
"Marilyn," Lew Soloff
"Marilyn," Les Wampas
"Marilyn," Zouk Time
"Marilyn," Dan Bern
"Marilyn," Nicolas Peyrac
"Marilyn," Lovebugs
"Marilyn," Donald Byrd
"Marilyn's Child," Seymores
"Marilyn and John," Vanessa Paradis
"Claiming Marilyn," Death in Vegas
"Marilyn," Gumball
"Marilyn and Joe," Kinky Friedman

## SOUTH AVON STREET
131 SOUTH AVON STREET, BURBANK, CALIFORNIA

Marilyn reputedly house-sat for a couple during the summer of 1947, after moving out of the STUDIO CLUB. This was the house where, Marilyn told friends, an intruder climbed through her bedroom window one night and sexually assaulted her. Although the man was arrested, because he was a policeman he was never charged. Doubt has been cast on the story by a number of biographers, though the incident was reported in a local paper.

## SPADA, JAMES

Lifelong Marilyn FAN who with GEORGE ZENO co-authored the handsome photographic biography of Marilyn called *Monroe: Her Life in Pictures*, published in 1982.

## SPERIGLIO, MILO

Private detective enlisted by ROBERT SLATZER to investigate alleged misdeeds surrounding Marilyn's DEATH. Speriglio's books *Marilyn Monroe: Murder Cover-Up* and *The Marilyn Conspiracy* squarely point the finger at ROBERT KENNEDY as the main culprit. Speriglio's main witness was a man who worked at the coroner's, LIONEL GRANDISON, who claimed that bruising on Marilyn body had not been reported in the autopsy.

A third book, *Crypt 33: The Saga of Marilyn Monroe*, which Speriglio co-authored with Adela Gregory, shifts the focus of blame to Joseph Kennedy, who, he claims, hired SAM GIANCANA to kill Marilyn because she was carrying Bobby's child.

Speriglio has also come up with a list of five organized crime bosses who allegedly banded together to have Marilyn murdered; the names figured on a so-called "Murder Chart" given to Speriglio by an informant named Jules Pappas.

BOOKS:
*Marilyn Monroe: Murder Cover-Up*, Milo Speriglio. New York: Seville Publishers, 1982.
*The Marilyn Conspiracy*, Milo Speriglio. New York: Pocket Books, 1986.
*Crypt 33: The Saga of Marilyn Monroe—The Final Word*, Adela Gregory and Milo Speriglio. New York: Carol Publishing, 1993.

## SPINDEL, BERNARD

A wiretap specialist who is said to have bugged Marilyn's home and obtained tapes of conversations between Marilyn and ROBERT KENNEDY. He reputedly also had recordings of them making love, and the events during the last night she was alive, including evidence that Marilyn was smothered to death. According to biographer ANTHONY SUMMERS, Spindel had been employed by JIMMY HOFFA, in an attempt to obtain information that could be used against Robert Kennedy. In 1966, after being investigated by the Manhattan District Attorney, Spindel went public that he had been BUGGING Marilyn's home, but said the resulting tapes had been stolen from him. In 1982 Los Angeles District Attorney officials listened to all the material sequestered from Spindel in 1966. Their official statement was that "none of the tapes contained anything relating to Marilyn Monroe."

## SPORTS

Marilyn may not have been known as a great sportswoman, but over the years she tried her hand at a number of sports and recreational activities. She was most active in her teenage years, during her marriage to first husband JAMES DOUGHERTY, who took her skiing, horseback riding, hiking, swimming, and canoeing. She also went with him a few times on fishing trips to Sherwood Lake (Ventura County), the first of which was in fact their HONEYMOON.

**Baseball**
Marilyn's 1951 publicity shot with Gus Zernial of the Chicago White Sox was Marilyn's first brush with baseball, and certainly not her last. JOE DIMAGGIO saw the photo and pulled strings until he managed to arrange a meeting with Marilyn.

She saw her first game on March 17, 1952: Hollywood Stars against Major League All-Stars at Gilmore Field (7750 Beverly Boulevard, Hollywood), a benefit game for the Kiwanis Club for Children. This was the only time Marilyn saw DiMaggio play—he hit a single and a home run.

During their marriage, Marilyn accompanied Joe a number of times to Yankee Stadium where he worked as a commentator. In 1961 they were back watching a game there. That year she also went with Joe to the Yankee spring training camp in Florida.

Marilyn's last ever public appearance was at Dodger Stadium in Los Angeles, on her thirty-sixth birthday, June 1, 1962, for a muscular dystrophy benefit. That day she threw out the first ball.

**Basketball**
Jack Hanson, owner of the Jax store, said that in her starlet days Marilyn played basketball in order to lose weight.

**Badminton**
In the late fifties, Marilyn played lawn tennis and badminton in the summer with PATRICIA ROSTEN, daughter of friends NORMAN and HEDDA ROSTEN.

**Golf**
One of the jobs Marilyn reputedly took when she was down on her luck in the late forties was serving as an assistant to trick golfer Joe Kirkwood Jr. Scantily clad, Marilyn's job was to hold a plastic ball out; she was so nervous on her first outing that her career as a trick golfer did not last beyond one performance.

Marilyn learned to play golf when she was with Joe DiMaggio. She told a journalist, "I was quite good at it as well, at least I could hit all right, but I never liked the things that went with it."

JEANNE CARMEN claimed she was scheduled to go golfing with Marilyn the day she died.

**Horseback-riding**
Marilyn went riding with Jim Dougherty in the early forties. She even rode ROY ROGERS' famous mount, Trigger, in LAS VEGAS in 1946. Many years later, she and ARTHUR MILLER bought a horse called Ebony, who lived with them at their country house in ROXBURY. Marilyn is said to have ridden this horse very few times.

**Running**
When Norma Jeane was eleven, she came first in running and jumping events at school. A probably apocryphal picture of a young Marilyn jogging through Hollywood back streets has appeared in the past.

**Soccer**
Marilyn made the ceremonial first kick in a soccer match between America and Israel, held at Ebbet's Field, New York, on May 12, 1957. Unfortunately, she kicked the soccer ball so hard in open-toed SHOES that she sprained two toes. This injury, however, did not prevent her from staying on until the end of the match, and then presenting the trophy to the winning captain.

Marilyn throws the opening pitch for the "Out of This World Series" with Ralph Edwards, 1952.

**Softball**
Norma Jeane was one of the strongest players on her ORPHANAGE softball team.

**Surfing**
According to ROBERT SLATZER and lifeguard TOMMY ZAHN, starlet Norma Jeane went surfing regularly at Malibu in 1946–7.

**Swimming**
There are conflicting reports about Marilyn's prowess as a swimmer. She reputedly learned to swim during her spell living at the Los Angeles Orphanage. Tommy Zahn says they often went together to the ocean for a swim. Early STUDIO BIOGRAPHIES list swimming among her interests. However, Marilyn is quoted as commenting on rushes of her swimming during shooting of *SOMETHING'S GOT TO GIVE* as being a surprise because, "I actually look like a good swimmer. Who'd guess that I'm just a dog paddler?"

By all accounts, Marilyn hardly ever swam in the pool at her last home, on FIFTH HELENA DRIVE.

**Weight Training**
In 1943, when her first husband was stationed with the Merchant Marine on CATALINA ISLAND, off the coast of California, Marilyn started working out with free weights. A 1952 feature in *Life* magazine shows her doing a forty-five-minute daily routine with barbells, part of the FITNESS regime which Marilyn followed for many years.

## SPOTO, DONALD

Entertainment BIOGRAPHER Donald Spoto published his Marilyn biography in 1993, to counter a "grim cyclorama of sensation." His extensive research included access for the first time to the private papers of a number of key people in Marilyn's life, including business partner MILTON GREENE, business manager INEZ MELSON, and genealogical research by archivist Roy Turner. He also conducted interviews with 150 people.

This work is regarded by many people as the best-researched Marilyn biography to date. Spoto refutes the many CONSPIRACY theories surrounding Marilyn's DEATH.

Spoto has also written biographies of Alfred Hitchcock, Ingrid Bergman, James Dean, MARLENE DIETRICH, LAURENCE OLIVIER, ELIZABETH TAYLOR, and Princess DIANA.

BOOK:
*Marilyn Monroe: The Biography*, Donald Spoto. New York: HarperCollins, 1993.

## SPRINGER, JOHN

Partner of ARTHUR JACOBS in the New York publicity agency which ran Marilyn's affairs from 1955 until her death, Springer personally took a great deal of responsibility for Marilyn's interviews in the last years of her life, as agency employee PAT NEWCOMB became more of a personal secretary than strictly a PR operative. He had first met Marilyn in 1952, while at the publicity department at RKO, where Marilyn was working on *CLASH BY NIGHT* (1952).

Springer set up Marilyn's famous interview with *Life* journalist RICHARD MERYMAN.

## *STAGE DOOR*

During her time with the Bliss-Hayden Theater Group, Marilyn had a small role in this play by Edna Ferber and George S. Kaufman, in the summer of 1948.

## STAMPS

Until 1995, Marilyn's likeness had only appeared on stamps issued by the African countries of Congo and Mali.

The Marilyn Monroe United States commemorative issue stamp.

This changed when a commemorative issue was brought out in the U.S.: 46.3 million stamps were bought and saved, and many millions bought and used. The only person commemorated on a stamp to outsell Marilyn is Elvis, whose 1993 stamp has sold an astonishing 124 million copies.

In recent years Marilyn stamps have been issued by, among others, Montserrat, Tanzania, Gambia, and Madagascar. She has also begun to appear on phonecards (SEE MEMORABILIA).

## STANISLAVSKY, KONSTANTIN
(1863–1938)

A Russian actor and director and co-founder of the influential Moscow Art Theater, whose theories on drama performance and actor training had an enormous influence on acting in the U.S. and around the world. Stanislavsky's teachings lay at the heart of THE METHOD, as taught by LEE STRASBERG at the ACTORS STUDIO.

According to Strasberg, the great contribution of Stanislavsky was, "to discover whether means could be found for consciously stimulating the creative process, which usually takes place unconsciously."

## STANLEY, KIM
(B. 1921, PATRICIA REID)

Kim Stanley was a renowned stage actress, a member of the ACTORS STUDIO, and a classmate of Marilyn's. Her greatest Broadway successes include the original version of *BUS STOP*, *Picnic*, and *A Touch of the Poet*.

Of Marilyn she said, "Anybody who had any largeness of spirit loved Marilyn. And she won us all... She had something about her that made you love her."

Stanley's "largeness of spirit" included seeing Marilyn in the audience for her performances of the stage version of *Bus Stop*, as her Hollywood colleague prepared for the screen interpretation of Cherie.

Stanley's movie debut had more than a little of Marilyn in it—she played the part of Rita Shawn in *The Goddess* (1958), a thinly-veiled Marilyn bio-pic, said to have been written by PADDY CHAYEFSKY as revenge for Marilyn reneging on a deal. *The Goddess* tells the story of a poor girl who becomes a huge Hollywood star and marries a sporting legend.

Although Kim Stanley acted in very few movies, she received two Academy Award nominations, for *Seance on a Wet Afternoon* (1964) and *Frances* (1982).

## STANWYCK, BARBARA
(1907–1990, B. RUBY STEVENS)

"She was awkward. She couldn't get out of her own way. She wasn't disciplined, and she was often late but there was a sort of magic about her which we all recognized at once. . . . Her phobias, or whatever they were, came later; she seemed just a carefree kid, and she owned the whole world."

Barbara Stanwyck's career spanned over fifty years, starting in the late twenties and including Oscar-nominated performances in movies such as *Stella Dallas* (1937), *Double Indemnity* (1944), and *Sorry Wrong Number* (1948). In 1952 Stanwyck headlined *CLASH BY NIGHT*, in which Marilyn had a supporting role, and though Marilyn was undoubtedly hard to work with on the set, Stanwyck offered her younger colleague nothing but encouragement. Unlike fellow star Paul Douglas, seasoned professional Stanwyck gallantly failed to take offence at the press' almost exclusive interest in her blonde co-star.

In 1957 Stanwyck reputedly beat out Marilyn to star in Samuel Fuller's *Forty Guns*.

## STAPLETON, MAUREEN (B. 1925)

A fellow student at the ACTORS STUDIO in the mid-fifties, Stapleton had achieved success on Broadway and later went on to a long career as a character actress in the movies.

In February 1956 Stapleton worked with Marilyn on a scene from Eugene O'Neill's *ANNA CHRISTIE*, to be performed onstage in front of LEE STRASBERG and the assembled student body. In 1992 Stapleton told biographer DONALD SPOTO, "She could have chosen a role that wasn't too well known, so that her performance could have been criticized only on its own merit. But to do *Anna Christie*, something that's been done by a dozen wonderful people—Garbo included!"

Stapleton's most famous movie performances are in *Lonelyhearts* (1959, Oscar-nominated), *Queen of the Stardust Ballroom* (1975), *Interiors* (1978, Oscar-nominated), and *Reds* (1981), for which she received an Academy Award.

## STEFFENS, LINCOLN (1866–1936)

An American journalist who in the early part of the twentieth century made a name for himself by writing exposés of corruption in business and local government, paving the way for a greater degree of awareness of civic responsibility. The *Autobiography of Lincoln Steffens*, published in 1931, was one of Marilyn's favorite BOOKS.

## STEINEM, GLORIA (B. 1934)

"It is the lost possibilities of Marilyn Monroe that capture our imaginations. It was the lost Norma Jeane, looking out of Marilyn's eyes, who captured our hearts."

A leading figure in the feminist movement and a political writer since 1960, Gloria Steinem was a founder of *Ms.* magazine in 1971. Since then, she has been one the most prominent feminist writers in America.

In 1986 Steinem brought a feminist perspective to the great amount of verbiage surrounding Marilyn. One of her insights is that Marilyn's DEATH changed her vulnerability, which in life had been an embarrassment to her sex, into a tragedy: "She personified many of the secret hopes of men and many secret fears of women."

BOOK:
*Marilyn*, Gloria Steinem, photos by George Barris. New York: Henry Holt, 1986.

## STENGEL, MARJORIE

Marjorie Stengel worked briefly as Marilyn's New York SECRETARY after MAY REIS left the job, possibly on the recommendation of MONTGOMERY CLIFT, for whom she had previously worked. Biographer FRED LAWRENCE GUILES writes that rather than following Marilyn to the West Coast in 1961, Stengel resigned. Biographer ANTHONY SUMMERS records her rather negative impressions of working for Marilyn, who she says was leading a lonely life in a filthy apartment strewn with half-empty pill bottles.

After moving west, Marilyn put Stengel's name on the bell of her DOHENEY DRIVE apartment to confuse fans and the press.

## STERN, BERT

Six weeks before her death, commercial and fashion PHOTOGRAPHER Bert Stern was sent by *Vogue* MAGAZINE to shoot a photo feature on Marilyn. Marilyn arrived five hours late, but in three sessions conducted over a two-week period at the BEL-AIR HOTEL, starting on June 23, 1962, Stern snapped just under 2,700 shots, spanning fashion, portrait, and nudes. Many fans consider these photographs to show Marilyn at her most mature, self-assured, and sensual.

A 464-page book of this event, containing 2,571 photographs and called *The Complete Last Sitting*, has been reprinted a number of times. More than any other book, *The Complete Last Sitting* gives an impression of what a photo session with Marilyn was like: the succession of slightly different poses, miniscule changes in how she held her posture, smiled, and moved.

However, if Marilyn had lived (or if Stern had not delayed in sending Marilyn the photographs), she would have exercised her right to destroy the images she did not approve for publication, as she had been doing for years with all other photographers and photo features. In fact, Stern only sent Marilyn a small proportion of the material he shot.

BOOK:
*The Last Sitting*, Bert Stern. Munich, Germany: Schirmer, 1992.
Selections from this material have appeared in book form over the years, and a full reprint is due in 1999.

## STRASBERG, ANNA

Two years after PAULA STRASBERG died, LEE STRASBERG married Anna Mizrahi, his third and final wife. They had two children. On Strasberg's death, Anna Strasberg inherited his estate, which included all of Marilyn's possessions, bequeathed to Lee in her final WILL, along with 75 percent of Marilyn's ESTATE after specific provisions had been settled.

Photograph by Bert Stern, 1962.

Lee and Paula Strasberg with Marilyn at a production of *Macbeth* in New York, 1962.

Handled by CMG, the Estate is worth an estimated annual income of over $1 million from film royalties, licensing, and merchandising revenues.

In 1999 Anna Strasberg commissioned Christie's to sell Marilyn's possessions, in the largest ever auction of its kind.

## STRASBERG, JOHN

Son of LEE and PAULA STRASBERG, an actor and drama teacher in his own right. When John was in his teens, Marilyn was a fixture in family life. When Marilyn went to stay with the Strasbergs in 1961, after her divorce from ARTHUR MILLER, she used John's bedroom, and John slept on the couch.

Marilyn gave John her black Thunderbird convertible for his eighteenth birthday.

## STRASBERG, LEE
(1901–1982, B. ISRAEL SRULKE)

"I saw that what she looked like was not what she really was, and what was going on inside was not what was going on outside, and that always means there may be something there to work with. It was almost as if she had been waiting for a button to be pushed, and when it was. . . . a door opened and you saw a treasure of gold and jewels."

ELIA KAZAN:
"The more naïve and self-doubting the actors, the more total was Lee's power over them. The more famous and the more successful these actors, the headier the taste of power for Lee. He found his perfect victim-devotee in Marilyn Monroe."

RUPERT ALLAN:
"The Strasbergs made it possible for her to work. They believed in her. They were like the parents she never had."

Arguably the best known ACTING coach of this century, whose teachings of THE METHOD for acting was espoused by famous names such as MARLON BRANDO, James Dean, Jane Fonda, and Paul Newman—to name just a few—Lee Strasberg became a very important figure in Marilyn's life after she moved to New York in 1955.

Born in Budzanow, Austria, (now known as Budanov, Ukraine), Strasberg's parents immigrated to America in 1909, and he grew up in Manhattan's Lower East Side Jewish community. He studied drama under Russian actress Maria Ouspenskaya and director Richard Boleslavski, a former colleague of KONSTANTIN STANISLAVSKY at the famous Moscow Art Theater. In 1931 Strasberg was a co-founder of the Group Theater, with partners Cheryl Crawford, Harold Clurman, and ELIA KAZAN. It was during this time that he developed The Method, his philosophy of acting. In 1937 he struck out on his own, before becoming artistic director of the ACTORS STUDIO in 1951, four years after it had been founded by Crawford, Kazan, and Robert Lewis.

The Actors Studio was a place for dramatic experimentation at an individual and group level. All actors were auditioned by Strasberg himself, and some received extra insruction from Strasberg at his home. ELI WALLACH said, "We were like converts to a new religion. We didn't understand anyone else's acting except our own. Everyone else was a pagan."

Marilyn began her professional association with Lee in February 1955, taking private lessons at his apartment at 225 West Eighty-sixth Street, just off Broadway, and then later at 135 Central Park West—curiously enough, in the very same building as her psychoanalyst Dr. MARIANNE KRIS.

Marilyn had already been introduced to Lee's wife, PAULA STRASBERG, six months earlier, by mutual friend SIDNEY SKOLSKY, but she was apparently too shy to approach Strasberg directly. Instead, she sought a recommendation from Kazan and Crawford, both of whom were in town for rehearsals of TENNESSEE WILLIAMS' latest play, *Cat on a Hot Tin Roof*. Alternative versions of who provided Marilyn with an introduction name MILTON GREENE.

Marilyn did not join the public sessions at the Actors Studio until she felt ready to do so, in May that year, though it is sometimes said that she did not join the studio until December. During the seven years of her association with Lee Strasberg, Marilyn never actually became a full member of the organization, though there is evidence that she was intending to become one of the dozen people of the 1962 class.

Deeply intertwined with Strasberg's approach to acting was a working and practicing knowledge of psychotherapy. As with her psychotherapists, Marilyn spent a good deal of time delving back into her past, dramatizing various stages of her unhappy childhood to add to the regular morning talk. Strasberg maintained that tapping these "sense-memories" was vital if she was to unleash her "real tragic power." A number of Marilyn's biographers have commented on the danger of this intense focus on Marilyn's childhood woes.

In his book *Conversations with Marilyn*, W. J. WEATHERBY writes of what a session with Strasberg at his Actors Studio was like: "Strasberg gave the impression of enormous self-assurance, the kind one associates not with a human being but with a messenger of the gods. . . . His comments were always thoughtful, sometimes ruthlessly analytical, his humor very much that of a pedagogue. . . . He behaved and was treated as though he were Moses come down from the mountain. This was the teacher as priest and psychiatrist."

Marilyn found Strasberg's approach very exciting, and very demanding. She told friend NORMAN ROSTEN, "Lee makes me think. Lee says I have to begin to face my problems in my work and life—the question of how or why I can act."

Particularly refreshing for Marilyn was the fact that Strasberg believed in her, and quickly became one of her staunchest public supporters. When JOSHUA LOGAN, considering an offer to direct Marilyn in *BUS STOP* (1956), contacted Strasberg to find out what he thought of Marilyn, Strasberg unhesitatingly told him that she and Brando were the two greatest talents ever to have passed through his school. Alone among her drama teachers, Strasberg instilled in Marilyn his belief that she had a future as a stage actress, though it must be said that despite her many years of instruction, and Strasberg's many contacts in the theater world, a stage role never materialized for Marilyn.

*Previous page*: Bert Stern and Marilyn during the famous "Last Sitting," 1962.

Marilyn soon became part of the family, sharing meals and staying overnight on many occasions, on nights when she felt lonely and couldn't sleep. She went with the family to their holiday home on Fire Island. DONALD SPOTO writes, "Lee gave Marilyn the strongest paternal-professional guidance of her life—a kind of total psychological mentorship." The ultimate expression of his role as a FATHER FIGURE to Marilyn came on July 1, 1956, when Strasberg gave the bride away at Marilyn's religious WEDDING ceremony to ARTHUR MILLER. Lee's fatherly regard for Marilyn has sometimes been placed in contrast to the rather absent parenting of his own children, John and Susan. John has said, "It was hard for anyone to have a relationship with [Lee] if you weren't a book, a record, a cat or Marilyn."

Susan Strasberg has described her feelings of rivalry in her two books on Marilyn. She said that the household which Marilyn joined as an occasional member, "revolved around my father, his moods, his needs, his expectations and his neuroses. He was teaching people how to act, but that was nothing compared to the drama in our house."

Aside from his influence on Marilyn's personal life, Strasberg's approach to acting, and Marilyn's diligent pursuit of The Method, was apparent in *Bus Stop* (1956), the first movie she made after switching from NATASHA LYTESS to Paula Strasberg, who as Lee's representative, served as her drama coach from this point on in her career.

For Marilyn's next project, *THE PRINCE AND THE SHOWGIRL* (1957), Strasberg personally went to Milton Greene to negotiate the fee for his wife's presence on the set in London. He demanded a total of $38,000 for ten weeks' work. This was far more than MARILYN MONROE PRODUCTIONS, whose financial situation was precarious to say the least, could afford. Marilyn suggested she could pass on some of her salary, and thus after star Marilyn and co-star/director LAURENCE OLIVIER, Paula was the third highest paid individual on the movie. Lee flew out with his wife at the start of production, and was on hand as relations quickly deteriorated between Marilyn and Olivier, in what many commentators have defined as a battle between two acting philosophies. FRED LAWRENCE GUILES writes that when Olivier gave Marilyn the fatal direction to "just be sexy," Marilyn ran off the set in tears and called Strasberg, not her husband. And when, in the often told story of the rupture that occurred in her marriage to Miller after just a few weeks, when Marilyn read an entry about herself in Miller's diary, the first person she called was Lee Strasberg.

After an initial period of grace, Miller began to voice his doubts about Strasberg and his almost religious hold on Marilyn. He had never had a great liking for what he described as the "cultish" aura around The Method, and he had not liked the way that just before he went to appear before the HOUSE UN-AMERICAN ACTIVITIES COMMITTEE, both Lee and Paula had suggested he present himself as a "friendly" witness, as Paula herself had done a few years earlier. Miller, like Elia Kazan, was skeptical about the way Strasberg appeared to make actors more rather than less dependent on him, though in a 1967 interview Miller told biographer FRED LAWRENCE GUILES that he never discussed Strasberg with her because he recognized her dependency on him.

Miller was also critical of Strasberg's behavior during the troubled shooting of *THE MISFITS* (1961). In his autobiography, he writes that even though Marilyn relied completely upon Strasberg for any self-confidence she could muster as an actress, he did not come out to location shooting for *The Misfits* until things were threatening to unravel completely. When he did arrive, his solution was to take Paula off the picture because JOHN HUSTON had failed to show her the respect Strasberg felt his wife was due.

The Strasbergs once more invited Marilyn into their home after the collapse of her marriage to Arthur. She spent Christmas 1960 with them. On some of the evenings she arrived to spend the night, Lee Strasberg would hold her until she was calm enough to get to sleep. He explained, "She wanted to be held, not to be made love to but just to be supported."

In early 1961, the Strasbergs were the first people Marilyn contacted when she found herself trapped on a locked psychiatric ward of the Payne-Whitney HOSPITAL. Later that year, Lee and Marilyn were planning a project for a TV version of Somerset Maugham's *Rain*, but when NBC refused to allow the unproven Strasberg to direct, Marilyn withdrew. She showed her generosity in other ways, not least of which was the prestige she brought to the Actors Studio, and a $10,000 gift for Lee to travel to Japan to study theater.

There are some signs that in the final year of her life, Marilyn's previously unshakable faith in Strasberg was weakening. By this time, she had moved back to Los Angeles. According to many commentators, her West Coast psychotherapist, DR. RALPH GREENSON, was keen on her starting afresh and rebuilding her life.

After Marilyn died, Strasberg was invited by JOE DIMAGGIO to read the eulogy at her FUNERAL. In her final WILL, Marilyn left Strasberg all her possessions and the bulk of her ESTATE, after personal provisions for close friends had been honored.

Lee Strasberg received an Academy Award nomination for his first foray into film, in *The Godfather Part II* (1974).

## STRASBERG, PAULA
(1911–1966, B. PAULA MILLER)

"People patronize Marilyn. They think she's weak in the head and in her character. They don't know her. She's very intelligent and sensitive and a fast learner. She is never satisfied. She examines everything she does."

"Marilyn has the fragility of a female but the constitution of an ox. She is a beautiful hummingbird made of iron. Her only trouble is that she is a very pure person in a very impure world."

PAT NEWCOMB:
"Paula was among the most loyal and helpful. She took the rap for Marilyn's lateness, but she gave Marilyn a great deal. And she never tried to own Marilyn, or to cut others out of Marilyn's life."

ARTHUR MILLER:
"She was a fantasy mother who would confirm anything that Marilyn wished to hear."

Paula and her then sixteen-year-old daughter Susan were first introduced to Marilyn by mutual friend SIDNEY SKOLSKY on the set of *THERE'S NO BUSINESS LIKE SHOW BUSINESS* in the summer of 1954. Marilyn already knew of husband Lee's reputation as an acting teacher, and told Paula that she had always wanted to study with him, particularly after hearing impressive first-hand reports from MARLON BRANDO.

After Marilyn moved to New York in 1955, she became the most famous star associated with the ACTORS STUDIO. She also became a surrogate member of the Strasberg family, in which, according to daughter Susan, there were no end of tensions. Lee

Marilyn and Paula Strasberg on the set of *Something's Got to Give*, 1962.

was used to being in charge, but Paula was a strong character who had to put her own career and aspirations in second place; in her younger days Paula had been one of the leading actresses at the Group Theater. Susan writes that Lee acted as daddy, while Paula mothered their friend and pupil, as well as dispensed the pills Marilyn needed to sleep.

In early 1956, Paula stepped into the shoes previously filled by NATASHA LYTESS as Marilyn's on-set coach and adviser, starting with *BUS STOP* (1956) and continuing right through until Marilyn's final movie. According to ARTHUR MILLER, "this subtly unstable woman was latest of a number of such matronly advisers in her life."

Typically, Marilyn prepared for her roles by breaking down scripts scene by scene, and then preparing every gesture and the delivery of every line. Paula did more than Marilyn's previous coaches to work on spontaneity, at least during rehearsals. For *Bus Stop*, they worked particularly hard on her Southern belle accent.

Paula was flown out to London to coach Marilyn during production of *THE PRINCE AND THE SHOWGIRL* (1957), but before long was dispatched to New York after director LAURENCE OLIVIER grew tired of her undermining his authority. After petitioning by Lee, Marilyn put her foot down and made sure that Paula was issued a new visa and allowed back. Arthur Miller, though, was equally skeptical about Paula's role: "Paula understood that what Marilyn needed to play this showgirl was what she already had when she arrived at Croydon airport; but between Marilyn's belief in a magical key, a flash of insight that would dispel all doubts, and Paula's inability to supply it, Paula had to keep talking."

Almost universally unpopular on the set, particularly with directors, Marilyn's black-clad drama coach acquired a whole series of nicknames, the most pleasant being "The Witch." Because of her insistence on wearing black at all times, even in the one hundred degree heat of the Nevada desert on *THE MISFITS* (1961), Paula was known as "Black Bart." However, BILLY WILDER, and to some extent JOHN HUSTON, acknowledged that Paula was a help in handling a very unstable lead actress.

A number of biographers have accused the Strasbergs of exploiting Marilyn. The significance of the nation's biggest star becoming an acolyte of the Actors Studio was parmount; but for her services on-set, Paula was paid handsomely, and some say extravagantly. LEE STRASBERG reputedly negotiated on behalf of his wife, and by the time Paula was coaching Marilyn through *LET'S MAKE LOVE* (1960), she was on a weekly salary of $3,000, which meant that she made even more out of the film than Marilyn. Her fees continued to rise, to $5000 per week for *SOMETHING'S GOT TO GIVE*, half of which Marilyn paid out of her own pocket.

Perhaps some of this money was for the emotional strain. The set of *The Misfits* was, by all accounts, a battleground, as Marilyn's marriage to Arthur went through its final scene. When Marilyn moved out of the hotel room she shared with her husband, it was to move in with Paula. In his autobiography, Miller is scathing about Paula's behavior: "She could hardly say what time it was without seeming to suggest it was secret information, and to engender awe in the innocent onlooker she wore several watches—a pendant hanging from her neck, a wrist watch, and another in her bag so she would know what time it was in London and Tokyo, Mexico City and Sydney, implying that she and Lee had important interests all over the world."

Paula, though, pressed on with what she was being paid for: getting a good performance out of Marilyn. At the time, she told author James Goode, "This is the most difficult part she has played. . . . I do believe it was essential for me to be with her on this picture . . . because so much of it was close to her, also because she is a creative actress, not a personality. . . . I feel that I have contributed to every frame of *The Misfits*. If it doesn't work out, that's something I must share with her. My work is not a mystery. This is my twenty-fourth picture. My work is evident on the screen." John Huston, for one, felt that Paula deserved at least some credit: "I think we're doing Paula a disservice. For all we know, she's holding this picture together."

Paula and Marilyn's closeness diminished somewhat after Marilyn moved back to Los Angeles in 1961. Undoubtedly, the strains of her role took their toll on Paula, who reportedly had a breakdown sometime that year. She returned to Los Angeles to coach Marilyn through *Something's Got to Give*, but when Marilyn was fired, she went back to New York. In some quarters it was said that Marilyn had, by this time, decided to dispense with Paula's services.

On August 8, 1962 Paula and Lee were in Los Angeles for Marilyn's FUNERAL. Paula died four years later, in 1966.

## STRASBERG, SUSAN (1938–1999)

"Marilyn was drawn to my father because although she had little formal education, she understood human nature. . . . Human nature, especially her own, fascinated her. They were really destined to meet and work together."

Susan Strasberg, daughter of Lee and Paula, was seventeen when Marilyn became a regular visitor to her home. An actress of some considerable and precocious success, she made her film debut in *Picnic* (1955), and earned glowing reviews for her debut Broadway performance as Anne Frank in *The Diary of Anne Frank* that same year. Marilyn was at the premiere and the party, held at Sari's restaurant.

Susan has written that Marilyn became like a SISTER to her, another sibling in the Strasberg household. There were moments when she "was convinced there was no love or energy left for me, and I felt guilty for even feeling that way, because I saw how lonely Marilyn was. She really had nobody she felt she could trust completely—not one person." As a testament to both their closeness and Marilyn's GENEROSITY, she gave Susan an original Chagall drawing for one of her birthdays.

Like her father, Susan Strasberg taught acting. She won a 1957 British Academy Award for *Picnic*, and worked extensively in film and television. She also appeared in a number of Marilyn Monroe documentaries.

BOOKS:

*Bittersweet*, Susan Strasberg. New York: G. P. Putnam, 1980.

*Marilyn and Me*, Susan Strasberg. New York: Warner Books, 1992.

She tells of her friendship and sibling rivalry with Marilyn, adopted into the family by her parents Lee and Paula Strasberg.

## *STREETCAR NAMED DESIRE, A*

One of the scenes Marilyn performed at the ACTORS STUDIO was the seduction scene in this TENNESSEE WILLIAMS play. John Strasberg acted opposite her.

## STRIKES

Marilyn joined many fellow stars (including Gary Cooper, GREGORY PECK, Paul Newman, ELIZABETH TAYLOR, DEBBIE REYNOLDS, and others) on a strike called by the Screen Actors Guild that stopped all work at Hollywood studios for weeks in early 1960. At the time, Marilyn was scheduled to start work on *LET'S MAKE LOVE* (1960). The dispute was resolved after an agreement was reached on residual rights for television showings of movies. The Screen Writers Guild came out in sympathy, but ARTHUR MILLER continued with script rewrites.

Years earlier, Marilyn humbled the powerful board of TWENTIETH CENTURY-FOX when she refused to work on the sub-standard material the studio was giving her. Marilyn was one of the first stars to stand up to the studios in this way.

## STUDIOS

MARILYN:
"Only the public can make a star. It's the studios who try to make a system out of it."

Marilyn made the vast majority of her twenty-nine completed films for TWENTIETH CENTURY-FOX. She also made three movies for MGM and two for RKO. UNITED ARTISTS financed later movies *SOME LIKE IT HOT* (1959) and *THE MISFITS* (1961). COLUMBIA Pictures only retained young Marilyn's services for one picture, *LADIES OF THE CHORUS* (1948).

Marilyn made a concerted attempt to escape the pervasive studio system by setting up her own production company, MARILYN MONROE PRODUCTIONS, which only made one movie, *THE PRINCE AND THE SHOWGIRL* (1957).

## STUDIO BIOGRAPHIES

**Twentieth Century-Fox, Issued by Harry Brand, December 30, 1946**

Eighteen-year-old Marilyn Monroe, Twentieth Century-Fox discovery, is being ballyhooed as a sort of a junior Lana Turner, and like the famous star, she's a Hollywood-born-and-bred youngster who didn't have to leave town to attract the attention of the talent scouts.

A Twentieth Century-Fox publicity photo of Marilyn, 1953.

Once named as the "Oomph" girl of Emerson Junior High School, Marilyn nevertheless had no screen ambitions. She wanted instead to be a secretary, went to work for a defense industry owned by Reginald Denny after her graduation from Van Nuys High School, and there was discovered by army public relations officers who asked her to do some army motion pictures.

As a result of that, she went to work as a photographer's model, worked for some of the biggest agencies in the Los Angeles area, and appeared on some of the fanciest magazine covers.

A short time later Miss Monroe, to add to her income, went to the home of a Twentieth Century-Fox talent scout to sit with the baby. He was so impressed with her beauty he arranged for her to have a screen test in black and white film. This was so good she was then tested in Technicolor and signed to a long-term contract.

That's fast action in Hollywood, where such behavior is usually considered "impulsive," but the studio execs didn't want to take a chance on a youngster they consider a terrific bet for stardom. . . .

Personal data: Loves swimming, horseback riding, yachting, but has a tendency to get seasick . . . writes poetry but won't show it to anyone . . . loves music, from the classics to boogie-woogie . . . hobby is photography, until her movie career hoped to become a woman photographer of baby animals, kittens, puppies, etcetera . . . hates untidiness, careless drivers, closed places, and cowboy music.

And she loves movies.

VITAL STATISTICS: Real name: Norma Jean Daugherty [sic]; Birthplace: Los Angeles California; Birthday: June 1; Foster Mother: Mrs. E. S. Goddard; Foster Father: E. S. Goddard; Height: 5 feet 5½ inches; Weight: 118 pounds; Hair: Blonde; Eyes: Blue; Education: Emerson Jr. High, Los Angeles; Van Nuys High, Van Nuys, California.

**Twentieth Century-Fox, Issued by Harry Brand, February 7, 1951**

One night not long ago Marilyn Monroe, beautifully groomed and dressed in expensive good taste, was escorted to a premiere at the Circle Theatre on El Centro Street in Hollywood by Charles Chaplin, Jr.

As they neared the theatre someone in the party called attention to a severe frame building sitting back from the street.

"That's the Los Angeles Orphanage," someone said. "You know, where they keep the kids that nobody wants."

Marilyn kept right on walking. She made no effort to conceal the fact that her early life was spent in a series of private homes and in the orphanage as a ward of Los Angeles Country, but this period of her life she prefers to forget. Her eyes are on a bright future in the make-believe world of the films, where anything can come true, and where it really is coming true for Marilyn. At twenty-two, she ranks as one of the cinema's most promising newcomers and her studio, Twentieth Century-Fox, is building her into a top-bracket star.

Big, sprawling Los Angeles Country did the best it could for Marilyn but it's a pretty impersonal sort of father and mother, and even though the various families who kept the little girl in their homes were good to her, she learned early in life to be self-sufficient

A Twentieth Century-Fox publicity photo for *Niagara* (1953)

A Twentieth Century-Fox publicity photo for *Love Nest* (1951).

and to make the best of whatever environment in which she found herself. Perhaps that accounts for the equanimity with which she faced the early disappointment of her Hollywood career after being "discovered" by a studio and then being dropped to await discovery all over again.

Marilyn's real name was Norma Jean Baker [sic] and her mother was a helpless invalid and her father was killed in an automobile accident shortly after her birth. Marilyn has never known either. She spent her childhood in a series of private homes as a ward of the County, and even now she finds it a trifle confusing to remember all of them. . . . Before she was ten, Marilyn was taken in by Mrs. E. Ana Lower, of West Los Angeles, whom Marilyn still thinks of as "Aunt Ana." Mrs. Lower was the nearest thing to 'family' that Marilyn has ever known. This wonderful woman, who has since died, treated Marilyn like a daughter and within the limits of her ability provided her with things she needed, plus an abundance of love and affections.

She was with "Aunt Anna" for two years and lived in what was then called the Sawtelle District, regarded by the more favored youngsters from Bel Air and Brentwood as the "wrong side of the tracks."

While living with Mrs. Lower she began to emerge from her shell and spend more time with other children. She took an interest in the school plays and being a lanky girl found herself playing boy's parts both in the school plays and in the out-of-school activities such as the little "radio" shows which she and her Sawtelle friends improvised. It was her fate to play the young prince when such productions as Jack and the Beanstalk were undertaken.

At fifteen and in high school, Marilyn experienced a short-lived marriage which she prefers to forget. Both were immature youngsters, the thing didn't work out, and the boy is now happily remarried and has a family.

After completing her schooling at Van Nuys High School in the San Fernando Valley, Marilyn went to work for the Radio Plane Co. inspecting parachutes for target planes. The firm was owned by Reginald Denny.

While working at the plant she augmented her income by modeling and one month had her picture on four magazine covers.

Howard Hughes, then convalescing from an airplane accident, saw them and became interested in her but before he could arrange a screen test, Twentieth Century-Fox had given her a color test and signed her for a year.

Marilyn worked in one picture, "Scudda Hoo! Scudda Hay!" but her tiny part ended up, in the best Hollywood tradition, on the cutting room floor. A year at Twentieth in which no suitable parts were found and Marilyn was dropped.

Columbia then signed her for a 9-day musical, "Ladies of the Chorus," in which she played a burlesque queen, and Marilyn was again dropped.

Things were tough. She decided she had better supplement her natural charms with acting ability, and engaged the coaching services of Natasha Lytess, one of Hollywood's best and who coincidentally is now a coach at Twentieth and continuing Marilyn's lessons.

Marilyn engaged a room at the Studio Club, home of many an aspiring starlet, and limited herself to two meals a day. She eked out a living modeling clothes and posing for fashion and cover photographers.

One day she was approached by an agent who told her Lester Cowan was producing "Love Happy" and needed a blonde for Groucho Marx to chase. She rushed over and was hired on the spot. The scene lasted for a full minute. It didn't get cut, either.

When the picture was released, Cowan persuaded Marilyn to go on tour and plug the picture in Chicago, Detroit, New York and other cities. She did everything—press interviews, TV appearances, charity shows, and picked up a lot of poise in the process.

When she returned from the tour, Twentieth sent for her again and gave her a part in "Ticket to Tomahawk," in which she played a dancing girl. The picture was filmed in Colorado and the day she returned she received a call from Arthur Hornblow, MGM producer, asking her to read for Director John Huston for a role in "Asphalt Jungle."

She got the part, and meantime had been taken into her home by Lucille Ryman,

A Twentieth Century-Fox publicity photo by Frank Powolny, 1950.

MGM talent director who had suggested her to Hornblow.

In "Asphalt Jungle" she played the 'niece' of Louis Calhern, a wide-eyed young lovely interested in an older man. The role was a minor one but when Marilyn came on the screen it made the audience gasp. Probably her greatest satisfaction came when Huston told her at the end of the picture, "You know, Marilyn, you're going to be a good actress."

Following the "Asphalt Jungle" role, Twentieth's Joseph Mankiewicz looked at the picture and picked her to play Miss Caswell in "All About Eve." It is another fat part since she appeared in support of Anne Baxter, George Sanders and Celeste Holm.

When Darryl Zanuck saw the rushes he sent for Marilyn's agent and signed her to a long-term contract. Her first picture on the new road to stardom was "Will You Love Me in December?" in which Monty Woolly, Constance Bennet, David Wayne, Jean Peters and Thelma Ritter complete the starring cast.

Marilyn is blue-eyed, blonde, 5 feet 5½ inches tall, and weighs 118 pounds.

After having grown up in an atmosphere of uncertainty and change, she is completely poised and takes each day's problems in stride.

Now, with a big studio behind her, a comfortable apartment, nice clothes and a world of friends, she is able to forget the early hardships.

Hollywood, which is often the scene of heartbreak, has been the scene of her success. It hasn't been easy, but at 22 Marilyn has little to complain about.

**RKO Radio Studios, Issued by Perry Lieber, November 30, 1951**

Date of birth: June 1, 1928 [sic]; Birthplace: Los Angeles, California; Real Name: Norma Jean Baker [sic]; Height: 5 feet 5½ inches; Weight: 118 Pounds; Hair: Silver Blonde; Eyes: Blue.

From lonely orphan to sought after motion picture star is the true life Cinderella story of Marilyn Monroe.

When Marilyn was nine years old she lived at the Los Angeles Orphan's Home, a single city block from the RKO Radio Pictures studios. From an upstairs window in the orphanage she could see the studio's big water tank, with the RKO Radio insignia. It was only a symbol, but it fired her child's imagination with dreams of what must be transpiring in the nearby glamourland.

Then came an unforgettable experience, one which doubtless influenced Marilyn's entire life. The children at the Orphanage were invited to a Christmas party at the RKO Studios. They were shown a movie on the lot, and each of the girls was given a string of imitation pearls as a gift. To Marilyn this party was sheer magic.

Fittingly, it was to the same RKO Radio Studios that Miss Monroe returned in the early autumn of 1951 to play her first starring role in motion pictures. She had, during the years that had intervened since the memorable Christmas party, won a foothold in pictures and become recognized as a personality to reckon with. Twentieth Century-Fox had placed her under contract, and was grooming her for stardom. It remained, however, for Jerry Wald and Norman Krasna to star her the first time in their picture "Clash by Night."

In that drama, produced for distribution by RKO Radio, Marilyn Monroe's name is placed above the title along with those of Barbara Stanwyck, Paul Douglas and Robert Ryan.

Thus the big film plant at Gower Street and Melrose Avenue was directly associated with a second major thrill in the life of a girl who can match every big moment of success with a heartache from a lonely childhood.

Marilyn's real name is Norma Jean Baker [sic], but she has no memory of the parents who bestowed it upon her. Her mother was a hopeless invalid and her father was killed in an automobile accident shortly after Marilyn's birth in Los Angeles on June 1, 1926. From infancy until the day she began earning her own living, Marilyn lived in a series of private homes, with an interlude in the orphanage already mentioned, as a ward of the county.

The first home in which she recalls being placed was in Hawthorne, Calif. She remembers little about this, as the family moved East when she was five. Marilyn's next move was to the home of British actors who had settled in Hollywood and were playing bits in pictures. She was picking up a British accent when she was again given a "new home", this time with a studio worker and his wife. They lived in a big house on a hill and were kind to her, but there were no other children around, and Marilyn found herself relying mainly for companionship upon a collection of exotic birds.

The kindly studio workers couldn't keep the little girl, and at the age of nine, the much buffeted Marilyn was taken to the Orphan's home. The superintendent was wonderful and sweet, the matrons were conscientious and kindly, but the simply couldn't provide enough motherly love to go around for so many children.

Before her tenth birthday, Marilyn was again placed as a boarder with a Los Angeles family, this time in the San Fernando Valley.

Then there was another move, to a family made up entirely of women—a great-grandmother, grandmother, mother and three young daughters. She stayed there but a short time.

Then came a move which was to have a most important effect upon the migratory child. She was taken in by a Mrs. Ana Lower, of West Los Angeles. Mrs. Lower was the nearest to "family" Marilyn has ever known. This fine woman, who has since died, treated her like a daughter, providing her with the love for which she was so starved. Marilyn remained with "Aunt Ana," as she still remembers Mrs. Lower, for two years. During that time she began to emerge from her protective shell and spend more time with other children. Remembering the wonderful Christmas party at the RKO studios, and still burning with the ambition to become a film actress, she took a lively interest in school plays.

At fifteen and while still in high school, Marilyn experienced a short-lived marriage which she prefers to forget. For two immature youngsters, marriage simply didn't work out. After completing her schooling at Van Nuys High School in San Fernando Valley, Marilyn went to work for the Radio Plane Company, owned by former film start Reginald Denny. Her job was inspecting parachutes. While working at the plant she augmented her income by modeling. In one month her picture adorned four magazine covers.

It was during this period that Marilyn adopted an attitude toward so-called "cheesecake photography" which she insists she'll never abandon. Most of her modeling was done in bathing suits, shorts and sweaters and playsuits.

The photographs, reproduced in magazines, attracted the attention of film scouts. Marilyn was tested by Twentieth Century-Fox, and signed to a year's contract. And that is why she insists she'll never refuse to do "cheesecake" pictures, so long as they are in good taste, no matter how big a dramatic star she may become. They gave her her big chance, and she isn't the kind who forgets.

In that first stop at Twentieth Century-Fox, Marilyn worked in one picture, "Scudda Hoo! Scudda Hay!" but her tiny part ended up, in familiar Hollywood tradition, on the cutting room floor. At the end of the year, her contract was not renewed.

Columbia then signed her for a musical, "Ladies of the Chorus," in which she played a burlesque queen. Then again, Marilyn was dropped.

At this point she decided she had better supplement her natural charms with acting technique, and she engaged the coaching service of Natasha Lytess.

Deadly serious in her determination to become an actress, Marilyn took a room at the Hollywood Studio Club, home of many an aspiring starlet, limited herself to two meals a day and eked out a living by modeling clothes and posing for fashion photography.

One day she was approached by an agent who told her Lester Cowan was producing a picture called "Love Happy," and needed a blonde for Groucho Marx to chase. Marilyn rushed over, was hired on the spot. When the film was released, Cowan engaged Marilyn to go on tour and plug it in Chicago, Detroit, New York and other cities. She did the complete routine—press interviews, TV appearances, radio shows and charity benefits. In doing so, she acquired confidence and poise.

When she returned form the tour, Twentieth sent for her again and gave her the part of a dancing girl in "Ticket to Tomahawk." The picture was filmed in Colorado, and the day she returned she received a call from MGM to read for Director John Huston for a role in "Asphalt Jungle." She got the part, which proved the real starting point of her film career.

In Asphalt Jungle," she played the niece of Louis Calhern. Her role, that of a wide-eyed lovely interested in older men, was comparatively minor, but when Marilyn came on the screen, the audience gasped. A new personality had "arrived."

Following "Asphalt Jungle," Marilyn got her second important chance in "All About Eve." Again, her role was comparatively minor, but she appeared in support of such stars as Bette Davis, Anne Baxter, George Sanders and Celeste Holm, and even in that fast company made herself noticed favorably.

When Twentieth's Darryl Zanuck saw the rushes of "All About Eve," he promptly signed Marilyn to a long-term contract, and ordered a stellar buildup for her. She appeared in three more pictures for her home studio before being borrowed by Jerry Wald and Norman Krasna for her first starring part in "Clash by Night."

The return to RKO studios ended a cycle in Marilyn's life, opened the doorway to another one in which the heartaches of the past will be remembered only as inspiration for the future.

## STUDIO CLUB
1215 NORTH LODI PLACE, HOLLYWOOD

MARILYN:
"The Studio Club had rules, but the women in charge were nice, and if you came home after they locked the doors at ten-thirty, a smile and apology would usually be enough to satisfy them."

Over the years, many successful actresses lived for a spell at this YWCA-affiliated residential hotel, including Barbara Eden, Linda Darnell, Donna Reed, and KIM NOVAK. Marilyn lived at this Spanish-style residence for aspiring actresses on two occasions.

It was the place she moved into after divorcing first husband JAMES DOUGHERTY, in 1946–7, when she was contracted to TWENTIETH CENTURY-FOX. Marilyn paid $12 per week to share room number 307 with an actress named Clarice Evans. Years later, Evans told the *Los Angeles Times* that Marilyn was as concerned about how much space there was for her books as for her clothes.

BEN LYON, who first brought Marilyn to Fox's attention in 1946, said, "I asked her where she lived, and when she said at the Studio Club, I was impressed, because I knew that a girl who looked like that could have the biggest house in Beverly Hills, she could have whatever she wanted because men would give it to her. Therefore, if she lived at the Studio Club it was because she had character."

Marilyn returned to the apartments on June 3, 1948. This time she had a room to herself, number 334; the first six months' rent, $300, was paid for by LUCILLE RYMAN. In some accounts, it is said that Marilyn agreed to pose nude for photographer TOM KELLEY because she needed the $50 to pay the rent for her Studio Club room.

## STYNE, JULE (1905–1994)

British-born composer, pianist, and conductor who wrote the songs for *GENTLEMEN PREFER BLONDES* (1953), including Marilyn's hallmark song "Diamonds Are a Girl's Best Friend." Styne's preference for Marilyn over BETTY GRABLE was apparently instrumental in persuading Fox chief DARRYL ZANUCK to give the studio's rising star this plum role. Other songs in his long career are "There Goes That Song Again," "Give Me Five Minutes More," "It's Magic," and "Three Coins in the Fountain."

In some reports Styne was preparing to work with Marilyn once more just before her death, writing songs for a project known at that stage as *A Tree Grows in Brooklyn*. Styne also wrote the songs for a 1974 stage musical *Sugar*, based on *SOME LIKE IT HOT* (1959).

## SUICIDE ATTEMPTS

MARILYN:
"[Suicide is] a person's privilege. I don't believe it's a sin or a crime. It's your right if you want to, though it doesn't get you anywhere."

Estimates on the number of times Marilyn attempted suicide vary wildly, though it is generally accepted that she did make attempts on her own life. Some biographers are of the opinion that she did not ever really intend to kill herself, but rather made these dramatic statements in order to obtain sympathy and attention. These tend to be the same biographers who believe that Marilyn's DEATH was murder, and not, as officially recorded by the Los Angeles CORONER, suicide.

Marilyn told friends she had twice attempted suicide before the age of twenty, once by leaving the gas on, and once by taking sleeping pills. Dr. Elliot Corday, who treated Marilyn up until mid-50s, stated that Marilyn had made many attempts on her life.

In 1950, grief-stricken at the death of mentor JOHNNY HYDE, Marilyn allegedly took twenty capsules of the BARBITURATE Nembutal. In a suicide note, she left her most valuable possessions—her car and a fur stole—to drama coach NATASHA LYTESS, who found her unconscious with a trail of pill residue coming out of her mouth. Marilyn later claimed that she had merely fallen asleep and a sleeping pill had dissolved in her mouth.

In 1953 Marilyn learned that her legal guardian GRACE MCKEE GODDARD killed herself with an overdose of barbiturates, after a long battle with alcohol and a couple of debilitating strokes.

During her marriage to ARTHUR MILLER, Marilyn is said to have made as many as three attempts on her life. Certainly, in Miller's play *AFTER THE FALL* the protagonist Maggie is saved several times by her partner, until she finally succeeds in taking her own life. Marilyn's documented suicide attempts during this period occurred when she was deeply depressed after losing the babies she was carrying. On these two occasions, Arthur found her in time.

Marilyn was taken to the hospital by PAULA STRASBERG in the fall of 1958 after taking too many sleeping pills with champagne. She was kept under observation for the weekend but returned to the set of *SOME LIKE IT HOT* (1959) on the next Monday.

The event which precipitated a ten-day suspension of shooting *THE MISFITS* (1961), when Marilyn went to rest at the Westside HOSPITAL in Los Angeles, may well have been a suicide attempt. At the time, Marilyn's DOCTOR Hyman Engelberg told the press, "My guess is that she will probably be able to go back to work in a week. She is just tuckered out."

She overdosed again after the break-up of her marriage with Miller; it seems that Dr. Engelberg was summoned in time to pump out Marilyn's stomach. Soon afterward, JOE DIMAGGIO came to nurse her back to health. This attempt, if it took place, occurred not long after reports that CLARK GABLE's widow Kay had blamed Marilyn for her husband's death, and after Marilyn had considered throwing herself out of the thirteenth-floor window of her New York apartment. Within weeks, Marilyn's psychoanalyst, DR. MARIANNE KRIS, recommended that Marilyn check in to the Payne-Whitney HOSPITAL.

Although details are sketchy, it has been claimed that Marilyn made an unspecified number of further attempts on her life requiring medical intervention, before her death on August 5, 1962. One such occasion, in some accounts of the last weeks of Marilyn's life, took place at the CAL-NEVA LODGE, where she allegedly stayed with FRANK SINATRA two weekends before she died.

A Suicide Investigation Team was set up by the Los Angeles Coroner's office to conduct a psychological profile of Marilyn. Dr. Robert Litman, who headed the team, has been quoted as saying that in no cases had anybody unknowingly committed suicide with barbiturates. The team concluded that Marilyn was not psychotic, nor physically addicted to drugs, but that Marilyn Monroe's death "was caused by self-administered sedative drugs, that the mode of death is 'probable suicide.'"

A verdict of suicide was passed by the coroner, bearing out the preliminary judgment by toxicologist R. J. Abernethy, who arrived at it after consultation with psychoanalyst Dr. RALPH GREENSON. Summing up in his official report, Coroner Theodore J. Curphey stated, "Miss Monroe had often expressed the wish to give up, withdraw, and even to die. On more than one occasion in the past, when disappointed and depressed, she had made suicide attempts by using sedative drugs. On these occasions she had called for help and had been rescued."

Marilyn biographers who subscribe to murder or accidental death theories share the belief that in the final months of her life, Marilyn had a degree of self-possession, a feeling of taking control of her life, which indicated a thirst for the future. People who are actively planning for the future, they assert, are not typical candidates for suicide. This is the opinion of many of Marilyn's FRIENDS and confidants of the time, such as RALPH ROBERTS, SUSAN STRASBERG, RUPERT ALLAN, and PAT NEWCOMB. Marilyn was busy arranging interviews, negotiating future film projects, organizing a trip to New York, and even, in some reports, planning an imminent WEDDING, either to former husband DiMaggio or to Sinatra.

## SUKARNO, PRESIDENT

Indonesian head of state whom Marilyn met on her thirtieth birthday, June 1, 1956 (or the day before, in some accounts), after the movie-mad president said that what would really make his trip to Los Angeles complete would be to meet Marilyn Monroe. JOSHUA LOGAN, directing Marilyn in *BUS STOP* (1956), did the honors and threw a party.

The president of Indonesia told Marilyn, "You are a very important person in Indonesia. Your pictures are the most popular of any that have ever played in my country. The entire Indonesian population is interested in my meeting you."

Marilyn later commented: "He kept looking down my dress. You'd think with five wives he'd have enough."

In one report of the occasion, Marilyn was

President Sukarno of Indonesia with Marilyn at her thirtieth birthday party, 1956.

presented to Sukarno and told him how pleased she was to meet the president of India. When Sukarno told her it was Indonesia, Marilyn replied that she had never heard of the place. Scandal-mongers have claimed that their evening together continued in the privacy of a bedroom.

Apparently when Sukarno ran into domestic trouble a year or so later, Marilyn wanted to offer him a safe haven, not something that husband ARTHUR MILLER would consider.

## SULLIVAN, ED (1902–1974)

Popular TV host Ed Sullivan was not one of Marilyn's greatest fans. After her performance of "Heat Wave," her big solo song and dance number in *THERE'S NO BUSINESS LIKE SHOW BUSINESS* (1954), on his show, Sullivan was quoted as saying, "Miss Monroe has just about worn the Welcome off this observer's mat . . . 'Heat Wave' is easily one of the most flagrant violations of good taste this observer has ever witnessed."

## SUMMERS, ANTHONY

A British investigative journalist who wrote the first major BIOGRAPHY to take a thorough look at the many rumors of KENNEDY involvement in Marilyn's DEATH. *Goddess: The Secret Lives of Marilyn Monroe* came out in 1985. The allegations in this book, many based on material made public by ROBERT SLATZER, led to a number of television documentaries, one of which, due to run on ABC's *20/20* news show in 1985, was cancelled at the last minute by network chief Roone Arledge, bringing accusations of censorship.

Between the hardcover and paperback publication of DONALD SPOTO's 1993 biography, the first of which was highly critical of Anthony Summers, Spoto omitted references to unscrupulousness after Summer let Spoto examine the tapes and transcripts of interviews he had conducted.

Summers has also written books on JFK and J. EDGAR HOOVER.

BOOK:

*Goddess: The Secret Lives of Marilyn Monroe*, Anthony Summers. New York: Macmillan, 1985.

## SUN VALLEY, IDAHO

In freezing conditions, the crew shot mountain exteriors for *BUS STOP* (1956) here during the last five days of March 1956. Marilyn and at least four of her fellow actors picked up a chest infection.

## SUPERSTITION

Very few biographers have anything to say about whether or not Marilyn was superstitious. She certainly had her superstitious rituals before appearing on set—warm-up exercises and stretches, and grooming and makeup rituals which made her infamously late.

It is known that she perceived the death of journalist MARA SCHERBATOFF on her wedding day as a bad omen for her marriage to ARTHUR MILLER.

## SUTTON PLACE
SUITE E8 (8TH FLOOR), NEW YORK

Marilyn moved out of the WALDORF-ASTORIA Hotel in late 1955, as financial reality began to sink in for MARILYN MONROE PRODUCTIONS. It was from this address that Marilyn made her return to Hollywood to shoot *BUS STOP* (1956). Following news of her engagement to ARTHUR MILLER, the building was besieged by reporters and photographers. Even without such portentous news, a reporter or two habitually staked out Marilyn's home, where she lived until, as Mrs. Arthur Miller, she rented a new New York apartment on East FIFTY-SEVENTH STREET.

(*see* HOMES)

## TALMADGE, NORMA (1893–1957)

The "Norma" in Norma Jeane was an homage to this doe-eyed star of the silent movie era, the favorite of Marilyn's mother GLADYS BAKER. She was regarded by many as the finest and most versatile actress of the silent era. The eldest of three actress sisters, Talmadge rose to fame in the 1914 movie *Battle Cry of Peace*. In 1917 she married producer JOSEPH M. SCHENCK, who helped her form Norma Talmadge Productions, before going to run UNITED ARTISTS and then set up his own studio in 1933, TWENTIETH CENTURY-FOX.

Talmadge was a major box office draw right through the twenties, until the advent of talkies, when her strong Brooklyn accent became an insurmountable liability. She retired from the cinema at the age of thirty-three.

## TARADASH, DANIEL (B. 1913)

Taradash was the SCREENWRITER who adapted *DON'T BOTHER TO KNOCK* (1952), in which Marilyn had her first starring role. Looking back at the movie, Taradash has said that although director ROY WARD BAKER was a nice man, he was a "bad choice to direct this picture. . . . someone who was more attuned to working with a young girl—and a young girl who was insecure, could probably have got a much better performance. . . . If they had spent more money and had got a better director, they might have had something. As it stands now, it is an oddity—a cult film."

Taradash won an Oscar the following year for *From Here to Eternity* (1953).

## TASHLIN, FRANK (1913–1972)

Tashlin was one of the very few writer/directors to make the transition from cartoons to live-action movies. After many years as the man behind Porky the Pig, Bugs Bunny, and Daffy Duck, Tashlin teamed up with the Marx brothers to write *A Night in Casablanca* (1946) and *LOVE HAPPY* (1950), in which up-and-coming actress Marilyn had a walk-on part.

In the mid-fifties Tashlin wrote, directed, and produced the movies which made JAYNE MANSFIELD, Marilyn's self-appointed biggest RIVAL, a household name: *The Girl Can't Help It* (1956) and *Will Success Spoil Rock Hunter?* (1957).

Tashlin was initially approached by TWENTIETH CENTURY-FOX to direct Marilyn's final movie project, *SOMETHING'S GOT TO GIVE*, but soon dropped out of the running when Marilyn said she preferred GEORGE CUKOR.

## TAYLOR, ELIZABETH (B. 1932)

MARILYN:
"Everybody says I can't act. They said the same thing about Elizabeth Taylor. And they were wrong. She was great in *A Place in the Sun*. I'll never get the right part, anything I really want. My looks are against me. They're too specific."

ELIZABETH TAYLOR ON MARILYN:
"She seemed to have a kind of unconscious glow about her physical self that was innocent, like a child. When she posed nude, it was 'Gee, I am kind of, you know, sort of dishy,' like she enjoyed it without being egotistical."

It has often been said that Marilyn's one true RIVAL in the star stakes was Elizabeth Taylor. British-born, Taylor's American parents took her back to the States at the onset of the Second World War. Taylor began her film career at the age of ten, and made a great splash with *National Velvet* (1944). Many of her performances from the late forties to the mid-sixties received rave reviews and Academy Award recognition: *Little Women* (1949), *A Place in the Sun* (1951), *Giant* (1956), three successive Oscar nominations for *Raintree County* (1957), *Cat On a Hot Tin Roof* (1958) and *Suddenly Last Summer* (1959), and then two Academy Awards for *Butterfield 8* (1960) and *Who's Afraid of Virginia Woolf* (1966). Taylor has continued to work over the years, but has often had a higher profile for her romantic entanglements (nine marriages) than for her screen performances. More recently, she has been a staunch campaigner for the fight against AIDS.

Most Marilyn biographers have something to say about the huge differences in remuneration these actresses commanded in 1962. At the end of her career, when Monroe was offered $100,000 for *SOMETHING'S GOT TO GIVE*, Elizabeth Taylor was paid $1 million for her part in *Cleopatra* (1963), a movie which almost bankrupted TWENTIETH CENTURY-FOX. Some biographers affirm that Marilyn's movie was cancelled by the studio because of the financial woes of Taylor's film. It is sometimes reported that at one stage, when Taylor was too ill to continue shooting on *Cleopatra*, Lloyd's of London suggested that Marilyn Monroe replace her.

## TAYLOR, FRANK AND FAMILY

Frank Taylor was ARTHUR MILLER's editor at Dell publishing, and for many years had been close friends with Marilyn's third husband.

Frank, his wife Nana, and their four boys often visited Marilyn and Arthur at their ROXBURY country home. Sometimes two of the boys, Mike and Curtice, went over to stay

A Twentieth Century-Fox publicity shot by Frank Powolny, ca. 1950.

with the Miller's, usually when Arthur's children Jane and Bobby were there. Taylor was Marilyn's escort on the trip to Los Angeles to meet NIKITA KHRUSCHEV.

In the summer of 1958, Miller asked his friend what he thought of the first draft of his screenplay for *THE MISFITS* (1961). Taylor suggested that JOHN HUSTON would make the ideal director, and demonstrated his personal enthusiasm by accepting Marilyn's request to leave his job as editorial director at Dell and produce the movie. Many years earlier Taylor had spent some time working in Hollywood, and had produced the movie *Mystery Street* (1950).

During shooting of *The Misfits*, Taylor was in the unenviable position of keeping the production together despite the internecine battles that engulfed the set. Biographer FRED LAWRENCE GUILES writes, "If *The Misfits* is the most important film Marilyn ever made, and many critics believe it is, surely the presence of Frank Taylor had much to do with the fact it exists—that it was finished at all. In Marilyn and Montgomery Clift he had two of the most self-destructive stars in the history of films."

Marilyn on *The Jack Benny Show*, 1953.

## TELEPHONE

MARILYN:
"You know who I've always depended on? Not strangers, not friends. The telephone! That's my best friend. I seldom write letters, but I love calling friends, especially late at night, when I can't sleep."

Marilyn jealously guarded the secrecy of her telephone number. Sometimes she made sure that the telephone was always turned to the wall, so that guests would not be able to memorize her number from the dial. At one address, she put a false telephone number on the dial; not just any old number, but the number, reportedly, of the Los Angeles Morgue.

DR. RALPH GREENSON told the police that when he found Marilyn's body, she was clutching the telephone receiver in her hand. The alleged disappearance of Marilyn's telephone records after her death has been seized upon by CONSPIRACY theorists as proof of skullduggery.

## TELEVISION

Marilyn's film career took off at the same time as television was beginning to make inroads into the primacy of the movies. By the early sixties, movie audiences had decreasd by half on what they had been when Marilyn was first signed by a Hollywood studio. TWENTIETH CENTURY-FOX used new star Marilyn and the new technology of Cinemascope to try and fight this new threat.

In her starlet years when work was scarce, Marilyn tried to find work on television too. Producer Stanley Rubin, who worked with Marilyn on *THERE'S NO BUSINESS LIKE SHOW BUSINESS* (1954) turned her down for a TV movie *The Necklace* at the very beginning of her career.

Marilyn only appeared on television a few times in her life. She felt that she was too nervous to risk putting across a poor image on live television, and live or studio shows were the only ones to which she was invited. Her first ever television appearance, however, was in a TV commercial for Royal Triton Oil (see ADVERTISEMENTS).

Marilyn's television debut was on the JACK BENNY show, broadcast on September 13, 1953, in which she joined the host for a sketch.

On April 8, 1955, Marilyn officially raised her head over the parapet after walking out on Hollywood with a live interview on EDWARD R. MURROW's "Person to Person" show. This was her last ever live appearance, despite lucrative offers. It is said that in 1957 a television network offered Marilyn $2 million to star in her own television series.

Marilyn's antipathy towards television was partly personal. She was not at all happy to find out that new husband JOE DIMAGGIO preferred to spend days on end watching the tube rather than talking to her. It was reported that DiMaggio checked in advance to make sure that the motel room where they spent their wedding night had a television.

Lucille Ball did a Marilyn impersonation in an episode called "Ricky's Movie Offer" broadcast of her "I Love Lucy" show on November 8, 1954. This was the first of many Marilyn take-offs and CAMEO appearances which continue to this day. And of course, ever since her mysterious death, Marilyn has featured in dozens of television DOCUMENTARIES; she is a fixture in any look back at Hollywood or glamour or sex symbols.

In the year before she died, Marilyn was in negotiations to headline a television version of *Rain*, by Somerset Maugham. Negotiations broke down when NBC refused to entrust LEE STRASBERG with directing, and Marilyn would not accept any alternative.

## THEATER

Norma Jeane was keen on acting as a young girl. The imaginary play-acting she indulged in as a child, in the privacy of her bedroom, found an outlet when she landed roles in a number of school plays: *Petronella* and a Valentine's Day musical show at EMERSON HIGH SCHOOL. However, it appears that she did not impress the drama society at her next school, Van Nuys High, sufficiently to get a part.

In 1947, after TWENTIETH CENTURY-FOX declined to renew the option on Marilyn's contract, Marilyn joined the Bliss-Hayden Miniature Theater acting company, located at 254 South Robertson Boulevard, Beverly Hills (now The Beverly Hills Playhouse). She appeared in two plays, *GLAMOUR PREFERRED* and *STAGE DOOR*. Other Hollywood actors who put in a stint at the theater included Veronica Lake, Jon Hall, DORIS DAY, DEBBIE REYNOLDS, and Craig Stevens.

Despite the plaudits Marilyn received from top drama coach LEE STRASBERG, and her undoubted dedication to the craft of ACTING, Marilyn was very much a screen actress. As many biographers have noted, she was not temperamentally suited to the rigors of day-in, day-out performance with no chance of a retake. Even consummately skilled stage actors, when converted to the film world for any length of time, can have trouble readjusting to an exacting theatrical regime.

During her time at the ACTORS STUDIO, Marilyn performed several scenes from well-known plays, including Eugene O'Neill's *ANNA CHRISTIE*, CLIFFORD ODETS' *The Golden Boy* and TENNESSEE WILLIAMS's *A STREETCAR NAMED DESIRE*.

Marilyn reputedly once did take a bow on Broadway. After a production of *Teahouse of the August Moon*, in which Marilyn's friend ELI WALLACH was appearing, Marilyn stepped onto the boards, in costume, during the curtain call at the Martin Beck Theater (302 West Forty-fifth Street, New York).

Marilyn is often used as theatrical shorthand for glamour, vulnerability, beauty and the smart dumb blonde. Since her death, hundreds of plays have included a Marilyn-esque character, usually costumed in a trademark Marilyn outfit, such as the white halter dress from *THE SEVEN YEAR ITCH* (1955).

The trend began in 1955, with Broadway smash *Will Success Spoil Rock Hunter?* in which JAYNE MANSFIELD played a Marilyn-type blonde. Perhaps the most famous—some would say infamous—Marilyn-based play was ARTHUR MILLER'S *AFTER THE FALL*, which premiered two years after Marilyn's death.

Many more stage productions ranging from fringe to mainstream have followed in countries around the world. The most successful thus far was Terry Johnson's 1982 play, *INSIGNIFICANCE*, brought to the screen by Nicholas Roeg in 1985.

### THEATER ROLES MARILYN WANTED

In the year when she became a household name, 1952, Marilyn confided in a reporter, "I'd like to do roles like Julie in *Bury the Dead*, Gretchen in *Faust* and Teresa in *Cradle Song*. I don't want to be a comedienne forever."

Marilyn had hopes of playing the heroines she briefly portrayed at the Actors Studio in fully-fledged stage versions. In 1956 Marilyn said that she would love to play Lady Macbeth, opposite Marlon Brando. She also said that there was a chance she might appear on stage in a musical version of *My Fair Lady*.

A Dutch poster for *There's No Business Like Show Business* (1954).

## *THERE'S NO BUSINESS LIKE SHOW BUSINESS* (1954)

Marilyn's supporting role in this tribute to composer IRVING BERLIN was a compromise which served a number of purposes. It smoothed over her refusal to appear in *Pink Tights*, which she had rejected despite studio insistence that they knew best what movies she should be doing; it brought her back to Los Angeles, after living for a couple of months with new husband JOE DIMAGGIO in SAN FRANCISCO; and it afforded Marilyn the kind of concessions, if not yet control, she was keen to obtain. She was allowed her own team of drama coach NATASHA LYTESS, voice coach HAL SCHAEFER, and dance director JACK COLE, who she apparently preferred over the choreographer hired by producer SOL C. SIEGEL, Robert Alton. Also, most biographers concur, she was promised a project she very much wanted to do, *THE SEVEN YEAR ITCH* (1955).

Original screenwriter LAMAR TROTTI died of a heart attack before he could complete the script. Husband and wife team Henry and Phoebe Ephron took over, but, in Henry's words, "I think it was the hardest job we ever had. From the nature of the story, all the scenes were clichés."

Marilyn's hastily-written character Vicky, added in after the original story was conceived, was given some of the songs originally assigned to Ethel Merman. The resulting mixture of talent in this movie was bizarre by any standards: Marilyn, baby-faced love interest DONALD O'CONNOR, and brassy Merman, was a combination judged by most critics to be well short of critical mass.

Marilyn's relations with director WALTER LANG were spectacularly bad, even by her standards. Lang is said to have denigrated Marilyn at every opportunity; Marilyn was customarily late and yet, as ever, worked hard with her coaches to give the best performance she could, anxious that she might not measure up to the practiced song and dance stars she was working with. Marilyn's SONG numbers in the movie are "A Man Chases a Girl" (with O'Connor), "After You Get What You Want You Don't Want It" (with Marilyn multiplied in a fan-like deployment of mirrors), the controversial "Heatwave," "Lazy," "You'd Be Surprised," and of course the title song. However, owing to Marilyn's recently-signed exclusive recording contract with RCA, the voice on the soundtrack of the show belonged to Broadway star Dolores Gray; Marilyn recorded separate versions for release by her record company.

Yet Marilyn remained optimistic. During production, Marilyn wrote a guest column for vacationing Washington columnist Drew Pearson: "Being neither a natural-born actress, singer, nor dancer, I still pinch myself as I drive to work on the lot in a very nice automobile and go into a singing, dancing and dramatic routine in Irving Berlin's *There's No Business Like Show Business*."

Shooting began on May 29, 1954. It did not run either to time or to intention; Marilyn was ill from the lingering bronchitis she had picked up during a trip to Korea, and suffering from anemia and the side-effects of the sleeping pills she had been taking. Marilyn is said to have had three fainting spells during filming. When the press got wind of this, rumors began to circulate that she was pregnant. More likely, her physical ailments were combined with the strains of her recent marriage to Joe DiMaggio.

The poor reception of the film upset Marilyn. LENA PEPITONE quoted her as saying, "I did what they said and all it got me was a lot of abuse. . . . Big breasts, big ass, big deal. Can't I be anything else? . . . The dance people kept making me flash the skirt wide open and jump around like I had a fever . . . it was ridiculous." As a result of overruns on this movie, shooting on *The Seven Year Itch* had to be postponed, and Marilyn didn't have a break between the two pictures.

MEMORABLE COSTUMES:

Enveloping sequined white gown layered over a flesh-colored body stocking, slit to the thigh, with strategically placed silver and white flowers.

Black and white two-piece "Heat Wave" costume with open flared skirt and strapless bikini top.

**Nominations:**

ACADEMY AWARD:
Best Costume Design (Color): Charles Le Maire, William Travilla, Miles White
Best Music, Scoring of a Musical Picture: Alfred Newman, Lionel Newman
Best Writing, Motion Picture Story: Lamar Trotti

**Credits:**

Twentieth Century-Fox, CinemaScope and DeLuxe Color
Length: 117 minutes
Release date: December 16, 1954

Directed by: Walter Lang
Produced by: Sol C. Siegel
Written by: Henry Ephron, Phoebe Ephron, Lamar Trotti (story)
Cinematography by: Leon Shamroy
Film Editing by: Robert E. Simpson
Music by: Irving Berlin
Costume Design by: Charles Le Maire, William Travilla, Miles White

**Cast (credits order):**

Ethel Merman . . . Molly
Donald O'Connor . . . Tim Donahue
Marilyn Monroe . . . Vicky
Dan Dailey . . . Tim Donahue
Johnnie Ray . . . Steve Donahue
Mitzi Gaynor . . . Kathy Donahue
Richard Eastham . . . Lew Harris
Hugh O'Brian . . . Charles Gibbs
Frank McHugh . . . Eddie Duggan
Rhys Williams . . . Father Dineen
Lee Patrick . . . Marge
Eve Miller . . . Hat-check girl
Robin Raymond . . . Lillian
Alvy Moore . . . Katy's boyfriend
Lyle Talbot . . . Stage manager
Chick Chandler . . . Harry
Gavin Gordon . . . Geoffrey
George Chakiris . . . Dancer
Nolan Leary . . . Archbishop
George Melford . . . Stagehand
Henry Slate . . . Dance director
Jimmy Baird . . . Steve, age six (uncredited)
Billy Chapin . . . Steve, age ten (uncredited)
Donald Gamble . . . Tim, age six (uncredited)
Matt Mattox . . . Dancer (uncredited)
Buzz Miller . . . Dancer (uncredited)

Donald O'Connor, Marilyn and Mitzi Gaynor in *There's No Business Like Show Business* (1954).

**Crew:**
Robert Alton . . . choreographer
Jack Cole . . . choreographer (uncredited)
John DeCuir . . . art director
Lyle R. Wheeler . . . art director
Alfred Newman . . . music supervision
Lionel Newman . . . music conducting

**Plot:**
The Five Donahues—mother Molly (Ethel Merman), father Terry (Dan Dailey), and children Tim (Donald O'Connor), Katy (Mitzi Gaynor), and Steve (Johnny Ray)—are a showbiz family, who one by one start to leave the family act.

Young Steve is the first to leave, to follow his faith as a priest. Tim meets and falls in love with night club hat-check girl Vicky (Marilyn Monroe). They subsequently meet up in a Florida hotel where both the Four Donahues and Vicky are on the bill, but there has been a mix-up as both acts are scheduled to do the same 'Heatwave' number. One scene cut from the film was Ethel Merman's Molly singing "Anything You Can Do, I Can Do Better." Originally back-to-back with Marilyn's "Heat Wave" number, the song carried a plot function, as for much of the film the characters are battling to do the headline "Heat Wave" number. Tim persuades mother Molly to let the young woman do it, and the mother's dislike of this brash young thing increases when Vicky persuades Tim and Katy to be in a Broadway show with her. The Five Donahues are now down to the original two, mom and pop.

Katy falls in love with lyric writer Charley Gibbs (Hugh O'Brian), but Tim is in for a shock when he gets the (wrong) idea that Vicky is two-timing him with Lew Harris (Richard Eastham), the show's producer. Spurned and jealous, he drowns his sorrows on opening night, fails to show, and is injured in a car accident. Molly, though, boldly goes on with the show. Brother Terry gets into a fight with Tim in the hospital, and then Tim disappears. Terry is badly affected by the whole episode, and loses all desire to perform. Molly Donahue remains distinctly cool toward Vicky, though Katy tries to reconcile them for an Actors' Fund benefit. At last Vicky tells Molly she still loves the boy Tim, and that she was completely innocent (of everything). The two women become friends, just in time for Steve to put in an appearance backstage (he is now an army chaplain), and Tim, now in the Navy, does likewise, allowing the Five Donahues plus Vicky, to perform once again, for the grand finale title number.

Marilyn and Donald O'Connor in *There's No Business Like Show Business* (1954).

**Reviews:**
*New York Daily Mirror*
"Marilyn Monroe, who shocks Donald out of show business and into uniform, is given a trio of tunes, sung and performed in her trademarked sexy manner. . . . 'There's No Business Like Show Business' is a big extravaganza, colorfully bright and melodic. Just lots of plain, wonderful sentiment."

*Variety*
"Miss Monroe's treatment of her vocal must be seen to be appreciated. It's not going to chase 'em away from the box office, on the other hand, as a song salesgirl, per se, she'll never worry Miss Merman. She's more competitive to Mae West in her delineations."

*New York Daily News*
" 'There's No Business Like Show Business' is full to overflowing with entertainment material. . . . Photographed in DeLuxe Color, it is a star-studded production with an Irving Berlin score that gives the film rhythm, bounce and a pleasant nostalgic quality . . . Marilyn stars in three specialty numbers amusingly, as she does a comic burlesque of the sexy singer of naughty songs."

*The New York Times*
"When it comes to spreading talent, Miss Gaynor has the jump on Miss Monroe, whose wriggling and squirming to 'Heat Wave' and 'Lazy' are embarrassing to behold."

## THORNDIKE, DAME (AGNES) SYBIL
(1882–1976)

"She has an innocence which is so extraordinary, whatever she plays, however brazen a hussy, it always comes out as an innocent girl. I remember Sir Laurence saying one day during filming: 'Look at that face—she could be five years old.'"

A distinguished British stage actress, the original star of George Bernard Shaw's *Saint Joan*, whose cinema outings were far more infrequent but included *THE PRINCE AND THE SHOWGIRL* (1957) with fellow Brit LAURENCE OLIVIER.

Before the end of the first week's shooting, Thorndike went over to Olivier and told him, "You did well in that scene, Larry, but with Marilyn up there, nobody will be watching you. Her manner and timing are just too delicious. And don't be too hard about her tardiness, dear boy. We need her desperately. She's really the only one of us who knows how to act in front of a camera!"

## TICKET TO TOMAHAWK, A (1950)

On the wise advice of paramour JOHNNY HYDE, Marilyn went for and landed a small part in this rather low-key musical Western. Dressed up in period costume, she plays one of four chorus girls who sing and dance the number "Oh, What a Forward Young Man!"

Marilyn reported for shooting in August or September 1949, depending on accounts. This was her first return to TWENTIETH CENTURY-FOX after they had turned her away in 1947. Marilyn and the crew spent five weeks shooting the movie's location scenes in Durango, Colorado.

The movie received only limited promotion from Fox, recently stung by poor audience response to BETTY GRABLE's color comic Western, *The Beautiful Blonde from Bashful Bend* (1949).

Marilyn worked with co-star Dan Dailey years later, on *THERE'S NO BUSINESS LIKE SHOW BUSINESS* (1954).

Memorable costume:
A yellow chorus girl dress with yellow ribbons and floppy-brimmed hat—the first costume Fox designed specially for Marilyn.

**Credits:**
Twentieth Century-Fox, Technicolor
Length: 90 minutes
Release date: May 19, 1950

Directed by: Richard Sale
Produced by: Robert Bassler
Written by: Mary Loos, Richard Sale
Cinematography by: Harry Jackson
Music by: Cyril J. Mockridge
Costume Design by: René Hubert
Film Editing by: Harmon Jones

**Cast (credits order):**
Dan Dailey . . . Johnny Behind-the-Deuces
Anne Baxter . . . Kit Dodge Jr.
Rory Calhoun . . . Dakota
Walter Brennan . . . Terence Sweeny
Charles Kemper . . . Chuckity
Connie Gilchrist . . . Madame Adelaide
Arthur Hunnicutt . . . Sad Eyes
Will Wright . . . Dodge
Chief Yowlachie . . . Pawnee
Mauritz Hugo . . . Dawson
Chief Thundercloud . . . Crooked Knife
Victor Sen Yung . . . Long Time
Raymond Greenleaf . . . Mayor
Harry Carter . . . Charley
Harry Seymour . . . Velvet Fingers
Marion Marshall . . . Annie
Joyce Mackenzie . . . Ruby
Marilyn Monroe . . . Clara
Barbara Smith . . . Julie
Jack Elam . . . Fargo
Edward Clark (uncredited)
Charles Stevens (uncredited)

**Crew:**
George W. Davis . . . art director
Lyle R. Wheeler . . . art director

**Plot:**
It's 1876. Dawson owns a stagecoach line and fears that his business will not survive long if Engine One, a locomotive called Emma Sweeney, gets to its destination of Tomahawk, Colorado, on time. His hired gunman, called Dakota, tries to derail progress in the form first of U.S. Marshal Dodge, and then after he is wounded, his granddaughter Kit (Anne Baxter). Marilyn is one of an assorted bunch of passengers on the eventful train journey; she is Clara, part of a showgirl troupe booked to perform in Tomahawk. On the way, she fits in a song and dance number "Oh, What a Forward Young Man You Are," (written by Ken Darby and John Read) with top billing star and her colleagues. Sabotage is attempted, unsuccessfully, and good defeats evil as the Indians come to the unlikely rescue.

**Reviews:**
*The New York Times*
"There's lots of pleasure in *A Ticket to Tomahawk*. Viewed as an uncompetitive venture (to *Annie Get Your Gun*), it offers surprising good fun. . . . Shot very largely on location in western Colorado, it does have an airiness and a beauty that you don't often find in such films. Likewise, the outdoor action of transporting a real old-fashioned iron horse, first by track and then by mule train, has flavour and humorous gusto."

## TIDES MOTOR INN, THE

Following the trauma of Marilyn's time on the psychiatric ward at the Payne-Whitney HOSPITAL, and then the more relaxed surroundings of the Columbia University Presbyterian Hospital Medical Center, in March 1961 JOE DIMAGGIO took Marilyn to Florida, where they stayed at the exclusive thirties-style Tides Hotel resort.

As well as relaxing and enjoying the sea air, Joe took Marilyn to the Yankee spring training camp in nearby St. Petersburg. Although they were booked in to separate rooms, PRESS speculation was rife that reconciliation and remarriage was in the air.

## TIME-LIFE BUILDING
1271 AVENUE OF THE AMERICAS, NEW YORK

In July 1957, during a period when she was more or less out of the public eye, Marilyn was flown into NEW YORK by helicopter from Long Island, where she was spending the summer with husband ARTHUR MILLER, to attend a ceremony marking the start of work on the Time-Life Building. Despite the fast method of transport, Marilyn arrived two hours late.

## TINKER BELL

Marilyn Monroe was the secret model for Walt Disney's fairy Tinker Bell in the 1953 animated classic *Peter Pan*.

## TOBEY BEACH

In 1949 photographer ANDRÉ DE DIENES brought Marilyn to this beach, on the north shore of Long Island, for a photo session. For many aficionados, these rank as some of the finest Marilyn photos ever taken.

Disney used pin-up pictures of Marilyn Monroe as inspiration for Tinker Bell.

## TOMMY (1975)

In the Who's celebrated rock opera, directed by Ken Russell, Marilyn is "the plastic miracle healer" icon in the temple to which deaf, dumb, and blind Tommy (Roger Daltrey) is taken to be cured by his mother (ANN-MARGRET).

## TORMÉ, MEL (1925–1999)

Popular singer and occasional actor Mel Tormé, who was one of Marilyn's favorites, gave her some last-minute coaching as she rehearsed her breathy rendition of "Happy Birthday" for president KENNEDY."

In his autobiography *It Wasn't All Velvet* he recounts the tale of a club act they once did together, and hints at a "bittersweet" personal relationship they had not long afterward.

## TRAVILLA, WILLIAM ("BILLY") (1920–1990)

"She liked to shock—she could look magnificent or hideous—like a dirty little bum or a sex queen."

"She was so childlike she could do anything, and you would forgive as you would forgive a seven-year old. She was both a woman and a baby, and both men and women adored her."

"On the surface, she was still a happy girl. But those who criticized her never saw her like I did, crying like a baby because she often felt herself so inadequate."

Leading costume designer William Travilla, known simply as "Travilla," first met Marilyn in 1950, when she asked if she could borrow his fitting room—he was one of several contract designers for TWENTIETH CENTURY-FOX—to try on a costume: "My introduction was the sight

One of André de Dienes's much-loved Tobey Beach photographs of Marilyn, 1949.

Jacques Cemas, Sammy Davis Jr., Marilyn, Milton Greene, and Mel Tormé, at The Mocambo in 1955 celebrating Davis's return to show business after his accident.

of her in a black bathing suit," he recalled. "She opened the sliding doors of my fitting room, and the strap fell off, and her breast was exposed . . . of course, she did it on purpose."

They worked together on eight movies: MONKEY BUSINESS (1952), DON'T BOTHER TO KNOCK (1952), GENTLEMEN PREFER BLONDES (1953), HOW TO MARRY A MILLIONAIRE (1953), THERE'S NO BUSINESS LIKE SHOW BUSINESS (1954), RIVER OF NO RETURN (1954), THE SEVEN YEAR ITCH (1955), and BUS STOP (1956). In his long career, Travilla won an Oscar for his work on the Errol Flynn drama *The Adventures of Don Juan* (1948); he was nominated for his work on two Marilyn movies, *There's No Business Like Show Business* and *Bus Stop*.

Travilla designed the vast majority of Marilyn's most memorable costumes, including the gowns she wore to such devastating effect at public events such as the 1953 PHOTOPLAY magazine awards. He helped to sew her into the sheer gold lamé dress she had worn (briefly—it was deemed too revealing to pass the censors) in *Gentlemen Prefer Blondes*, to go and claim her award for Hollywood's "Fastest Rising Star of 1952." The way Travilla tells it, Marilyn set out to make a splash. Travilla's last words to her before she left in the dress were, "Walk like a lady." Her passage from the hall to the dais to pick up her award had JERRY LEWIS howling, and JOAN CRAWFORD later publicly castigating Marilyn for her vulgarity.

Three years after they first met, Travilla says that while working together on *Gentleman Prefer Blondes* (1953) they had an affair. He squired her around town on a number of occasions, and Marilyn sometimes called him in the middle of the night to ask him over. He has never told biographers what excuse he managed to give his wife.

Marilyn autographed a nude calendar for Travilla with the words, "Billy Dear, please dress me forever. I love you, Marilyn."

Travilla last saw Marilyn dining with PETER LAWFORD and PAT NEWCOMB, a week before her death, though in some accounts it's the last evening she was alive. He said she was looking drawn and haggard, and when he went over to her table to say hello, she didn't recognize him immediately. He was offended, and decided to write a letter to tell her as much. She died before he had the chance.

William Travilla and Marilyn during a wardrobe test for *Gentlemen Prefer Blondes* (1952).

## TRILLING, DIANA (1905–1996)

"She was alive in a way not granted the rest of us. She communicated such a charge of vitality as altered our imagination of life, which is the job and wonder of art."

"I think it would be more precise to call this kind of death incidental rather than purposeful—incidental to the desire to escape the pain of living..."

This American author and critic, married to writer and critic Lionel Trilling, is widely quoted for her observations on Marilyn's life and death.

Trilling also commented on the general "mockery of the wish to be educated," which

Marilyn suffered in her life, and the bane of her dependence on sexual artifice.

## TROTTI, LAMAR (1900–1952)

Trotti was a prolific writer and producer, responsible for such movies as *In Old Chicago* (1938), *The Ox Bow Incident* (1942), *Wilson* (1943, Oscar) and *Cheaper by the Dozen* (1950).

Trotti was involved as writer and/or producer on three Marilyn productions: *AS YOUNG AS YOU FEEL* (1951), the Marilyn segment in O. *HENRY'S FULL HOUSE* (1952), and he conceived the story for *THERE'S NO BUSINESS LIKE SHOW BUSINESS* (1954) but died before he had time to complete the script. Trotti nevertheless received a posthumous Oscar nomination for this last piece of work.

## TWENTIETH CENTURY-FOX
10201 WEST PICO BOULEVARD, BEVERLY HILLS (NOW CENTURY CITY)

The studio for which Marilyn Monroe made all but eight of her twenty-nine movies was created in 1935 by the merger of Fox Film Corporation, founded by Hungarian-born William Fox, and Twentieth Century Pictures, founded by JOSEPH M. SCHENCK and DARRYL F. ZANUCK in 1933. Zanuck headed the studio's production arm from the company's creation to 1956, while SPYROS SKOURAS was company president from 1942 to 1962. One of the Hollywood "Big Five," Fox discovered and promoted stars such as Shirley Temple, Tyrone Power, Will Rogers, Don Ameche, BETTY GRABLE, and the biggest female star in movie history, Marilyn Monroe.

By the time aspiring starlet Norma Jeane first signed on to the studio's books, it was the dominant production facility in Hollywood, and under the stewardship of legendary producer Darryl F. Zanuck, continued to lead the field for two more decades, introducing the CinemaScope widescreen process to stay ahead of the pack, and stave off the inevitable competition of television.

Norma Jeane came to the studio's attention through BEN LYON, head of talent, who arranged a SCREEN TEST after colleague Ivan Kahn initially met her. On the strength of this test, unusually shot in color on July 23, 1946, she was offered a standard six-month contract, at a salary of $75 per week, with an option for the studio to renew for another six months at double the original salary. Because Norma Jeane was still under age, legal guardian GRACE MCKEE GODDARD had to sign her first contract.

Renamed "Marilyn Monroe," she became one of several dozen hopefuls on a minimum contract. During her first six months Marilyn was not assigned a single picture, not even as an extra. Instead, she learned about makeup, costumes, lighting, and camera techniques, took acting and singing lessons, tried to get herself noticed, and spent a lot of time in contact with the press office, which could always find PHOTOGRAPHERS for a pretty blonde in a tight sweater. Head publicist HARRY BRAND and his staff concocted a sanitized studio biography for Marilyn, excising her mentally unstable mother and turning Marilyn officially into an orphan; the publicity department also concocted a story of how Marilyn had been discovered one day when she went to babysit for the child of a talent scout.

Marilyn's first role was as a high school student in B-picture *SCUDDA HOO! SCUDDA HAY!* (1948). A couple of months later she shot her second picture *DANGEROUS YEARS* (1948), though this movie was actually released first. It has sometimes been suggested that Marilyn made walk-on appearances in other FILMS in production on the Fox lot at the time, but nobody has ever succeeded in making a positive Marilyn identification.

Neither *Scudda Hoo! Scudda Hay!* nor *Dangerous Years* were particularly successful for Fox or for Marilyn. The studio declined to renew her contract for a third six-month term. When Marilyn's agent HARRY LIPTON broke the news to her that Fox had not taken up its option, Marilyn simply said, "Well, I guess it really doesn't matter—it's a case of supply and demand."

Disappointed but not discouraged, Marilyn continued with her MODELING work, and earnestly began to cultivate the contacts which would get her back into the movie industry. She befriended MGM talent scout LUCILLE RYMAN and, more importantly, co-founder Joseph Schenck.

A year at Columbia Pictures brought a third movie appearance, and a meeting with drama coach NATASHA LYTESS, who was to be an important figure for Marilyn over the next seven years. Then Marilyn met JOHNNY HYDE, one of Hollywood's top agents. It was Hyde who gave her career the push it needed to get her back to Fox. By cajoling his friends and calling in favors, Hyde succeeded in getting Marilyn roles in three Fox movies released in 1950—*A TICKET TO TOMAHAWK*, *THE FIREBALL*, and *ALL ABOUT EVE*—the last being one of the highest profile movies of the year.

Marilyn was finally offered a long-term contract, which took effect on May 11, 1951. Gossip-mongers have claimed that when Marilyn signed on the dotted line, she muttered under her breath something to the effect that at last this meant she would never have to do another blow-job again.

Biographers delight in commenting on the timing of this new, long-term contract, coming as it did immediately after Marilyn made a dramatic entrance to the studio's 1951 exhibitors party. Fox president Spyros Skouras asked his aides who the blonde in the black cocktail gown was, and invited her to join him at the top table. Thereafter, the word went out around the studio that Marilyn was to be put into as many pictures as possible.

Marilyn's contract was in fact a one-year option on a seven-year contract. She was to be paid $500 per week, guaranteed for forty weeks of the year, whether she worked on a film or not. If the studio renewed the contract her weekly salary would rise to $750 in the second year, $1250 in the third, $1500 in the fourth, $2000 in the fifth, $2500 in the sixth, and $3500 in the seventh and final year. The studio had the right to cancel the contract at the end of any year without having to give a reason, and Marilyn could work only for Fox, unless the studio decided to loan her out for another production; Marilyn was also forbidden from seeking employment in any other medium, unless approved by Fox. Alongside the standard contract clauses, Marilyn asked for and obtained agreement for drama coach Natasha Lytess to be put on the studio payroll.

In the year that followed, Marilyn appeared on seven mostly forgettable movies, but as Fox's publicity machine moved into high gear, her name began creeping up the billing order. Then, in late 1951, Fox loaned Marilyn out to RKO for its production of *CLASH BY NIGHT* (1952), directed by FRITZ LANG, the first role of any dramatic weight Marilyn was ever given.

The advance press on this movie was so good that word filtered down from studio stockholders to Skouras, and from Skouras to Darryl Zanuck, that the time had come to give Marilyn a chance in a lead role. The studio renewed its option on her contract on April, 18 1952. That year Marilyn featured in five releases (*Clash by Night* that June, *WE'RE NOT MARRIED* and *DON'T BOTHER TO KNOCK* in July, *MONKEY BUSINESS* in September, and O. *HENRY'S FULL HOUSE* in October), and achieved PRESS notoriety thanks to two scandals and a romance: her nude CALENDAR, her mother surfacing when she was supposed to have died long ago, and Marilyn's fairytale romance with the nation's favorite baseball hero, JOE DIMAGGIO.

Harry Brand and his publicity department found themselves in the curious position of having to work to keep their latest star out of the news, in order not to impinge upon the delicate moral climate of the early fifties.

1953 was Marilyn's year. *NIAGARA* confirmed Marilyn as a top box-office talent. In *GENTLEMEN PREFER BLONDES* she may have been the second string star, but she was the only one the public talked about. In *HOW TO MARRY A MILLIONAIRE* she was cast alongside BETTY GRABLE, until then Fox's undisputed top blonde, in a Technicolor CinemaScope extravaganza. Grable reputedly told her younger co-star, "Honey, I've had it. Go get yours. It's your turn now."

Once Marilyn had hit the top, the studio seemed to be unsure how to make the most of its latest, greatest asset. Her next project, the Western *RIVER OF NO RETURN* (1954), like *Niagara*, pitched Marilyn once more into dramatic scenery, rather than putting her in dramatic situations. Marilyn began to grow frustrated with the material she was given, and by the paltry sums of MONEY she was earning.

After *River of No Return*, the studio was anxious to pitch Marilyn into a new vehicle as soon as possible, a movie called *The Girl in Pink Tights*. Marilyn did not like the idea that co-star FRANK SINATRA was set to earn $5000 a week against her $1500; even more insulting to her was Fox's refusal to even allow her to preview the script, a reworking of the 1943 Betty Grable movie *Coney Island*.

Marilyn went on a one-woman strike. She failed to turn up for the first day of shooting. She ignored studio threats and an official suspension. The studio told her she was being replaced by SHEREE NORTH. Marilyn blithely went up to SAN FRANCISCO to spend Christmas with Joe DiMaggio. The studio sent Marilyn the script, and her worst fears were confirmed. Marilyn began 1954 by marrying DiMaggio, and was on her HONEYMOON when another Fox-imposed deadline passed.

For the first time, Marilyn succeeded in calling the studio's bluff. Faced with losing the

hottest property on celluloid, Fox recanted. They agreed to drop *Pink Tights* on the condition that Marilyn take a supporting role in the planned musical *There's No Business Like Show Business* (1954). As an inducement, Marilyn was promised the lead role in the Billy Wilder project *The Seven Year Itch* (1955), a screen version of the Broadway hit by George Axelrod. Marilyn's grievances about her low pay were addressed in a new contract that started in August 1954, another seven-year deal, plus an extra $100,000 bonus for the Wilder film. But a precedent had been created: Marilyn had stared the studio down. More wrangles halted production of *There's No Business Like Show Business*. Marilyn's agent at the time, Charles K. Feldman, announced that his client was "tired of having to fight the studio when all she was interested in was getting great parts."

In the summer of 1954, Marilyn traveled to New York to shoot the skirt scene for *The Seven Year Itch*. This trip marked the rupture of her marriage to Joe DiMaggio, and saw Marilyn conducting secret meetings with photographer Milton Greene to start up her own production company, and at last have proper control over her material and finances.

A month after announcing her divorce, Marilyn dropped out of sight. She re-emerged on the East Coast, where she had been staying with new business partner Greene. In January 1955 they held a press conference to announce the formation of Marilyn Monroe Productions. As soon as they went public, the studio immediately suspended her—though she still had to return to Los Angeles that January for the final retakes necessary for *The Seven Year Itch*.

Throughout 1955 Milton Greene's team of lawyers, Frank Delaney and Irving Stein, and Marilyn's new talent agency, MCA, battled it out with the studio's legal representatives, co-ordinated by Zanuck's right-hand man, Lew Schreiber. Fox held firm and maintained that Marilyn was contracted to work exclusively for them for the four remaining years of her contract, but their resolve was severely weakened by the huge box-office success of *The Seven Year Itch* that summer. As Marilyn told Susan Strasberg at the time, "Hollywood will never forgive me—not for leaving, not for fighting the system—but for winning, which I'm going to do."

Marilyn's representation countered the studio's position by citing non-payment of the $100,000 bonus negotiated for *The Seven Year Itch*. Bolstering their case was a letter confirming that an oral agreement had been reached to rescind Marilyn's original 1951 contract. But as the year progressed, it became increasingly evident to Greene that he could not find sufficient funding for Marilyn Monroe Productions to survive long enough to actually make a picture.

Marilyn and Fox signed a new contract on December 31, 1955. The four-movie, seven-year deal provided for $100,000 per film plus a percentage of the profits. More important for Marilyn, she finally wrested control over the types of movies she would do: not just script approval, but director and cinematographer approval too—an almost unprecedented amount of power for a performer. Marilyn also stood to receive a weekly $500 allowance during filming. No longer did Fox have exclusivity over their star; Marilyn was permitted to take on one independent film project each year, and appear on up to six radio and television shows each year. In addition, she received a $100,000 annual retainer, with a further annual salary of $75,000 to be paid to Greene. Marilyn's new contract with Fox even had a specific fever clause, whereby Marilyn agreed to turn up to work with a fever up to 101° F (or 98.8° F in some accounts)—this proved to be a source of confusion in Marilyn's dismissal from her last movie project, *Something's Got to Give*.

The first movie Marilyn made under the new regime was *Bus Stop* (1956), followed a year later by *The Prince and the Showgirl* (1957), the only title made by Marilyn Monroe Productions before Marilyn fell out with partner Milton Greene. Next came a movie "on loan" to United Artists, *Some Like It Hot* (1959), and it was 1960 before Marilyn returned to her home studio, for *Let's Make Love*. *The Misfits* (1961) was another project conducted outside Fox. By the time Marilyn moved back to Los Angeles in 1961, following the breakdown of her marriage to Arthur Miller, she had only done two out of the four movies she owed Fox, with only one year remaining on her contract.

The situation at the summit of Twentieth Century-Fox had changed considerably. In 1956, Darryl Zanuck had stepped down from his post as head of production and moved to Europe, where he worked as an independent producer. Zanuck was replaced by Buddy Adler, who personally produced *Bus Stop*. After Adler died in 1960, Spyros Skouras took over increasing responsibility, and later blame, for production. By this time the Studio was in a perilous financial state, the result of a long, slow decline and then the enormous cost overrun of the Elizabeth Taylor film *Cleopatra*. The company front office put pressure on Skouras, who moved from president to the less powerful position of chairman of the board. A man named Robert Goldstein briefly took over as head of production at the behest of the studio's New York-based committee of financiers, only to be replaced by Peter Levathes.

It was in this climate that Marilyn began work on *Something's Got to Give*. Although she reportedly had little enthusiasm for the much-rewritten script, she, like original director George Cukor, owed Twentieth Century-Fox movies on her contract.

As *Cleopatra* burst through the $30 million barrier, Fox was forced to make drastic cuts or

A Twentieth Century-Fox publicity photograph by Frank Powolny, 1952.

face bankruptcy. The studio sold off its real estate holdings, slashed its staffing bills, and closed down studio facilities to save money. Levathes, under intense pressure, took an axe to the most expensive project underway at Fox, apart from *Cleopatra*, and fired Marilyn for breach of contract not long after she returned from singing "Happy Birthday" to President JOHN F. KENNEDY, blaming her poor attendance on set for filming—twelve out of thirty-three shooting days.

Marilyn's lawyer, Milton Rudin, and her psychoanalyst, DR. RALPH GREENSON, met with Fox executives on June 8, 1962 for eleventh-hour talks. Greenson pleaded his client's case, saying that she had been incapacitated by a virus but was ready and willing to work. The studio was unimpressed, and that same day notified Rudin that they were launching a lawsuit and suing Marilyn Monroe Productions for $500,000. Fox had already been casting about for a replacement, and announced that filming would continue with LEE REMICK. But co-star DEAN MARTIN, who had approval of the leading lady written into his contract, refused to work with anyone but Marilyn.

Meanwhile, Skouras, in the last six months of his tenure at Fox, was arguing the case to reinstate Marilyn. Behind-the-scenes negotiations were conducted between the studio and Marilyn's representatives. Two weeks before her death, Marilyn was told by Levathes that she was to be rehired at an improved salary of $250,000 (or up to $500,000 in some reports) and all lawsuits were to be dropped. It is estimated that by the time Marilyn began work on her final movie, her previous pictures had made Twentieth Century-Fox over sixty million dollars.

Before the end of 1962, Spyros Skouras was replaced as president by Darryl Zanuck. He appointed his son Richard as vice-president in charge of production. They remained in control until the early seventies. Alan Ladd Jr. had a successful run through the rest of the seventies, most memorably issuing the *Star Wars* trilogy. In 1981 the company was sold off, and then in 1985 Rupert Murdoch added it as the jewel in the crown of his worldwide media empire.

BOOK:

*Marilyn at Twentieth Century-Fox*, Lawrence Crown. London: Comet Books, 1987.

Marilyn's career at Fox illustrated in over two hundred photographs.

U/V

## UCLA
University of California at Los Angeles
405 Hilgard Avenue, Westwood

In her ongoing quest for self-EDUCATION, Marilyn attended evening classes in art and literature appreciation in early 1951. Backgrounds of Literature was taught by Claire Seay. Remembering her former student, Seay explains, "She was so modest, so humble, so attentive, that she could have been some girl who had just come from a convent."

## Underwear

Marilyn:
"I never wear girdles, and bras as rarely as possible. I feel encumbered by them. . . . When I wear a girdle, it flattens me out. Can you give me one good reason why I should flatten myself out?"

George Masters:
"When she was dressed she wore no bra or panties. If she had to wear a brassiere, it was always a skimpy affair with two strings and a sheer half-cup called a no-no bra. But usually she wore none. She didn't have a huge bust. She looked good with no bra; not vulgar or trashy but different."

One of the things people generally know about Marilyn is that she eschewed underwear whenever she could. This was perhaps less a matter of choice than a way of fitting into clothing that was up to two sizes too small for her voluptuous contours. Marilyn's lack of undergarments became part of her growing legend in 1952, when columnist EARL WILSON wrote of her admission that she wore no undergarments at all, because "I like to feel unhampered." From then on, press reports of her publicity engagements frequently carried comments that she had "absolutely nothing on underneath" whatever she was wearing. One such occasion, the source of a minor scandal, was the exceedingly low-cut dress Marilyn wore to the MISS AMERICA PAGEANT as part of the promotion tour for *MONKEY BUSINESS* (1952).

On many occasions, Marilyn's NUDITY beneath her clothes was paraded as a sign of her dangerous and uncontrollable sensuousness. Marilyn would remove her undergarments before photo sessions, to make sure panty lines would not mar the result.

Marilyn is famously remembered by a number of directors for the "perfection" of her bust and her lack of need of evident support. However, many incidents have been recorded showing that Marilyn and underwear were not perfect strangers. In 1947 when living with JOHN CARROLL and LUCILLE RYMAN, Lucille recalled finding Marilyn one evening looking at two dozen bras on which she had lavished what was meant to be a full week's allowance. Marilyn was stuffing tissue into each cup, because, as she told her friend, "This is all anyone ever looks at. When I walk down Hollywood Boulevard, everyone will notice me now!" There is a story that Marilyn turned up to her audition with JOHN HUSTON for *THE ASPHALT JUNGLE* (1950) with one of these stuffed bras. Huston is reputed to have reached in, pulled out the wadding, and told her she had the part regardless.

A Twentieth Century-Fox publicity shot features Marilyn in a negligee, 1953.

The famous dress that designer Orry-Kelly created for Marilyn to wear in *Some Like It Hot (1959)* had a nude-colored mesh heart outlined in red on its backside.

Marilyn knew how to use underwear to good effect. In 1951, before she had won star billing and was still just one the hopeful blondes on the Fox lot, she walked six blocks from the wardrobe department to the photo studio, wearing nothing but a silky negligee. The news spread like wildfire around the studios, and made it as far as the Hollywood press. Reporter Robert Cahn wrote, "People were leaning out of every window. And there was Marilyn, naive and completely unperturbed, smiling and waving up at everybody she knew, didn't know or hoped to know."

Though Marilyn may rarely have worn a bra (reportedly she was a 36D, though her MEASUREMENTS do vary depending on sources) when going out, it is known that in later years she commissioned Hulda Dombek to make her custom-made bras. As AMY GREENE revealed, Marilyn wore a bra at night because she believed it would help to prevent her bust from sagging.

There is a (possibly apocryphal) story that one warm New York day Marilyn was walking down the street in the mink coat husband JOE DIMAGGIO had given her, when a friend asked her how she managed to wear the mink when it was so warm. Marilyn's response was to flash her naked body underneath the coat.

## United Artists
1918 South Vermont Avenue, Hollywood

United Artists, the studio set up by Mary Pickford, CHARLIE CHAPLIN, and Douglas Fairbanks to give them an independent vehicle for their own movies, released the Marx brothers' final film, *LOVE HAPPY* (1950), in which Marilyn had a small part. Notwithstanding the fact that she only appeared on screen for one minute, the studio sent her on a nationwide promotional tour.

Years later, UA made Marilyn's most commercially successful movie, *SOME LIKE IT HOT* (1959), and provided finance and distribution for *THE MISFITS* (1961) through subsidiary company Seven Arts Productions.

## University High School

Norma Jeane attended her last high school from February to June 1942. Perhaps it was the fact she was going steady with older boyfriend JAMES DOUGHERTY, perhaps it was a general improvement in self-confidence, but classmates at University High remembered her as "loud" and "wild," a far cry from just a couple of years earlier, when she was so shy she was known as "The Mouse."

In mid-March, a couple of days after legal guardian GRACE MCKEE GODDARD and her husband moved to West Virginia, Norma Jeane announced to her teachers and classmates that she was leaving school to be married in June, and that was the last they saw of her.

# V

## Van Doren, Mamie
(b. 1933, Joan Lucille Olander)

Scouts at Universal Studios came up with former model Mamie Van Doren to try to compete with rival studio TWENTIETH CENTURY-FOX's Marilyn Monroe. Van Doren built up quite a following, but struggled to progress

In 1945 a nineteen-year-old Norma Jeane had embarked on a modeling career.

beyond B-movie fare. She made her debut in *Two Tickets to Broadway* (1951), and starred in movies such as *The Second Greatest Sex* (1955), *Running Wild* (1955), *Untamed Youth* (1957), and *Sex Kittens Go to College* (1960).

## VAN NUYS HIGH SCHOOL
6535 CEDROS AVENUE, VAN NUYS
(LATER VAN NUYS SENIOR HIGH)

Norma Jeane spent half of her tenth grade year at this school, from September 1941 to February 1942, while she was still living with the GODDARD family. This was the same school that JAMES DOUGHERTY had attended a few years earlier. Another former student, with whom Norma Jeane was to later work, was JANE RUSSELL.

## VIRGINIA CITY, NEVADA

This is where the cast of *THE MISFITS* (1961) went for R&R during free time (or enforced breaks) from shooting near RENO. Virginia City was more or less a ghost town, abandoned after the gold rush.

## VISTA DEL MONTE STREET

In 1942 Norma Jeane and JAMES DOUGHERTY began their married life together in a one-room bungalow at 4524 Vista Del Monte Street, Sherman Oaks. The place was so small that they had a fold-up bed.

## VOICE

MARILYN:
"It isn't necessary to use your voice in any special way. If you think something sexy the voice just naturally goes along."

ARTHUR MILLER:
"Her voice [was] so soft and soothing that grown men went limp as lichens at the living sound of it."

Through her CHILDHOOD of shifting adult influences and instability, Norma Jeane was a very quiet and shy girl. In her own words, she "figured early in life that if I didn't talk I couldn't be blamed for anything."

Norma Jeane suffered from low self-esteem, and developed a stammer. Marilyn recalled that at junior high school she was class secretary, and would open class meetings by saying "M-m-minutes of the last m-m-meeting." She was still battling this problem during her early years as an actress. It has been suggested that the frustration of stammering was one of the reasons why Marilyn was so nervous about learning and delivering her lines. At times like this, her voice was described by drama coach NATASHA LYTESS as a "tight squeak."

During her years as an aspiring actress, one of the many pieces of advice she received, useful or spurious, was to "lower her tone." This she duly did. She also studied singing, quickly developing her distinctive style. Phil Moore, who coached Marilyn for *GENTLEMEN PREFER BLONDES* (1953), pinpointed Marilyn's special appeal in SONG: "She always sounds as if she's just waking up. You'd be surprised what kind of effect that has on male listeners."

To a large extent, the Marilyn voice of the first half of her career, with its exaggerated clarity and staccato stressing of "d" and "t," was the result of tutoring from Lytess. Marilyn was, more than once, lampooned by her directors for what OTTO PREMINGER described as her "grave ar-tic-yew-lay-shun." Stylized as this may have been, it finally helped Marilyn overcome her tendency to stutter. It is this breathy whisper which generations of later actresses have employed as a surefire signifier of sexual attraction and availability.

Only on very few occasions did Marilyn publicly use her real voice: in a few press conferences, press announcements, and in interviews with journalists, recordings of which have found their way into collectors' hands. However, in her last, unfinished movie, *SOMETHING'S GOT TO GIVE*, Marilyn took a new direction and spoke in her normal voice.

Journalist W. J. WEATHERBY, who met Marilyn a number of times in the last years of her life, wrote that her voice "could range from the seductive to the girlish to the intonations of a granddame."

Sondra Locke, a former lover of Clint Eastwood, claimed that the Western hero based his gravelly drawl on Marilyn's breathy baby-doll whisper.

Marilyn outside the Voltaire Apartments, 1954.

### VOICE COACHES

Billie Daniels (for "That Old Black Magic" in *Bus Stop*)
Ken Darby
Fred Karger
Margaret McLean
Phil Moore
Hal Schaefer

## VOLTAIRE APARTMENTS
1424 NORTH CRESCENT HEIGHTS BOULEVARD, WEST HOLLYWOOD
(NOW CALLED GRANVILLE APARTMENTS)

Marilyn's hideaway after leaving JOE DIMAGGIO, where she gathered herself before making her secret move to NEW YORK. While the press frantically searched Los Angeles, Marilyn was right under their noses in Hollywood, with friend Anne Karger.

W

## WAGENKNECHT, EDWARD

"Marilyn played the best game with the worst hand of anybody I know."

Biographer of many leading figures of the nineteenth and twentieth century, in 1969 Wagenknecht compiled a book on Marilyn that brought together the insights of several of Marilyn's friends and colleagues. Ernest Cunningham, author of *The Ultimate Marilyn*, makes this book one of his choices for the Essential Marilyn Library.

BOOK:
*Marilyn Monroe: a Composite View*, Edward Wagenknecht, ed. New York: Chilton Books, 1969.

## WAGNER, ROBERT (B. 1930)

"Nothing happened easily for Marilyn. It took a lot of time and effort to create the image that became so famous."

Wagner was signed by TWENTIETH CENTURY-FOX as a twenty-year-old while still at college. After making his debut in *Halls of Montezuma* (1950), Wagner screen-tested with aspiring actress Marilyn, which led to them teaming up in *LET'S MAKE IT LEGAL* (1951), one of the many movies in which Marilyn had a supporting role before stardom arrived in 1953.

Wagner progressed to leading roles. His 1957 marriage to fellow Fox star NATALIE WOOD was billed by the studio as "the most glittering union of the twentieth century." His movie career tailed off a little in the sixties, when he switched to television in long-running series such as *It Takes a Thief* and *Hart to Hart*. Most recently he has appeared as Number Two in the *Austin Powers* movies.

## WALD, JERRY (1911–1962)

"She walks like a young antelope, and when she stands up it's like a snake uncoiling."

"She is the greatest farceuse in the business, a female Chaplin. In the right kind of picture she is superb and the public will go to see her. It is only when she plays a serious role that she has trouble. The audience doesn't believe her."

A prolific and energetic figure around Hollywood, Wald began his film career in the thirties as a writer, then became a writer-producer, and in the latter part of his career he concentrated on producing. Wald was reputedly the inspiration for Budd Schulberg's novel *What Makes Sammy Run?*

Over a lunch interview arranged by SIDNEY SKOLSKY, Marilyn impressed producer Jerry Wald sufficiently to be given the biggest role she had yet landed, in CLIFFORD ODETS' movie *CLASH BY NIGHT* (1952). Marilyn arrived at lunch in a low-cut blouse with a strategic red rose in her cleavage, over a pair of pedal pushers Skolsky described as clinging "so tightly they looked as though they were painted on."

Wald later showed that he knew how to exploit Marilyn's body almost as well as she did. In the most commonly reported account of how the world got wind of Marilyn's nude CALENDAR photos, it was a leak circulated by Wald to garner extra publicity for *Clash by Night*. In some accounts, though, Wald tipped off journalist Aline Mosby rather than pay the ten thousand dollars asked of him by a blackmailer to keep this news a secret before release of the film.

By 1959 Wald was working at TWENTIETH CENTURY-FOX. He sought to interest Marilyn in *The Story on Page One*, another project written by Clifford Odets. After Marilyn turned it down, Wald returned with a new project, *LET'S MAKE LOVE* (1960).

Wald unsuccessfully tried to interest Marilyn in a later project, *The Stripper* (1963), which proved to be the last movie he made before he died. Wald's other notable projects included *Mildred Pierce* (1945), *Johnny Belinda* (1948), *Peyton Place* (1957), and *Sons and Lovers* (1960).

## WALDORF-ASTORIA HOTEL
301 PARK AVENUE, NEW YORK

From April 1955 Marilyn's New York home was at this luxurious New York hotel. MILTON GREENE, as partner in MARILYN MONROE PRODUCTIONS, sublet the twenty-seventh-floor three-room suite, number 2728 from its owner, actress Leonora Corbett, for the sum of $1,000 per week.

Biographer FRED LAWRENCE GUILES writes, "She was often acutely lonely in her Waldorf Towers apartment, as only a famed movie star cut off from ordinary mortals can be."

JAMES HASPIEL describes Marilyn's living quarters in his book *Marilyn: The Ultimate Look at the Legend*:

> You entered Marilyn's apartment directly into the living room, and on a bulletin board there on the right-hand wall . . . were items that stay even today in my memory. Pages from foreign magazines; a picture of Albert Einstein, of his face; and another picture of Einstein walking down a road, seen from behind. There was another page that appeared to me to be a picture of a cluster of hungry orphans all huddled together. Sitting on a little table on the left side of the room was a sketch of Marilyn that was quite wonderful . . . executed by actor Zero Mostel. . . . Marilyn's bed was against the wall that bordered the living room, and hung over her bed was this enormous painting of Abraham Lincoln. . . . Marilyn's telephone was turned into the bed's headboard, so that her private number was not readily obvious to just anyone who might be passing through…

By the end of 1955, this luxurious suite was too much of a financial drain for Marilyn Monroe Productions, so Marilyn moved to an apartment on SUTTON PLACE. Over the following years she had occasion to return for a radio show recording (1956), for the post-premiere party for *THE PRINCE AND THE SHOWGIRL* (1957), and a fashion show held by the March of Dimes in 1958.

## THE WALK

MARILYN:
"I've never deliberately done anything about the way I walk. People say I walk all wiggly and wobbly, but I don't know what they mean. I just walk. I've never wiggled deliberately in my life, but all my life I've had trouble with people who say I do."

"I use walking just to get me around."

HARMON JONES:
"She can squeeze more meaning out of a few steps than most actresses can get out of six pages of dialogue."

Columnist Elsa Maxwell with Marilyn in her suite at the Waldorf-Astoria Hotel, 1956.

Marilyn's "longest walk in film history" in *Niagara* (1953) generated a great deal of commentary. This publicity photo was released to the press and articles appeared all over the world describing Marilyn's particular way of walking. (The dress Marilyn wears in this picture actually never made it into the film.)

Marilyn's way of moving from A to B was not simply what mere mortals did. After she performed what was claimed to be the longest walk in film history, measuring 116 feet, in NIAGARA (1952), it became known as "The Walk," and Marilyn was dubbed by columnist SIDNEY SKOLSKY (or rival Pete Martin, who also claimed credit) "the girl with the horizontal walk."

And yet Marilyn's eye-popping ambulation had been captured on screen as early as 1950, in the Marx brothers' caper *LOVE HAPPY*. In fact, it had been turning heads for years, not necessarily for the right reasons. EMMELINE SNIVELY, who ran the BLUE BOOK MODELING AGENCY where Marilyn began her MODELING career, admitted in 1954: "The first thing we tried to do was change that horrible walk. That wiggle wasn't good for fashion models but it was Marilyn and we couldn't change it."

After *Niagara*, everybody wanted to know whether Marilyn's walk was natural or invented. According to ALLAN "WHITEY" SNYDER, Marilyn first developed her walk accidentally, one day when her high heels met uneven cobblestones. Another suggestion was that she secretly filed down one heel until it was half an inch shorter than the other. Marilyn's masseur, RALPH ROBERTS, said that Marilyn worked out the walk after reading *The Thinking Body* by Mabel Ellsworth Todd, a book containing an exercise which involved shifting the weight from one buttock to the other while sitting.

The Walk, it turns out, is simplicity itself. Marilyn's stand-in EVELYN MORIARTY learned the art from the master craftswoman herself. She said the trick is, "Shoulders back, fanny hoisted and lots of shimmy."

Whether it came naturally or through artifice, a whole generation of women practiced Marilyn's savvy sashay and tried it out on the local boys on Saturday nights. One woman who was not impressed, however, was MAE WEST, who claimed Marilyn's walk was just a poor copy of her own, which had apparently evolved because she teetered onto theater stages on six-inch heels.

Perhaps the best description of Marilyn's trademark walk—a phenomenon best studied from behind—comes from JACK LEMMON in *SOME LIKE IT HOT* (1959). Struggling to master high heels on a station platform, he spots Marilyn up ahead, and explains to fellow cross-dresser TONY CURTIS, "It's like Jell-O with springs!"

## WALLACH, ELI (B. 1915)

Marilyn cemented her friendship with Brooklyn-born Eli Wallach at the ACTORS STUDIO, where they both studied through the mid- to late-fifties. A friend of ARTHUR MILLER's too, during her New York years Marilyn and Arthur saw a lot of Eli and his wife, actress Anne Jackson. SHELLEY WINTERS' accounts of the MEN Marilyn found most sexy, drawn up in the early fifties, included Wallach.

According to biographer FRED LAWRENCE GUILES, their long friendship did not survive a tussle over rewrites on *THE MISFITS* (1961). There was also trouble during the filming of a dance scene in which Marilyn thought Wallach deliberately had tried keep her face hidden from the camera. In the bitter aftermath of Marilyn and Miller's break-up, Marilyn is said to have felt that Wallach took Miller's side.

An accomplished stage actor before moving into film, Wallach's screen debut was in *Baby Doll* (1956), in which Marilyn unsuccessfully lobbied for a role, followed by *The Magnificent Seven* (1960) and *The Misfits* (1961). He has appeared, often as a villain, in films like *The Good, the Bad and the Ugly* (1967), *MacKenna's Gold* (1969), and *The Godfather Part III* (1990).

## WARHOL, ANDY (1928–1987, B. ANDREW WARHOLA)

"She was a fool to kill herself . . . she could have been the first great woman director because she understood how to make movies."

Andy Warhol is perhaps the most famous exponent of pop art, the sixties' movement which turned everyday objects into art. One of Warhol's most famous images is the pouting Marilyn Monroe, serially repeated in silk-

Andy Warhol chose this publicity portrait by Frank Powolny as the basis for his famous silkscreen series.

screen prints and on show in modern art museums around the world.

## WARNER BROTHERS

Although Marilyn never made a picture for Warner Brothers Studios, in 1956 MARILYN MONROE PRODUCTIONS announced that it had struck a distribution deal with Warner Brothers for *THE PRINCE AND THE SHOWGIRL* (1957), the only film that Marilyn's independent production company ever made. At the March 1, 1956 press conference, Marilyn and Jack Warner jointly announced this news.

Marilyn receives the key to Warner Brothers from Jack Warner, 1956.

Madame Tussaud's wax statue of Marilyn Monroe.

## WASSERMAN, LEW (LOU)
(B. 1913)

Head of MCA from 1946 and Universal Studios from 1962 to 1995, Wasserman wielded much influence in Hollywood, and personally looked after client Marilyn Monroe in the mid-fifties after she set up her own production company, MARILYN MONROE PRODUCTIONS.

Wasserman, known for negotiating the first ever contract in which an actor waived a portion of the up-front fee for a percentage of film profits, put Marilyn on this type of contract for her later movies. The Marilyn ESTATE continues to receive income from these deals more than forty years later.

## WAXWORKS

Marilyn appears round-the-clock, cast in wax, in practically every wax museum around the globe, including Madame Tussaud's in London, and the Hollywood Wax Museum. She's also represented, without clothes, in her nude CALENDAR pose at the Sex Museum in Amsterdam.

## WAYNE, DAVID
(1914–1995, B. WAYNE MCKEEKAN)

Character actor David Wayne appeared in more films with Marilyn than any other actor: *AS YOUNG AS YOU FEEL* (1951), *WE'RE NOT MARRIED* (1952), *O. HENRY'S FULL HOUSE* (1952), and *HOW TO MARRY A MILLIONAIRE* (1953).

Wayne was a successful stage actor who transferred to the movies in 1948, when he shone in *Adam's Rib*. He worked often in television and film right up to his death.

## WEATHERBY, W. J.

"She had an ability, unique in my experience, to appear to be what you wanted her to be and therefore the real person remained elusive."

A British journalist whom Marilyn befriended after they met on the set of *THE MISFITS* (1961).

They subsequently met up a number of times in a bar on Eighth Avenue in New York. Ten years after Marilyn's death, Weatherby went back to the notes he took after his chats with Marilyn, and put them together to make a book, *Conversations with Marilyn*.

Weatherby's contacts in the U.S. told him that ROBERT KENNEDY had made a statement to the Los Angeles POLICE about Marilyn's DEATH—the statement, however, had remained secret. Much as he did not want to believe the rumors because of the danger to Marilyn, who always took rejection so badly, Weatherby does not discount the possibility that in the final year of her life, Marilyn had a relationship with one or both Kennedy brothers.

BOOK:
*Conversations with Marilyn*, W. J. Weatherby. New York: Mason/Charter, 1976.

## WEDDINGS

Marilyn's three weddings were all low-key affairs, and they were all, in their way, snap decisions. Marilyn was also married three times on film in *WE'RE NOT MARRIED* (1952), *GENTLEMEN PREFER BLONDES* (1953), and *HOW TO MARRY A MILLIONAIRE* (1953).

JAMES DOUGHERTY—June 19, 1942
The home of the Chester Howells,
432 Bentley Avenue, West Los Angeles

Norma Jeane's first marriage was an arranged union, contracted to keep her out of the ORPHANAGE after legal guardian GRACE MCKEE GODDARD and her husband "DOC" GODDARD moved to West Virginia for work reasons. As well as choosing the husband—the son of her good friend and neighbor Ethel Dougherty—Goddard also chose the venue, the home of Chester Howell, apparently because she thought that its spiral staircase would make a dramatic entrance for the bride. The Howells, who had known Norma Jeane since she was little, and in one report had once considered adopting her, were happy to oblige.

Norma Jeane picked a school friend as her maid of honor; James chose his brother Marion as best man. The limited guest list of twenty-five included Norma Jeane's first foster parents (with whom she lived for seven years), IDA and WAYNE BOLENDER.

The ceremony began at 8:30 P.M. Norma Jeane's embroidered white gown was made for her by "Aunt" ANA LOWER, who performed the role of giving the bride away before Reverend Benjamin Lingenfelder of the CHRISTIAN SCIENCE Church. Neither Norma Jeane's mother, GLADYS BAKER, nor guardian Grace McKee Goddard, were present at the ceremony.

JOE DIMAGGIO—January 14, 1954
San Francisco City Hall, Polk Street

Initially Joe DiMaggio had wanted to marry Marilyn in a church ceremony. But the archbishop of San Francisco, John Mitty, refused to recognize the validity of his divorce from first wife Dorothy Arnold, so a civil wedding was the only alternative.

On January 14, 1954 in the chambers of Judge Charles S. Peery, Marilyn and Joe were pronounced man and wife in a barebones three minute service that began at 1:48 P.M. Marilyn, in dispute with her studio TWENTIETH CENTURY-FOX at the time, only informed the chief studio publicist minutes before the event, but that was enough time for a crowd of over a hundred PHOTOGRAPHERS and reporters to congregate outside. They

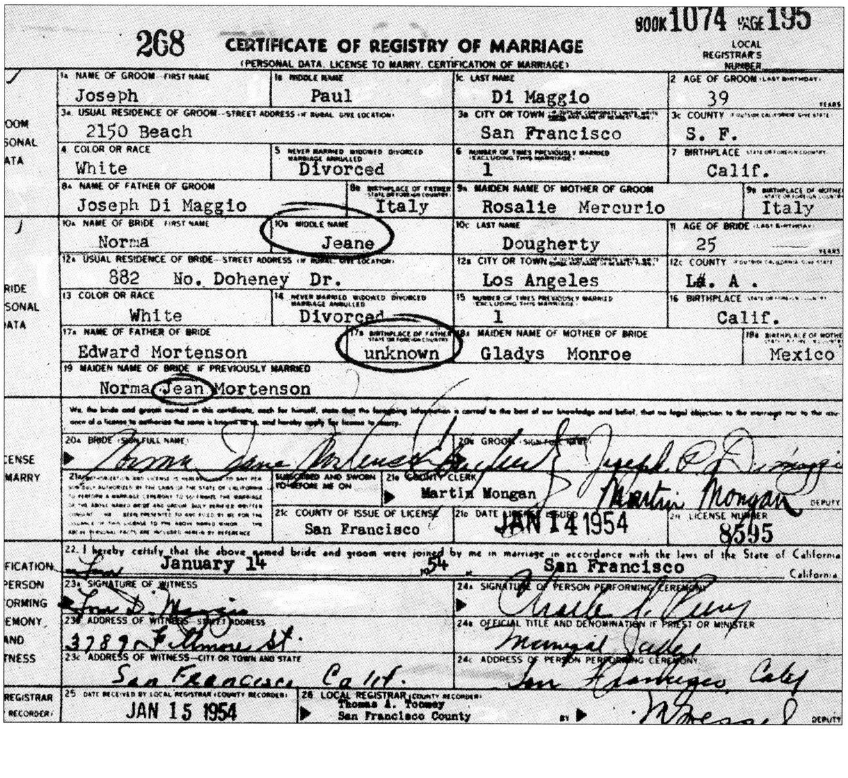

268 CERTIFICATE OF REGISTRY OF MARRIAGE
(PERSONAL DATA. LICENSE TO MARRY. CERTIFICATION OF MARRIAGE)
BOOK 1074 PAGE 195
LOCAL REGISTRAR'S NUMBER

1a NAME OF GROOM—FIRST NAME: Joseph
1b MIDDLE NAME: Paul
1c LAST NAME: Di Maggio
2 AGE OF GROOM: 39 YEARS
3a USUAL RESIDENCE OF GROOM—STREET ADDRESS: 2150 Beach
3b CITY OR TOWN: San Francisco
3c COUNTY: S. F.
4 COLOR OR RACE: White
5 NEVER MARRIED, WIDOWED, DIVORCED, MARRIAGE ANNULLED: Divorced
6 NUMBER OF TIMES PREVIOUSLY MARRIED (EXCLUDING THIS MARRIAGE): 1
7 BIRTHPLACE: Calif.
8a NAME OF FATHER OF GROOM: Joseph Di Maggio
8b BIRTHPLACE OF FATHER: Italy
9a MAIDEN NAME OF MOTHER OF GROOM: Rosalie Mercurio
9b BIRTHPLACE OF MOTHER: Italy
10a NAME OF BRIDE—FIRST NAME: Norma
10b MIDDLE NAME: Jeane
10c LAST NAME: Dougherty
11 AGE OF BRIDE: 25 YEARS
12a USUAL RESIDENCE OF BRIDE—STREET ADDRESS: 882 No. Doheney Dr.
12b CITY OR TOWN: Los Angeles
12c COUNTY: L. A.
13 COLOR OR RACE: White
14 NEVER MARRIED, WIDOWED, DIVORCED, MARRIAGE ANNULLED: Divorced
15 NUMBER OF TIMES PREVIOUSLY MARRIED (EXCLUDING THIS MARRIAGE): 1
16 BIRTHPLACE: Calif.
17a NAME OF FATHER OF BRIDE: Edward Mortenson
17b BIRTHPLACE OF FATHER: unknown
18a MAIDEN NAME OF MOTHER OF BRIDE: Gladys Monroe
18b BIRTHPLACE OF MOTHER: Mexico
19 MAIDEN NAME OF BRIDE IF PREVIOUSLY MARRIED: Norma Jean Mortenson
20a BRIDE (SIGN FULL NAME)
20b GROOM (SIGN FULL NAME)
SUBSCRIBED AND SWORN TO BEFORE ME ON
21a COUNTY CLERK: Martin Mongan
DEPUTY
21c COUNTY OF ISSUE OF LICENSE: San Francisco
21d DATE LICENSE ISSUED: JAN 14 1954
21e LICENSE NUMBER: 8595
22. I hereby certify that the above named bride and groom were joined by me in marriage in accordance with the laws of the State of California January 14 1954 at San Francisco California.
23a SIGNATURE OF WITNESS
23b ADDRESS OF WITNESS—STREET ADDRESS
23c ADDRESS OF WITNESS—CITY OR TOWN AND STATE
24a SIGNATURE OF PERSON PERFORMING CEREMONY
24b OFFICIAL TITLE AND DENOMINATION IF PRIEST OR MINISTER
24c ADDRESS OF PERSON PERFORMING CEREMONY
25 DATE RECEIVED BY LOCAL REGISTRAR (COUNTY RECORDER): JAN 15 1954
26 LOCAL REGISTRAR (COUNTY RECORDER): Thomas A. Toomey, San Francisco County
BY DEPUTY

Marilyn and Joe DiMaggio's wedding certificate.

Joe DiMaggio and Marilyn Monroe on their wedding day at San Francisco City Hall, January 14, 1954.

recorded Marilyn in a chocolate-brown high-necked suit, edged with a high ermine collar, wearing a corsage of three white orchids; husband Joe superstitiously wore the same polka-dotted tie he had sported the night he first met Marilyn, setting off his somber dark blue suit. Practically all the people at the wedding were from Joe's side: best man Reno Barsocchini, Lefty and Jean O'Doul, and brother Tom DiMaggio and his wife.

Despite the brevity of the actual service, it took some time for the judge to get things ready. First of all, there was no typewriter to fill out the marriage license. Then the noise of the crowd three floors below threatened to drown out the vows. On the official documents Marilyn signed her name as Norma Jeane Mortenson Dougherty, and removed three years from her age. She promised to "love, honor and cherish" her husband, but the wording omitted "obey." After taking their vows, the newlyweds went to meet the fans and give glowing responses to the massed ranks below, before driving off in Joe's own blue Cadillac.

ARTHUR MILLER—June 29, 1956
White Plains Court House, New York
"Egghead weds Hourglass" ran the headline after this civil wedding ceremony performed by Judge Seymour Rabinowitz at the White Plains Court House of Westchester County, New York. For this, her third wedding, Marilyn dressed casually, in a sweater and skirt suit. The four-minute evening ceremony began at 7:21 P.M., and was attended by MILTON H. GREENE, LEE AND PAULA STRASBERG, JOHN MOORE, and on Miller's side, his cousin Morton Miller and wife Florence. Marilyn was distraught just before the ceremony because journalist MARA SCHERBATOFF had been killed in a road accident earlier that day.

Two days later, on 1 July 1956, the Millers married in a Jewish ceremony at the home of Arthur's agent, Kay Brown, in Katonah, New York. Rabbi Robert Goldberg officiated at this ceremony, after taking Marilyn through the process of conversion to Judaism that morning. Lee Strasberg gave Marilyn away. She wore a beige wedding dress with matching veil. It is said that Marilyn dyed the veil to match the dress by dunking it in coffee. Marilyn chose a number of maids of honor that day: HEDDA ROSTEN, AMY GREENE, and Judy Kantor.

NORMAN ROSTEN wrote, "The bride was both beautiful and nervous. Really ecstatic. She gave off a luminosity like the Rodin marble. . . . It was the culmination of a dream and carried within it the danger of all dreams."

ROBERT SLATZER
Alleged wedding, October 4, 1952
Tijuana, Mexico

Robert Slatzer has long claimed that he was married to Hollywood's hottest star for three days after a passionate dash over the border. The only witness who has corroborated this was Slatzer's pal, former boxer "Kid" Chissell, who later told a journalist that he only backed up Slatzer's claim because he wanted to help a friend—and because he needed the $100 Slatzer gave him. Slatzer claims the wedding was sanctioned by a local lawyer, cost $5, and was annulled on studio insistence three days later, when all traces of the marriage document was destroyed.

## WEIGHT

Marilyn's weight generally stayed between 115 and 120 pounds. At her most voluptuous, during filming of *LET'S MAKE LOVE* (1960), she reached 140 pounds. In her early STUDIO BIOGRAPHIES, Marilyn's weight was put at 118 pounds. After she separated from ARTHUR MILLER, she slimmed down again, to the point where some old friends thought she looked gaunt. At her death she weighed 117 pounds.

Marilyn as a beauty contestant in *We're Not Married* (1952).

## WEINSTEIN, HENRY

Henry Weinstein was the producer on Marilyn's abandoned last movie, *SOMETHING'S GOT TO GIVE*. FRED LAWRENCE GUILES writes that he was appointed simply on the strength of his friendship with Marilyn's psychoanalyst, DR. RALPH GREENSON. The logic followed that with Marilyn, the main thing was to get her to work on time, and if she couldn't on her psychoanalyst's recommendation, then she never would.

Although some biographers have ventured that the relatively inexperienced Weinstein (he had produced only one movie, *Tender Is the Night* in 1961), did not have the clout to keep Marilyn in line, no producer found it easy to get Marilyn to do what they wanted. In May 1962 Marilyn directly disobeyed Weinstein by going to New York to sing "Happy Birthday" to PRESIDENT KENNEDY, and on the last day's shooting, she went to a charity benefit against his advice.

In ANTHONY SUMMERS' biography, Weinstein says that he once saved Marilyn from an overdose of BARBITURATES.

## WELLES, ORSON (1915–1985)

The *enfant terrible* of American cinema, whose Oscar-winning first movie, *Citizen Kane* (1941), established him as one of the most ambitious and precocious filmmakers of all time, has sometimes been named as an early LOVER of starlet Marilyn Monroe.

## *WE'RE NOT MARRIED* (1952)

A compilation move in which, according to screenwriter NUNNALLY JOHNSON, Marilyn's role as a beauty contestant—who discovers that she cannot compete in the Mrs. America pageant because her wedding was not technically valid—was created solely because it gave the opportunity to put her on screen in not one but two bathing suits. This was one of the main movies Marilyn was written into in order to cash in on her rising popularity, but before TWENTIETH CENTURY-FOX was ready to entrust her with a leading role.

**Credits:**
Twentieth Century-Fox, Black and White
Length: 85 minutes
Release date: July 12, 1952

Directed by: Edmund Goulding
Produced by: Nunnally Johnson
Written by: Nunnally Johnson (screenplay), Dwight Taylor (adaptation), Jay Dratler (story), Gina Kaus (story)
Cinematography by: Leo Tover
Film Editing by: Louis R. Loeffler
Music by: Cyril J. Mockridge
Production Design by: Leland Fuller, Lyle R. Wheeler
Costume Design by: Eloise Jensson

**Cast (credits order):**
Ginger Rogers . . . Ramona Gladwyn
Fred Allen . . . Steve Gladwyn
Victor Moore . . . Justice of the Peace Melvin Bush
Marilyn Monroe . . . Annabel Norris
David Wayne . . . Jeff Norris
Eve Arden . . . Katie Woodruff
Paul Douglas . . . Hector Woodruff
Eddie Bracken . . . Willie Fisher
Mitzi Gaynor . . . Patsy Fisher
Louis Calhern . . . Freddie Melrose
Zsa Zsa Gabor . . . Eve Melrose
James Gleason . . . Duffy
Paul Stewart . . . Attorney Stone
Jane Darwell . . . Mrs. Bush

**Uncredited:**
Harry Antrim . . . Justice of the Peace
Al Bridge . . . Detective Magnus
Richard Buckley . . . Mr. Graves
James Burke . . . Willie's Sergeant
Harry Carter . . . Postman
Maurice Cass . . . Organist
Robert Dane . . . MP at Railroad Station
Ralph Dumke . . . Twitchell
Kay English . . . Wife
Eddie Firestone . . . Man in Radio Station
Robert Forrest . . . MP
Byron Foulger . . . License Bureau Clerk
Harry Golder . . . Radio Announcer
Alvin Greenman . . . Man in Radio Station
Dabbs Greer . . . Man at the Miss Mississippi Contest
Harry Harvey . . . Ned
Selmer Jackson . . . Chaplain Hall
Margie Liszt . . . Irene
Lee Marvin . . . Pinky
Edwin Max . . . Counterman
Emile Meyer . . . Beauty Contest Announcer
Forbes Murray . . . Governor of Mississippi
Tom Powers . . . Attorney General
Victor Sutherland . . . Governor Bush
Maude Wallace . . . Autograph Hunter
Marjorie Weaver . . . Ruthie
O. Z. Whitehead . . . Postman

**Crew:**
Claude E. Carpenter . . . set decorator
W. D. Flick . . . sound recordist
Leland Fuller . . . art director
Paul Helmick . . . assistant director
Roger Heman . . . sound recordist
Ray Kellogg . . . special effects
Charles Le Maire . . . wardrobe director
Thomas Little . . . set decorator
Bernard Mayers . . . orchestration
Lionel Newman . . . musical director
Ben Nye . . . makeup
Helen Turpin . . . hair styles
Lyle R. Wheeler . . . art director

**Plot:**
An ensemble piece with five interwoven stories about five married couples, who, two and a half years after tying the knot, find out that they are not (and never have been) married because the justice of the peace who married them, Melvin Bush (played by Victor Moore), performed the ceremonies a few days before his license actually became valid.

Marilyn plays Mississippi beauty Annabel Norris, current Mrs. Mississippi and eligible for the Mrs. America beauty contest. Husband Jeff (David Wayne) is less than happy that her "career" is distracting her from her duties as a housewife and mother. The bombshell that they are not married makes Jeff happy—his wife is no longer eligible for the "Mrs." competition—but he then finds out that Annabel intends to take part in (and win) the Miss Mississippi pageant. The Marilyn segment of this movie ends with the couple's second wedding.

The other four couples who find they are in a similar unmarried predicament are played by Ginger Rogers and Fred Allen, Paul Douglas and Eve Arden, Eddie Bracken and Mitzi Gaynor, and Louis Calhern and Zsa Zsa Gabor.

**Reviews:**
*New York Post*
"Chalk up a direct hit for producer-writer Nunnally Johnson, director Edmund Goulding and their all-star cast in 'We're Not Married' at the Roxy. This happy compilation of the five episodes . . . studies marriage with admirable changes of pace and content. . . . There isn't a dud in the lot of them."

*Variety*
"The Monroe-Wayne sequence is pretty lightweight, but shows off the Monroe form to full advantage in a bathing suit, offering certain exploitation for film."

*The New York Times*
"Hands less skillful than those of Nunnally Johnson, who produced and wrote the script, and Edmund Goulding, who directed, might as easily have botched this jape. . . . Marilyn Monroe and David Wayne display the ironic dilemma of a beauty-contest winner and her mate."

*New York Herald Tribune*
"Nunnally Johnson has a picnic with marriage in 'We're Not Married' at the Roxy, and his good time is shared by all. . . . With David Wayne and Marilyn Monroe (who looks as though she had been carved out of cake by Michelangelo), it becomes a reason for a kitchen-bound husband to demand that his wife drop her busy activities as a beauty contest winner and return to the home."

## WEST, MAE (1893–1980)

Mae West was one of the first women to put the sex into sex symbol, and certainly the first to have so much control over her own image: she wrote most of her own scripts and had a firecracker wit to match.

Born into an entertainment family, by the age of fourteen West was billed as "The Baby Vamp" on the vaudeville circuit. She wrote her own plays, one of which, entitled *SEX*, led to a ten-day spell in prison on obscenity charges. Although she only made eight films during the thirties, from her opening exchange she was unique. By 1936 she was reputedly the highest-paid woman in the United States West's best-known roles were in *She Done Him Wrong* (1933), *I'm No Angel* (1933), and My *Little Chickadee* (1939).

Marilyn once told a reporter that she had learned a few tricks from the indomitable Mae West, particularly the impression of mocking her own sexuality.

## WESTON, CONNECTICUT

In early 1955 Marilyn had her own room at MILTON and AMY GREENE's home on Fanton Hill Road, just outside this Connecticut town. The house was a converted stable which had been extended and made into a welcoming home.

This was the perfect place to live incognito, at least until April 8, 1955, when EDWARD R. MURROW interviewed Marilyn here for his "Person to Person" show.

## WESTWOOD MEMORIAL PARK/ CEMETERY AND CHAPEL

1218 GLENDON AVENUE, WESTWOOD, LOS ANGELES

Founded in 1904, the Pierce Brothers' Westwood Memorial was a quiet neighborhood cemetery until 1962, when Marilyn Monroe was buried here, near former guardian GRACE MCKEE GODDARD and beloved foster parent ANA LOWER.

After her death, the owner of the Westwood Memorial Cemetery, Guy Hockett, removed Marilyn's body from her home to the mortuary at 7:30 A.M. on August 5, 1962. Her body lay unclaimed for some hours. Marilyn's FUNERAL, restricted to a few close mourners, was conducted at the then brand new Westwood Village Mortuary Chapel.

Marilyn's simple wall crypt is located on the Corridor of Memories, at number twenty-four. Just opposite is a memorial bench with a plaque dedicated to Marilyn by FAN clubs "Marilyn Remembered" and "All About Marilyn" on the thirtieth anniversary of her death.

When Marilyn was buried here, it was considered a rather "unfashionable" last resting place. Now it is one of the most expensive in the United States, reputedly costing $22,000 to be interred near Eve Arden, Jim Backus, Fanny Brice, John Cassavetes, TRUMAN CAPOTE, Will Durant, Eva Gabor, Armand Hammer, NUNNALLY JOHNSON, Stan Kenton, PETER LAWFORD, Irving Lazar, Burt Lancaster, DEAN MARTIN, Roy Orbison, Buddy Rich, MEL TORMÉ, Josef Von Sternberg, NATALIE WOOD, DARRYL ZANUCK, and Frank Zappa.

The crypt next to Marilyn's was purchased by HUGH HEFNER, who reputedly paid $85,000 for the privilege of lying next to Marilyn for eternity.

## WHITE PIANO

Marilyn's many moves from one HOME to another were made more cumbersome by the white baby grand piano she owned from 1951 onward. The object held a special significance for Marilyn: the only brief time, when she was seven years old, that Norma Jeane lived with her mother, GLADYS BAKER, was in a house on ARBOL STREET, Hollywood. Biographers relate different accounts about whether the piano, a white Franklin baby grand, was already at the property before Gladys moved in, or if Gladys purchased it specially for her daughter. She had previously paid for Norma Jeane to have piano lessons while living with the foster family, the

Marilyn Monroe's grave at Westwood Memorial Park Cementary, Los Angeles.

BOLENDERS. In most accounts, the instrument is said to have previously belonged to actor FREDRIC MARCH.

After Gladys was taken into psychiatric care, the piano was sold off to clear the outstanding debts on the property. By 1951 Marilyn was on a contract wage with TWENTIETH CENTURY-FOX and living at the BEVERLY CARLTON HOTEL. Despite the restricted size of this apartment, Marilyn's possessions included a white baby grand piano which she was paying for in installments; many biographers affirm that Marilyn had somehow managed to track the earlier instrument down. By 1953, the piano was installed in Marilyn's three-room apartment on DOHENY DRIVE.

The piano adorned Marilyn's NEW YORK homes from the mid-fifties. Accounts differ, but the most common story is that Marilyn shipped the instrument across country, and gave it pride of place in the living room at the FIFTY-SEVENTH STREET apartment she shared with husband ARTHUR MILLER, and then retained after they separated.

However, in at least one account, it is stated that this piano had in fact been purchased by business partner MILTON GREENE, and that when he was ousted from MARILYN MONROE PRODUCTIONS he made a claim for the instrument.

## WIDMARK, RICHARD (B. 1914)

"We had a hell of a time getting her out of the dressing room and on to the set. At first we thought she'd never get anything right. . . . But something happened between the lens and the film, and when we looked at the rushes she had the rest of us knocked off the screen!"

Marilyn's first leading man (as a leading lady) made his movie debut with an Oscar-nominated performance as a psychopath of uncommon evil in *Kiss of Death* (1947). Typecast as a bad guy, he began to emerge as a hero a couple of years later. He was cast as airline pilot Jed Towers, opposite psychotic babysitter Marilyn in *DON'T BOTHER TO KNOCK* (1952). Like so many actors who worked with Marilyn, he was amazed at the difference between the difficult experience of actually shooting the film and the finished product.

Other notable Widmark movies are *Saint Joan* (1957), *Judgment at Nuremberg* (1961), and *The Bedford Incident* (1965). In 1972 he starred in the TV series *Madigan*.

Widmark narrated the 1986 DOCUMENTARY *Marilyn Monroe: Beyond the Legend.*

## WILDER, BILLY
(B. 1906, SAMUEL WILDER)

MARILYN:
"He's a brilliant moviemaker, but he worries too much about the box office."

A publicity photo of Richard Widmark and Marilyn, 1952.

BILLY WILDER:
"Unique is an over-worked word, but in her case it applies. There will never be another like her, and Lord knows there have been plenty of imitations."

"I have never met anyone as utterly mean as Marilyn Monroe. Nor as utterly fabulous on the screen, and that includes Garbo."

"She has breasts like granite and a brain like Swiss cheese, full of holes. Extracting a performance from her is like pulling teeth."

"The greatest thing about Monroe is not her chest. It is her ear. She is a master of delivery. She can read comedy better than anyone else in the world."

"She is a very great actress. Better Marilyn late than most of the others on time."

"I'm the only director who ever made two films with Monroe. I think the Screen Directors Guild owes me a purple heart."

Wilder directed Marilyn in her two most successful comedies, *THE SEVEN YEAR ITCH* (1955) and *SOME LIKE IT HOT* (1959). In his many statements to biographers and journalists, his full appreciation for her talents, and despair at the strains of working with her, are eloquently and directly expressed. Wilder defined Marilyn's special magnetism on camera as "flesh impact—she looks on the screen as if you could reach out and touch her. . . . she had a quality no one else ever had on the screen except Garbo."

Dubbed "Hollywood's most mischievous immigrant," Wilder was born in Austro-Hungary and immigrated to America in 1933, after giving up his law studies for journalism and then working as a scriptwriter in Berlin. A few years later, he began writing for PARAMOUNT. The partnership he developed with Charles Brackett, which lasted until 1950, brought an early Oscar-nomination for *Ninotchka* (1939). This and subsequent writing collaborations—notably with I. A. L. DIAMOND—led to many works which turned conventional wisdom on its head with sly dialogue and ingenious situations. Wilder co-wrote and directed *Double Indemnity* (1944), *A Foreign Affair* (1948), *Sunset Boulevard* (1950), *Stalag 17* (1953), *Sabrina* (1954), all of which were Oscar-nominated; as well as *The Lost Weekend* (1945) and *The Apartment* (1960), both of which won Oscars. In 1986 Wilder received a Life Achievement Award from the American Film Institute.

Marilyn was very keen to work with Wilder on *The Seven Year Itch* (1955). She only agreed to do *THERE'S NO BUSINESS LIKE SHOW BUSINESS* (1954) after receiving assurances from TWENTIETH CENTURY-FOX that she could at last have some control over the projects she did, and that the studio would purchase the rights for GEORGE AXELROD's original Broadway play. Shooting was, as ever, complicated by Marilyn's FEARS and foibles. Marilyn required multiple retakes even when Wilder was happy; the location shooting of the famous skirt scene precipitated the collapse of her marriage to JOE DIMAGGIO; and by the time it came to the final soundstage shots, Marilyn had walked out on Fox, and had to fly back to Los Angeles from New York even though she was entering a dispute with the studio which lasted a year.

Marilyn's revised contract with Fox included approval of the director. Wilder was on the list. In late 1957, he sent her a two-page synopsis for *Some Like It Hot*, and was, by his own admission, pleasantly surprised at her interest in a role which was only a supporting one. Since *Itch*, Marilyn had become a devotee of THE METHOD, undoubtedly matured as an actress, and endured the frustrations of the failure of her independent production company, MARILYN MONROE PRODUCTIONS. On *Some Like It Hot*, Marilyn's expected intransigence during shooting reportedly reached new heights, as she missed entire mornings, was too groggy to remember her lines, required as many as fifty retakes for simple sequences, and looked right through Wilder to acting coach PAULA STRASBERG for guidance. Wilder is said to have been put under such stress that his back seized up. His succinct description of what it was like filming *Some Like It Hot:* "We were in mid-flight, and there was a nut on the plane."

After finishing *Some Like It Hot*, Wilder declined to invite Marilyn to the party he threw to celebrate completion. At this time, a relieved Wilder quipped to a journalist, "I am able for the first time to look at my wife again without wanting to hit her because she's a woman." Marilyn read the remarks and was deeply hurt. Arthur Miller leapt to his wife's defense, accusing Wilder of deliberately overworking Marilyn even though he knew she was pregnant (and subsequently miscarried). Wilder retorted, "I am deeply sorry that she lost her baby but I must reject the implication that overworking . . . was in anyway responsible." Miller counterattacked: "The simple truth is that whatever the circumstances she did her job and did it superbly, while your published remarks create the contrary impression without any mitigation." Wilder had the last word: "I hereby acknowledge that good wife Marilyn is a unique personality and I am the beast of Belsen but in the immortal words of Joe E. Brown quote nobody is perfect unquote."

Wilder publicly vowed he would never work with Marilyn again: "I have discussed this project with my doctor and my psychiatrist and they tell me I'm too old and too rich to go through this again."

Marilyn and Wilder's frostiness thawed in September 1959, when they met at the reception Fox gave for visiting Soviet premier NIKITA KHRUSCHEV. Wilder claims that he was so shocked at seeing her arrive early that he unthinkingly threw his arms around her: "I vowed then that if I did another picture with her I'd hire Khruschev to hang around the set so she'd show up on time." The last vestiges of their feud vanished in 1960, when Marilyn went to a preview of Wilder's *The Apartment* (1960) and later attended the party at Romanoff's restaurant.

When journalist Art Buchwald asked Wilder to comment on some of the more disparaging things he had said about Marilyn, Wilder responded, "I was speaking under duress and the influence of barbiturates and I was suffering from high blood pressure and I had been brainwashed."

But by 1962, Wilder was ready to try for a third Marilyn success. He told trade publication *Show Business Illustrated*, "I can tell you my mouth is watering to have her in another picture. The idea that she may be slipping is like saying a model is out of fashion when 100 sculptors are just waiting to get their chisels in a choice piece."

Wilder initially approached Marilyn to act in *Irma La Douce*. He explained exactly why he was willing to put himself through the mill once more: "Marilyn is very talented and a huge box office star. And that's what matters. After all, if her picture is running in Manchester and a man tells his wife, 'there's a Monroe picture showing,' the wife doesn't turn around and say, 'We don't want to see her, she's always rowing with directors.' They go and see her, and that's why I want her."

Years after her death, he summed up his feelings: "I miss her. It was like going to the dentist, making a picture with her. It was hell at the time, but after it was over, it was wonderful."

BOOK:
*Billy Wilder in Hollywood*, Maurice Zolotow. New York: Putnam, 1977.

Billy Wilder and Marilyn on the set of *The Seven Year Itch* (1955). With them is Hollywood columnist Sidney Skolsky.

## WILL

The main benefactors after Marilyn's DEATH were her mother GLADYS BAKER, half-sister BERNIECE MIRACLE, business manager MAY REIS (legal guardian to Marilyn's mother, who was deemed incompetent due to mental illness), LEE STRASBERG, and a charity appointed by psychiatrist MARIANNE KRIS. A sum was bequeathed as a college fund for PATRICIA ROSTEN, daughter of friends NORMAN and HEDDA ROSTEN, and provisions were made for XENIA CHEKHOV, the widow of drama coach MICHAEL CHEKHOV.

Marilyn's first will, written in February 1956, divided up an estate valued at $200,000 as follows: $100,000 to ARTHUR MILLER, $25,000 to Lee and Paula Strasberg, $20,000 to Dr. MARGARET HOHENBERG, $10,000 to Mrs. Michael Chekhov, $10,000 to the ACTORS STUDIO, plus $10,000 for the education of Patricia Rosten. She also left enough money to pay for lifelong sanitarium expenses (up to a total of $25,000) for her mother, Gladys Baker. As she signed the document before LAWYER Irving Stein, she quipped that on her tombstone should be written: "Marilyn Monroe, Blonde—37-23-36."

When Marilyn married Arthur Miller in June 1956, she changed the will to leave everything to her husband, plus a trust fund to provide for care of her mother.

Marilyn wrote her final will on January 14, 1961, soon after announcing her divorce from Arthur Miller, and three weeks before she entered the Payne Whitney psychiatric HOSPITAL.

### MARILYN'S WILL

I, MARILYN MONROE, do make, publish and declare this to be my Last Will and Testament.
FIRST: I hereby revoke all former Wills and Codicils by me made.

Marilyn in the iconic white dress from Billy Wilder's
*Some Like It Hot.*

A calendar photo of Marilyn by Laszlo Willinger, 1950.

SECOND: I direct my Executor, hereinafter named, to pay all of my just debts, funeral expenses and testamentary charges as soon after my death as can conveniently be done.
THIRD: I direct that all succession, estate or inheritance taxes which may be levied against my estate and/or against any legacies and/or devises hereinafter set forth shall be paid out of my residuary estate.
FOURTH: (a) I give and bequeath to BERNICE MIRACLE, should she survive me, the sum of $10,000.00.
(b) I give and bequeath to MAY REIS, should she survive me, the sum of $10,000.00.
(c) I give and bequeath to NORMAN and HEDDA ROSTEN, or to the survivor of them, or if they should both predecease me, then to their daughter, PATRICIA ROSTEN, the sum of $5,000.00, it being my wish that such sum be used for the education of PATRICIA ROSTEN.
(d) I give and bequeath all of my personal effects and clothing to LEE STRASBERG, or if he should predecease me, then to my Executor hereinafter named, it being my desire that he distribute these, in his sole discretion, among my friends, colleagues and those to whom I am devoted.
FIFTH: I give and bequeath to my Trustee, hereinafter named, the sum of $100,000.00, in Trust, for the following uses and purposes:
(a) To hold, manage, invest and reinvest the said property and to receive and collect the income therefrom.
(b) To pay the net income therefrom, together with such amounts of principal as shall be necessary to provide $5,000.00 per annum, in equal quarterly installments, for the maintenance and support of my mother, GLADYS BAKER, during her lifetime.
(c) To pay the net income therefrom, together with such amounts of principal as shall be necessary to provide $2,500.00 per annum, in equal quarterly installments, for the maintenance and support of MRS. MICHAEL CHEKHOV during her lifetime.
(d) Upon the death of the survivor between my mother, GLADYS BAKER, and MRS. MICHAEL CHEKHOV to pay over the principal remaining in the Trust, together with any accumulated income, to DR. MARIANNE KRIS to be used by her for the furtherance of the work of such psychiatric institutions or groups as she shall elect.
SIXTH: All the rest, residue and remainder of my estate, both real and personal, of whatsoever nature and wheresoever situate, of which I shall die seized or possessed or to which I shall be in any way entitled, or over which I shall possess any power of appointment by Will at the time of my death, including any lapsed legacies, I give, devise and bequeath as follows:
(a) to MAY REIS the sum of $40,000.00 or 25% of the total remainder of my estate, whichever shall be the lesser,
(b) To DR. MARIANNE KRIS 25% of the balance thereof, to be used by her as set forth in ARTICLE FIFTH (d) of this my Last Will and Testament.
(c) To LEE STRASBERG the entire remaining balance.
SEVENTH: I nominate, constitute and appoint AARON R. FROSCH Executor of this my Last Will and Testament. In the event that he should die or fail to qualify, or resign or for any other reason be unable to act, I nominate, constitute and appoint L. ARNOLD WEISSBERGER in his place and stead.
EIGHTH: I nominate, constitute and appoint AARON R. FROSCH Trustee under this my Last Will and Testament. In the event he should die or fail to qualify, or resign or for any other reason be unable to act, I nominate, constitute and appoint L. Arnold Weissberger in his place and stead.
Marilyn Monroe (L.S.)
SIGNED, SEALED, PUBLISHED and DECLARED by MARILYN MONROE, the Testatrix above named, as and for her Last Will and Testament, in our presence and we, at her request and in her presence and in the presence of each other, have hereunto subscribed our names as witnesses this 14th day of January, One Thousand Nine Hundred Sixty-One.
Aaron R. Frosch residing at 10 West 86th St. NYC
Louise H. White residing at 709 E. 56 St., New York, NY.

Some sources contend that Marilyn was considering making changes to her will at the time of her death. Marilyn's business manager, INEZ MELSON, contested Marilyn's final will (in which she did not feature) in October 1962, claiming that her client had drawn it up while under invalidating influence from either Lee Strasberg or Marianne Kris. At the time, the ESTATE in question was estimated at around $1 million. Judge Samuel DiFalco dismissed Melson's claim, but further legal problems resulted in no payments being made to Marilyn's beneficiaries until almost ten years after her death.

The greatest legacy bequeathed in this will—all of her possessions, and the remainder of Marilyn's estate after all provisions were settled—fell to Lee Strasberg. On his death in 1974, it passed to his second wife, ANNA STRASBERG, whom Lee had married after Paula died in 1966. The Marilyn Monroe estate is estimated to generate an income in excess of one million dollars a year in royalties from films and licensing of the Marilyn image. The remaining 25 percent funds the Monroe Young Family Unit at the Tavistock Center, London.

## WILLIAMS, TENNESSEE
(1911–1983, B. THOMAS LANIER WILLIAMS)

There are conflicting reports whether Marilyn met Pulitzer Prize-winning playwright Tennessee Williams through ARTHUR MILLER or RUPERT ALLAN, but it seems that Williams initiated the contact. Marilyn had already seen a number of Williams's plays, which include *The Glass Menagerie* (1945), *A Streetcar Named Desire* (1947), *The Rose Tattoo* (1950), *Cat On a Hot Tin Roof* (1954), and *Suddenly Last Summer* (1958). All of these plays became highly successful screen adaptations.

Marilyn never had the opportunity to act in a film version of one of Williams's plays, nor in a stage play. The closest she came was performing a scene from *A Streetcar Named Desire* at an ACTORS STUDIO class. It has also been said that Williams wanted Marilyn to star in his only original screenplay, *Baby Doll* (1956), but was overruled by director ELIA KAZAN.

At a dinner party thrown by Rupert Allan to celebrate her thirty-fourth birthday, Marilyn spent much of evening talking with Williams and his mother Edwina.

## WILLINGER, LASZLO (1906–1989)

"She had a talent to make people feel sorry for her, and she exploited it to the best of her ability—even people who had been around and knew models fell for this 'Help me' pose."

One of the photographers in Norma Jeane's early MODELING career, Hungarian-born Willinger was certainly not the most complimentary. Even after she became a famous film star, he quibbled "Marilyn Monroe is not a raving beauty, and her legs are too short for the rest of her."

Perhaps his best-known Marilyn shot is a CALENDAR photo of Norma Jeane, as she was still known, in a gold bathing suit. He was responsible for many of her early magazine covers.

In 1986 he told *LA Style* magazine that Marilyn responded to his inquiry as to why she had such chemistry with the camera, by answering, "It's like being screwed by a thousand guys and you can't get pregnant."

## WILLOUGHBY, BOB

For many decades Willoughby did stills work on movie shoots, commissioned by the major glossy picture MAGAZINES such as *Life* and *Look*. He photographed Marilyn on *NIAGARA* (1953) and *LET'S MAKE LOVE* (1960).

## WILSHIRE BOULEVARD
LOS ANGELES, CALIFORNIA

Baby Norma Jeane was brought home from the Los Angeles General HOSPITAL by her mother GLADYS BAKER to her then HOME, 5454 Wilshire Boulevard. Within two weeks the baby had been placed with foster parents IDA and WAYNE BOLENDER, on the recommendation of grandmother DELLA MAE HOGAN.

## WILSON, EARL (1907–1987)

This syndicated Hollywood columnist and writer first met Marilyn in July 1949, while she was in New York promoting *LOVE HAPPY* (1950). He interviewed her at the SHERRY-NETHERLAND HOTEL and wrote a piece spreading the word about the "MMMMM GIRL," as Marilyn had been nicknamed by the studio.

Wilson often featured gossip on Marilyn, sometimes nuggets placed by Marilyn herself. Wilson was one of Marilyn's PRESS allies, to whom she fed little tidbits. In recognition of this, she once made a gift to him of an autographed copy of her nude CALENDAR photograph, inscribed, "I hope you like my hairdo."

In 1955 Wilson quizzed Marilyn about her love interests, at the very moment when she was secretly dating ARTHUR MILLER. Marilyn answered: "No serious interests, but I'm always interested." Six years later, Wilson was the first columnist to break the news that Marilyn and Miller were to get a divorce.

Wilson's several books on Hollywood, notably *The Show Business Nobody Knows*, (1971), have proven to be a rich source of anecdote for Marilyn biographers.

## WINCHELL, WALTER (1897–1972)

Gossip columnist and broadcaster Walter Winchell was an old friend of JOE DIMAGGIO's. Whether or not it was a friendly gesture to bring his pal along to witness the crowd ogling his wife as she shot the billowing skirt scene from *THE SEVEN YEAR ITCH* (1955), is another matter. Winchell escorted a fuming and jealous DiMaggio back to the ST. REGIS HOTEL. The next day Joe flew back to Los Angeles, alone.

After the divorce, Winchell made references to Marilyn which provoked controversy. Around the time the new man in her life, ARTHUR MILLER, was called to testify before the HOUSE UN-AMERICAN ACTIVITIES COMMITTEE, the journalist informed his radio listeners that the "subpoena will check into [Miller's] entire inner circle, which also happens to be the inner circle of Miss Monroe—and all of them are former Communist sympathizers!"

It has been said that Winchell was in league with friend J. EDGAR HOOVER, and was happy to use his column to try and tar Miller's reputation. It has also been rumored that at one time Marilyn slept with the columnist—though perhaps this rumor was spread by the columnist himself.

In the wake of Marilyn's death, Winchell was apparently contacted by FBI chief Hoover to provide additional information about the movements of ROBERT KENNEDY on the weekend of Marilyn's DEATH.

In the August 1963 issue of *PHOTOPLAY*, Winchell amplified the allegations which had appeared in the foreign press about a "married man" allegedly involved in Miss Monroe's death. The scenario he illustrates has Marilyn taking an overdose of pills after learning that this famous and admired man, at the height of his career, refused to see her any more. This material provided ammunition for right-wing political allies—such as FRANK A. CAPELL—to cast suspicion on Bobby Kennedy.

Like many significant media figures of his day, Winchell made a few cameos on the silver screen, and served as a model for the columnist portrayed by Burt Lancaster in *Sweet Smell of Success* (1957). He also provided the voice for the narrator of popular sixties television series *The Untouchables*.

## WINTERS, SHELLEY
(B. 1922, SHIRLEY SCHRIFT)

"Marilyn is a moonwalker. When she used to live in my house, I often felt like she was a somnambulist walking around."

"She'd come out of our apartment in a shleppy old coat, looking like my maid, and all the people would push her aside to get *my* autograph. She loved it."

Shelley Winters' career spans more than five decades, from Academy Awards for *The Diary of Anne Frank* (1959) and *A Patch of Blue* (1965), to made-for-television movies to theater appearances. Her haul of over 100 movie roles also includes *A Double Life* (1948), *A Place in the Sun* (1951, Oscar-nominated), *The Night of the Hunter* (1955), and *The Poseidon Adventure* (1972).

Winters recalls the first times she saw the young starlet at the studio: Marilyn "used to sit in the corner and watched us working actresses at lunch. Her name was Norma Jeane Something. She rarely spoke to us, and when she did, she would whisper. We would shout back at her, 'What did you say?' and that would scare her more. She always wore halter dresses one size too small and carried around a big library book like a dictionary or encyclopaedia."

According to Winters, she and Marilyn became friends in the late 1940s, and shared an apartment on HOLLOWAY DRIVE, Hollywood, in 1951. It was at this time that both women wrote down a list of the MEN they regarded as being the most sexy.

As an early member of the ACTORS STUDIO, Winters was one of the first to recommend to Marilyn the man who for many years would be her guiding light in the dramatic arts, LEE STRASBERG. Winters also says that she tried to get Marilyn to join the informal drama courses held by CHARLES LAUGHTON, but Marilyn was too awed by the stars in attendance to open her mouth. It has also been said that Winters was attending the ACTORS LAB when Marilyn first arrived there in 1947.

Winters has written three autobiographical books which contain references to Marilyn.

Walter Winchell and Marilyn at his birthday party at Ciro's restaurant, 1953.

## WOLFE, DONALD H.

Author of 1998 Marilyn BIOGRAPHY, entitled *The Last Days of Marilyn Monroe*, and, more directly, *The Assassination of Marilyn Monroe*. Using material from, among others, ROBERT SLATZER and JEANNE CARMEN, the book favors the CONSPIRACY theory view and calls for a full new investigation into the circumstances of her DEATH.

Wolfe's thesis hinges upon a sighting of ROBERT KENNEDY on the night of Marilyn's death:

> Shortly before midnight, a dark Mercedes sped east on Olympic Boulevard in Beverly Hills. Estimating the car to be driving in excess of 55 miles per hour (88km/hr), Beverly Hills police officer Lynn Franklin flipped on his siren and lights and gave chase. When the Mercedes pulled to a stop, Franklin cautiously walked to the driver's side and directed his flashlight towards the three occupants. He immediately recognized that the driver was actor Peter Lawford. Aiming his flashlight at the two men seated in the rear, he was surprised to see the Attorney-general of the United States, Robert Kennedy, seated next to a third man he later identified as Dr Ralph Greenson. Lawford explained that he was driving the attorney-general to the Beverly Hills Hotel on an urgent matter. Franklin waved them on.

Wolfe also cites material from an off-the-record interview given by Marilyn's psychoanalyst DR. RALPH GREENSON. He claims that in a massive COVER-UP, secret service agents methodically destroyed all but one photograph of Marilyn with the Kennedy brothers at the reception after the president's 1962 MADISON SQUARE GARDEN birthday bash.

## WOMEN

MARILYN:
"I have always had a talent for irritating women since I was fourteen. Sometimes I've been to a party when no one spoke to me for a whole evening. The men, frightened by their wives or sweeties, would give me a wide berth. And the ladies would gang up in a corner to discuss my dangerous character."

It was Marilyn's enormous sexual charge, the effect she had on MEN, that helped her build her film career, not her renown as a sympathetic girlfriend. Her reputation as a sexual

Shelley Winters and Marilyn at the Golden Globe Awards, 1959.

predator, whether it was deserved or not, meant that women of her own generation tended to see her as a competitor or a threat. Marilyn candidly acknowledged this in later years: "I was sorry in a way to do this, but I had a long way to go and I needed a lot of advertising to get there."

Marilyn had very few close women FRIENDS her own age. She did, however, have a number of long-lasting friendships with older women, and enthusiastically threw herself into a big-sister role with her stepchildren and the CHILDREN of friends.

GLORIA STEINEM's biography did something to redress the almost exclusively male bias of Marilyn hagiography. Certainly, after her death, for some people Marilyn has become a symbol of vulnerability and the perils of a woman viewing herself only in terms of her desirability to the opposite sex.

## WOOD, NATALIE (1938–1981, B. NATASHA NIKOLAEVNA GURDIN)

"When you look at Marilyn on the screen, you don't want anything bad to happen to her. You really care that she should be all right—happy."

Natalie Wood was a seasoned child actress with six years' experience by the time she landed her supporting role in SCUDDA HOO! SCUDDA HAY! (1948), the first movie Marilyn appeared in.

Wood made the transition successfully from child star to adult actress. Three times nominated for Academy Awards, in *Rebel without a Cause* (1955), *Splendor in the Grass* (1961), and *Love with the Proper Stranger* (1964), Wood also made memorable performances in *Miracle on 34th Street* (1947), *West Side Story* (1961), and in *Bob and Carol and Ted and Alice* (1969). She died in 1981 after slipping off the yacht she was sailing on with husband ROBERT WAGNER.

## WRIGHT, FRANK LLOYD (1867–1959)

In the summer of 1957 Marilyn went to the PLAZA HOTEL to see one of the fathers of modern architecture—creator of, among other buildings, the Guggenheim Museum—to ask him if he would design a new house for her and ARTHUR MILLER on the site of their country place at ROXBURY, in Connecticut.

The tour Marilyn gave him was lavish: an enormous home on a new hilltop site (offering stunning views), and a building with its own projection room, children's nurseries, a big study for Arthur to work in, a walk-in wardrobe, and of course a swimming pool. In some accounts Lloyd Wright never completed his design; in others, the cost of this dream home was so exorbitant that Marilyn and Arthur decided to renovate the existing property.

## WRITING

Marilyn was left-handed. According to ARTHUR MILLER, her handwriting was a riot of slanting lines, sometimes running up and down margins, and she wrote him notes sometimes using two or three different pens.

Marilyn was also a correspondent, though perhaps not the most reliable. She wrote letters to friends, and kept in touch by telgram too. She often signed her letters, "Love and kisses, Marilyn."

Marilyn frequently wrote down things she learned during classes at the ACTORS STUDIO, and things that occurred to her during shoots. There also has been some dispute about whether or not she kept diaries. It has been alleged that in the last year of her life she kept a DIARY which has been kept hidden or was destroyed because it contained material incriminating about the KENNEDYS.

Marilyn also wrote POETRY: "The few poems I do write are very private."

### SOME OF MARILYN'S THOUGHTS

"My problem of desperation in my work and life—I must begin to face it continually, making my work routine more continuous and of more importance than my desperation."

"Doing a scene is like opening a bottle. If it doesn't open one way, try another—perhaps even give it up for another bottle? Lee wouldn't like that."

"How or why I can act—and I'm not sure I can—is the thing for me to understand. The torture, let alone the day to day happenings—the pain one cannot explain to another."

"How can I sleep? How does this girl fall asleep? What does she think about?"

"What is there I'm afraid of? Hiding in case of punishment? Libido? Ask Dr. H."

"How can I speak naturally onstage? Don't let the actress worry, let the character worry."

"Learn to believe in contradictory impulses."

## "WRONG DOOR RAID"

A week after Marilyn's first divorce hearing, JOE DIMAGGIO and FRANK SINATRA concocted a plan to catch Marilyn with voice coach HAL SCHAEFER, with whom they suspected she was having an affair. According to ROBERT SLATZER, however, DiMaggio had evidence that Marilyn was having a lesbian affair with her another actress, and not with the voice coach they shared.

On November 5, 1954, DiMaggio and Sinatra came to the apartment building at 8122 Waring Avenue in Hollywood to meet private detectives Barney Ruditsky and Phil Irwin. The four of them, and possibly more hired help, smashed their way into the apartment, and clicked away with cameras they had brought to gather proof. The only problem was that they had broken into the next door apartment, home of thirty-seven-year-old Florence Kotz.

The racket was enough to alert the people next door—reputedly the other actress, Schaefer, and Marilyn—and give them time to escape. Although this incident was reported in the press in the following days, Sinatra somehow managed to keep his and DiMaggio's names out of the reports. He was not, however, successful in preventing the full story from coming out in *Confidential* magazine ten months later.

Ms. Kotz filed a $200,000 damages claim against her famous intruders. Sinatra denied having any part in the business, and proceedings dragged on for several years. In the end, DiMaggio settled out of court and paid her $7,500 in damages.

It has been speculated that Sinatra deliberately took DiMaggio to the wrong door. Their friendship was severely shaken by the episode, and is said to have never really recovered.

## WYMAN, JANE
(B. 1914, SARAH JANE FAULKS)

Wyman worked her way out of her early dumb blonde roles to win an Oscar for *Johnny Belinda* (1948) in the year that young Marilyn fell head over heels in love with voice coach FRED KARGER. Wyman was, that year, divorcing second husband RONALD REAGAN. In 1952, though, Wyman married Fred Karger.

Marilyn had not forgotten her old love, and made a point of turning up, uninvited, at their wedding reception. It is said that some time later, Marilyn set up a life-size cut-out of herself in the halter dress from *THE SEVEN YEAR ITCH* (1955) on Wyman's lawn, though by the time *Itch* came out, Wyman and Karger had divorced. The couple married a second time in 1961, but that marriage also was destined to end in divorce within four years.

As well as her Oscar-winning exploits, Wyman put in appreciated performances in *The Lost Weekend* (1945), *Magnificent Obsession* (1954), and *Pollyanna* (1960). Throughout the eighties she was a regular on the TV series *Falcon Crest*.

# X Y Z

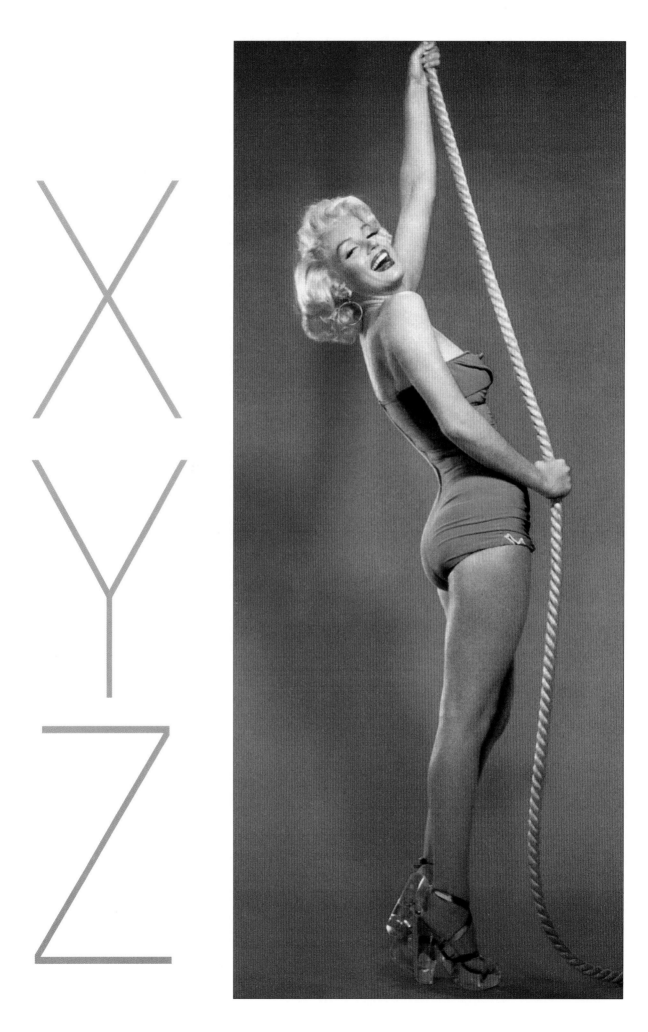

## YANK

This weekly U.S. Army MAGAZINE was the first to run a cover featuring Norma Jeane, in mid-1945, photographed by DAVID CONOVER.

## YOGA

Marilyn took lessons from Virginia Dennison in 1962.

(*see* SPORTS)

## *YOU WERE MEANT FOR ME* (1948)

TWENTIETH CENTURY-FOX movie in which Marilyn reputedly had a part as an extra—but her appearance as a peripheral dancer in a bandstand sequence did not make it past the cutting room.

This musical starring Jeanne Craine and Dan Dailey is about a bandleader and his new hometown bride, and their tough life on the road in Depression-era America.

During filming of *Ladies of the Chorus* (1948) Columbia Pictures took publicity photos of the young starlet exercising for a piece on "How to Exercise." Fourteen years later Marilyn took Yoga classes.

# Z

## ZAHN, TOMMY

According to biographer ANTHONY SUMMERS, in 1946 this twenty-two-year-old lifeguard on "Muscle Beach," who also happened to be under contract to TWENTIETH CENTURY-FOX, befriended starlet Norma Jeane. They often went surfing together—Zahn recalls she was very much at ease in the water—and enjoyed each other's company on and off the beach.

## ZANUCK, DARRYL F. (1902–1979)

MARILYN:
"Mr. Zanuck had never seen me as an actress with star quality. He thought I was some kind of freak."

DARRYL ZANUCK:
"I do not claim to have discovered Marilyn Monroe. Nobody discovered her. She discovered herself. I was merely an instrument that provided her with the vehicles in which she was able to reach the theatregoing public of the world."

For more than three decades Darryl Zanuck was one of the men who ran Hollywood, a cigar-chomping movie mogul who co-founded and masterminded the success of TWENTIETH CENTURY-FOX. After a succession of jobs, he began in the industry as a writer, and had his first hit by coming up with the idea for the twenties police dog film series *Rin Tin Tin*. Zanuck moved into production, and at the age of just twenty-three was running the production department at Warner Brothers. In 1933 he left to set up Twentieth Century Films, with JOSEPH M. SCHENCK, and then two years later merged the company with the ailing Fox company. As well as taking the production decisions, Zanuck personally produced over 150 movies during his long career, including *The Grapes of Wrath* (1940), *How Green Was My Valley* (1942), *Gentleman's Agreement* (1947), and *ALL ABOUT EVE* (1950). Under his guidance, Fox collected over thirty Oscars.

Among Zanuck's recorded quotes, he is famously known for uttering the ultimate megalomaniac studio boss put-down, "Don't say yes until I finish talking." He also had a reputation as a proponent of the casting couch theory of success for young actresses, though in his case the couch was actually a bedroom built behind his office, ostensibly because he so often stayed late for screenings. Zanuck did not deny his famous sexual appetite, though he did say, in his defense, "Any of my indiscretions were with people, not actresses."

All biographers remark on Zanuck's ongoing skepticism about Marilyn's talents, not just when Fox first hired her, but even after she had risen to prominence in 1953 with massive box-office hits *NIAGARA*, *GENTLEMEN PREFER BLONDES*, and *HOW TO MARRY A MILLIONAIRE*. One reason provided for this was that Marilyn was not "his" girl: her protectors at Twentieth Century-Fox were Schenck, and then SPYROS SKOURAS, whose desires were strong enough to win over the head of production. Nevertheless, it has been ventured that either Zanuck made a play for Marilyn and she spurned his advances, or that Marilyn made herself available but Zanuck wasn't interested.

Zanuck was shown Marilyn's first SCREEN TEST, filmed in July 1946 by BEN LYON. In most versions, he was not convinced that the untested actress had any star qualities, but he was won over by the enthusiasm of both talent manager Lyon and cinematographer LEON SHAMROY. Marilyn was signed to her first film contract on August 26, 1946.

Zanuck's own recollection of his first meeting with Marilyn was at his home in PALM SPRINGS, when Schenck turned up with her: "I didn't jump up and say, 'oh, this is a great star,' or anything like that. Later on, Joe said, 'if you can work her in some role or something, some, you know, supporting role, do so.' I did, but I didn't think that I had found any gold mine. John Huston gave her a hell of a good role in *The Asphalt Jungle*. Jesus, she was good in that. I thought, it must have been the magic of Huston, because I didn't think she had all that in her. But then I put her in *All About Eve*, and she was an overnight sensation."

Marilyn's initial year-long contract was allowed to lapse. Reportedly, she tried to speak directly with Zanuck to find out what he thought was wrong with her, but did not manage to get past his secretary.

Two years passed before JOHNNY HYDE succeeded in getting Marilyn's foot back in the door. The appearance in *THE ASPHALT JUNGLE* (1950) was worth a six-month contract, which was extended to a seven-year deal in May 1951. Despite the petitions of Schenck and Skouras, Zanuck continued to resist putting Marilyn in a major role, though her film appearances to date were creating quite a stir in the press. Marilyn appeared in half a dozen movies, in minor parts. Before entrusting her with a lead role, Zanuck loaned her out to RKO for a supporting role in the drama *CLASH BY NIGHT* (1952). Then, finally, he took the plunge with the woman he privately thought was "empty-headed," and cast her as a lead in *DON'T BOTHER TO KNOCK* (1952). His comments on the rushes were scathing: "She's an amateur. Her voice is too small and her body is too stiff. You've got to work hard on training. You got to make an

Photograph by George Barris, 1962.

actress of her. She's a tremendous personality. But that's it."

The next film Zanuck cast her in, *Niagara* (1953), confirmed her as a top-ranked star. Although Marilyn didn't seem to "do it" for him, Zanuck could not deny the effects she had on others, especially on fellow executives and most American males who saw her on the screen. He cast her as a ditzy blonde in every big production the studio was running: *Gentlemen Prefer Blondes*, *How to Marry a Millionaire* (both 1953), *River of No Return* (1954), and *THERE'S NO BUSINESS LIKE SHOW BUSINESS* (1954).

Zanuck was the studio executive who always berated Marilyn or chastised her. According to biographer FRED LAWRENCE GUILES, when JOAN CRAWFORD launched her scathing attack on Marilyn's brazenness following the 1953 *PHOTOPLAY* Awards, Zanuck wrote to Crawford advising her, despite press pressures, not to apologize to Marilyn for her comments.

In 1954, as Marilyn's marriage to JOE DIMAGGIO fell apart, Zanuck complained about her LATENESS and the vast number of retakes required when she was involved. But he also told her he thought she was "incredibly good" in *THE SEVEN YEAR ITCH* (1955).

Meanwhile, Marilyn was beginning to bridle at the tough terms of her 1951 contract, her lack of power over the roles Zanuck was offering, and the small amount of MONEY she was earning compared to fellow stars. When Marilyn finally walked out on Twentieth Century-Fox, Zanuck told the press, "This [*The Seven Year Itch*] will be her last picture for anyone but Twentieth Century-Fox for three years and four months. She's under contract to this studio, and she'll fulfill it."

Marilyn had the courage to battle it out with the studio. Business partner MILTON GREENE helped to set up MARILYN MONROE PRODUCTIONS, while lawyers renegotiated a new contract in which almost all her demands were met. Marilyn returned to Hollywood to shoot *BUS STOP* (1956) in February 1956. In March 1956, Zanuck stepped down from his position as chief of production, and went to live in Europe where he worked as an independent producer. In 1962 he was called back as President of Fox, just in time to oversee Marilyn's re-hiring for *SOMETHING'S GOT TO GIVE*. He managed to turn the company back from the brink, and installed his son Richard as vice president in charge of production. His tenure finally came to an end in 1971, when he was ousted as president—making him the last of the old-school moguls to succumb.

On Marilyn's death, Zanuck stated, "Like everyone who knew Marilyn Monroe or worked with her, I am shocked. Marilyn was a star in every sense of the word."

## ZENO, GEORGE

A FAN and collector of Marilyn MEMORABILIA, Zeno co-authored a book with JAMES SPADA in 1982 called *Monroe: Her Life in Pictures*.

## ZOLOTOW, MAURICE

"A great force of nature, she was becoming a victim of the propaganda machine, of her own struggle to build herself up. About her swirled a hurricane, and she was its eye. She longed for privacy, but she had murdered privacy, as Macbeth had murdered sleep. Her time was not hers. And her personality was not hers."

In 1960 Maurice Zolotow published *Marilyn Monroe*, a BIOGRAPHY of Marilyn based on a series of interviews he conducted with her in 1955.

According to *Marilyn Unabridged*, Zolotow's biography stands at the head of the pack: "There have been many unworthy imitators over the years, but Maurice Zolotow's *Marilyn Monroe* has remained the bible for every post-1960 book published on the life and times of Marilyn Monroe."

Zolotow has also written biographies of BILLY WILDER and John Wayne.

BOOK:
*Marilyn Monroe*, Maurice Zolotow. New York: Harcourt Brace, 1960.

Photograph by Milton Greene, 1955.

# A MARILYN BIBLIOGRAPHY


Agan, Patrick. *The Decline and Fall of the Love Goddesses*. Los Angeles: Pinnacle, 1979.

Alfonso, Alfonso, ed. *Monroe & DiMaggio*. Miami: Conquest Comics, 1992.

Alien, Jack, ed. *Marilyn by Moonlight*. New York: Barclay, 1996.

Anderson, Janice. *Marilyn Monroe*. London: Hamlyn, 1983.

———, and Marilyn Monroe, *"Quote Unquote"*. New York: Crescent, 1995.

Arnold, Eve. *The Unretouched Woman*. New York: Alfred A Knopf, 1976.

———. *Marilyn Monroe: An Appreciation*. New York: Alfred A Knopf, 1987.

Archer, Robyn and Diana Simmonds. *A Star Is Torn*. New York: Dutton/ Signet, 1986.

Avedon, Richard. "Fabled Enchantresses" photo feature. *Life*, December 22, 1958.

———. "Color Essay of the Year." *1960 Photography Annual*.

———. "The Persistence of Marilyn." *American Photographer*, July 1984.

———. "Photos by Richard Avedon." *The New Yorker*, March 21, 1994.

Axelrod, George. *Will Success Spoil Rock Hunter?* New York: Random House, 1956.

Bacall, Lauren. *By Myself*. New York: Alfred A Knopf, 1979.

Bacon, James. *Hollywood Is a Four-Letter Town*. Chicago: Regnery, 1976.

Baker, Roger. *Marilyn Monroe*. New York: Portland, 1990.

Barker, Clive. *Son of Celluloid*. Forestville, CA: Eclipse, 1991.

Barris, George. *Her Life in Her Own Words*. New York: Henry Holt & Co.,1995.

Baty, S. Paige. *American Monroe, The Making of a Body Politic*. Berkeley: University of California Press, 1995.

Beaton, Cecil. Cecil Beaton, *Photographs 1920-1970*. New York: Stewart, Tabori & Chang, 1995.

Beauchamp, Antony. *Focus on Fame*. London: Odhams, 1958.

Bellavance-Johnson, Marsha. *Marilyn Monroe in Hollywood*. Computer Lab, Idaho: Ketchum, 1992.

Bergala, Alain, text. *Magnum Cinema, photographs from 50 years of movie-making*. London: Phaidon, 1995.

Bernard, Susan, ed. *Bernard of Hollywood's Marilyn*. New York: St. Martin's Press, 1993.

Bernau, George. *Candle in the Wind*. New York: Warner Books,1990.

Bessie, Alvah. *The Symbol*. New York: Random House, 1966.

Birnbaum, Agnes, ed. *Marilyn's Life Story*. New York: Bantam Doubleday Dell, 1962.

Blanpied, John W. ed. *Movieworks*. Rochester, NY: Little Theatre Press, 1990.

Bowering, Marilyn. *Anyone Can See I Love You*. Ontario: Porcupine's Quill, 1987.

Boyd, Herb, ed. *Marilyn Monroe: Seductive Sayings*. Stamford, CT: Longmeadow, 1994.

Brambilla, Giovan Battista and Gianni Mercurio, Stefano Petricca. *Marilyn Monroe: the Life, the Myth*. New York: Rizzoli International Publications, 1996.

Brandon, Henry. *As We Are*. New York: Bantam Doubleday Dell, 1961.

Brown, Peter and Patte B. Barham. *Marilyn: The Last Take*. New York: Dutton/Signet, 1992.

Bruno of Hollywood (Bruno Bernard). *Requiem for Marilyn*. London: Kensal, 1986.

Burke, Phyllis. *Atomic Candy*. New York: Atlantic, 1989.

Buskin, Richard. *The Films of Marilyn Monroe*. Lincolnwood, IL: Publications International, 1992.

Cabanas, Frederic. *Marilyn Monroe, A Bibliography*. Barcelona: Ixia Libres, 1992.

Cahill, Marie. *Forever Marilyn*. London Bison, 1991.

Canevari, Leonore and Jeanette van Whye, Christian Dimas, Rachel Dimas. *The Murder of Marilyn Monroe*. New York: Carrol & Graf Publishers, 1992.

Capell, Frank A. *The Strange Death of Marilyn Monroe*. Staten Island, NY: Herald of Freedom, 1964.

Capote, Truman. *Music for Chameleons*. New York: Random House, 1980.

Cardiff, Jack. *Magic Hour*. London/Boston: Faber & Faber, 1996.

Carpozi, George Jr. *Marilyn Monroe: "Her Own Story"*. Belmont, New York 1961. (Published in England as *The Agony of Marilyn Monroe.)*

Carroll, Jock. *The Shy Photographer*. New York: Stein and Day, 1964.

———. *Falling for Marilyn: The Lost Niagara Collection*. Michael New York: Friedman Publishing Group, 1996.

Cawthorne, Nigel. *Sex Lives of the Hollywood Goddesses*. London: Prion, 1997

Chayefsky, Paddy. *The Goddess, a screenplay*. New York: Simon & Schuster, 1957.

Clark, Colin. *The Prince, the Showgirl and Me*. New York: St. Martin's Press, 1996.

Collins, Peter. *I Remember ... Marilyn*. Vestal, NY: Vestal, 1995.

Conover, David. *Finding Marilyn*. New York: Grosset & Dunlap Publishers, 1981.

———. *The Discovery Photos, Summer 1945*. Ontario, Canada: Norma Jeane Enterprises, 1990

Conway, Michael and Mark Ricci. *The Films of Marilyn Monroe*. New York: Citadel Press, 1964, 1988.

Crivello, Kirk. *Fallen Angels*. Secaucus, NJ: Citadel Press,1988.

Crown, Lawrence. *Marilyn at Twentieth Century-Fox*. London: Comet, 1987.

Cunningham, Ernest W. *The Ultimate Marilyn*, Los Angeles: Renaissance Books, 1998.

Curtis, Tony. *Tony Curtis, the Autobiography*. New York: William Morrow & Co., 1993.

De Dienes, André. *Marilyn, Mon Amour*. St. Martin's Press, New York 1985.

———, and Bernard, Susan. *Marilyn–My Prayer for You*. New York: St. Martin's Press, 1999

Denker, Henry. *The Director*. New York: Baron, 1970.

DePaoli, Geri, ed. *Elvis + Marilyn: 2 x Immortal*. New York: Rizzoli International Publications, 1994.

Dillinger, Nat. *Unforgettable Hollywood*. New York: William Morrow & Co., 1982.

Doll, Susan, ed. *Marilyn: Her Life and Legend*. New York: Beekman Publishers, 1990.

Dougherty, James E. *The Secret Happiness of Marilyn Monroe*. Chicago: Playboy, 1976.

Douglas, Carole Nelson, ed. *Marilyn: Shades of Blonde*. New York: Forge, 1997.

Dyer, Richard. *Heavenly Bodies: Film Stars and Society*. New York: St. Martins Press, 1986.

Eisenstaedt, Alfred. *Eisenstaedt's Album*. New York: Viking,1976.

Engelmeier, Regine and Peter W. *Fashion in Film*. Munich: Prestel, 1990.

Epstein, Edward Z. and Lou Valentine. *Those Lips, Those Eyes*. New York: Carol Publishing Group, 1992.

Evans, Liz. *Who Killed Marilyn Monroe?* London: Orion, 1997.

Fahey, David and Linda Rich. *Masters of Starlight: Photographers in Hollywood*. Los Angeles: County Museum of Art, 1987.

Fast, Jonathan. *The Inner Circle*. Delacorte Press, New York 1979.

Feingersh, Ed. *Marilyn: March 1955*. New York: Delta Books, 1990.

Finn, Michelle. *Marilyn's Addresses*. London: Smith Gryphon, 1995.

Fowler, Christopher. *How to Impersonate Famous People*, New York: Crown Books, 1984.

Fox, Patty. *Star Style: Hollywood Legends as Fashion Icons*. Los Angeles: Angel City, 1995.

Franklin, Joe and Laurie Palmer. *The Marilyn Monroe Story*. New York: Field, 1953.

Freeman, Lucy. *Why Norma Jean Killed Marilyn Monroe*. Chicago: Global Rights, 1992.

French, Philip and Ken Wlaschin, eds. *The Faber Book of Movie Verse*. London/ Boston: Faber & Faber, 1993.

Garnett, Tay. *Light Your Torches and Pull Up Your Tights*. New Rochelle, NY: Arlington, 1973.

Giancana, Sam and Chuck. *Double Cross*. New York: Warner Books, 1992.

Giles, Nicki. *The Marilyn Album*. New York: Gallery,1991.

Goldman, William. *Tinsel*. New York: Delacorte Press, 1979.

Goode, James. *The Story of The Misfits*. Indianapolis: Bobbs-Merrill, 1961.

Goodman, Ezra. *The Fifty Year Decline and Fall of Hollywood*. New York: Simon & Schuster, 1961.

Gorman, E. J. *The Marilyn Tapes*. New York: Doherty, 1995.

Graham, Sheilah. *Hollywood Revisited*. St. New York: Martin's Press, 1985.

Grant, Neil. *Marilyn In Her Own Words*. New York: Crescent, 1991.

Greene, Milton. *Of Women and Their Elegance*. New York: Simon & Schuster, 1980.

———. *Milton's Marilyn*. Munich: Schirmer, 1994.

Griffith, Corinne. *Hollywood Tales*. Los Angeles: Fell, 1962.

Grumbach, Doris. *The Missing Person*. New York: The Putnam Berkley Group, 1981.

Guilaroff, Sydney. *Crowning Glory*. Los Angeles: General, 1996.

Guiles, Fred Lawrence. *Norma Jean: The Life of Marilyn Monroe*. New York: McGraw-Hill, 1969.

———. *Legend: The Life and Death of Marilyn Monroe*. New York: Stein and Day, 1984.

Hall, Allan. *The World's Greatest Secrets*. London: Hamlyn, 1989.

Hall, James E. "Marilyn Was Murdered: An Eyewitness Account." *Hustler*, May 1986.

Halliday, Brett. *Kill All the Young Girls*. New York: Bantam Doubleday Dell, 1973.

Halsman, Philippe. *Philippe Halsman's Jump Book*. New York: Simon & Schuster, 1959.

Hamblett, Charles. *The Hollywood Cage*. New York: Hart, 1959. (Originally published in England as *Who Killed Marilyn Monroe?)*.

Harris, Radie. *Radie's World*. New York: The Putnam Berkley Group, 1975.

Harrison, Jay. *Marilyn* Surrey, UK: Colour Library, 1992.

Harvey, Diana Karanikas. *Marilyn (Life in Pictures)*. London: Metro Books, 1999.

Haspiel, James. *Marilyn: The Ultimate Look at the Legend*. New York: Henry Holt & Co., 1991.

———. *The Young Marilyn: Becoming the Legend*. New York: Hyperion, 1994.

Hawkins, G. Ray. *The Marilyn Monroe Auction*, a catalog. Los Angeles: G. Ray Hawkins Gallery, 1992.

Hayes, Suzanne Lloyd, ed. *3-D Hollywood, photos by Harold Lloyd*. New York: Simon & Schuster, 1992.

Hecht, Ben. *The Sensualists*. New York: Messner, 1959.

Hegner, William. *The Idolaters*. New York: Trident, 1973.

Hembus, Joe. *Marilyn*. London: Tandem, 1973.

Heymann, C. David. *A Woman Named Jackie*. New York: Stuart, 1989.

Hoyt, Edwin P. *Marilyn: The Tragic Venus*. New York: Chilton,1965.

Hudson, James A. *The Mysterious Death of Marilyn Monroe*. New York: Volitant, 1968.

Huston, John. *An Open Book*. New York: Alfred A Knopf, 1980.

Hutchinson, Tom. *Marilyn Monroe*. London: Optimum, 1982.

Hyatt, Kathryn. *Marilyn, The Story of a Woman*. New York: Seven Stories, 1996.

Janis, Sidney, text. *Homage to Marilyn Monroe*, exhibition catalog. New York: Sidney Janis Gallery, 1967.

Jasgur, Joseph. *The Birth of Marilyn: the lost photographs of Norma Jean*. New York: St. Martin's Press, 1991.

Johnson, Terry. *Insignificance: the book*, with the screenplay. London: Sidgwick, 1985.

———. *Insignificance*, the play. London: Methuen, 1982.

Jordan, Ted: *Norma Jean: My Secret Life With Marilyn Monroe*. New York: William Morrow & Co., 1989.

Kahn, Roger. *Joe & Marilyn: A Memory of Love*. New York: William Morrow & Co., 1986.

Kanin, Garson. *Come On Strong*. New York: Dramatists Play Service, 1962.

———. *Moviola*. New York: Simon & Schuster, 1979.

Kazan, Elia. *A Life*. New York: Alfred A Knopf, 1988.

Kidder, Clark, ed. *Marilyn Monroe unCovers*. Alberta, Canada: Quon, 1994.

———. *Marilyn Monroe: Cover to Cover*. Iola, WI: Krause Publications, 1999.

———. *Marilyn Monroe Collectibles: A Comprehensive Guide to the Memorabilia of an American Legend*. New York: Avon Books, 1999.

Kirkland, Douglas. *Light Years*. Thames, New York 1989.

———. *Icons: Creativity with Camera and Computer*. San Francisco: HarperCollins, 1993.

Kobal, John, ed. *Marilyn Monroe: A Life on Film*. Hamlyn, London 1974. (U.S. edition, Exeter, New York 1984.)

Korda, Michael. *The Immortals*. Poseidon, New York 1992.

Krohn, Katherine E. *Marilyn Monroe: Norma Jeane's Dream*. Lerner, Minneapolis 1997.

Leaming, Barbara. *Marilyn Monroe*. New York: Crown Publishing, 1998.

Leese, Elizabeth. *Costume Design in the Movies*. England: BCW, 1976.

Lefkowitz, Frances. *Marilyn Monroe*. New York: Chelsea House, 1995.

Lembourn, Hans Jorgen. *Diary of a Lover of Marilyn Monroe*. New York: Arbor, 1979.

Levinson, Robert S. *The Elvis and Marilyn Affair*. New York: Forge, 1999.

Levy, Alan, interviewer. "A Good Long Look at Myself." *Redbook*, August 1962.

Lifshin, Lyn. *Marilyn Monroe*. Portland: Quiet Lion, 1994.

Lloyd, Ann. *Marilyn: A Hollywood Life*. New York: Mallard, 1989.

Logan, Joshua. *Movie Stars, Real People and Me*. New York: Delacorte Press, 1978.

Loney, Glenn. *Unsung Genius* (Jack Cole). New York: Watts, 1984.

Loren, Todd, ed. *The Marilyn Monroe Conspiracy*. San Diego: Conspiracy Comics, 1991.

Luitjers, Guus, ed. *Marilyn Monroe: A Never-Ending Dream*. New York: St. Martin's Press, 1987.

———. *Marilyn Monroe in Her Own Words*. New York: Omnibus, 1991.

McBride, Joseph. *Hawks on Hawks*. Berkeley: University of California Press, 1982.

McCann, Graham. *Marilyn Monroe*. New Brunswick: Rutgers University Press, 1988.

Macavoy, Elizabeth and Susan Israelson. *Lovesick: The Marilyn Syndrome*. New York: Fine, 1991

McClung, Nellie. "My Sex Is Ice Cream," *The Marilyn Monroe Poems*. Victoria, B. C. Canada: Ekstasis, 1996.

Mailer, Norman. *Marilyn*. New York: Grosset & Dunlap Publishers, 1973.

———. *Of Women and Their Elegance*. Photos by Milton Greene. New York:; Simon & Schuster, 1980.

———. *Strawhead*, a play. Excerpted in *Vanity Fair*, April 1986.

Mankiewicz, Joseph L. *All About Eve*, the screenplay. New York: Random House, 1951.

———. *More About All About Eve*. Screenplay, plus interview. New York: Random House, 1972.

Margener, Vardis. *Double Take*. Chicago: Playboy, 1982.

Mars, Julie ed. *Marilyn Monroe*. Kansas City, MO: Andrews McMeel, 1995.

Martin, Pete. *Pete Martin Calls On....* Simon & Schuster, New York 1962.

———. *Will Acting Spoil Marilyn Monroe?* New York: Bantam Doubleday Dell, 1956.

Meaker, M.J. *Sudden Endings*. Garden City, NY: Bantam Doubleday Dell, 1964.

Mellen, Joan. *Marilyn Monroe*. New York: Pyramid, 1973.

Meryman, Richard, interviewer. "Fame may go by and so long, I've had you." *Life*, August 3, 1962.

Messick, Hank. *The Beauties & the Beasts*. New York: McKay, 1973.

Miller, Arthur. *After the Fall*. New York: Viking, 1964.

———. *The Misfits*, "synthesis of screenplay and novel." New York: Viking, 1961.

———. *Timebends*. New York: Grove, 1987.

Miller, George. *Marilyn: Her Tragic Life*. New York: Escape Magazines, 1962.

Mills, Bart. *Marilyn on Location*. London: Sidgwick, 1989.

Miracle, Berniece Baker. *My Sister Marilyn*. Chapel Hill, NC: Algonquin Books, 1994.

Monroe, Marilyn. *My Story*. New York: Stein and Day, 1974.

Montand, Yves. *You See, I Haven't Forgotten*. New York: Alfred A Knopf, 1992.

Moore, Robin and Gene Schoor. *Marilyn and Joe DiMaggio*. New York: Manor, 1977.

Morley, Sheridan and Ruth Leon, *Marilyn Monroe*. Gloucester: Sutton Publishing, 1999

Murray, Eunice with Rose Shade. *Marilyn: The Last Months*. New York: Pyramid, 1975.

Negulesco, Jean. *Things I Did... and Things I Think I Did*. New York: Simon & Schuster, 1984.

Noguchi, Thomas T. *Coroner*.New York: Simon & Schuster, 1983.

Oates, Joyce Carol. *Blonde*. NY: Ecco Press/ HC, 2000.

Olivier, Laurence. *Confessions of an Actor*. New York: Simon & Schuster, 1982.

Oppenheimer, Joel. *Marilyn Lives!* New York: Delilah, 1981.

Ott, Frederick W. *The Films of Fritz Lang*. Secaucus, NJ: Citadel Press, 1979.

Pall, Gloria. *The Marilyn Monroe Party*. Los Angeles: self-published, 1992.

Paris, Yvette. *Dying To Be Marilyn*. Wyoming: Lagurno, 1996.

Parish, James Robert. *The Fox Girls*. New Rochelle, NY: Arlington, 1971.

Parsons, Louella. *Tell It to Louella*. New York: The Putnam Berkley Group, 1961.

Pascal, John. *Marilyn Monroe: The Complete Story of Her Life, Her Loves and Her Death*. New York: Popular, 1962.

Peabody, Richard and Lucinda Ebersole, eds. *Mondo Marilyn: An Anthology of Fiction and Poetry*. New York: St. Martin's Press, 1995.

Pepitone, Lena with William Stadiem. *Marilyn Monroe Confidential*. New York: Simon & Schuster, 1979.

Post, Adam. *Tragic Goddess: Marilyn Monroe*. Westport, CT: POP Comics, 1995.

Preminger, Otto. *Preminger: an autobiography*. New York: Bantam Doubleday Dell,1977.

"Her psychiatrist friend." *Violations of the Child Marilyn Monroe*. New York: Bridgehead, 1962.

Quirk, Lawrence. *The Kennedys in Hollywood*. Dallas: Taylor, 1996.

Rechy, John. *Marilyn's Daughter*. New York: Carroll & Graf Publishers, 1988.

Renaud, Ron. *Fade to Black*. New York: Pinnacle, 1980.

Riese, Randall and Neal Hitchens. *The Unabridged Marilyn: Her Life from A to Z*. New York: Congdon and Weed, 1987.

Rollyson, Carl E., Jr. *Marilyn Monroe: A Life of the Actress*. Ann Arbor: UMIP, 1986.

Rooks-Denes, Kathy. *Marilyn*. New York; Bantam Doubleday Dell, 1993.

Rooney, Mickey. *Life Is Too Short*. New York: Villard, 1991.

Rosten, Norman. *Marilyn: An Untold Story*. New York: Signet, 1973.

———. *Marilyn Among Friends*. Photos by Sam Shaw. New York: Henry Holt & Colt, 1987.

Russell, Jane. *Jane Russell: My Path & My Detours*. New York: Watts, 1985.

St. Pierre, Roger. *Marilyn Monroe*. London: Anabas, 1985.

Sanford, Jay, ed. *Marilyn Monroe: Suicide or Murder?* San Diego: Revolutionary Comics, 1993.

Schiller, Lawrence, ed. *Marilyn*. With biography by Norman Mailer. New York: Grosset & Dunlap Publishers, 1973.

Schirmer, Lothar, ed. *Marilyn Monroe and the Camera*. Boston: Little, Brown, 1989.

———. *Marilyn Monroe, Photographs 1945-1962*. Munich: Schirmer, 1994.

Schonauer, David, ed. "Rare Marilyn: a portfolio of work." *American Photo*, May/June, 1997.

Sciacca, Tony (Anthony Scaduto). *Who Killed Marilyn?* New York: Manor, 1976.

Shaw, Sam. *Marilyn Monroe as The Girl*. New York; Ballantine, 1955.

———. *The Joy of Marilyn in the Camera Eye*. New York: Exeter, 1979.

Shevey, Sandra. *The Marilyn Scandal*. New York :William Morrow & Co., 1987.

Signoret, Simone. *Nostalgia Isn't What It Used to Be*. New York: HarperCollins, 1978.

Sinyard, Neil. *Marilyn*. New York: Gallery, 1989.

Skolsky, Sidney. *Marilyn*. New York: Bantam Doubleday Dell, 1954.

———. *Don't Get Me Wrong—I Love Hollywood*. New York: The Putnam Berkley Group, 1975.

Slatzer, Robert. *The Life and Curious Death of Marilyn Monroe*. New York: Pinnacle, 1974.

———. *The Marilyn Files*. New York: Shapolsky, 1992.

Smith, Mathew. *The Men Who Murdered Marilyn*. London: Bloomsbury, 1996.

Smith, Milburn, ed. *Marilyn*. New York: Barven, 1971.

Smith, Milburn. *The Marilyn Chronicles*. New York: Starlog,1994.

Spada, James with George Zeno. *Monroe: Her Life in Pictures*. New York: Bantam Doubleday Dell, 1982.

Spada, James. *Peter Lawford: The Man Who Kept the Secrets*. New York: Bantam Doubleday Dell, 1991.

Speriglio, Milo. *The Marilyn Conspiracy*. New York: Pocket Books, 1986.

———. *Marilyn Monroe: Murder Cover-Up*. New York: Seville, 1982.

——— with Adela Gregory. *Crypt 33: The Saga of Marilyn Monroe—The Final Word*. New York: Carol Publishing Group, 1993.

Spire, Steven. "Marilyn Monroe." *Personality Classics #2*. Massapequa, 1991.

Spoto, Donald. *Marilyn Monroe, the Biography*. New York: HarperCollins, 1993.

Staggs, Ben. *MMII, the Return of Marilyn Monroe*. New York: Fine, 1991.

Steinem, Gloria. *Marilyn*. Photos by George Barris. New York: Henry Holt & Co., 1986.

Stempel, Tom. *Screenwriter, the life and times of Nunnally Johnson*. New York: Barnes & Noble Books, 1980.

Stern, Bert. *The Last Sitting*, a selection. New York: William Morrow & Co., 1982.

———. *The Last Sitting*, 101 selected photos. Munich: Schirmer, 1993.

———. *Marilyn Monroe: The Complete Last Sitting*. Munich: Schirmer, 1992.

Strasberg, Susan. *Bittersweet*. New York; The Putnam Berkley Group, 1980.

———. *Marilyn and Me: Sisters, Rivals, Friends*. New York: Warner Books, 1992.

Sullivan, Steve. *Va Va Voom! Bombshells, Pin-Ups, Sexpots and Glamour Girls*. Los Angeles: General, 1995.

Summers, Anthony. *Goddess: The Secret Lives of Marilyn Monroe*. New York: Macmillan, 1985.

Taylor, Roger G. *Marilyn in Art*. Salem, NH: Salem, 1984.

———. *Marilyn Monroe: In Her Own Words*. London: Kwintner, 1983.

Thomas, Roseanne Daryl. *The Angel Carver*. New York: Random House, 1993.

Thomson, David. *A Biographical Dictionary of Film*. London: André Deutsch, 1994

Tierney, Tom. *Marilyn Monroe Paper Dolls*. New York: Dover, 1979.

Toperoff, Sam. *Queen of Desire*. New York: HarperCollins, 1992.

Wagenknecht, Edward. *Marilyn Monroe: A Composite View*. Philadelphia: Chilton, 1969.

Walker, Alexander. *The Celluloid Sacrifice*. New York: Hawthorne, 1967.

Walker, John, ed. *Halliwell's Film Guide and Filmgoer's Companion*. New York: HarperCollins, 1997.

Wayne, Jane Ellen. *Marilyn's Men: The Private Life of Marilyn Monroe*. St. Martin's Press, New York 1992.

Weatherby, W. J. *Conversations with Marilyn*. New York: Mason, 1976.

Weiner, Leigh. *Marilyn: A Hollywood Farewell*. Los Angeles: 7410 Publishing, 1990.

Willoughby, Bob. *The Hollywood Special*. New York: Takarajima, 1993.

Wilson, Earl. *The Show Business Nobody Knows*. Washington, DC: Regnery, 1971

Winters, Shelley. *Shelley: Aka Shirley*. Ballantine, New York, 1980

———. *Shelley II, the Middle of My Century*. New York: Simon & Schuster, 1989.

Wolhart, Dayna. *Marilyn Monroe*. Mankato, MN: Capstone Press, 1991

Woog, Adam. *Mysterious Deaths: Marilyn Monroe*. San Diego Lucent, 1997.

Zolotow, Maurice. *Marilyn Monroe*. New York Harcourt Brace & Co., 1960; Revised Edition. New York: HarperCollins, 1990.


# INDEX OF NAMES

NOTE: This is an index of people's names, Hollywood and TV movies, and plays. **Bold** page numbers refer to primary discussions of people or movies. *Italicized* page numbers refer to people named in picture captions.

*Next page*: Marilyn on Tobey Beach. Photograph by André de Dienes, 1949.